THE PRACTICE OF
ENTERPRISE ARCHITECTURE

THE PRACTICE OF
ENTERPRISE ARCHITECTURE

A Modern Approach to Business and IT Alignment

Svyatoslav Kotusev

First published in 2018 by SK Publishing, Melbourne, Australia 3000

ISBN (Kindle): 978-0-6483098-0-2
ISBN (ePub): 978-0-6483098-1-9
ISBN (Paperback): 978-0-6483098-2-6
ISBN (Hardcover): 978-0-6483098-3-3

A catalogue record for this book is available from the National Library of Australia

ACM Computing Classification System (2012): Applied computing ~ Enterprise architectures

Printed in the United States of America

10 9 8 7 6 5 4 3 2 1

Visit http://kotusev.com

In memory of Leonard (Len) Fehskens

Contents

Contents..vii

Complete Table of Contents...ix

Preface...xix

PART I: Introduction to Enterprise Architecture 1

Chapter 1: Introduction 3

Chapter 2: The Concept of Enterprise Architecture 15

Chapter 3: The Role of Enterprise Architecture Practice 35

Chapter 4: Enterprise Architecture and City Planning 45

Chapter 5: The Dialog Between Business and IT...63

Chapter 6: Processes of Enterprise Architecture Practice 85

Chapter 7: IT Initiatives and Enterprise Architecture 101

PART II: Enterprise Architecture Artifacts..111

Chapter 8: The CSVLOD Model of Enterprise Architecture 113

Chapter 9: Considerations 127

Chapter 10: Standards 143

Chapter 11: Visions...159

Chapter 12: Landscapes...181

Chapter 13: Outlines..201

Chapter 14: Designs 215

Chapter 15: The CSVLOD Model Revisited...229

PART III: Other Aspects of Enterprise Architecture 243

Chapter 16: Architects in Enterprise Architecture Practice...............................245

Chapter 17: Architecture Functions in Organizations 261

Chapter 18: Instruments for Enterprise Architecture 281

Chapter 19: The Lifecycle of Enterprise Architecture Practice.........................307

Afterword 331

Appendix: The Origin of EA and Modern EA Best Practices............................333

Notes..357

References 399

Index..435

About the Author..441

Complete Table of Contents

Contents vii

Complete Table of Contents ix

Preface xix

    The Subject of This Book.. xxiii

    The Uniqueness of This Book.. xxiii

        Based on Original Research and Direct Empirical Evidence....................... xxiv

        Descriptive and Analytical Attitude... xxiv

        Describes Industry-Born Best Practices... xxiv

        Both Practical and Conceptual Perspective.. xxv

        Systematic and Comprehensive Approach.. xxv

        Introduces Novel Conceptualizations xxv

        Reflects the Perspective of Organizations, Not of External Consultants...... xxv

        Placed in the Context of the Existing Literature xxvi

    The Intended Audience of This Book xxvi

    Materials for This Book xxvii

    The Structure of This Book.. xxviii

    A Note on the Used Terminology xxix

    Acknowledgements xxx

PART I: Introduction to Enterprise Architecture 1

Chapter 1: Introduction 3

    The Role of IT in Modern Organizations... 3

    Organizations as Socio-Technical Systems.. 6

    The Problem of Business and IT Alignment 8

        Diversity of Actors Involved in Business and IT Alignment....................... 9

        Main Groups of Actors Involved in Business and IT Alignment 10

        Miscommunication Between Actors as a Reason of Misalignment.............. 11

    Enterprise Architecture as a Solution.. 12

    Chapter Summary.. 14

Chapter 2: The Concept of Enterprise Architecture 15
What Is Enterprise Architecture? 15
    The Essence of Enterprise Architecture 15
    Domains of Enterprise Architecture.. 18
The Practice of Enterprise Architecture 19
Enterprise Architecture Artifacts.. 20
    Informational Contents of Enterprise Architecture Artifacts...................... 21
    Duality of Enterprise Architecture Artifacts 21
    Two Meanings of Enterprise Architecture Artifacts: Decisions and Facts ...23
    Two Lifecycles of Enterprise Architecture Artifacts: Permanent and Temporary........25
    Examples of Enterprise Architecture Artifacts 25
The Role of Architects in Enterprise Architecture Practice 27
    General Responsibilities of Architects... 27
    Architects as Developers of Enterprise Architecture Artifacts 27
    Enterprise Architecture Artifacts, Architects and Other Actors................. 31
Architecture Functions in Organizations... 32
Chapter Summary... 33

Chapter 3: The Role of Enterprise Architecture Practice..............................35
The Need for Enterprise Architecture 35
The Benefits of Practicing Enterprise Architecture.. 36
What Organizations Practice Enterprise Architecture? 38
The Historical Origin of Enterprise Architecture and Modern Best Practices 38
What Enterprise Architecture Practice Is Not 40
    Not a Purely Technical Planning... 40
    Not a One-Size-Fits-All Methodology 40
    Not an Automated Planning 41
    Not a Substitute for Competence 41
    Not a Work of Dedicated Experts 41
    Not a One-Time Planning Project 42
    Not a Technology-Specific Practice.. 42
    Not an Enterprise Modeling 42
    Not an Enterprise Engineering 43
    Not an Implementation of Enterprise Architecture Frameworks 43
Chapter Summary... 43

Chapter 4: Enterprise Architecture and City Planning.................................45
Enterprise Architecture Practice as City Planning 45
Six Types of Enterprise Architecture Artifacts and City Planning Documents 47
    Considerations... 48

Standards..49
Visions 50
Landscapes...52
Outlines..53
Designs...54
Relationship Between Different Types of Enterprise Architecture Artifacts......................55
Complementarity of Different Types of Enterprise Architecture Artifacts.........................58
The CSVLOD Model of Enterprise Architecture...60
Chapter Summary..61

Chapter 5: The Dialog Between Business and IT **63**
Problems with the Business Strategy as the Basis for IT Planning.....................63
Business Strategy Is Often Vague, Unknown or Merely Absent...............................63
Business Strategy Rarely Provides a Clear Direction for IT...................................64
Business Strategy Is Often Unstable and Frequently Changes 64
Business Strategy Often Requires Non-Reusable IT Systems...................................65
The Role of Business Strategy for Enterprise Architecture Practice 65
Key Discussion Points Between Business and IT 66
Operating Model 68
Business Capabilities 74
Specific Business Needs 76
Business Processes..77
Business Requirements 78
The Hierarchy of Key Discussion Points 79
Enterprise Architecture Uncertainty Principle 82
Chapter Summary..84

Chapter 6: Processes of Enterprise Architecture Practice **85**
Processes Constituting Enterprise Architecture Practice 85
Strategic Planning 85
Initiative Delivery 87
Technology Optimization 89
Relationship Between EA-Related Processes 91
Strategic Planning and Initiative Delivery 93
Initiative Delivery and Technology Optimization 94
Technology Optimization and Strategic Planning 95
A High-Level Process View of Enterprise Architecture Practice 96
Chapter Summary..99

Chapter 7: IT Initiatives and Enterprise Architecture.................................. **101**
   The Role of IT Initiatives in Enterprise Architecture Practice 101
   Different Types of IT Initiatives... 103
      Fundamental Initiatives.. 104
      Strategic Initiatives... 104
      Local Initiatives.. 105
      Urgent Initiatives.. 105
      Architectural Initiatives.. 106
   The Flow of Different Types of IT Initiatives... 107
   Chapter Summary.. 110

PART II: Enterprise Architecture Artifacts... **111**

Chapter 8: The CSVLOD Model of Enterprise Architecture..................... **113**
   Dimensions for Classifying Enterprise Architecture Artifacts........................ 113
      Dimension One: What?... 113
      Dimension Two: How?.. 115
   Six General Types of Enterprise Architecture Artifacts................................ 116
      Considerations.. 118
      Standards.. 119
      Visions 119
      Landscapes.. 120
      Outlines 121
      Designs... 121
   The Resulting CSVLOD Model of Enterprise Architecture 122
   Chapter Summary.. 124

Chapter 9: Considerations **127**
   Considerations as a General Type of Enterprise Architecture Artifacts........... 127
      Informational Contents... 127
      Development and Usage 129
      Role and Benefits 130
      Difference from the Adjacent Types 131
   Specific Enterprise Architecture Artifacts Related to Considerations 131
      Principles (Essential).. 131
      Policies (Common)... 133
      Conceptual Data Models (Uncommon).. 135
      Analytical Reports (Uncommon) 136
      Direction Statements (Uncommon)... 138
   Additional Concerns Regarding Considerations 140

Chapter Summary... 141

Chapter 10: Standards **143**
Standards as a General Type of Enterprise Architecture Artifacts.................... 143
    Informational Contents 143
    Development and Usage 144
    Role and Benefits... 146
    Difference from the Adjacent Types 147
Specific Enterprise Architecture Artifacts Related to Standards 148
    Technology Reference Models (Essential) 148
    Guidelines (Essential) 150
    Patterns (Common) 151
    IT Principles (Common) 152
    Logical Data Models (Uncommon) 154
Additional Concerns Regarding Standards 155
Chapter Summary... 157

Chapter 11: Visions **159**
Visions as a General Type of Enterprise Architecture Artifacts 159
    Informational Contents 159
    Development and Usage 160
    Role and Benefits... 162
    Difference from the Adjacent Types 163
Specific Enterprise Architecture Artifacts Related to Visions 163
    Business Capability Models (Essential).. 163
    Roadmaps (Essential)... 167
    Target States (Common) 170
    Value Chains (Uncommon) 172
    Context Diagrams (Uncommon)... 174
    Less Popular Enterprise Architecture Artifacts Related to Visions 175
Additional Concerns Regarding Visions.. 177
Chapter Summary... 178

Chapter 12: Landscapes..**181**
Landscapes as a General Type of Enterprise Architecture Artifacts.................. 181
    Informational Contents 181
    Development and Usage 182
    Role and Benefits... 184
    Difference from the Adjacent Types 185
Specific Enterprise Architecture Artifacts Related to Landscapes.................... 185
    Landscape Diagrams (Essential)... 185

Inventories (Common) 187

Enterprise System Portfolios (Common) 189

IT Roadmaps (Common)... 191

Less Popular Enterprise Architecture Artifacts Related to Landscapes..... 194

Additional Concerns Regarding Landscapes... 197

Chapter Summary... 199

Chapter 13: Outlines 201

Outlines as a General Type of Enterprise Architecture Artifacts.................... 201

Informational Contents... 201

Development and Usage 203

Role and Benefits 206

Difference from the Adjacent Types 206

Specific Enterprise Architecture Artifacts Related to Outlines...................... 207

Solution Overviews (Essential)... 207

Options Assessments (Common) 209

Initiative Proposals (Uncommon) 210

Less Popular Enterprise Architecture Artifacts Related to Outlines........... 211

Additional Concerns Regarding Outlines... 213

Chapter Summary... 214

Chapter 14: Designs... 215

Designs as a General Type of Enterprise Architecture Artifacts..................... 215

Informational Contents... 215

Development and Usage 217

Role and Benefits 219

Difference from the Adjacent Types... 220

Specific Enterprise Architecture Artifacts Related to Designs 220

Solution Designs (Essential) 220

Preliminary Solution Designs (Uncommon)... 222

Less Popular Enterprise Architecture Artifacts Related to Designs............ 223

Additional Concerns Regarding Designs 225

Chapter Summary... 226

Chapter 15: The CSVLOD Model Revisited...................................... 229

Continuous Nature of the CSVLOD Taxonomy 229

Mapping of Specific EA Artifacts to the CSVLOD Taxonomy....................... 231

Decision Path of the EA-Enabled Strategy Execution 234

Descriptive Nature of the CSVLOD Model 237

Exceptions to the CSVLOD Model... 238

Enterprise Architecture on a Page 239

Chapter Summary 241

PART III: Other Aspects of Enterprise Architecture 243

Chapter 16: Architects in Enterprise Architecture Practice 245

General Skills and Qualities of Architects 245

Knowledge of Business and IT 245

Effective Communication 247

Collaborative Attitude 248

Innovative Mindset 248

Systems Thinking 249

Five Common Archetypes of Architects 250

Solution Architects 251

Domain Architects 251

Business Unit Architects 253

Enterprise Architects 253

Architecture Managers 254

Hierarchy of Architecture Positions 254

Organizational Mapping of Architecture Positions 256

Process Mapping of Architecture Positions 257

Chapter Summary 260

Chapter 17: Architecture Functions in Organizations 261

The Role of Architecture Functions in Organizations 261

The Structure of Architecture Functions 263

Dependence on the Size of an Organization 263

Dependence on the Degree of Decentralization 266

Governance Bodies of Architecture Functions 268

The Role of Governance Committees 269

Four Types of Governance Committees 270

Exemption and Escalation Procedures 273

The Structure of Governance Committees 276

Chapter Summary 278

Chapter 18: Instruments for Enterprise Architecture 281

Modeling Languages for Enterprise Architecture 281

ArchiMate 281

UML 282

BPMN 284

ARIS..285
Applicability of Modeling Languages...285
The Role of Modeling Languages..287
Software Tools for Enterprise Architecture 289
Capabilities of Specialized Software Tools 289
Applicability of Software Tools...290
The Role of Specialized Software Tools...296
Templates for Enterprise Architecture Artifacts 297
Straw-Man Architecture...298
Architecture Debt 299
Measurements in Enterprise Architecture Practice 302
Chapter Summary..305

Chapter 19: The Lifecycle of Enterprise Architecture Practice 307
Establishing Enterprise Architecture Practices in Organizations.............307
The Historical Path to Establishing Enterprise Architecture Practice.........310
The Deliberate Path to Establishing Enterprise Architecture Practice.........312
Facilitating the Organizational Acceptance of an EA Practice 316
Maturity of Enterprise Architecture Practice 318
Signs of Mature Enterprise Architecture Practices 318
Maturity of an EA Practice as a Factor of Sustainable Competitive Advantage.........321
Enterprise Architecture Practice and Enterprise Architecture Consulting 322
Initiative-Based Engagements...324
Strategic Engagements 325
Developmental Engagements...325
Productive and Counterproductive Relationships with Consultancies.......326
Chapter Summary..329

Afterword 331

Appendix: The Origin of EA and Modern EA Best Practices.......................333
The Origin of Enterprise Architecture: Myths and Facts 333
The History of Architecture-Based Planning Methodologies 333
Information Systems Plans Epoch...334
Information Systems Architecture Epoch 337
Enterprise Architecture Epoch 341
Conclusions of the Historical Analysis 346
The Application of Architecture-Based Planning Methodologies.............349
Problems of Architecture-Based Planning Methodologies 349
Prevalence of Architecture-Based Planning Methodologies...............351

Conclusions of the Application Analysis 352

Appendix Summary 356

Notes **357**

References **399**

Index **435**

About the Author **441**

Preface

In 2013 after several years of practical software development and architecture experience in industry I started my PhD research program at RMIT University, Melbourne, Australia. The focus of my PhD research was the notion of enterprise architecture (EA) as an instrument for organization-wide information systems planning.

By the time I started my PhD studies I was already TOGAF-certified and aware of other popular EA frameworks including Zachman, FEAF and DoDAF. Similarly to all other PhD students, I started my research from studying existing academic and practitioner literature on enterprise architecture. Very soon I realized that the vast majority of available EA publications are based on the ideas of well-known EA frameworks. Probably like most people familiar with the EA literature, at the early stage of my study I concluded that the entire EA discipline is rooted in EA frameworks[1], which reflect proven EA best practices, and originates from the seminal Zachman Framework[2].

However, during my further analysis of the available EA literature I identified some other approaches to using enterprise architecture advocating significantly different ideas inconsistent with the essential recommendations of EA frameworks[3]. Moreover, the authors of these alternative approaches criticized the ideas of EA frameworks for their impracticality[4]. This curious situation raised the initial suspicions regarding the role and value of EA frameworks for the EA discipline. If EA frameworks really represent widely acknowledged EA best practices, as the EA literature generally suggests, then why are their ideas harshly criticized? If the ideas of EA frameworks are so important and fundamental, then why have other different approaches to using enterprise architecture been proposed? If the basic ideas of an EA practice are so clear and well understood, then why does the phenomenon of an EA practice have multiple inconsistent and even mutually exclusive descriptions? If several profoundly different approaches have been recommended, then what are their advantages and disadvantages?

My further in-depth comprehensive review of the available EA literature revealed a number of even more curious facts around EA frameworks. Firstly, I was not able to find even a single publication demonstrating how exactly the essential ideas of any EA framework can be successfully implemented in real organizations[5]. Secondly, I realized that almost every qualitative EA research dealing with practical down-to-earth questions concludes that the ideas of EA frameworks can hardly be successfully implemented[6]. Thirdly, I noticed that all qualitative descriptions of successful EA practices barely resemble the main prescriptions of EA frameworks[7]. Fourthly, I realized that all discussions of the value of EA frameworks sooner or later come to the point when even their passionate proponents admit that frameworks cannot be implemented directly, but rather should be "adapted" to the needs of specific organizations[8]. However, I was not able to find even a single attempt to explain how exactly EA frameworks should be adapted, when and why[9]. All these curious facts strengthened my initial suspicions regarding the real nature of EA frameworks. If EA frameworks are so widely used, as generally suggested by the popular EA literature, then why cannot documented examples of their real practical implementation be found? If EA frameworks really emerged from the practical experience of numerous EA practitioners, as often argued by their advocates, then why do multiple independent studies consistently conclude that their ideas cannot be implemented in practice? If EA frameworks are based on real EA best practices, then why do successful EA practices barely resemble their essential prescriptions? If it is widely acknowledged that EA frameworks should be adapted to specific organizations, then why does nobody try to explain how exactly it should be done?

My later broader studies of information systems planning and management literature helped resolve the mysterious puzzle with EA frameworks. Firstly, my inquiries into the history of information systems planning methodologies revealed that the lineage of all popular EA frameworks can be clearly traced back to the seminal Business Systems Planning (BSP) methodology introduced by IBM in the end of the 1960s[10]. Secondly, my analysis of the problems with early BSP-like planning methodologies[11] revealed that these problems are essentially identical to the reported problems with modern EA frameworks[12]. Moreover, BSP and other similar methodologies were consistently found to be ineffective approaches to information systems planning[13]. Thirdly, my studies of the available literature on the phenomenon of management fads[14] (i.e. flawed management-related ideas of passing interest aggressively promoted by management consultancies) revealed that the curious phenomenon of EA frameworks is far from unique, but rather is merely yet another management fad invented and successfully "sold" to the public by consultants and gurus[15], along with quality circles (QC), business process reengineering (BPR) and many other once-fashionable but now discredited managerial techniques[16]. These findings instantly elucidated the mystery of EA frameworks and clarified the general picture of the EA discipline. On the one hand, the notion of EA frameworks is only a grand mystification created by talented gurus and consultancies[17]. EA frameworks essentially represent merely the next attempt of consulting companies to sell under a new fresh title the same 50-years-old flawed BSP-based planning approach with a long history of expensive failures. EA frameworks, as well as their numerous conceptual predecessors, were created artificially by consultancies and positioned as best practices in information systems planning, but actually never reflected genuine best practices and cannot be successfully implemented[18]. On the other hand, the entire EA discipline, including both practitioner and academic publications, is largely based on the unproven ideas of popular EA frameworks. The validity of these EA frameworks is not questioned and typically taken for granted even without any empirical validation[19]. It is widely assumed in the EA literature that the existing EA frameworks define current EA best practices, which is very far from the truth[20].

These conclusions, though dispelled my initial doubts regarding the dubious nature of EA frameworks, naturally raised a number of new questions of different sort. If popular EA frameworks are only successfully promoted management fads, then is there any real value in the very concept of enterprise architecture? If the recommendations of EA frameworks cannot be successfully implemented, then are there any successful value-adding EA practices in industry? If the prescriptions of EA frameworks are impractical, then what is actually practiced in real organizations under the title of enterprise architecture? If EA frameworks still convey some valuable ideas, then to what extent do successful EA practices correlate with their original prescriptions?

By the time I completed the first year of my PhD research program, I studied tens of books and nearly a thousand other publications on enterprise architecture[21]. From my comprehensive analysis of the available EA literature I got a long list of troublesome questions regarding the current status of the EA discipline and only a vague conjecture of how successful EA practices work in real organizations. Descriptions of an EA practice provided by the existing literature were simply too obscure, theoretical, fragmentary or even inconsistent to explain how enterprise architecture is really used. As a result, at the beginning of the second year of my PhD program, right before the initial empirical data collection, I had essentially no idea regarding what I will encounter in organizations practicing enterprise architecture. When I started to interview different participants of established EA practices I realized that my initial suspicions and later conclusions on the status of the EA discipline were generally correct. The recommendations of popular EA frameworks were indeed not implemented anywhere, while the actual activities of practicing architects were simply unrelated to their key prescriptions. For example, even the organizations included in the "official" list of TOGAF users provided by The Open Group[22] did not follow the essential recommendations of TOGAF in any real sense (e.g. did not follow the ADM steps and did not develop recommended deliverables), but rather implemented something else instead. At this stage, both my practical observations and literature studies unequivocally indicated that all EA frameworks, as well as all other conceptually similar EA methodologies[23], are purest management fads based only on anecdotal promises and self-proclaimed authority of their own authors, but having no examples of successful practical implementation.

At the same time, in real organizations I discovered an entirely new unexplored world of actual EA best practices significantly different from the "imaginary" best practices recommended by EA frameworks[24]. Moreover, my observations from visiting multiple different organizations with established EA practices also suggested that solid EA best practices existed in industry for a pretty long time and were successfully adopted by many organizations, though they were not formally studied, conceptualized or codified anywhere. Instead, genuine EA best practices were conveyed only in the minds of individual architects, learned from practical experience, transferred verbally and spread gradually from architects to architects, from organizations to organizations. To my further amazement, unlike the chaos I witnessed in the EA literature, these EA best practices turned out remarkably consistent even across diverse organizations. These curious observations raised a new series of surprising questions regarding the inexplicable relationship between the EA literature and practice. If the typical frameworks-inspired recommendations found in literature are impractical, then why does nobody try to openly criticize and reject them as ineffective?[25] If consistent EA best practices exist in industry for many years, then why does nobody try to analyze, document and spread them? If the gaps between the EA literature and practice are so evident, then why does nobody try to close them? If information systems and their effective planning are so important to modern organizations, then why is the existing literature on information systems planning still largely based on management fads?

My further academic experience and a deeper understanding of the consulting market revealed that the uncovered paradoxical situation in the EA discipline is, in fact, perfectly natural and unsurprising, rather than accidental or astonishing. This situation logically follows from the very essence of the current consulting industry and academia. On the one hand, consultancies are merely commercial organizations. Their main goal is to make profits, rather than study and disseminate best practices. Consultancies are generally eager to sell whatever can be successfully sold regardless of its real practical effectiveness[26]. The main purpose of their publication activities is to create hype and promote their own services, rather than critically and objectively analyze the industry situation[27]. Numerous self-proclaimed "acknowledged thought leaders", "highly demanded speakers", "sought-after international experts", "globally recognized trainers", "certified consultants", "presidents", "fathers", witchdoctors and snake oil salesmen earn considerable profits in the muddy waters of EA frameworks by means of speculating on non-existing best practices, magical recipes and silver bullets. Obviously, these people may not be interested in spreading genuine evidence-based EA best practices and in demystifying the concept of enterprise architecture in general. On the other hand, academics are generally interested only in publishing their research in the top ranking academic journals in order to get their promotions and secure their positions in universities[28]. However, the current mechanism of peer-reviewed academic journals in information systems is pathologically obsessed with so-called theoretical contributions and does not favor any practically valuable research[29]. Unsurprisingly, academic researchers are much more interested in developing new, more advanced theories infinitely distant from the practical realities than in discussing problems with the existing theories or realigning the established theoretical foundation to new empirical facts. Essentially, most EA academics feel perfectly comfortable with EA frameworks, while the unpleasant fact that their recommendations are simply impractical only distracts academics from more important theorizing and does not attract any significant attention in the EA research community[30]. As a result, for the last fifteen years of active research[31] academic EA scholars were generally unable not only to develop an alternative evidence-based EA guidance instead of impractical EA frameworks, but even to acknowledge the faddish nature of popular frameworks and identify the existence of considerable gaps between the current EA theory and practice. This sad fact arguably signifies that the current academic research in information systems is simply ill-organized and hardly brings any real practical value.

Essentially, everybody on the market of EA-related ideas is merely doing his own work. Consultants sell faddish innovative approaches of questionable quality to increase their profits, while academics in their "ivory towers" publish semi-philosophical theories to increase their citation indices. However, seemingly no one seriously cares about the essential needs of real practitioners, organizations and societies[32]. In particular, no one aims to analyze and spread actual best practices in using enterprise architecture for improving business and IT alignment, which can help EA practitioners be more effective, help organizations be more profitable and help societies be more prosperous. Surprisingly, it turns out that studying genuine time-proven EA best practices is simply no one's job.

This fact served as the main motivation for writing this book. In the 21st century the use of enterprise architecture for IT planning is arguably essential for all large organizations, including private, public and even non-profit ones. However, a meaningful conceptualization and detailed description of an EA practice in the EA literature is still missing[33]. Despite the critical importance of effective information systems planning for modern organizations, the existing practitioner and academic EA literature, with some notable exceptions[34], essentially has nothing to show except useless management fads, speculative theories and vague consultant-speak[35]. Systematic, comprehensive and evidence-based descriptions of working EA practices are incredibly hard to find. Moreover, with the current academic traditions and consulting approaches sensible descriptions of EA best practices might never appear in print[36].

Presently actual EA best practices are known only to a pretty narrow and closed community of experienced architects, while for all other "unprivileged" people an EA practice still remains largely an inscrutable black magic practiced by wizards and surrounded by endless gossips, myths and speculations. Unsurprisingly, essentially the only possible way for a newbie architect to acquire an understanding of the established EA best practices is to join an organization successfully using enterprise architecture and learn these best practices from more senior colleagues, who intuitively know what to do based on their own practical experience. Put it simply, at the present moment the only way to understand enterprise architecture is to start working with people who already understand enterprise architecture[37].

Ironically, while the use of enterprise architecture for information systems planning can be considered among the most noticeable management innovations of the last two decades, the available EA literature generally more resembles typical marketing puffery and is shamefully shallow, esoteric and unrealistic. While proven EA best practices exist in industry and familiar to many experienced architects, a meaningful description and analysis of these best practices is currently not available on the bookshelves. This book intends to finally close this important gap and present a systematic, comprehensive and research-based description of established industry best practices in the EA discipline.

The Subject of This Book

The main subject of this book is what is now generally known as "enterprise architecture". However, the very term "enterprise architecture" is rather vague and used inconsistently. It has multiple different definitions in literature, means different things to different people and is often confused with the closely related terms "IT architecture" and "information systems architecture" (each of these terms is arguably even more obscure and used even more inconsistently). Without diving into complex terminological disputes, it would be fair to say that the key subject of this book is effective organization-wide information systems planning. In other words, regardless of the preferred terminology, this book describes how global IT planning is carried out in modern organizations. This book considers the multifaceted phenomenon of organization-wide information systems planning in its full complexity and intends to cover all relevant aspects of information systems planning in organizations, including all involved actors, documents and processes, as well as their interrelationship.

At the same time, business strategy, decision-making, enterprise modeling, system architecture and information systems themselves are not the subject of this book. Even though this book touches all these topics to the extent to which it is necessary from the perspective of information systems planning, the real subject of this book is somewhere "between" these topics and essentially represents a complex overlapping of all these topics. From this point of view, the subject of this book can be formulated as an effective translation of the organizational business strategy through specific decision-making procedures leveraging enterprise modeling techniques into the implementable system architectures of concrete information systems.

The Uniqueness of This Book

The general attitude taken in this book makes it a rather unique product on the bookshelves. On the one hand, this book represents arguably the first deliberate attempt to provide a research-based, consistent and comprehensive description of EA best practices in their full complexity from both the conceptual and practical perspectives. On the other hand, this book specifically intends to study, analyze and describe existing EA best practices that proved effective in industry, rather than trying to invent, propose, prescribe or "sell" some new best practices. Due to its distinctive approach, this book has a number of specific features distinguishing it from most other available books on enterprise architecture.

Based on Original Research and Direct Empirical Evidence

This book is entirely based on a comprehensive analysis of the empirical evidence provided by EA practitioners from real organizations with established EA practices. Unlike many other speculative books on enterprise architecture, which often describe unseen anecdotal best practices invented by their own authors, provide superficial overviews of existing EA frameworks and methodologies or merely retranslate some ideas proposed earlier by other authors, this book relies mostly on the first-hand evidence collected directly from numerous architects. Essentially, this book reports on what has actually been discovered in multiple organizations practicing enterprise architecture. All the essential conclusions of this book are based on the original empirical research conducted by the author. Importantly, this book does not include any descriptions or conceptual models of questionable empirical validity abundant in the existing EA literature, but relies only on what has been proven to work more or less successfully with available empirical evidence.

Descriptive and Analytical Attitude

This book is analytical and descriptive in nature. It analyzes and documents the current EA best practices existing in industry. Unlike many other available books on enterprise architecture providing simplistic step-by-step prescriptions, which usually signify shallow management fads, this book intends to describe EA practices in their full complexity and offers no quick recipes or easy answers to complex questions[38]. This book also does not attempt to speculate on what should be, what should happen or how organizations must work, but rather describes what actually is. Moreover, this book does not propose any novel EA methodologies or new better approaches competing with other approaches. Instead, the purpose of this book is to analyze and describe as objectively as possible what enterprise architecture is and how successful EA practices work in real organizations.

Describes Industry-Born Best Practices

This book describes authentic time-tested best practices in using enterprise architecture for achieving business and IT alignment that were born in industry. Unlike many other available books on enterprise architecture, which describe various branded EA methodologies "proposed" by different consultancies, academics and gurus, this book describes the approaches to using enterprise architecture that emerged, gradually matured and proved effective in industry[39]. These approaches, even if resemble branded EA methodologies in some aspects, crystallized naturally out of the practical experience, successes and failures of numerous architects in organizations, rather than were created artificially in any consulting companies or university labs.

Both Practical and Conceptual Perspective

This book offers practical descriptions of an EA practice in real organizational terms as well as high-level conceptual models explaining the overall mechanics of an EA practice in general. In line with Kurt Lewin's famous saying that "there is nothing more practical than a good theory", this book intends to present theoretically sound conceptual models describing an EA practice of immediate practical value to down-to-earth EA practitioners. On the one hand, this book has a very practical attitude and deliberately avoids any discussions of pure philosophy irrelevant to practice. It attempts to provide easy-to-understand and well-structured descriptions of complex EA-related questions to shape the pragmatic practical thinking around enterprise architecture. On the other hand, key descriptions provided by this book also represent interrelated conceptual models intended to deepen our theoretical understanding of enterprise architecture. The full set of these conceptual models arguably presents a consistent and comprehensive theoretical view of an EA practice explaining the existing logical connections between its different elements and aspects, e.g. documents, processes and actors. Essentially, one of the main aims of this book is to bridge the evident gap between the current EA theory and practice by providing a set of theoretical models very closely aligned to the practical realities and needs of enterprise architecture.

Systematic and Comprehensive Approach

This book takes a holistic perspective and provides a systematic and comprehensive description of an EA practice. Unlike many other available books on enterprise architecture, which often focus on specific narrow aspects of an EA practice and discuss them in isolation, this book attempts to cover all practically significant aspects of an EA practice and their relationship with each other. On the one hand, this book considers an EA practice as a complex socio-technical system of interrelated actors, documents, processes and other elements, describes the connections and interactions between all relevant elements of this system and thereby explains how the entire system of an EA practice works as a single mechanism. On the other hand, this book intends to provide a comprehensive end-to-end description of an EA practice including all important EA-related topics. However, certainly not all aspects of an EA practice have been studied and understood sufficiently to provide their evidence-based in-depth descriptions. For these aspects this book provides only high-level descriptions corresponding to the current level of understanding of these aspects.

Introduces Novel Conceptualizations

This book introduces brand new theoretical conceptualizations of enterprise architecture and an EA practice, which resulted directly from the analysis of the first-hand empirical evidence. Due to the questionable and non-empirical nature of most existing EA-related theoretical models, many of which have been derived directly from popular faddish EA frameworks, these models cannot be trusted or taken as the basis for a meaningful analysis of real EA practices[40]. Essentially, this book attempts to reconceptualize the notion of enterprise architecture from scratch in order to align the theoretical understanding of EA practices to empirical realities.

Reflects the Perspective of Organizations, Not of External Consultants

This book discusses an EA practice from the perspective of organizations practicing enterprise architecture, rather than from the perspective of external consultants engaged by organizations to develop EA documents. This difference in perspectives between organizations and consultancies is extremely important for the EA discipline. External EA consultants often treat consulting engagements as one-shot planning projects and get paid merely for producing some EA documents, but may be not really interested in the ultimate fate of these documents, i.e. what will eventually happen with these documents after they leave the organization and go to the next client. Consequently, an EA practice from the perspective of consulting companies can be essentially equated with creating EA documents[41]. However, organizations can hardly get any business value simply from having some EA documents, but only from using these documents for specific purposes. Investments in developing useless EA documents represent pure profits for consultancies and pure losses for organizations. Hence, the best practices of EA consultants naturally focus on creating and "selling" more EA documents regardless of their real usefulness, while the best practices of organizations focus on maintaining and using pragmatic sets of value-adding EA documents. Unsurprisingly, the best practices of EA consulting engagements may be significantly different from the best practices of organizations using enterprise architecture internally. Consultants' EA best practices may even be organizations' EA worst practices[42]. This book is focused on describing the perspective of organizations as the actual end users of enterprise architecture.

Placed in the Context of the Existing Literature

This book is placed in the context of the current EA literature and refers to other available EA publications where appropriate. Specifically, references to other relevant publications with explanatory comments are generally provided in four difference cases. Firstly, references to other publications are provided when some information provided in the book is taken from these original publications. Secondly, references to other publications are provided when similar ideas have been expressed earlier by other authors. Thirdly, references to other publications are provided when some notable ideas in these publications evidently contradict the established empirical facts. Fourthly, references to other publications are provided to connect the ideas expressed in the book with broader research streams and position them in the overall theoretical context. The text of this book contains ample references to other EA publications, which explain the relationship between the ideas expressed in this book and the existing body of knowledge.

The Intended Audience of This Book

This book is intended for a broad readership, including EA practitioners, academics, students and all other people interested in modern approaches to information systems planning. It does not require any previous theoretical knowledge or practical experience with enterprise architecture, though some general understanding of business and IT is highly desirable.

Firstly, this book may be valuable for EA practitioners and other senior IT specialists. It is written in a practical language accessible to down-to-earth architects and intends to offer reasonable actionable suggestions for establishing successful EA practices in organizations. It provides a comprehensive set of reference models and "tools for thinking" covering all the essential aspects of an EA practice from the practical perspective.

Secondly, this book may be valuable for EA academics and researchers. It consolidates the available theoretical knowledge and provides a number of solid, research-based conceptual models explaining the notion of enterprise architecture which can be taken as the basis for further

EA research. Moreover, it contains a rich bibliography and, where appropriate, explains the relationship between the presented ideas and earlier EA publications putting the narrative in the context of the existing EA literature.

Thirdly, this book may be valuable for students interested in enterprise architecture and their teachers. It is written in a sequential manner, does not require any prior knowledge of enterprise architecture and can provide a sound introduction to the EA discipline for beginners. It can be also used by lecturers for developing EA curricula and teaching enterprise architecture courses to undergraduate and postgraduate students in universities.

Materials for This Book

The materials underpinning this book come from the extensive empirical research and comprehensive literature analysis conducted by the author. In particular, the key conclusions of this book are based on the following main sources:

- Analysis of more than 1700 diverse publications on enterprise architecture and more than 500 earlier pre-EA publications on information systems planning that appeared in print since the 1960s, including available books, academic papers, conference proceedings, industry reports, vendor materials, web pages and some other publications
- Initial in-depth case studies of six large Australian organizations practicing enterprise architecture for at least 3-5 years from the banking, telecom, retail, delivery and education industry sectors, including one organization with an award-winning EA practice
- Subsequent mini-case studies of 21 diverse Australian, New Zealand and international organizations with established and reasonably mature EA practices from different industry sectors
- Additional mini-case studies of four Australian consulting companies providing EA-related services and four Australian organizations with rudimentary or immature EA practices
- More than 20 finalizing interviews with Australian, European and U.S. architects and EA academics where the key resulting findings have been discussed, validated and confirmed

In total, the empirical part of the research undertaken for this book includes more than a hundred interviews with architects from 35 different organizations (27 with more or less mature EA practices, four with immature EA practices and four consulting companies) of various sizes (ranging from only ~35 to several thousand IT staff and from only one to a few hundred architects) representing diverse industry sectors (banking, insurance, telecom, energy, utilities, manufacturing, delivery, marketing, food, retail, education, healthcare, emergency services, government agencies and some other industries). Generally, the content of this book is based either on the primary data collected directly by the author in the studied organizations, or on the secondary data found in other research-based EA publications substantiated by empirical evidence. The core conceptual model of this book, the CSVLOD model of enterprise architecture, has been confirmed by multiple independent EA practitioners and academics.

The Structure of This Book

This book consists of nineteen consecutive chapters organized into three core parts and a separate complementary appendix. Part I (Introduction to Enterprise Architecture) provides a general introduction to the concept of enterprise architecture and other relevant topics. In particular, Chapter 1 (Introduction) discusses the role of IT in modern organizations, explains the problem of business and IT alignment and introduces the notion of enterprise architecture as a potential solution to this problem. Chapter 2 (The Concept of Enterprise Architecture) explains the general meaning of enterprise architecture, EA practice and EA artifacts as well as the role of architects and architecture functions in organizations. Chapter 3 (The Role of Enterprise Architecture Practice) discusses the need for enterprise architecture, the benefits of practicing enterprise architecture, the historical origin of modern EA best practices and clarifies what enterprise architecture practice is not. Chapter 4 (Enterprise Architecture and City Planning) explains the key mechanisms of an EA practice and six essential types of EA artifacts based on the close analogy between enterprise architecture and city planning practices. Chapter 5 (The Dialog Between Business and IT) discusses the typical problems associated with using a business strategy as the basis for IT planning and describes five convenient discussion points for establishing a productive dialog between business and IT. Chapter 6 (Processes of Enterprise Architecture Practice) describes three key processes constituting an EA practice, explains the relationship between these processes and provides a high-level process-centric view of an EA practice. Finally, Chapter 7 (IT Initiatives and Enterprise Architecture) discusses the role of IT initiatives in the context of an EA practice, describes five different types of IT initiatives and explains the flow of these initiatives through the processes of an EA practice.

Part II (Enterprise Architecture Artifacts) focuses specifically on EA artifacts as the core elements of an EA practice. Firstly, Chapter 8 (The CSVLOD Model of Enterprise Architecture) describes in detail the CSVLOD model of enterprise architecture defining six general types of EA artifacts: Considerations, Standards, Visions, Landscapes, Outlines and Designs. Then, the subsequent chapters provide an in-depth discussion of these key types of EA artifacts. Specifically, Chapter 9 (Considerations) discusses Considerations as a general type of EA artifacts and describes in detail popular narrow subtypes of Considerations including Principles, Policies, Conceptual Data Models, Analytical Reports and Direction Statements. Chapter 10 (Standards) discusses Standards as a general type of EA artifacts and describes in detail popular narrow subtypes of Standards including Technology Reference Models, Guidelines, Patterns, IT Principles and Logical Data Models. Chapter 11 (Visions) discusses Visions as a general type of EA artifacts and describes in detail popular narrow subtypes of Visions including Business Capability Models, Roadmaps, Target States, Value Chains and Context Diagrams. Chapter 12 (Landscapes) discusses Landscapes as a general type of EA artifacts and describes in detail popular narrow subtypes of Landscapes including Landscape Diagrams, Inventories, Enterprise System Portfolios and IT Roadmaps. Chapter 13 (Outlines) discusses Outlines as a general type of EA artifacts and describes in detail popular narrow subtypes of Outlines including Solution Overviews, Options Assessments and Initiative Proposals. Chapter 14 (Designs) discusses Designs as a general type of EA artifacts and describes in detail popular narrow subtypes of Designs including Solution Designs and Preliminary Solution Designs. Finally, Chapter 15 (The CSVLOD Model Revisited) revisits the CSVLOD model of enterprise architecture introduced earlier and provides an advanced discussion of some important aspects of this model including the continuous nature of the classification taxonomy, the mappings of specific EA artifacts and the known exceptions to the model.

Part III (Other Aspects of Enterprise Architecture) provides a high-level discussion of other important aspects of enterprise architecture and an EA practice. In particular, Chapter 16 (Architects in Enterprise Architecture Practice) discusses the role and skills of architects, common architecture positions often found in organizations, their differences and relationship. Chapter 17 (Architecture Functions in Organizations) discusses the general role and structure of architecture functions in organizations as well as the roles and different types of architecture governance bodies. Chapter 18 (Instruments for Enterprise Architecture) discusses specialized modeling languages and software tools for enterprise architecture, templates for EA artifacts, architecture debt and quantitative measurements for an EA practice. Finally, Chapter 19 (The Lifecycle of Enterprise Architecture Practice) discusses the initiation of an EA practice in organizations, maturity of an EA practice and the role of external consultants in an EA practice.

Additionally, Appendix (The Origin of EA and Modern EA Best Practices) provides an extended discussion and analysis of the complex historical origin of the modern EA discipline and corresponding best practices described in this book.

A Note on the Used Terminology

Unfortunately, the EA discipline currently suffers from the lack of a consistent, clearly defined and commonly accepted terminology. An ongoing controversy in the EA community suggests that it is often hard to reach an agreement between two architects even on the basic EA-related questions. For example, it is still debatable where exactly the boundaries of an EA practice are, which exactly documents should be considered as EA artifacts, where exactly the border between "true enterprise architecture" and "just IT architecture" lies and whether enterprise architecture is mostly about IT or, on the contrary, not about IT at all. It is arguably hard to come up even with a clear definition of the very term "enterprise architecture" everyone can agree on[43]. Similarly, the interviewing experience gained as part of the data collection process for this book shows that numerous more specific EA-related terms, including the titles of particular EA artifacts, EA-related processes and architecture positions, also can be very organization-specific, individual-specific and even country-specific. Moreover, even more general terms playing important roles in the context of an EA practice (e.g. "business strategy", "IT strategy" and "operating model") often mean different things to different people in different situations. At the same time, excessive commercial hype and endless Chinese whispers around enterprise architecture further aggravated this situation, lead to more serious semantic diffusion of the EA-related terminology and even engendered new paradoxical reinterpretations of some basic notions[44].

Due to these terminological problems existing in the EA discipline, it is simply impossible to stick with the one widely accepted set of EA-related terms intuitively understandable to everyone. Hence, readers may find the terminology used in this book somewhat different from the terminology used in their organizations or in other available sources on enterprise architecture. However, the utmost care has been taken to achieve a solid terminological consistency within this book. Readers are encouraged to pay close attention to definitions and descriptions of the key notions used in the book (bolded when first introduced), which may not always accurately correspond with the intuitive understanding of their one-word or two-word titles. In other words, some terms found on these pages may not always be interpreted literally. For better coherence the titles of the most important concepts introduced in this book are capitalized. These concepts include general types of EA artifacts (e.g. Visions and Landscapes), narrow subtypes of EA artifacts (e.g. Business Capability Models and Landscape Diagrams) as well as main EA-related processes (e.g. Strategic Planning and Initiative Delivery).

Acknowledgements

With the rare exceptions explicitly acknowledged in endnote comments, I am the sole author of this book and all the ideas presented on these pages are mine. However, I am extremely grateful to numerous people who helped shape these ideas and thereby implicitly contributed to this book. Firstly, for the core empirical part of my research, or field studies, I am deeply indebted to more than 80 EA practitioners and other IT professionals who kindly agreed to spend their precious time to participate in my inquiry, answer my questions, share their best practices and validate the resulting conceptualizations. Without the crucial contribution of all these people this book would have never been written. Due to strict confidentially requirements and anonymity guaranteed to each interviewee, I cannot thank personally all the architects who participated in my research, but only those people who gave me their explicit written permission to mention their names on these pages. Accordingly, I would like to wholeheartedly thank Adam Hart, Adrian van Raay, Andrew Schafer, Chao Cheng-Shorland, Dan Maslin, Darren Sandford, David Johnston-Bell, Eetu Niemi, Frank Amodeo, George Hobbs, Graeme Grogan, Ian Edmondstone, Igor Aleksenitser, Jayshree Ravi, Jeetendra Bhardwaj, Justin Klvac, Ken Ke, Mark Virgin, Martin van den Berg, Michael Baird, Michael Gill, Michael Lambrellis, Michael Scales, Niall Smith, Nic Bishop, Nick Malik, Peter Mitchell, Ralph Foorthuis, Roy Cushan, Sarath Chandran, Scott Draffin, Simon Peisker, Stephen Oades, Suresh Venkatachalaiah, Sven Brook and Tim Liddelow for their truly invaluable contribution to my study.

Secondly, for the historical part of my research I am very grateful to the staff of the RMIT library and specifically to the team of its document delivery services (DDS) unit. Most notably, I would like to thank Adrian Thomas, Alice Davies, Jennifer Phillips, Kirsty Batchelor and especially Marina Zovko and Tony Foley who somehow managed to provide heaps of ancient "antediluvian" texts on information systems planning required for my research often published about a half of a century ago. These rare books and articles, in some cases magically delivered at my request even from the overseas libraries of other universities and organizations, were of critical importance for untangling and systematizing the current curious situation in the EA discipline. Without the excellent work of these people my historical investigation of the EA discipline and its origins might have never been conducted. In particular, the unique appendix of this book (The Origin of EA and Modern EA Best Practices) would have been missing.

Finally, I would like to express a special thank and gratitude to my friend Mikhail Efremov for all the good things.

Svyatoslav Kotusev (kotusev@kotusev.com)
Melbourne, Australia
December 2017

PART I: Introduction to Enterprise Architecture

Part I of this book provides a general introduction to the concept of enterprise architecture and other relevant topics. This part discusses the meaning of enterprise architecture, the place and role of enterprise architecture in the overall organizational context, key constituting elements and core mechanisms of an EA practice as well as the business value and benefits of using enterprise architecture in organizations.

Part I consists of seven consecutive chapters. Chapter 1 discusses the role of IT in modern organizations, explains the problem of business and IT alignment and introduces the notion of enterprise architecture as a potential solution to this problem. Chapter 2 explains the general meaning of enterprise architecture, EA practice and EA artifacts as well as the role of architects and architecture functions in organizations. Chapter 3 discusses the need for enterprise architecture, the benefits of practicing enterprise architecture, the historical origin of modern EA best practices and clarifies what enterprise architecture practice is not. Chapter 4 explains the key mechanisms of an EA practice and six essential types of EA artifacts based on the close analogy between enterprise architecture and city planning practices. Chapter 5 discusses the typical problems associated with using a business strategy as the basis for IT planning and describes five convenient discussion points for establishing a productive dialog between business and IT. Chapter 6 describes three key processes constituting an EA practice, explains the relationship between these processes and provides a high-level process-centric view of an EA practice. Chapter 7 discusses the role of IT initiatives in the context of an EA practice, describes five different types of IT initiatives and explains the flow of these initiatives through the processes of an EA practice.

Chapter 1: Introduction

This chapter provides a general introduction to this book and specifically to the notion of enterprise architecture. In particular, this chapter starts from discussing the critical importance of IT for modern business. Then, this chapter discusses modern organizations as complex socio-technical systems of business and IT and describes the problem of achieving business and IT alignment. Finally, this chapter introduces the concept of enterprise architecture as a potential solution to the problem of business and IT alignment.

The Role of IT in Modern Organizations

Most organizations in the 21st century are critically dependent on information technology (IT) in their daily operations. In most private and public, commercial and non-commercial organizations IT systems became an essential infrastructure required to execute day-to-day business activities. Even small organizations cannot operate in the modern competitive environment without leveraging the support provided by information systems, while large organizations are often running and maintaining thousands of various IT systems enabling their businesses. Information systems help run business processes, store business data and facilitate internal communication within organizations.

Due to the steadily growing computing power and functional capabilities of available IT systems, their influence on business models of various organizations is continuously increasing. Since their inception in the end of the 1950s, the role of information systems in organizations gradually evolved from a purely technical and supporting function (e.g. numerical calculations and batch data processing) to a more strategic or even business-enabling function[1]. As a result, many financial and telecommunication organizations essentially already turned into IT companies specializing in finance and telecommunications. Even more traditional industries, including agriculture, construction or education, are profoundly impacted by groundbreaking IT-driven trends.

Emerging IT technologies constantly open new opportunities for organizations to optimize current business processes, eliminate known inefficiencies and restructure existing business units. Due to their innovative potential and transformative capacity, information systems often become a backbone of major organizational changes and reorganizations. For many modern organizations the successful execution of any business strategy may be largely equivalent to the successful delivery of corresponding information systems implementing this strategy.

Unsurprisingly, capital investments in IT systems and infrastructure in organizations are steadily increasing over the last decades. For instance, in the United States private business investments in IT, including hardware, software and communications equipment, increased from less than 100 billion dollars in 1980 to more than 500 billion dollars in 2010. Moreover, the proportion of IT investments in total capital investments grew from 32% in 1980 to 52% in 2010[2]. IT budgets of private and public organizations in different industry sectors are growing accordingly. For instance, over the decade from 2007 to 2017 average IT budgets as a percentage of overall revenue increased almost by 75%, from 3.50% of revenue in 2007 to 6.08% of revenue in 2017[3].

Over the time, information systems become more powerful, ubiquitous, diverse and affordable. The computing power and storage capacity of IT systems are increasing exponentially[4]. Complex business applications now can be deployed on dedicated mainframe servers, hosted in the cloud, run in web browsers or even installed on handheld mobile devices of thousands of users. Available packaged business-oriented information systems include customizable enterprise resource planning (ERP), customer relationship management (CRM), supply chain management (SCM), business intelligence (BI), enterprise content management (ECM), knowledge management (KM) and many other systems from various global and local vendors[5]. At the same time, the relative price of information systems is gradually decreasing making different IT systems more accessible to organizations than ever before. Even smallest organizations now can benefit from using simple cloud-hosted subscription-based IT solutions for accounting, finance and human resource management.

The productive use of information systems for improving the quality of business processes in organizations is not equivalent merely to installing the appropriate software and hardware, but always requires consistent and coordinated changes in three broad organizational aspects: people, processes and technology[6]. In order to successfully introduce any new high-impact IT system, an organization should properly address each of these three essential aspects. Specifically, addressing the people aspect may include, among others, the following actions:

- Providing the necessary education and training to future users of the new IT system
- Explaining the benefits of using the new IT system and coping with resistance
- Dealing with political and power redistribution issues associated with the new IT system
- Modifying attitudes and cultural prejudices regarding the new IT system

Addressing the process aspect may include, but is not limited to, the following actions:

- Introducing new business processes enabled by the new IT system
- Modifying existing business processes affected by the new IT system
- Discontinuing redundant business processes automated by the new IT system
- Modifying decision-making procedures and rules related to the new IT system

Finally, addressing the technology aspect may include, among many others, the following actions:

- Setting up the new IT system and required underlying infrastructure
- Making the new IT system available to its end users and granting proper access rights
- Providing help desk support to end users of the new IT system
- Ensuring technical support, monitoring and maintenance of the new IT system

The proper use of information systems can deliver numerous business benefits and open multiple innovative opportunities to organizations. For instance, IT systems can help improve business processes, reduce costs and delays, enable analytical capabilities, support executive decision-making, enable timely information sharing with partners, facilitate effective knowledge exchange between employees, support collaboration and cooperation, provide new customer communication channels, create new innovative products and services or even develop entirely new business models. Essentially, appropriate information systems can bring tangible business value to virtually any organization in any industry sector.

Information systems can help organizations execute their business strategies and gain strategic competitive advantage. In particular, organizations can use their IT systems to achieve the competitive advantage in the following areas[7]:

- Operational excellence and cost leadership – IT systems can be used to fully automate operations, eliminate delays and deviations, avoid manual labor and achieve standardized, fine-tuned and predictable business processes
- Product differentiation and leadership – IT systems can be used to facilitate the design of new products, support teamwork, collaboration and creativity and provide unique innovative products or services to the market
- Customer intimacy and focus – IT systems can be used to collect and store customer data, analyze customer needs and preferences, identify broad customer segments, target specific customer groups and even develop highly customized offers for particular customers

However, the dynamic technological environment of the 21st century not only creates the opportunities for improving existing and developing new products and services, but also poses considerable threats to many organizations[8]. So-called **disruptive technologies** have the potential to make entire industries ineffective or even irrelevant, displace current market leaders and reshape the global competitive landscape[9]. For instance, recently the publishing industry has been significantly disrupted by electronic books (e-books), while the recording industry has been disrupted by the Internet-based delivery of audio files[10]. Similarly, the emergence of radio-frequency identification (RFID) tags represented a disruptive technological trend for logistic, shipping and delivery companies. Today the rapid propagation of mobile devices, big data, Facebook, Twitter, YouTube and other social media can be considered as a dangerous and potentially disruptive trend for many industries. Tomorrow the Internet of things, industrial 3D printing, artificial intelligence, blockchain-based technologies, electric and driverless cars may disrupt many conventional industries. Unsurprisingly, disruptive technologies are of critical interest to business executives and can dramatically change the business strategies of many organizations[11].

Due to the critical importance and impact of information on the modern society, the proper use of information systems in organizations became a subject of strict regulatory control. National governments of many countries have enacted legislative **compliance acts** intended to regulate access, sharing, transfer and protection of sensitive information stored in corporate IT systems. For instance, the Sarbanes-Oxley Act (SOX) and Health Insurance Portability and Accountability Act (HIPAA) in the United States, the General Data Protection Regulation (GDPR) in the European Union, as well as analogous legal acts existing in other countries, prescribe a complex set of norms for dealing with financial, private and health-related information. Organizations are liable for incompliance with various data protection acts established in their jurisdictions and might be subjected to heavy fines for the inappropriate use or handling of personal and commercially sensitive information. Moreover, the inability of organizations to provide required information for computer forensic procedures in a timely manner, as obliged by law in case of investigation, can lead to considerable fines as well.

Hence, information systems provide numerous benefits, opportunities, threats and obligations to organizations and their importance for business is only going to increase in the future. For this reason, effective control and conscious management of IT is extremely important for most organizations in the 21st century. The management and planning of information systems in organizations is no longer simply an IT job, but rather a direct responsibility of business executives[12].

Organizations as Socio-Technical Systems

Due to the ubiquitous use, proliferation and penetration of information systems in business, many or even most organizations in the 21st century essentially experience the convergence of business and IT. Currently even simplest routine business activities in most companies, large and small, are totally dependent on the underlying information systems. In many organizations no business operations whatsoever can be carried out without the appropriate support of IT. Business capabilities of a modern organization are often determined largely by the capabilities of its IT systems.

This convergence of business and IT implies an inextricable interrelationship between organizational business processes and information systems. From this perspective, modern organizations represent very complex **socio-technical systems** consisting of diverse but interacting human actors, business processes and IT systems united by a common purpose and goals[13]. The business of an organization can be viewed as a comprehensive set of all business capabilities that this organization can fulfill, where each business capability includes all the related roles, processes, information systems, data assets and physical facilities required to perform this capability. Essentially, business activities and IT landscapes enabling these activities in modern organizations represent "two sides of the same coin" and the one cannot exist without the other.

Moreover, modern organizations represent decentralized, dynamic and constantly evolving socio-technical systems. Typically organizations do not have a single center of power and decision-making accountable for all planning decisions. Instead, decision-making processes in organizations are usually distributed across multiple global and local decision-makers with different and often conflicting interests. Organizations can be also considered as self-evolving entities, where numerous actors belonging to the organizational system gradually modify the structure of this system by their daily decisions and actions. Separate actors, processes and IT assets in organizations get periodically modified and replaced without stopping or interrupting their routine business operations. Due to these reasons, organizations always evolve organically, rather than mechanically.

Business managers and IT specialists in modern organizations are mutually dependent partners with significantly different duties. On the one hand, business managers can be collectively considered roughly as a "frontend" of an organization responsible for analyzing the external business environment (e.g. market opportunities, customer needs and competitive moves) and determining the desirable direction for evolving the entire organizational system. On the other hand, IT specialists essentially constitute a "backend" of an organization responsible for modifying the IT landscape to enable the evolution of the organizational system towards the direction defined by business managers. Put it simply, business decides what needs to be done, while IT responds to these decisions. The view of a modern organization as a complex, decentralized, socio-technical system of business and IT is shown in Figure 1.1.

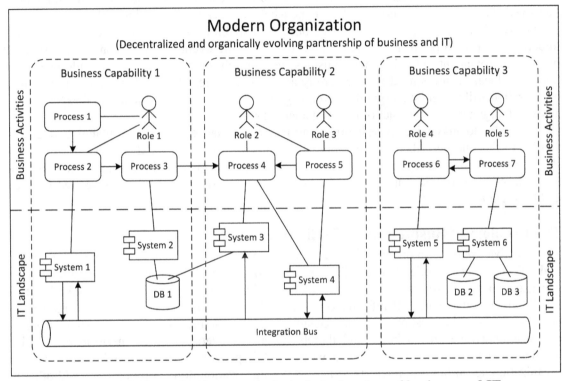

Figure 1.1. Organization as a socio-technical system of business and IT

The complex and decentralized nature of modern organizations consisting of closely interrelated business and IT components has at least two critical implications from the perspective of their planning. Firstly, one of the most important consequences of the convergence of business and IT is the necessity to synchronize all the ongoing changes in business and IT parts of an organization[14]. Incremental improvements in separate business processes usually correspond to limited modifications in the underlying information systems, while considerable business transformations often correspond to significant reorganizations of the entire IT landscape.

Secondly, as complex systems consisting of multiple parts, organizations should be planned based on the balance of global and local interests. On the one hand, some planning decisions can be optimal for particular business units or areas, but suboptimal for an organization as a whole. On the other hand, some planning decisions can be desirable from the organization-wide perspective, but ignore the vital needs of specific business units. Effective planning decisions should take into account and respect the strategic needs of an entire organization as well as the tactical needs of separate business units.

For example, local business leaders can decide to optimize a particular business process to substantially improve the corresponding business capability, which may be a very good idea on its own. However, if the desirable process changes require developing an additional information system, introducing a completely new technology or duplicating master data, then these business improvements might be unreasonably expensive or technically undesirable from the IT perspective. Furthermore, if the respective business capability is not considered as strategically important from the organization-wide perspective, then the overall contribution of the proposed process improvement to the long-term business goals might be negligible. As a result, even if an important local business need is successfully addressed, the resulting added value for the whole organization still might be marginal or even negative depending on the incurred IT expenses and an overall organizational impact of the implemented solution.

In order to maximize overall organizational performance, ineffective planning decisions similar to the one described above should be avoided. Organizations should try to align both short-term and long-term changes in their IT landscapes to their business plans, strategies and goals. In other words, it is imperative for modern organizations to strive for so-called business and IT alignment[15].

The Problem of Business and IT Alignment

The effective use of IT in organizations requires achieving business and IT alignment[16]. **Business and IT alignment** implies that the IT goals, IT plans and IT systems in an organization are consistent with its business goals, business plans and business processes[17]. Put it simply, business and IT alignment is when all information systems in an organization correspond to its genuine business needs in the most optimal way. Business and IT alignment increases the payoff from the organizational investments in IT and thereby improves overall business performance[18]. Ideal business and IT alignment is achieved when all IT specialists working on IT projects in an organization act in the best interests of the whole organization defined by its CEO and other C-level executives, i.e. when all IT projects enhance the general quality of the entire organizational system (see Figure 1.1). More specifically, perfect business and IT alignment is achieved when each IT project:

- Fulfills local short-term business needs and requirements
- Contributes to global long-term strategic goals and objectives
- Is implemented in a predictable, cost-effective and risk-free manner
- Leverages and reuses available IT assets existing in an organization
- Does not create redundant IT assets that need to be maintained in the future
- Can be leveraged as an IT asset in next IT projects if appropriate
- Is built on technologies that the organization plans to continue using in the future
- Is implemented consistently with other similar IT projects
- Does not introduce complexity beyond necessity

In order to achieve business and IT alignment, the whole organization should strive to act essentially as a single "big brain" always making best globally and locally optimized business and IT decisions in all areas based on all available information from both the internal and external environments. However, no organizational actors are competent enough to make such optimal planning decisions alone on behalf of the whole organization and powerful enough to enact the subsequent implementation of these decisions. For this reason, business and IT alignment requires *collective* decision-making with the involvement of multiple organizational actors. Specifically, the alignment between business and IT in practice can be achieved only through the effective coordination of all business and IT-related changes between all relevant stakeholders of these changes. Ideally, all proposed changes in organizations should be understood and approved by their key business and IT stakeholders to ensure that these changes satisfy their essential concerns and interests.

Diversity of Actors Involved in Business and IT Alignment

Perfect business and IT alignment is not easily achievable in practice. In real organizations ideal business and IT alignment requires achieving complete mutual understanding and agreement between all relevant actors involved in business and IT decision-making as well as in implementation of IT systems. These actors work in different areas of the organization and occupy different levels of the organizational hierarchy. They have different positions, responsibilities, backgrounds, education, competences, expertise, goals, objectives, interests, concerns, planning horizons, personalities, mindsets and perceptions of reality. Essentially, from the perspective of business and IT alignment relevant actors include almost all business managers and IT specialists in an organization, ranging from the CEO to junior software developers. Moreover, even IT departments of largest organizations typically do not employ IT specialists knowledgeable in all the technologies required to develop, run and maintain the entire IT landscape. As a result, many IT projects in organizations are delivered via consulting or outsourcing arrangements by competent partners and vendors specialized in corresponding technologies. These external third parties involved in the implementation of IT systems on behalf of client organizations can be considered as relevant actors from the perspective of business and IT alignment as well.

Unsurprisingly, achieving meaningful coordination between a large number of very diverse actors poses a significant challenge for organizations. Specifically, three different aspects of diversity between relevant actors can be accountable for most problems with poor coordination of plans and activities from the perspective of business and IT alignment. Firstly, all relevant actors can be roughly separated into business actors and IT actors. On the one hand, **business actors** are knowledgeable in business strategy and processes, business opportunities and problems, customer needs and preferences, competitive advantages and disadvantages, relevant laws and regulations, market share and profits. Business actors barely understand IT and typically consider IT-related talks as a meaningless techno-babble. On the other hand, **IT actors** are knowledgeable in technologies, systems, vendor packages, applications, programming languages, databases, operating systems, servers, networks and other hardware. IT actors, even if they are able to understand the business terminology, may not understand the relative importance or irrelevance of different software and hardware for the overall business performance of an organization from the perspective of its business actors. This disparity of knowledge and backgrounds impedes the mutual understanding between business and IT actors[19].

Secondly, all relevant actors can be roughly separated into strategic actors and tactical actors. On the one hand, **strategic actors** are concerned with a long-range strategic business and IT planning, global emerging trends in the business and IT environments, organization-wide business and IT capabilities, strategic partnerships, disruptive influences and other fundamental factors that might influence the business of an entire organization in the long run. Strategic actors may be unaware of how exactly their high-level plans can be implemented "on the ground" or ignorant of the critical tactical needs, demands and problems of separate business units. On the other hand, **tactical actors** are concerned with tactical business and IT planning, carrying out particular business processes in business units, introducing specific local changes, making incremental improvements, implementing concrete IT systems or projects and solving other urgent problems on a short time horizon. Tactical actors may not understand how exactly their activities aimed at achieving critical local short-term objectives contribute to the global long-term vision developed by strategic actors. This difference in planning horizons and scopes inhibits the agreement between strategic and tactical actors regarding the balance between long-term and short-term objectives, global and local needs, important and urgent demands.

Finally, all relevant actors can be roughly separated into internal actors and external actors. On the one hand, **internal actors** are well aware of the specifics of their own organization. They understand how their organization works, what roles, business processes, systems and technologies they have. Internal actors may be unaware of new prospective technologies, latest vendor offerings, specific features of available products or established industry best practices. On the other hand, **external actors** (e.g. consultants, partners, vendors and outsourcers) are well aware of the situation in their niche markets or areas. They are experts in their specific technologies, products or approaches and tend to implement latest industry best practices. External actors may not know organization-specific features of their client companies including their unique needs or opportunities, histories or cultures, peculiarities of their business processes or IT landscapes, legacy-driven standards or path-dependent limitations. This difference in perspectives impedes the effective communication between internal and external actors.

Main Groups of Actors Involved in Business and IT Alignment

The three aspects of diversity discussed above represent the main boundaries disconnecting and alienating different groups of decision-makers from each other. These boundaries prevent effective communication, mutual understanding and collaborative partnership between different actors undermining overall business and IT alignment in organizations[20]. Specifically, all relevant actors involved in strategic decision-making and implementation of IT systems can be loosely separated by these boundaries into five broad groups: business executives, IT executives, business unit managers, IT project teams and third parties. **Business executives** include all senior business managers responsible for strategic planning and making investment decisions, e.g. CEOs, other C-level executives and heads of business units. **IT executives** include all senior IT managers responsible for organizing the IT department according to the business needs, e.g. CIOs, IT directors, heads of IT delivery and support. **Business unit managers** include all business managers and operators responsible for running local routine business processes on a daily basis, e.g. ordinary sales managers, marketing specialists and product designers. **IT project teams** include all project managers and IT specialists responsible for implementing new IT projects, e.g. business analysts, software developers and infrastructure engineers. Finally, **third**

parties include all external consultants, vendors and outsourcers engaged to deliver specific IT solutions for organizations according to industry best practices. These five groups of relevant actors with their essential concerns separated by the three main boundaries are shown in Figure 1.2[21].

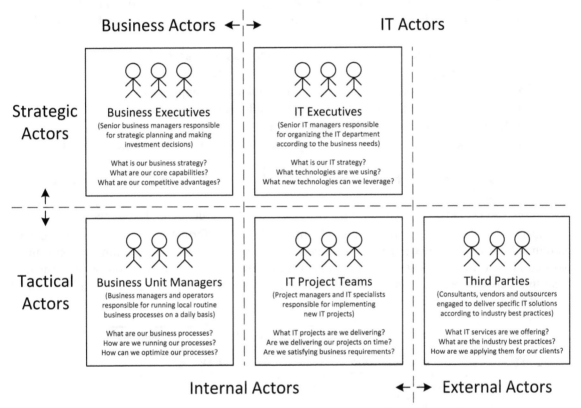

Figure 1.2. Main groups of actors and boundaries between them

Miscommunication Between Actors as a Reason of Misalignment

The three main boundaries shown in Figure 1.2 significantly complicate the communication, collaboration and mutual understanding between different groups of relevant actors in organizations from the perspective of business and IT alignment. At the same time, poor communication and the lack of mutual understanding between different actors often lead to inadequate information systems planning decisions, where the essential interests of relevant stakeholders, often conflicting ones, are not taken into account and neglected. Inadequate information systems planning in its turn eventually results in the general misalignment between business and IT, when IT projects address only some immediate needs, but unable to optimize the organizational system as a whole (see Figure 1.1). Poor business and IT alignment manifests itself in all kinds of IT-related inefficiencies in organizations, including the following and many other similar symptoms:

- IT projects uplift the least important business capabilities

- IT projects address urgent needs of local business units, but do not move the whole organization towards its long-term strategic business vision
- Business executives do not understand where IT budget is spent, what IT is delivering and when
- Different business units implement same business processes in different ways
- Different business units are unable to access the data they need for their operations
- The most commercially sensitive data is stored in the least secure IT systems
- Fragile legacy systems threaten critical business operations
- Frequent outages caused by unproven technologies or approaches
- The IT landscape is overly complex, inflexible and hard to change
- Each new IT project introduces a new expensive vendor product or technology
- Available platforms are not leveraged, all IT initiatives are implemented from scratch
- Established best practices are not reused, each new IT project "reinvents the wheel"
- The IT budget is spent on supporting duplicated or redundant IT systems

The list of potential problems caused by the inadequate information systems planning can be continued further, but the persistent misalignment between business and IT ultimately ends up in wasted IT investments, general disappointment in IT and reduced overall business performance. The link between poor communication, inadequate IT planning and the resulting misalignment between business and IT is shown in Figure 1.3.

Figure 1.3. Link between poor communication and business and IT misalignment

The problem of business and IT alignment is an unavoidable, inherent and natural problem of establishing effective communication between multiple heterogeneous groups of people with conflicting objectives and concerns. Unfortunately, this is an intractable problem with no easy and straightforward solutions. Improving business and IT alignment in organizations is a highly challenging, but important practical goal. Unsurprisingly, for the last four decades achieving business and IT alignment and improving information systems planning have consistently been among the top most important issues for IT executives[22].

Enterprise Architecture as a Solution

A set of special documents is often used in organizations to facilitate communication between different groups of relevant actors, improve information systems planning and thereby achieve business and IT alignment[23]. These special documents are collectively titled as enterprise architecture (EA). In other words, enterprise architecture is a collection of documents helping establish effective communication between all relevant actors involved in strategic decision-making and implementation of IT systems.

For each group of relevant actors (see Figure 1.2) EA documents provide the necessary information that satisfies their interests, reflects their concerns and answers their questions. EA documents help different actors collaborate and achieve mutual understanding despite their disparate roles, interests and expertise[24]. For instance, to business actors EA documents provide relevant information regarding the business impact of particular planning decisions, while to IT actors the same EA documents provide relevant information regarding the IT-related implications of these planning decisions. To strategic actors EA documents provide relevant information regarding the long-term consequences of particular planning decisions, while to tactical actors the same EA documents provide relevant information regarding the short-term outcomes of these planning decisions. To internal actors EA documents provide relevant information regarding the planned solutions based on established industry best practices, while to external actors the same EA documents provide relevant information regarding the internal details and specifics of an organization.

Hence, enterprise architecture helps close the communication gaps existing between all groups of relevant actors and eliminate the three main boundaries preventing effective collaboration in organizations (see Figure 1.2). By enabling better communication between different actors of the organizational network, enterprise architecture accelerates the propagation of information and knowledge sharing inside an organization. Essentially, the use of enterprise architecture moves an organization, as a decentralized network of diverse, independent and interacting actors, closer to the ideal desirable state of the single "big brain" capable of making best globally and locally optimized business and IT decisions in all areas based on all available information[25]. As a result, the essential interests of all relevant stakeholders are respected and taken into account in each planning decision. The improved quality of information systems planning in its turn leads to better business and IT alignment, when all IT projects tend to optimize the structure of the organizational system as a whole (see Figure 1.1).

The mechanism described above explains why organizations using enterprise architecture are able to achieve better business and IT alignment, i.e. increase the payoff from their IT investments, improve the general satisfaction with IT and enhance overall business performance. The link between the use of enterprise architecture, effective communication, adequate IT planning and the resulting alignment between business and IT is shown in Figure 1.4.

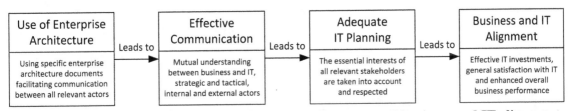

Figure 1.4. Link between the use of enterprise architecture and business and IT alignment

In short, by facilitating effective communication between all relevant actors involved in business and IT planning, enterprise architecture enables successful translation of the high-level strategic plans defined by global business executives into the corresponding low-level tactical activities of specific IT project teams across the organization.

Chapter Summary

This chapter discussed the general role of IT in modern organizations, described the nature of a modern organization as a complex socio-technical system of business and IT, explained the problem of achieving business and IT alignment and introduced the concept of enterprise architecture as a potential solution to the longstanding alignment problem. The key message of this chapter can be summarized into the following essential points:

- In the 21st century the effective control, management and planning of IT in organizations is a direct concern and responsibility of business executives that can no longer be simply delegated to IT managers
- Modern organizations represent complex socio-technical systems of business and IT, where business and IT components can be changed only synchronously and all planning decisions should take into account both global and local interests
- The effective organizational use of IT requires achieving so-called business and IT alignment, when the IT goals, IT plans and IT systems in an organization are consistent with its business goals, business plans and business processes
- Significant diversity of the actors involved in strategic decision-making and implementation of IT systems undermines productive communication between these actors, leads to inadequate planning decisions and eventually results in the misalignment between business and IT
- Enterprise architecture, as a collection of special documents enabling effective communication between different groups of actors, helps improve the quality of information systems planning and thereby achieve better business and IT alignment in organizations

Chapter 2: The Concept of Enterprise Architecture

The previous chapter introduced the problem of business and IT alignment in organizations as well as the notion of enterprise architecture as a potential solution to this problem. This chapter focuses specifically on the concept of enterprise architecture and discusses in more detail its key aspects. In particular, this chapter starts from formally introducing the concept of enterprise architecture and the practice of using enterprise architecture for improving business and IT alignment. Then, this chapter discusses enterprise architecture artifacts as fundamental components of enterprise architecture and their essential properties. Finally, this chapter discusses the role of architects in enterprise architecture practices as well as the place of architecture functions in organizations.

What Is Enterprise Architecture?

Enterprise architecture (EA) can be defined as a collection of special documents (artifacts) describing various aspects of an organization from an integrated business and IT perspective intended to bridge the communication gap between business and IT stakeholders, facilitate information systems planning and thereby improve business and IT alignment[1]. Enterprise architecture typically describes business, applications, data, infrastructure and sometimes other domains of an organization relevant from the perspective of business and IT, e.g. integration or security. Even though enterprise architecture often covers specific aspects related directly to business planning (e.g. business processes, organizational roles or even corresponding business unit structures), it still generally revolves largely around IT, offers mostly IT-related views and is currently associated primarily with IT planning or, more precisely, with joint business and IT planning. For example, enterprise architecture can describe how specific business processes and roles will be modified when a new IT system is introduced.

The Essence of Enterprise Architecture

Enterprise architecture, as a collection of specific documents, provides effective instruments facilitating communication, collaboration and mutual understanding between different groups of actors involved in strategic decision-making and implementation of IT systems. Using specific EA documents for supporting discussions helps alleviate communication problems resulting from disparate knowledge, responsibilities, interests and goals of business and IT actors, strategic and tactical actors, internal and external actors (see Figure 1.2)[2]. Essentially, enterprise architecture can be considered as a *communication medium* between diverse business and IT stakeholders in organizations enabling effective knowledge sharing, collaborative decision-making and balanced planning.

By enabling effective communication and cooperation between relevant actors, enterprise architecture helps organizations make optimal planning decisions taking into account the interests and concerns of all key business and IT stakeholders involved in strategic decision-making and implementation of IT systems. Specifically, to business executives EA documents explain the implications of each planning decision for the organizational business strategy. For example, to business executives EA documents may provide the answers to the following essential questions:

- How does the decision contribute to our long-term business strategy?
- What financial investments are required to implement the decision?
- When can the decision be implemented?

To IT executives EA documents explain the implications of each planning decision for the organizational IT strategy. For example, to IT executives EA documents may provide the answers to the following essential questions:

- What technologies need to be introduced or reused to implement the decision?
- What is the overall impact of the decision on our IT landscape?
- What teams and partners should be involved to implement the decision?

To business unit managers EA documents explain the implications of each planning decision for their local business processes. For example, to business unit managers EA documents may provide the answers to the following essential questions:

- How does the decision meet our local requirements and needs?
- How does the decision modify our specific business processes?
- How does the decision change the information systems we use on a daily basis?

To IT project teams EA documents explain the implications of each planning decision for the design of a specific IT project. For example, to IT project teams EA documents may provide the answers to the following essential questions:

- What exactly needs to be done to implement the decision?
- What approaches can be used to implement the decision?
- How exactly does the decision modify our IT landscape?

Finally, to third parties EA documents explain the implications of each planning decision for the structure of a specific contract or outsourcing agreement. For example, to third parties EA documents may provide the answers to the following essential questions:

- What essential requirements need to be met to implement the decision?
- What products or technologies can we offer to implement the decision?
- How does the existing IT landscape facilitate or stop the implementation of the decision?

The information provided by EA documents to different business and IT stakeholders described above is far from complete and exhaustive. However, it illustrates the general intention of EA documents to provide the critical information regarding each planning decision relevant to the key concerns of all main actors involved in information systems planning (see Figure 1.2). The use of enterprise architecture for discussing and balancing the interests of all relevant stakeholders helps organizations implement well-coordinated changes and make optimal planning decisions, i.e. decisions that achieve both short-term and long-term goals with minimal costs in a technically optimal and risk-free manner without introducing excessive complexity or undermining overall consistency. The essence of enterprise architecture, as the instrument for supporting communication between different groups of relevant actors, is shown in Figure 2.1.

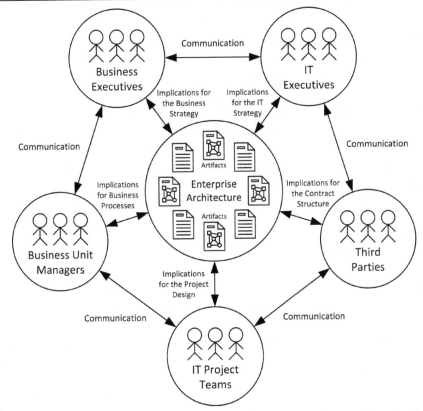

Figure 2.1. Enterprise architecture as an instrument for communication

Despite that the notion of architecture is usually associated with buildings and other construction objects, enterprise architecture has not much in common with building architecture[3]. Unlike buildings, organizations as dynamic socio-technical systems (see Figure 1.1) cannot be designed or engineered and then built[4]. Instead, organizations can be considered as extremely complex, organic and living entities that gradually evolve or grow over time[5], rather than get constructed in a well-planned manner[6]. In the real world there are no perfectly planned organizations. Successful organizations are the results of well-managed evolutions, rather than the results of careful, deliberate and detailed planning.

From this point of view, enterprise architecture cannot be considered as a comprehensive detailed plan of an organization similar to building architecture[7], but rather as a pragmatic set of descriptions useful for managing and controlling the evolution of an organization from the business and IT perspective[8]. Moreover, since organizations as organic entities cannot have architecture in the same sense in which buildings have architecture, the very term "enterprise architecture" seemingly gained its widespread popularity only because of some complex historical reasons[9], but now is purely metaphorical, conceptually meaningless, highly confusing and largely misguiding[10]. Essentially, the term "enterprise architecture" today can be considered only as a conditional and peculiar umbrella term representing the whole collection of diverse documents used in organizations for information systems planning, but having no other conceptual or practical meaning.

Domains of Enterprise Architecture

The informational contents of enterprise architecture, as a collection of documents describing an organization from an integrated business and IT perspective, cover various organizational aspects important for business and IT usually called as **EA domains**. In particular, typical facets of organizations reflected in EA documents include, but are not limited to, the following six common domains:

- Business – the **business domain** views an organization from the perspective of its business operations, e.g. customers, capabilities, processes, roles, etc.
- Applications – the **applications domain** views an organization from the perspective of its end-user applications, e.g. programs, systems, custom software, vendor products, etc.
- Data – the **data domain** views an organization from the perspective of its core data, e.g. data entities, structures, storage and representation formats, sources, etc.
- Integration – the **integration domain** views an organization from the perspective of its system integration mechanisms, e.g. interfaces and connections, interaction protocols, integration platforms, messaging middleware, etc.
- Infrastructure – the **infrastructure domain** views an organization from the perspective of its underlying IT infrastructure, e.g. hardware, servers, operating systems, networks, etc.
- Security – the **security domain** views an organization from the perspective of its security mechanisms, e.g. firewalls, authentication approaches, identity and access management systems, cryptographic protocols, etc.

The set of these common EA domains can be loosely represented as a multilayered stack of domains, where lower layers underpin higher layers. For instance, applications from the applications domain automate business processes from the business domain. Data from the data domain is used by applications from the applications domain. Integration mechanisms from the integration domain link all applications and data from the corresponding domains. Infrastructure from the infrastructure domain is used to host all applications, databases and integration platforms from the respective domains. Finally, security mechanisms from the security domain permeate all business processes, applications, data, integration mechanisms and infrastructure from the corresponding domains.

While the business domain is unrelated to any specific technology and can be considered as non-technical and technology-neutral, all other EA domains are directly related to respective technologies and can be considered as **technical domains**. All common EA domains can be also loosely separated into business-enabling domains and business-supporting domains. On the one hand, **business-enabling EA domains** occupy the top layers of the stack and can be considered as functional domains. Common business-enabling EA domains include the business, applications and data domains. These domains essentially define the core business functionality provided by IT systems. They are of direct interest and "visible" to most business stakeholders. For instance, business managers are naturally interested in how their business processes work, what applications they can use and what data is available to them. All planning decisions relevant to business-enabling EA domains and affecting business functionality are normally agreed with business stakeholders. On the other hand, **business-supporting EA domains** occupy the bottom layers of the stack and can be considered as non-functional domains. Common business-supporting EA domains include the integration, infrastructure and security domains. These domains are essentially unrelated to specific business functionality of IT systems. They are largely irrelevant and invisible to most business stakeholders. For instance, business managers are generally not interested in the integration, infrastructure and security aspects of their information systems, as long as these systems are adequately integrated, run on reliable infrastructure and are reasonably secure. Most planning decisions relevant to business-supporting EA domains usually do not affect any business functionality and might be not discussed with business stakeholders. The stack of common EA domains with business-enabling and business-supporting domains is shown in Figure 2.2.

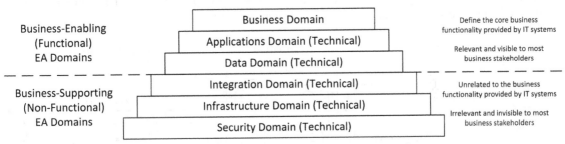

Figure 2.2. The stack of common EA domains

Generally, enterprise architecture can describe any domains considered as important from the perspective of the relationship between business and IT in a particular organization. The six EA domains shown in Figure 2.2 are merely the most common domains which are often described in enterprise architecture in many organizations.

The Practice of Enterprise Architecture

The practice of enterprise architecture, or simply an **EA practice**, is an organizational practice of using specific documents called EA artifacts for improving communication between business and IT stakeholders, facilitating information systems planning and improving business and IT alignment[11]. An EA practice is a complex and multifaceted organizational practice embracing all EA-related artifacts, people, processes, software and their interaction. The strict boundaries of an EA practice are extremely hard to define. An EA practice essentially penetrates an entire organization, involves numerous actors ranging from the CEO to ordinary project team members and significantly modifies most IT-related decision-making processes. Generally, an EA practice can arguably be considered as one of the most sophisticated, hard-to-explain and even inscrutable organizational practices[12].

An EA practice is not a separate standalone activity, but rather an integral part of the organizational organism. Initiating an EA practice implies introducing profound and complex changes to an organization affecting its people, processes and technology aspects[13]. An EA practice cannot work in isolation and requires integration with other organizational processes, most importantly with strategic management and project management[14]. Essentially, an EA practice "sits" between strategic management and project management and the role of an EA practice is to continuously translate abstract business considerations into the designs of specific IT solutions implementing these considerations in the most optimal manner.

The strategic management process carried out by business executives takes relevant information from the external business environment as an input and produces abstract business considerations guiding an organization as an output, e.g. goals, objectives, plans and needs. An EA practice takes these abstract business considerations as an input and produces specific implementable designs of IT solutions describing what exactly needs be done, how and when to satisfy the business considerations as an output. Finally, the project management process carried out by IT project teams takes these implementable designs as an input and produces optimal IT solutions corresponding to these designs as an output thereby implementing the abstract business considerations defined by business executives. Importantly, all these processes are continuous, carried out simultaneously and imply constant feedback. The position of an EA practice in the context of regular organizational processes is shown in Figure 2.3.

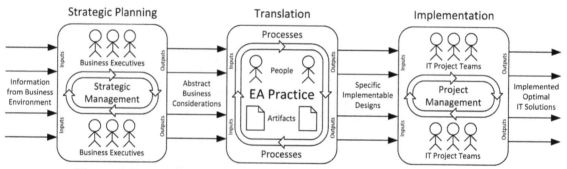

Figure 2.3. An EA practice in the context of organizational processes

An EA practice provides a connecting link between high-level strategic business planning and low-level IT systems implementation. By acting as a mediator between the strategic management and projects management processes, an EA practice enables effective coordination of plans and activities between all relevant actors involved in strategic decision-making and implementation of IT systems resulting in improved business and IT alignment.

Enterprise Architecture Artifacts

Separate documents constituting enterprise architecture are typically called as **EA artifacts**[15]. EA artifacts provide descriptions of an organization from different perspectives important for the various actors involved in strategic decision-making and implementation of IT systems. They can be considered as key elements and cornerstones of an EA practice. Essentially, an EA practice revolves around using specific sets of EA artifacts for improving communication between different actors. EA artifacts are main "workhorses" of an EA practice enabling effective decision-making and IT planning in organizations. The systematic use of EA artifacts for collective decision-making distinguishes a disciplined approach to information systems planning from an ad hoc and ill-organized one.

Different EA artifacts are used by different actors at different moments for different purposes and fulfill different roles in organizations. Unsurprisingly, EA artifacts can be very diverse in their basic properties and attributes. In particular, from the perspective of their properties all EA artifacts can differ in their informational contents, general meanings and lifecycles in the context of an EA practice.

Informational Contents of Enterprise Architecture Artifacts

From the perspective of their informational contents, various EA artifacts can use different representation formats, provide different levels of detail, cover different scopes, describe different EA domains and focus on different points in time.

Firstly, EA artifacts can have different representation formats. Specifically, EA artifacts can be represented in textual, graphical and sometimes tabular formats, or as a mix of these formats. Purely textual EA artifacts contain only plain text. Purely graphical EA artifacts contain only diagrams and models sometimes created using special modeling languages or notations. Purely tabular EA artifacts contain only tables with rows and columns. Mixed EA artifacts can contain the elements of all these representation formats in different proportions.

Secondly, EA artifacts can provide different levels of detail. Descriptions contained in EA artifacts can range in their granularity from very high-level abstractions (e.g. business and IT capabilities, overarching conceptual rules and executive-level considerations) to pretty low-level details (e.g. specific business activities, concrete IT systems and their components).

Thirdly, EA artifacts can cover different organizational scopes. From the perspective of their scopes, coverage of EA artifacts ranges from entire organizations, lines of business and business functions to narrow organizational areas, separate change initiatives and even single IT projects. Typically EA artifacts covering wider scopes are less detailed, while EA artifacts covering narrower scopes are more detailed.

Fourthly, EA artifacts can describe different domains of enterprise architecture. EA domains often described in EA artifacts include, but are not limited to, business, applications, data, integration, infrastructure and security domains (see Figure 2.2), as well as all possible combinations of multiple different EA domains.

Fifthly, EA artifacts can focus on different temporal states of an organization, i.e. describe an organization at different points in time. All states typically described in EA artifacts can be roughly separated into the current state (now), short-term future state (<1 year), mid-term future state (2-3 years) and long-term future state (3-5 years). Additionally, some EA artifacts can describe a combination of all these states in different proportions or can even be essentially stateless, i.e. do not focus on specific points in time. For example, some EA artifacts can describe the current state of an organization as well as the planned changes to this state in both the short-term and mid-term future, while other EA artifacts can describe some timeless imperatives for an organization which were relevant in the past, are relevant now and will be relevant in the future.

Duality of Enterprise Architecture Artifacts

One of the most important properties of EA artifacts is the duality of their informational contents. **Duality of EA artifacts** implies that the information provided by these artifacts is relevant to two different audiences simultaneously, satisfies the information needs of both these audiences and presented in a convenient format appealing to both audiences. Their duality allows using EA artifacts as a means of communication and partnership between different groups of actors involved in strategic decision-making and implementation of IT systems (see Figure 2.1). Duality of EA artifacts can be considered as one of the most fundamental mechanisms underpinning an EA practice and enabling effective collaboration between diverse stakeholders[16].

Duality of EA artifacts can be explicit or implicit. On the one hand, **explicit duality** is when different parts of EA artifacts are relevant to different groups of actors, e.g. some sections of an EA artifact are intended primarily for business stakeholders, while other sections of the same artifact are intended primarily for IT stakeholders. On the other hand, **implicit duality** is when same parts of EA artifacts are interpreted differently by different actors, e.g. the same diagram in an EA artifact is relevant to both business and IT stakeholders, but has significantly different implications for each of these parties. In other words, duality of EA artifacts implies either providing different information to different actors, or providing same information having different meanings for different actors. However, explicit and implicit dualities in EA artifacts are often combined.

The duality of EA artifacts discussed above, and specifically explicit duality, can be clearly illustrated with a specific example of a popular EA artifact often called as solution overview providing a high-level description of a proposed IT solution from both the business and IT viewpoints. This EA artifact typically has a number of different sections intended for business and IT stakeholders, where these stakeholders can find the answers to their most critical questions regarding an IT solution. Duality of EA artifacts illustrated based on the example of a solution overview is shown in Figure 2.4.

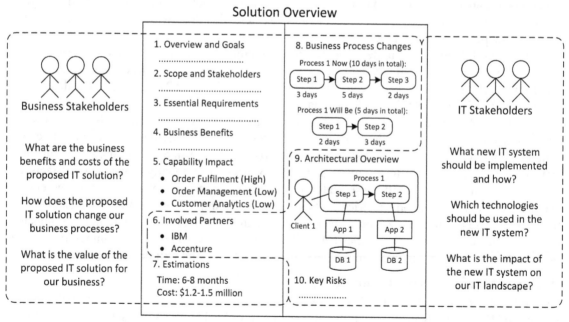

Figure 2.4. Duality of EA artifacts

Due to its evident duality, the solution overview shown in Figure 2.4 helps business and IT stakeholders make optimal collective planning decisions regarding the launch of a new IT initiative. In particular, based on this dual EA artifact business stakeholders can evaluate and assure the positive business value of a proposed IT solution, whereas IT stakeholders can assess and approve its general technical feasibility. A comprehensive assessment of complex planning decisions enabled by dual EA artifacts improves the quality of these decisions from both the business and IT perspectives and, thereby, enhances the overall organizational effectiveness of IT planning. However, not all useful EA artifacts are dual in nature.

Two Meanings of Enterprise Architecture Artifacts: Decisions and Facts

From the perspective of their general meaning in an EA practice all EA artifacts can be separated into decisions EA artifacts and facts EA artifacts. On the one hand, **decisions EA artifacts** represent made planning decisions, i.e. achieved and formalized agreements between various stakeholders regarding the desired future course of action. For instance, these EA artifacts can embody all sorts of IT-related planning decisions in organizations including, among many others, the following decisions:

- How an organization needs to work from the IT perspective
- Where an organization should invest its IT dollars
- How a particular IT solution should be implemented

Decisions EA artifacts always have certain implications for the future and usually imply some changes in an organization. Since all planning decisions regarding the future require the discussion and consensus between their stakeholders, these EA artifacts are always developed or updated *collaboratively* by all relevant stakeholders and represented in formats convenient for these stakeholders. For example, they are often optimized for productive teamwork, ease of editing and distribution. Decisions EA artifacts are inherently subjective, speculative and people-specific in nature. They are based only on informed opinions of their contributors regarding the desirable future course of action and shaped primarily by the key interests of their stakeholders[17]. Essentially, decisions EA artifacts play the primary role in an EA practice by providing the instruments for effective communication, balanced decision-making and collaborative IT planning (most decisions EA artifacts are dual in nature, see Figure 2.4). Their general purpose is to help make optimal planning decisions approved by all relevant stakeholders. After decisions EA artifacts are created and approved, all their stakeholders should be ready to act according to the corresponding planning decisions reflected in these artifacts. Since any ideas regarding the desired future always imply collective decisions, all EA artifacts describing the future state, as well as all stateless EA artifacts also having specific implications for the future, can be automatically considered as decisions EA artifacts from the perspective of their general meaning in an EA practice.

On the other hand, **facts EA artifacts** represent documented objective facts, i.e. reflections of the actual current situation in an organization as it is. For instance, these EA artifacts usually document some aspects of the existing organizational IT landscape including, among others, the following objective facts:

- What technologies the organizational IT landscape uses
- What IT assets an organization possesses, runs and maintains

- How the existing IT systems and databases are interconnected

Unlike decisions EA artifacts, facts EA artifacts do not imply any planning decisions and have no implications for the future. Since objective facts are normally not debatable and do not require any real decision-making, these EA artifacts may be developed or updated solely by specific actors, but represented in formats convenient for their future users. For example, they are often optimized for long-term storage, searchability and analysis of information. Facts EA artifacts are based only on acknowledged "hard" data and largely independent of specific people involved in their development. Essentially, facts EA artifacts play the supporting role in an EA practice by providing the information base required for developing decisions EA artifacts. Their general purpose is to help capture and store the objective facts regarding an organization important from the perspective of IT planning. After facts EA artifacts are created, they can be used by any actors as reference materials for planning purposes. Since a mere documentation of the current situation does not imply any real decisions, all EA artifacts describing only the current state can be automatically considered as facts EA artifacts from the perspective of their general meaning in an EA practice. The main differences between decisions and facts EA artifacts described above are summarized in Table 2.1.

Artifacts	Decisions EA artifacts	Facts EA artifacts
State	Either the future state or stateless	Only the current state
Represent	Made planning decisions	Documented objective facts
Implications	Always have implications for the future	Have no implications for the future
Developed	Collaboratively by all stakeholders	Solely by specific actors
Format	Optimized for productive teamwork, ease of editing and distribution	Optimized for long-term storage, searchability and analysis of information
Nature	Subjective, i.e. based on the interests and opinions of specific people	Objective, i.e. based on acknowledged facts and independent of specific people
Role	Primary, i.e. provide instruments for communication, decision-making and planning	Supporting, i.e. provide the information base required for developing decisions EA artifacts
Purpose	Help make optimal planning decisions	Help store the facts important for IT planning
Outcome	Stakeholders act according to the made decisions	Can be used by any actors as reference materials

Table 2.1. Decisions and facts EA artifacts

However, as discussed earlier, some EA artifacts can describe both the current and future states together. Consequently, these rare EA artifacts can combine the properties of both decisions and facts EA artifacts simultaneously. For example, EA artifacts can describe the current state, and therefore automatically belong to facts EA artifacts, as well as some recommended future changes in this current state, and therefore also belong to decisions EA artifacts at the same time. In this case the respective EA artifacts should be considered as either facts or decisions EA artifacts depending on the situation. Specifically, these EA artifacts should be treated as facts EA artifacts from the perspective of all updates of the current state, but as decisions EA artifacts from the perspective of all updates of the recommended future changes.

However, in some cases descriptions of the future state can still be included in facts EA artifacts as well if these descriptions have been approved earlier via other decisions EA artifacts, i.e. reflect the planning decisions that have already been made previously elsewhere.

Two Lifecycles of Enterprise Architecture Artifacts: Permanent and Temporary

From the perspective of their lifecycles in an EA practice all EA artifacts can be separated into permanent EA artifacts and temporary EA artifacts. On the one hand, **permanent EA artifacts** are long-lived EA artifacts often existing for many years. They live and evolve together with an organization. Permanent EA artifacts are created once and then updated when necessary according to the ongoing changes in an organization and its business environment. They may be either developed at once in a proactive manner, or produced reactively on an as-necessary basis, i.e. accumulated in organizations gradually over time. After being developed these EA artifacts are constantly used, continuously maintained and occasionally discarded when become irrelevant. Most EA artifacts covering wider scopes beyond specific IT initiatives or projects tend to be permanent EA artifacts.

On the other hand, **temporary EA artifacts** are short-lived EA artifacts often existing for several months or even weeks. They are transitory, single-purposed and disposable. Temporary EA artifacts are created at specific moments for particular purposes, used as intended and then immediately discarded or archived. Due to their short lifespan, the very need to update or maintain temporary EA artifacts is usually absent. All EA artifacts covering narrow scopes (e.g. separate IT initiatives or projects) tend to be temporary EA artifacts. At the same time, all temporary EA artifacts tend to be decisions EA artifacts (see Table 2.1). The main differences between permanent and temporary EA artifacts described above are summarized in Table 2.2.

Artifacts	Permanent EA artifacts	Temporary EA artifacts
Scope	Wide scope, beyond specific IT initiatives	Narrow scope, limited to specific IT initiatives
Lifespan	Long-lived, often exist for years	Short-lived, exist for months or even weeks
Usage	Created once, periodically updated, constantly used and occasionally discarded	Created for particular purposes, used as intended and then immediately discarded

Table 2.2. Permanent and temporary EA artifacts

Examples of Enterprise Architecture Artifacts

The informational contents, general meanings and lifecycles of EA artifacts discussed above can be illustrated with specific examples of popular EA artifacts: principles, landscape diagrams and solution designs (these and many other types of EA artifacts are discussed in great detail later in Chapters 9-14). Examples of these typical EA artifacts and their analysis from the perspective of their informational contents, meanings and lifecycles are shown in Figure 2.5.

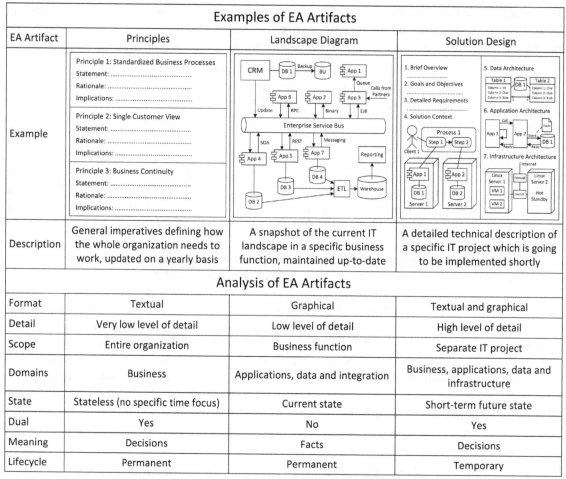

Figure 2.5. Examples of popular EA artifacts and their analysis

Although various EA artifacts can be very diverse from the perspective of their informational contents, meanings and lifecycles, all EA artifacts still share the single common property of critical importance. Specifically, all EA artifacts without any exceptions, like any other tools, are valuable only when they are used for certain purposes by specific people to facilitate particular activities. For this reason, all EA artifacts should be produced with a clear idea regarding their intended future usage and intent.

Even though it is possible to develop a potentially infinite number of diverse EA artifacts describing an entire organization with all its business units from all perspectives, EA artifacts merely describing some aspects of organizations for unclear purposes are useless and should be avoided. Unused EA artifacts represent only wasted investments of time and money for organizations. Instead, from the overall set of all possible descriptions successful EA practices select only a limited number of the most valuable descriptions helpful for decision-making purposes and develop them as EA artifacts. EA artifacts in an EA practice are not mere descriptions, but fully-fledged working instruments of information systems planning.

The Role of Architects in Enterprise Architecture Practice

The key actors of an EA practice are **architects**[18]. Architects act as chief IT planners in organizations. Ideal architects are effective communicators, team players, innovators and systems thinkers knowledgeable in both business and IT. These qualities allow architects to communicate with relevant business and IT stakeholders, understand their concerns and propose optimal planning decisions satisfying the essential interests of all these stakeholders. Even though architects usually come from IT departments and have IT-centric backgrounds, they do not belong wholly to IT specialists or to business specialists. Instead, architects are "T-shaped" professionals in connecting business and IT, i.e. specialists in finding optimal IT strategies and solutions satisfying business strategies and needs.

General Responsibilities of Architects

Architects are the chief owners of EA artifacts and facilitators of the dialog between business and IT. They play the critical role in organizing, establishing and running an EA practice. Even though architects themselves cannot be the sponsors or ultimate beneficiaries of an EA practice, they are among the main actors of most EA-related processes. Typical responsibilities of architects include:

- Communicating with various business and IT stakeholders and understanding their concerns
- Acting as intermediaries or "translators" between diverse stakeholders
- Facilitating the dialog and conversation between different stakeholders
- Finding, proposing and discussing optimal planning decisions satisfying the concerns of different stakeholders
- Developing and updating EA artifacts for supporting discussions and documenting the achieved agreements
- Peer-reviewing and approving EA artifacts developed by other architects
- Establishing and maintaining a repository of EA artifacts
- Setting up necessary software tools for working with EA artifacts
- Establishing, running and optimizing EA-related processes

Even though the responsibilities of architects in organizations are usually diverse and complex, the most critical responsibility of any architect is the development of necessary EA artifacts underpinning an EA practice.

Architects as Developers of Enterprise Architecture Artifacts

Architects are the key developers of all EA artifacts in an EA practice. They are personally responsible for involving relevant stakeholders, collecting necessary data and completing all other activities required to develop EA artifacts. However, the typical process of developing and updating EA artifacts differs significantly for decisions EA artifacts and facts EA artifacts due to their disparate meanings, purposes and nature (see Table 2.1).

On the one hand, the development and update of decisions EA artifacts is a complex, creative and tricky process. Since all modifications of decisions EA artifacts, including their initial development and possible subsequent updates, require reaching the consensus among all relevant stakeholders on the future course of action, these artifacts are always developed *collaboratively* by architects and their stakeholders[19]. The presence of multiple groups of stakeholders exerting different power and representing different or even conflicting viewpoints often turns the development of decisions EA artifacts into a highly politicized process. Essentially, the collaborative development of decisions EA artifacts is the actual process of IT planning. Even though architects usually act as facilitators or drivers of their development, fundamentally decisions EA artifacts are products of a collective teamwork. These EA artifacts are normally created in a proactive manner.

The development or update of decisions EA artifacts typically starts from the need for specific planning decisions. As the first step, architects organize an informal preliminary dialog with all relevant stakeholders of these decisions. During these discussions the stakeholders and architects achieve a basic mutual understanding regarding the possible planning decisions. Then, architects formalize the proposed planning decisions as new or updated EA artifacts and collaborate with the relevant stakeholders to elaborate these artifacts with necessary details. During this collaboration the resulting EA artifacts get completed and informally agreed with all their direct stakeholders. As the last step, the completed and finalized EA artifacts undergo the procedure of a formal collective approval and eventually become official documents representing the planning decisions made jointly by all the involved stakeholders and architects. From this moment all the involved parties are committed to act according to these decisions. For example, to develop principles or a solution design (see Figure 2.5) an architect may schedule a series of meetings with relevant stakeholders (business executives and IT project teams respectively) to discuss their views and concerns, based on the collected opinions propose the initial versions of EA artifacts, organize workshops with the stakeholders to elaborate and complete these EA artifacts, and then distribute the final versions of these artifacts to all the stakeholders for their formal approval and sign-off. After the EA artifacts are signed-off, all the involved parties are committed to align their decision-making to the newly established principles or to implement an IT solution exactly as described in the developed solution design.

Importantly, the main value of decisions EA artifacts is realized during the process of their development. The collective teamwork of multiple stakeholders on developing decisions EA artifacts helps these stakeholders communicate, achieve a mutual understanding and produce optimal planning decisions taking into account the essential interests of all the stakeholders. By the time the actual EA artifacts are completed, the critical planning decisions formalized in these artifacts have already been made. Essentially, finalized decisions EA artifacts merely document the agreements between the stakeholders reached in the process of their development. From this perspective, the collaborative efforts of stakeholders to develop decisions EA artifacts are much more valuable than the actual resulting artifacts as tangible formal documents. In other words, for these EA artifacts the process is more important than the product itself. The most critical success factor related to decisions EA artifacts is the timely involvement and active participation of all relevant stakeholders in the process of their development.

On the other hand, the development and update of facts EA artifacts is a more simple, routine and straightforward process. Unlike decisions EA artifacts developed collaboratively by all stakeholders, facts EA artifacts usually may be developed by individual architects alone or with only a minimal involvement of other actors (see Table 2.1). These EA artifacts are often created in a reactive manner on an as-necessary basis.

The development or update of facts EA artifacts typically starts from the need for specific documented facts. As the first step, architects collect the necessary raw data from all relevant sources, which may include studying available documents, asking competent people and extracting data from the existing IT systems or repositories. When the sufficient information on the required facts is collected, architects create new or update existing EA artifacts to accurately document the uncovered facts with the necessary level of detail. Since facts EA artifacts merely describe what is, do not imply any planning decisions and do not have any implications, the completed facts EA artifacts normally do not need to be approved by any other actors. However, architects may still decide to go back to the people who provided the original information to verify the resulting EA artifacts and ensure their correctness. After these EA artifacts are created, all actors can use them for planning purposes. For example, to develop or update a landscape diagram (see Figure 2.5) an architect may read the available documentation from recent IT projects, interview members of the IT support department, search the central configuration management database (CMDB) and then produce the landscape diagram depicting all the collected facts in a compact one-page drawing. The architect may also return to the IT support team to double-check and confirm the accuracy of the resulting description. From this moment anybody can use the new landscape diagram as a reference baseline of the current state for decision-making.

Unlike decisions EA artifacts, the main value of facts EA artifacts is realized after their development. The development process of facts EA artifacts is highly mechanistic in nature and does not have any intrinsic value. However, after the development of facts EA artifacts is completed, these artifacts are valuable as the information base supporting the development of decisions EA artifacts. From this perspective, the actual resulting facts EA artifacts as tangible formal documents are much more valuable than the efforts of architects to develop these artifacts. In other words, for these EA artifacts the product is more important than the process. The most critical success factor related to facts EA artifacts is the accuracy and up-to-dateness of the corresponding descriptions. The processes for developing or updating decisions and facts EA artifacts discussed above and their comparison are summarized in Figure 2.6.

Decisions EA Artifacts

(Represent made planning decisions)

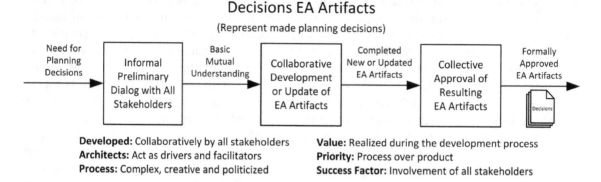

Developed: Collaboratively by all stakeholders
Architects: Act as drivers and facilitators
Process: Complex, creative and politicized

Value: Realized during the development process
Priority: Process over product
Success Factor: Involvement of all stakeholders

Facts EA Artifacts

(Represent documented objective facts)

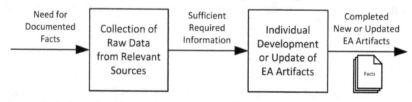

Developed: By individual architects alone
Architects: Act as sole developers
Process: Straightforward and routine

Value: Realized after development is completed
Priority: Product over process
Success Factor: Accuracy of all descriptions

Figure 2.6. Development of decisions and facts EA artifacts

The profound difference between decisions EA artifacts and facts EA artifacts is hard to overemphasize. Using the appropriate development processes for decisions and facts EA artifacts is absolutely critical for the success of an EA practice. While developing facts EA artifacts as decisions EA artifacts simply does not make any sense, developing decisions EA artifacts as facts EA artifacts can be easily considered as a tempting "shortcut" way to develop these artifacts as well as to practice enterprise architecture in general. However, all the attempts to develop decisions EA artifacts similarly to facts EA artifacts are misleading, extremely dangerous and may have catastrophic consequences for an EA practice.

Developing decisions EA artifacts in a similar way to facts EA artifacts (i.e. merely by interviewing relevant stakeholders and then creating decisions EA artifacts for them) inevitably substitutes real practical IT planning with wishful thinking, benevolent phantasies and idealistic imaginations. All significant planning decisions in organizations must be discussed and agreed with their key stakeholders, rather than made by someone else on their behalf. For this reason, decisions EA artifacts created with little or no involvement of their real stakeholders are typically ignored and never get acted upon. Therefore, taking shortcuts in developing decisions EA artifacts by producing them alone on behalf of their true stakeholders essentially transforms an entire EA practice from the driver of communication into the factory of useless documents. Excluding stakeholders from the discussions of relevant decisions EA artifacts eradicates the very essence of using enterprise architecture as an instrument for communication (see Figure 2.1). Put it simply, developing decisions EA artifacts as facts EA artifacts can easily ruin an EA practice.

Enterprise Architecture Artifacts, Architects and Other Actors

An EA practice includes architects and other actors communicating via developing and using EA artifacts. However, the roles of architects and other actors, as well as their communication and interaction patterns in the context of an EA practice, are significantly different from the perspective of decisions EA artifacts and facts EA artifacts (see Table 2.1).

On the one hand, as part of the general development process of all decisions EA artifacts (see Figure 2.6) architects continuously communicate with various business and IT stakeholders, analyze their interests and needs, propose optimal planning decisions satisfying all relevant stakeholders, formalize these initial decisions as EA artifacts and then go through iterative cycles of further discussions, refinements and clarifications of these artifacts until the final agreement between the stakeholders is achieved and the proposed planning decisions are formally approved by all the involved parties. Even though architects are still the primary developers of decisions EA artifacts, various stakeholders providing their input and approving resulting artifacts essentially act as their co-developers.

On the other hand, as part of the general development process of all facts EA artifacts (see Figure 2.6), architects collect all the required data from various sources and then create or update the corresponding EA artifacts acting as their sole developers. The relationship between EA artifacts, architects and other actors of an EA practice described above is shown in Figure 2.7.

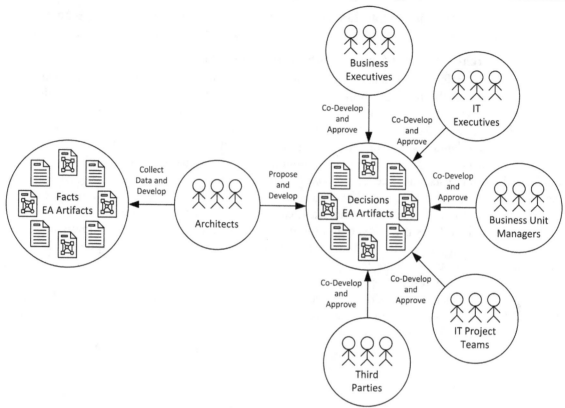

Figure 2.7. The relationship between EA artifacts, architects and other actors

By leading continuous discussions with relevant stakeholders, proposing optimal planning decisions expressed in decisions EA artifacts and getting these decisions approved, architects achieve the balance of interests between all key stakeholders in every planning decision. The resulting planning decisions take into account the critical interests of all relevant business and IT stakeholders improving business and IT alignment in organizations. Since the active participation of key stakeholders is absolutely essential for developing decisions EA artifacts representing corresponding IT planning decisions, an EA practice fundamentally cannot be carried out by architects alone without involving other stakeholders. Consequently, the effectiveness of organizational information systems planning is not the concern of architects alone, but the concern of an entire organization.

Architecture Functions in Organizations

Organizationally, an EA practice is typically implemented by an **architecture function**. An architecture function is a separate organizational function usually reporting directly to the CIO and responsible for an EA practice and for organization-wide IT planning in general. Essentially, architecture functions in organizations can be considered as specialized planning subunits of their IT departments.

An architecture function is a supporting organizational function which does not add any direct business value to the organizational value chain. Similarly to other supporting functions (e.g. accounting and human resource management), the main purpose of an architecture function is to enable and support primary value-adding organizational activities (e.g. production and sales).

All architects employed by an organization typically reside in its architecture function. Depending on the size, structure and complexity of an organization, its architecture function may employ different types of architects and architecture managers, i.e. managers of other architects. Different types of architects usually have different responsibilities and may focus on different EA domains (e.g. applications, data or infrastructure, see Figure 2.2) or scopes, ranging from entire organizations to specific IT solutions. For instance, common types of architects often found in organizations include chief architects, enterprise architects, principal architects, lead architects, domain architects, platform architects, program architects, solution architects and some other less popular denominations. However, the exact meaning of these positions and titles is very organization-specific and can vary significantly across different organizations.

Besides employing individual architects, an architecture function typically also includes one or more **architecture governance bodies**, i.e. special decision-making committees involving architects and other relevant business and IT stakeholders. These governance bodies are responsible for ensuring the adequate level of engagement between different stakeholders, making collective architecturally significant planning decisions, formally reviewing and approving all decisions EA artifacts (see Table 2.1).

Chapter Summary

This chapter discussed the phenomenon of enterprise architecture in general and the practice of using enterprise architecture, EA artifacts as separate components of enterprise architecture and their key properties as well as the role of architects and architecture functions in organizations. The key message of this chapter can be summarized into the following essential points:

- Enterprise architecture is as a collection of specific documents, or EA artifacts, describing various aspects of an organization from an integrated business and IT perspective intended to bridge the communication gap between business and IT stakeholders
- An EA practice is a complex and multifaceted organizational practice of using EA artifacts for enabling effective collaboration between business and IT stakeholders, facilitating information systems planning and improving business and IT alignment
- EA artifacts are separate documents constituting enterprise architecture and providing different views of an organization important for various actors involved in strategic decision-making and implementation of IT systems
- EA artifacts can be very diverse from the perspective of their informational contents and use different representation formats, provide different levels of detail, cover different scopes, describe different domains and focus on different points in time

- Many EA artifacts are dual in nature, i.e. information provided by these artifacts is relevant to two different groups of actors simultaneously, satisfies the information needs of both these groups and enables productive communication between them
- Some EA artifacts represent made planning decisions developed collectively by all relevant stakeholders and have certain implications for the future, while other EA artifacts represent only documented objective facts having no implications for the future
- Permanent EA artifacts are created once, periodically updated, constantly used and occasionally discarded, while temporary EA artifacts are created for particular purposes, used as intended and then immediately discarded
- Architects are the key actors of an EA practice responsible for IT planning and chief developers of EA artifacts, although all decisions EA artifacts are always co-developed by all the stakeholders of corresponding planning decisions
- Architecture functions are specialized supporting organizational functions responsible for an EA practice that employ all architects, host some architecture governance bodies and are usually embodied as planning subunits of IT departments

Chapter 3: The Role of Enterprise Architecture Practice

The previous chapter discussed in detail the concept of enterprise architecture and specific aspects of this concept. This chapter discusses the position of enterprise architecture and an EA practice in the broader organizational, managerial and historical context. In particular, this chapter starts from explaining the natural need for enterprise architecture in modern organizations, benefits of practicing enterprise architecture and applicability of enterprise architecture across various industries and organizations. Then, this chapter discusses the historical origin of enterprise architecture and modern EA best practices described in this book. Finally, this chapter dispels popular misconceptions related to enterprise architecture and clarifies what an EA practice is not.

The Need for Enterprise Architecture

Enterprise architecture is not an accidental phenomenon, but rather is a natural solution to natural problems of many modern organizations. Large international organizations employ thousands or even tens of thousands of IT specialists, who develop and maintain hundreds or even thousands of diverse information systems supporting the daily business operations of these organizations. Even organizations of a much smaller scale can maintain tens or hundreds of information systems critically important for their businesses. Moreover, the competitive advantages of many, if not most, modern organizations are heavily dependent on the effective use of IT. A successful execution of any business strategy in modern organizations often implies, or sometimes is even equivalent to, the implementation of the corresponding information systems supporting this strategy. This critical interdependence between business and IT functions requires a disciplined approach to coordinating business and IT plans. Achieving a mutual understanding between business and IT stakeholders in modern organizations becomes imperative[1]. However, business and IT are disparate areas of knowledge and establishing the effective communication between diverse business and IT stakeholders have always been troublesome. Hence, the emergence of the phenomenon of enterprise architecture is a natural reaction of modern organizations to the desperate need to optimize their extensive IT landscapes as well as to improve collaboration, communication and mutual understanding between various stakeholders with disparate business and IT backgrounds[2].

Furthermore, enterprise architecture is here to stay and its importance seemingly is only going to increase in the future because of three ongoing industry trends. Firstly, IT systems are continuously getting more sophisticated, comprehensive and diverse. If typical business managers barely understood IT before, then in the future it will be even harder for an ordinary business person to understand how IT works. Secondly, the general dependence of business on IT is constantly increasing. More and more manual operations become automated, more and more analytical capabilities get implemented in software, more and more traditional human roles in organizations get substituted with computers. Thirdly, the innovative potential of IT for business

---

is incessantly growing. New strategic opportunities for gaining competitive advantage from the effective use of IT emerge with a very quick pace. If typical business managers were not completely aware of the full innovative potential of IT before, then in the future it will be even harder for an ordinary business person to understand what new strategic opportunities IT can offer to their business. Consequently, for business managers it will be only harder to understand IT in the future, while their dependence on IT and on competitive advantages offered by IT is only going to increase. These trends suggest that the importance of enterprise architecture as an instrument for bridging the gap between business and IT is likely to increase in the future.

The use of enterprise architecture affects multiple organizational processes from strategic planning to project implementation, involves multiple actors ranging from the CEO to project team members and profoundly modifies the general mechanism of planning and executing organizational changes. As noted earlier, the practice of using enterprise architecture can be considered as one of the most sophisticated organizational practices. Moreover, enterprise architecture seemingly represents one of the most significant and widely applicable management innovations of the last two decades, which engendered a completely new organizational function and even a separate dedicated profession, reflecting the fundamental importance of IT for modern organizations.

The Benefits of Practicing Enterprise Architecture

Practicing enterprise architecture in a disciplined manner can bring numerous benefits to organizations. Different EA artifacts provide powerful instruments for facilitating communication, improving the quality of decision-making and achieving more effective information systems planning. Direct benefits resulting from the proper usage of particular types of EA artifacts include, but are not limited to:

- Improved effectiveness of IT investments – specific EA artifacts help focus IT investments on the most strategically important business areas and ensure that organizations achieve their critical long-term business objectives by investing in IT
- Improved efficiency of IT investments – specific EA artifacts help estimate the short-term business value of separate IT investments and ensure that each IT initiative has positive financial returns and delivers reasonable business value for its money
- Reduced costs of IT operations – specific EA artifacts help limit the number of supported technologies, products and vendors and ensure that proposed IT solutions do not introduce unnecessary additional maintenance expenses
- Reduced technical and compliance risks – specific EA artifacts help follow consistent implementation approaches based on proven technologies and compliant with relevant legislative norms and ensure that proposed IT solutions do not introduce any unacceptable risks
- Reduced complexity of the IT landscape – specific EA artifacts help reduce the diversity of used technologies and approaches, untangle the IT landscape and ensure that new IT solutions do not introduce any excessive complexity

- Increased reuse of available IT assets – specific EA artifacts help manage and reuse existing corporate IT assets and ensure that new IT solutions leverage available systems, platforms or databases whenever possible
- Reduced numbers of duplicated and legacy systems – specific EA artifacts help identify potential duplication, manage the lifecycle of IT assets and ensure that redundant and legacy IT systems are decommissioned in a timely manner
- Increased agility of IT planning – specific EA artifacts help plan the changes in the IT landscape, explore available implementation options in a timely manner and ensure that new IT solutions seamlessly fit into the existing IT environment
- Increased speed of the project delivery – specific EA artifacts help accelerate the delivery of new IT projects and ensure that all IT solutions are implemented with minimal unnecessary delays
- Improved quality of the project delivery – specific EA artifacts help deliver new IT projects in a more consistent, smooth and predictable manner and ensure that all IT solutions meet essential business and architectural requirements
- Improved overall conceptual consistency – specific EA artifacts help avoid making inconsistent or incompatible planning decisions and ensure that all IT solutions align to the fundamental business and IT considerations

These direct benefits of utilizing certain types of EA artifacts for effective communication, balanced decision-making and disciplined planning eventually help organizations achieve overall business and IT alignment, when IT goals, plans and systems are consistent with business goals, plans and processes. The improved business and IT alignment, in its turn, leads to numerous organizational benefits which can be considered as indirect general benefits of practicing enterprise architecture. These indirect business benefits of an EA practice include, but are not limited to:

- Better operational excellence, customer intimacy and product leadership[3]
- Increased speed to enter new markets and overall organizational agility[4]
- Improved managerial satisfaction[5]

The link between the use of enterprise architecture, direct benefits of using specific EA artifacts and the resulting indirect general benefits of an EA practice is shown in Figure 3.1.

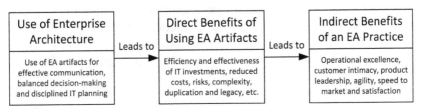

Figure 3.1. Benefits of practicing enterprise architecture

Importantly, similarly to other supporting organizational functions like accounting or human resource management (HRM), the business value of an architecture function and of an EA practice in general cannot be easily calculated, measured or otherwise quantified in financial terms. An architecture function, like an accounting or HRM function, represents a cost center and adds no direct business value to the organizational value chain. Moreover, analogously to an accounting or HRM practice, an EA practice is a continuous organizational activity rather than a one-time project. It is hardly possible to estimate the total investments in enterprise architecture as well as the returns (ROI) from EA efforts. For this reason, it is arguably impossible to evaluate quantitatively the exact contribution of an EA practice to the bottom line[6]. The benefits of practicing enterprise architecture are qualitative in nature and cannot be converted into dollars in a straightforward manner. Similarly to an accounting or HRM practice, there cannot be any real business case in its classical meaning for an EA practice[7].

On the other hand, in the modern world it is hard to build a large successful organization without a disciplined accounting practice (e.g. by writing down annual sales figures on napkins) or without a disciplined HRM practice (e.g. by hiring and promoting random people). Likewise, it is also hard to build a large successful organization without a disciplined EA practice, e.g. by implementing arbitrary IT systems on an ad hoc basis. It is arguably impossible to manage thousands, hundreds and even tens of information systems without using enterprise architecture to control and drive their evolution. In large organizations enterprise architecture is perceived as valuable not because it offers some specific extra benefits, but because it allows these organizations to change and evolve in a controlled manner[8]. There are no alternatives to using enterprise architecture in large organizations. Like accounting or HRM, enterprise architecture can be considered essentially as a "necessary evil" in the modern world. An EA practice is simply not an option any longer[9].

What Organizations Practice Enterprise Architecture?

The use of enterprise architecture seemingly can benefit all organizations employing more than 30-50 IT specialists where IT is used to support main business activities. For example, enterprise architecture is widely practiced in various commercial companies across the globe working in diverse industry sectors including banking, agriculture, insurance, retail, high-tech and even oil industry[10]. Moreover, enterprise architecture is widely practiced even in non-profit organizations including hospitals, universities and police departments as well as in national governments, ministries, agencies, bureaus and customs services[11]. The general idea of using EA artifacts for improving communication between business and IT stakeholders is not industry-specific and widely applicable to most organizations globally. There are arguably little or no articulate differences between the mechanisms of an EA practice in different industries.

Almost two-thirds of large organizations practiced enterprise architecture in 2010[12]. Currently it would be arguably fair to say that the overwhelming majority of large organizations in developed countries either already practice enterprise architecture, or plan to start practicing enterprise architecture in the near future.

The Historical Origin of Enterprise Architecture and Modern Best Practices

The widespread commercial adoption of information systems in business seemingly started around 1959 when IBM introduced its first transistorized mainframe computers, IBM 1401 and 7090 series[13]. At that time a considerable disruptive potential of computers for the business of many organizations, for established management practices and even for the society in general was already widely understood[14]. The commercial use of mainframe computers in organizations further expanded in 1965 after the introduction of the innovative IBM 360 series with a powerful operating system, time sharing and multitasking support. By the end of the 1960s computers had been already widely used in many leading U.S. companies and most of these companies established permanent positions for top computer executives (prototype of modern CIOs)[15]. Since that time the issue of organization-wide information systems planning gained significant attention and first planning approaches had been proposed accordingly[16].

The growing importance of information systems for the business of many organizations intensified the persistent problem of achieving business and IT alignment as well as the need for effective strategic information systems planning[17]. In order to address the pressing issue of business and IT alignment, different vendors, consulting companies and individual experts since the early 1960s proposed numerous formal, detailed, step-by-step **architecture-based planning methodologies**, initially positioned as strategic information systems planning methodologies and later as EA frameworks, intended to translate the business strategy of an organization into an actionable plan for its information systems[18]. The most widely known of these methodologies and frameworks promoted during different time periods include early Business Systems Planning (BSP)[19] and Method/1[20] in the 1970s, Information Engineering[21] and Strategic Data/Information Planning[22] in the 1980s, later Enterprise Architecture Planning (EAP)[23] and TAFIM[24] in the 1990s, FEAF[25] in the 2000s and now TOGAF[26] in the 2010s. These planning approaches have been marketed under different titles including strategic information systems planning, then strategic data planning, information architecture and finally enterprise architecture.

However, all these methodologies and frameworks essentially represent slightly different variations of the same step-wise formal planning approach, which in some form or the other implies analyzing the current support of IT systems, defining the required future architecture aligned to strategic business goals and then developing an action plan, or roadmap, for migrating from the current state to the desired target state. Despite being very widely promoted for decades under various titles as industry "best practices" by their commercially motivated vendors, none of these architecture-based planning methodologies actually worked successfully in practice[27]. For example, seemingly inspired by the advice of "leading industry experts" the U.S. Federal Government in 1999 initiated the infamous Federal Enterprise Architecture (FEA) program to develop enterprise architecture for all government agencies, which eventually delivered only the heaps of largely useless architectural documents and reportedly wasted more than one billion dollars[28]. As a natural result of the endless aggressive promotion of flawed architecture-based methodologies and numerous resulting practical failures, the concept of architecture has been largely discredited and even the very word "architecture" subsequently became a bad word in many organizations[29].

To summarize, numerous architecture-based planning methodologies and frameworks, though created significant hype around architecture, promoted the notion of enterprise architecture in general and stimulated architectural thinking, still did not offer much valuable advice regarding the practical usage of architectural documents, i.e. EA artifacts. As it usually happens in management, genuine managerial innovations and best practices gradually emerge and crystallize in industry as a result of countless attempts of multiple practitioners to address the most pressing business problems[30]. Similarly, in the case of enterprise architecture real EA best practices seemingly emerged and matured *in industry* as numerous IT planners tried for decades to address the perennial problem of poor business and IT alignment existing in many organizations[31]. In other words, the emergence of consistent EA best practices is a natural industry reaction caused by the dire need for business and IT alignment, rather than a deliberate product of some consultants, gurus or "fathers"[32]. Numerous EA methodologies and frameworks might have inspired current EA best practices, but certainly did not invent or prescribe them in any real sense[33]. From this perspective, EA frameworks arguably contributed to the development of actual EA best practices only in the same sense in which wars contributed to the development of modern medicine, i.e. stimulated or even forced their development without providing any particularly useful ideas on their own. Due to their fundamentally disparate nature, genuine industry-born EA best practices barely overlap with the recommendations of branded EA frameworks and methodologies, with the exception that some EA artifacts are indeed developed and used for information systems planning. Paradoxically, even though for many people the very concept of enterprise architecture is closely associated with, if not synonymous to, popular EA frameworks (e.g. TOGAF, Zachman and FEAF), all these frameworks have surprisingly little to do with the actual EA best practices described in this book which emerged some time ago, crystallized over the years and matured to their present state in industry[34]. These best practices simply cannot be derived from any existing EA frameworks or methodologies. Moreover, systematic descriptions of most EA best practices presented in this book can hardly be found in any other available sources on enterprise architecture. An exhaustive historical analysis of the origin of the EA discipline and corresponding best practices is provided in Appendix (The Origin of EA and Modern EA Best Practices).

What Enterprise Architecture Practice Is Not

Since the early 2000s enterprise architecture has been a "hot", widely discussed and overly hyped topic. As a result of prolonged and excessive EA-related speculations, many descriptions of an EA practice available today are unsubstantiated, misguiding, unrealistic or even completely fictitious[35]. In order to dispel numerous myths and rumors around an EA practice, it is important to understand what an EA practice is not.

Not a Purely Technical Planning

An EA practice should not be confused with a purely technical planning accomplished inside IT departments. Even though most architects are former IT specialists and most architecture functions report to CIOs, the general purpose of an EA practice is to bridge the gap between business planning and IT planning and thereby improve business and IT alignment. Successful EA practices naturally require to be closely integrated with business planning, while the separate planning of IT disconnected from business planning can lead only to misalignment.

Not a One-Size-Fits-All Methodology

Even though an EA practice can be beneficial to most large organizations depending on IT regardless of their sectors or industries as noted earlier, there are no easily replicable one-size-fits-all approaches or universal step-by-step methodologies for organizing a successful EA practice[36]. EA practices in successful organizations, though generally follow the same high-level patterns described in this book, are always idiosyncratic in many lower-level details, e.g. specific EA artifacts, roles of architects or peculiarities of EA-related processes. Successful EA practices cannot be simply copied "verbatim" from other organizations, but need to be established in-house and then continuously adapted or fine-tuned to unique organizational needs. In this light, this book should be considered as purely descriptive, rather than prescriptive. The purpose of this book is merely to describe the general regularities of successful EA practices found in multiple organizations, rather than provide a set of exact to-do instructions or "silver bullets" for an EA practice.

Not an Automated Planning

An EA practice is a practice of using specific EA artifacts for effective communication, balanced decision-making and disciplined information systems planning. However, the usage of EA artifacts does not make the planning in organizations happen automatically. In other words, an EA practice itself is unable to translate the business strategy into specific information systems in an automated quasi-mechanical manner. EA artifacts are merely the tools that help different actors collaborate, achieve mutual understanding and develop reasonable planning decisions taking into account the best interests of all stakeholders. In EA practices the planning work itself is still carried out only by human actors, not by EA artifacts. EA artifacts only facilitate, but not automate the information systems planning process. EA artifacts, though useful for planning, are unable to make any tough planning decisions for people, e.g. select appropriate technologies, determine strategic investment priorities or define rational solution structures. They can neither substitute the human ability to plan and achieve agreements, nor automate the actual planning work.

Not a Substitute for Competence

An EA practice helps people in organizations make optimal planning decisions and implement these decisions. However, an EA practice is unable to transform incompetent decisions and actions into competent ones. For instance, an EA practice cannot help develop winning business strategies to incompetent business executives, who are unaware of the current business trends and opportunities on the market[37]. An EA practice cannot help develop successful IT strategies to incompetent IT leaders, who are not knowledgeable in the latest available technologies and their capabilities. Similarly, an EA practice cannot help implement IT solutions to incompetent IT specialists, who are not well-acquainted with relevant technologies or unable to deliver high-quality work on time. In other words, an EA practice, though facilitates information systems planning and delivery, is unable to compensate for the incompetence of involved actors.

Not a Work of Dedicated Experts

An EA practice requires active involvement and participation of multiple business and IT stakeholders in the planning processes. Architectural planning cannot be carried out solely by an isolated group of architects or other highly qualified experts on behalf of the whole organization. Any plans, regardless of their quality, are useless unless all the essential stakeholders of these plans clearly understand how these plans were developed, why certain decisions have been taken and how these plans should be modified when circumstances change. Therefore, successful EA practices require collaborative planning efforts involving both business and IT representatives. Even though the key actors of an EA practice are architects, the role of architects implies involving all relevant business and IT stakeholders into planning activities, rather than being their sole actors. Any architectural plans produced by a narrow group of architects on behalf of their real stakeholders typically end up laying on shelves, not improving business and IT alignment[38].

Not a One-Time Planning Project

An EA practice is a continuous organizational activity that requires constant communication and collaboration between various actors, not a one-time planning project or exercise resulting in some perfect plans[39]. In successful EA practices the ongoing process of planning and communication itself is more important than the actual plans represented by EA artifacts produced as an outcome of this process[40]. Successful EA practices require continuous discussion and readjustment of plans involving all relevant stakeholders, while EA artifacts can be considered merely as tools supporting this discussion, or even as byproducts of this discussion[41]. An EA practice implies intensive organizational learning and matures over time as its main stakeholders learn to cooperate by means of using EA artifacts. At the same time, heaps of EA artifacts describing a snapshot of the ideal future produced as a single one-shot planning effort usually end up laying on shelves, rather than improving business and IT alignment[42]. Even discrete or intermittent bursts of planning can have only a limited efficacy compared to successful EA practices with continuous readjustments of plans.

Not a Technology-Specific Practice

An EA practice is a technology-agnostic and vendor-neutral practice. It is not related to any particular technologies, technical approaches or paradigms. From this perspective, an EA practice can be considered as a universal organizational practice facilitating information systems planning regardless of what specific systems, products or technologies an organization is willing to use. Since an EA practice intends to enable effective communication, knowledge sharing and balanced decision-making, its primary focus is not technologies but people (and for this reason respective EA best practices are rather stable in nature and evolve much slower than technologies). Hence, it is essentially irrelevant to an EA practice whether an organization is going to leverage big data, artificial intelligence or any other recent technical novelties, purchase particular products from IBM, HP or Oracle, or adhere to service-oriented architecture (SOA), microservices or other architectural styles. The role of an EA practice is only to help make optimal decisions regarding the selection of appropriate systems, products, technologies and approaches fitting the organizational needs.

Not an Enterprise Modeling

An EA practice should not be confused with enterprise modeling[43]. Even though an EA practice implies some form of modeling and can benefit from using specialized modeling languages or notations, the actual overlap between an EA practice and enterprise modeling is relatively small. Successful EA practices include not only and not so much modeling. Firstly, an EA practice is a much more complex and broader activity than just modeling. Successful EA practices require not only developing EA artifacts, but also involving multiple diverse actors, organizing productive communication between them, establishing consistent decision-making processes and governance bodies. Modeling itself is only a narrow and relatively insignificant part of an EA practice. Secondly, all EA artifacts created as part of an EA practice are developed in a pragmatic manner for clear and specific aims, typically to facilitate communication between different stakeholders or support decision-making on particular problems[44]. These EA artifacts should be adequate for their purposes, rather than perfectly correct. Creating comprehensive models accurately describing an organization in every detail is not the goal of an EA practice. Modeling for the sake of modeling is a useless activity that should be avoided in EA practices[45]. Thirdly, diagrams created with sophisticated modeling languages or notations are hardly understandable to most business stakeholders and have only a limited application in the context of an EA practice. The majority of practically useful EA artifacts use simplistic and intuitive representation formats that do not rely on any formal modeling approaches. Advanced or "correct" modeling is not particularly important for an EA practice[46].

Not an Enterprise Engineering

An EA practice should not be confused with enterprise engineering. Even though an EA practice includes some analytical work with quantitative estimations, it does not imply any rigid analysis-synthesis procedures similar to the ones used in traditional engineering[47]. An EA practice typically does not require producing any formal blueprints or using any sophisticated calculations[48]. Compared to "hard" mechanical engineering, an EA practice can be considered as a "soft" organic planning approach, which relies on pragmatic documents, informal discussions and quick approximations instead of rigorous drawings, strict processes and precise computations[49]. Real organizations are extremely complex living systems, or organisms, that cannot be designed with traditional engineering methods[50]. For the most part, enterprise engineering can be considered only as a utopian idea unfit for the real world, while an EA practice is a pragmatic and widely adopted approach to managing the evolution of real organizations.

Not an Implementation of Enterprise Architecture Frameworks

As discussed earlier, an EA practice should not be confused with implementing popular EA frameworks, e.g. TOGAF, Zachman, FEAF and DoDAF. Though actively promoted and closely associated with the very notion of enterprise architecture, these frameworks are merely marketing-driven *management fads* unrelated to successful EA practices and having no examples of their successful implementation[51]. All the attempts to follow the actual recommendations of EA frameworks in practice result in failures[52]. From this perspective, popular EA frameworks can be considered only as proven anti-patterns, i.e. impractical approaches that should be avoided. EA practices in successful organizations do not resemble the prescriptions of these frameworks in any real sense, neither in specific details nor even in general ideas. For instance, successful EA practices never fill the cells of the Zachman Framework, never follow the steps of the TOGAF architecture development method (ADM) and never develop the heaps of EA artifacts recommended by TOGAF, even in the organizations included in the list of TOGAF users provided by The Open Group itself[53]. Moreover, successful EA practices do not follow even the general high-level sequential logic advocated by most EA frameworks to develop a comprehensive plan of the desired future state and then implement this plan[54]. While popular EA frameworks are useless products of marketing specialists and management gurus, genuine EA best practices discussed in this book emerged and matured in industry and do not have much in common with these frameworks[55].

Chapter Summary

This chapter discussed the need for enterprise architecture in modern organizations, the benefits of practicing enterprise architecture, the applicability of enterprise architecture across different industries, the historical origin of enterprise architecture and modern EA best practices and finally clarified what enterprise architecture practice is not. The key message of this chapter can be summarized into the following essential points:

- Enterprise architecture is not an accidental or artificially created phenomenon, but rather is a natural solution to natural problems of many modern organizations struggling to manage their extensive IT landscapes
- Practicing enterprise architecture brings numerous benefits to organizations eventually leading to better operational excellence, customer intimacy and product leadership, increased speed-to-market, overall organizational agility and improved managerial satisfaction
- Enterprise architecture is widely applicable, industry-agnostic and arguably can benefit all organizations employing at least 30-50 IT specialists where IT systems are used to support main business operations
- Modern EA best practices emerged some time ago in organizations, evolved over the years, matured to their current state in industry and have no real relationship to aggressive promoted but utterly useless EA frameworks
- An EA practice should not be confused with enterprise modeling, enterprise engineering, purely technical and automated planning, one-shot planning efforts and implementation of EA frameworks

Chapter 4: Enterprise Architecture and City Planning

The previous chapters provided a rather high-level introductory overview of the problem of business and IT alignment, the concept of enterprise architecture and the practice of using enterprise architecture for improving the alignment between business and IT. This chapter descends to the next level of detail and explains the core mechanisms of an EA practice, including its documents, actors and processes, based on the close analogy between enterprise architecture and city planning practices. In particular, this chapter starts from discussing the similarity between organizations and cities from the perspective of their planning. Then, this chapter describes in great detail six general types of EA artifacts and city planning documents as well as their type-specific roles in the context of enterprise architecture and city planning practices. Finally, this chapter explains the relationship and complementarity between different types of EA artifacts and city planning documents.

Enterprise Architecture Practice as City Planning

An EA practice is a complex and multifaceted organizational practice representing a sophisticated interaction of various people, EA artifacts and processes. The general mechanics of an EA practice is far from trivial and can be best explained using close analogies from other, more intuitive areas[1]. Specifically, the practice of using enterprise architecture for managing the evolution of organizations can be compared to the practice of city planning[2].

The close analogy between city planning and EA practices provides a lucid and elegant illustration of what enterprise architecture is and how enterprise architecture works. The purpose of a city planning practice is to organize the urban landscape of a city, enable its sustainable development and make the city more livable. Similarly, the purpose of an EA practice is to organize the IT landscape of an organization, enable its sustainable development and make the organization more effective.

Using the metaphor of city planning, business executives can be compared to city governors willing to develop their city in the interests of its inhabitants. IT project teams can be compared to construction project teams, including bricklayers, plumbers and other workers, responsible for constructing separate buildings. Finally, architects can be compared to city planners responsible for the technical aspects of urban planning. The commonalities between main actors of EA and city planning practices are summarized in Table 4.1.

Enterprise architecture	City planning	Commonalities between enterprise architecture and city planning
Business executives	City governors	Both business executives and city governors are interested in the long-term prosperity of their organizations or cities from the perspective of their ultimate value, but unaware of their technical infrastructure
IT project teams	Construction project teams	Both IT project teams and construction project teams are responsible for completing their technical projects on time, but may be unaware of their long-term ultimate value
Architects	City planners	Both architects and city planners are responsible for translating the long-term ultimate value perspective of business executives or city governors into the short-term technical perspective of IT project teams or construction project teams

Table 4.1. Commonalities between main actors of EA and city planning practices

Both city planning and EA practices are continuous activities intended to control the ongoing evolution of very complex dynamic systems of a semi-organic nature (see Figure 1.1), rather than design some static physical objects. Moreover, cities and organizations share a number of common properties important from the perspective of their planning:

- Both cities and organizations have some valuable objects "visible" for their end users as well as some "invisible" technical infrastructure supporting these objects
- Both cities and organizations cannot be perfectly planned in every detail
- The future needs of both cities and organizations can be anticipated in principle, but cannot be described in detail
- Both cities and organizations cannot be designed and built from scratch
- Both cities and organizations run and evolve simultaneously, they cannot be stopped, modified and then resumed
- Both cities and organizations cannot be changed entirely, but only through step-wise sequences of small incremental modifications of a limited scope
- Major changes in both cities and organizations do not happen quickly overnight, but require considerable time to be implemented
- Both cities and organizations evolve slowly in a continuous and path-dependent manner
- The future evolution of both cities and organizations is always limited by their current structures, previous planning decisions and other natural constraints
- Poor planning decisions, even if they successfully solve current problems, can significantly hinder the further development of both cities and organizations
- The evolution of both cities and organizations is endless in nature and has no definite ultimate or final state
- Both cities and organizations have no single best ways to evolve, but rather sets of multiple available development options with different advantages and disadvantages, benefits and costs

Due to these analogous properties of cities and organizations, all planning decisions in city planning and EA practices have to take into account a number of similar concerns, which are often in conflict with each other. These concerns include, but are not limited to, the following planning considerations:

- Each planning decision should be satisfactory from both the visible ultimate value perspective and the invisible technical infrastructure perspective
- Each planning decision should fulfill specific short-term needs and solve current problems
- Each planning decision should also contribute to abstract long-term goals
- Each planning decision should take into account the current structures and leverage them when possible
- Each planning decision should not create obstacles for the future evolution

Essentially, cities and organizations face very similar problems from the perspective of their planning. In order to overcome these problems both city planning and EA practices employ specific instruments to balance the conflicting interests of different stakeholders and facilitate optimal decision-making. The practice of city planning revolves around specific planning documents helping manage the balanced development of a city. Likewise, the practice of enterprise architecture revolves around specific EA artifacts helping manage the balanced evolution of an organization from the business and IT perspective.

Six Types of Enterprise Architecture Artifacts and City Planning Documents

Enterprise architecture is a collection of specific EA artifacts for managing different aspects of the evolution of an organization. Similarly, city planning documents are intended for managing different aspects of the evolution of a city. All EA artifacts used in successful EA practices can be separated into six general fundamental types: Considerations, Standards, Visions, Landscapes, Outlines and Designs. These six general types of EA artifacts play pivotal roles in an EA practice and also have direct analogs in a city planning practice as well.

In successful EA practices, as well as in city planning practices, Considerations and Standards describe certain rules defining an organization or city, Visions and Landscapes describe the high-level structure of an organization or city, while Outlines and Designs describe specific planned incremental changes to an organization or city. On the one hand, Considerations, Visions and Outlines describe an organization or city from the perspective of its "visible" ultimate value, i.e. from the perspective of business for organizations and from the perspective of livability for cities. Considerations, Visions and Outlines are used by business executives or city governors to manage their IT or urban landscape. On the other hand, Standards, Landscapes and Designs describe an organization or city from the perspective of its "invisible" technical infrastructure supporting the primary value-adding entities, i.e. from the perspective of IT infrastructure for organizations and from the perspective of urban infrastructure for cities. Standards, Landscapes and Designs are used by architects or city planners to organize their IT or urban landscape.

Each of the six general types of EA artifacts and city planning documents answers different questions regarding an organization or city and provides a unique view of it. Specifically, Considerations answer the question on how an organization or city is organized from the business or livability perspective. Standards answer the question on how an organization or city is organized from the IT or urban infrastructure perspective. Visions answer the question on what the high-level structure of an organization or city is from the business or livability perspective. Landscapes answer the question on what the high-level structure of an organization or city is from the IT or urban infrastructure perspective. Outlines answer the question on what specific changes to an organization or city are proposed from the business or livability perspective. Finally, Designs answer the question on what specific changes to an organization or city are proposed from the IT or urban infrastructure perspective. The taxonomy defining the six general types of EA artifacts and city planning documents described above is shown in Figure 4.1.

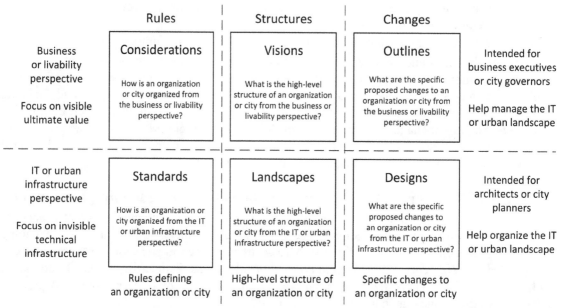

Figure 4.1. Taxonomy for EA artifacts and city planning documents

Considerations, Standards, Visions, Landscapes, Outlines and Designs are the six general types of EA artifacts and city planning documents. Each of these fundamental types has a unique role, purpose, usage and value in the context of an EA or city planning practice.

Considerations

Considerations are abstract high-level guidelines or imperatives defining an entire organization or city. These overarching imperatives are important for business executives and city governors at the same time also having significant technology-related consequences for the whole IT or urban landscape. For instance, for a city Considerations can be represented by urbanism principles defining transport policies, preferences for a particular architectural style or general scaling requirements, while for an organization Considerations are often represented by architecture principles defining process standardization and data centralization policies or business continuity requirements. Typical examples of EA artifacts and city planning documents related to the Considerations general type are shown in Figure 4.2.

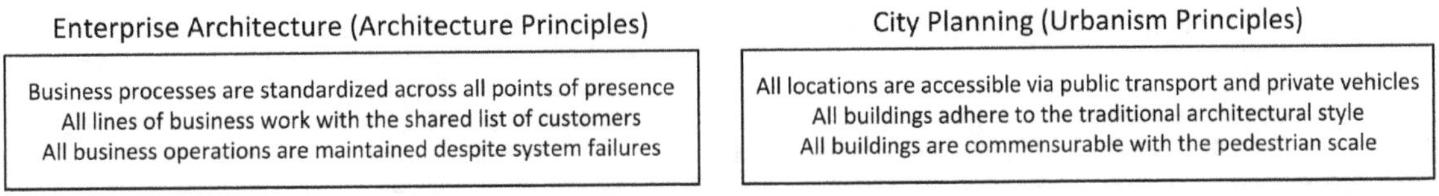

Enterprise Architecture (Architecture Principles)	City Planning (Urbanism Principles)
Business processes are standardized across all points of presence All lines of business work with the shared list of customers All business operations are maintained despite system failures	All locations are accessible via public transport and private vehicles All buildings adhere to the traditional architectural style All buildings are commensurable with the pedestrian scale

Figure 4.2. EA artifacts and city planning documents related to Considerations

Considerations represent planning decisions (see Table 2.1 and Figure 2.6) and, therefore, are always established collaboratively by business executives and architects for an organization or by city governors and city planners for a city based on their overall strategic vision. Considerations articulate the most fundamental rules and essential requirements for an entire organization or city shared by all senior stakeholders that change infrequently. Due to their implicit duality (see Figure 2.4), Considerations convey one value-related meaning to business executives or city governors, but another infrastructure-related meaning to architects or city planners. For example, the architecture principle stating that "all lines of business work with the shared list of customers" (see Figure 4.2) has different implications for business executives and architects. To business executives this principle means that their organization is able to cross-sell products offered by different lines of business to the same customers, while to architects the same principle means that all IT systems supporting the activities of different lines of business should access the same shared customer database[3]. Considerations are permanent and very long-lived in nature (see Table 2.2). They are established for an organization or city only once and then periodically updated to stay relevant.

After being agreed upon, Considerations provide a common basis for all further discussions and influence all planning decisions. The dual nature of Considerations allows business executives and city governors to implicitly shape their IT or urban landscape, even though Considerations often do not mention explicitly the IT or urban infrastructure. Considerations help all relevant stakeholders tune on the same "wavelength" and thereby improve the overall conceptual consistency and mutual alignment of all plans produced for an organization or city.

Standards

Standards are highly specialized low-level technical guidelines prescribing how the IT or urban landscape should be organized and built. These guidelines are critically important for architects and city planners, but largely irrelevant and meaningless for business executives and city governors. For instance, for a city Standards can be represented by construction standards prescribing specific building materials for particular purposes, special requirements for certain types of buildings or the width of traffic lanes, while for an organization Standards are often represented by technology standards prescribing the use of particular application platforms, specific database management systems or proven integration patterns. Typical examples of EA artifacts and city planning documents related to the Standards general type are shown in Figure 4.3.

Enterprise Architecture (Technology Standards)   City Planning (Construction Standards)

All applications should be implemented on the Java EE platform
All databases should use the Oracle RDBMS platform
Enterprise Service Bus should be used to integrate all applications

High alumina cement must be used for brick masonry
Plastic glasses should be used for all residential buildings
All traffic lanes must be 3.0 meters wide

Figure 4.3. EA artifacts and city planning documents related to Standards

Standards represent technical planning decisions and are always established collectively by architects or city planners based on their understanding of the best interests and concerns of business executives or city governors. Unlike dual Considerations, which are always agreed with business executives or city governors, Standards are essentially invisible to business executives and city governors since they reflect highly technology-specific rules incomprehensible and irrelevant to them. Standards are permanent and rather stable. They are updated periodically with the emergence of new promising technologies or better approaches and represent acknowledged best practices in IT system or building construction.

After being established, Standards influence the designs of all individual IT systems or buildings as well as the overall structure of the IT or urban landscape. They help reduce complexity and achieve homogeneity of the IT or urban landscape, reuse proven technical best practices and ensure compliance with the existing regulatory norms. Moreover, Standards can accelerate the construction of new IT systems or buildings, lower their construction costs and reduce the associated risks.

Visions

Visions are abstract, often one-page diagrams providing high-level views of an entire organization or city. Usually they describe the strategic development plan of an organization or city up to 3-5 years ahead in the future. The long-term strategy reflected in Visions is critical for business executives and city governors at the same time also having direct implications for the IT or urban landscape from the technology perspective. For instance, for a city Visions can be represented by zoning maps showing which areas of the city should be built in the future, while for an organization Visions are often represented by business capability maps showing which capabilities should be uplifted in the future. Typical examples of EA artifacts and city planning documents related to the Visions general type are shown in Figure 4.4.

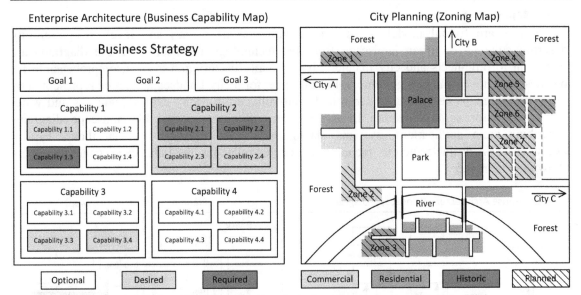

Figure 4.4. EA artifacts and city planning documents related to Visions

Visions represent planning decisions developed collaboratively by business executives and architects for an organization or by city governors and city planners for a city based on the long-term strategy. Visions are consistent with Considerations, reflect the general future direction and suggest what should be done in order to execute the business or city development strategy. In particular, Visions typically articulate specific business capabilities or city zones where future IT or construction investments should go. Essentially they represent an abstract and commonly agreed view of the desired future approved by all senior stakeholders. Due to their implicit duality, Visions convey one meaning to business executives or city governors and another meaning to architects or city planners. For example, to business executives the business capability map shown in Figure 4.4 suggests that their organization is going to uplift certain business capabilities consistent with its business strategy and goals, while to architects the same business capability map suggests that their IT departments should focus on delivering new IT systems improving these "heatmapped" business capabilities[4]. Visions are permanent, but evolving in nature. They are established for an organization or city only once and then continuously updated according to the latest changes in strategic plans.

After being developed, Visions provide a sound basis for directing future investments and prioritizing proposed IT or construction projects. The dual nature of Visions allows business executives and city governors to implicitly develop their IT or urban landscape in the right direction, even though Visions often do not mention explicitly the IT or urban infrastructure. Visions facilitate strategic planning, help achieve a common understanding of the long-term development priorities of an organization or city among all relevant stakeholders and thereby improve the strategic effectiveness of future IT or construction investments.

Landscapes

Landscapes are formal models or diagrams with various scopes and levels of granularity describing the IT or urban landscape from the technology perspective. These diagrams are important for architects and city planners, but virtually useless and even incomprehensible for business executives and city governors. For instance, for a city Landscapes can be represented by infrastructure maps describing underground high-voltage electricity cables, main gas and water pipes, while for an organization Landscapes are often represented by landscape diagrams describing main applications, systems, databases and connections between them. Typical examples of EA artifacts and city planning documents related to the Landscapes general type are shown in Figure 4.5.

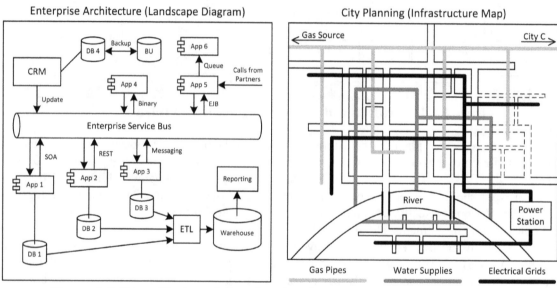

Figure 4.5. EA artifacts and city planning documents related to Landscapes

Landscapes represent documented facts (see Table 2.1 and Figure 2.6) and, therefore, may be developed and maintained for an organization or city by individual architects or city planners alone. Unlike dual Visions, which are always co-developed and approved by business executives or city governors, Landscapes are purely technical diagrams focusing predominantly on the IT or urban infrastructure. They are usually considered as a meaningless techno-babble by business executives and city governors and do not reflect directly any of their strategic concerns. While Visions typically focus on the future and represent the outcomes of proactive planning efforts, Landscapes more often aim to depict accurately the current "as-is" state of the IT or urban landscape. Essentially, they provide a baseline or inventory of the existing IT or urban infrastructure. Landscapes are permanent, long-lived and evolve together with an organization or city. They are updated in a reactive manner to stay current after some changes in the landscape occur, e.g. after a new IT system or building is constructed or deconstructed.

Landscapes are used mostly by architects or city planners and typically serve several different purposes. Firstly, they help understand which IT or urban infrastructure is redundant, unfit for purpose or aging and plan the replacement. Secondly, they help plan the designs of individual IT or construction projects and find the optimal ways of connecting new projects to the existing infrastructure. Landscapes help rationalize the IT or urban infrastructure, reuse existing assets, reduce the unnecessary duplication of supporting facilities and accelerate the planning of new IT systems or buildings.

Outlines

Outlines are high-level descriptions of separate IT or construction projects understandable to business executives and city governors. They provide decision-makers with the relevant summary information regarding a proposed new IT system or building, but do not contain sufficient technical details to actually implement it. For instance, for a city Outlines can be represented by building models showing the sketch of the building, its total area, approximate cost and completion date, while for an organization Outlines are often represented by solution overviews describing the essence of the proposed IT solution, its overall impact, estimated cost, time and risks. Typical examples of EA artifacts and city planning documents related to the Outlines general type are shown in Figure 4.6.

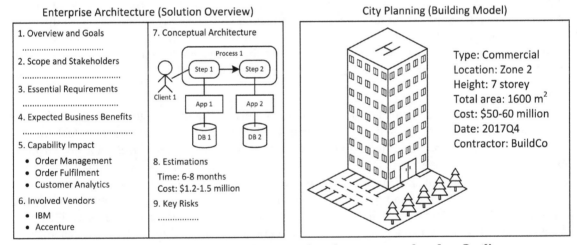

Figure 4.6. EA artifacts and city planning documents related to Outlines

Outlines represent planning decisions and are always created collaboratively by architects and business executives for all proposed IT projects or by city planners and city governors for all proposed construction projects based on their basic requirements. Outlines are often initiated from Visions in order to implement the overall strategic direction approved by business executives or city governors. At the same time, they are initiated in a manner consistent with Considerations in order to be aligned with the agreed organization-wide or city-wide general principles[5]. For developing Outlines architects or city planners also leverage Standards and Landscapes in order to reuse established best practices and plan the connection of the new IT system or building to the existing infrastructure. Due to their explicit duality (see Figure 2.4), Outlines convey one meaning to business executives or city governors and another meaning to architects or city planners. For example, to business executives the solution overview shown in

Figure 4.6 describes how the proposed IT solution will impact their business, which business processes will be improved, what financial investments are required and when the solution can be delivered, while to architects the same solution overview provides a high-level description of the IT solution that needs to be delivered if the project is approved by business executives.

After being developed, Outlines inform business cases for IT or construction projects and serve as main discussion points for these projects. On the one hand, Outlines allow business executives and city governors to understand the tactical value, timelines and costs of specific IT systems or buildings without diving into the complex technical details of their implementation. On the other hand, based on Outlines business executives and city governors can ensure that all proposed IT or construction projects are consistent with Considerations and aligned to the general strategic direction reflected in Visions. Thereby, Outlines facilitate informed judgment and enable sound decision-making regarding the funding of all proposed projects. They help business executives and city governors approve specific IT or construction projects based on the balance of their tactical and strategic benefits and ensure that money is spent wisely. Outlines are temporary and short-lived in nature (see Table 2.2). They are created at the early stages of IT or construction projects to support decision-making, but then discarded after these projects are approved or rejected. The dual nature of Outlines allows business executives and city governors to control all IT or construction investments, even though Outlines only briefly mention the IT or urban infrastructure. Outlines help ensure that a reasonable tactical and strategic value is delivered with each new IT or construction project for a reasonable price, maximize the cost-benefit ratio and thereby improve the efficiency of all investments.

Designs

Designs are detailed technical descriptions of separate IT systems or buildings actionable for their implementers. They provide IT or construction specialists with the precise technology-specific information required to deliver the project, but are largely irrelevant to business executives and city governors. For instance, for a city Designs can be represented by formal architectural drawings of the building with the accurate measures of its geometry, while for an organization Designs are often represented by solution designs describing in detail all the typical "layers" of the IT system including its applications, data, technology and security elements. Typical examples of EA artifacts and city planning documents related to the Designs general type are shown in Figure 4.7.

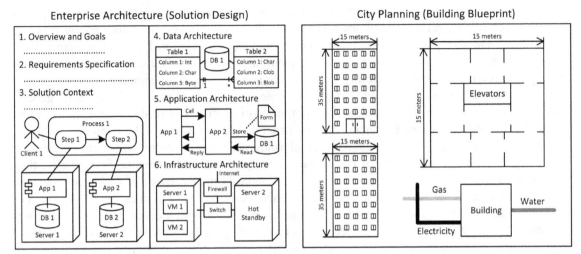

Figure 4.7. EA artifacts and city planning documents related to Designs

Designs represent rather technical planning decisions developed collectively by architects and IT project teams for all IT projects or by city planners and construction project teams for all construction projects based on the corresponding Outlines previously approved by business executives or city governors[6]. Designs provide very detailed and specific technical information regarding the IT or construction project required to implement it. They also explain how exactly the new IT system or building follows the established technical guidelines prescribed by Standards and how exactly this new system or building connects to the existing infrastructure described in Landscapes. Due to their duality, Designs convey one meaning to architects or city planners and another meaning to IT or construction project teams. For example, to architects the solution design shown in Figure 4.7 describes how the IT system adheres to established organization-wide principles, standards and approaches, reuses appropriate strategic IT assets and decommissions redundant, duplicate or legacy systems, while to IT project teams the same solution design specifies detailed business requirements for the IT system as well as the exact plan for their practical implementation.

After being developed, Designs are "consumed" by IT or construction project teams, who are responsible for implementing the project as planned. Designs are temporary and limited in their active lifespan to the duration of respective projects. They are created at the later stages of IT or construction projects to support their implementation, but then discarded after these projects are delivered. The dual nature of Designs allows IT or construction project teams to implicitly deliver globally optimized IT systems, even though Designs typically do not describe explicitly any organization-wide or city-wide considerations. Designs help assure decent technical quality of individual IT systems or buildings and guarantee that all the essential requirements of business executives or city governors are met.

Relationship Between Different Types of Enterprise Architecture Artifacts

Considerations, Standards, Visions, Landscapes, Outlines and Designs are the six general types of EA artifacts and city planning documents playing fundamental roles in EA and city planning practices. These EA artifacts represent six cornerstones of an EA practice and provide six pivots around which all EA-related processes revolve. As discussed above, these six general types of EA artifacts and city planning documents have complex interrelationships and influence each other. The alignment of one EA artifacts to the planning decisions reflected in other EA artifacts enables the connection and traceability between the business and IT perspectives, strategic and tactical plans, organization-wide and project-level decisions, global and local concerns, generic and specific views. A clear understanding of the existing interrelationships between different types of EA artifacts helps better understand the general mechanics of an EA practice.

Considerations, as overarching conceptual rules defining an entire organization or city, essentially impact all other types of EA artifacts or city planning documents. Specifically, they influence the development of Visions, selection of Standards and evolution of Landscapes as well as the architectures of all IT systems or buildings described in Outlines and Designs. For example, Considerations requiring all lines of business to work with a common list of customers may drive the creation of Visions aligned to this requirement, inform the selection of appropriate database and integration Standards suitable for all business units, influence the evolution of Landscapes towards having a centralized customer repository and oblige all Outlines and Designs to connect to the same customer database.

Standards, as global technical rules defining an entire organization or city, provide implementation-specific guidelines for developing Outlines and Designs for specific IT systems or buildings. By shaping individual IT or construction projects, Standards eventually also shape Landscapes describing the IT or urban landscape resulting from these projects. For example, Standards requiring all applications to be implemented on the Java EE platform naturally guide the technology choices made in Outlines and Designs for new IT projects, which ultimately leads to the formation of Java-based Landscapes.

Visions, as high-level views of the desired future for an entire organization or city, initiate the creation of new Outlines for specific IT or construction projects required to achieve this future. They also guide the selection of proper Standards, evolution of Landscapes and development of Designs. For example, Visions implying strategic improvements of the order management capability will inspire Outlines for new IT projects intended to uplift this capability, guide the choice of appropriate Standards related to order management, suggest the general future direction for Landscapes and may also impact on particular project-level decisions in corresponding Designs.

Landscapes, as high-level descriptions of the existing IT or urban landscape from the technology perspective, provide the environment for all new IT systems or buildings described in Outlines and Designs. For example, Landscapes describing the structure of the current IT landscape allow planning the interaction between the existing and new IT systems in their Outlines and Designs.

Outlines, as high-level descriptions of separate IT or construction projects, provide the initial basis for developing more detailed Designs describing how to implement these IT systems or buildings. For example, Outlines describing what a new IT system should do and how approximately it should work offer a starting point for the further planning of technical Designs explaining how exactly this system should work at the physical level.

Designs, as low-level technical descriptions of separate IT systems or buildings, represent the most specific, detailed and local planning decisions. They are shaped and influenced by the "previous", higher-level planning decisions reflected in all other types of EA artifacts or city planning documents, but do not influence directly any of these artifacts or documents. However, Designs provide the basis for updating existing Landscapes after the completion of corresponding IT or construction projects. The essential relationships between different types of EA artifacts described above are shown in Figure 4.8[7].

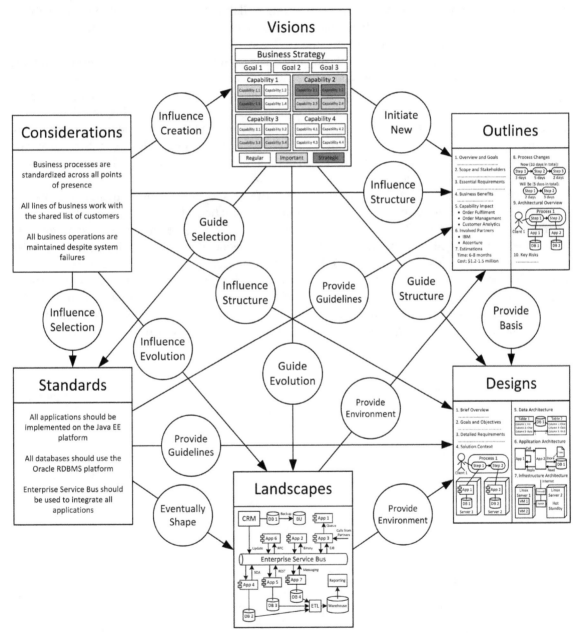

Figure 4.8. The relationship between different types of EA artifacts

Complementarity of Different Types of Enterprise Architecture Artifacts

As discussed above, each of the six general types of EA artifacts and city planning documents (i.e. Considerations, Standards, Visions, Landscapes, Outlines and Designs) fulfills a specific purpose in the context of an EA or city planning practice. Essentially, Considerations, Visions and Outlines provide communication "interfaces" between business executives and architects or between city governors and city planners supporting collaborative decision-making and enabling effective partnership. These interfaces allow business executives or city governors to shape, direct and control the development of their IT or urban landscape by means of setting overarching fundamental principles through Considerations, defining the overall strategic direction through Visions and approving specific tactical steps towards this direction through Outlines. Designs also provide a similar communication interface between architects and IT project teams or between city planners and construction project teams. This interface allows architects or city planners to optimize their IT or urban landscape by means of embedding globally optimized technical decisions into specific local IT projects. However, Standards and Landscapes are used largely as reference materials only by architects and city planners to facilitate optimal technical decision-making.

Since each of the six general types of EA artifacts and city planning documents plays a unique role in the context of an EA or city planning practice, these six general types of EA artifacts and city planning documents can be considered as complementary or even synergistic to each other. The unique and complementary roles of Considerations (e.g. architecture principles and urbanism principles, see Figure 4.2), Standards (e.g. technology standards and construction standards, see Figure 4.3), Visions (e.g. business capability maps and zoning maps, see Figure 4.4), Landscapes (e.g. landscape diagrams and infrastructure maps, see Figure 4.5), Outlines (e.g. solution overviews and building models, see Figure 4.6) and Designs (e.g. solution designs and building blueprints, see Figure 4.7) in EA and city planning practices are summarized in Figure 4.9.

Considerations	**Visions**	**Outlines**
(Architecture principles and urbanism principles)	(Business capability maps and zoning maps)	(Solution overviews and building models)
Who Uses Them?	**Who Uses Them?**	**Who Uses Them?**
Business executives and architects or city governors and city planners	Business executives and architects or city governors and city planners	Business executives and architects or city governors and city planners
How They Are Used?	**How They Are Used?**	**How They Are Used?**
Established collaboratively and then influence all planning decisions	Developed collaboratively and then direct future investments and projects	Developed collaboratively and then inform project funding decisions
Why They Are Used?	**Why They Are Used?**	**Why They Are Used?**
Improve the overall conceptual consistency and mutual alignment	Improve the strategic effectiveness of future investments	Improve the cost-benefit ratio and efficiency of all investments
Dual: Yes **Meaning:** Decisions **Lifecycle:** Permanent	**Dual:** Yes **Meaning:** Decisions **Lifecycle:** Permanent	**Dual:** Yes **Meaning:** Decisions **Lifecycle:** Temporary
Standards	**Landscapes**	**Designs**
(Technology standards and construction standards)	(Landscape diagrams and infrastructure maps)	(Solution designs and building blueprints)
Who Uses Them?	**Who Uses Them?**	**Who Uses Them?**
Only architects or city planners	Only architects or city planners	Architects and IT project teams or city planners and construction project teams
How They Are Used?	**How They Are Used?**	**How They Are Used?**
Established and then influence all project designs as well as the landscape structure	Maintained current to support technical decision-making and project planning	Developed collaboratively and then guide project implementation
Why They Are Used?	**Why They Are Used?**	**Why They Are Used?**
Reduce complexity, risks and costs, achieve homogeneity and compliance	Rationalize infrastructure, reuse assets and accelerate project planning	Improve quality of the project delivery according to requirements
Dual: No **Meaning:** Decisions **Lifecycle:** Permanent	**Dual:** No **Meaning:** Facts **Lifecycle:** Permanent	**Dual:** Yes **Meaning:** Decisions **Lifecycle:** Temporary

Figure 4.9. Complementarity of different types of EA artifacts

Figure 4.9 emphasizes the complementary nature of the six general types of EA artifacts. Although different types of EA artifacts are used differently by different people for different purposes, when used together in mature EA practices these six general types of EA artifacts reinforce each other and improve overall business and IT alignment in organizations. In particular, the proper combined usage of these EA artifacts ensures that all IT projects in an organization:

- Fulfill local short-term needs and requirements – all IT projects are intentionally approved by business executives based on Outlines and their detailed requirements are documented and addressed in Designs
- Contribute to long-term strategic goals and objectives – Outlines of all IT projects are aligned to and prioritized based on Considerations and Visions by architects and business executives

- Implemented rapidly in a predictable, cost-effective and risk-free manner – architects ensure that Designs of all IT projects follow proven implementation approaches and best practices prescribed by Standards
- Reuse and leverage available IT assets – architects ensure that Outlines and Designs of all IT projects leverage the reusable IT assets described in Landscapes
- Do not create redundant IT assets – based on Landscapes architects ensure that Outlines and Designs of new IT projects do not duplicate existing systems
- Can be reused and leveraged as IT assets in the future if appropriate – architects ensure that Designs of IT projects allow reusability when necessary
- Built on technologies that the organization wants to continue using in the future – architects ensure that Outlines and Designs of all IT projects are based on technologies allowed by Standards
- Implemented consistently with other similar projects – architects ensure that Outlines and Designs of all IT projects follow established approaches recommended by Standards and suggested by Considerations
- Do not introduce complexity beyond necessity – based on Standards and Landscapes architects ensure that Designs of new IT projects do not deviate from established approaches and do not complicate the IT landscape

The introductory explanation of the concept of enterprise architecture provided above offers a simplified, but reasonably accurate view of all the main types of EA artifacts and their practical usage. Based on simple, direct and intuitive analogies from city planning, this description provides an easily understandable, straightforward and holistic model explaining what enterprise architecture is, how enterprise architecture works, how enterprise architecture benefits organizations and how the value of enterprise architecture is delivered in practice.

The CSVLOD Model of Enterprise Architecture

Considerations, Standards, Visions, Landscapes, Outlines and Designs (CSVLOD) are the core fundamental components of enterprise architecture at the same time also having direct analogs in city planning. On the one hand, Considerations, Visions and Outlines help business executives or city governors manage their IT or urban landscape. Specifically, Considerations help define the fundamental rules of work, Visions help determine the long-term strategic direction, while Outlines help undertake right tactical steps towards this strategic direction. On the other hand, Standards, Landscapes and Designs help architects or city planners organize their IT or urban landscape. In particular, Standards help reuse proven technical approaches, Landscapes help leverage existing technology assets, while Designs help plan individual technical changes in detail.

The six-type model described above, or the **CSVLOD model of enterprise architecture**, explains the notion of enterprise architecture as a set of six complementary types of EA artifacts (see Figure 4.9) and provides a robust evidence-based conceptualization of enterprise architecture[8]. Despite its apparent simplicity, the CSVLOD model of enterprise architecture reflects the essence of all key EA artifacts, actors and activities constituting successful EA practices. The CSVLOD model and its close analogy to city planning make the fundamental mechanisms of an EA practice easy to understand even to people unrelated to IT. The CSVLOD model of enterprise architecture briefly introduced in this chapter will be used further in this book as the basis for explaining various aspects of an EA practice and described in more detail later in Chapter 8 (The CSVLOD Model of Enterprise Architecture).

Chapter Summary

This chapter explained the key mechanisms of an EA practice and illustrated six essential types of EA artifacts with their interrelationship at work based on the close analogy between enterprise architecture and city planning practices. The key message of this chapter can be summarized into the following essential points:

- The practice of enterprise architecture is conceptually similar to the practice of city planning due the similarity of the typical challenges associated with planning both organizations and cities
- Both EA and city planning practices are based on the six fundamental types of documents: Considerations, Standards, Visions, Landscapes, Outlines and Designs (CSVLOD)
- Considerations are abstract high-level guidelines or imperatives defining an entire organization or city, providing a common basis for all further discussions and influencing all planning decisions
- Standards are highly specialized low-level technical guidelines prescribing how the IT or urban landscape should be constructed and influencing the designs of all individual IT systems or buildings as well as the overall landscape structure
- Visions are abstract, often one-page diagrams depicting high-level views of an entire organization or city and providing a sound basis for directing future investments and prioritizing proposed IT or construction projects
- Landscapes are formal models or diagrams with various scopes and levels of granularity describing the IT or urban landscape from the technology perspective, helping rationalize the IT or urban infrastructure and accelerate the planning of new IT systems or buildings
- Outlines are high-level non-technical descriptions of separate IT or construction projects understandable to business executives or city governors and used to discuss, evaluate, approve and fund proposed projects
- Designs are detailed technical descriptions of separate IT systems or buildings actionable for IT or construction project teams and used to implement corresponding projects after they have been approved by business executives or city governors
- Considerations, Standards, Visions, Landscapes, Outlines and Designs are interrelated, complementary and even synergistic to each other

Chapter 5: The Dialog Between Business and IT

The previous chapter illustrated the practice of using enterprise architecture for achieving business and IT alignment at work based on the analogy between enterprise architecture and city planning. This chapter focuses specifically on the communication aspects of an EA practice and discusses in detail the dialog between business and IT stakeholders. In particular, this chapter starts from describing the most typical practical problems associated with using a business strategy as the basis for IT planning, i.e. as an input for an EA practice. Then, this chapter discusses five common discussion points providing a convenient middle ground meaningful to both business and IT representatives and suitable for establishing a productive dialog between them. Finally, this chapter analyzes the hierarchy and relationship between these discussion points and introduces the so-called EA uncertainty principle.

Problems with the Business Strategy as the Basis for IT Planning

As discussed earlier in Chapter 2, the general organizational role of an EA practice is to translate the abstract business considerations defined by business executives as part of the strategic management process into specific implementable designs of new IT solutions (see Figure 2.3). In most organizations the key product of the strategic management process is a high-level **business strategy**, which defines the overall long-term direction for the whole organization. A formal organizational business strategy often includes, but is not limited to, the following common elements:

- Core mission statement
- Organizational vision and values
- Competitive and environmental analysis, e.g. SWOT, PEST, Five Forces, etc.
- Strategic goals and objectives
- Quantitative and measurable key performance indicators (KPIs)

From the naive common-sense perspective it would be logical to start information systems planning directly from the formal business strategy to achieve better business and IT alignment. In other words, the intuitive assumption suggests that an EA practice should take the business strategy as the key input for all further IT-related planning efforts[1]. Even though this assumption may sound reasonable and rational at the first sight, the real-world practical experience in IT planning shows that the business strategy in a narrow sense, as a general plan for the next 3-5 years with some goals, objectives and KPIs, rarely provides an adequate basis for information systems planning because of at least four different reasons.

Business Strategy Is Often Vague, Unknown or Merely Absent[2]

Even though a business strategy is generally intended to provide some formal long-range plan for the whole organization, the actual guidance provided by the business strategy may be too vague, unclear or abstract for many senior business stakeholders[3]. For example, many business strategies proclaim largely meaningless generic motherhood statements, e.g. to be the industry leading service provider or to offer superior products to customers. Often a business strategy, even if expressed in a sufficiently clear manner, is misunderstood or interpreted differently by different executive-level stakeholders. Some business executives might formally approve, but secretly disagree with the declared strategy. In some cases an organizational business strategy may be miscommunicated or merely unknown to some senior decision-makers[4]. Moreover, in the most extreme cases a commonly agreed, formal and documented business strategy might be simply missing in an organization altogether, even if some long-term objectives do exist in the minds of its business leaders[5]. An unclear, elusive or absent business strategy may often result from the lack of commitment of senior executives to stick with any particular strategy or even from a deliberate decision to stay flexible[6]. In any case, the lack of a clearly defined, mutually agreed and widely understood business strategy, which is often observed in practice, essentially undermines the strategy-based IT planning efforts[7].

Business Strategy Rarely Provides a Clear Direction for IT[8]

Even when an organizational business strategy is clearly defined, known, agreed and shared by all business executives, this business strategy is still often unable to offer any clear guidance for IT. In other words, a business strategy often does not contain any specific suggestions regarding its practical implementation from the IT perspective[9]. For instance, inspiring mission statements, motivating corporate values, ambitious market-share goals, target indicators of financial performance, decisions on brand positioning and even intentions to expand into particular markets typically provide little or no guidance on what types of new information systems might be required to achieve these objectives[10]. Surprisingly, but even a clearly formulated business strategy and objectives can be essentially useless for IT planners to act upon[11]. These problems associated with translating business strategies into actionable IT plans often force IT planners to make significant planning decisions on behalf of the whole organization based mostly on their own guesswork[12]. The inconsistency of perspectives between the business planning and IT planning described above minimizes the actual value of the business strategy as an input for an EA practice and for IT planning in general[13].

Business Strategy Is Often Unstable and Frequently Changes[14]

Even if an organizational business strategy is specific enough and allows deriving some actionable plans for IT, it is still often unable to provide a robust foundation for IT planning due to its unstable and volatile nature[15]. In other words, in many organizations a business strategy changes too often to offer a sound basis for IT planning[16]. Constantly changing business objectives quickly make any strategy-based plans for IT outdated. For example, strategic priorities of an organization can be rapidly changed as a result of its attempts to seize new business opportunities or respond to the recent initiatives of its competitors. At the same time, these changes in the business priorities can immediately destroy all the IT plans based on the previous priorities[17]. In the most extreme cases, strategy-based plans for IT might become obsolete even before they are completed. The unpredictable, volatile and unstable nature of the business strategy in many organizations makes a meaningful strategy-based IT planning essentially impossible and reduces the importance of the business strategy for an EA practice.

Business Strategy Often Requires Non-Reusable IT Systems[18]

Even if an organizational business strategy is reasonably clear, stable and actionable for IT, this business strategy often requires the implementation of highly strategy-specific information systems, which might be essential for the current strategy, but useless for an organization in the long run. In other words, specific IT systems delivered to execute the current business strategy are often idiosyncratic and cannot be leveraged in the future after this business strategy fades away. Even stable and long-lasting business strategies may be active only for 3-5 years, but the information systems implemented to support these strategies often "live" in organizations for ten years or even longer. These systems gradually complicate the organizational IT landscape, impede its modification and reduce strategic IT agility. Moreover, all these IT systems also need to be supported by IT staff and naturally lead to increased maintenance costs and bloated IT budgets. Since IT systems generally have much longer lifetimes than the specific business strategies they are intended to enable, these systems might be considered as an asset for the current business strategy, but as a liability for the next strategies[19]. Essentially, when some business strategy decays, all the information systems delivered specifically for this strategy turn into an IT burden for an organization. After switching several business strategies over a period of years organizations often accumulate numerous isolated legacy IT systems, which were once considered as strategic during the previous strategies, but now are simply irrelevant and redundant.

As a result of this effect, chasing latest business strategies often leads to proliferation of countless legacy IT systems, which create significant problems for organizations in the long-term future. Constant focus on delivering new IT systems aligned to the current strategic needs eventually leads to the situation of "alignment trap", when the organizational IT landscape gradually becomes increasingly complex, fragile and inefficient[20]. Furthermore, the IT planning focused exclusively on the current business strategy does not allow organizations to develop any truly reusable IT capabilities lasting beyond individual strategies[21]. But when IT is always reacting to the latest business strategies, it becomes a persistent bottleneck rather than a strategic asset supporting future opportunities[22].

The Role of Business Strategy for Enterprise Architecture Practice

Due to the four problems described above a business strategy in a narrow sense, as a general business plan, mission, goals and objectives, rarely provides a very useful input for an EA practice[23]. A business strategy may be simply too obscure, vague or irrelevant to IT. For example, the mission statements to "become the most trusted service provider on the market" or "turn into a perfectly customer-centric organization" as well as the strategic objectives to "increase the gross annual revenue by 10% over the next three years" or "extend the market share in the retail segment to 20% by 2020" on their own are virtually meaningless and useless from the IT perspective.

Paradoxically, but even a stable and articulate business strategy can be considered as both too abstract and too specific at the same time for the purposes of IT planning. On the one hand, even if the business strategy is pretty detailed, it still might be too abstract and high-level for launching specific IT initiatives and even for determining what types of IT systems are required, let alone for specifying the details of these systems. On the other hand, even if the business strategy is reasonably stable for the period of the next 3-5 years, it still might be too specific and short-sighted for identifying fundamental IT capabilities required by an organization beyond the current strategy, over a period of time commensurate with the full lifecycle of IT systems from their initial deployment to final retirement. In other words, a business strategy might be too "broad" for IT systems from the perspective of their development, but at the same time too "narrow" for IT systems from the perspective of their support and maintenance. Essentially, a business strategy specifies neither what IT should do right now, nor what IT should provide after the next 3-5 years. The problems with the business strategy as the basis for IT planning discussed above are summarized in Figure 5.1.

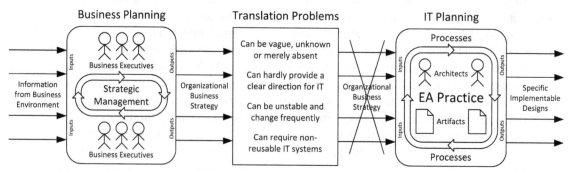

Figure 5.1. Problems with the business strategy as the basis for IT planning

The four described typical problems with the business strategy hinder the strategy-based IT planning efforts and minimize the actual role of the business strategy as an input for an EA practice. A business strategy, though sets the overall "soft" context for an EA practice and for IT planning in general, rarely provides enough "hard" data for concrete IT-related planning activities. For this reason, an EA practice and IT planning in most organizations cannot be carried out based only on a business strategy alone. In order to circumvent the typical problems associated with the strategy-based IT planning, business stakeholders and architects typically focus on discussing other considerations unrelated directly to the business strategy and providing a more solid basis for making specific IT-related planning decisions[24].

Key Discussion Points Between Business and IT

Since a business strategy itself can hardly be used as a sound foundation for IT planning (see Figure 5.1), some other aspects and elements of an organization should be taken into account and discussed for developing optimal IT-related planning decisions. These elements and aspects should offer a more stable, clear and actionable input for an EA practice than an ambiguous, elusive and volatile business strategy. Moreover, these elements and aspects should be able to provide a middle ground relevant to both business and IT, which can be suitable for establishing effective communication and achieving a mutual understanding between business and IT stakeholders.

In order to enable a productive partnership between business and IT, the middle ground for business and IT alignment should be equally meaningful from both the business and IT viewpoints and clearly address both business and IT concerns. In other words, the middle ground between business and IT should be clearly understandable and valuable to both business and IT stakeholders from the planning perspective. Specifically, to business stakeholders this middle ground should explain the business value of corresponding planning decisions, while to IT stakeholders this middle ground should provide some actionable suggestions. However, most purely business-specific notions (e.g. competitive advantages, strengths, opportunities, market segments and customer experience), similarly to the business strategy, do not provide any clear actionable implications for IT and, therefore, are essentially meaningless to most IT stakeholders. Likewise, most purely IT-specific notions (e.g. applications, systems, databases, infrastructure and networks) are not clearly traceable to the resulting business value and, therefore, are essentially meaningless to most business stakeholders. Consequently, neither typical business notions nor typical IT notions are able to provide an adequate middle ground meaningful to both parties. In other words, these typical business and IT notions are generally unsuitable for establishing a productive dialog between business and IT stakeholders.

Furthermore, the middle ground between business and IT should be suitable for discussions with different planning horizons. On the one hand, the middle ground considerations should reflect some immediate and short-term business priorities, be traceable to the organizational business strategy and also provide a longer-term business outlook beyond the current strategy. On the other hand, the middle ground considerations should reflect some immediate and short-term IT-related needs, be reducible to more or less specific IT-related plans for the next 3-5 years and also provide a longer-term view of the required IT capabilities.

Essentially, these middle ground planning considerations should be able to provide certain **discussion points** important for both business and IT across the entire time spectrum, from the immediately actionable short-term (<1-2 years) time horizons to the long-term (3-5 years) and very long-term (>3-5 years) time horizons. These discussion points should allow making collaborative IT-related planning decisions aligned to the business strategy and to the longer-term business vision without discussing the business strategy directly.

Even though different organizations, teams and individuals often find their own unique organization-specific, initiative-specific or even individual-specific discussion points for establishing a constructive dialog between business and IT, common discussion points playing significant roles in many organizations include, but are not limited to, the following five key discussion points:

- Operating model – global process standardization and data sharing requirements
- Business capabilities – specific capabilities of an organization that require improvements
- Specific business needs – specific needs of an organization that require to be addressed
- Business processes – high-level process change requirements to specific IT solutions
- Business requirements – detailed business requirements to specific IT systems

These five key discussion points and their relationship to common business notions and IT notions are shown in Figure 5.2.

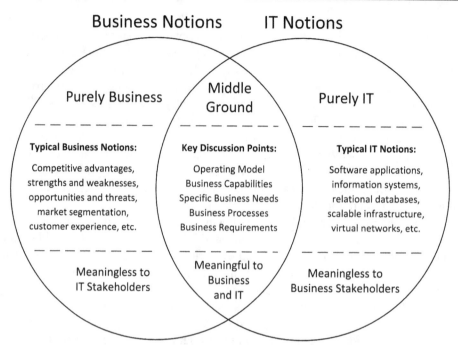

Figure 5.2. Key discussion points between business and IT

Importantly, the list of five discussion points described above is far from complete and exhaustive. The key discussion points shown in Figure 5.2 are certainly not the only possible discussion points, but rather the most typical and commonly used discussion points for different planning horizons facilitating communication between business and IT stakeholders in numerous organizations. Essentially, these discussion points offer convenient shared topics around which business and IT stakeholders can start a conversation, establish an effective dialog and achieve a mutual understanding.

The core underlying ideas behind convenient discussion points are very similar conceptually to the mechanism of dual EA artifacts discussed earlier (see Figure 2.4). By analogy with dual EA artifacts, these discussion points can be considered as dual notions equally meaningful to both business and IT stakeholders at the same time.

Operating Model[25]

An **operating model** is the desired level of organization-wide process standardization and data integration[26]. The operating model of an organization defines what business processes are standardized and what business data is shared across its major business units. Since standardized business processes also imply standardized underlying applications, an operating model essentially determines global standardization and integration requirements for the key business-enabling EA domains, i.e. business, applications and data (see Figure 2.2).

Depending on the highest-level structure of an organization, its major business units may represent different lines of business, business functions, product divisions, market segment divisions, regional offices or any other separate business departments. On the one hand, the required level of **process standardization** indicates the degree to which these business units should perform same business processes in the same way. Standardization of business processes across business units has both advantages and disadvantages for organizations. In particular, it facilitates brand recognition, global efficiency and predictability, but at the same time limits local opportunities for customization and innovation. To determine the desired level of process standardization across business units, senior business and IT stakeholders should collectively decide to what extent an organization can benefit from having its business units run their operations in the same way.

On the other hand, the required level of **data integration** indicates the degree to which these organizational business units should share business data between each other. Similarly to process standardization, data sharing across business units also has both advantages and disadvantages for organizations. For instance, it allows presenting a "single face" to customers, enables end-to-end transaction processing, increases transparency, coordination and agility. However, data integration increases coupling between different organizational units, requires achieving a common understanding of shared data entities across diverse business divisions and developing their standard, commonly agreed definitions and formats. To determine the desired level of data integration across business units, senior business and IT stakeholders should collectively decide to what extent the successful completion of transactions in business units depends on the availability, integrity, accuracy and timeliness of data from other business units.

Decisions regarding the necessary level of standardization and integration have critical and far-reaching implications for the whole organization from both the business and IT perspectives. These decisions are mutually independent and the combination of these two decisions defines four possible operating models: diversification, coordination, replication and unification. Each of these operating models implies different structure of the business, requires different organization of the IT landscape and supports different types of business strategies[27].

The **diversification model** is an operating model with low process standardization and low data integration. The diversification model is appropriate for highly decentralized organizations consisting of diverse and independent business units, e.g. separate lines of business or even subsidiary companies. From the business perspective, business units in these organizations are often managed autonomously, perform unique business operations, design their own business processes, have independent transactions and share little or no common customers and suppliers. From the IT perspective, the IT landscapes of these organizations often consist of global IT services and infrastructure shared by all business units and local applications and databases owned by specific business units. Core organization-wide elements of these IT landscapes are lean layers of shared infrastructure and technology services supporting all local IT systems in business units. The key IT capability expected from these landscapes is providing economies of scale through sharing IT services and infrastructure without limiting local independence. From the strategic perspective, the diversification model largely relies on the independence, flexibility and local autonomy of separate business units in serving customers and generating profits. However, the diversification model may be unsuitable for any centrally orchestrated business innovations. In their business strategies these organizations can leverage natural synergies from related, but not integrated, business units as well as economies of scale and cost reductions from using shared technical standards, IT infrastructure and services. Moreover, they can also introduce and benefit from some shared organization-wide business services or functions, e.g.

human resources, finance or procurement. Organic growth in these organizations is often achieved through the local growth of their existing business units or via establishing new business units. These organizations can also easily grow through acquisitions since only a minimal integration of new businesses into the existing structures is required. However, some strategic market synergy between existing and new business units is necessary to benefits from these acquisitions.

The **coordination model** is an operating model with low process standardization and high data integration. The coordination model is appropriate for decentralized organizations consisting of diverse but interdependent business units, e.g. different business functions or product divisions. From the business perspective, business units in these organizations are often managed autonomously, perform unique business operations, design their own business processes and may offer their own local products or services, but depend on transactions in other business units and have shared customers, products, suppliers or partners. From the IT perspective, the IT landscapes of these organizations often consist of global databases (e.g. customers, products and suppliers), IT services and infrastructure shared by all business units and local applications owned by specific business units. Core organization-wide elements of these IT landscapes are central data hubs storing common information accessible to all local applications in business units. The key IT capability expected from these landscapes is providing easy global access to the shared data through standard technology interfaces. From the strategic perspective, the coordination model largely relies on the ability to offer superior customer service, encourage local innovation, enable cross-selling and upselling opportunities, achieve transparency across key transactions and supply chain processes. However, the coordination model may be unsuitable for competing based on lower costs. In their business strategies these organizations can leverage the deep process expertise of their business units to attract new customers or sell more products to existing customers as well as the available IT infrastructure for global data sharing between the business units. For instance, a comprehensive shared customer repository may enable the intimate knowledge of customers, their needs and buying patterns thereby helping develop better-targeted products and improve the overall business decision-making. Organic growth in these organizations is often achieved via reaching new customer segments or even new markets, offering innovative products to existing customers through established selling channels or extending current services to meet new customer demands. These organizations can also grow through acquisitions, often by obtaining either new customers for existing products or new products for existing customers. However, the information systems of acquired organizations should be adapted to common data standards and integrated with the existing global databases.

The **replication model** is an operating model with high process standardization and low data integration. The replication model is appropriate for decentralized organizations consisting of similar but independent business units, e.g. separate regional offices marketing same products or services. From the business perspective, business units in these organizations are often managed autonomously but follow centrally defined business processes, perform similar business operations, have independent transactions, manage their customers locally and share little or no common customers. From the IT perspective, the IT landscapes of these organizations often consist of globally standardized applications and databases owned locally by specific business units and global IT services and infrastructure shared by all business units. Core organization-wide elements of these IT landscapes are replicable IT systems supporting core business processes and deployed in all business units. The key IT capability expected from these landscapes is providing standard sets of information systems for standardized business processes optimized for global efficiency. From the strategic perspective, the replication model largely relies on efficient, predictable and repeatable business processes enabling consistent customer experience as well as on the capacity for organization-wide process innovation. However, the replication model may be unsuitable for building complex customer relationships. In their business strategies these organizations can leverage standardized business processes and underpinning IT systems to quickly expand into new markets, offer new products or services. For instance, standard business practices and information systems can be rapidly installed in new business units or locations to replicate the business with minimal start-up costs and generate new profits. Organic growth in these organizations is often achieved via replicating established best practices in new markets or regions and introducing new global products or services. These organizations can also grow through acquisitions by "ripping and replacing" local business processes and IT systems of the acquired competitors with the globally standardized ones.

The **unification model** is an operating model with high process standardization and high data integration. The unification model is appropriate for centralized organizations consisting of similar and interdependent business units, e.g. interrelated geographical or market segment divisions. From the business perspective, business units in these organizations are often managed centrally, perform similar or overlapping business operations, run standardized business processes, have globally integrated transactions, shared customers, products or suppliers. From the IT perspective, the IT landscapes of these organizations often consist of global applications, databases, IT services and infrastructure shared by all business units. Essential organization-wide elements of these IT landscapes are globally accessible information systems enabling core business processes in all business units, often implemented as comprehensive ERP systems[28]. The key IT capability expected from these landscapes is providing standard IT systems with global data access reinforcing standardized business processes. From the strategic perspective, the unification model largely relies on maximizing efficiency and reducing variability of business processes, using integrated data, minimizing costs and ensuring consistent customer experience. While the unification model is generally appropriate for providing commodity products and services, it may be unsuitable for competing based on highly innovative offerings since it may be too restrictive and essentially disable any local experimentation in business units. In their business strategies these organizations can leverage primarily the significant economies of scale resulting from the global standardization and integration of all applications, data and IT infrastructure across all business units. Organic growth in these organizations is often achieved via extending their product lines and introducing existing products or services in new markets. These organizations can also grow through acquisitions by ripping and replacing custom information systems of the acquired competitors with the standard organization-wide IT systems. The key properties of the four operating models described above are summarized in Figure 5.3.

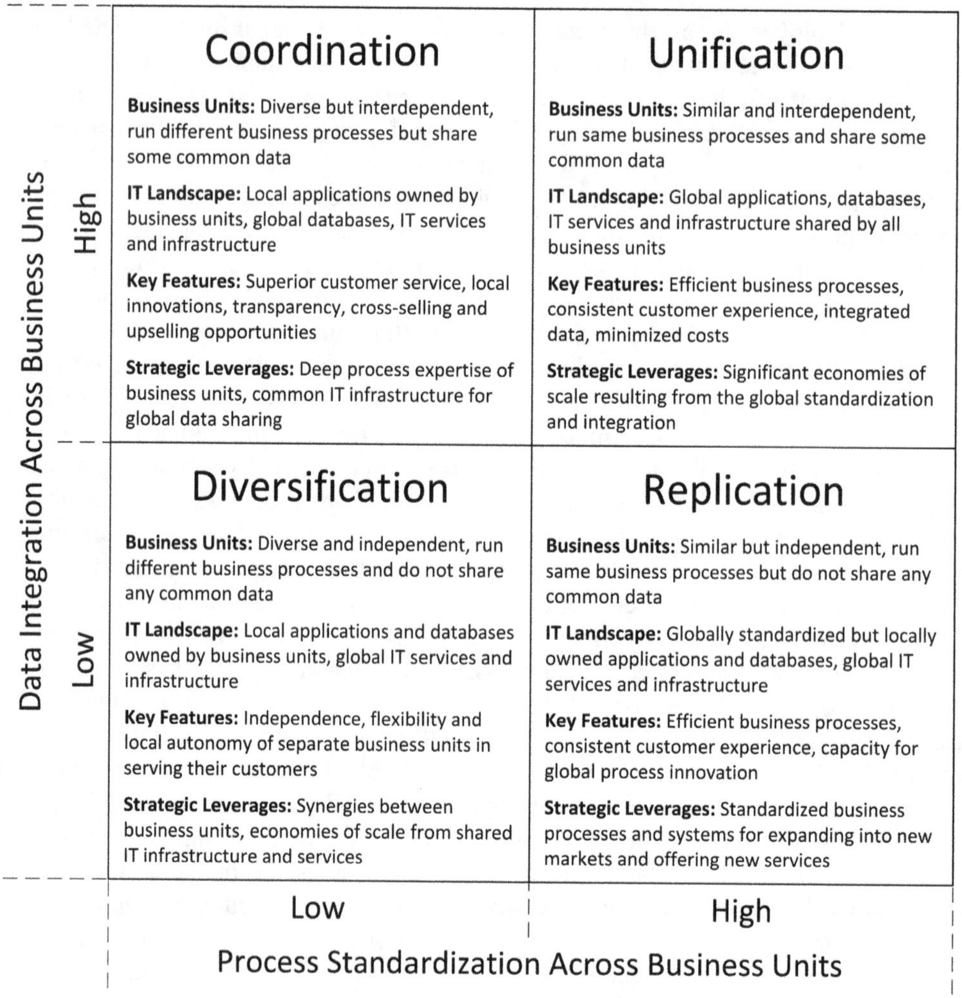

Coordination	**Unification**	

Coordination

Business Units: Diverse but interdependent, run different business processes but share some common data

IT Landscape: Local applications owned by business units, global databases, IT services and infrastructure

Key Features: Superior customer service, local innovations, transparency, cross-selling and upselling opportunities

Strategic Leverages: Deep process expertise of business units, common IT infrastructure for global data sharing

Unification

Business Units: Similar and interdependent, run same business processes and share some common data

IT Landscape: Global applications, databases, IT services and infrastructure shared by all business units

Key Features: Efficient business processes, consistent customer experience, integrated data, minimized costs

Strategic Leverages: Significant economies of scale resulting from the global standardization and integration

Diversification

Business Units: Diverse and independent, run different business processes and do not share any common data

IT Landscape: Local applications and databases owned by business units, global IT services and infrastructure

Key Features: Independence, flexibility and local autonomy of separate business units in serving their customers

Strategic Leverages: Synergies between business units, economies of scale from shared IT infrastructure and services

Replication

Business Units: Similar but independent, run same business processes but do not share any common data

IT Landscape: Globally standardized but locally owned applications and databases, global IT services and infrastructure

Key Features: Efficient business processes, consistent customer experience, capacity for global process innovation

Strategic Leverages: Standardized business processes and systems for expanding into new markets and offering new services

Vertical axis: **Data Integration Across Business Units** (High / Low)

Horizontal axis: Low / High — **Process Standardization Across Business Units**

Figure 5.3. Key properties of the four operating models

Large and complex organizations often establish different operating models at different organizational levels[29]. For example, an organization may adopt the diversification model at the highest organization-wide level in order to grant full independence to its three core business units, while these business units in their turn may adopt the coordination, replication and unification models respectively according to their specific local needs[30].

Since each operating model has profound and long-lasting consequences for an entire organization from both the business and IT viewpoints (see Figure 5.3), an operating model provides a very convenient discussion point for senior business and IT stakeholders. On the one hand, each operating model implies a specific way of structuring the business of an organization. By sticking with a particular operating model, business executives decide how their organization needs to operate to thrive in its business environment. Essentially, the choice of an operating model determines what an organization can do well and cannot do well. Each operating model facilitates the successful execution of some business strategies, but at the same time inhibits the execution of others. Moreover, each operating model also shapes an overall organizational reporting structure and defines the level of autonomy and decision-making responsibilities of separate business units[31]. For these reasons, business executives should clearly understand the implications of their operating model for the long-term future of their organization. On the other hand, each operating model requires a specific way of structuring the IT landscape of an organization. By understanding and sticking with a particular operating model, architects and IT executives can align the IT landscape to the most fundamental and long-term needs of the business. Essentially, the selection of a certain operating model by business executives provides clear suggestions to architects regarding what their organizational IT landscape should do well and should not do well. Aligning the IT landscape to the operating model facilitates the IT-enabled execution of the whole range of different business strategies supported by the operating model. Furthermore, the operating model of an organization also shapes the general high-level structure of its architecture function as well as specific architecture roles within the architecture function, as discussed later in Chapter 17 (Architecture Functions in Organizations).

An operating model is the most abstract of all common discussion points between business and IT stakeholders. The choice of a specific operating model is a much more fundamental and far-reaching organizational decision than the choice of a specific business strategy. While any business strategy reflects some speculative expectations that will inevitably change in the future, the choice of an operating model reflects more fundamental considerations that are not expected to change in the foreseeable future. In other words, a business strategy is based on the assumptions of what is going to change, while an operating model is based on the assumptions of what is not going to change. Moreover, each of the four operating models essentially delineates a range of compatible business strategies available to organizations[32]. Any operating model can support a rapid implementation of the business strategies consistent with its core assumptions, but the same operating model may also hinder the business strategies inconsistent with these assumptions. For instance, the entire family of business strategies based on price leadership may be perfectly appropriate for the replication model, but inappropriate for the coordination model where the IT landscape consists of diverse applications customized specifically for local needs and does not imply substantial economies of scale from global standardization. At the same time, the entire family of business strategies based on customer intimacy may be perfectly appropriate for the coordination model, but inappropriate for the replication model where the IT landscape consists of numerous siloed, locally owned databases and does not imply any global sharing of the customer information between different business units. Similarly, the choice of an operating model has significant implications for the ability of an entire organization to introduce new products or services, expand into new markets and integrate new acquisitions. An operating model thereby suggests which strategic opportunities an organization should and should not pursue. Each operating model provides a different foundation for strategy execution and offers different opportunities and challenges for growth. From this perspective, an operating model can be considered as a driver of the business strategy.

Even though most organizations can identify some processes and data related to every operating model, organizations can arguably benefit from selecting a single operating model and sticking with it in the future[33]. By stipulating the most basic conceptual requirements to the organizational IT landscape, the preferred operating model provides a stable and actionable view of an organization to IT. Specifically, the target operating model helps senior business and IT stakeholders determine which exactly core processes and data should be globally standardized or integrated across all business units and plan the IT landscape accordingly. The clear understanding of standard processes and shared data allows establishing truly reusable IT capabilities supporting not only the current business strategy, but also all the next business strategies in the long-term future. Essentially, the IT landscape closely aligned to the required operating model represents a digitized platform that can be leveraged by an organization in the future for executing all subsequent business strategies, rather than merely for providing isolated IT solutions for the current strategy[34]. Sticking with a particular target operating model helps organizations build reusable IT platforms and avoid the common problem of turning today's strategic IT assets into tomorrow's legacy IT liabilities described earlier. Moreover, these digitized platforms reflecting the essential requirements of the operating model may enable proactive, rather than reactivate, identification of potential strategic opportunities. Due to its profound and far-reaching organizational impact, the notion of operating model is naturally appropriate for a very long-range global IT planning with a horizon of longer than 3-5 years. Decisions on the desired operating model as part of an EA practice are often expressed through architecture principles (see Figure 4.2) or other dual EA artifacts helping executive-level business and IT stakeholders document key organization-wide process standardization and data sharing requirements.

Selecting a specific operating model essentially represents a commitment of an entire organization to a certain way of doing business. Although sticking with any particular operating model might be risky, not sticking with any operating model at all might be even more risky for an organization in the long run. In particular, the lack of focus on any specific operating model inhibits the growth of permanent IT capabilities lasting beyond individual, ever-changing strategies. Organizations with uncertain operating models are simply incapable of accumulating and reusing any global IT assets. As a result, these organizations, being unable to leverage established IT platforms, often have to start the implementation of any business strategies from scratch every time. Switching operating models is a significant organizational undertaking which usually requires deep and fundamental transformations in an organization. Even though sometimes these changes might be necessary, organizations normally do not change their operating models too often.

Business Capabilities[35]

A **business capability** is a general ability or capacity of an organization to perform a specific business activity. The full set of all organizational business capabilities represents everything that an organization can do or needs to do to run its business. Business capabilities are multifaceted notions. They encompass all underlying business processes, procedures, people, knowledge, incentives and other resources, including information systems, required to fulfill these capabilities[36]. For example, business capabilities "marketing campaign management", "customer behavior tracking" and "financial reporting" reflect the ability of an organization to manage marketing campaigns, track the behavior of its customers and report its financial results respectively. At the same time, each of these capabilities also abstracts all the related business processes, roles and IT systems enabling these capabilities. This multidimensional nature of business capabilities helps position IT projects in the overall organizational context, i.e.

understand them as business projects that imply not only installing new information systems, but also addressing other aspects of respective capabilities in a complementary manner, e.g. modifying established operational procedures or providing appropriate training to system users.

Business capabilities can be considered as consistent, independent and unique building blocks of an organization corresponding to its different business functions. Essentially, a set of all organizational business capabilities provides a high-level overarching structure of the whole business. Moreover, basic business capabilities of an organization change pretty rarely, only in case of significant transformations of its core business model. For this reason, business capabilities offer a stable view of the business, which is typically more durable than specific business strategies or organizational structures, let alone specific projects, processes or IT systems.

Since each business capability represents both a capacity of the business to do something valuable and a set of all underlying IT assets enabling this capacity, business capabilities provide very convenient discussion points for senior business and IT stakeholders. On the one hand, business capabilities resonate with the thought processes of most business executives. For instance, business leaders normally understand the relationship between their business strategy and business capabilities. Instead of discussing mission statements, market-share or financial objectives, which are typically unable to provide any real basis for IT planning, business executives can specify which exactly business capabilities should be improved in order to achieve these goals. This focus on business capabilities allows business executives to express their business strategy in more clear, specific and actionable terms. On the other hand, business capabilities also resonate with the thought processes of most architects. For instance, architects normally understand the relationship between business capabilities and underlying information systems. Instead of guessing what IT systems might be necessary to achieve some vague strategic objectives, architects can use the set of strategic business capabilities identified by senior business leaders as the basis for IT planning. Specific business capabilities typically provide reasonably clear suggestions to architects regarding the types of new IT capabilities and systems that might need to be introduced to uplift the requested business capabilities. However, not all capability enhancements can be achieved with IT since many required improvements often lay in other dimensions of business capabilities unrelated to IT, e.g. people, motivation or skills.

As discussion points between business and IT stakeholders, business capabilities are more detailed than an operating model. While the operating model only defines the fundamental "permanent" structure of the business and its IT landscape, business capabilities suggest where exactly business and IT improvements are required according to the current business strategy. However, business capabilities are still concepts of a high abstraction level somewhat commensurable with the abstraction level of a business strategy. Due to their highly conceptual nature, business capabilities provide convenient wide-scope abstractions suitable for describing entire organizations or their major business units, e.g. lines of business, business functions or divisions. Since business capabilities are largely ignorant of specific details of their underlying processes, actors and systems, they may be very useful for coarse-grained conceptual planning, typically with the long-term planning horizons up to 3-5 years ahead. Specifically, business capabilities, as very high-level abstractions of the business, can be discussed as part of the organization-wide strategic planning efforts to decide where in an organization future improvements are required. At the same time, as highly abstract concepts, business capabilities are unsuitable and useless for more detailed planning at the level of specific business processes or IT systems. Discussions of business capabilities as part of an EA practice are often supported by business capability maps (see Figure 4.4) or other similar dual EA artifacts helping senior business and IT stakeholders decide which business capabilities should be uplifted in the future.

While the business strategy itself is typically unable to provide an actionable basis for IT planning, as discussed earlier (see Figure 5.1), the same business strategy translated into the set of strategic business capabilities usually provides a much more clear, unambiguous and sound basis for IT planning. Essentially, business capabilities provide the appropriate level of detail (i.e. the next level of detail beneath the business strategy) to facilitate strategic IT planning. From this perspective, business capabilities offer a valuable mechanism for translating the business strategy into action. In many cases the set of specific business capabilities that need to be improved essentially substitutes the business strategy in the discussions on business and IT alignment. This feature often makes business capabilities key discussion points of the strategic dialog between business and IT leaders helping bridge the gap between high-level business interests and key IT concerns. However, in some organizations other conceptually similar and closely related notions (e.g. business activities) might be used instead of business capabilities for analogous purposes during strategic IT planning.

Specific Business Needs

A **specific business need** is a general idea to address a particular business problem using IT to achieve some business improvements. Essentially, specific business needs can be considered as proposed business initiatives or projects with necessary IT components. For example, specific business needs to "accelerate the mortgage lending process", "enable order tracking for customers" and "improve the accuracy of demand forecasting" describe some business problems to be solved. At the same time, each of these business needs usually implies specific changes in the organizational IT landscape enabling the solutions of the corresponding problems.

Since specific business needs represent opportunities for particular business improvements and also suggest specific modifications of the IT landscape, they provide very convenient discussion points for business and IT stakeholders. On the one hand, business executives generally understand the relative importance of specific business needs for the business of an organization. Business leaders, who identify specific business needs, are able to evaluate the anticipated organizational benefits ensuing from addressing these needs and assess the overall business value resulting from solving the corresponding problems. For instance, senior business stakeholders can roughly estimate what cost savings, service quality improvements, time-to-market reductions or increases in customer satisfaction can be achieved if specific business needs are successfully addressed. On the other hand, architects understand what types of changes in the IT landscape might be required to implement specific business needs. Architects are usually able to articulate and offer a number of possible technical options for addressing the requested business needs with IT. For instance, architects can explore the potential approaches that might be suitable for solving specific business problems, assess the status of the currently available IT assets and roughly estimate the magnitude of changes in the existing IT landscape required to address these problems.

As discussion points between business and IT stakeholders, specific business needs are more detailed than business capabilities. While required business capabilities only suggest where in an organization improvements should be made, specific business needs suggest what approximately should be done. They provide the appropriate abstractions for negotiating the changes and improvements required in certain business areas. In particular, discussing specific business needs helps understand what types of IT solutions might be required in the future in different parts of an organization. However, specific business needs are rather detailed abstractions, which are often considered as too narrow for the purposes of organization-wide strategic IT planning. At the same time, specific business needs still offer only very high-level suggestions regarding the required IT solutions, which are typically considered as too broad for more detailed IT planning. Essentially, specific business needs are mid-level abstractions bridging the gap between highly conceptual strategic plans and their actual practical implementation. The scope of discussions around specific business needs is usually limited to separate business areas, e.g. individual business units, functions or capabilities. Since specific business needs provide moderate abstractions of the organizational plans, they are often used for planning the mid-term future up to 2-3 years ahead, in some cases for longer planning horizons. Discussions of specific business needs as part of an EA practice are often facilitated by IT investment roadmaps or other similar dual EA artifacts helping senior business and IT stakeholders prioritize and schedule candidate business needs to be addressed with IT in the future.

Business Processes

A **business process** is a sequence of concrete activities carried out by specific actors, often using supporting information systems, intended to produce some valuable business outcomes. Business processes are also characterized by certain inputs and outputs, material or immaterial, e.g. physical goods or information. Running established processes is a routine daily organizational activity. For example, business processes "issue an insurance policy", "ship an ordered product" and "produce an annual report" define the essential steps and tasks accomplished by the employees on a regular and repeatable basis to issue a policy, ship a product and produce a report respectively. At the same time, each of these processes usually leverages some specialized IT systems for facilitating or automating separate steps of these processes or even entire processes.

Since business processes represent collections of specific business activities and also explicitly reflect the role of the underlying information systems enabling these activities, they provide very convenient discussion points for business and IT stakeholders. On the one hand, business leaders generally understand the role of separate business processes for the business of an organization. Business sponsors of IT initiatives are normally able to evaluate the business impact of specific changes in established business processes and appreciate the business benefits of improving these processes. For instance, senior business stakeholders can assess the overall business value of accelerating or even completely automating specific business processes via leveraging new information systems. On the other hand, architects understand the role of information systems in supporting specific business processes. Architects of IT initiatives are able to articulate what the IT department should deliver to enable the desired changes in business processes. For instance, architects can determine what IT systems might need to be deployed to underpin specific business processes, what basic business functionality these systems should provide, what business data might be necessary for these systems to operate and what infrastructure capacity is required to run them smoothly.

As discussion points between business and IT stakeholders, business processes are more detailed than specific business needs. While business needs provide only rough suggestions regarding the types of IT solutions that might be required to solve particular problems, business processes suggest how approximately these solutions should work and how exactly specific organizational activities should be changed. They focus on pretty detailed notions of a tangible and down-to-earth nature. Business processes offer the appropriate abstractions for negotiating the expected business impact of separate IT solutions. Specifically, discussing desirable changes in certain business processes helps understand what approximately new IT solutions should do and how they should work at a high level. However, business processes are too detailed and fine-grained to facilitate organization-wide strategic planning efforts and still too abstract for specifying detailed functional requirements to new IT systems. For this reason, the scope of discussions around specific business processes is usually limited to separate IT initiatives. Since business processes provide rather detailed descriptions of organizational activities, they can be used only for relatively short-term planning up to 1-2 years ahead in the future, but can hardly be useful for a longer-term planning. Discussions of business processes as part of an EA practice are often based on solution overviews (see Figure 4.6) or other dual Outlines helping business and IT stakeholders decide how exactly current business processes should be modified by new IT solutions.

Business Requirements[37]

Business requirements, or system requirements, are detailed functional and non-functional specifications for concrete IT systems. Business requirements describe the expected behavior of a particular IT system from the business perspective. For example, business requirements may specify what input data should be provided by users, what should happen when a user presses a specific button, how exactly a particular number should be calculated or how many transactions should be processed per second. At the same time, each of these business requirements also implies certain underlying system components implementing these requirements in software or hardware.

Since business requirements explicitly reflect the desired behavior of IT systems from both the business and IT perspectives, they provide very convenient discussion points for business and IT stakeholders. On the one hand, business stakeholders generally understand the role and purpose of specific business requirements to IT systems. Business sponsors of IT projects, or their competent representatives, are normally able to formulate reasonably detailed business requirements for their projects and prioritize these requirements based on their perceived business importance. For instance, business stakeholders usually can describe their expectations on how new IT systems should work from the purely functional perspective and explain which functionality is more critical for the business. On the other hand, architects also understand the role of specific business requirements to IT systems. Architects of IT projects are able to propose and describe the detailed structure of new IT systems addressing the necessary business requirements. For instance, based on business requirements to IT systems, architects can specify what technologies should be used in these systems, what system components should be developed, how these components should interact with each other and which data entities should be used by these components.

Business requirements are the most detailed of all common discussion points between business and IT stakeholders, more detailed than business processes. While business processes provide only approximate suggestions regarding required IT solutions, business requirements provide very specific descriptions of desired IT systems. They offer appropriate implementation-level abstractions for negotiating the expected business behavior of separate IT systems. Specifically, discussing business requirements helps understand what exactly new IT systems should look like and how exactly they should work. Due to their very low abstraction level, business requirements are naturally suitable only for the short-term IT planning typically covering the immediately actionable perspective up to 6-12 months ahead. For the same reason, the scope of discussions around specific business requirements is naturally limited only to separate IT projects. Detailed business requirements, as discussion points between business and IT, can hardly be helpful for wider organizational scopes as well as for a longer-term IT planning. Discussions of business requirements as part of an EA practice often revolve around solution designs (see Figure 4.7) or other dual Designs helping project-level business and IT stakeholders agree on specific functional and non-functional requirements to new IT systems.

The Hierarchy of Key Discussion Points

An operating model, business capabilities, specific business needs, business processes and business requirements are arguably the most common discussion points relevant for respective organizational scopes and time horizons, but far from the only possible convenient discussion points between business and IT stakeholders[38]. Put it simply, they are merely the most typical things that business leaders and architects can negotiate together to plan IT. These key discussion points help business and IT stakeholders initiate a conversation, achieve a mutual understanding and eventually improve business and IT alignment. Essentially, these discussion points provide an actionable input for an EA practice instead of a business strategy, which is often found unsuitable for this purpose (see Figure 5.1). The role of key discussion points as an input for an EA practice is shown in Figure 5.4.

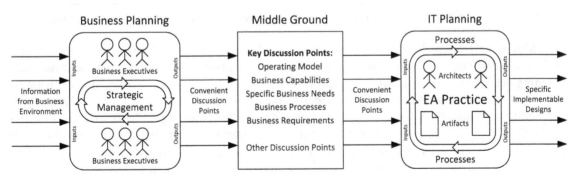

Figure 5.4. The role of key discussion points as an input for an EA practice

The five key discussion points described above are significantly different in their abstraction levels, appropriate organizational scopes and planning horizons. For instance, an operating model provides a very abstract discussion point appropriate for a very long-range, global IT planning at the highest organizational level, while business requirements provide very detailed discussion points appropriate for a very short-term, local IT planning at the project level. Main properties of the five key discussion points between business and IT are summarized in Table 5.1.

Discussion point	Abstraction level	Planning scope	Planning horizon	Key business concerns	Key IT concerns
Operating model	Very abstract	Very wide (entire organization)	Very long-term (>3-5 years)	What operating model should be appropriate for the business of an entire organization?	What general structure of the IT landscape is required to enable the adopted operating model?
Business capabilities	Abstract	Wide (entire organization or major business units)	Long-term (3-5 years)	What business capabilities should be improved to execute the business strategy?	What IT capabilities are required to improve the strategic business capabilities?
Specific business needs	Moderate	Moderate (separate business areas)	Mid-term (2-3 years)	What specific business needs should be addressed in the future?	What types of IT solutions are required to address the identified business needs?
Business processes	Detailed	Narrow (separate IT initiatives)	Short-term (1-2 years)	How should specific business processes be changed?	What systems, data and infrastructure are required to change the business processes as requested?
Business requirements	Very detailed	Very narrow (separate IT projects)	Very short-term (<1 year)	What specific business functionality should be provided?	What technical structure of IT systems is required to provide the necessary functionality?

Table 5.1. Main properties of the five key discussion points between business and IT

Moreover, the key discussion points described above can be considered as different "layers" of decision-making, where the planning decisions at more abstract levels shape all the subsequent planning decisions at more detailed levels. For instance, the highest-level overarching decision on the target operating model suggests a specific range of compatible business strategies to be pursued in the future (see Figure 5.3)[39]. However, due to the common problems with the strategy-based IT planning discussed earlier (see Figure 5.1), business strategies can be considered as purely business notions playing critical roles in business discussions, but not providing convenient discussion points between business and IT. In its turn, the decision to pursue a particular organization-wide business strategy suggests a number of specific business capabilities to be uplifted in the future in order to execute this business strategy. Similarly, the decision to uplift a set of strategic business capabilities suggests specific business needs to be addressed in the future in order to improve these business capabilities. The decision to address specific business needs suggests particular changes in current business processes to be implemented in the future in order to resolve these business needs. Finally, the decision to modify the business processes in particular way suggests specific business requirements to new IT systems to be delivered in the future in order to enable the required modifications in business processes.

Essentially, the sequence of planning decisions described above represents a chain of related decisions permeating and going through all organizational levels, where more local and short-term planning decisions are aligned to more global and long-term planning decisions. These planning decisions and corresponding key discussion points supporting them form a hierarchy of planning decisions important at different organizational levels. This hierarchy of discussion points, associated planning decisions and their relationships can be conveniently represented as a pyramid. The lower levels of the pyramid represent more fundamental, global and long-lasting planning decisions made at higher organizational levels, while the higher levels of the pyramid represent more volatile, local and short-term decisions made at lower organizational levels[40]. The lower levels of the pyramid naturally underpin and provide the conceptual basis for all the higher levels. The pyramid of key discussion points and corresponding planning decisions described above is shown in Figure 5.5 (a business strategy, as an important planning decision but not a convenient discussion point between business and IT, is also shown for completeness purposes as an intermediate link between an operating model and business capabilities).

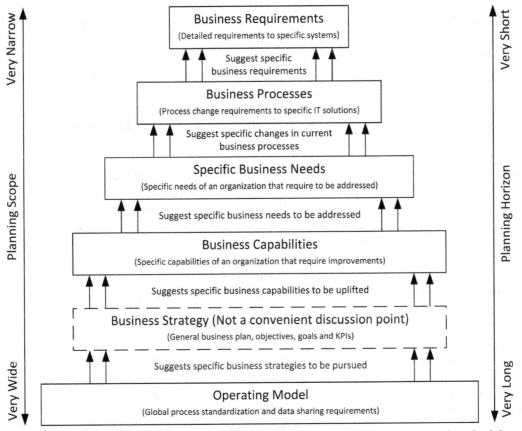

Figure 5.5. The pyramid of key discussion points and corresponding planning decisions

Enterprise Architecture Uncertainty Principle

The main properties of the five key discussion points between business and IT demonstrate the evident negative correlation between the abstraction levels of discussion points and their appropriate planning scopes and horizons (see Table 5.1). In particular, the discussion points and respective planning decisions appropriate for the widest organizational scopes and longest time horizons are the most abstract ones, while the most detailed discussion points and respective planning decisions are appropriate for the most narrow scopes and shortest time horizons. Since most IT-related planning decisions are reflected in corresponding decisions EA artifacts (see Table 2.1), exactly the same conclusion is naturally relevant for EA artifacts as well, i.e. EA artifacts covering the widest organizational scopes are the least detailed ones, and vice versa (see Figure 2.5).

This general conceptual pattern explaining the essential properties of all discussion points and corresponding EA artifacts can be formulated as the EA uncertainty principle. The **EA uncertainty principle** suggests that organizations can be either planned for wider scopes and longer horizons in less detail, or planned for narrower scopes and shorter horizons in more detail, but they cannot be planned for wide scopes and long horizons in great detail[41]. This universal principle is generally valid for all possible discussion points and EA artifacts in the context of an EA practice.

Essentially, the EA uncertainty principle delineates the practical boundaries of all IT-related planning efforts in organizations since all discussion points and EA artifacts significantly deviating from this principle can be considered as impractical. However, different deviations from this fundamental principle are impractical because of two very different reasons. On the one hand, highly abstract discussion points and EA artifacts focused on narrow organizational scopes and short planning horizons are simply useless for all practical purposes since they are too high-level and vague for their intended scopes and horizons. For example, discussing general business needs (e.g. to accelerate the mortgage lending process), let alone required business capabilities or a target operating model, during the implementation steps of separate IT initiatives is largely meaningless since these discussions are lacking the critical implementation-level details expected at this stage by IT project teams. In other words, highly abstract descriptions of the local short-term future have no practical value. On the other hand, the attempts to use highly detailed discussion points and EA artifacts focused on wide organizational scopes and long planning horizons are simply unachievable in practice due to the significant inherent uncertainty associated with these scopes and horizons. For example, discussing the vision of the five-year future for an entire organization in terms of specific business needs (e.g. to enable order tracking for customers), let alone in terms of specific business processes or business requirements, is essentially impossible since all these details cannot be predicted for the whole organization in advance for five years ahead. In other words, highly detailed descriptions of the global long-term future state are practically impossible to develop.

Consequently, all the discussion points and EA artifacts inconsistent with the EA uncertainty principle are either useless or unachievable, and in both cases should not be used as part of an EA practice. Based on the five common discussion points described earlier (see Table 5.1), the EA uncertainty principle is illustrated in Figure 5.6.

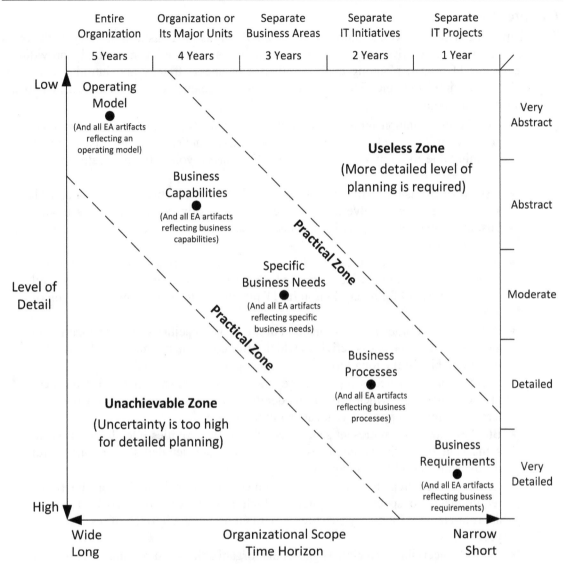

Figure 5.6. Enterprise architecture uncertainty principle

Since possible discussion points that might be helpful for facilitating the dialog between business and IT are not limited only to the five key discussion points shown in Figure 5.6, as noted earlier, the EA uncertainty principle essentially defines the entire practical zone for discussion points and EA artifacts, i.e. the range of all potentially useful discussion points and EA artifacts. Moreover, this principle also suggests that organizations generally cannot be comprehensively planned in a formal manner, but can only be planned by means of deriving more short-term, detailed and local plans from more long-term, abstract and global plans[42].

Chapter Summary

This chapter discussed the typical problems associated with using a business strategy as the basis for IT planning, described five convenient discussion points between business and IT providing a better basis for IT-related planning decisions than a business strategy and introduced the so-called EA uncertainty principle. The key message of this chapter can be summarized into the following essential points:

- Despite the common intuitive assumption, a business strategy in a narrow sense actually rarely provides a useful input for an EA practice or a sound basis for IT planning due to its inherent vagueness, elusiveness, volatility and irrelevancy to IT

- Instead of a business strategy, productive discussions between business and IT stakeholders often revolve around five key discussion points: operating model, business capabilities, specific business needs, business processes and business requirements

- An operating model represents the desired level of organization-wide process standardization and data integration which provides an overarching highest-level abstraction useful for a very long-term IT planning often exceeding the horizon of 3-5 years

- Business capabilities represent general abilities or capacities of an organization to perform specific business activities which offer convenient high-level abstractions indispensable for the long-term IT planning up to 3-5 years ahead

- Specific business needs represent general ideas to address particular business problems using IT which provide moderate abstractions appropriate for the mid-term IT planning up to 2-3 years ahead in the future

- Business processes represent sequences of specific activities intended to produce some valuable business outcomes which offer rather detailed abstractions useful for the short-term IT planning up to 1-2 years ahead

- Business requirements represent detailed functional and non-functional requirements to specific IT systems which provide very detailed abstractions appropriate only for a very short-term IT planning with a horizon of less than one year

- The EA uncertainty principle suggests that organizations can be either planned for wider scopes and longer horizons in less detail, or planned for narrower scopes and shorter horizons in more detail

Chapter 6: Processes of Enterprise Architecture Practice

The previous chapter addressed the communication aspects of an EA practice and discussed specifics of the dialog between business and IT. This chapter focuses specifically on the process aspects of an EA practice and provides an in-depth discussion of key EA-related processes. In particular, this chapter starts from describing three core processes constituting an EA practice and their meaning in the organizational context. Then, this chapter discusses the relationship and information exchange between these processes enabling their coordination and synergy. Finally, this chapter provides a comprehensive high-level process view of an EA practice explaining the interaction between all its major elements including different actors, EA artifacts, EA-related processes, the external business environment and the organizational IT landscape.

Processes Constituting Enterprise Architecture Practice

An EA practice is a complex organizational practice including multiple various activities of its diverse participants. Due to the complex and parallel nature of these activities, an EA practice cannot be represented as a single sequential step-wise process with a certain number of steps[1], but only as a set of several different processes revolving around the six general types of EA artifacts described by the CSVLOD model of enterprise architecture: Considerations, Standards, Visions, Landscapes, Outlines and Designs (see Figure 4.1 and Figure 4.9).

Specifically, all the activities constituting successful EA practices can be grouped into three distinct high-level EA-related processes with different goals, participants and outcomes: Strategic Planning, Initiative Delivery and Technology Optimization[2]. These three processes are carried out simultaneously by different actors and interrelated with each other. Each of these processes implies developing and using specific types of EA artifacts. The Strategic Planning process revolves around Considerations and Visions (see Figure 4.2 and Figure 4.4), the Initiative Delivery process revolves around Outlines and Designs (see Figure 4.6 and Figure 4.7), while the Technology Optimization process revolves around Standards and Landscapes (see Figure 4.3 and Figure 4.5).

On the one hand, the Strategic Planning and Technology Optimization processes are continuous, largely unstructured and somewhat informal. These processes can hardly be broken down into repeatable linear sequences of separate steps with specific inputs and outputs, but only the general essence and meaning of these processes can be explained. On the other hand, the Initiative Delivery process is a finite linear step-wise process with rather specific inputs and outputs.

Strategic Planning[3]

Strategic Planning is the EA-related process translating relevant fundamental factors of the external business environment into more specific Considerations and Visions providing the general rules and directions for IT[4]. Organizations often have only a single instance of the

Strategic Planning process encompassing an entire organization. However, highly decentralized organizations with a significant degree of local decision-making autonomy (e.g. organizations with the diversification or coordination operating model, see Figure 5.3) besides having central organization-wide Strategic Planning may also have several independent but interrelated instances of the Strategic Planning process covering separately their major business units, e.g. lines of business, business functions or divisions.

Relevant fundamental factors incoming from the external environment often include various economic, social, demographic, legal, political, ecological and any other factors important for the business of an organization. While these fundamental factors may be very abstract and have no obvious implications for IT (e.g. new markets are opening, competitors shift their strategies, consumers change their habits, inflation is growing, etc.), Considerations and Visions provide conceptual bridges connecting these abstract business factors with the ensuing plans for IT. Both Considerations and Visions, though use business language meaningful to business executives, provide a high-level direction and guidance for IT as well. Essentially, the main goal of Strategic Planning (i.e. of developing Considerations and Visions) is to derive general long-range IT-related plans from the fundamental environmental business factors and articulate the approximate future course of action for IT, including some suggestions regarding specific desired future IT initiatives to be executed. From this perspective, the overall meaning of this process can be best summarized as strategy-to-portfolio.

The Strategic Planning process is tightly integrated with regular strategic management activities (e.g. environmental analysis, identification of competitive advantages, formulation of goals, etc.), incorporated into the annual business planning cycle and carried out collaboratively by business executives and architects. Strategic Planning is generally driven by the question "How is the business environment changing and what should we do to react on these changes?" As part of this process business leaders and architects discuss relevant fundamental environmental factors influencing their organization, articulate the implications of these factors for IT, achieve agreements on the desired future course of action for IT and document the resulting planning decisions as Considerations and Visions[5]. On the one hand, Considerations help articulate and document the most general agreements on how an organization needs to work from the IT perspective in order to prosper in its environment. These decisions may include the answers to the following and similar essential IT-related questions:

- What role should IT play in an organization?
- Which IT capabilities should be provided organization-wide?
- What IT-related policies should be complied with?
- What level of business continuity and security is required?
- Which IT-related innovations should be adopted?

On the other hand, Visions help articulate and document more specific agreements on what an organization needs to do in the long term from the IT perspective in order to prosper in its environment. These decisions may include the answers to the following and similar strategic IT-related questions:

- What should IT deliver in the long run?
- Where should future IT investments go?
- What types of IT investments should be made?

- When should IT investments be made?
- In what sequence should IT investments be made?

The Strategic Planning process is continuous in nature, loosely structured and cannot be reduced to a predefined sequence of steps. It consists mostly of numerous meetings, presentations, workshops and even informal "elevator" discussions involving both business executives and architects where various planning decisions are made[6]. However, Strategic Planning also implies periodical formal approvals and sign-offs of finalized Considerations and Visions by all relevant stakeholders, often on a yearly basis. From the temporal perspective, activities of this process can be aligned to important business dates, periods and events, e.g. budgeting cycles, board meetings or updates of a business strategy. As part of Strategic Planning senior business leaders and architects usually discuss the desired operating model (i.e. potential synergies between business units, organization-wide process standardization and data sharing requirements, see Figure 5.3), required business capabilities as well as specific business needs to be addressed with IT (see Table 5.1). Since both Considerations and Visions are decisions EA artifacts (see Table 2.1), the entire Strategic Planning process can be considered as an intertwined set of multiple simultaneous development and update processes of separate Considerations and Visions representing specific collective strategic planning decisions (see Figure 2.6).

The ultimate result of Strategic Planning is a set of Considerations and Visions agreed by both business and IT, defining the general rules and long-term directions for IT and aligned to the strategic demands of the external business environment. Considerations and Visions, though still very high-level, offer more specific guidance for the strategic development of IT than abstract fundamental environmental factors. They provide a common basis for further, more detailed IT planning and help articulate specific IT-related business needs to be addressed in the future.

Initiative Delivery[7]

Initiative Delivery is the EA-related process translating specific business needs, or more rarely specific technical needs, into tangible IT solutions implementing these needs in an optimal manner[8]. Organizations typically have multiple instances of the Initiative Delivery process (i.e. multiple separate IT initiatives) running in parallel and delivering different IT solutions simultaneously. Each IT initiative (or simply an IT project for small initiatives), as a single instance of the Initiative Delivery process, delivers its own IT solution intended to address a specific business or technical need[9].

Initiative Delivery is an end-to-end process delivering IT solutions for specific business, and sometimes technical, needs from the initial idea-level concepts to the final deployment of working IT systems. Since each specific need can be implemented in multiple different ways with various IT solutions having potential advantages and disadvantages, the main goal of the Initiative Delivery process is to select the best available implementation option for a particular need and then deliver the actual solution based on the preferred option in a timely and risk-free manner. From this perspective, the overall meaning of this process can be best summarized as need-to-solution. Initiative Delivery is generally driven by the question "What is the best way to address the requested need and all the associated requirements?"

The Initiative Delivery process is tightly integrated with regular project management activities (e.g. scoping, estimating, scheduling, budgeting, monitoring, etc.) and follows a typical step-wise project delivery lifecycle with several sequential phases and control gates, e.g. scope, evaluate, plan, build, test and deploy[10]. However, regardless of organization-specific phases and gates of the project lifecycle, the Initiative Delivery process always consists of two inherent steps: initiation and implementation. Firstly, the initiation step implies formulating the goals and objectives of the IT initiative, generating potential implementation options, evaluating their pros and cons, selecting the most appropriate option and then getting the proposed high-level IT solution approved by all relevant business stakeholders. Secondly, the implementation step implies the actual technical implementation, testing and deployment of the approved IT solution by competent IT specialists.

The **initiation step**, as the first stage of the Initiative Delivery process, involves business executives and architects. During this step business leaders formulate specific goals and essential requirements for new IT solutions, while architects offer possible solution implementation options addressing these goals and requirements. Outlines are the key EA artifacts enabling effective communication between business executives and architects at the initiation step. Specifically, Outlines provide the answers to the following and similar essential questions regarding the proposed IT solutions:

- What do the proposed IT solutions look like conceptually?
- How will the proposed IT solutions modify established business processes?
- What is the immediate and long-term business value of the proposed IT solutions?
- What is the overall business impact of the proposed IT solutions?
- What is the cost of the proposed IT solutions and when can they be delivered?

By providing this and other critical information Outlines help business executives make informed approval decisions regarding the proposed IT solutions and ensure that each solution brings considerable strategic and tactical business value for a reasonable price. Outlines allow business leaders either to select the most desirable solution implementation options based on their trade-off analysis, or to cancel IT initiatives at their early stages if no options seem acceptable. Discussions between business executives and architects at the initiation step often revolve around particular business processes that should be modified with new IT solutions (see Table 5.1). Since Outlines are decisions EA artifacts (see Table 2.1), the entire initiation step of the Initiative Delivery process can be considered as a collaborative development process of new Outlines representing high-level planning decisions regarding specific IT initiatives (see Figure 2.6).

Outlines are complementary to business cases for IT initiatives[11]. While business cases are purely business-specific documents providing only detailed financial justifications for new IT initiatives, Outlines address both the business and IT aspects of the initiatives briefly explaining how the corresponding IT solutions will be implemented and where the benefits from these solutions will come from. Outlines are usually elaborated in parallel with the corresponding business cases for new IT initiatives and inform the time and cost estimates included in these business cases. Outlines and business cases are the key documents approved by senior business leaders for all IT initiatives to start their actual implementation. After these two documents are approved and signed-off, the implementation step begins.

The **implementation step**, as the second stage of the Initiative Delivery process, involves architects, IT project teams and some business representatives. During this step architects, project teams and business representatives collectively elaborate the business requirements for the approved high-level IT solutions described in Outlines, develop their detailed implementation plans and then project teams deliver these solutions according to the agreed plans. Designs are the key EA artifacts enabling detailed planning and effective collaboration between architects, project teams and business representatives at the implementation step. In particular, Designs describe all architecturally significant decisions related to the implementation of new IT systems including the answers to the following and similar essential questions:

- What business requirements should be addressed?
- What new software should be developed or installed?
- Which data types and entities should be used?
- What servers and hardware should be deployed?
- How exactly should new IT systems interact with the existing systems?

By providing this and other critical information Designs help architects, IT project teams and business representatives develop optimal implementation plans for new IT systems satisfying both the business and architectural requirements. Discussions between architects, project teams and business representatives at the implementation step typically focus on detailed business requirements that should be fulfilled by new IT systems (see Table 5.1). Since Designs are decisions EA artifacts, the beginning of the implementation step can be considered as a collaborative development process of new Designs representing detailed planning decisions regarding specific IT systems.

Developed Designs are then used by project teams to deliver the approved IT solutions, while architects supervise project teams and ensure the adherence of the implemented solutions to their Designs. The ultimate result of each instance of the Initiative Delivery process is a new working IT solution satisfying a particular business need, addressing specific business requirements and bringing both the long-term and short-term business value.

Technology Optimization

The Strategic Planning process, among other suggestions, articulates specific IT-related business needs aligned to the strategic demands of the business environment, while the Initiative Delivery process turns these business needs into tangible IT solutions simultaneously addressing local business requirements and contributing to the overall business strategy. However, from the long-term perspective simply addressing strategic business needs is not enough. Constant delivery of new IT solutions, even if these solutions are perfectly aligned to the business strategy, inevitably complicates the IT landscape, gradually tangles the connections between various IT systems, multiplies IT assets, proliferates supported technologies, introduces legacy and redundancy. These negative side effects inflate the IT budget, reduce the strategic agility and flexibility of IT, increase IT-related risks and eventually create substantial problems for organizations in the long run[12]. The last EA-related process intended to alleviate these adverse effects is the Technology Optimization process.

Technology Optimization is the EA-related process translating the information on the current structure of the organizational IT landscape into specific technical rationalization suggestions intended to optimize the landscape. Organizations often have only a single instance of the Technology Optimization process covering the entire IT landscape. However, highly decentralized organizations with a significant degree of local technical autonomy (e.g. organizations with the diversification or coordination operating model, see Figure 5.3), may have several interrelated instances of the Technology Optimization process encompassing separately the IT landscapes of their major business units, e.g. lines of business, business functions or divisions.

The Technology Optimization process intends to identify potential inefficiencies, problems, risks and other technical bottlenecks in the current IT landscape (e.g. duplicated, inadequate, misused or legacy IT systems, aging infrastructure, excessive complexity, etc.) and propose specific corrective actions to improve the overall quality and fitness of the landscape. These actions often include streamlining troublesome areas of the IT landscape, decommissioning or replacing inappropriate IT assets and consolidating redundant technologies. Technology Optimization also aims to reduce the volume of a so-called "architecture debt", as discussed later in Chapter 18 (Instruments for Enterprise Architecture). Essentially, the main goal of the Technology Optimization process is to simplify and rationalize the entire organizational IT landscape and technology portfolio. From this perspective, the overall meaning of this process can be best summarized as structure-to-rationalization.

Unlike Strategic Planning and Initiative Delivery, Technology Optimization is an "internal" IT-specific housekeeping process which is relatively independent and might be not integrated with any other regular organizational processes or activities. The Technology Optimization process is carried out mostly by architects inside the IT department with some involvement of other IT experts and leaders, including the CIO. Technology Optimization is generally driven by the question "What is wrong with the current IT landscape and what should we do to improve it?" Standards and Landscapes help architects conduct a "health check" of the current IT landscape, analyze its strategic capabilities and constraints, control its complexity, relevancy and diversity. On the one hand, Standards provide the information regarding the current technology stack, implementation approaches and best practices including the answers to the following and similar questions:

- What technologies and vendor products are used?
- What approaches and best practices are followed?
- Which technologies and products are redundant or fulfill similar purposes?
- Which technologies, products or approaches cause problems?
- Do the current technologies and approaches meet the general business needs?

On the other hand, Landscapes provide the information regarding the existing IT assets, their status and interrelationship including the answers to the following and similar questions:

- What IT assets are maintained by an organization?
- Which IT assets are not actively used or provide duplicated functionality?
- Which IT assets are no longer supported by their vendors?
- Which IT assets may cause problems in the future?
- Are the existing IT assets adequate for the general business needs?

Similarly to Strategic Planning, the Technology Optimization process is continuous and largely unstructured in nature. It consists mostly of numerous meetings and informal discussions between architects, IT executives and technical subject-matter experts, but requires little or no involvement of business stakeholders. As part of this process architects periodically review, analyze and update Standards and Landscapes. Specifically, in Standards architects mark some technologies, approaches and practices as desirable, current or strategic, whereas others are tagged as undesirable, deprecated or retiring. Architects can also introduce some new promising Standards or remove some old and irrelevant ones. In Landscapes architects mark some IT assets as "healthy", reusable or strategic, while others are flagged as "unhealthy", non-reusable or to-be-decommissioned. Architects can also develop more detailed improvement plans for Landscapes. The Technology Optimization process often implies periodical formal approvals of updated Standards and Landscapes by the CIO or other IT executives, often on a yearly basis. Since most Standards are decisions EA artifacts and most Landscapes are facts EA artifacts (see Table 2.1), the entire Technology Optimization process can be considered as a set of diverse processes, including both documenting the current state of the IT landscape by individual architects and making collective decisions on the desired future of the landscape (see Figure 2.6). From this perspective, the Technology Optimization process can be viewed as the process of formulating the organizational IT strategy, or architecture strategy.

The ultimate result of Technology Optimization is a set of technical rationalization suggestions reflected in Standards and Landscapes and helping achieve a more adequate, consolidated and lean IT landscape. These suggestions can be either implemented later in an opportunistic manner as part of regular business-oriented IT initiatives or, in some cases, delivered separately as special architectural initiatives.

Relationship Between EA-Related Processes

The three key EA-related processes driving successful EA practices are Strategic Planning, Initiative Delivery and Technology Optimization. As discussed above, Strategic Planning produces high-level rules and directions for IT helping articulate specific IT-related business needs, Initiative Delivery implements IT solutions addressing specific business needs, while Technology Optimization produces technical rationalization suggestions to optimize the entire IT landscape. The essential properties of the Strategic Planning, Initiative Delivery and Technology Optimization processes are summarized in Table 6.1.

Process	Strategic Planning	Initiative Delivery	Technology Optimization
Instances	Single, or several for highly decentralized organizations	Multiple, i.e. one instance for each IT initiative	Single, or several for highly decentralized organizations
Goal	Articulate the long-term future course of action for IT	Deliver optimal IT solutions for specific needs	Improve the overall quality of the organizational IT landscape
Meaning	Strategy-to-portfolio	Need-to-solution	Structure-to-rationalization
Question	How is the business environment changing and what should we do to react on these changes?	What is the best way to address the requested need and all the associated requirements?	What is wrong with the current IT landscape and what should we do to improve it?
Nature	Continuous and unstructured	Sequential with two main steps: initiation and implementation	Continuous and unstructured
Integration	Integrated with regular strategic management activities	Integrated with regular project management activities	Not integrated with any regular processes or activities
Actors	Business leaders and architects	Initiation step: Business leaders and architects Implementation step: Architects and project teams	Architects alone
EA artifacts	Considerations and Visions	Initiation step: Outlines Implementation step: Designs	Standards and Landscapes
Inputs	Fundamental factors of the external business environment	Specific business, and sometimes technical, needs	Current structure of the organizational IT landscape
Activities	Informal discussions, meetings, presentations and workshops as well as periodical formal approvals and sign-offs	Initiation step: Discussion of possible implementation options Implementation step: Actual technical implementation	Numerous informal discussions and periodical formal approvals
Discussion points	Operating model, business capabilities and specific business needs	Initiation step: Business processes Implementation step: Business requirements	Little or no discussion between business and IT
Outputs	High-level strategic plans for IT reflected in Considerations and Visions	New working IT solutions	Technical rationalization suggestions reflected in Standards and Landscapes

Table 6.1. Strategic Planning, Initiative Delivery and Technology Optimization processes

All the three key EA-related processes described in Table 6.1 are carried out largely independently from each other and pursue different goals in the context of an EA practice. However, these processes are synergistic and imply intensive information exchange between each other. Even though each of these EA-related processes alone can arguably deliver only some limited benefits to an organization, a combination of these processes working together allows developing and maintaining the optimal organizational IT landscape closely aligned to the strategic and tactical demands of the business environment. Specifically, successful EA practices require effective bidirectional information flows between all the corresponding pairs of these EA-related processes: Strategic Planning and Initiative Delivery, Initiative Delivery and Technology Optimization, and Technology Optimization and Strategic Planning.

Strategic Planning and Initiative Delivery

The Strategic Planning process alone neither delivers any IT solutions nor even describes what exactly needs to be delivered, but provides only some high-level rules and strategic directions for IT reflected in Considerations and Visions agreed by both business and IT. Initiative Delivery is the "next" downstream EA-related process which turns these abstract plans into tangible IT solutions implemented in an optimal manner. Essentially, Initiative Delivery closes the gap between Strategic Planning and the actual practical implementation of working IT solutions.

Considerations and Visions resulting from Strategic Planning provide the appropriate basis for launching new IT initiatives, i.e. for starting new instances of the Initiative Delivery process. In particular, Visions provide a long-term guidance for future IT investments suggesting what types of IT initiatives should be implemented, while Considerations provide conceptual rules suggesting how these initiatives should be implemented. In other words, Visions represent planned business needs for certain IT solutions and Considerations provide the initial requirements for them. For example, Visions may suggest that a certain business capability should be uplifted in the future (see Figure 4.4), while Considerations may suggest that all business operations should be resilient and failsafe (see Figure 4.2). These suggestions form a planned business need to deliver a highly available and reliable IT solution enhancing the requested business capability. As a result of this planned business need, a new IT initiative is launched to explore the need, discuss potential implementation options and deliver the best possible IT solution addressing the business need. In other words, the planned business needs and requirements outlined in Visions and Considerations are elaborated into specific IT initiatives implementing these needs according to these requirements.

Since Considerations and Visions are agreed with business executives and implicitly reflect the strategic demands of the external business environment, all IT initiatives emerging from Visions and consistent with Considerations automatically become aligned to the long-term business goals. Ideally, all IT initiatives should be launched from Visions and aligned to Considerations to deliver strategic competitive advantages. However, the real world is very dynamic and often forces an organization to react in a timely manner on unexpected urgent needs due to unpredictable business demands, lucrative short-term opportunities, unanticipated regulatory changes and other reasons. For this reason, in the real world new IT initiatives are launched either from the planned business needs provided by Visions, or from the urgent business needs incoming directly from the external business environment. IT investment portfolios in real organizations typically represent mixes of both planned and urgent IT initiatives.

However, not all planned business needs initially identified in Visions can always be implemented with reasonable means. For instance, a more thorough Outlines-based discussion of possible IT solutions for a specific business need as part of the Initiative Delivery process may conclude that all the available implementation options are too expensive, too risky, require too much time or undesirable due to some other reasons. For business executives it may mean that there are no easy ways to implement the approved business strategy as initially planned, strategic plans might need to be reviewed and corrected. Cancelled IT initiatives essentially trigger back the Strategic Planning process and may force business leaders and architects to adjust the previously agreed Considerations and Visions to new realities.

The main result of the synergy between the Strategic Planning and Initiative Delivery processes is the strategic effectiveness of delivered IT initiatives. All IT solutions initiated from Visions not only address short-term business requirements and bring immediate business value, but also make a substantial contribution to the long-term business goals. These IT solutions incrementally build the organizational IT landscape closely aligned to both the strategic and tactical business needs.

Initiative Delivery and Technology Optimization

Most IT initiatives in real organizations are not "greenfield" efforts implemented from scratch for specific business needs. Instead, new IT initiatives are typically constrained by the current IT environment, its features and peculiarities. They have to take into account the existing IT landscape and incrementally modify it to deliver the requested business functionality. Consequently, the Initiative Delivery process does not merely implement new IT solutions for particular business needs in a vacuum, but rather introduces certain long-lasting changes to the entire organizational IT landscape.

At the same time, the uncontrolled complexity of the IT landscape increases maintenance costs, reduces agility and creates additional risks to the business of an organization. To restrain the complexity of the IT environment, the Technology Optimization process produces specific technical rationalization suggestions intended to streamline and optimize the existing IT landscape. However, these rationalization suggestions do not get implemented automatically, but have to be delivered via specific IT initiatives.

Due to this duality of their purposes, many IT initiatives essentially pursue two different "orthogonal" goals simultaneously and intend both to address specific business needs and to make some technical improvements in the current IT landscape. Effective information exchange between the Initiative Delivery and Technology Optimization processes helps organizations successfully combine these goals. In successful EA practices regular business-oriented IT initiatives often fulfill the required business needs and maintain, cleanup or even improve the IT landscape along the way as well.

The simultaneous accomplishment of these two goals is achieved via incorporating relevant technical rationalization suggestions resulting from the Technology Optimization process into the designs of regular IT initiatives addressing specific business needs. For instance, at the early initiation step of the Initiative Delivery process architects propose possible solution implementation options taking into account the rationalization suggestions regarding the appropriate utilization of the available IT assets and technologies provided by Landscapes and Standards. As a result, Outlines of new IT solutions discussed with business executives implicitly reflect certain technical considerations of architects intended to optimize the IT landscape. At the later implementation step of the Initiative Delivery process architects also ensure that the final system implementation plans reflected in Designs incorporate relevant technical suggestions provided by Landscapes and Standards. Specifically, Designs of new IT systems should seamlessly fit into the existing IT environment and be consistent with the recommended implementation approaches and established best practices. Moreover, in some cases Designs may also include some additional actions or extra work intended to improve the IT landscape.

Various technical rationalization suggestions provided by the Technology Optimization process to the Initiative Delivery process might be very diverse. For example, they may include, among many others, the following recommendations:

- Reuse specific IT assets, products or technologies
- Follow certain implementation approaches or practices
- Integrate with particular existing IT systems
- Substitute the functionality of specific legacy IT systems
- Migrate, transform or enrich the data from some legacy databases
- Decommission specific IT assets replaced by the new IT solution
- Create a reusable IT asset for future IT initiatives
- Pioneer the introduction of new technologies or products
- Try a new proof-of-concept approach or practice

The incorporation of various technical rationalization suggestions into the designs of regular business-oriented IT initiatives allows these initiatives to fit harmoniously into the existing IT environment, sometimes even improving it, and still deliver the requested business functionality with minimal overhead expenses. In order to ensure that relevant technical suggestions are taken into account in new IT solutions, their Outlines and Designs are typically peer-reviewed by other architects responsible for Technology Optimization. In some cases, when specific technical rationalization suggestions of critical importance cannot be implemented as part of regular IT initiatives, separate architectural initiatives of a purely technical nature might be launched to implement these suggestions, as discussed later in Chapter 7 (IT Initiatives and Enterprise Architecture).

However, the Initiative Delivery process also feeds back to the Technology Optimization process. For instance, Landscapes describing the current state of the IT environment are incrementally updated at the completion stages of all IT initiatives to reflect the recent changes of the IT landscape. Likewise, Standards are often updated after the successful delivery of innovative IT initiatives pioneering the use of new technologies or approaches that proved particularly effective. Existing Standards might be also updated to document some new best practices learned from the implementation of specific IT initiatives.

The main result of the synergy between the Initiative Delivery and Technology Optimization processes is the technical optimality of delivered IT solutions. All IT solutions incorporating relevant technical rationalization suggestions not only satisfy specific planned or urgent business needs using proven technologies, approaches and best practices, but also maintain or even improve the overall quality of the organizational IT landscape. These IT solutions incrementally build a simplified, consistent and up-to-date IT landscape.

Technology Optimization and Strategic Planning

The Technology Optimization process aims to rationalize the IT landscape, improve its overall quality and increase its general relevancy to the business needs. As part of Technology Optimization architects make numerous technical decisions regarding the future evolution of the

IT landscape. In particular, architects often decide what technologies should be introduced, used or retired as well as which IT assets should be considered as strategic, current or legacy.

In order to make informed decisions regarding the desired evolution of the organizational portfolio of IT assets and technologies, architects should be aware of the desired strategic direction of an organization from the business perspective. This general strategic direction is provided by the Strategic Planning process and reflected in Considerations and Visions. Considerations describe how business executives want their organization to work, while Visions describe what business leaders want from IT in the future. This information serves as the basis for the Technology Optimization process and helps architects make sound technical decisions corresponding to the anticipated future business plans. Essentially, Considerations and Visions guide the evolution of Standards and Landscapes in the right strategic directions.

However, the Technology Optimization process also influences Strategic Planning. Even though IT can facilitate the execution of a business strategy, typically not all strategic directions can be effectively supported with the currently available portfolio of IT assets and technologies. In other words, the existing IT landscape may enable or disable specific strategic business directions. For example, the IT landscape closely aligned to a certain operating model (see Figure 5.3) may boost the business strategies that leverage core IT capabilities of the adopted operating model, but essentially disable all the strategies inconsistent with the key assumptions of this operating model. Consequently, reasonable business strategies cannot be based only on wishful idealistic desires of business executives, but rather should take into account the actual capabilities and constraints of their IT platforms. The information regarding strategic IT capabilities and constraints provided by the Technology Optimization process helps architects better understand what IT can or cannot deliver to the business. Informed by Standards and Landscapes, architects are unlikely to approve unfeasible or unrealistic Considerations and Visions. Thereby, the Technology Optimization process supports Strategic Planning and facilitates the development of sober and realistic business strategies.

The main result of the synergy between the Technology Optimization and Strategic Planning processes is the effective mutual interrelationship between strategic business directions and strategic IT capabilities. All strategic business decisions not only guide the evolution of the organizational portfolio of IT assets and technologies, but are also informed and influenced by the current IT portfolio. Effective decision-making enabled by the linkage between Strategic Planning and Technology Optimization helps build relevant IT landscape corresponding to the long-term business goals.

A High-Level Process View of Enterprise Architecture Practice

Essentially, an entire organizational EA practice consists of three main EA-related processes described above: Strategic Planning, Initiative Delivery and Technology Optimization. These processes are interrelated with each other and exchange specific information enabling their synergy. These processes also interact with the external business environment and with the organizational IT landscape thereby establishing a desired dynamic connection between the external and internal environments. The three main EA-related processes with their essential actors, underpinning EA artifacts and mutual interrelationships are shown in Figure 6.1.

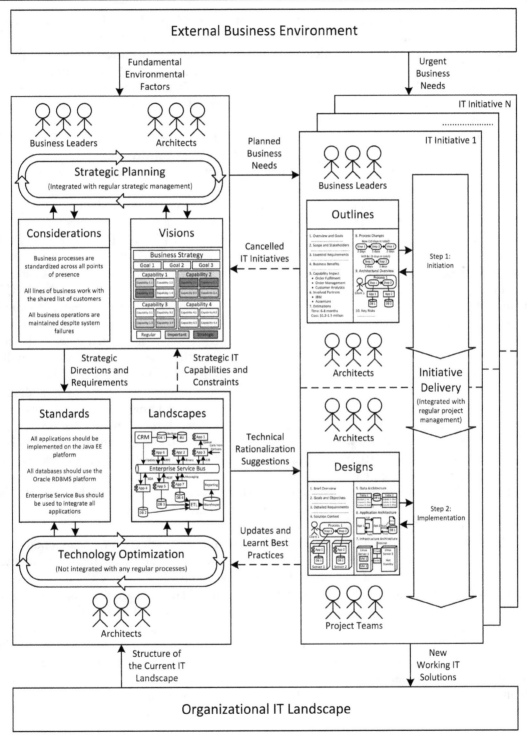

Figure 6.1. The relationship between the three EA-related processes

Figure 6.1 represents a high-level process view of an EA practice. This view shows main EA-related processes and describes who performs these processes, what EA artifacts are essential to these processes and what information these processes exchange with each other. On the one hand, this process view explains how exactly an EA practice connects relevant actors involved in strategic decision-making and implementation of IT systems (see Figure 1.2). On the other hand, this process view shows the general end-to-end information flow of an EA practice and explains how exactly an EA practice translates fundamental factors and urgent needs of the external business environment into the effective organizational IT landscape. As noted earlier and now further clarified in Figure 6.1, a successful EA practice always implies complex and comprehensive organizational changes including various people-related, process-related and technology-related aspects.

Importantly, even though architects are the key actors and facilitators of an EA practice and all its processes, a significant involvement of other relevant stakeholders in corresponding EA-related processes, as shown in Figure 6.1, is absolutely essential for the success of an EA practice. While the Technology Optimization process can be carried out largely by architects alone inside the IT department, the Strategic Planning and Initiative Delivery processes cannot be carried out solely by architects and require conscious participation of relevant stakeholders. For instance, if senior business executives do not participate adequately in the Strategic Planning process, then architects alone have to make critical strategic business decisions on behalf of the whole organization. These decisions will never be treated seriously and acted upon by business leaders, while the planning efforts invested in developing Considerations and Visions will be wasted. If business executives do not participate adequately at the initiation step of the Initiative Delivery process, then architects alone have to make critical business decisions regarding the necessity and value of specific IT initiatives and their preferable implementation options. These decisions will never be sponsored and funded by business leaders, while the proposed IT initiatives described in Outlines will never proceed further to the implementation step. Finally, if IT project teams do not participate adequately at the implementation step of the Initiative Delivery process, then architects alone have to make project-level implementation-specific decisions on behalf of all project participants. These decisions will never be respected and committed to by project teams, while the proposed implementation plans described in Designs, even perfect ones, will be simply ignored.

Generally, the insufficient involvement of relevant stakeholders in corresponding EA-related processes leads to the "ivory tower" syndrome, when EA artifacts created by architects are inexplicable, irrelevant and useless to their potential stakeholders. Since the majority of EA artifacts, with the exception of most Landscapes and some Standards, are decisions EA artifacts (see Table 2.1), an active participation of their stakeholders is essential to their development (see Figure 2.6). For this reason, any EA artifacts created in "ivory towers" without a substantial involvement of their real stakeholders are typically ignored and shelved. They neither facilitate decision-making nor improve business and IT alignment, while the efforts invested in these EA artifacts are merely wasted. In this case, the development of EA artifacts essentially becomes an end unto itself, i.e. architecture is produced for the sake of architecture[13].

Chapter Summary

This chapter described in detail three key processes constituting an EA practice, explained the relationship existing between these processes and provided a high-level view of an EA practice from the process perspective. The key message of this chapter can be summarized into the following essential points:

- An EA practice consists of three distinct processes with different goals, participants and outcomes and revolving around different types of EA artifacts: Strategic Planning, Initiative Delivery and Technology Optimization
- The Strategic Planning process revolves around Considerations and Visions, the Initiative Delivery process revolves around Outlines and Designs, while the Technology Optimization process revolves around Standards and Landscapes
- Strategic Planning is the EA-related process translating relevant fundamental factors of the external business environment into more specific Considerations and Visions providing the general rules and directions for IT
- Initiative Delivery is the EA-related process translating specific business needs, or more rarely specific technical needs, into tangible IT solutions implementing these needs in an optimal manner
- Technology Optimization is the EA-related process translating the information on the current structure of the organizational IT landscape into specific technical rationalization suggestions intended to optimize the landscape
- Although the three key EA-related processes are carried out largely independently from each other and pursue different goals in the context of an EA practice, these processes are synergistic and imply intensive information exchange between each other

Chapter 7: IT Initiatives and Enterprise Architecture

The previous chapter addressed the process aspects of an EA practice and discussed in great detail three main EA-related processes. This chapter focuses specifically on the role of separate IT initiatives in the context of an EA practice and their flow through the key EA-related processes. In particular, this chapter starts from discussing the role of IT initiatives in an EA practice and their relationship to EA artifacts, discussion points and EA-related processes. Then, this chapter describes five different types of IT initiatives having a distinct meaning, origin, purpose and other important properties in the context of an EA practice. Finally, this chapter explains the type-specific flow of these IT initiatives through the corresponding EA-related processes.

The Role of IT Initiatives in Enterprise Architecture Practice

An **IT initiative** is the key unit of work in the context of an EA practice. All IT-related plans of an organization can be materialized only through executing concrete IT initiatives. A successful execution of any IT initiative results in a deployed IT solution, or some other desirable modifications of the IT landscape, and ensuing business improvements enabled by these changes in IT. The typical purpose of an IT initiative is to address a specific business need, e.g. to accelerate the mortgage lending process or enable order tracking for customers[1]. From this perspective, most IT initiatives directly correspond to specific business needs as discussion points between business and IT stakeholders (see Table 5.1). In other words, most IT initiatives actually represent business initiatives with significant IT components. Each IT initiative is characterized by a number of properties including, but not limited to, the following attributes:

- Core business need or problem that the IT initiative intends to address
- Main goals and objectives of the IT initiative
- Specified and limited scope delineating the magnitude of expected changes
- Business case describing the financial details associated with the IT initiative, including required initial investments and anticipated future returns
- Business sponsors interested in the implementation of the IT initiative and providing the necessary funding
- Separate budget allocated to finance the implementation of the IT initiative

Small IT initiatives may be equivalent to single IT projects, while larger initiatives might be considered as full-fledged change programs requiring multiple related projects to be implemented. However, even multi-project IT initiatives usually have one general purpose and business case uniting all their sub-projects into a single articulate effort.

Essentially, the general meaning of an EA practice can be roughly reduced to addressing two different questions related to IT initiatives. Firstly, an EA practice is intended to understand what IT initiatives should be implemented in the future. This question implies shaping the most optimal portfolio of desired IT initiatives to bring the maximum business value to an organization. Secondly, an EA practice is intended to understand how exactly these IT initiatives should be implemented. This question implies finding the most optimal ways to deliver each of these IT initiatives from the technical point of view.

From this perspective, IT initiatives can be considered as the "middle link" of an EA practice connecting high-level abstract plans with their low-level practical implementation. For instance, specific business needs, as the key discussion points corresponding to separate IT initiatives, represent "average" discussion points in terms of their scope, horizon and level of detail (see Figure 5.6). All discussion points more abstract than specific business needs, including an operating model and business capabilities, can be considered as organization-wide discussion points, while all discussion points more detailed than specific business needs, including business processes and business requirements, can be considered as initiative-specific discussion points (see Table 5.1). Essentially, discussing an operating model and business capabilities, among other possible high-level discussion points, helps business executives and architects decide what IT initiatives are desirable for an organization, while discussing business processes and business requirements, among other possible low-level discussion points, helps architects and business stakeholders decide how exactly these IT initiatives should be implemented (see Figure 5.5).

The pivotal role of IT initiatives in an EA practice described above allows clarifying the process view of an EA practice discussed earlier (see Figure 6.1). Firstly, the Strategic Planning process generally can be considered as a joint effort of business executives and architects to shape the organization-wide portfolio of desired IT initiatives. As part of this process, among other planning decisions, they may select the target operating model, determine required business capabilities and eventually formulate, prioritize and schedule specific business needs to be addressed with respective IT initiatives in the foreseeable future. All these planning decisions are reflected in corresponding Considerations and Visions. Secondly, the Initiative Delivery process generally can be considered as a joint effort of architects, business stakeholders and IT project teams to find the most optimal implementation options and then deliver the IT initiatives addressing the business needs formulated as a result of Strategic Planning. As part of this process, among other planning decisions, they may identify the required changes in business processes, stipulate specific business requirements to new IT solutions and then implement these solutions. All the planning decisions made for specific IT initiatives are reflected in their Outlines and Designs. Thirdly, the Technology Optimization process generally can be considered as an effort of architects to inform the decision-making around all IT initiatives. As part of this process, they analyze the organizational IT landscape and identify its potential influence on future IT initiatives. All significant facts on the current IT landscape and some plans regarding its future evolution are reflected in corresponding Standards and Landscapes. Since the Technology Optimization process is carried out largely by architects alone and requires little or no involvement of business stakeholders, this process typically does not imply any specific discussion points between business and IT. The relationship between EA-related processes, IT initiatives and discussion points described above is shown in Figure 7.1.

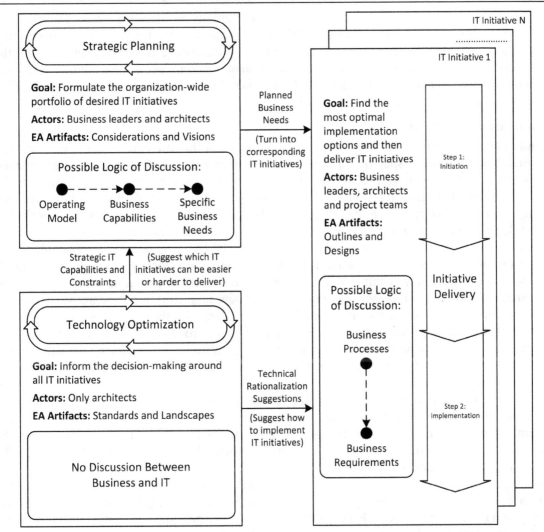

Figure 7.1. The relationship between EA-related processes, IT initiatives and discussion points

The transition from the general list of candidate IT initiatives to the detailed elaboration of separate initiatives essentially delineates the border between the Strategic Planning and Initiative Delivery EA-related processes. While the Strategic Planning process suggests what IT initiatives are desirable, the Initiative Delivery process elaborates and delivers each of them.

Different Types of IT Initiatives

From the perspective of an EA practice, all IT initiatives are delivered generally in the same way through the sequential Initiative Delivery process implying two natural steps: initiation and implementation (see Figure 6.1). However, different IT initiatives may have different origin and motivation. Although ideally all IT initiatives should originate only from the Strategic Planning process, in real organizations due to a number of practical reasons this process cannot be considered as the single possible source of new IT initiatives. Moreover, even IT initiatives originating directly from the Strategic Planning process may have different underlying motivation. Specifically, five general types of IT initiatives can be articulated from the perspective of their origin and motivation: fundamental initiatives, strategic initiatives, local initiatives, urgent initiatives and architectural initiatives. These types of IT initiatives are handled somewhat differently as part of an EA practice.

Fundamental Initiatives

Fundamental initiatives are IT initiatives originating from the Strategic Planning process with an intention to address specific fundamental or "permanent" business needs. Fundamental initiatives are strategy-agnostic in nature. They do not address any business needs dictated by the current strategy, but rather focus on some more profound business needs that can be considered as important for an organization regardless of any business strategy. These needs are identified in a top-down manner by global business leaders (e.g. C-level executives) and architects, often based on the requirements of the adopted operating model (see Figure 5.3). For example, if the target operating model implies standardized business processes for managing suppliers in all business units, then a new IT initiative may be proposed directly by global business executives to automate some of these processes (e.g. registration of new suppliers) in a standard way across all business units, even though the approved business strategy for the next three years may not require significant improvements in supplier management processes. Similarly, if some basic product management or accounting processes in an organization are performed manually, then it might be beneficial in the long run to have all these processes digitized regardless of the current business strategy.

Every organization arguably has a definite set of "permanent" business capabilities (e.g. customer relationship management or supply chain management), which should be well-automated with IT to operate the business in an efficient manner and eventually bolster the execution of any business strategies. These strategy-neutral business capabilities provide the primary targets for fundamental initiatives and corresponding IT investments. Put it simply, fundamental initiatives implement something that will always be necessary and useful for the business. Essentially, they help organizations abstract from ever-changing business strategies and start growing permanent IT-enabled capabilities instead. The periodical execution of fundamental initiatives allows building truly reusable digitized platforms supporting all further business strategies[2]. However, while implementing fundamental initiatives business executives and architects should ensure that these initiatives also have positive business cases and bring some strategic and tactical business value.

Strategic Initiatives

Strategic initiatives are IT initiatives originating from the Strategic Planning process with an intention to address specific strategic business needs. These initiatives are closely related to the current business strategy and address the key business needs required to execute it. In other words, they stem directly from the business strategy as part of its execution. Strategic business needs are identified in a top-down manner by global business executives and architects, often based on the required business capabilities. For example, if the current business strategy requires uplifting the customer relationship management capability, then a new IT initiative may be proposed directly by global business leaders to streamline some processes related to this capability (e.g. issuing customer invoices) and thereby immediately contribute to the strategy execution.

Essentially, strategic initiatives can be considered as key "workhorses" of the strategy execution helping organizations implement their business strategies. However, while implementing strategic initiatives business executives and architects should ensure that these initiatives will not become burdensome legacies for the potential next business strategies after the current strategy fades away. For this purpose, strategic initiatives might be aligned to some more stable planning considerations, e.g. to the target operating model (see Figure 5.3). Furthermore, if the business strategy is subject to constant or radical change, then business executives and architects may consider retreating from strategic to fundamental initiatives for securing the long-term business value of their IT investments.

Local Initiatives

Local initiatives are IT initiatives originating from the Strategic Planning process with an intention to address specific local business needs. These initiatives may be unrelated to the organization-wide business strategy, but focus on the critical tactical needs of specific business units[3]. Unlike fundamental and strategic initiatives, they are proposed in a bottom-up manner by local business executives responsible for managing particular business units (e.g. heads of these business units) based on the perceived importance of the respective tactical needs for their business units. After being proposed, local initiatives are discussed with global business executives and architects, who decide whether these initiatives should be implemented based on their perceived importance for the business of the whole organization and their overall organizational fitness.

Often proposed local initiatives are registered via formal business proposal forms capturing the general idea, intent and justification behind these initiatives. These forms are filled by local business leaders and submitted for senior executive consideration. All the proposal forms incoming from different business units are collected in the common pool of proposed IT initiatives and then the most valuable of these initiatives are picked out by global business leaders to be further elaborated, funded and executed.

For example, if the head of the direct marketing department needs an IT solution to enable email marketing campaigns and submits the corresponding formal business proposal, then global business executives and architects should estimate to what extent this local initiative contributes to the current business strategy and to the organization in general (e.g. how it improves strategic business capabilities and aligns to the adopted operating model) and then decide whether this IT initiative should be delivered. Approved local initiatives are prioritized and scheduled for implementation along with other fundamental and strategic initiatives as part of the Strategic Planning process.

Urgent Initiatives

Urgent initiatives are IT initiatives implemented with an intention to address specific urgent business needs. These urgent business needs may emerge due to a multitude of various reasons including the previously overlooked critical problems, new operational demands, recent changes in relevant government regulations or unexpected tactical moves of competitors[4]. All these business needs are unanticipated and unpredictable in nature. Consequently, corresponding urgent initiatives are fundamentally unplanned IT initiatives.

Unlike fundamental, strategic and local initiatives originating from the Strategic Planning process, these initiatives essentially originate directly from the external business environment. Urgent business needs may be identified in a bottom-up manner by any business leaders in an organization and, if considered as critical, corresponding IT initiatives may be immediately kicked off to address these needs. However, if these business needs are not very critical or can be postponed, then they should be handled as typical planned local initiatives through the regular Strategic Planning process, i.e. discussed with global business executives, prioritized and scheduled for implementation at some moment in the future.

Since urgent initiatives are usually dictated by certain compelling business needs that cannot be ignored, their implementation is often considered as non-optional and mandatory. For this reason, the best that business executives and architects can do is to try to align urgent initiatives to the general strategic direction of an organization as much as possible and ensure that these initiatives do not undermine overall technical and business consistency.

Ideally organizations should avoid urgent initiatives altogether and "sift" all identified business needs through the disciplined Strategic Planning process for their formal alignment, prioritization and scheduling. However, in real organizations urgent initiatives are far from uncommon and often constitute a substantial portion of all implemented IT initiatives. Depending on various factors, including the industry-specific nature of competition, general volatility of the business environment and the maturity of an EA practice, the overall ratio of urgent initiatives among all IT initiatives can vary significantly across organizations[5].

Architectural Initiatives

Architectural initiatives are IT initiatives implemented with an intention to improve the overall quality of the organizational IT landscape. Unlike the four other types of IT initiatives discussed above, these initiatives do not address directly any specific business needs and do not provide any new business functionality, but rather deliver some highly desirable technical enhancements[6]. In other words, while all other types of IT initiatives represent some business initiatives with IT components, architectural initiatives do not represent any business initiatives. Even though they may be essentially invisible to business stakeholders, architectural initiatives might still be very important for the business of an organization. For example, these initiatives may consolidate duplicated systems, decommission legacy IT assets, replace aging hardware, upgrade obsolete software or install new technical infrastructure necessary for maintaining uninterrupted operations and meeting future business needs. Often architectural initiatives address some of the existing architecture debts, as discussed later in Chapter 18 (Instruments for Enterprise Architecture).

Architectural initiatives originate as technical rationalization suggestions directly from the Technology Optimization process (see Figure 6.1). In particular, they are proposed in a top-down manner by architects based on their analysis of the existing IT landscape, its problems, bottlenecks and limitations. After being proposed, architectural initiatives are discussed with relevant IT executives, who decide whether these initiatives should be implemented based on their perceived importance for the quality of the IT landscape and for the business of an organization. Unlike all other types of IT initiatives addressing specific business needs and funded by corresponding senior business stakeholders, architectural initiatives are often funded directly by the CIO or other senior IT leaders. From the delivery perspective, architectural initiatives typically follow the regular two-step Initiative Delivery process with the single exception that IT stakeholders of these initiatives act instead of their missing business stakeholders, i.e. approve high-level implementation options during their initiation steps and then provide more detailed requirements during their implementation steps.

Since architectural initiatives do not deliver any new business functionality or capabilities, they essentially offer little or no noticeable strategic or tactical business value to an organization, with the exception of possible cost savings. From this perspective, ideally organizations should avoid executing purely architectural initiatives altogether and try to optimize their IT landscapes as part of regular business initiatives to minimize unnecessary overhead IT expenses, i.e. periodically incorporate the desirable technical improvements into the designs of fundamental, strategic and local initiatives to achieve both the business and technical goals with each IT initiative. However, in real organizations not all optimizations of the IT landscape can be conveniently implemented as part of normal business initiatives. As a result, even organizations with mature EA practices periodically execute some purely architectural initiatives, even though the number of these initiatives is relatively small compared to the number of regular business initiatives.

The Flow of Different Types of IT Initiatives

The five types of IT initiatives described above (i.e. fundamental, strategic, local, urgent and architectural initiatives) are the key types of initiatives distinguishable from the perspective of an EA practice[7]. Although all these types of IT initiatives are implemented through the Initiative Delivery process, each of these types still has a unique flow in the context of an EA practice. Main properties of these five types of IT initiatives are summarized in Table 7.1.

Initiatives	Origin	Motivation	Initiation	Nature	Concerns
Fundamental initiatives	Strategic Planning process	Grow permanent capabilities and build a reusable digitized platform	Initiated directly by global business executives	Top-down and planned	Ensure positive business case, strategic and tactical value
Strategic initiatives	Strategic Planning process	Execute the current business strategy	Initiated directly by global business executives	Top-down and planned	Ensure lasting business value beyond the current strategy
Local initiatives	Strategic Planning process	Address important tactical needs of business units	Proposed by local executives and approved by global executives	Bottom-up and planned	Ensure alignment to the business strategy and fitness to the organization
Urgent initiatives	External business environment	Address critical, unexpected and urgent business needs	Identified by any business leaders and immediately executed	Bottom-up and unplanned	Align to the general strategic direction as much as possible, ensure overall consistency
Architectural initiatives	Technology Optimization process	Optimize the structure of the IT landscape	Proposed by architects and approved by IT executives	Top-down and planned	Try to incorporate required architectural improvements into regular business initiatives

Table 7.1. Main properties of the five types of IT initiatives

The flow of different types of IT initiatives through an EA practice can be illustrated via mapping these types of initiatives to the process view of an EA practice (see Figure 6.1). Specifically, fundamental initiatives, strategic initiatives and local initiatives arrive to the Initiative Delivery process from the Strategic Planning process, which intends to determine what IT initiatives are required to support the business of an organization. Urgent initiatives arrive to the Initiative Delivery process directly from the external business environment, which is the primary source of uncertainty in organizations. Architectural initiatives arrive to the Initiative Delivery process from the Technology Optimization process, which intends to determine what IT initiatives are required to improve the technical quality of the IT landscape. Finally, the role of the Initiative Delivery process for all types of IT initiatives is to determine how exactly these initiatives should be implemented and then implement the resulting IT solutions. The flow of different types of IT initiatives described above is shown in Figure 7.2.

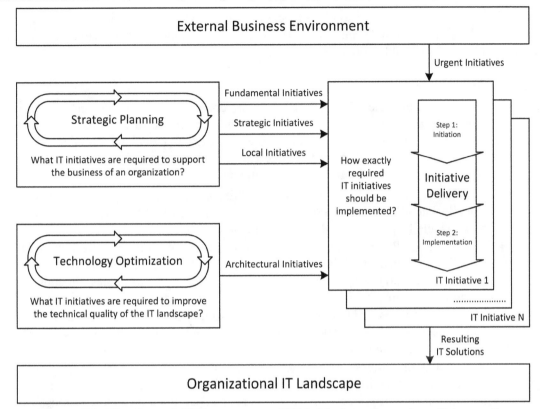

Figure 7.2. The flow of different types of IT initiatives through an EA practice

Fundamental, strategic, local, urgent and architectural initiatives define the essence of the actual implementation work completed as part of an EA practice to modify the organizational IT landscape. Organizations arguably should try to maximize the number of more value-adding fundamental and strategic initiatives and minimize the number of other less value-adding IT initiatives, especially urgent and architectural initiatives. However, due to many practical reasons initiative portfolios of most organizations typically include all the five types of IT initiatives in different proportions. On the one hand, all real organizations operate in inherently uncertain business environments and are often forced to launch urgent initiatives in order to instantly react on the critical environmental changes. On the other hand, all real organizations have imperfect IT landscapes and are often forced to execute purely architectural initiatives in order to deliver required technical enhancements that cannot be implemented as part of regular business initiatives. Generally, organizations should plan their portfolios of IT initiatives with an intention to improve their overall strategic position and general fitness to the demands of the external business environment[8].

Importantly, many IT initiatives in organizations often combine the properties of multiple different types of initiatives and can be related to more than one general type. For instance, IT initiatives can often address both fundamental and strategic, or strategic and local, business needs simultaneously. Moreover, while focusing on specific business needs, all these IT initiatives can, and ideally should, also introduce some technical improvements to the existing IT landscape. For this reason, the five types of IT initiatives discussed above should be considered only as pure archetypes of various possible initiatives.

Chapter Summary

This chapter discussed the role of IT initiatives in the context of an EA practice, analyzed the meaning of the three key EA-related processes from the perspective of IT initiatives, described five different types of IT initiatives distinguishable in an EA practice and explained the type-specific flow of these initiatives through the three EA-related processes. The key message of this chapter can be summarized into the following essential points:

- An IT initiative is the key unit of work in the context of an EA practice which is typically intended to address a specific business need and may vary in its size from a single IT project to a multi-project change program
- The Strategic Planning process intends to formulate the organization-wide portfolio of desired IT initiatives, the Initiative Delivery process aims to deliver each of these initiatives, while the Technology Optimization process intends to inform the decision-making around all IT initiatives
- Five different types of IT initiatives can be distinguished in an EA practice from the perspective of their origin and motivation: fundamental initiatives, strategic initiatives, local initiatives, urgent initiatives and architectural initiatives
- Fundamental initiatives are planned IT initiatives proposed directly by global business executives in a top-down manner with an intention to address specific fundamental business needs, grow permanent capabilities and build a reusable digitized platform
- Strategic initiatives are planned IT initiatives proposed directly by global business executives in a top-down manner with an intention to address specific strategic business needs and execute the current business strategy
- Local initiatives are planned IT initiatives proposed by local executives in a bottom-up manner with an intention to address specific tactical needs of separate business units and approved by global executives
- Urgent initiatives are unplanned IT initiatives identified by any business leaders and then immediately executed with an intention to address specific critical, unexpected and urgent business needs
- Architectural initiatives are planned IT initiatives proposed by architects in a top-down manner with an intention to optimize the structure of the organizational IT landscape and approved by IT executives
- Fundamental, strategic and local initiatives arrive to the Initiative Delivery process from the Strategic Planning process, architectural initiatives arrive to the Initiative Delivery process from the Technology Optimization process, while urgent initiatives arrive to the Initiative Delivery process directly from the external business environment

PART II: Enterprise Architecture Artifacts

Part II of this book focuses specifically on EA artifacts as the core elements of an EA practice. This part discusses the most tangible and "hard" aspects of an EA practice including specific physical documents constituting enterprise architecture, their typical informational contents and representation formats, development and usage as part of an EA practice, practical roles and purposes in the organizational context.

Part II consists of eight consecutive chapters. Chapter 8 describes in detail the CSVLOD model of enterprise architecture defining six general types of EA artifacts: Considerations, Standards, Visions, Landscapes, Outlines and Designs. Then, the subsequent chapters provide an in-depth discussion of these key types of EA artifacts. In particular, Chapter 9 discusses Considerations as a general type of EA artifacts and describes in detail popular narrow subtypes of Considerations including Principles, Policies, Conceptual Data Models, Analytical Reports and Direction Statements. Chapter 10 discusses Standards as a general type of EA artifacts and describes in detail popular narrow subtypes of Standards including Technology Reference Models, Guidelines, Patterns, IT Principles and Logical Data Models. Chapter 11 discusses Visions as a general type of EA artifacts and describes in detail popular narrow subtypes of Visions including Business Capability Models, Roadmaps, Target States, Value Chains and Context Diagrams. Chapter 12 discusses Landscapes as a general type of EA artifacts and describes in detail popular narrow subtypes of Landscapes including Landscape Diagrams, Inventories, Enterprise System Portfolios and IT Roadmaps. Chapter 13 discusses Outlines as a general type of EA artifacts and describes in detail popular narrow subtypes of Outlines including Solution Overviews, Options Assessments and Initiative Proposals. Chapter 14 discusses Designs as a general type of EA artifacts and describes in detail popular narrow subtypes of Designs including Solution Designs and Preliminary Solution Designs. Finally, Chapter 15 revisits the CSVLOD model of enterprise architecture introduced earlier and provides an advanced discussion of some important aspects of this model including the continuous nature of the classification taxonomy, the mappings of specific EA artifacts and the known exceptions to the model.

Chapter 8: The CSVLOD Model of Enterprise Architecture

Previously Chapter 4 briefly introduced the CSVLOD model of enterprise architecture using the close analogy between enterprise architecture and city planning. This chapter provides a more formal, detailed and comprehensive description of the CSVLOD model and its various aspects important for an EA practice. In particular, this chapter starts from explaining two orthogonal dimensions of the CSVLOD model for classifying EA artifacts, what and how, and their essential properties. Then, this chapter describes six general types of EA artifacts defined by the CSVLOD model ensuing from the intersection of these two dimensions: Considerations, Standards, Visions, Landscapes, Outlines and Designs. Finally, this chapter discusses the resulting CSVLOD model of enterprise architecture used further in this book, its key features and explanatory value.

Dimensions for Classifying Enterprise Architecture Artifacts

Leveraging the evident analogy between enterprise architecture and city planning, Chapter 4 illustrated the core mechanisms of an EA practice and introduced six general types of EA artifacts fulfilling pivotal roles in the context of an EA practice: Considerations, Standards, Visions, Landscapes, Outlines and Designs (see Figure 4.1 and Figure 4.9). These six types of EA artifacts constitute the overarching CSVLOD model of enterprise architecture providing the basis for this book and widely used for explaining various aspects of an EA practice.

The CSVLOD model offers a comprehensive conceptual description of the notion of enterprise architecture[1]. In particular, the CSVLOD model defines fundamental types of EA artifacts and their main properties in the context of an EA practice. The key element of the CSVLOD model is the taxonomy for EA artifacts providing a classification scheme for grouping diverse EA artifacts into six consistent groups according to their essential roles and properties.

Specifically, the CSVLOD taxonomy has two orthogonal dimensions for classifying EA artifacts. These dimensions help better understand the general properties of different types of EA artifacts. The first dimension classifies all EA artifacts into rules, structures and changes. The second dimension classifies all EA artifacts into business-focused and IT-focused.

Dimension One: What?

The first dimension of the CSVLOD taxonomy classifies EA artifacts based on *what* objects they describe. According to this dimension all EA artifacts can be classified into rules, structures and changes. **Rules EA artifacts** describe broad global *rules* defining an organization or its divisions. They are often represented in textual formats. Rules typically do not refer to any specific instances (e.g. concrete capabilities, initiatives, processes, systems or databases), but rather apply to all instances of a certain type. For example, rules may define how all business processes in an organization should be run or how all IT systems in an organization should be implemented. Rules are permanent EA artifacts (see Table 2.2), which are usually created once and then periodically updated. They are the most stable and infrequently changing EA artifacts. Rules provide the basis for all other planning decisions and usually answer the question "How do we work or want to work?" They are typically intangible and uncountable. For instance, rules may prescribe to install Linux operating systems on all servers, but at the same time there might be zero, one, 50 or 1000 Linux-based servers actually running in an organization. The general purpose of all rules is to help achieve consistency and homogeneity of all planning decisions and approaches used in an organization.

Structures EA artifacts describe high-level *structures* of an organization or its parts. They are usually represented in graphical formats. Unlike rules, structures typically refer to specific, but relatively abstract instances (e.g. concrete capabilities, initiatives, processes, systems and databases) and often describe the relationship between different instances. For example, structures may describe how different IT systems relate to specific business capabilities or how these systems are connected to each other. Structures are permanent EA artifacts, which are usually created once and then continuously updated. They are relative stable, but change together with an organization and its plans. Structures provide high-level "maps" facilitating decision-making and usually answer the question "What approximately do we have or want to have?" Structures are typically tangible and countable since they describe specific instances and their relationship. The general purpose of all structures is to help understand what changes are desirable in an organization and how to implement them.

Changes EA artifacts describe specific proposed incremental *changes* to an organization, i.e. separate change initiatives or projects[2]. They are usually represented in mixed textual and graphical formats. Unlike structures, changes thoroughly describe concrete instances with their internal details, e.g. separate process steps, system components, functional specifications, data objects and communication interfaces. For example, changes may describe how exactly a new IT system needs to be implemented and how exactly this system will modify particular business processes. In contrast to rules and structures, changes are temporary EA artifacts (see Table 2.2), which are usually created for specific purposes and then discarded. They are the most volatile EA artifacts having relatively short lifespans essentially limited to the timeframes of corresponding change initiatives. Changes represent tactical plans of an organization and usually answer the question "What exactly are we going to change right now?" Changes are typically tangible since they describe specific "palpable" instances in great detail. The general purpose of all changes is to help plan separate organizational changes in detail. The main differences between rules, structures and changes EA artifacts are summarized in Table 8.1.

Artifacts	Rules	Structures	Changes
Describe	Broad global rules defining an organization or its divisions	High-level structures of an organization or its parts	Specific proposed incremental changes to an organization
Scope	Very wide, often cover an entire organization	Wide, often cover large parts of an organization	Narrow, limited to separate IT initiatives or projects
Format	Often textual	Usually graphical	Mix of textual and graphical
Question	How do we work or want to work?	What approximately do we have or want to have?	What exactly are we going to change right now?
Lifecycle	Permanent, created once and then periodically updated	Permanent, created once and then continuously updated	Temporary, created for specific purposes and then discarded
Role	Basis for all other planning decisions	High-level "maps" facilitating decision-making	Tactical plans of an organization
Purpose	Help achieve consistency and homogeneity of all planning decisions	Help understand what changes are desirable and how to implement them	Help plan separate changes in detail

Table 8.1. Rules, structures and changes EA artifacts

Dimension Two: How?

The second dimension of the CSVLOD taxonomy classifies EA artifacts based on *how* they describe objects. According to this dimension all EA artifacts can be classified into business-focused and IT-focused. On the one hand, **business-focused EA artifacts** tend to be technology-neutral and use plain business language, e.g. money, customers, capabilities, business goals and competitive advantages. Naturally, these EA artifacts typically cover the business domain. However, they may also cover other relevant domains, and especially business-enabling EA domains (e.g. applications and data, see Figure 2.2), at the superficial level understandable even to non-IT-savvy people. Business-focused EA artifacts provide rather "soft" descriptions. They tend to be brief, largely informal, use highly intuitive presentation formats and contain only the most essential information relevant to executive-level audience. Business-focused EA artifacts are intended largely for business executives[3]. They are always dual EA artifacts (see Figure 2.4) aiming to facilitate effective collaboration and partnership between business and IT stakeholders. Essentially, these EA artifacts can be considered as communication "interfaces" between business and IT. All business-focused EA artifacts are either developed collaboratively by architects and business executives, or at least consciously approved by business leaders. The general purpose of all business-focused EA artifacts is to help business leaders manage IT without understanding its technical details.

On the other hand, **IT-focused EA artifacts** tend to be purely technical and use highly IT-specific language, e.g. systems, applications, databases, platforms and networks. These EA artifacts typically cover various technical EA domains (e.g. applications, data, integration, infrastructure and security, see Figure 2.2) and sometimes the business domain as well (e.g. specific business processes or requirements). IT-focused EA artifacts represent mostly "hard" descriptions. Unlike business-focused EA artifacts, they can be more formal, voluminous and detailed to provide all the relevant implementation-specific information, sometimes using specialized and sophisticated modeling notations. IT-focused EA artifacts are intended primarily for architects and other IT specialists. They are used largely as reference materials for decision-making and project implementation within the IT department. Essentially, these EA artifacts can be considered as internal IT tools invisible to business. All IT-focused EA artifacts are developed predominantly by architects with the involvement of other IT stakeholders when necessary. The general purpose of all IT-focused EA artifacts is to help architects organize IT according to their best understanding of the business interests. The main differences between business-focused and IT-focused EA artifacts are summarized in Table 8.2.

Artifacts	Business-focused	IT-focused
Language	Technology-neutral business language	Technical IT-specific language
Domains	Business domain and often other relevant domains at a high level	Applications, data, integration, infrastructure, security domains and sometimes business domain
Format	Brief, intuitive, largely informal and include only the most essential information	Can be voluminous, formal, use strict notations and include comprehensive details
Stakeholders	Business leaders and architects	Architects and other IT specialists
Role	Communication interfaces between business and IT	Internal IT tools invisible to business
Purpose	Help business leaders manage IT	Help architects organize IT

Table 8.2. Business-focused and IT-focused EA artifacts

Six General Types of Enterprise Architecture Artifacts

The intersection of the two orthogonal dimensions described above (i.e. what and how) produces a six-cell taxonomy for classifying EA artifacts. This taxonomy defines six general types of EA artifacts playing fundamental roles in successful EA practices. Specifically, all business-focused rules EA artifacts are collectively titled as Considerations since all these artifacts describe some general overarching business *considerations* defining the architectural decision-making in an organization. All IT-focused rules EA artifacts are collectively titled as Standards since all these artifacts describe some IT-specific technical *standards* shaping the designs of all IT systems in an organization. All business-focused structures EA artifacts are collectively titled as Visions since all these artifacts describe some abstract business *visions* of an organization usually in its long-term future state. All IT-focused structures EA artifacts are collectively titled as Landscapes since all these artifacts describe some significant parts of the organizational IT *landscape* from the technical perspective. All business-focused changes EA artifacts are collectively titled as Outlines since all these artifacts describe some brief *outlines* of specific IT-driven change initiatives understandable to business executives. Finally, all IT-focused changes EA artifacts are collectively titled as Designs since all these artifacts describe some detailed technical *designs* of specific IT-enabled change initiatives. The CSVLOD taxonomy defining the six general types of EA artifacts is shown in Figure 8.1.

What Artifacts Describe?

	Rules	Structures	Changes	
Business-Focused	**Considerations** (Business-Focused Rules)	**Visions** (Business-Focused Structures)	**Outlines** (Business-Focused Changes)	**Language:** Technology-neutral business language **Domains:** Business domain and often other relevant domains at a high level **Format:** Brief, intuitive, largely informal and include only the most essential information **Stakeholders:** Business leaders and architects **Role:** Communication interfaces between business and IT **Purpose:** Help business leaders manage IT
IT-Focused	**Standards** (IT-Focused Rules)	**Landscapes** (IT-Focused Structures)	**Designs** (IT-Focused Changes)	**Language:** Technical IT-specific language **Domains:** Various technical domains and sometimes also business domain **Format:** Can be voluminous, formal, use strict notations and include comprehensive details **Stakeholders:** Architects and other IT specialists **Role:** Internal IT tools invisible to business **Purpose:** Help architects organize IT
	Describe: Broad global rules defining an organization or its divisions **Scope:** Very wide, often cover an entire organization **Format:** Often textual **Question:** How do we work or want to work? **Lifecycle:** Created once and then periodically updated **Role:** Basis for all other planning decisions **Purpose:** Help achieve consistency and homogeneity	**Describe:** High-level structures of an organization or its parts **Scope:** Wide, often cover large parts of an organization **Format:** Usually graphical **Question:** What approximately do we have or want to have? **Lifecycle:** Created once and then continuously updated **Role:** High-level "maps" facilitating decision-making **Purpose:** Help understand what changes are desirable and how to implement them	**Describe:** Specific proposed changes to an organization **Scope:** Narrow, limited to separate IT initiatives or projects **Format:** Mix of textual and graphical **Question:** What exactly are we going to change right now? **Lifecycle:** Created for specific purposes and then discarded **Role:** Tactical plans of an organization **Purpose:** Help plan separate changes in detail	

*(Left vertical axis label: **How Artifacts Describe?**)*

Figure 8.1. The CSVLOD taxonomy for EA artifacts

The CSVLOD taxonomy explains the essential conceptual differences between different types of EA artifacts. The main properties of each general type of EA artifacts are largely determined by its position in the taxonomy, i.e. by its column and row. For instance, all EA artifacts related to Considerations share the common properties of both rules and business-focused EA artifacts, while all EA artifacts related to Designs share the common properties of both changes and IT-focused EA artifacts. However, each of the six general types of EA artifacts also has its own refined, type-specific properties defining its unique role and usage in the context of an EA practice.

Each general type of EA artifacts defined by the taxonomy represents a variety of different EA artifacts with similar properties and purposes. Even though the variety of specific EA artifacts related to any general type can be very wide (potentially infinite), for each general type there is a limited set of specific subtypes of EA artifacts having a very close meaning across different organizations. These narrow subtypes of EA artifacts are consistently found in more or less successful EA practices and share the basic properties of their general types. Although all EA artifacts can be allocated to one of the six general types, many useful EA artifacts are unique, organization-specific and cannot be allocated to any specific subtypes within these general types.

All narrow subtypes of EA artifacts can be conditionally grouped into three categories based on their relative popularity in reasonably mature and successful EA practices[4]:

- **Essential EA artifacts** – the subtypes of EA artifacts used in the majority (more than 50%) of established EA practices
- **Common EA artifacts** – the subtypes of EA artifacts used in approximately ~25-50% of established EA practices
- **Uncommon EA artifacts** – the subtypes of EA artifacts used in approximately ~10-25% of established EA practices

Since most narrow subtypes of EA artifacts do not have any consistent standardized titles adopted across the industry and are often used under different titles in different organizations, the titles of these subtypes used further in this book represent either the most commonly used titles of respective EA artifacts, or the most descriptive titles accurately conveying their perceived practical meaning.

Considerations

Considerations describe global conceptual rules and fundamental considerations important for business and relevant for IT. They are dual EA artifacts (see Figure 2.4) relevant to both business leaders and architects. Considerations usually either do not focus on specific points in time or focus on the long-term future. They are typically expressed in simple intuitive formats, often as brief written statements. Specific EA artifacts related to Considerations used in successful EA practices include, but are not limited to, the following five articulate subtypes:

- Principles (essential) – global high-level guidelines influencing all decision-making and planning in an organization
- Policies (common) – overarching organizational norms typically of a restrictive nature providing compulsory prescriptions in certain areas
- Conceptual Data Models (uncommon) – abstract definitions of the main data entities critical for the business of an organization and their relationship
- Analytical Reports (uncommon) – executive-level analyses of relevant technology trends and their potential impact on the business of an organization
- Direction Statements (uncommon) – conceptual messages communicating major organization-wide decisions with far-reaching consequences

Considerations represent planning decisions on how an organization needs to work from the IT perspective (see Table 2.1 and Figure 2.6). They are developed collaboratively by senior business executives and architects and then used to influence all "downstream" architectural decisions. As permanent EA artifacts (see Table 2.2), Considerations are developed once and then updated according to the ongoing changes in the business environment.

Considerations can be considered as the overarching organizational context for information systems planning. The general purpose of all Considerations is to help achieve the agreement on basic principles, values, directions and aims. The proper use of Considerations leads to improved overall conceptual consistency between business and IT.

Standards

Standards describe global technical rules, standards, patterns and best practices relevant for IT systems. They are not dual EA artifacts and relevant mostly to architects. Standards usually either do not focus on specific points in time or focus on the current state. They can be expressed in various formats, often using strict notations. Specific EA artifacts related to Standards used in successful EA practices include, but are not limited to, the following five articulate subtypes:

- Technology Reference Models (essential) – structured graphical representations of all technologies used in an organization
- Guidelines (essential) – IT-specific implementation-level prescriptions applicable in narrow technology-specific areas or domains
- Patterns (common) – generic reusable solutions to commonly occurring problems in the design of IT systems
- IT Principles (common) – global high-level IT-specific guidelines influencing all IT-related decisions and plans in an organization
- Logical Data Models (uncommon) – logical or even physical platform-specific definitions of the key data entities and their relationship

Standards represent mostly planning decisions on how all IT systems should be implemented and some facts on the current approaches and technologies (see Table 2.1 and Figure 2.6). They are developed collaboratively by architects and technical subject-matter experts and used to shape architectures of all IT initiatives. As permanent EA artifacts, Standards are developed on an as-necessary basis and updated according to the ongoing technology progress.

Standards can be considered as proven reusable means for IT systems implementation. The general purpose of all Standards is to help achieve technical consistency, technological homogeneity and regulatory compliance. The proper use of Standards leads to faster delivery of new IT initiatives and reduced IT-related costs, risks and complexity of the IT landscape in general.

Visions

Visions provide high-level conceptual descriptions of an organization from the business perspective. They are dual EA artifacts relevant to both business leaders and architects. Visions often focus on the long-term future up to 3-5 years ahead. They are typically expressed in brief informal formats, often as simple one-page diagrams. Specific EA artifacts related to Visions used in successful EA practices include, but are not limited to, the following five articulate subtypes:

- Business Capability Models (essential) – structured graphical representations of all organizational business capabilities, their relationship and hierarchy
- Roadmaps (essential) – structured graphical views of all planned IT initiatives in specific business areas having direct business value
- Target States (common) – high-level graphical descriptions of the desired long-term future state of an organization
- Value Chains (uncommon) – structured graphical representations of the added value chain of an organization
- Context Diagrams (uncommon) – high-level graphical descriptions of the current operational flows of an organization

Visions represent mostly planning decisions on what IT should deliver to an organization in the long run. They are developed collaboratively by senior business executives and architects and then used to guide IT investments, identify, prioritize and launch new IT initiatives. As permanent EA artifacts, Visions are developed once and then updated according to the ongoing changes in strategic business priorities.

Visions can be considered as shared views of an organization and its future agreed by business and IT. The general purpose of all Visions is to help achieve the alignment between IT investments and long-term business outcomes. The proper use of Visions leads to improved strategic alignment and effectiveness of IT investments.

Landscapes

Landscapes provide high-level technical descriptions of the organizational IT landscape. They are not dual EA artifacts and relevant predominantly to architects. Landscapes more often focus on the current state. They are typically expressed in strict formats, often as complex one-page diagrams using formal modeling notations, e.g. ArchiMate. Specific EA artifacts related to Landscapes used in successful EA practices include, but are not limited to, the following four articulate subtypes:

- Landscape Diagrams (essential) – technical "boxes and arrows" schemes of different scopes and granularities describing the organizational IT landscape
- Inventories (common) – structured catalogs of currently available IT assets describing their essential properties and features
- Enterprise System Portfolios (common) – structured high-level mappings of all essential IT systems to relevant business capabilities
- IT Roadmaps (common) – structured graphical views of all planned IT initiatives of a purely technical nature having no visible business impact

Landscapes represent mostly facts on the current IT landscape and some planning decisions on its future evolution (see Table 2.1 and Figure 2.6). They are developed and maintained by architects and used to rationalize the IT landscape, manage the lifecycle of IT assets and plan new IT initiatives. As permanent EA artifacts, Landscapes are developed on an as-necessary basis and updated according to the ongoing evolution of the IT landscape.

Landscapes can be considered as a knowledge base of reference materials on the IT landscape. The general purpose of all Landscapes is to help understand, analyze and modify the structure of the IT landscape. The proper use of Landscapes leads to increased reuse and reduced duplication of IT assets, improved IT agility and decreased dependence on legacy IT systems.

Outlines

Outlines provide high-level descriptions of separate IT initiatives understandable to business leaders. They are dual EA artifacts relevant to both business executives and architects. Outlines usually focus on the mid-term future up to 1-2 years ahead. They are typically expressed as a mix of textual descriptions and simple diagrams. Specific EA artifacts related to Outlines used in successful EA practices include, but are not limited to, the following three articulate subtypes:

- Solution Overviews (essential) – high-level descriptions of specific proposed IT solutions understandable to business leaders
- Options Assessments (common) – lists of available high-level implementation options for specific IT initiatives with their pros and cons
- Initiative Proposals (uncommon) – very early idea-level descriptions of proposed IT initiatives and their justifications

Outlines represent planning decisions on how approximately specific IT initiatives should be implemented. They are developed collaboratively by architects and business executives and then used to evaluate, approve and fund specific IT initiatives. As temporary EA artifacts (see Table 2.2), Outlines are developed at the early stages of IT initiatives to support decision-making and then archived.

Outlines can be considered essentially as benefit, time and price tags for proposed IT initiatives. The general purpose of all Outlines is to help estimate the overall business impact and value of proposed IT initiatives. The proper use of Outlines leads to improved efficiency and ROI of IT investments.

Designs

Designs provide detailed technical and functional descriptions of separate IT projects actionable for project teams. They are dual EA artifacts relevant to both project teams and architects. Designs usually focus on the short-term future up to one year ahead. They are typically expressed as a mix of text, tables and complex diagrams, can be voluminous and often use formal modeling notations, e.g. UML. Specific EA artifacts related to Designs used in successful EA practices include, but are not limited to, the following two articulate subtypes:

- Solution Designs (essential) – detailed technical and functional specifications of approved IT solutions actionable for project teams
- Preliminary Solution Designs (uncommon) – preliminary high-level technical and functional designs of specific approved IT solutions

Designs represent planning decisions on how exactly specific IT projects should be implemented. They are developed collaboratively by architects, IT project teams and business representatives and then used by project teams to implement IT projects. As temporary EA artifacts, Designs are developed at the later stages of IT initiatives to support implementation and then archived.

Designs can be considered as communication interfaces between architects and project teams. The general purpose of all Designs is to help implement approved IT projects according to business and architectural requirements. The proper use of Designs leads to improved quality of the IT project delivery.

The Resulting CSVLOD Model of Enterprise Architecture

The six general types of EA artifacts described above (i.e. Considerations, Standards, Visions, Landscapes, Outlines and Designs) constitute the CSVLOD model of enterprise architecture. These six types of EA artifacts are fundamental for an EA practice. All the six types of EA artifacts can be found in the vast majority of mature and successful EA practices. Of all the six general types only most Landscapes and some Standards are facts EA artifacts, while all other types, including most Standards and some Landscapes, are decisions EA artifacts (see Table 2.1 and Figure 2.6).

Even though specific EA artifacts related to each general type are highly organization-specific and can be very diverse, each general type has a small number of consistent subtypes of EA artifacts described above: five subtypes of Considerations, five subtypes of Standards, five subtypes of Visions, four subtypes of Landscapes, three subtypes of Outlines and two subtypes of Designs (24 different subtypes in total, including eight essential, eight common and eight uncommon subtypes). However, successful EA practices typically use limited pragmatic sets of ~10-15 different EA artifacts, rather than all imaginable EA artifacts. Although all EA artifacts found in successful EA practices belong to the six general types of EA artifacts defined by the CSVLOD model, not all EA artifacts belong to the 24 narrow subtypes since many organizations "invent" and use unique organization-specific EA artifacts. The CSVLOD model of enterprise architecture is shown in Figure 8.2.

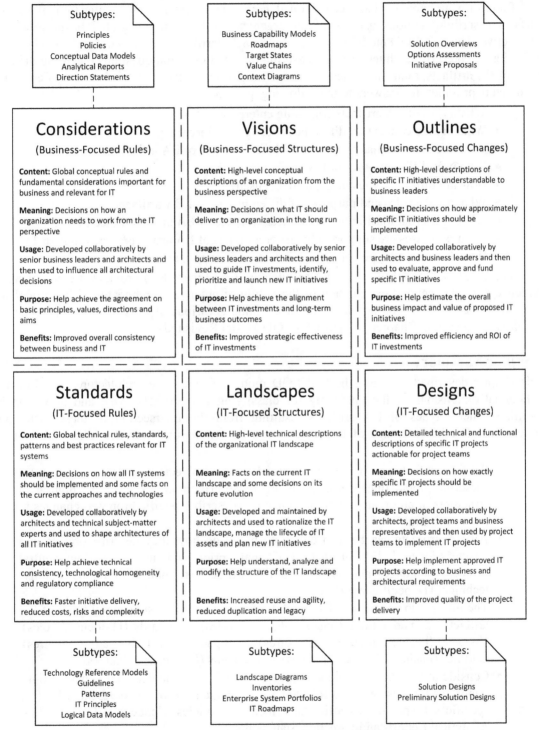

Subtypes:

Principles
Policies
Conceptual Data Models
Analytical Reports
Direction Statements

Considerations
(Business-Focused Rules)

Content: Global conceptual rules and fundamental considerations important for business and relevant for IT

Meaning: Decisions on how an organization needs to work from the IT perspective

Usage: Developed collaboratively by senior business leaders and architects and then used to influence all architectural decisions

Purpose: Help achieve the agreement on basic principles, values, directions and aims

Benefits: Improved overall consistency between business and IT

Subtypes:

Business Capability Models
Roadmaps
Target States
Value Chains
Context Diagrams

Visions
(Business-Focused Structures)

Content: High-level conceptual descriptions of an organization from the business perspective

Meaning: Decisions on what IT should deliver to an organization in the long run

Usage: Developed collaboratively by senior business leaders and architects and then used to guide IT investments, identify, prioritize and launch new IT initiatives

Purpose: Help achieve the alignment between IT investments and long-term business outcomes

Benefits: Improved strategic effectiveness of IT investments

Subtypes:

Solution Overviews
Options Assessments
Initiative Proposals

Outlines
(Business-Focused Changes)

Content: High-level descriptions of specific IT initiatives understandable to business leaders

Meaning: Decisions on how approximately specific IT initiatives should be implemented

Usage: Developed collaboratively by architects and business leaders and then used to evaluate, approve and fund specific IT initiatives

Purpose: Help estimate the overall business impact and value of proposed IT initiatives

Benefits: Improved efficiency and ROI of IT investments

Standards
(IT-Focused Rules)

Content: Global technical rules, standards, patterns and best practices relevant for IT systems

Meaning: Decisions on how all IT systems should be implemented and some facts on the current approaches and technologies

Usage: Developed collaboratively by architects and technical subject-matter experts and used to shape architectures of all IT initiatives

Purpose: Help achieve technical consistency, technological homogeneity and regulatory compliance

Benefits: Faster initiative delivery, reduced costs, risks and complexity

Landscapes
(IT-Focused Structures)

Content: High-level technical descriptions of the organizational IT landscape

Meaning: Facts on the current IT landscape and some decisions on its future evolution

Usage: Developed and maintained by architects and used to rationalize the IT landscape, manage the lifecycle of IT assets and plan new IT initiatives

Purpose: Help understand, analyze and modify the structure of the IT landscape

Benefits: Increased reuse and agility, reduced duplication and legacy

Designs
(IT-Focused Changes)

Content: Detailed technical and functional descriptions of specific IT projects actionable for project teams

Meaning: Decisions on how exactly specific IT projects should be implemented

Usage: Developed collaboratively by architects, project teams and business representatives and then used by project teams to implement IT projects

Purpose: Help implement approved IT projects according to business and architectural requirements

Benefits: Improved quality of the project delivery

Subtypes:

Technology Reference Models
Guidelines
Patterns
IT Principles
Logical Data Models

Subtypes:

Landscape Diagrams
Inventories
Enterprise System Portfolios
IT Roadmaps

Subtypes:

Solution Designs
Preliminary Solution Designs

Figure 8.2. The CSVLOD model of enterprise architecture

Enterprise architecture has been defined earlier in Chapter 2 as a collection of specific artifacts describing various aspects of an organization from an integrated business and IT perspective. The CSVLOD model shown in Figure 8.2 clarifies, complements and completes this definition of enterprise architecture by answering the most essential questions regarding different types of EA artifacts, their properties and usage. In particular, the CSVLOD model of enterprise architecture provides the answers to the following questions:

- What types of EA artifacts constitute enterprise architecture?
- What are the conceptual differences between different types of EA artifacts?
- What are the essential properties of different types of EA artifacts?
- Who uses different types of EA artifacts?
- How are different types of EA artifacts used?
- What are the roles and purposes of different types of EA artifacts?
- What is the relationship between different types of EA artifacts? (see Figure 4.8)
- What processes are supported by different types of EA artifacts? (see Figure 6.1)
- How do different types of EA artifacts benefit organizations?

The CSVLOD model of enterprise architecture (see Figure 8.2) provides a comprehensive evidence-based conceptual explanation of the notion of enterprise architecture. This model will be used further in this book as the basis for explaining various aspects of an EA practice and revisited again later in Chapter 15 (The CSVLOD Model Revisited).

Chapter Summary

This chapter described in detail the CSVLOD model of enterprise architecture including two orthogonal dimensions of the taxonomy for classifying EA artifacts, what and how, and six resulting general types of EA artifacts resulting from the intersection of these orthogonal dimensions. The key message of this chapter can be summarized into the following essential points:

- All EA artifacts can be classified based on what objects they describe into rules (describe global rules defining an organization), structures (describe high-level structures of an organization) and changes (describe specific proposed changes to an organization)
- All EA artifacts can be also classified based on how they describe objects into business-focused EA artifacts (informal, brief and use technology-neutral business language) and IT-focused EA artifacts (formal, voluminous and use technical IT-specific language)
- The intersection of these orthogonal dimensions produces six general types of EA artifacts: Considerations (business-focused rules), Standards (IT-focused rules), Visions (business-focused structures), Landscapes (IT-focused structures), Outlines (business-focused changes) and Designs (IT-focused changes)
- Considerations describe global conceptual rules and fundamental considerations important for business and relevant for IT, which are often represented by five specific subtypes of EA artifacts: Principles, Policies, Conceptual Data Models, Analytical Reports and Direction Statements

- Standards describe global technical rules, standards, patterns and best practices relevant for IT systems, which are often represented by five specific subtypes of EA artifacts: Technology Reference Models, Guidelines, Patterns, IT Principles and Logical Data Models
- Visions provide high-level conceptual descriptions of an organization from the business perspective, which are often represented by five specific subtypes of EA artifacts: Business Capability Models, Roadmaps, Target States, Value Chains and Context Diagrams
- Landscapes provide high-level technical descriptions of the organizational IT landscape, which are often represented by four specific subtypes of EA artifacts: Landscape Diagrams, Inventories, Enterprise System Portfolios and IT Roadmaps
- Outlines provide high-level descriptions of separate IT initiatives understandable to business leaders, which are often represented by three specific subtypes of EA artifacts: Solution Overviews, Options Assessments and Initiative Proposals
- Designs provide detailed technical and functional descriptions of separate IT projects actionable for project teams, which are often represented by two specific subtypes of EA artifacts: Solution Designs and Preliminary Solution Designs

Chapter 9: Considerations

The previous chapter provided an in-depth description of the CSVLOD model of enterprise architecture defining six general types of EA artifacts. This chapter discusses in great detail various aspects of Considerations as the first general type of EA artifacts (business-focused rules) as well as their more specific subtypes often used in EA practices. In particular, this chapter starts from describing the common properties of all Considerations including their type-specific informational contents, development and usage scenarios, role in an EA practice and associated organizational benefits. Then, this chapter discusses in detail popular narrow subtypes of Considerations including Principles, Policies, Conceptual Data Models, Analytical Reports and Direction Statements. Finally, this chapter provides additional concerns and recommendations regarding the practical use of Considerations as part of an EA practice.

Considerations as a General Type of Enterprise Architecture Artifacts

Considerations are business-focused rules EA artifacts (see Figure 8.1). They describe global business-related rules defined collaboratively by senior business and IT stakeholders and share the essential common properties of both business-focused EA artifacts and rules EA artifacts. Specific examples of EA artifacts related to Considerations include Principles, Policies, Conceptual Data Models, Analytical Reports and Direction Statements (see Figure 8.2)[1].

Informational Contents

Considerations describe global conceptual rules and fundamental considerations important for business and relevant for IT. Essentially, Considerations document some significant organization-wide business decisions having a direct impact on IT. The global decisions reflected in Considerations address the following and similar foundational questions:

- How should an entire organization work?
- Which operating model is desirable for an organization?
- Which business processes should be standardized across business units?
- Which types of data should be standardized and shared organization-wide?
- What is the general role and purpose of IT in an organization?
- How should, and should not, an organization use information systems?
- What technology trends may be disruptive for the business of an organization?
- What IT innovations may be strategic for an organization?

All these questions represent critical business decisions of organization-wide significance that should not be made by IT executives alone on behalf of the whole organization[2]. For example, the intuitive decision of IT executives to replace local IT systems customized for specific business units with a single centralized ERP system for the sake of cost optimization may be inconsistent with the actual business strategy to provide highly customized and flexible services in the premium price segment. Likewise, the decision of IT executives to maintain local customer databases for the sake of greater agility may be inconsistent with the actual business strategy to leverage cross-selling opportunities between different lines of business. On the one hand, the decision of IT executives to adopt a certain cutting-edge innovative technology may be inconsistent with the perceived strategic potential of this technology from the business perspective as well as with the overall organizational attitude and risk appetite for innovations. On the other hand, the decision not to adopt a particular "hot" technology may undermine the strategic positioning of an organization in the long run.

In order to avoid these and other similar inconsistencies, Considerations document the essential agreements reached between business and IT on the most profound questions regarding an organization and its business. For this reason, all Considerations are dual EA artifacts (see Figure 2.4) of direct interest to both senior business executives and architects. They represent the consensus understanding of the fundamental business needs shared by both business and IT. Considerations reflect both the desire of business to operate in a particular way and the ability of IT to enable this way of working. Often Considerations are relevant to an entire organization. However, in large, complex and decentralized organizations major business units (e.g. lines of business, business functions or divisions) can also develop their own Considerations reflecting local unit-specific strategies consistent with global organization-wide Considerations.

However, far from all significant decisions important for the business have articulate implications for IT. For example, human resource strategies defining the desired qualities of potential candidates, promotion criteria and salary ranges for different positions, though critical for the business, are essentially irrelevant to IT and may not have any real IT-related consequences. Similarly, legal and financial strategies of an organization usually do not influence its IT-related decision-making. Unlike the strategic decisions regarding the requirements to business processes, data handling and technology adoption, strategic decisions in these areas are rarely represented in Considerations due to the absence of their direct connection with IT.

Considerations typically either do not focus on specific points in time or focus on the long-term future. On the one hand, many Considerations, especially Policies and most Principles, are essentially timeless in nature and do not refer to any specific points in time. They define certain fundamental rules which are active now, might have been active in the past and will be active in the future as well, unless revised or removed as irrelevant. On the other hand, some Considerations, including Direction Statements, most Analytical Reports and even some Principles, may focus on the long-term future. Essentially, these Considerations may define some worthwhile strategic IT-related goals and objectives for an entire organization.

Considerations are usually expressed in simple intuitive formats easily understandable to executive-level business audience. Since they provide very abstract suggestions of a conceptual nature, which often can be interpreted differently in different contexts and situations, Considerations typically do not require accurate details, exact numbers or voluminous descriptions. Essentially, they can use any reasonable representation formats suitable and convenient for conveying their conceptual messages. However, most often Considerations are expressed as brief statements written in plain technology-neutral language. Physically, they are most often stored and distributed as ordinary MS Word documents.

Development and Usage

Considerations represent collective planning decisions (see Table 2.1) on how an organization needs to work from the IT perspective. They are developed as part of the Strategic Planning process (see Figure 6.1) collaboratively by senior business executives and architects (see Figure 2.6) based on their common understanding of how an organization should operate in the future to achieve its long-term goals and objectives. When developing Considerations, business executives and architects, among other things, often discuss and reach an agreement on the key elements of the target operating model, i.e. desired synergies between major business units, global process standardization and data integration opportunities (see Figure 5.3). Some Considerations, especially Policies, may be derived directly from the requirements of external compliance laws or industry regulations. Business leaders should clearly understand the implications of Considerations for their business, while architects should clearly understand the implications of Considerations for their IT. Moreover, business executives and architects should be able to make a conscious commitment to act according to established Considerations. Often they are explicitly signed-off by both parties. Importantly, even though Considerations as physical documents are created primarily by architects, their real meaning is based mostly on the desire of business executives to work in a particular way. Key planning decisions reflected in Considerations are always made by senior business stakeholders, while the role of architects is only to facilitate their development, i.e. help business executives make right planning decisions, understand their implications and clearly formulate them in a way appropriate for the purposes of IT planning.

After being established, Considerations influence all IT-related decision-making processes in an entire organization or in its major business units. For example, the requirement to provide a single customer view documented in Considerations may have numerous and diverse implications for IT planning at different organizational levels including the selection of reliable and secure storage technologies for creating a shared customer repository, the deployment of an appropriate integration infrastructure for accessing the central customer database from all running IT systems, the cancellation of current or planned IT initiatives contradicting the very idea of a single customer view and even the modification of the designs of all new IT projects to make them work with the same customer database. The decision to adopt a new strategic technology documented in Considerations may stimulate the development of corresponding guidelines regulating the usage of this technology, initiate new pilot projects to test the technology and highlight the necessity to upgrade the current IT landscape to achieve compatibility with the new technology. Likewise, the policy restricting the storage of commercially sensitive data in offshore datacenters documented in Considerations may also have considerable implications for IT planning at both the organization-wide and project levels.

While staying in background, Considerations provide a sound basis for IT-related planning decisions and continuously underpin all architectural thought processes involving both business leaders and architects. However, the alignment of IT-related plans to Considerations can be also assessed more formally as part of regular EA-related processes. For instance, all Outlines and Designs are typically peer-reviewed by other architects and evaluated against Considerations during their approval and sign-off governance procedures, as discussed later in Chapter 17 (Architecture Functions in Organizations). For that purpose, Outlines and Designs can contain specific subsections explicitly explaining the alignment of corresponding IT initiatives to

Considerations. Similarly, the alignment of Visions to Considerations is often evaluated during their yearly formal approval by senior business executives, while the alignment of Standards to Considerations can be evaluated during their approval by the CIO.

Although Considerations provide universal rules for IT planning, reasonable and substantiated deviations from Considerations are usually tolerated, probably with the exception of Policies, as discussed later in this chapter. For example, even if Considerations require business processes in all business units to use standardized organization-wide IT systems, some unit-specific systems still can be implemented if a conscious decision to depart from Considerations is made by business leaders due to extremely profitable short-term opportunities or critical local requirements. This and other similar decisions to temporarily deviate from Considerations may be informed and guided by the volume of the associated architecture debt, as discussed later in Chapter 18 (Instruments for Enterprise Architecture).

Considerations, with the exception of temporary Direction Statements and some Analytical Reports, are permanent EA artifacts (see Table 2.2) with a very long lifetime. Once established, they evolve slowly according to the changes in the organizational business strategy and external business environment. Specifically, Considerations are usually reviewed and reapproved on a periodical basis, often yearly after the re-approval of a business strategy by the executive committee, to reflect the latest shifts in strategic business priorities as well as the recent changes in technological, legislative and other relevant environmental factors. As part of the regular annual review process established Considerations may be revised and even occasionally discarded if recognized as irrelevant, counterproductive or no longer appropriate for an organization. For example, some Principles might be cancelled if they are found inconsistent with the current business strategy, while some Policies might be discontinued if the respective regulatory norms have been amended.

Role and Benefits

Considerations represent the overarching organizational context for information systems planning. They setup a common intellectual environment for all relevant actors involved in strategic decision-making and implementation of IT systems. Essentially, Considerations can be considered as a global "compass" for the whole organization and its major business units showing which general direction is right or wrong and what planning decisions are desirable or unacceptable. Although they provide little or no guidance regarding where specifically an organization needs to go and what exactly it needs to accomplish, Considerations still determine the proper ways of achieving the envisioned organizational objectives and set the guardrails to keep an organization on the right track along the entire journey.

The general purpose of all Considerations is to help achieve the agreement on basic principles, values, directions and aims between all relevant stakeholders. By means of using Considerations for discussions, senior business and IT stakeholders can achieve a shared understanding of what is important for their organization and how it should work. This shared understanding underpins all IT-related plans and stops architects from making inappropriate planning decisions detrimental to the best business interests.

The proper use of Considerations leads to improved overall conceptual consistency between business and IT. In other words, Considerations help ensure that all IT systems in an organization are implemented generally according to how business executives want them to be implemented.

This conceptual consistency between IT plans and business needs has numerous positive manifestations in various aspects of planning and eventually leads to multiple indirect benefits for the whole organization.

Difference from the Adjacent Types

Considerations, as business-focused rules EA artifacts, are adjacent to Standards and Visions (see Figure 8.1). Although Standards also describe some global rules defining an organization similar to Considerations, the rules described in Standards are purely technical in nature, incomprehensible and useless to business executives. While the influence of Standards is largely limited only to rather narrow IT-specific decisions (e.g. what is the best way to implement a particular IT initiative), Considerations represent overarching organization-wide rules influencing both business and IT decisions at the portfolio level (e.g. what IT initiatives are desirable for the business as a whole). Unlike Standards, Considerations directly reflect the essential business interests of an organization endorsed by its business leaders. Considerations thereby provide an important means of controlling IT to senior business stakeholders. Essentially, Considerations allow business leaders to govern IT indirectly, without understanding how exactly IT works.

Although Visions also provide some conceptual business-oriented descriptions of an organization similar to Considerations, the descriptions offered by Visions are more specific, situational and volatile. Unlike Visions, Considerations focus on the most profound business aspects that are rather stable in nature and less dependent on the latest business priorities, e.g. relationships between key business units or the attitude towards particular disruptive technologies. Considerations typically describe how an organization wants to work, rather than what an organization wants to do. Considerations, though influence Visions, usually do not direct future IT investments and do not provide any real guidance for launching new IT initiatives, but rather define the general context for all future investments and offer a sound decision-making framework for the whole organization.

Specific Enterprise Architecture Artifacts Related to Considerations

Articulate subtypes of Considerations often used in established EA practices include Principles, Policies, Conceptual Data Models, Analytical Reports and Direction Statements. Principles can be considered as essential EA artifacts, Policies as common EA artifacts, while Conceptual Data Models, Analytical Reports and Direction Statements as uncommon EA artifacts.

Principles (Essential)

Principles (sometimes can be also called maxims or drivers) are specific Considerations defining global high-level guidelines influencing all decision-making and planning in an organization[3]. Principles can be considered as an essential subtype of Considerations found in the majority of successful EA practices.

Principles are formulated as brief written statements defining what is important for an organization and how an organization needs to work. Principles are very abstract and can be interpreted broadly depending on the context. They often apply differently in different situations and in some aspects may even contradict each other. Due to their conceptual nature, Principles may border with philosophy and values of an organization.

The definition of a single Principle often includes its statement, rationale and implications. The statement provides a more extended definition of the Principle, the rationale explains the underlying reasons justifying this Principle, while the implications describe the consequences of the Principle. For instance, for the Principle "Business Continuity" its statement may clarify that "Critical business operations should not be interrupted even in case of severe emergency", its rationale may explain that "Uninterrupted 24/7 business operations are required to provide flawless customer experience and establish the reputation of the most trusted service provider according to the business strategy", while its implications may describe that "All critical information systems and databases should have geographically dispersed, readily available reserve copies in place".

Among other numerous purposes, Principles are commonly used to define the integration and standardization requirements of the adopted operating model (see Figure 5.3), i.e. to indicate which data should be shared and which business processes should be standardized across all business units[4]. For example, the Principle "Single Customer View" represents an explicit specification of the requirement to share customer data between all business units corresponding to the coordination or unification operating model, while the Principle "Standardized Business Processes" represents an explicit specification of the requirement to standardize specific business processes across all business units corresponding to the replication or unification operating model.

Organizations usually establish ~10-20 global guiding Principles agreed by senior business and IT stakeholders, and in some cases even formally endorsed by the board of directors, to support IT-related decision-making. These Principles can be grouped for better convenience into a few related categories (e.g. business, data and systems) and stored in a simple MS Word file. Large organizations often establish a hierarchy of Principles, including organization-wide overarching Principles and more specific local Principles relevant for particular business units derived from the global Principles. The schematic graphical representation of Principles is shown in Figure 9.1.

```
┌─────────────────────────────────────────────┐
│ Principle 1: Standardized Business Processes  │
│                                               │
│ Statement: ...........................................  │
│                                               │
│ Rationale: ...........................................   │
│                                               │
│ Implications: .......................................   │
├─────────────────────────────────────────────┤
│ Principle 2: Single Customer View             │
│                                               │
│ Statement: ...........................................  │
│                                               │
│ Rationale: ...........................................   │
│                                               │
│ Implications: .......................................   │
├─────────────────────────────────────────────┤
│ Principle 3: Business Continuity              │
│                                               │
│ Statement: ...........................................  │
│                                               │
│ Rationale: ...........................................   │
│                                               │
│ Implications: .......................................   │
└─────────────────────────────────────────────┘
```

Figure 9.1. Principles

Once established, Principles act as underpinning drivers of all IT-related decision-making processes. Alignment to Principles is required for all plans and decisions reflected in other EA artifacts. This alignment is often evaluated more or less formally during the approval of newly developed EA artifacts. For instance, in most formal cases Outlines and Designs for all IT initiatives may contain specific subsections with the checklists of relevant Principles and explicit explanations of how exactly these Principles have been taken into account in the corresponding IT solutions. Principles may be also used to evaluate and prioritize proposed IT initiatives, as well as their possible implementation options, based on their overall organizational fitness. Often they provide the basis for developing more technical IT Principles (see Figure 10.4).

Policies (Common)

Policies (can be called security policies, cloud policies, access policies, etc.) are specific Considerations defining overarching organizational norms typically of a restrictive nature providing compulsory prescriptions in certain areas. Policies can be considered as a common subtype of Considerations often found in successful EA practices.

Policies are formulated as textual descriptions usually specifying what an organization must not do under any circumstances. Unlike Principles, which are often very abstract and can be interpreted broadly, Policies are generally more clear, definite and unambiguous. Typically they are not a subject of much debate, reinterpretation or controversy. While Principles often provide "positive" guidance (i.e. what an organization should do), Policies usually provide "negative" guidance (i.e. what an organization should not do). Essentially, Policies define the boundaries and limits of possible IT-related planning decisions.

Policies are usually restrictive in nature and often related to security, compliance and risk. For instance, they may specify how organizational information systems should be accessed by internal and external users, how the duties of these users should be separated, which information can be shared with partners and what types of applications can be hosted outside of corporate datacenters or in the cloud.

Policies can either document some internal organization-specific decisions controlling the use of information and IT systems, or be derived from external compliance policies common for all organizations working in specific industries or dealing with particular types of sensitive data. For example, national privacy protection legislation existing in most countries (e.g. GDPR across the European Union), country-specific governmental acts (e.g. Sarbanes-Oxley[5], Gramm-Leach-Bliley and HIPAA in the United States) and international compliance standards (e.g. PCI DSS) impose strict limitations on handling, storing and sharing specific types of information. All these external regulations have significant implications for the planning and usage of information systems in organizations[6].

Due to their inherently restrictive nature, Policies are more often used in organizations processing more sensitive types of data (e.g. financial and personal information) and operating in more regulated industries from the informational perspective (e.g. banking and healthcare). They are often represented as high-level textual MS Word documents listing and describing key external and internal regulatory norms relevant to an organization. The schematic graphical representation of Policies is shown in Figure 9.2.

External	National Privacy Policies	Policy 1: Personal Data Must Be Stored Onshore Description: ....
		Policy 2: Destroy Personal Data When Not Needed Description: ....
	Sarbanes-Oxley Policies	Policy 3: Log All Accesses to Accounting Systems Description: ....
		Policy 4: Retain Audit Trails and Emails for 5 Years Description: ....
Internal	Data Security Policies	Policy 5: No Sensitive Data on Mobile Devices Description: ....
		Policy 6: Store Credit Cards in Encrypted Formats Description: ....
	Data Exchange Policies	Policy 7: Do Not Share Key Data with Third Parties Description: ....
		Policy 8: Share Client Data with Trusted Partners Description: ....
	Cloud Hosting Policies	Policy 9: Use Only the PCI DSS Compliant Cloud Description: ....
		Policy 10: Do Not Store Health Data in the Cloud Description: ....

Figure 9.2. Policies

Once established, Policies act as limiting constraints of all IT-related decision-making processes. Unlike Principles, which provide merely highly desirable guidelines, Policies are typically more strict and compulsory. For this reason deviations from Policies are usually not discussable and not tolerated. While Principles can be considered as a weak form of rules for driving decision-making, Policies can be considered as a stronger form of rules for restricting inadmissible planning decisions.

Adherence to Policies is often checked and ensured during the approval of other more specific EA artifacts. For instance, all Outlines and Designs of new IT initiatives must be strictly compliant with the enacted Policies. Moreover, Policies often provide the basis for developing more detailed and IT-specific Standards translating high-level regulatory norms into actionable implementation-level prescriptions. For example, if established compliance Policies require logging all accesses to the corporate accounting system, then Standards may specify how exactly this requirement should be implemented from the technical perspective.

Conceptual Data Models (Uncommon)

Conceptual Data Models (can be also called enterprise data models, information models, etc.) are specific Considerations providing abstract definitions of the main data entities critical for the business of an organization and their relationship. Conceptual Data Models can be considered as an uncommon subtype of Considerations relatively rarely found in EA practices.

Conceptual Data Models are expressed as simple intuitive data diagrams describing essential information entities used in an organization. In particular, Conceptual Data Models often describe significant data types, their main properties and relationships with each other in a business-oriented manner. Sometimes they may also include glossaries defining the meaning of key data objects. Conceptual Data Models provide executive-level conceptual descriptions of data entities abstracting their storage-specific technical details. They are rather stable in nature and more often used in highly information-dependent organizations.

Conceptual Data Models allow business executives to explicitly specify what information is important for the business, propose standard naming conventions and agree on the semantic meaning of core data entities, e.g. decide what exactly is understood under "customer" or "product" in the context of their organization. On the one hand, the structure and availability of data assets may have substantial business-related consequences. For example, the availability of dates of birth for all customers enables effective birthday marketing campaigns, while the availability of home addresses for all customers allows creating customized location-specific offers. On the other hand, definitions of the critical information provided by Conceptual Data Models shape the design of all IT systems handling the corresponding data. For example, if Conceptual Data Models define the customer data entity as a set of name, date of birth, location and phone properties, then every IT system capturing customer data should capture name, date of birth, location and phone properties, while all customer databases should store these properties in appropriate formats.

Conceptual Data Models also provide a common vocabulary and definitions for business discussions, promote a shared understanding of the critical data entities, help eliminate data silos caused by inconsistent language and allow comparing "apples to apples". Moreover, Conceptual Data Models can improve the organization-wide consistency of data across all business units as well as facilitate effective data exchange between partner organizations. The schematic graphical representation of Conceptual Data Models is shown in Figure 9.3.

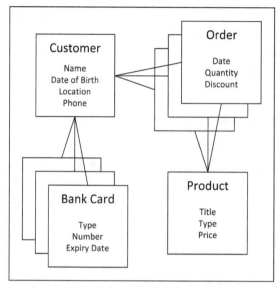

Figure 9.3. Conceptual Data Models

Once developed, Conceptual Data Models provide high-level data-centric rules shaping all architectural decisions in an organization related to data management. In particular, Conceptual Data Models influence the logical design of all business applications, storage systems and underlying integration platforms manipulating with data. All IT systems should be compliant with the established Conceptual Data Models, which is necessary for maintaining purity and consistency of data across the organization. Conceptual Data Models typically also provide the basis for developing more detailed, low-level and platform-specific Logical Data Models (see Figure 10.5).

Analytical Reports (Uncommon)

Analytical Reports (can be called whitepapers, position papers, strategy papers, etc.) are specific Considerations providing executive-level analyses of relevant technology trends and their potential impact on the business of an organization. Analytical Reports can be considered as an uncommon subtype of Considerations relatively rarely found in EA practices.

Analytical Reports typically represent the results of a business-oriented analysis of the technology environment in which an organization operates. Analytical Reports intend to describe the potential influence of important technology trends on the business of an organization as well as the desirable reaction of the organization on these trends. These descriptions may include the answers to the following and similar questions:

- What new technologies might be important for the business of an organization?
- What new technologies should be adopted or ignored by an organization?
- What are the strengths and weaknesses of an organization from the technology perspective?
- What opportunities and threats does the technology environment provide to an organization?

- What product vendors or service providers should be selected by an organization for strategically important technologies?

Analytical Reports are more often developed in relatively large organizations heavily dependent on IT. They facilitate the early detection of "tectonic shifts" in the technology environment, prompt identification of disruptive technologies and their timely adoption by an organization. Analytical Reports can take multiple different forms including hype cycles, technology radars, SWOT analyses and vendor analyses.

Hype cycles and technology radars focus primarily on evaluating emerging technologies from the perspective of their maturity and readiness for the adoption in an organization. Specifically, hype cycles help assess emerging technologies according to their five maturity lifecycle phases (technology trigger, peak of inflated expectations, trough of disillusionment, slope of enlightenment and plateau of productivity)[7], while technology radars help assess emerging technologies according to their four stages of readiness for adoption (hold, assess, trial and adopt)[8]. These forms of Analytical Reports facilitate informed decision-making regarding the adoption of new technologies in an organization. Technology adoption decisions are usually made collaboratively by business executives and architects taking into account the relevancy and potential strategic importance of the corresponding technology for an organization, its overall maturity and associated risks of adoption[9]. The schematic graphical representation of Analytical Reports (hype cycles and technology radars) is shown in Figure 9.4.

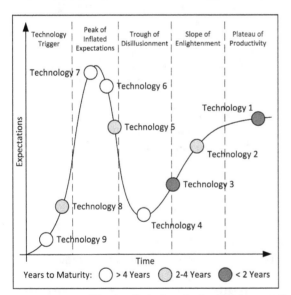
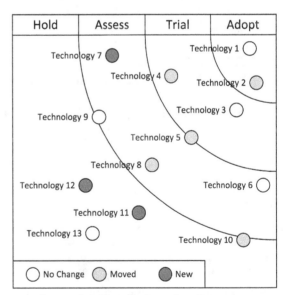

Figure 9.4. Analytical Reports (hype cycles and technology radars)

SWOT analyses and vendor analyses focus respectively on the overall technological position of an organization and on the selection of strategic vendors or providers. In particular, SWOT analyses focus on identifying the organizational strengths, weaknesses, opportunities and threats from the technology perspective. They analyze the general alignment of the IT capabilities of an organization to the current situation and future trends in the business and technology environments. Vendor analyses are more narrow-purposed and focus specifically on the assessment and selection of appropriate strategic vendors, partners or service providers. They evaluate and range available offerings on the technology market based on their suitability in the context of an organization, often using analytical techniques similar to the Gartner Magic Quadrant and Forrester Wave[10]. The schematic graphical representation of Analytical Reports (SWOT analyses and vendor analyses) is shown in Figure 9.5.

Figure 9.5. Analytical Reports (SWOT analyses and vendor analyses)

Similarly to all other Considerations, Analytical Reports provide an overarching decision-making framework for an organization. They inform and influence various business-related and IT-related decisions, including strategic decisions with significant long-term consequences as well as project-level decisions with local implications.

Direction Statements (Uncommon)

Direction Statements (can be called architecture strategies, governance papers, position papers, strategic papers, etc.) are specific Considerations describing conceptual messages communicating major organization-wide decisions with far-reaching consequences. Direction Statements can be considered as an uncommon subtype of Considerations relatively rarely found in EA practices.

Direction Statements typically represent the results of strategic decision-making processes regarding the desired future direction of an entire organization or its major business units. They can declare an organization-wide intention to go in a specific way, follow a particular approach, address a specific global need, do a certain thing or merely propose to leverage some new promising opportunity. For example, Direction Statements may articulate the desire of an organization to migrate all non-business-critical applications into the cloud, to consolidate all organizational information systems on the basis of a single global ERP platform or, on the contrary, to develop custom IT systems tailored specifically for unique needs of individual business units. Often Direction Statements communicate strategic directives intended to improve the overall fitness of an organization from the technology perspective, e.g. close significant IT capability gaps undermining the business.

Direction Statements are the most action-oriented EA artifacts of all Considerations. While other Considerations merely describe how an organization needs to work or analyze the technology environment, Direction Statements point to a certain direction where an organization needs to go in the future and explain the rationale for this direction. However, they still do not provide any specific details regarding how exactly it should be done. Essentially, Direction Statements only indicate where an entire organization needs to go without specifying how.

Direction Statements can be considered as EA artifacts complementary to Analytical Reports. While Analytical Reports analyze the general positioning of an organization from the technology perspective, Direction Statements propose high-level strategies for addressing the suggestions of Analytical Reports. The schematic graphical representation of Direction Statements is shown in Figure 9.6.

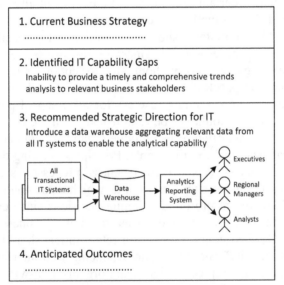

Figure 9.6. Direction Statements

Once approved by senior executives, strategic imperatives provided by Direction Statements drive all subsequent decision-making processes in an organization. In particular, Direction Statements often provide the basis for developing more specific Visions. However, they may also influence on technology selection processes as well as on the overall evolution of the IT landscape. The alignment of all lower-level planning decisions to the endorsed Direction Statements is often evaluated during the approval of corresponding EA artifacts. Unlike other Considerations, which are normally permanent and long-lived, Direction Statements are temporary EA artifacts (see Table 2.2) with a limited lifespan. They are developed and widely communicated to disseminate specific global and far-reaching IT-related planning decisions across the whole organization, but then lose their value and get archived.

Additional Concerns Regarding Considerations

The single biggest threat associated with the practical use of Considerations is arguably the development of trivial and universal Considerations which may be applied equally well to all organizations. These Considerations only distract attention, but add no real value from the perspective of IT planning. Considerations can be useful only if they are able to guide other IT-related decision-making processes, i.e. help understand which specific planning decisions may be suitable for the needs of an organization and which decisions might be unacceptable. In other words, valuable Considerations allow clearly distinguishing appropriate IT planning decisions from inappropriate ones. Essentially, useful Considerations themselves represent certain conceptual, global and overarching planning decisions guiding more specific, local and low-level planning decisions.

In order to understand whether proposed Considerations represent real planning decisions or merely universal truisms, they can be subjected to a simple "smoke" test: meaningful Considerations always imply certain trade-offs, can be potentially disagreed with and stay meaningful when negated. For example, Principles proclaiming that "All IT systems should be effective and efficient", "All IT systems should be developed for specific purposes" or "All IT systems should be driven by the essential business needs" are evident motherhood statements equally applicable to all organizations without any exceptions since no organizations need ineffective, inefficient and purposeless systems, which are not driven by their business needs. These and similar Principles are essentially useless for all practical purposes, do not represent any real planning decisions and should not be established[11]. On the contrary, effective Principles are usually organization-specific, often reflect unique organizational needs and cannot be simply borrowed from other organizations[12]. For example, Principles defining the essential requirements of the desired operating model (i.e. which business processes should or should not be standardized across different business units as well as which data should or should not be shared globally, see Figure 5.3) represent profound planning decisions since each of these options has certain long-term and far-reaching consequences for both business and IT. Analogously, Principles stating that "All IT systems deployed in retail outlets should work correctly with the intermittent Internet connectivity" and "All customer-facing web interfaces should be accessible via a single sign-on mechanism" represent significant organization-wide planning decisions with clear trade-offs and implications for both business and IT[13]. In some cases, meaningful Principles can articulate organization-specific decisions on the required core IT capabilities critical for the adopted business model[14].

At the same time, some Principles at the first sight might sound as trivial, but actually represent important business decisions. For instance, Principles declaring that "All IT systems should be designed for high availability and business continuity" and "All IT systems should be highly secure" might seem universal since no organizations want to have unavailable or insecure systems. However, in reality these and similar Principles typically indicate that an organization needs IT systems with the increased levels of fault tolerance and security (i.e. beyond some reasonable default levels) and its business executives are ready to invest additional amounts of money in the necessary IT infrastructure to achieve these desired levels[15]. Despite their apparent triviality, each of these Principles represents a significant global planning decision with specific requirements, pros and cons for both business and IT. For example, using hot standby servers, real-time data backups or multi-factor authentication (MFA) mechanisms for business-critical systems always implies a certain tradeoff between business continuity, information security, user convenience, development timelines and costs. After being agreed upon, these Principles guide all "downstream" technology selection and project-level planning decisions.

Likewise, Analytical Reports suggesting that an organization should adopt the recent release of the Windows operating system and install it on all its Windows-based computers, or that all its web-based applications should embrace the capabilities of the latest versions of popular Internet browsers are essentially trivial and useless. They do not contain any significant planning decisions and should not be produced. On the contrary, Analytical Reports evaluating the overall readiness, maturity, suitability and possible opportunities of adoption, as well as the risks of non-adoption, of potentially disruptive technologies represent key technology-related business concerns. For example, comprehensive assessments of the long-term consequences associated with introducing cloud, big data, RFID or block chain technologies and corresponding decisions regarding their adoption might be critical for the whole organization[16]. Each of these adoption or non-adoption decisions entails considerable risks, opportunities and far-reaching implications for both business and IT.

Chapter Summary

This chapter discussed Considerations as a general type of EA artifacts from the perspective of their informational contents, development, usage, purpose and benefits and then described in more detail popular narrow subtypes of Considerations including Principles, Policies, Conceptual Data Models, Analytical Reports and Direction Statements. The key message of this chapter can be summarized into the following essential points:

- Considerations describe global conceptual rules and fundamental considerations important for business and relevant for IT representing the overarching organizational context for information systems planning
- Considerations are permanent decisions EA artifacts that are developed once collaboratively by business executives and architects, periodically updated according to the ongoing changes in the business environment and used to influence all other architectural decisions
- Considerations help achieve the agreement on basic principles, values, directions and aims eventually leading to improved overall conceptual consistency between business and IT in an organization
- Principles are essential Considerations defining global high-level guidelines influencing all decision-making and helping business executives and architects agree on the most fundamental imperatives regarding the use of IT in an organization
- Policies are common Considerations defining overarching organizational norms and compulsory prescriptions of a restrictive nature and helping business leaders and architects agree on how an organization must not use its IT resources
- Conceptual Data Models are uncommon Considerations providing abstract definitions of the key data entities with their relationship and helping business

leaders and architects achieve a shared understanding of the required structure of corporate data assets

- Analytical Reports are uncommon Considerations providing executive-level analyses of relevant technology trends and helping business leaders and architects develop a common attitude towards innovative and disruptive technologies
- Direction Statements are uncommon Considerations communicating major organization-wide planning decisions with far-reaching consequences and helping business executives and architects agree on the most general future course of action for IT

Chapter 10: Standards

The previous chapter focused on Considerations as the first general type of EA artifacts defined by the CSVLOD model of enterprise architecture. This chapter discusses in great detail various aspects of Standards as the next general type of EA artifacts (IT-focused rules) as well as their more specific subtypes often used in EA practices. In particular, this chapter starts from describing the common properties of all Standards including their type-specific informational contents, development and usage scenarios, role in an EA practice and associated organizational benefits. Then, this chapter discusses in detail popular narrow subtypes of Standards including Technology Reference Models, Guidelines, Patterns, IT Principles and Logical Data Models. Finally, this chapter provides additional concerns and recommendations regarding the practical use of Standards as part of an EA practice.

Standards as a General Type of Enterprise Architecture Artifacts

Standards are IT-focused rules EA artifacts (see Figure 8.1). They describe global IT-specific rules defined by architects and share the essential common properties of both IT-focused EA artifacts and rules EA artifacts. Specific examples of EA artifacts related to Standards include Technology Reference Models, Guidelines, Patterns, IT Principles and Logical Data Models (see Figure 8.2).

Informational Contents

Standards describe global technical rules, standards, patterns and best practices relevant for IT systems. Essentially, Standards define how all IT systems in an organization are implemented from the technology perspective. The implementation-level guidelines reflected in Standards address the following and similar technical questions:

- What technologies and products should be used in IT solutions?
- How exactly should the available technologies be used in IT solutions?
- What implementation approaches should be followed in IT solutions?
- What system components should be reused in IT solutions?
- How should IT systems be organized and integrated?
- What protocols should be used for the interaction between IT systems?
- How should main data entities be stored in IT systems?
- What legislative prescriptions should be followed in IT solutions?

All these questions reflect very IT-specific concerns irrelevant and even incomprehensible to most business stakeholders. Business executives are usually unaware of particular programming languages, system implementation approaches, integration patterns, technical best practices or server operating systems supporting business processes in their organization. Even though Standards are based on best business interests, they are developed exclusively by architects and other senior IT experts inside the IT department and may have no evident or easily traceable connections to the underlying business needs. Since Standards are purely technical EA artifacts intended largely for architects alone, they cannot be considered as dual EA artifacts (see Figure 2.4).

Standards rarely describe the business domain, but predominantly focus on various technical EA domains including applications, data, integration, infrastructure and security (see Figure 2.2). Standards are very technology-specific in nature and heavily depend on the current technology environment. A single set of Standards may be applicable to an entire organization, especially in small organizations. However, different subunits of the IT department focused on particular technologies often develop their own sets of Standards addressing their technology-specific practices. In large, complex and decentralized organizations IT departments of major business units (e.g. lines of business, business functions or divisions) can also develop their own Standards addressing local unit-specific needs consistent with global organization-wide Standards.

Standards typically either do not focus on specific points in time or focus on the current state. On the one hand, many Standards, including IT Principles and Guidelines, do not refer to any specific points in time and can be considered as timeless. They recommend specific implementation approaches that are followed now, might have been followed in the past and will be followed in the future as well, unless modified or removed as inappropriate. On the other hand, some Standards, most notably Technology Reference Models, are more focused on the current state of the technology portfolio. Essentially, these Standards provide an inventory of existing technologies, approaches and best practices currently used in an organization.

Standards can be expressed in various formats from the perspective of their representation, volume and notation. Depending on the nature of their content, Standards can be textual or graphical, brief or voluminous, formal or informal. Since they are intended for competent, specialized and IT-savvy audience, Standards can use essentially any reasonable formats required to convey their meaning in the most accurate way. They often use very IT-specific terminology and strict notations. Physically, Standards can be stored either in simple MS Office formats (e.g. Word and less often Visio), or in architectural repositories offered by specialized software tools for enterprise architecture, as discussed later in Chapter 18 (Instruments for Enterprise Architecture).

Development and Usage

Standards represent mostly planning decisions on how all IT systems should be implemented and some facts on the current approaches and technologies (see Table 2.1). They are developed as part of the Technology Optimization process (see Figure 6.1) collaboratively by architects and technical subject-matter experts (see Figure 2.6). The primary developers of most Standards are architects. Architects discuss, select and document the most appropriate technologies and system implementation approaches on behalf of the whole organization based on their best understanding of its business interests. However, architects usually also involve knowledgeable subject-matter experts competent in specific technologies or areas, who contribute their expertise and facilitate the development of adequate Standards. Additionally, Standards are often formally approved by senior IT managers and signed-off by the CIO.

New Standards are usually introduced in a reactive bottom-up manner as they become necessary for particular IT initiatives, often along with the delivery of IT projects pioneering the practical use of a new technology or implementation approach. Moreover, Standards are usually not developed from scratch in an organization-specific manner, but rather based on established industry standards and best practices. Architects can study available industry standards, assess their applicability in the context of their organization, adapt these standards to unique organization-specific needs if necessary and then introduce them to their organization. Some Standards, especially related to information security, encryption and retention, may be prescribed by or derived from the requirements of mandatory legislative acts reflected in Policies (see Figure 9.2). For example, if regulatory Policies require preserving all audit trails, access logs and electronic documentation for a certain number of years, then specific Patterns or other Standards may be developed to provide recommended ways of addressing these requirements in all information systems across the entire IT landscape

After being established, Standards influence architectures of all IT initiatives. They are used predominantly as technical reference materials by architects during the planning of Outlines and Designs for new IT solutions. Essentially, Standards can be considered as "backend" EA artifacts used mostly inside the IT department. They are developed largely by architects for architects to facilitate IT project planning, but may have little or no external stakeholders outside of the architecture function. For instance, IT project teams may be unaware that the projects they are implementing are aligned to some approaches defined by Standards, reuse specific components described in Standards or based on particular technologies recommended by Standards. However, some Standards, especially Guidelines and Logical Data Models, often provide highly specific implementation-level prescriptions that can be used directly by project teams during the development of Designs and their subsequent implementation.

By providing recommended technical means for developing Outlines and Designs, Standards shape architectures of all new IT solutions including their internal structure as well as their integration with the existing IT systems. At the same time, by shaping the structure of individual IT solutions, Standards eventually shape the overall structure of the entire organizational IT landscape. For instance, the persistent usage of specific technologies in all new IT solutions eventually creates the IT landscape based on the corresponding technologies, while the consistent adherence to specific system integration approaches in all new solutions eventually creates the landscape structured according to the respective interaction patterns. Essentially, the prolonged use of certain Standards shapes the entire IT landscape via shaping separate IT solutions constituting it.

Adherence to Standards is typically achieved by means of formal architectural reviews of all the plans for specific IT initiatives and projects. Specifically, Outlines and Designs for all proposed IT solutions are typically peer-reviewed and approved by other architects as part of regular governance procedures in order to enforce their compliance with the established Standards, as discussed later in Chapter 17 (Architecture Functions in Organizations). Architects also often supervise IT project teams during the subsequent project implementation to ensure the actual adherence to Standards. Similarly to Considerations, reasonable deviations from Standards are usually acceptable when sound justifications for these deviations are provided. For example, if the intended business objectives of a new IT project can be achieved only via using a unique technology or specific implementation approach inconsistent with the existing Standards, then the deviation from Standards in this particular project may be consciously approved by architects, depending on the business importance of the project. The decision to depart from Standards may be informed by the estimated architecture debt ensuing from this departure, as discussed later in Chapter 18 (Instruments for Enterprise Architecture).

Standards are permanent EA artifacts (see Table 2.2) normally with a lengthy lifespan. They are relatively stable in nature and, once established, do not change particularly often. However, Standards still should be periodically reviewed and updated according to the ongoing evolution in the technology environment to stay current and relevant. For instance, they may be revised by architects and technical subject-matter experts on a yearly basis to reflect the latest cutting-edge technology developments. As part of the annual review process established Standards might be occasionally discarded if considered as obsolete or no longer relevant.

Role and Benefits

Standards represent proven reusable means for IT systems implementation. They document effective, reliable and regulatory compliant implementation approaches that proved useful in previous IT projects for their further reuse. Thereby, Standards facilitate organizational learning, accumulate and allow reusing the experience and wisdom of multiple senior IT specialists. The recommendations of Standards offer experience-based advice regarding the design of new IT solutions in the context of an organization. Standards essentially provide numerous time-tested IT tools and recipes for solving organizational business problems.

The general purpose of all Standards is to help achieve technical consistency, technological homogeneity and regulatory compliance. The use of Standards for planning new IT solutions can ensure that all IT systems in an organization use similar approaches in similar situations, similar solutions to similar problems, same property fields for same data entities and same technologies at all layers of the technology stack. Furthermore, the inclusion of relevant legislative requirements into a regular set of Standards also ensures that all IT systems are compliant with mandatory industry regulations.

The proper use of Standards allows consolidating, simplifying and standardizing the organizational IT landscape as well as "pipelining" the delivery of new IT initiatives. Main ensuing organizational benefits of using Standards can be summarized into faster initiative delivery, reduced costs, risks and complexity. Firstly, the use of Standards leads to faster delivery of new IT initiatives due to a number of reasons, including the following ones:

- Standards help accumulate and leverage existing technical expertise of IT staff in new IT initiatives
- Standards help establish reusable components or building blocks for creating new IT systems
- Standards help avoid unnecessary learning curves associated with using untried technologies and approaches

Secondly, the use of Standards leads to reduced IT-related costs due to a number of reasons, including the following ones:

- Standards help limit the number of supported technologies, products and vendors
- Standards help minimize the license fees for proprietary software
- Standards help streamline the skill sets of IT staff and optimize the workforce

Thirdly, the use of Standards leads to mitigated IT-related risks due to a number of reasons, including the following ones:

- Standards help reuse proven implementation approaches reducing the typical risks associated with the IT project delivery
- Standards help reuse proven technologies increasing the general stability and security of the organizational IT landscape
- Standards help adhere to the requirements of relevant regulatory acts reducing the potential corporate risks related to compliance

Fourthly, the use of Standards leads to lowered complexity of the organizational IT landscape due to a number of reasons, including the following ones:

- Standards help restrain the overall technological diversity of the IT landscape
- Standards help control the diversity of adopted implementation approaches
- Standards help minimize the number of interaction patterns between different IT systems and avoid the "spaghetti" of connections

Additionally, the use of Standards leads to improved technical and logical interoperability between different IT systems due to a number of reasons, including the following ones:

- Standards help eliminate the technological disparity between IT systems
- Standards help leverage common system integration approaches and protocols
- Standards help achieve logical data compatibility and consistency by defining common data types, structures and formats

Difference from the Adjacent Types

Standards, as IT-focused rules EA artifacts, are adjacent to Considerations and Landscapes (see Figure 8.1). Although Considerations also describe some global rules defining an organization similar to Standards, the rules described in Considerations have significant business importance and represent critical business decisions. While Considerations are very abstract in nature, expressed in business language and reflect the essential concerns of business executives, Standards are rather narrow, use highly IT-specific terminology and do not reflect any business interests directly. Accordingly, Considerations influence both business and IT decision-making, but the impact of Standards is largely limited only to technical decisions related to the implementation of new IT solutions. However, Considerations provide only general conceptual suggestions for decision-making, while Standards offer more specific prescriptions directly applicable in particular situations or projects. Business leaders do not understand Standards and cannot use them to manage IT. Unlike collaboratively developed Considerations, Standards are developed largely by architects alone based on their best understanding of business interests. Essentially, business executives can control Standards only indirectly by establishing Considerations, which in their turn influence the selection of Standards, and by hiring trustworthy architects, who are able to establish appropriate Standards reflecting the genuine business needs.

Although Landscapes also provide some high-level technical descriptions of an organization similar to Standards, the descriptions offered by Landscapes are more specific in nature and refer to particular instances of IT assets. Unlike Landscapes, Standards do not distinguish individual IT assets (e.g. separate systems or databases), but rather provide some overarching rules related to all assets or instances of a certain type (e.g. to all applications or servers). Even though Standards describe proven approaches for implementing IT systems, they do not explain which or how many existing systems are actually implemented based on these approaches. Standards only recommend how to develop new IT systems, but do not describe what systems exist in the current IT landscape and how they are related to each other.

Specific Enterprise Architecture Artifacts Related to Standards

Articulate subtypes of Standards often used in established EA practices include Technology Reference Models, Guidelines, Patterns, IT Principles and Logical Data Models. Technology Reference Models and Guidelines can be considered as essential EA artifacts, Patterns and IT Principles as common EA artifacts, while Logical Data Models as uncommon EA artifacts.

Technology Reference Models (Essential)

Technology Reference Models (can be also called technology standards, technical reference models, technology reference architectures or split into separate domain-specific reference models, e.g. infrastructure reference models and application reference models) are specific Standards providing structured graphical representations of all technologies used in an organization. Technology Reference Models can be considered as an essential subtype of Standards found in the majority of successful EA practices.

Technology Reference Models represent comprehensive views of the whole organizational technology stack. They map all technologies and products used in an organization to the respective technical functions they fulfill or support. Essentially, Technology Reference Models structure and describe the technology portfolio of an entire organization.

Technology Reference Models usually organize the technology stack into typical technical layers (e.g. networks, servers, databases, applications, etc.) and show what technologies are used in an organization at each of these layers. The structured nature of Technology Reference Models helps architects identify redundant and duplicated technologies fulfilling same or highly similar technical functions. In organizations relying predominantly on available packaged solutions Technology Reference Models may be rather high-level and focus mostly on the corresponding products, providers and vendors, while in organizations developing their own homegrown information systems Technology Reference Models may also contain some lower-level underlying elements including programming languages, major libraries and key frameworks, e.g. Spring, Hibernate or AngularJS.

Technology Reference Models are often color-coded to indicate the status of different technologies and products. In particular, technologies and products can be classified from the perspective of their lifecycle phases and opportunities for future reuse into different groups including, but not limited to, the following categories:

- Current – up-to-date technologies and products that are currently in use, not planned to be retired in the future and can be safely reused in new IT solutions
- Emerging – cutting-edge technologies and products that are not actively used at the current moment, but planned for future adoption and can be used in new IT solutions
- Unsupported – outdated technologies and products that are currently in use, but are no longer supported by their vendors and should not be reused in new IT solutions

- Retiring – legacy technologies and products that are currently in use, but planned to be retired in the near future and should not be reused in new IT solutions

Technology Reference Models provide a perfect example of EA artifacts representing both decisions and facts (see Table 2.1) and combining their properties. On the one hand, as facts EA artifacts they list all the technologies currently deployed and used in an organization, which is a mere reflection of the objective reality. On the other hand, as decisions EA artifacts they specify which of these technologies will be supported, expanded or retired in the future, which is a purely subjective planning decision. Put it simply, the set of utilized technologies represents objective facts, whereas their color-coding represents planning decisions. Different types of updates of Technology Reference Models also differ accordingly in their nature, i.e. the updates of facts can be accomplished by individual architects, while the updates of decisions require achieving a collective consensus (see Figure 2.6). For example, if a previously unidentified technology is found to be used somewhere in an organization, then this technology can be simply added to Technology Reference Models by a single architect to reflect the newly uncovered fact. However, an authoritative decision to reuse, support or decommission this technology in the future can be made only collaboratively with the involvement of all relevant architects, senior IT managers and subject-matter experts.

In some cases comprehensive Technology Reference Models can be split into two-three more narrow reference models covering different layers of the technology stack, for example into application reference models, infrastructure reference models and security reference models. In the simplest cases Technology Reference Models, or their separate components, can be maintained as one-page MS Visio diagrams. The schematic graphical representation of Technology Reference Models is shown in Figure 10.1.

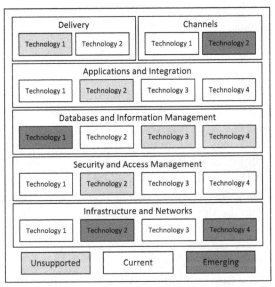

Figure 10.1. Technology Reference Models

Technology Reference Models help architects select the most appropriate available technologies and products for new IT solutions at both the early Outline and later Design stages of IT initiatives. Compliance with Technology Reference Models is typically achieved via peer-reviewing Outlines and Designs of all IT solutions and discussing possible deviations. The mechanism of color-coding (i.e. marking technologies as deprecated, current or strategic) also helps architects manage the lifecycle of different technologies and optimize the entire technology portfolio of an organization. Technology Reference Models play especially important roles in organizations having significant in-house software development resources and producing custom applications and systems, rather than in organizations relying on standard commercial off-the-shelf (COTS) products supplied by external vendors.

Guidelines (Essential)

Guidelines (can be also called standards) are specific Standards providing IT-specific implementation-level prescriptions applicable in narrow technology-specific areas or domains. Guidelines can be considered as an essential subtype of Standards found in the majority of successful EA practices.

Guidelines are formulated as brief written statements providing actionable recommendations regarding the usage of particular technologies in IT solutions. They are typically very concrete, unambiguous and technical in nature. Guidelines focus mostly on the internal structure of separate IT solutions, rather than on the overall structure of the IT landscape. They are usually grouped according to multiple narrow technology-specific domains (e.g. network protocols, data encryption, server deployment, etc.) and maintained by different groups of IT experts specialized in different technologies.

Guidelines are complementary to Technology Reference Models and often used in conjunction with them. While Technology Reference Models only specify what technologies should be used in IT solutions, Guidelines provide more detailed prescriptions specifying how exactly these technologies should be used. Unlike Technology Reference Models, which are often used only by architects, Guidelines might be relevant to both architects and IT project teams.

Organizations often develop numerous Guidelines of all sorts covering various technical EA domains (see Figure 2.2). These Guidelines are typically introduced over time as architects and project teams learn new best practices reflecting the effective use of specific technologies in IT solutions. However, architects may also leverage the established body of time-proven industry best practices and develop organization-specific Guidelines on their basis. Moreover, Guidelines might be derived from high-level normative Policies (see Figure 9.2). For example, if regulatory Policies require handling personal information and credit card data in encrypted formats, then corresponding Guidelines may be developed to specify how exactly these types of data must be encrypted, transmitted, stored and protected in all IT systems.

Since Guidelines are very detailed and specific, for most organizations of a considerable size it is impractical to maintain a single unified list of Guidelines relevant to all IT solutions in an entire organization. In these cases multiple separate lists of local Guidelines may be developed and maintained by the groups of IT specialists working in different parts of an organization. For instance, architects and project teams implementing IT solutions for different business units may establish highly unit-specific lists of Guidelines reflecting their local best practices. As a result, different business units of an organization often have differing Guidelines regarding the proper use of the same technology closely aligned to their needs. Alternatively, technology-specific Guidelines may be owned by architects and senior subject-matter experts from the centers of excellence in respective technologies, e.g. data warehousing or mobile applications.

Established Guidelines can be most easily stored in a number of simple MS Word documents related to corresponding technologies and, if necessary, to different business units. The schematic graphical representation of Guidelines is shown in Figure 10.2.

Server Deployment Standards	Guideline 1: Run Applications as OS Services Description: ....
	Guideline 2: Store Deployment Packages in VCS Description: ....
Network Protocol Standards	Guideline 3: Avoid Using UDP Multicast Description: ....
	Guideline 4: Prefer REST Over SOAP Description: ....
Data Encryption Standards	Guideline 5: Use 256-Bit Encryption Keys Description: ....
	Guideline 6: Store MD5 Hashes of Passwords Description: ....
Interface Design Guidelines	Guideline 7: Use Web-Safe Colours Description: ....
	Guideline 8: Place Menu in the Top Right Corner Description: ....
Secure Coding Guidelines	Guideline 9: Initialize Variables to Safe Defaults Description: ....
	Guideline 10: Validate All Incoming Data Description: ....

Figure 10.2. Guidelines

Guidelines help architects and IT project teams follow proven best practices during the planning and implementation of new IT solutions. Many Guidelines provide very detailed and low-level prescriptions which are often too specific to be reflected in Designs, let alone in Outlines. Furthermore, some Guidelines (e.g. secure coding standards) cannot be enforced at the solution planning stage. For this reason, the adherence to Guidelines is more often achieved via supervising project teams at the solution implementation stage, than via peer-reviewing Designs. For example, the adherence to secure coding standards can be ensured by architects only by means of reviewing the actual program code produced by project teams.

Patterns (Common)

Patterns (can be also called reference architectures) are specific Standards providing generic reusable solutions to commonly occurring problems in the design of IT systems[1]. Patterns can be considered as a common subtype of Standards often found in successful EA practices.

Patterns represent proven organization-specific reusable technical components for IT solutions addressing some common problems or needs. They describe how the most typical problems related to the design of new IT solutions should be solved in an organization. For example, Patterns can provide readily available solutions to the problem of creating failover clusters, deploying firewall-protected servers or structuring distributed IT systems. Particularly often Patterns deal with the information exchange issues and provide recommended organization-wide integration approaches for connecting disparate applications with each other. Essentially, patterns offer complete logical "bricks" or building blocks from which new IT solutions can be constructed. Same Patterns can be successfully reused in the design of multiple different IT solutions facing similar design problems.

The definition of a single Pattern often includes its description, applicability, rationale and solution sections. In particular, the description section explains what common problem the Pattern intends to solve and how. The applicability section clarifies in which situations the Pattern should be and should not be applied. The rationale section explains why the Pattern provides a preferred solution to the stated problem. Finally, the solution section describes in detail the structure of the solution recommended by the Pattern.

Although Patterns describe some tangible components of IT solutions, on their own they can be considered only as purely conceptual constructions or rules. Patterns do not physically exist independently of specific IT solutions embodying these Patterns. In other words, Patterns themselves are intangible in nature and can be instantiated and materialized only via following their prescriptions in actual IT solutions. The schematic graphical representation of Patterns is shown in Figure 10.3.

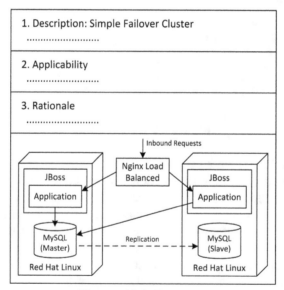

Figure 10.3. Patterns

A catalog of Patterns helps architects select and reuse proven implementation approaches during the planning of specific IT solutions, more often at the later Design stages of IT projects. Adherence to established Patterns is typically achieved via peer-reviewing Outlines and Designs of all IT solutions and negotiating possible deviations.

IT Principles (Common)

IT Principles (can be often called simply principles) are specific Standards defining global high-level IT-specific guidelines influencing all IT-related decisions and plans in an organization. IT

Principles can be considered as a common subtype of Standards often found in successful EA practices.

IT Principles are conceptually similar, or even identical, IT-oriented counterparts of business-focused Principles (see Figure 9.1). IT Principles are formulated as brief written statements defining what is important for IT and how IT needs to work. Similarly to Principles, they can be very abstract and interpreted differently in different situations. The definition of a single IT Principle may also include its statement, rationale and implications.

Unlike Principles, IT Principles define purely IT-specific rules, which are irrelevant to most business stakeholders and do not directly reflect any business decisions. However, IT Principles can be derived from business-focused Principles. For instance, if Principles require high business continuity, then IT Principles may require hosting backup copies of all critical IT systems and databases in separate datacenters.

IT Principles can be also considered as broad, abstract and high-level versions of Guidelines. While Guidelines define narrow technology-specific rules usually shaping only the internal details of separate IT solutions, IT Principles define overarching technology-agnostic rules usually having a broad impact on IT and shaping the designs of all solutions as well as the overall structure of the organizational IT landscape.

Organizations often establish ~10-20 or more guiding IT Principles agreed by architects and other senior IT stakeholders, including the CIO. For better convenience these IT Principles are usually grouped according to their domains, e.g. applications, data, integration, infrastructure and security. Large organizations often establish a hierarchy of IT Principles, including global organization-wide IT Principles and more specific local IT Principles in particular areas consistent with the global ones. The schematic graphical representation of IT Principles is shown in Figure 10.4.

Applications	IT Principle 1: Prefer Open Source Solutions Description: ....
	IT Principle 2: Log All Main Operations Description: ....
Data	IT Principle 3: Use Scalable Storage Description: ....
	IT Principle 4: Backup All Permanent Data Description: ....
Integration	IT Principle 5: Use Middleware for Integration Description: ....
	IT Principle 6: Avoid Binary Integration Protocols Description: ....
Infrastructure	IT Principle 7: Host in the Cloud Description: ....
	IT Principle 8: Dedicated Server for Each System Description: ....
Security	IT Principle 9: Place Public Systems in DMZ Description: ....
	IT Principle 10: Secure by Default Description: ....

Figure 10.4. IT Principles

Once established, IT Principles act as underpinning drivers of all IT-specific decisions. IT Principles help architects select the most appropriate implementation approaches for all IT initiatives, often at the early Outline stages of IT projects. Alignment to IT Principles is required for all IT plans and decisions. This alignment is typically achieved by means of peer-reviewing and discussing Outlines, Designs and Landscapes.

Logical Data Models (Uncommon)

Logical Data Models (can be also called logical information models, canonical data models, data schemas, etc.) are specific Standards providing logical or even physical platform-specific definitions of the key data entities and their relationship. Logical Data Models can be considered as an uncommon subtype of Standards relatively rarely found in EA practices.

Logical Data Models are expressed as formal IT-oriented data diagrams describing common data entities used in an organization. Usually they define the structure of main data types with all their fields in accurate detail, often including exact field titles, types, formats, lengths and their relationships with each other. Sometimes Logical Data Models also explain where and when the corresponding data objects are generated, where and when they are consumed and which systems use these objects for communication.

Since detailed Logical Data Models are pretty hard to maintain, these models tend to focus only on the most critical shared data entities of organization-wide significance that exist separately from specific applications and are often passed between different services and systems, e.g. customer, product or order entities. Similarly to business-focused Conceptual Data Models (see Figure 9.3), Logical Data Models are rather stable and more commonly used in highly information-dependent organizations. Often they represent more detailed and IT-specific versions of abstract Conceptual Data Models agreed with business executives, i.e. the next level of detail underneath them. While Conceptual Data Models might look somewhat generic and organization-neutral, Logical Data Models are typically very organization-specific. Due to their direct relationship, Logical Data Models are normally updated synchronously with Conceptual Data Models.

Unlike simple and intuitive Conceptual Data Models, Logical Data Models usually use special entity-relationship modeling notations intended primarily for IT specialists and hardly understandable to most business stakeholders, e.g. UML. These diagrams provide purely technical descriptions of data entities, or classes, and may contain peculiar storage-specific details or fields. For instance, Logical Data Models often include primary keys and foreign keys specific for tables in relational databases. Moreover, they can even describe physical platform-specific representations of data entities. For example, Logical Data Models may provide separate recommended definitions of same data entities in an XML schema definition (XSD) format for integration platforms and in an SQL data definition language (DDL) format for Oracle and DB2 database platforms.

Similarly to Technology Reference Models, Logical Data Models can represent a mix of both decisions and facts (see Table 2.1). On the one hand, they can establish the desirable standardized structure of the key organization-wide data entities which all new IT systems are expected to use. On the other hand, they can simply document the existing structure of the most widely used data objects in different IT systems to facilitate their further reuse or to be helpful merely as common data reference materials for architects.

Logical Data Models help achieve better technical data consistency between different IT systems and ensure that all systems in an organization capture and store exactly the same data in same formats. Thereby, Logical Data Models ease data exchange, improve interoperability and facilitate integration between different IT systems. The schematic graphical representation of Logical Data Models is shown in Figure 10.5.

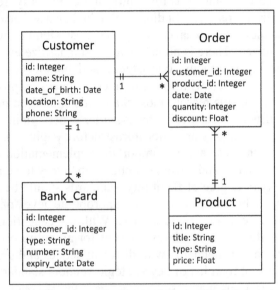

Figure 10.5. Logical Data Models

Similarly to all other Standards, Logical Data Models provide global IT-specific rules relevant to all IT systems in an organization. Specifically, all new IT systems handing common data entities are expected to use standard definitions of these entities provided by Logical Data Models in their Designs. Essentially, Logical Data Models shape the architectural requirements for all applications dealing with shared data. Instead of creating different versions of same data objects in different applications, architects and project teams should reuse established data definitions to achieve logical consistency, enable interoperability and ease the integration between various IT systems, especially between customized in-house systems and commercial off-the-shelf (COTS) products. Compliance with Logical Data Models is typically achieved via peer-reviewing Designs of all IT systems and via supervising the IT project teams implementing these systems.

Additional Concerns Regarding Standards

The single biggest threat associated with the practical use of Standards is arguably the development of overly strict and inflexible Standards which might be harmful for an organization. Excessively rigid Standards essentially paralyze the delivery of new IT initiatives with endless negotiations, bureaucracy and red tape. The pursuit of standardization for the sake of standardization typically leads to the creation of a superfluous number of Standards trying to formally regulate all imaginable aspects of information systems. This obsession with setting and enforcing Standards often prevents project teams from doing their normal daily work, i.e. implementing new IT projects. At the same time, architecture functions constantly inspecting and stopping ongoing IT projects for even minor deviations from countless Standards are infamously known as "architecture police". In relation to Standards, "the more, the better" is an inappropriate and detrimental attitude.

Instead, the effective use of Standards for controlling complexity, reducing costs, mitigating risks and accelerating delivery requires finding the right balance between standardization and flexibility. In order to achieve this balance, only the most significant aspects of information systems should be standardized. There is no necessity to standardize everything, but only what is truly important for achieving simplicity, consistency and homogeneity. Moreover, reasonable Standards should be closely aligned with the real practical needs of project teams delivering IT solutions in specific areas. For this reason, most Standards should be developed with the direct involvement of IT specialists and technical subject-matter experts doing a hands-on work on the ground, e.g. lead software developers or senior infrastructure engineers. Standards developed by architects alone without taking into account important implementation-level concerns are often found too clumsy by project teams and eventually end up in "ivory towers".

To achieve the necessary degree of flexibility Standards should be also defined specifically for particular technology or business areas at the appropriate level of abstraction and closely aligned to the specific needs existing in these areas. With the exception of small organizations, which may maintain a single set of Standards relevant for an entire organization, organizations typically establish a hierarchy of Standards with different scopes and granularities. For instance, large organizations may have only a list of key strategic vendors standardized organization-wide, while medium-sized organizations may also standardize a kit of concrete vendor products to be used by all their business units. More fine-grained Standards in large and medium-sized organizations are typically developed at the level of specific business units or subunits of the IT department to reflect their unique needs. For example, different lines of business may establish their own technical Standards taking into account their process-specific requirements, while the subunits of the IT department responsible for different technologies may develop their own technology-specific Standards. Furthermore, separate IT project teams may accumulate their own local implementation-level Standards relevant only for certain types of projects. Some lowest-level Standards, for example variable naming conventions and other coding standards, may be even largely informal and undocumented, i.e. agreed and communicated verbally between different team members or learned directly from the existing codebase. The hierarchical approach to defining Standards described above helps standardize the right things at the appropriate organizational levels with the necessary degree of granularity and formality. This hierarchical approach allows combining the desired levels of standardization and flexibility, i.e. realize the main benefits associated with standardization and still retain sufficient leeway.

At the same time, all irrelevant and obsolete Standards should be removed in a timely manner to avoid excessive rigidity and clumsiness. For that purpose, Standards should be periodically reviewed, revised and cleaned up, which is often done on a yearly basis. There are no reasons to accumulate Standards beyond pragmatic necessity. Additionally, reasonable and substantiated deviations from established Standards should be tolerated. These deviations should be documented, possibly as architecture debts, and then analyzed to facilitate organization learning and guide the evolution of Standards.

Chapter Summary

This chapter discussed Standards as a general type of EA artifacts from the perspective of their informational contents, development, usage, purpose and benefits and then described in more detail popular narrow subtypes of Standards including Technology Reference Models, Guidelines, Patterns, IT Principles and Logical Data Models. The key message of this chapter can be summarized into the following essential points:

- Standards describe global technical rules, standards, patterns and best practices relevant for IT systems representing proven reusable means for solution implementation
- Standards are permanent decisions EA artifacts that are developed on an as-necessary basis collaboratively by architects and technical subject-matter experts, periodically updated according to the ongoing technology progress and used to shape architectures of all IT initiatives
- Standards help achieve technical consistency, technological homogeneity and regulatory compliance eventually leading to faster delivery of new IT initiatives, reduced IT-related costs, risks and complexity
- Technology Reference Models are essential Standards providing structured graphical representations of all technologies used in an organization and helping architects control, manage and consolidate the corporate technology portfolio
- Guidelines are essential Standards providing IT-specific implementation-level prescriptions applicable in narrow technology-specific areas or domains and helping architects and subject-matter experts document, share and reuse corresponding best practices in the use of IT
- Patterns are common Standards providing generic reusable solutions to commonly occurring problems in the design of IT systems and helping architects provide standardized approaches or building blocks for constructing new IT projects
- IT Principles are common Standards defining global high-level IT-specific guidelines influencing all IT-related planning decisions in an organization and helping architects implicitly shape architectures of all IT systems
- Logical Data Models are uncommon Standards providing logical or even physical platform-specific definitions of the key data entities and their relationship and helping architects stipulate common data formats and achieve better interoperability between IT systems

Chapter 11: Visions

The previous chapter focused on Standards as the second general type of EA artifacts defined by the CSVLOD model of enterprise architecture. This chapter discusses in great detail various aspects of Visions as the next general type of EA artifacts (business-focused structures) as well as their more specific subtypes often used in EA practices. In particular, this chapter starts from describing the common properties of all Visions including their type-specific informational contents, development and usage scenarios, role in an EA practice and associated organizational benefits. Then, this chapter discusses in detail popular narrow subtypes of Visions including Business Capability Models, Roadmaps, Target States, Value Chains and Context Diagrams. Finally, this chapter provides additional concerns and recommendations regarding the practical use of Visions as part of an EA practice.

Visions as a General Type of Enterprise Architecture Artifacts

Visions are business-focused structures EA artifacts (see Figure 8.1). They provide high-level business-oriented descriptions of an organization developed collaboratively by senior business and IT stakeholders and share the essential common properties of both business-focused EA artifacts and structures EA artifacts. Specific examples of EA artifacts related to Visions include Business Capability Models, Roadmaps, Target States, Value Chains, Context Diagrams and some other similar, but less popular EA artifacts (see Figure 8.2)[1].

Informational Contents

Visions provide high-level conceptual descriptions of an organization from the business perspective. Essentially, Visions describe in an abstract manner what an organization looks like or needs to look like in the future. The business-oriented descriptions provided by Visions address the following and similar strategic questions:

- What does an entire organization do?
- What are the business activities and capabilities of an organization?
- What is the relationship between main customers, processes, data and systems?
- What should IT deliver for an organization in the long term?
- Which business areas should receive future IT investments?
- Which business capabilities should be uplifted with IT in the future?
- What types of IT investments should be made in the future?
- Which specific business needs should be addressed with IT and when?

All these questions represent critical organization-wide business interests, concerns and plans that should be agreed between senior business and IT stakeholders, rather than merely delegated to IT executives[2]. For example, the intuitive decision of IT executives to implement a new IT system solving some pressing business problems may be inconsistent with the executive-level business understanding of what is really important for an entire organization in the long run.

The decision of IT executives to establish IT infrastructure supporting a particular business capability may be inconsistent with the relative importance of this capability for the business of an organization from the viewpoint of its business executives. Similarly, the decision of IT executives to accelerate the implementation of a seemingly critical IT initiative or postpone the implementation of a presumably unimportant IT solution may be inconsistent with the actual priorities of the senior business leaders aligned to their business strategy.

In order to avoid these and other similar inconsistencies between business and IT, Visions document a shared view of how an organization works today, how it needs to work in the future and what should be done to enable the desired way of working from the IT perspective. For this reason, all Visions are dual EA artifacts (see Figure 2.4) intended for both senior business executives and architects. They describe the consensus understanding of an organization, its general future direction and tentative further steps in this direction agreed by both business and IT. Visions reflect both the desire of business to transform an organization in a particular direction and the ability of IT to enable this transformation. Often Visions are relevant to an entire organization. However, in large, complex and decentralized organizations major business units (e.g. lines of business, business functions or divisions) can also develop their own Visions reflecting local unit-specific strategies consistent with global organization-wide Visions.

Visions often focus on the long-term future up to 3-5 years ahead[3]. With the notable exception of Context Diagrams, which normally focus on the current state of an organization, most Visions provide some descriptions of the future explaining what should happen with an organization in the long run and what long-term contribution to the business is expected from IT. However, even if some Visions describe the current state, these descriptions are still change-oriented, i.e. intended to facilitate the discussion of what should be changed in the future. Essentially, all Visions regardless of their time focus are intended to support the strategic dialog between business and IT.

Visions are usually expressed in brief informal formats easily understandable to executive-level business audience. Since they are intended to provide very conceptual and high-level descriptions, Visions typically focus only on the most essential relevant information, rather than on specific details. They tend to use simplistic schematic pictures instead of sophisticated full-fledged wiring diagrams with numerous boxes and arrows incomprehensible to most business executives. Moreover, in order to be more attractive to business stakeholders, Visions usually provide full-colored stylish descriptions, rather than monotonous black-and-white "boring" technical drawings. Due to these properties, Visions are often expressed as simple, neat and appealing one-page diagrams with the most critical executive-level information. Physically, all Visions are most typically created, maintained and distributed as plain drawings in MS Visio.

Development and Usage

Visions, with the exception of Context Diagrams depicting current operational flows, represent collective planning decisions (see Table 2.1) on what IT should deliver to an organization in the long run. They are developed as part of the Strategic Planning process (see Figure 6.1) collaboratively by senior business executives and architects (see Figure 2.6). When developing Visions, business leaders and architects, among other things, usually discuss and achieve an agreement on which general business capabilities should be improved in the long run as well as what specific business needs should be addressed with IT in the future (see Table 5.1). Business executives should clearly understand how Visions are aligned to their business strategy, while architects should clearly understand what IT needs to deliver according to Visions. Visions thereby help align future IT investments to the business strategy and synchronize business and IT plans. Both business executives and architects should be able to make a conscious commitment to act according to Visions. Analogously to Considerations, they are physically created by architects, but mentally shaped by senior business stakeholders. Visions are based mostly on the ideas of business executives and represent their understanding of the business and its desirable future, while architects merely facilitate their development by helping business leaders formalize their views. Essentially, Visions facilitate day-to-day strategic communication between business executives and architects.

After being agreed upon, Visions are used to guide IT investments, identify, prioritize and launch new IT initiatives. Firstly, Visions are used to focus future IT investments on strategically important business areas. High-level descriptions of an organization and its future provided by Visions help business executives determine where IT investments should go to support the long-term business strategy. Strategic business capabilities often emphasized by Visions provide a relatively clear guidance regarding the desired direction and type of required IT investments.

Secondly, Visions are used to identify potential IT initiatives to be executed in the future. By providing general high-level suggestions on what an organization wants to achieve with IT, Visions help business leaders and architects come up with a list of candidate IT initiatives that need to be implemented. For example, if Visions present the abstract long-term future state that an organization is trying to achieve, then a number of specific IT initiatives required to reach the envisioned target state in a step-by-step manner may be identified.

Thirdly, Visions are used to prioritize IT initiatives according to their actual importance for the business of an organization. They help senior business leaders decide when and in what sequence future IT initiatives should be implemented. Specifically, Visions can be used for prioritizing fundamental, strategic and local initiatives (see Table 7.1). On the one hand, they can be used to arrange fundamental and strategic initiatives identified in a top-down manner by global business executives and directly contributing to the long-term organizational goals. On the other hand, Visions can be also used to select and prioritize the most appropriate IT initiatives from the pool of local initiatives proposed in a bottom-up manner by local business leaders based on their alignment to the general strategic direction defined by global business executives, sometimes being informed by respective Outlines. In cases when local initiatives of significant importance imply substantial deviations from the approved organization-wide Visions the notion of architecture debt may be used by architects to evaluate the consequences of these deviations and inform the decision-making regarding the necessity of these initiatives, as discussed later in Chapter 18 (Instruments for Enterprise Architecture).

Fourthly, Visions are used to determine which IT initiatives should be launched in the near future or immediately. Although Visions themselves offer only a high-level guidance for future IT investments that cannot be implemented directly, they suggest specific business needs to be addressed at particular moments in time, thereby providing the basis for launching new IT initiatives addressing these planned business needs (see Figure 6.1). For example, if Visions suggest that a business need to uplift a certain business capability should be addressed in the immediate future, then a new IT initiative intended to improve this capability is kicked off and discussed with relevant business stakeholders based on its early Outlines. In other words, a new instance of the Initiative Delivery process is launched from a planned business need indicated in Visions. Thereby, Visions help translate a high-level business strategy into specific executable IT initiatives.

Visions, and especially Business Capability Models and Value Chains, are permanent EA artifacts (see Table 2.2) with an "infinite" lifetime, i.e. once created, they generally exist as long as an organization exists. They can be updated multiple times a year if necessary to reflect the latest strategic priorities and ongoing shifts in the external business environment. Typically Visions are also formally reviewed, approved and signed-off by business executives and architects on a periodical basis, usually yearly after the re-approval of a business strategy by the executive committee. However, some Visions might still be discarded after major organizational restructurings or redeveloped from scratch after significant transformations of the business model.

Role and Benefits

Visions represent shared views of an organization and its future agreed by business and IT. They establish a common general future direction for all relevant actors involved in strategic decision-making and implementation of IT systems. Essentially, Visions can be considered as a global "map" for an entire organization and its major business units showing where exactly an organization needs to go in the long run and what steps are required to get there. Visions explain how to execute the organizational business strategy with IT and provide a rather detailed guidance for future IT investments.

The general purpose of all Visions is to help achieve the alignment between IT investments and long-term business outcomes. Via using Visions for strategic discussions, business executives and architects can agree on the future course of action for IT and make sure that all planned IT investments contribute to the strategic business goals. In particular, Visions help address four critical aspects of the alignment between IT expenditures and business results:

- How much money to invest in IT – Visions can give an approximate idea regarding what magnitude of IT expenses is necessary or desirable to accommodate with the strategic business demands
- Where to invest IT dollars – Visions allow focusing future IT investments on the most strategically important business areas while minimizing ineffective or unnecessary IT expenses
- What types of IT investments are needed – Visions help identify the critical types of new IT systems required by an organization to execute its business strategy
- When IT investments should be made – Visions allow allocating and scheduling future IT investments according to the strategic business priorities and organization-wide investment plans

The proper use of Visions leads to improved strategic alignment and better effectiveness of IT investments. Since senior business executives ensure that Visions are aligned to their business strategy, all IT investments aligned to Visions are automatically aligned to the business strategy as well. All IT initiatives implied by Visions, including fundamental, strategic and local initiatives, are explicitly mapped to tangible strategic business outcomes and, therefore, are effective in nature. By bridging the gap between the business goals and planned IT investments,

Visions help increase the transparency of IT expenses and achieve better traceability between IT expenditures and declared long-term business objectives.

Difference from the Adjacent Types

Visions, as business-focused structures EA artifacts, are adjacent to Considerations, Landscapes and Outlines (see Figure 8.1). Although Considerations also provide some conceptual business-oriented descriptions of an organization similar to Visions, the descriptions offered by Considerations are less specific, directive and actionable. Unlike Considerations, which describe only how an organization wants to work, Visions provide a high-level direction suggesting what an organization wants to do in the future and offer rather articulate plans regarding the long-term course of action for IT. Essentially, Considerations only define some general conceptual requirements for all IT systems in an organization, while Visions go further and specify where future IT investments should focus, when these investments should be made and what types of IT projects should be initiated.

Although Landscapes also describe the high-level structure of an organization similar to Visions, the descriptions provided by Landscapes are highly technical in nature, incomprehensible and irrelevant to business leaders. While Landscapes focus mostly on documenting the current state of the organizational IT landscape, Visions focus on the strategic long-term direction of an organization endorsed directly by its business executives. Unlike Landscapes, Visions provide important instruments for directing IT to senior business stakeholders. Essentially, Visions allow business leaders to guide IT initiatives indirectly, without understanding what specific IT systems may be implemented.

Although Outlines also provide some high-level business-oriented descriptions similar to Visions, the descriptions offered by Outlines are more specific, narrow and actionable. While Outlines focus on describing in detail separate IT initiatives with limited scopes and timelines, Visions focus on describing the global strategic direction of IT. Unlike Outlines, Visions do not explain what exactly needs to be done, but provide only a general long-term guidance for IT investments. Essentially, Visions articulate the organization-wide future course of action for IT without specifying the details of proposed IT initiatives.

Specific Enterprise Architecture Artifacts Related to Visions

Articulate subtypes of Visions often used in established EA practices include Business Capability Models, Roadmaps, Target States, Value Chains and Context Diagrams. Business Capability Models and Roadmaps can be considered as essential EA artifacts, Target States as common EA artifacts, while Value Chains and Context Diagrams as uncommon EA artifacts.

Business Capability Models (Essential)

Business Capability Models (sometimes can be also called business capability maps, business capability canvases or capability reference models) are specific Visions providing structured graphical representations of all organizational business capabilities, their relationship and hierarchy[4]. Business Capability Models can be considered as an essential subtype of Visions found in the majority of successful EA practices.

Business Capability Models represent holistic high-level views of an organization from the perspective of its business capabilities. Essentially, they briefly describe everything that an organization can do. Business Capability Models are very stable and organizationally neutral in nature. They are largely independent of specific organizational structures, reporting relationships, political agendas and cultural aspects of individual business leaders, current initiatives and projects. Furthermore, most changes happening in organizations do not affect the fundamental structure of their Business Capability Models.

Business Capability Models are structured in a hierarchical manner, i.e. each higher-level business capability includes multiple constituting lower-level capabilities. They can have several nested levels of depth and granularity, typically from two to four distinct abstraction levels depending on the size, complexity and experience of an organization. At the highest level, often considered as level zero, all business capabilities can be separated into customer-facing ("front office") capabilities and operational ("back office") capabilities. Top-level business capabilities can be also organized according to main organizational functions (e.g. enable, manage and run) or aligned to the core activities of the value chain (e.g. logistics, operations, sales and service). Underlying lower-level business capabilities are naturally more numerous and fine-grained[5]. Specific business capabilities in Business Capability Models can be titled using either a noun-verb style or a verb-noun style, e.g. "product development" or "develop products".

In their simplest form Business Capability Models can show only structured sets of nested business capabilities and sub-capabilities. However, more sophisticated versions of these EA artifacts can also provide additional information regarding an organization and its environment relevant for strategic decision-making. For example, complex Business Capability Models often include an organizational mission, strategy and vision, document its long-term goals, objectives and constraints and even show the most important elements of its external business environment that should be taken into account during strategic planning, e.g. key competitors, strategic partners, major suppliers, target markets, core customer groups, industry regulators or some other critical elements of the organizational context.

Since Business Capability Models offer only a very high-level view of an organization, usually they can be created rather quickly. Perfect accurateness and correctness are not among their most important or critical qualities. Moreover, more intuitive and simple Business Capability Models are more likely to resonate with the thought processes of business executives. In many industries the development of Business Capability Models can be accelerated via taking openly available industry-standard reference models or even proprietary generic reference models provided by commercial vendors as the basis for producing customized, organization-specific capability models[6]. In some cases, separate parts of Business Capability Models representing common groups of the most typical capabilities (e.g. customer management or product management) can be borrowed from other industries and adapted to the organizational needs. Put it simply, organization-specific Business Capability Models can be often composed of the elements taken from other capability models.

Business Capability Models can be considered as key EA artifacts underpinning all conversations around specific business capabilities, which typically provide very convenient discussion points between senior business and IT stakeholders (see Table 5.1). Since business capabilities, as high-level planning abstractions, are perfectly suitable for a long-range planning on the horizon of 3-5 years, Business Capability Models are naturally used for strategic planning up to 3-5 years ahead in the future. Specifically, as part of the Strategic Planning process (see Figure 6.1) business executives and architects usually discuss the relative importance of different business capabilities from the strategic perspective, identify the capabilities requiring the most significant enhancements in the long run and then employ the so-called technique of "heatmapping", i.e. explicitly highlighting or color-coding the business capabilities that should become the primary focus of future IT investments. Often the necessary strategic capability improvements can be also classified into different types reflecting the nature of these improvements (e.g. fundamentally new business operations should be added to the capability, the quality of current operations should be raised or the existing capability should be performed at lower cost) and then color-coded appropriately in Business Capability Models. In some cases completely new business capabilities that need to be developed from scratch may be added to Business Capability Models and heatmapped accordingly, while some existing capabilities that lost their importance may be removed as irrelevant.

The identification and subsequent heatmapping of the most high-priority business capabilities can be accomplished in various more or less formal ways. On the one hand, the most straightforward approach to heatmapping implies simple marking of some capabilities as strategic by business executives based on their intuitive judgment and in-depth understanding of the business, its problems and opportunities. On the other hand, more complex approaches to heatmapping imply the initial evaluation of the current maturity levels of relevant business capabilities, determination of the required levels of these capabilities, estimation of the gaps between the current and required maturity levels and subsequent heatmapping based on a detailed analysis of the existing capability gaps. For example, an organization may assess the present maturity level of a particular business capability as two (on a five-point scale), characterize its desirable target level as four, then estimate the volume of change required to achieve this level (delta) and finally highlight in Business Capability Models where the biggest IT investments should be made. In this case, the current and desired maturity levels of business capabilities, as well as the identified capability gaps, can be also reflected in Business Capability Models for analytical purposes by means of appropriate color-coding. However, a formal assessment of the current and required capability levels in an organization may require comprehensive performance benchmarking, i.e. comparing the levels of organizational business capabilities either with the corresponding capability levels of its key competitors, or more broadly with the industry-average levels of these capabilities.

The set of heatmapped business capabilities in Business Capability Models represents a consensus understanding of the organizational focus and strategic priorities agreed by business and IT. In their turn, these business capabilities provide a sound basis for further, more detailed IT planning. Using heatmapped business capabilities as a starting point for IT planning, architects and business leaders can propose candidate IT initiatives intended to uplift these capabilities and thereby directly contribute to the execution of a business strategy. By means of heatmapping, Business Capability Models offer very effective instruments for translating an abstract business strategy into more specific and actionable plans for IT. Essentially, they help view an entire organization as an investment portfolio with different types of assets, proactively focus IT investments on the assets with highest returns and achieve the greatest possible strategic impact. However, not all enhancements of business capabilities can be relevant to IT, especially the ones related to people aspects, as noted earlier.

Besides highlighting the most critical target capabilities for future IT investments and indicating respective maturity levels and capability gaps, Business Capability Models can be also color-coded in many other useful ways to facilitate strategic decision-making. For example, they can be color-coded to distinguish differentiating capabilities from non-differentiating ones and thereby identify the needs for custom IT systems. While non-differentiating capabilities may be often supported by low-cost packaged systems or ERP modules embodying standardized business processes, differentiating capabilities may require highly organization-specific applications developed in-house[7]. Similarly, Business Capability Models can be color-coded to distinguish core capabilities from non-core ones and thereby identify the opportunities for outsourcing. While core capabilities should be cultivated and mastered within an organization, non-core capabilities can be considered as good candidates for outsourcing with minimal business risk. Color-coding business capabilities based on the safety and regulatory requirements to the information they handle can help decide which applications should be and should not be migrated into the cloud or which systems must employ strengthened authentication mechanisms.

Business Capability Models have many other helpful uses in organizations. Firstly, they enable the so-called initiative "footprinting", i.e. mapping of specific IT initiatives to the affected business capabilities. This footprinting helps understand the contribution of corresponding IT initiatives to the overall strategic direction, identify their potential sponsors and stakeholders, determine their scope, effect and disruption. Better understanding of specific IT initiatives and their impact, in its turn, enables a more informed comparison between different initiatives as well as between different possible implementation options of the same initiative. Secondly, mapping of the accomplished or planned IT investments to Business Capability Models helps understand how the IT budget is allocated and where IT dollars are going, as discussed later in Chapter 18 (Instruments for Enterprise Architecture). Finally, Business Capability Models provide a common language, shared vocabulary and unified organization-wide reference points to all stakeholders involved in decision-making processes.

Business Capability Models often describe an entire organization. However, large and decentralized organizations can develop separate Business Capability Models for their major business units, e.g. lines of business, business functions or divisions. Fundamentally, Business Capability Models are one-page EA artifacts, though they may often also include some additional supporting information, e.g. exact definitions and detailed descriptions of all business capabilities from the perspective of their different dimensions including processes, systems, facilities, people, skills and information. The schematic graphical representation of Business Capability Models (simple models and complex models) is shown in Figure 11.1.

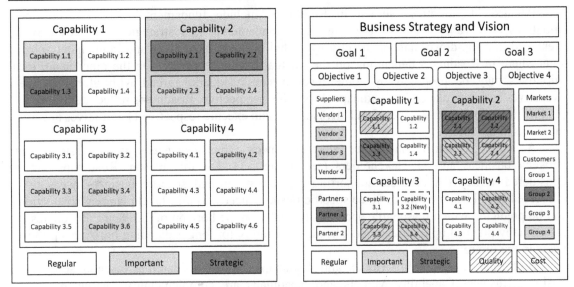

Figure 11.1. Business Capability Models (simple models and complex models)

Business Capability Models are often considered as an "entry point" to IT for business executives. Every change that business leaders want to make ultimately relates to improving a particular business capability. Unsurprisingly, many strategic conversations between business and IT revolve around business capabilities and start from identifying the capabilities that should be enhanced with IT. On the one hand, a clear understanding of the most critical business capabilities allows proposing effective strategic initiatives intended to improve these capabilities in a top-down manner. On the other hand, this understanding also allows selecting the most appropriate local initiatives emerging in a bottom-up manner (see Table 7.1) based on their expected contribution to the heatmapped business capabilities.

By focusing IT efforts on the most important business capabilities, Business Capability Models boost the strategic effectiveness of IT investments. However, due to their simplicity Business Capability Models are more suitable for guiding incremental capability improvements, rather than organizational transformations of a structural nature.

Roadmaps (Essential)

Roadmaps (can be called investment roadmaps, capability roadmaps, application roadmaps, technology roadmaps, etc.) are specific Visions providing structured graphical views of all planned IT initiatives in specific business areas having direct business value. Roadmaps can be considered as an essential subtype of Visions found in the majority of successful EA practices.

Roadmaps describe tentative IT delivery schedules for different business areas agreed by senior business and IT stakeholders. Essentially, they show everything that IT plans to deliver for the business in the foreseeable future. Roadmaps present all planned IT initiatives with their approximate start dates and completion timelines. They also often show the current point in time to explicitly indicate which IT initiatives are active right now and what their implementation stages are.

Planned IT initiatives shown in Roadmaps include fundamental, strategic and local initiatives (see Table 7.1). On the one hand, fundamental and strategic initiatives may be identified in a top-down manner directly by global business executives and immediately placed somewhere in Roadmaps depending on their actual business priority. On the other hand, local initiatives may be proposed by some local business leaders, agreed with global business executives and then placed in Roadmaps. From this perspective, Roadmaps reflect deliberate and planned intentions to make specific IT investments and execute respective IT initiatives at certain moments in the future.

As noted earlier, IT initiatives represent specific business needs as discussion points between business and IT stakeholders (see Table 5.1). For this reason, Roadmaps can be considered as key EA artifacts supporting discussions around specific business needs to be addressed with IT in the future. Since specific business needs, as mid-level planning abstractions, can be predicted with a reasonable accuracy typically on the horizon of 2-3 years, Roadmaps are also usually planned up to three years ahead, more rarely for longer planning horizons up to five years in the future.

Both Business Capability Models and Roadmaps can be considered as essential subtypes of Visions. Business Capability Models and Roadmaps are complementary instruments of IT planning and normally used in conjunction with each other. While Business Capability Models operate with business capabilities and help business executives decide where future IT investments should go, Roadmaps operate with specific initiatives and help business executives decide when these investments should be made. For this reason IT initiatives in Roadmaps are often considered as business capability increments. Unsurprisingly, Roadmaps are often aligned to separate business capabilities, or cohesive groups of related capabilities, and map specific IT initiatives to the corresponding capabilities or sub-capabilities they intend to uplift. However, in some cases Roadmaps may be aligned to major IT systems or platforms having an intuitive business meaning, e.g. ERP, CRM or BI. Roadmaps are also complementary to and used in conjunction with Target States, as discussed later in this chapter.

All IT initiatives placed in Roadmaps can be roughly estimated by means of an educated guess, conditionally separated into different groups based on their relative order-of-magnitude size estimates (e.g. large or small) and color-coded accordingly for better convenience. Moreover, IT initiatives in Roadmaps can be also color-coded to indicate their approval status, beneficiaries or sponsors. For instance, Roadmaps often distinguish IT initiatives at different stages of their approval including, but not limited to, the following stages:

- Planned – the IT initiative has been proposed as an idea, preliminarily approved by business leaders and placed in the Roadmap, but any further work on this initiative has not yet started
- Approved – the IT initiative has been discussed in more detail and the development of Outlines to explore possible implementation options has been started
- Funded – the IT initiative has been sufficiently elaborated, finally approved based on its Outlines, signed-off by business executives and funded for further implementation

Roadmaps can range in their complexity from very simple timetables to rather complex graphical EA artifacts with rich informational contents. On the one hand, simplest Roadmaps merely show all planned IT initiatives with their timelines aligned to corresponding business capabilities or areas. On the other hand, the most sophisticated versions of Roadmaps can also provide plenty of additional supporting information regarding these IT initiatives and their connection to the overall organizational context. For example, complex Roadmaps often include key strategic business drivers, goals and objectives, explain the expected contribution and outcomes of planned IT initiatives, link these initiatives to business priorities, problems and pain points, clarify the dependencies existing between different initiatives and even describe at a high level the current and desired future states in respective business areas, though these descriptions are usually very abstract and limited either to listing the most essential systems constituting the IT landscape in these business areas, or to defining the present and target maturity levels of corresponding business capabilities.

Small organizations may maintain a single Roadmap describing all planned IT initiatives in an entire organization. However, larger organizations typically develop a set of multiple Roadmaps related to different business units or capabilities. Large and decentralized organizations often maintain a hierarchy of Roadmaps including separate local Roadmaps for major business units (e.g. lines of business, business functions or divisions) and a single, or a few, organization-wide consolidated Roadmaps intended for C-level executives aggregating the most significant IT initiatives across all the business units. Additionally, for budgeting and portfolio planning purposes organizations can also create separate truncated versions of Roadmaps, sometimes called as investment slides, showing only the approved and funded IT initiatives to be delivered during the next financial year.

Although Roadmaps are often one-page EA artifacts, they may also include some more detailed supporting information, e.g. high-level descriptions and basic justifications of all planned IT initiatives. The schematic graphical representation of Roadmaps (simple roadmaps and complex roadmaps) is shown in Figure 11.2.

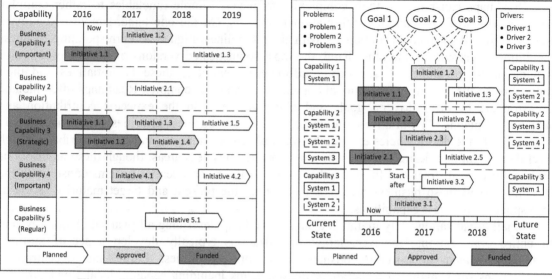

Figure 11.2. Roadmaps (simple roadmaps and complex roadmaps)

Roadmaps, along with Business Capability Models, are essential instruments for supporting the strategic dialog between business and IT. However, Roadmaps enable more fine-grained and detailed IT planning than Business Capability Models. Specifically, they help business executives and architects prioritize planned IT initiatives, ensure the alignment between specific IT investments and required business capabilities and connect future initiatives with respective business and financial plans.

Ultimately, all IT initiatives from Roadmaps provide planned business needs as an input to the Initiative Delivery process (see Figure 6.1). When the time to implement particular planned IT initiatives comes, these initiatives from Roadmaps turn into full-fledged instances of the Initiative Delivery process. As part of this process, planned IT initiatives and corresponding business needs are further elaborated and transformed into more detailed Outlines. In other words, each IT initiative placed in Roadmaps is eventually discussed in more detail with relevant business stakeholders and elaborated with Outlines when its time comes. Essentially, Roadmaps are the main suppliers of planned business needs to the Initiative Delivery process.

Besides their primary purpose (i.e. facilitating the internal planning of future IT initiatives), Roadmaps sometimes might be also necessary for external regulatory compliance purposes. For instance, in some heavily regulated industries (e.g. energy, utilities and public sector) organizations may be legislatively obliged to develop long-term IT investment Roadmaps and submit them to the corresponding regulatory bodies for notification purposes, i.e. to inform the industry regulators on the organizational intents and future capital investment plans.

Target States (Common)

Target States (can be called target architectures, future state architectures, business reference architectures, etc.) are specific Visions providing high-level graphical descriptions of the desired long-term future state of an organization. Target States can be considered as a common subtype of Visions often found in successful EA practices[8].

Target States represent the ultimate planned destination of an organization from the perspective of its business and IT. Essentially, Target States explain what an organization is trying to achieve with IT in the long-term future. They are often planned for a horizon up to three years ahead, less often for longer planning horizons up to five years ahead.

Target States primarily focus on describing how future information systems will solve current business problems, what the strategic business value of these systems is and how these systems align to the long-term organizational goals and objectives. Target States often give a high-level idea regarding what types of IT systems will be delivered to improve the required strategic business capabilities. They may also provide additional relevant information regarding the desired "to-be" state, e.g. its key drivers, motivating factors, assumptions or outcomes. Even though Target States often describe the current "as-is" state of an organization as well, these current state descriptions are typically intended only to clarify the nature of the proposed changes and better explain the anticipated benefits of these changes.

Target States are more sophisticated and powerful planning instruments than Business Capability Models and Roadmaps. While Business Capability Models only highlight the most critical business capabilities and Roadmaps only explain what IT initiatives are planned towards these capabilities, Target States provide explicit descriptions of the ultimate desired state that an organization is trying to implement in the future. Unsurprisingly, Target States are more often found in mature EA practices. The successful usage of Target States for IT planning arguably requires more experienced architects as well as longer overall organizational experience with enterprise architecture. Additionally, Target States are seemingly more appropriate and valuable for organizations pursuing large-scale structural transformations of a qualitative nature (e.g. modifying an operating model (see Figure 5.3) or consolidating information systems after a merger or acquisition), rather than just seeking evolutionary improvements of the existing business capabilities[9].

Target States are developed as products of strategic communication between business executives and architects. They are often updated once a year and signed-off by all relevant business and IT leaders. In small organizations Target States can describe an entire organization. However, in large and decentralized organizations multiple separate Target States are typically developed for different organizational areas, e.g. individual business functions, departments or capabilities.

Although Target States can be one-page EA artifacts stored as simple MS Visio drawings, they may often also include some more detailed supporting information, e.g. explanation of the underlying logic behind the proposed target state. The schematic graphical representation of Target States is shown in Figure 11.3.

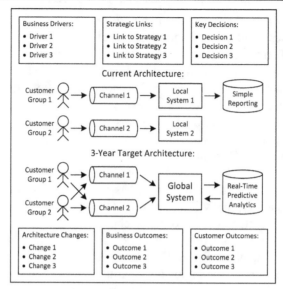

Figure 11.3. Target States

Target States are powerful instruments for guiding future IT investments. Once developed and approved by senior business executives, they provide a reasonably clear description of what IT needs to deliver in the long run. In particular, Target States provide an input for developing more detailed IT investment Roadmaps. Overarching Target States are broken down into a number of smaller components, these components are placed in Roadmaps as separate IT initiatives, prioritized based on their tactical importance and possible interdependences between each other and then implemented as regular IT solutions. At the same time, new local initiatives proposed in a bottom-up manner by business unit leaders (see Table 7.1) can be evaluated for their alignment and contribution to strategic Target States in order to decide whether these IT initiatives should be implemented and if yes, how and when.

Essentially, Target States represent the intermediate level of planning between very abstract Business Capability Models and rather specific Roadmaps. In many organizations the Strategic Planning process (see Figure 6.1) generally progresses from Business Capability Models to Target States and then to Roadmaps. In this case firstly Business Capability Models are heatmapped based on strategic business priorities to specify what capability improvements are required, then long-term Target States are planned with an intention to show how approximately the necessary capability enhancements should be realized in the future and finally fine-grained Roadmaps are developed to explain how exactly the desired future should be achieved step-by-step.

Value Chains (Uncommon)

Value Chains (can be called value reference models, business activity models, etc.) are specific Visions providing structured graphical representations of the added value chain of an organization. Value Chains can be considered as an uncommon subtype of Visions relatively rarely found in EA practices[10].

Value Chains represent holistic high-level views of an organization from the perspective of its value-adding business activities. Value Chains structure all organizational business activities according to their positions in the value chain, e.g. inbound logistics, operations, outbound logistics, marketing and sales, and service[11]. Essentially, they briefly describe all primary and supporting activities that an organization performs to deliver valuable products or services to the market.

Value Chains are conceptually similar to Business Capability Models, but describe an organization from a slightly different perspective. While Business Capability Models focus on business capabilities and offer largely a static picture of an organization, Value Chains focus on key business activities of the organizational value chain and provide a more dynamic view of its operational flows. These business activities, as alternative discussion points between business and IT stakeholders, offer approximately the same level of abstraction as business capabilities (see Table 5.1) and, naturally, are also perfectly suitable for an organization-wide strategic planning up to 3-5 years ahead.

Depending on organization-specific needs, Value Chains can be used either in a complementary combination with or instead of Business Capability Models to facilitate the strategic dialog between business executives and architects. Analogously to Business Capability Models, Value Chains are often color-coded or heatmapped to indicate which organizational activities should be improved in the long run and receive more IT dollars in the future[12]. For this purpose, business activities of the value chain may be also benchmarked against acknowledged best practices, industry-average levels or key competitors according to time, quality, cost and any other relevant performance indicators.

Similarly to Business Capability Models, Value Chains are largely timeless in nature and normally survive most changes in the organizational structure and business strategy. Although strategic priorities of an organization may shift very frequently, the fundamental structure of its core value chain changes pretty rarely, only in case of profound business transformations. Moreover, since different organizations working in same industry sectors usually have rather similar value chains, architects can often leverage existing standard reference models for their industries and adapt them to develop customized Value Chains for their organizations.

A relative advantage of Value Chains (e.g. over Business Capability Models) is their better comprehensibility and attractiveness to business stakeholders. The concept of a value chain is well known to many business executives. Value chains are popular instruments of strategic management, which are widely taught at business schools and may be easily understandable to most business stakeholders with MBA degrees. Due to this quality, Value Chains can cause less confusion, discomfort and resistance among senior business leaders and, therefore, may be easier to introduce as part of an EA practice. The schematic graphical representation of Value Chains is shown in Figure 11.4.

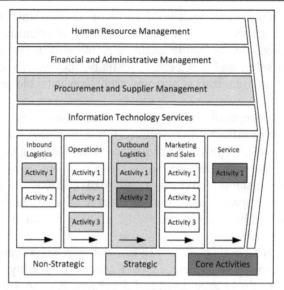

Figure 11.4. Value Chains

Similarly to Business Capability Models, Value Chains are one-page EA artifacts supporting the conversations between business leaders and architects regarding the desired long-term future course of action for IT. Specifically, Value Chains help senior business and IT stakeholders identify the most strategically important business activities or areas and then focus IT investments on these areas.

Context Diagrams (Uncommon)

Context Diagrams (can be called business context diagrams, application diagrams, concepts of operations, etc.) are specific Visions providing high-level graphical descriptions of the current operational flows of an organization. Context Diagrams can be considered as an uncommon subtype of Visions relatively rarely found in EA practices.

Context Diagrams represent high-level views of an organization describing its essential elements and relationship between them. Essentially, they explain on a single page how the business operates and clarify how an entire organization or its major business units work. Context Diagrams may contain any elements critical for understanding the main operational flows in an organization. These elements might be very diverse and include customers, products, services, activities, physical production and storage facilities, business units and functions, geographical locations, workforce, information, IT systems and any other relevant entities.

Unlike all other Visions, which represent planning decisions and usually reflect some long-term future plans, Context Diagrams are facts EA artifacts depicting the existing business as it is seen by business executives and focusing mostly on the current "as-is" state of an organization (see Table 2.1). However, like all Visions, Context Diagrams also facilitate the strategic dialog between senior business and IT stakeholders regarding the best possible opportunities for future IT investments. The schematic graphical representation of Context Diagrams is shown in Figure 11.5.

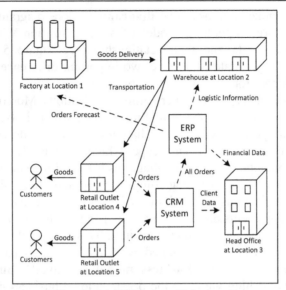

Figure 11.5. Context Diagrams

Similarly to all other Visions, Context Diagrams are intended to support the strategic communication between business executives and architects. In particular, Context Diagrams help discuss the problems, bottlenecks, pain points and limitations of current operations as well as better understand the long-term consequences of different strategic IT-related planning decisions. Additionally, they allow identifying the drivers, owners and stakeholders of separate IT initiatives and determining their overall organizational impact. These and other similar discussions supported by Context Diagrams help decide what IT investments should be done in the future, why and when.

Less Popular Enterprise Architecture Artifacts Related to Visions

Besides Business Capability Models, Roadmaps, Target States, Value Chains and Context Diagrams described above, some other noteworthy subtypes of Visions are occasionally found in organizations practicing enterprise architecture. Firstly, some organizations actively use **process models**, or maps. Process models provide very high-level views of all organizational business processes, their relationship and hierarchy. Process models are conceptually similar to Business Capability Models and may also have several nested levels of scope, depth and granularity. While Business Capability Models focus on business capabilities representing narrow business functions and encompassing all underlying processes, roles and IT systems, process models focus specifically on describing business processes, i.e. specific sequences of activities carried out by a particular role. Process models are complementary to Business Capability Models and used in a very similar manner to facilitate the strategic dialog between business executives and architects. Specifically, process models can be heatmapped to articulate the priorities for future IT investments and thereby translate the business strategy into specific IT initiatives. Process models help all the involved stakeholders decide what high-level business processes should be added, improved or removed.

Secondly, some organizations use **core diagrams**[13]. Core diagrams provide explicit one-page depictions of the target operating model of an organization with its key standardized processes, shared business data and their relationship (see Figure 5.3). Core diagrams are conceptually similar to Target States, but have two important differences. Unlike Target States, which are often developed for specific areas of an organization, core diagrams are more overarching in their scope and typically cover entire organizations. Moreover, while Target States focus on describing some specific long-term future state, which is typically a moving target routinely changing from year to year, core diagrams focus on describing the fundamental structure of an organization and its IT landscape, which is normally very stable and does not change every year. The main purpose of core diagrams is to facilitate the strategic dialog between senior business and IT stakeholders regarding a very long-term direction of the whole organization. Using core diagrams helps align all IT initiatives to the essential structure of an organization, focus IT investments on its "permanent" needs which are not expected to change in the future, identify and launch new fundamental initiatives (see Table 7.1) and thereby build a reusable digitized platform that can be leveraged by all subsequent business strategies[14].

Thirdly, some organizations use **business model canvases**[15]. Business model canvases provide very abstract overarching views of the organizational business model including its nine key elements: partners, activities, resources, value propositions, customer relationships, channels, customer segments, cost structure and revenue streams. Business model canvases are somewhat similar to Context Diagrams and also explain how an organization generally works and makes its profits. However, they offer highly structured and semi-textual descriptions of organizations focused strictly on their nine definitive aspects, while Context Diagrams present free-form graphical depictions using any appropriate elements to explain the business of an organization. Business model canvases provide a convenient platform for strategic communication between business and IT as well as a solid basis for achieving long-term business and IT alignment in general. In particular, they help business executives and architects understand what is really important for the business of an organization in the long run, identify weaknesses and improvement opportunities in the current business model, prioritize future business development efforts and corresponding IT initiatives.

Fourthly, some organizations use various EA artifacts providing high-level views of an organization from highly specific perspectives, e.g. from the perspective of its organizational structure or from the perspective of its key products[16]. These EA artifacts are somewhat similar to Context Diagrams and typically describe only the current state, but focus specifically on some narrow aspects of an organization. Analogously to Context Diagrams, these EA artifacts facilitate mutual understanding between business leaders and architects by providing a common context for IT planning. For example, **organizational structures** may describe which business units are responsible for specific activities or which business units produce specific products. Organizational structures may also provide the mapping between business units and specific capabilities shown in Business Capability Models. These EA artifacts can help senior business and IT stakeholders understand which parts of an organization will drive specific IT initiatives, who might be the primary stakeholders and business owners of these initiatives as well as who might be involved in their implementation. **Product catalogs** may describe what products an organization produces, where they are produced, what source materials are required for these products and who eventually consumes them. These EA artifacts can help senior business and IT stakeholders better understand how business units at different locations operate and identify potential similarities, differences and synergies between them. Similarly to Context Diagrams, all these EA artifacts give an overall idea of how the business is structured, how it works and how an organization relates to its key activities. The usage of these EA artifacts for supporting communication between business and IT stakeholders may improve the quality of strategic IT-related decision-making and effectiveness of resulting IT investments.

Additional Concerns Regarding Visions

The single biggest threat associated with the practical use of Visions is arguably the attempts to develop overly detailed and fine-grained Visions that might be essentially useless for all practical purposes. Visions are intended to establish a commonly agreed long-term course of action for both business and IT. However, the external business environment is very dynamic in nature and the future is volatile. Consequently, most strategic plans for the next 3-5 years might be based essentially only on certain expectations on what will happen, or not happen, in the future. Even technologies that might be available after 3-5 years are rarely known. Due to the inherent environmental uncertainty, any future plans are naturally highly speculative and may often quickly change when some new relevant information comes in[17]. As a result, all long-range plans for the future represented in Visions are fundamentally tentative and should not be particularly detailed[18]. As suggested by the EA uncertainty principle (see Figure 5.6), all the attempts to develop detailed plans for long-term time horizons can be considered as impractical or even unachievable[19]. For instance, there are no practical reasons for investing significant efforts in describing the desired long-term Target States in great detail when even slight shifts in the business environment might instantly invalidate these plans and render them obsolete[20]. Even if based on the essential requirements of the desired operating model (see Figure 5.3), which are more stable than any particular business strategy and normally not expected to change in the future, any long-term future plans still can be only very abstract in nature.

At the same time, the commonly used representation formats of Business Capability Models and Roadmaps (shown in Figure 11.1 and Figure 11.2 respectively) naturally do not imply any detailed future planning unsuitable for Visions. Although both of these formats may have different levels of granularity, the corresponding Visions usually can be modified in a timely manner according to the ongoing changes in the business environment. For instance, in the case of considerable changes in the external environment business capabilities in Business Capability Models might be relatively quickly re-heatmapped, while IT initiatives in Roadmaps might be relatively quickly reprioritized, added or removed accordingly. Due to these qualities, Business Capability Models and Roadmaps are often found to be very convenient instruments for a tentative long-range IT planning.

Generally, Visions are represented as very high-level diagrams, oftentimes even as one-page diagrams. On the one hand, this format allows discussing and achieving agreements on conceptual IT-related planning decisions with a profound long-term impact. On the other hand, this format does not imply any detailed planning, focuses only on the most essential aspects and can be changed reasonably quickly if necessary. However, different Visions have different levels of granularity and are often developed or updated in a loose logical sequence from more abstract ones to more detailed ones. For instance, Business Capability Models might be considered as the most abstract Visions suggesting only which business capabilities should be uplifted with IT in the future. They are typically heatmapped as the first logical step of the long-term IT planning to understand where improvements are required. Target States might be considered as next more detailed Visions. When they are used, they are typically created as the second logical step (i.e. after the required business capabilities are identified) to describe how approximately these capabilities will be improved. Finally, Roadmaps might be considered as the most detailed Visions suggesting what specific IT initiatives need to be implemented and when they should be implemented to achieve the desired Target States (if they are explicitly defined) and uplift the required business capabilities. Visions usually do not imply any more detailed planning than merely specifying the list of required IT initiatives, while more specific details of these initiatives are elaborated later on a closer time horizon in Outlines and then in Designs.

Chapter Summary

This chapter discussed Visions as a general type of EA artifacts from the perspective of their informational contents, development, usage, purpose and benefits and then described in more detail popular narrow subtypes of Visions including Business Capability Models, Roadmaps, Target States, Value Chains and Context Diagrams. The key message of this chapter can be summarized into the following essential points:

- Visions provide high-level conceptual descriptions of an organization from the business perspective representing shared views of the company and its future agreed by business and IT
- Visions are permanent decisions EA artifacts that are developed once collaboratively by business executives and architects, continuously updated according to the ongoing changes in strategic business priorities and used to guide IT investments, identify, prioritize and launch new IT initiatives
- Visions help achieve the alignment between IT investments and long-term business outcomes eventually leading to improved strategic effectiveness of IT investments
- Business Capability Models are essential Visions providing structured graphical representations of all organizational business capabilities and helping business executives and architects focus future IT investments on the most critical business areas
- Roadmaps are essential Visions providing structured graphical views of planned IT initiatives in specific business areas and helping business leaders and architects prioritize corresponding IT investments according to their perceived business importance
- Target States are common Visions providing high-level graphical descriptions of the desired long-term future state of an organization and helping business executives and architects explicitly define where their company is going in the long run
- Value Chains are uncommon Visions providing structured graphical representations of the added value chain of an organization and helping business

executives and architects focus future IT investments on the most strategic business activities

- Context Diagrams are uncommon Visions providing high-level graphical descriptions of the current operational flows of an organization and helping business leaders and architects identify best opportunities for improving their business with IT

Chapter 12: Landscapes

The previous chapter focused on Visions as the third general type of EA artifacts defined by the CSVLOD model of enterprise architecture. This chapter discusses in great detail various aspects of Landscapes as the next general type of EA artifacts (IT-focused structures) as well as their more specific subtypes often used in EA practices. In particular, this chapter starts from describing the common properties of all Landscapes including their type-specific informational contents, development and usage scenarios, role in an EA practice and associated organizational benefits. Then, this chapter discusses in detail popular narrow subtypes of Landscapes including Landscape Diagrams, Inventories, Enterprise System Portfolios and IT Roadmaps. Finally, this chapter provides additional concerns and recommendations regarding the practical use of Landscapes as part of an EA practice.

Landscapes as a General Type of Enterprise Architecture Artifacts

Landscapes are IT-focused structures EA artifacts (see Figure 8.1). They provide high-level IT-specific descriptions of the organizational IT landscape useful for architects and share the essential common properties of both IT-focused EA artifacts and structures EA artifacts. Specific examples of EA artifacts related to Landscapes include Landscape Diagrams, Inventories, Enterprise System Portfolios, IT Roadmaps and some other similar, but less popular EA artifacts (see Figure 8.2).

Informational Contents

Landscapes provide high-level technical descriptions of the organizational IT landscape. Essentially, Landscapes describe what IT assets exist in an organization, how they are related to each other and how they are used. The IT-oriented descriptions provided by Landscapes address the following and similar technical questions:

- What IT systems, databases and infrastructure are available in an organization?
- How are existing IT assets connected to each other?
- What is the information flow and interaction between different IT assets?
- How are existing IT assets used to support business capabilities and processes?
- Which IT assets are duplicated, unused or redundant?
- Which IT assets are considered as strategic or legacy?
- Which IT assets should be reused or decommissioned in the future?
- What technical improvements of IT assets are required in the future and when?

All these questions reflect purely IT-specific concerns irrelevant and even incomprehensible to most business stakeholders. Even though all IT assets in an organization exist to enable certain business capabilities, business executives may be unaware of which specific IT systems support their business processes or which specific databases store their corporate data. Landscapes essentially reflect strategic IT capabilities and assets of an organization that may have a considerable impact on its business strategy, e.g. enable some business strategies and obstruct the execution of other strategies. However, they are maintained largely by architects alone inside the IT department to facilitate technical decision-making and cannot be considered as dual EA artifacts (see Figure 2.4).

Landscapes are IT-specific in nature and describe mostly common technical EA domains including applications, data, infrastructure and integration (see Figure 2.2). However, Landscapes often cover the business domain as well, for instance, to indicate which business processes or capabilities are supported by specific IT assets. Even if the business domain is described in some Landscapes, these descriptions are usually still technical in nature and often unsuitable for discussions with senior business stakeholders due to their overly strict, formal and detailed representation formats.

Landscapes often focus on the current state of an organization. With the notable exception of IT Roadmaps, which naturally focus on the planned future changes, most Landscapes provide various descriptions of the existing IT landscape and currently available IT assets with only a limited and discreet outlook for the future. In other words, Landscapes are generally more intended to accurately capture the current IT environment, than to speculate on the desired future of this environment. However, all Landscapes regardless of their time focus provide the instruments for understanding, controlling and modifying the organizational IT landscape.

Landscapes are usually expressed in strict formats understandable mostly to IT specialists. Since Landscapes are intended to provide exact and reasonably detailed descriptions of the IT landscape, they can use any representation formats suitable for capturing the "hard" data. Depending on their specific purpose, Landscapes can be pretty abstract or rather detailed, brief or voluminous, formal or largely informal. Unlike stylish and tidy Visions intended for business audience, Landscapes are purely technical in nature and might be very meticulous, thorough and complex. For instance, they can be represented as extensive wiring schemes including all the necessary "gory" details of IT systems required for IT specialists to understand how the IT landscape works. Due to these properties, Landscapes, and especially Landscape Diagrams, are often expressed as complex and dense one-page diagrams with rich technical information using strict and formal modeling notations, often branded ones like ArchiMate or ARIS. Physically, Landscapes can be stored and maintained in a variety of ways via using standard MS Office tools (typically Visio and in some cases Excel), configuration management databases (CMDBs) or specialized software tools for enterprise architecture, as discussed later in Chapter 18 (Instruments for Enterprise Architecture).

Development and Usage

Landscapes represent mostly facts on the current IT landscape and some planning decisions on its future evolution (see Table 2.1). They are developed and maintained as part of the Technology Optimization process (see Figure 6.1) largely by architects alone. However, some Landscapes dealing with desirable future changes in the IT landscape and containing certain planning decisions, most notably IT Roadmaps, are developed collaboratively by architects, senior IT managers and other relevant stakeholders (see Figure 2.6).

Since Landscapes are irrelevant to most business stakeholders, they are created and used inside the architecture function to accumulate the knowledge on the structure of the organizational IT landscape and share this knowledge between architects and other relevant IT stakeholders, permanent employees or temporary contractors, often including IT operations and support teams. For example, they allow both newly hired internal architects and external architects engaged for specific initiatives (e.g. product vendors or delivery partners) to smoothly join the architecture team, transfer relevant knowledge and quickly understand the existing IT environment.

Due to significant initial efforts required to develop comprehensive Landscapes encompassing the entire IT landscape, especially Landscape Diagrams and Inventories, new Landscapes are usually created in a reactive manner when they are necessary for specific practical purposes, but then carefully maintained up-to-date. For example, if a new IT initiative implies substantial changes in a particular area of the IT landscape but the current state of the landscape in this area is not reflected in the existing Landscapes, then new Landscapes are created to initially capture the current state in this area and continually maintained in the future to stay relevant. For this reason, the full set of Landscapes is rarely developed at once, but rather accumulated gradually over time along with other EA-related activities. Organizations typically start their EA practices with very patchy Landscapes, slowly fill the gaps as required and eventually cover the entire IT landscape comprehensively.

Landscapes are used predominantly by architects to rationalize the IT landscape, manage the lifecycle of IT assets and plan new IT initiatives. Firstly, Landscapes are used to rationalize the overall structure the organizational IT landscape. They show architects all the existing IT assets and help understand which IT systems are duplicated, unused or redundant. They also show architects the connections and dependencies between different IT systems and help understand which parts of the IT landscape are overly complex, messy or problematic. This understanding provides the basis for producing specific technical rationalization suggestions intended to optimize the IT landscape (see Figure 6.1), which are often implemented later either opportunistically as part of regular IT initiatives (i.e. fundamental, strategic, local or urgent initiatives), or more rarely as separate architectural initiatives (see Table 7.1).

Secondly, Landscapes are used to manage the lifecycle of the available IT assets. They show architects the lifecycle phases of different IT systems, applications or platforms and help understand which of these IT assets should be retained, removed or considered as strategic in the future. The use of Landscapes allows identifying "healthy" IT assets that can be safely reused in new IT systems as well as legacy assets that should be decommissioned, rather than reused. Landscapes also help architects identify IT systems based on obsolete technologies or unsupported by their vendors and retire these systems in a planned and timely manner without creating significant disturbance for daily business operations. This understanding of the status of different IT assets also provides the basis for producing technical rationalization suggestions intended to optimize the organizational IT landscape and improve its overall fitness.

Thirdly, Landscapes are used to plan Outlines and Designs for new IT initiatives. They show architects the general structure of the surrounding IT environment and help understand how exactly new IT solutions should be integrated with the existing IT systems. Specifically, during the development of Outlines and Designs of new IT solutions Landscapes provide the information on what other systems these solutions can interact with, where the required input data can be taken from, where the resulting output data can be sent to, where the new solutions can be deployed and other similar technical questions. From this perspective, the role of Landscapes during the planning of new IT initiatives is complementary to the role of Standards.

While Standards provide prescriptions mostly regarding the internal structure of new IT solutions (i.e. recommended technologies and implementation approaches), Landscapes help fit new solutions into the external environment. In other words, Standards more focus on the "interior" of IT solutions, whereas Landscapes more focus on their "exterior". Additionally, technical rationalization suggestions provided by Landscapes (e.g. to reuse some existing IT assets or decommission some legacy systems) can be also incorporated into the designs of new IT solutions to improve the overall quality of the IT landscape.

Landscapes are permanent EA artifacts (see Table 2.2) living together with the organizational IT landscape and mirroring its evolution. Due to their primary focus on the current state, Landscapes are mostly maintained up-to-date, rather than "developed", by architects after some structural changes occur, e.g. after the implementation and deployment of new IT projects based on their Designs, as discussed later in Chapter 14 (Designs). However, they may be also periodically reviewed in order to reflect the latest considerations and prospects regarding the status of the available IT assets. For example, some existing IT assets can be marked as strategic, redundant or unsupported. Although the chief owners of Landscapes are architects, some Landscapes, especially Inventories, might be also updated by other IT specialists, including IT operations, maintenance and support staff. Landscapes are almost never discarded, unless a considerable part of the IT landscape is decommissioned at once.

Role and Benefits

Landscapes represent a knowledge base of reference materials on the IT landscape. Essentially, a set of Landscapes can be considered as a shared organizational repository of documents describing the overall structure and high-level technical details of the IT landscape. Landscapes enable the accumulation and storage of the technical knowledge on the IT landscape as well as the exchange of this knowledge between architects and other IT specialists. As a common knowledge base for IT stakeholders, Landscapes provide the information on what IT systems, applications, databases and infrastructure exist in an organization, how they are connected and used. Instant access to this information helps architects make better technical planning decisions and find more optimal IT responses to specific business needs.

The general purpose of all Landscapes is to help understand, analyze and modify the structure of the IT landscape. Landscapes serve as a starting point and reference materials for technical decision-making to architects. Instead of exploring the current structure of the IT landscape on an as-necessary basis, architects use Landscapes to get the initial high-level view of the existing IT environment in particular areas of interest. They provide a certain baseline to start planning with instead of starting from scratch every time. Informed by Landscapes, architects are able to make better planning decisions regarding the designs of specific IT initiatives as well as regarding the organization of the entire IT landscape in general.

The proper use of Landscapes enables better understanding, management and optimization of the organizational IT landscape. Main ensuing consequences of using Landscapes include, but are not limited to, the following benefits:

- Increased reuse of IT assets – Landscapes help architects identify suitable IT assets to be reused in new IT initiatives
- Reduced duplication of IT assets – Landscapes help architects identify duplicated or redundant IT assets and eliminate them

- Decreased dependence on legacy IT systems – Landscapes help architects identify fragile legacy IT systems and decommission them in a timely manner
- Improved IT agility – Landscapes provide a baseline of the current IT landscape thereby accelerating the planning of new IT solutions

Difference from the Adjacent Types

Landscapes, as IT-focused structures EA artifacts, are adjacent to Standards, Visions and Designs (see Figure 8.1). Although Standards also provide some high-level technical descriptions of an organization similar to Landscapes, the descriptions offered by Standards are less specific and refer to the IT landscape in general, rather than to particular instances of IT assets. While Standards define broad rules applicable to all IT assets of a certain type, Landscapes distinguish specific tangible instances of these assets and describe their connections to each other. Unlike Standards, Landscapes provide snapshots of the organizational IT landscape and explain the logical relationship between different servers, platforms, databases, applications, processes and capabilities.

Although Visions also describe the high-level structure of an organization similar to Landscapes, the descriptions provided by Visions are very conceptual, speculative and future-focused. While Visions are intended to support the communication between architects and senior business stakeholders regarding the desired future direction of an organization, Landscapes are mostly intended to document its actual current state from the purely technical perspective. Landscapes are largely useless for business-related discussions, but provide very important instruments for facilitating the IT planning and optimization inside the IT department useful to architects and other senior IT stakeholders, including the CIO.

Although Designs also provide some technical descriptions of specific IT instances similar to Landscapes, the descriptions offered by Designs are more granular, narrow and actionable. While Designs provide in-depth descriptions of separate IT projects with their low-level implementation-specific details actionable for project teams, Landscapes provide higher-level descriptions of the entire organizational IT landscape or its major parts, e.g. separate business units or areas. In other words, Designs focus on describing a single IT system in great detail, while Landscapes focus on describing a cohesive set of multiple systems and connections between them. Landscapes provide only the general technical context and environment for new IT systems, but do not offer enough implementation-level details required by project teams to deliver any new system.

Specific Enterprise Architecture Artifacts Related to Landscapes

Articulate subtypes of Landscapes often used in established EA practices include Landscape Diagrams, Inventories, Enterprise System Portfolios and IT Roadmaps. Landscape Diagrams can be considered as essential EA artifacts, while Inventories, Enterprise System Portfolios and IT Roadmaps as common EA artifacts.

Landscape Diagrams (Essential)

Landscape Diagrams (can be called simply an architectural repository or used under very diverse titles including relational diagrams, system interaction diagrams, one-page diagrams, platform architectures, enterprise system models, integration contexts, etc.) are specific

Landscapes providing technical "boxes and arrows" schemes of different scopes and granularities describing the organizational IT landscape. Landscape Diagrams can be considered as an essential subtype of Landscapes found in the majority of successful EA practices.

Landscape Diagrams represent snapshots of different parts of the organizational IT landscape. Essentially, Landscape Diagrams show what IT assets support different business areas and how these assets are related to each other. They focus mostly on describing connections and interactions between different IT assets. Due to the reasons explained later in this chapter, Landscape Diagrams often describe only the current structure of the IT landscape. However, in some cases they may also show the planned future structure as well. For instance, Landscape Diagrams may describe desirable structural optimizations of a technical nature or show new IT systems planned for implementation as part of specific IT initiatives already approved by business executives.

Landscape Diagrams can be very diverse in nature. Firstly, Landscape Diagrams can provide different levels of granularity in their descriptions. The granularity of Landscape Diagrams can vary from focusing only on the most critical information systems to describing all existing IT systems, even the minor and inessential ones. Secondly, Landscape Diagrams can describe different scopes of the organizational IT landscape. The scope of Landscape Diagrams can vary from pretty narrow parts of the IT landscape supporting separate business capabilities to very broad landscape areas enabling the operations of entire lines of business. In small organizations they can even provide a high-level one-page view of the entire IT landscape. Thirdly, Landscape Diagrams can describe any EA domains as well as all possible combinations of these domains, e.g. business, applications, data, integration, infrastructure and security (see Figure 2.2). Although in some cases they may focus on a single EA domain, more often they describe a mix of multiple domains, combine objects from different logical layers and explain the relationship between these layers. For example, they can depict the relationship between specific business processes, underlying applications and databases in a particular business area. Fourthly, Landscape Diagrams can use any appropriate elements from different EA domains in their descriptions. These elements may include customers, business processes, roles, services, applications, communication interfaces, databases, data types, integration platforms, physical and virtual servers, network equipment, interaction protocols and any other relevant elements important for understanding the structure and workflow of the organizational IT landscape.

Landscape Diagrams are typically formal and IT-specific in nature. They can use sophisticated modeling languages or notations incomprehensible to most business stakeholders, e.g. ArchiMate or less often ARIS. Landscape Diagrams can be maintained either as a set of multiple simple MS Visio drawings, or as a comprehensive graph of interconnected entities stored in specialized tool-based EA repositories or less often in configuration management databases. The schematic graphical representation of Landscape Diagrams is shown in Figure 12.1.

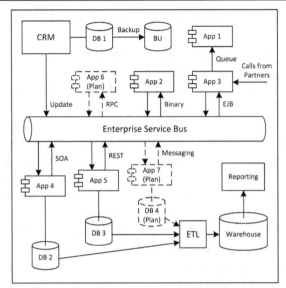

Figure 12.1. Landscape Diagrams

Landscapes Diagrams are created primarily by architects for other architects. They are initially developed with an intention to document a particular area of the IT landscape when it is necessary for planning purposes and then maintained up-to-date to accurately reflect the ongoing landscape evolution. Landscapes Diagrams help architects identify and eliminate redundant IT assets, simplify the overall structure of the IT landscape and integrate new IT systems into the existing IT environment. For instance, during the development of new Outlines and Designs they show architects what applications are impacted, which interfaces are modified and where necessary master data sources are located.

Inventories (Common)

Inventories (can be also called asset registers, architectural repositories or split into separate domain-specific inventories, e.g. application inventories and infrastructure inventories) are specific Landscapes providing structured catalogs of currently available IT assets describing their essential properties and features. Inventories can be considered as a common subtype of Landscapes often found in successful EA practices.

Inventories represent comprehensive directories of organizational IT assets with their detailed descriptions. Essentially, they list all IT assets owned and maintained by an organization and describe their key attributes. Unlike Landscape Diagrams, which focus on explaining the connections between different IT assets, Inventories predominantly focus on describing the main properties of individual assets.

All IT assets in Inventories are often organized into consistent logically related groups of assets, e.g. into applications, systems and databases. In some cases, separate Inventories can be established for different classes of IT assets, e.g. system Inventory and infrastructure Inventory. Regardless of their specific structure, Inventories list available IT assets and describe the core properties of these assets from the perspective of their usage in an organization. The properties described in Inventories for each IT asset may include, among others, the following common attributes:

- Purpose – the general purpose of the IT asset from the business perspective
- Technology – the full technology stack of the IT asset and its components
- Owners – business and IT owners responsible for maintaining the IT asset
- Lifetime – the lifetime of the IT asset in an organization since its introduction
- Cost – the estimated annual maintenance cost of the IT asset, e.g. license fees, hardware costs and the number of full-time IT staff required to support it
- Fitness – the fitness of the IT asset for its current and future business purpose
- Problems – identified problems and potential risks associated with the IT asset

Different types of IT assets in Inventories can have their own, type-specific properties[1]. Moreover, all IT assets in Inventories can be also tagged and color-coded, or have respective regular attributes, to indicate their overall "health" and status in the IT landscape. In particular, IT assets are often classified from the perspective of their lifecycle phases and suitability for future reuse into different groups including, but not limited to, the following categories:

- Reuse – "healthy" IT assets that are currently in use, will be maintained in the future and can be safely reused in new IT solutions
- Invest – strategic IT assets that are currently in use, will be further enhanced in the future and reuse of these assets in new IT solutions is highly encouraged
- Maintain – "toxic" IT assets that are currently in use, will still be maintained in the future, but reuse of these assets in new IT solutions is highly discouraged
- Decommission – legacy or problematic IT assets that are currently in use, but will be decommissioned in the near future and should not be reused in new IT solutions

Similarly to Technology Reference Models (see Figure 10.1), Inventories also provide a good example of EA artifacts blending the properties of both decisions and facts (see Table 2.1). On the one hand, as facts EA artifacts they accurately capture the list and properties of the existing IT assets and can be easily updated by individual architects if new assets are identified. On the other hand, as decisions EA artifacts they suggest which IT assets should be reused in the future and the corresponding decisions to consider particular assets as strategic or legacy can be made only collectively by all relevant stakeholders and asset owners.

Inventories are the only EA artifacts that are typically represented in a tabular form. They can be maintained either as ordinary MS Excel spreadsheets, or as lists of entities with properties and attributes stored in configuration management databases, tool-based EA repositories or any other "handmade" searchable registers. The schematic graphical representation of Inventories is shown in Figure 12.2.

Asset	Purpose	Owners	Cost	Problems
Application 1	....	....	....	....
Application 2	....	....	....	....
Application 3	....	....	....	....
Application 4	....	....	....	....
System 1	....	....	....	....
System 2	....	....	....	....
System 3	....	....	....	....
System 4	....	....	....	....
System 5	....	....	....	....
Database 1	....	....	....	....
Database 2	....	....	....	....
Database 3	....	....	....	....
Database 4	....	....	....	....

Decommission	Reuse	Invest

Figure 12.2. Inventories

Inventories are typically initially filled when it is necessary to document a particular area of the IT landscape and then maintained up-to-date to reflect the actual current state of the landscape. Inventories are often created and owned solely by architects. However, they may be also populated, maintained and used by IT operations and support teams responsible for running existing IT systems in a business-as-usual (BAU) mode, especially if Inventories are based on configuration management databases.

Inventories help architects review the available IT assets, analyze their status and manage their lifecycle. They allow reusing appropriate IT assets in new IT solutions and decommissioning legacy or problematic assets in a timely manner. Furthermore, Inventories also help synchronize the changes to specific IT assets and plan the temporal sequencing of all IT initiatives. For instance, during the planning of Roadmaps (see Figure 11.2) and IT Roadmaps architects can mark the IT assets affected by the corresponding IT initiatives with their estimated start and completion dates in order to ensure that two different initiatives do not attempt to modify same assets at the same time.

Enterprise System Portfolios (Common)

Enterprise System Portfolios (can be called application portfolios, application models, IT system value maps, IT strategy maps, etc.) are specific Landscapes providing structured high-level mappings of all essential IT systems to relevant business capabilities. Enterprise System Portfolios can be considered as a common subtype of Landscapes often found in successful EA practices.

Enterprise System Portfolios represent comprehensive 10,000-feet abstract views of the entire organizational IT landscape. They map all core IT systems and applications used in an organization to specific business capabilities they support. Enterprise System Portfolios structure and describe the information systems portfolio of the whole organization and present its full IT landscape in an extremely condensed form. Essentially, they can be considered as a "landscape on a page".

Enterprise System Portfolios explain connections between business capabilities and the key information systems enabling these capabilities. Hence, they naturally describe both the business and application domains and provide a high-level mapping between them. Unlike Landscape Diagrams, which usually depict specific parts of the IT landscape in a more or less detailed manner, Enterprise System Portfolios focus only on the most significant information systems and applications critical from the organization-wide perspective. Enterprise System Portfolios primarily show the currently running IT systems, but in some cases they may also outline planned systems that should be introduced in the foreseeable future.

Enterprise System Portfolios are somewhat similar to Technology Reference Models (see Figure 10.1). While Technology Reference Models provide the mapping between technical functions and underlying technologies, Enterprise System Portfolios provide the mapping between business capabilities and underlying IT systems. However, the technologies described in Technology Reference Models are potentially relevant to all systems in an organization, while Enterprise System Portfolios describe specific instances of IT systems.

Since Enterprise System Portfolios deal with business capabilities, they typically highly resemble corresponding Business Capability Models (see Figure 11.1) and often accurately mirror their structure. However, in rare cases when Value Chains (see Figure 11.4) are used for guiding IT investments instead of Business Capability Models, Enterprise System Portfolios can be structured as Value Chains as well and map information systems to the value-adding business activities they support.

While Business Capability Models focus solely on business capabilities and color-code them according to their perceived strategic importance, Enterprise System Portfolios are more focused on underpinning IT systems and color-code them according to their general status in the IT landscape. In particular, IT systems can be classified from the perspective of their strategic adequacy and lifecycle phases into different groups including, but not limited to, the following categories:

- Active – IT systems that are actively used, adequately fit for current purpose and will be maintained in the future
- Strategic – IT systems that are actively used, adequately fit for strategic business needs and will be further expanded in the future
- Legacy – IT systems at their "sunset" that are actively used, but unfit for purpose and need to be replaced with more adequate systems in the future
- Inactive – IT systems that are currently deployed, but not actively used and can be safely decommissioned in the future

Like Technology Reference Models and Inventories, Enterprise System Portfolios also combine the evident distinct features of both decisions and facts EA artifacts (see Table 2.1). On the one hand, as facts EA artifacts they merely depict which information systems currently support different business capabilities and can be easily updated by individual architects. On the other hand, as decisions EA artifacts they indicate which of these IT systems should be invested in, reused or retired in the future, which always requires collective decision-making and approval.

Similarly to Business Capability Models, Enterprise System Portfolios are fundamentally one-page EA artifacts, though they may also include some additional more detailed supporting information as well. They can be either maintained as plain MS Visio drawings, or less often generated in a semi-automatic manner by specialized software tools based on the architectural information stored in underlying EA repositories. The schematic graphical representation of Enterprise System Portfolios is shown in Figure 12.3.

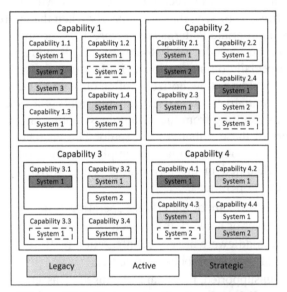

Figure 12.3. Enterprise System Portfolios

Enterprise System Portfolios are developed and then maintained by architects to be used for strategic technical decision-making within the architecture function. Specifically, Enterprise System Portfolios help architects identify duplicated, redundant, misused and inadequate IT systems, recognize the legacy systems nearing the end of support and creating risks for the business, control the lifecycle and transition of core applications, assess the overall "health" and strategic fitness of the organizational information systems portfolio and plan corrective actions if necessary. They can also inform the development of complex Roadmaps (see Figure 11.2) via showing current and suggesting future IT systems for particular business capabilities. However, Enterprise System Portfolios might be too abstract for detailed planning of new IT solutions.

IT Roadmaps (Common)

IT Roadmaps (can be called technology roadmaps, platform roadmaps, infrastructure roadmaps, integration roadmaps, etc.) are specific Landscapes providing structured graphical views of all planned IT initiatives of a purely technical nature having no visible business impact. IT Roadmaps can be considered as a common subtype of Landscapes often found in successful EA practices.

IT Roadmaps are conceptually similar or even identical IT-oriented counterparts of regular business-focused Roadmaps (see Figure 11.2). Analogously to Roadmaps, IT Roadmaps show planned IT initiatives with their approximate start dates and completion timelines as well as the current point in time indicating which initiatives are active right now. However, these IT initiatives reflect "internal", purely IT-specific efforts intended primarily to improve the technical quality of the IT landscape without delivering any new business functionality or evident business benefits. Put it roughly, initiatives in business-focused Roadmaps intend to generate some business value, while initiatives in IT Roadmaps intend to enhance intrinsic IT efficiency and reduce IT-related risks. For example, IT Roadmaps may indicate when specific technologies marked as emerging or unsupported in Technology Reference Models (see Figure 10.1) will be actually introduced or retired. Similarly, they may specify when the entire IT landscape should be switched to newer, more appropriate Patterns (see Figure 10.3) or updated versions of Guidelines (see Figure 10.2). Unlike business-focused Roadmaps, IT Roadmaps focus predominantly on technical EA domains, especially on integration and infrastructure (see Figure 2.2). Additionally, they are usually planned for shorter time horizons, often only up to 1-2 years ahead in the future.

Essentially, all IT initiatives in IT Roadmaps represent specific planned technical rationalization suggestions resulting from the Technology Optimization process (see Figure 6.1). The primary stakeholders of these initiatives are senior IT managers, often including the CIO, rather than business leaders. These initiatives imply certain IT-specific optimizations and housekeeping activities scheduled in the foreseeable future which may include, among many others, the following types of operations:

- Upgrade end-user software or underlying operating systems to newer versions
- Replace aging server or network infrastructure with newer equivalents
- Introduce a new middleware or service integration platform
- Relocate active IT systems to better datacenters
- Decommission unsupported, redundant or unused IT assets
- Consolidate IT systems providing similar business functionality
- Streamline overly complex areas of the organizational IT landscape
- Apply software patches to close potential security breaches

These and other possible technical rationalization suggestions planned in IT Roadmaps can be either aligned to and implemented as part of regular business initiatives (i.e. fundamental, strategic, local or urgent initiatives), or launched independently as separate architectural initiatives (see Table 7.1). Unlike planned IT initiatives in business-focused Roadmaps having direct business value and sponsors among business executives, many initiatives in IT Roadmaps, though may lead to potential cost savings, often have no reasonable business cases and cannot attract any significant interest of senior business stakeholders. Due to their irrelevance to business leaders, most initiatives in IT Roadmaps have to be sponsored by other stakeholders and funded from other sources. Firstly and most preferably, many initiatives in IT Roadmaps can be implemented opportunistically as part of regular business initiatives and in this case may not require considerable extra funding. Secondly, initiatives in IT Roadmaps may be launched as separate architectural initiatives sponsored directly by the CIO, who often controls a small pool of funding, or even a separate budget, intended specifically for internal optimizations and routine housekeeping activities irrelevant to business executives. Thirdly, some initiatives in IT Roadmaps might still be "sold" to and then sponsored by senior business stakeholders who understand the importance of these initiatives for an organization despite their lack of a clear business value and positive business cases. Unsurprisingly, initiatives in IT Roadmaps typically represent only a small fraction of all organizational IT investments and require much less funding compared to business-focused Roadmaps.

Initiatives in IT Roadmaps are often color-coded to indicate their sponsorship status and funding needs. For instance, IT Roadmaps can distinguish IT initiatives with different sponsorship status including, but not limited to, the following categories:

- CIO – IT initiatives agreed, sponsored and funded by the CIO
- Business – IT initiatives sponsored and funded by business stakeholders understanding their importance
- Not Sponsored – IT initiatives which require separate funding, but sponsors are missing
- Not Required – IT initiatives for which sponsorship and separate funding is not required

Separate IT Roadmaps are more often used in large organizations with a considerable number of planned IT initiatives to clearly distinguish business-value-adding IT investments from purely technical investments required just to "keep the lights on". In small organizations housekeeping IT initiatives are often placed in business-focused Roadmaps along with regular business initiatives, but color-coded to indicate their inherent technical nature and stand out from all other initiatives.

Unlike all other Landscapes, which are mostly facts EA artifacts focused primarily on describing the current state of the organizational IT landscape, IT Roadmaps are decisions EA artifacts representing the future plans regarding the landscape rationalization developed based on the consensus agreement of all relevant IT stakeholders (see Table 2.1). However, like all Landscapes, IT Roadmaps are also intended to help architects modify the IT landscape, optimize its overall structure and manage the lifecycle of IT assets.

While business-focused Roadmaps are usually aligned to business capabilities, IT Roadmaps are typically aligned to technology-specific areas or domains. Similarly to business-focused Roadmaps, IT Roadmaps are often one-page EA artifacts, though they may also include some additional more detailed supporting information regarding the planned IT initiatives. Most often they are maintained as simple MS Visio drawings. The schematic graphical representation of IT Roadmaps is shown in Figure 12.4.

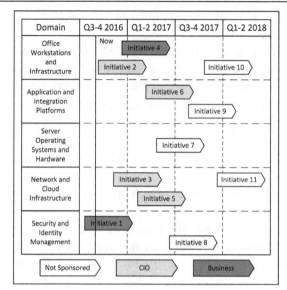

Figure 12.4. IT Roadmaps

Similarly to all other Landscapes, IT Roadmaps are used by architects as reference materials for planning the changes and technical improvements in the organizational IT landscape. Essentially, IT Roadmaps help architects eliminate the anticipated technical problems and bottlenecks in a proactive manner and schedule the planned maintenance of the IT landscape. IT Roadmaps also help discuss housekeeping IT initiatives with relevant IT stakeholders and align these initiatives to the timelines of planned regular business initiatives.

Less Popular Enterprise Architecture Artifacts Related to Landscapes

Besides Landscape Diagrams, Inventories, Enterprise System Portfolios and IT Roadmaps described above, some other noteworthy subtypes of Landscapes are occasionally found in organizations practicing enterprise architecture. Firstly, some organizations actively use EA artifacts which might be considered as **domain-specific landscape diagrams**. These EA artifacts provide in-depth technical descriptions of different parts of the organizational IT landscape from the perspective of specific EA domains. Domain-specific landscape diagrams are conceptually similar to regular Landscape Diagrams, but focus specifically on describing a single EA domain in greater detail, e.g. only applications, only data or only infrastructure (see Figure 2.2). For example, **application interaction diagrams** may describe the interaction between all applications running in an organization and explain how exactly these applications "talk" to each other. Likewise, **master data maps** may provide a detailed view of all master data sources and their accurate replicas existing in an organization for different types of data and explain where specific information can be found and how it can be retrieved. Analogously to regular Landscape Diagrams, domain-specific landscape diagrams help architects understand the current structure of the IT landscape, identify inefficiencies, complexities and deficiencies of the existing structure and plan new IT initiatives.

Secondly, some organizations actively use **asset roadmaps**. Asset roadmaps provide a detailed view of the existing IT assets from the perspective of their lifecycles. These EA artifacts show available IT assets and explain when each of these assets will be supported, upgraded, decommissioned or replaced. On the one hand, asset roadmaps are similar to Inventories. Like Inventories, they offer a rather fine-grained view of the IT landscape and describe separate IT assets (e.g. applications, systems and hardware equipment), but focus specifically on the lifecycle of these assets. While Inventories list available IT assets, describe their properties and indicate their current status or lifecycle phases, asset roadmaps are more future-oriented and specify approximate planned timelines of the major milestones in their lifecycles. On the other hand, asset roadmaps also resemble regular IT Roadmaps. However, they are more granular and distinguish specific IT assets, rather than focusing on the IT landscape in general. Unlike IT Roadmaps, which align to broad technical areas or domains, asset roadmaps are inseparably linked to corresponding IT assets. From this perspective, these EA artifacts might be considered as a mixture of Inventories and IT Roadmaps. The key purpose of asset roadmaps is providing a specialized precise instrument for controlling the lifecycle of IT assets. They are maintained and used by architects to discuss what should happen with particular IT assets and when, decide how the IT landscape should evolve, understand which assets can be reused in the future and plan the timelines of new IT initiatives. Asset roadmaps inform the decision-making inside the IT department and facilitate communication between architects, senior IT managers, asset owners and external vendors, but are largely irrelevant to senior business stakeholders due to their overly detailed and technical nature.

Thirdly, some organizations use EA artifacts which might be considered as **IT target states**. These EA artifacts provide high-level views of the desired long-term future state of an organization from the technical perspective. IT target states are conceptually similar to business-focused Target States (see Figure 11.3), but primarily focus on various technical aspects of the organizational IT landscape. Specifically, they often describe only business-supporting EA domains, e.g. integration, infrastructure and security (see Figure 2.2). While Target States are developed collaboratively by architects and business executives, IT target states are largely irrelevant to business leaders and developed collaboratively by architects and other senior IT stakeholders, including the CIO. They allow all relevant IT stakeholders to plan the desired future evolution of the entire IT landscape and produce specific technical rationalization suggestions for new IT initiatives (see Figure 6.1). Like all Landscapes, IT target states help understand and rationalize the high-level structure of the IT landscape, optimize and consolidate the portfolio of available IT assets. However, due to the reasons explained later in this chapter, they should be developed with a great caution.

Fourthly, some organizations use EA artifacts which might be considered as **enterprise data portfolios**. These EA artifacts provide structured high-level mappings of all essential data entities to relevant business capabilities. Enterprise data portfolios are conceptually similar to Enterprise System Portfolios, but focus primarily on data types instead of IT systems. They offer a convenient one-page view of the organizational IT landscape from the data perspective. In particular, enterprise data portfolios explain what data is possessed by an organization and where this data can be found. For instance, they often show which key data types are owned and mastered by different business capabilities. From this perspective, enterprise data portfolios might be considered as very high-level master data maps. Analogously to Enterprise System Portfolios, enterprise data portfolios are maintained and used by architects to understand the overall structure of the existing IT landscape, manage its data assets, identify its potential problems and plan its future evolution according to strategic business needs.

Fifthly, some organizations use EA artifacts which might be considered as **IT capability models**. These EA artifacts provide structured graphical representations of all organizational IT capabilities, their relationship and hierarchy. IT capability models are conceptually similar to business-focused Business Capability Models (see Figure 11.1). While Business Capability Models describe what an organization can do from the business perspective, IT capability models describe what an organization can do from the IT perspective. IT capability models usually focus on different technical EA domains, e.g. applications, data or infrastructure (see Figure 2.2), and explain what application, data or infrastructure capabilities exist in an organization. Essentially, they provide highly abstracted descriptions of the organizational IT landscape from the perspective of its technical capacity. IT capability models are used primarily by architects to understand the current capabilities of the existing IT landscape, assess the overall strategic fitness of the available IT assets, identify and "heatmap" potential problems or capability gaps and then plan specific measures to improve the relevancy of the landscape to the required business capabilities highlighted in Business Capability Models.

Sixthly, some organizations use EA artifacts which might be considered as **extended inventories**. These EA artifacts provide catalogs of the existing groups of related IT assets with their comprehensive descriptions. Extended inventories are conceptually similar to regular Inventories, but have two important differences. On the one hand, unlike Inventories, which focus on describing separate IT assets (e.g. applications, databases, servers and other equipment), extended inventories describe consistent groups of multiple logically related assets. For instance, they may describe the clusters of all interrelated IT assets providing a specific service or fulfilling a particular function. On the other hand, extended inventories provide more comprehensive information regarding these clusters of IT assets. For example, in addition to the typical properties described in regular Inventories (e.g. definition, purpose, owners, maintenance cost, etc.), extended inventories may also provide the following descriptions for each cluster of IT assets:

- Detailed textual descriptions explaining how the whole cluster works
- Short-term or long-term development strategy for the entire cluster
- Graphical descriptions explaining the current high-level structure of the cluster
- Graphical descriptions showing the planned future state of the cluster

From this perspective, extended inventories might be considered as a mix of regular Inventories and Landscape Diagrams. Extended inventories are created and maintained by architects to capture the current state of the IT landscape and plan its future rationalization. As a shared knowledge base of reference materials, these EA artifacts help architects understand the structure of the IT landscape and control the overall portfolio of IT assets.

Additionally, architecture debt registers used in many organizations to track and manage existing architecture debts can be loosely related to Landscapes as well, as discussed later in Chapter 18 (Instruments for Enterprise Architecture).

Additional Concerns Regarding Landscapes

The practical use of Landscapes is associated mainly with two significant threats. The first considerable threat associated with Landscapes is arguably the attempts to use Landscapes for describing desired long-term future states or, more broadly, for a full-fledged strategic IT planning in general. The inappropriateness of Landscapes for strategic planning is not accidental and rooted in the typical structure of organizational decision-making processes and governance arrangements. Specifically, in most organizations business executives define the long-term future direction for an organization and control the budget, while IT executives largely respond to the predefined business direction within the allocated IT budget. In this situation all general IT-related future plans, as well as specific ensuing IT investments, are normally supported, approved and sponsored by business leaders, who need to clearly understand how exactly these plans and investments contribute to their business strategy. However, due to their inherent technical and IT-centric nature, Landscapes can hardly be used for discussions with senior business stakeholders. For this reason, any future states described in Landscapes usually cannot be understood, consciously approved and sponsored by business executives to be implemented, whereas IT executives typically do not control a sufficient budget to fund the implementation of large-scale initiatives understandable only to IT stakeholders. Unsurprisingly, idealistic global future-state Landscapes created by architects and senior IT stakeholders alone or with insufficient involvement of business leaders, though might be considered as an "easier" way of IT planning, often end up in an "ivory tower" and never get implemented.

Strategic business planning is always proactive in nature, while IT planning is more reactive and responsive to strategic business goals. Most IT-related plans in organizations normally follow their general business plans. For this reason, senior IT stakeholders cannot plan the future of IT independently or ahead of senior business stakeholders. In other words, all significant future plans for IT should be firstly agreed with business executives. In organizations practicing enterprise architecture these agreements are achieved as part of the collaborative development of business-focused EA artifacts (i.e. Considerations, Visions and Outlines) essentially representing communication interfaces between business and IT (see Figure 8.1). Consequently, when Landscapes occasionally describe desired future states, these future states typically either represent relatively minor improvements of a purely technical nature (e.g. possible optimizations and simplifications), or provide IT-centric views of the planning decisions already approved earlier in some other business-focused EA artifacts. For example, only after business executives have specified key business capabilities to be uplifted in the future via using Visions (e.g. Business Capability Models, see Figure 11.1), architects can place new planned information systems required to uplift these capabilities in Enterprise System Portfolios, but not in the opposite order. Similarly, new planned applications or databases can be placed in Landscape Diagrams only after their implementation has been explicitly approved by business leaders based on their Outlines, but not in the opposite order. Even though strategic planning generally cannot start from Landscapes, they can still reflect specific future plans earlier approved by business leaders elsewhere, in rare cases future plans for 2-3 years ahead. All significant future plans described in Landscapes should be based on the previously agreed plans reflected in business-focused EA artifacts, otherwise they might be never executed.

For the reasons explained above, Landscapes represent primarily the instruments for capturing knowledge, rather than the means of strategic IT planning. With the notable exception of IT Roadmaps, they focus mostly on describing the current state of the IT landscape, rather than its desirable future. Even if Landscapes provide some limited descriptions of the desired future state, these descriptions are usually derived from other planning decisions approved earlier, often as part of Visions or Outlines. The difference between business-focused future-oriented Visions and IT-focused present-oriented Landscapes is rather fundamental and naturally reflects the leading role of business stakeholders in strategic decision-making processes of most organizations. On the contrary, all the attempts to develop future-state Landscapes ahead of Visions essentially represent the attempts of IT to lead business and can be considered as risky and dangerous. Put it simply, IT-specific target states either should not be developed at all, or at least should be developed with a great caution.

The second considerable threat associated with Landscapes is arguably the attempts to maintain excessively detailed and find-grained Landscapes, especially Landscape Diagrams and Inventories. Even though the current state, unlike the future state, is not a subject of uncertainty, accurately describing the current state of the IT landscape in detail and then maintaining these descriptions up-to-date is still not an easy task. On the one hand, the development of highly detailed Landscapes is a tedious and very time-consuming process. Taking into account that documenting the current structure of the IT landscape is not a particularly productive and value-adding activity on its own, architects spending a substantial portion of their time merely describing the existing IT environment instead of doing some "real work" might be considered as futile and lose their credibility in the eyes of senior business and IT stakeholders. On the other hand, the maintenance of highly detailed Landscapes is even more problematic than their initial development and often aggravated by another typical problem. While major changes of the organizational IT landscape are normally accomplished with the involvement of architects and can be easily tracked, minor changes often might be accomplished without their involvement or notification. Consequently, numerous ongoing small changes in the IT landscape can be essentially invisible from the perspective of an architecture function and happen unnoticed. In other words, even when architects can afford to incorporate all the ongoing minor changes into the existing Landscapes, they are often simply unable to keep track of these changes. For this reason excessively detailed Landscapes tend to inevitably become stale. At the same time, when Landscapes are likely to be obsolete, the very trust in the information they provide can be undermined reducing their overall usefulness as a shared knowledge base for architects.

In order to avoid the typical challenges associated with the development and maintenance of Landscapes, their level of abstraction should not be overly detailed. Pragmatic Landscapes should focus primarily on architecturally significant details of the organizational IT landscape which do not change very often and are not expected to change without the involvement of architects. At the same time, more detailed and relevant information on the low-level structure of particular IT systems or narrow areas of the IT landscape, when required, usually can be extracted from their archived Designs, as discussed later in Chapter 14 (Designs), obtained directly from their daily users and the operations teams supporting these systems or even reverse-engineered from their actual source code and hardware configuration. Selection of the appropriate abstraction level for Landscapes helps mitigate the common problems associated with their development, maintain resulting Landscapes up-to-date with reasonable efforts and keep track of all relevant changes.

Generally, higher-level and up-to-date Landscapes are more preferable and useful than more detailed but outdated ones.

Chapter Summary

This chapter discussed Landscapes as a general type of EA artifacts from the perspective of their informational contents, development, usage, purpose and benefits and then described in more detail popular narrow subtypes of Landscapes including Landscape Diagrams, Inventories, Enterprise System Portfolios and IT Roadmaps. The key message of this chapter can be summarized into the following essential points:

- Landscapes provide high-level technical descriptions of the organizational IT landscape representing a knowledge base of detailed reference materials on its overall structure
- Landscapes are permanent facts EA artifacts that are created on an as-necessary basis by individual architects, continuously updated according to the ongoing evolution of the IT landscape and used to rationalize the landscape, manage the lifecycle of IT assets and plan new IT initiatives
- Landscapes help understand, analyze and modify the structure of the IT landscape eventually leading to increased reuse and reduced duplication of IT assets, improved IT agility and decreased dependence on legacy IT systems
- Landscape Diagrams are essential Landscapes providing technical "boxes and arrows" schemes of different scopes and granularities describing the organizational IT landscape and helping architects manage connections between different IT assets
- Inventories are common Landscapes providing structured catalogs of currently available IT assets, describing their essential properties and helping architects keep track of the existing systems constituting the organizational IT landscape
- Enterprise System Portfolios are common Landscapes providing structured high-level mappings of all essential IT systems to relevant business capabilities and helping architects understand potential capabilities and constraints of the current IT landscape
- IT Roadmaps are common Landscapes providing structured graphical views of all planned IT initiatives of a purely technical nature having no visible business impact and helping architects schedule the required improvements of the IT landscape

Chapter 13: Outlines

The previous chapter focused on Landscapes as the fourth general type of EA artifacts defined by the CSVLOD model of enterprise architecture. This chapter discusses in great detail various aspects of Outlines as the next general type of EA artifacts (business-focused changes) as well as their more specific subtypes often used in EA practices. In particular, this chapter starts from describing the common properties of all Outlines including their type-specific informational contents, development and usage scenarios, role in an EA practice and associated organizational benefits. Then, this chapter discusses in detail popular narrow subtypes of Outlines including Solution Overviews, Options Assessments and Initiative Proposals. Finally, this chapter provides additional concerns and recommendations regarding the practical use of Outlines as part of an EA practice.

Outlines as a General Type of Enterprise Architecture Artifacts

Outlines are business-focused changes EA artifacts (see Figure 8.1). They provide business-oriented descriptions of specific IT initiatives developed collaboratively by business and IT stakeholders and share the essential common properties of both business-focused EA artifacts and changes EA artifacts. Specific examples of EA artifacts related to Outlines include Solution Overviews, Options Assessments, Initiative Proposals and some other similar, but less popular EA artifacts (see Figure 8.2)[1].

Informational Contents

Outlines provide high-level descriptions of separate IT initiatives understandable to business leaders. Essentially, Outlines describe what approximately will be implemented as part of a particular IT initiative and what business value is anticipated from its execution. The business-oriented descriptions provided by Outlines address the following and similar initiative-related questions:

- What business need is fulfilled by the proposed IT initiative?
- What solution will be implemented as a result of the proposed IT initiative?
- How will the proposed IT solution change current business processes?
- What is the tactical and strategic value of the proposed IT initiative?
- What is the overall organizational impact of the proposed IT solution?
- What financial investments are required to implement the proposed IT initiative?
- When can the proposed IT initiative be delivered?
- What risks are associated with the proposed IT initiative?

All these questions regarding a specific IT initiative satisfy natural interests of the senior business stakeholders sponsoring this initiative. The decision to start the implementation of an IT initiative cannot be made by IT executives alone, but rather should be approved and signed-off by business executives based on their evaluation of the overall business value, impact, timelines and costs of the initiative. Many proposed IT initiatives might seem desirable at the early idea stage, but eventually be rejected by business leaders because of multiple different reasons. For example, important tactical IT initiatives may be considered as unimportant from the strategic perspective. Excessively long implementation timelines may diminish, or even completely destroy, the business value of IT initiatives. Even if IT initiatives can bring considerable business value, business executives may find them prohibitively costly. The overall impact of IT initiatives on an organization and its business processes may be considered by business executives as undesirable. Even technically feasible and risk-free IT solutions might be considered as too risky from the business perspective. For this reason, all Outlines are dual EA artifacts (see Figure 2.4) of direct interest to both business leaders and architects. They describe the business value of proposed IT solutions as well as their high-level technical structures.

As noted earlier in Chapter 7, IT initiatives can vary in their scope and range from small IT projects to full-fledged change programs consisting of multiple related projects. However, regardless of its size, the decision to implement any specific IT initiative should be taken consciously by business executives based on a careful analysis of the expected outcomes and required investments. Outlines help business leaders make informed decisions regarding proposed IT initiatives and then, if initiatives are approved, provide the initial basis for developing more detailed Designs for these initiatives. Outlines are critical EA artifacts informing the executive decision-making and facilitating the dialog between business executives and architects during the early initiation steps of IT initiatives.

Outlines usually focus on the mid-term future up to 1-2 years ahead, sometimes on longer-term planning horizons in case of large transformation programs. Since all Outlines describe some proposed IT initiatives at different stages of their approval, their focus on the future is inherent and fundamental. However, even the high-level details of specific IT solutions, as well as the corresponding business cases for these solutions, usually cannot be planned with an acceptable precision for a horizon of longer than 2-3 years. For this reason, Outlines generally focus only on the relatively short-term foreseeable future, where the architecture, business value and financial details of specific IT initiatives can be planned and estimated with a reasonable accuracy, while the strategic IT planning for longer time horizons is typically accomplished via more abstract Visions.

Outlines are usually expressed as a mix of textual descriptions and simple diagrams. Since they are intended to provide only high-level descriptions of IT initiatives understandable to "average" business stakeholders, Outlines typically avoid using long descriptions, complex explanations, sophisticated diagrams and technical details. For instance, textual descriptions included in Outlines tend to provide only the most essential information regarding the proposed IT initiatives, their general motivations, goals, benefits and basic requirements. Graphical diagrams included in Outlines also tend to be rather intuitive and describe the proposed IT solutions only at the conceptual level sufficient to understand and assess their overall business impact. Due to their intentional simplicity, Outlines generally avoid using any strict and formal modeling notations intimidating for many business stakeholders. However, some Outlines, especially Solution Overviews, may occasionally benefit from using a simplified version of BPMN understandable to a wide business audience for explaining the anticipated changes in business processes. Physically, Outlines are most often created and presented either as more official MS Word documents, or as less formal MS PowerPoint presentations.

Development and Usage

Outlines represent collective planning decisions (see Table 2.1) on how approximately specific IT initiatives should be implemented. They are developed for all proposed IT initiatives at the initiation step of the Initiative Delivery process (see Figure 6.1) by architects with a significant involvement of relevant senior business stakeholders (see Figure 2.6), e.g. executive sponsors of these initiatives. The participation of business leaders is critical for developing Outlines to discuss the general idea of new IT solutions, define their essential executive-level requirements, delineate their scope and negotiate the overall desirable effect of corresponding IT initiatives on the organizational activities. Specifically, as part of developing Outlines business leaders and architects, among other things, often discuss and reach an agreement on how exactly new IT solutions should modify current business processes (see Table 5.1). For instance, business leaders may specify what process changes are expected from these IT initiatives, while architects may recommend specific high-level IT solutions to realize the requested improvements. In order to achieve better mutual understanding, architects and business stakeholders may employ some sophisticated techniques for clarifying the conceptual structure of desired IT solutions, e.g. formal business process modeling or customer journey mapping for customer-facing initiatives[2]. Outlines usually start their existence from early informal discussions of the general idea of an IT initiative between architects and business leaders, often based on the original business proposal submitted previously by its business owners. Then, Outlines are elaborated with more detail during the ongoing discussions with relevant business stakeholders and get more formalized, substantive and "meaty". Finally, Outlines are completed, reviewed and officially approved by their executive sponsors.

IT initiatives and corresponding Outlines typically focus on addressing specific business needs, or more rarely specific technical needs. Outlines are normally developed for all types of IT initiatives, i.e. for fundamental, strategic, local, urgent and architectural initiatives (see Table 7.1). However, since different types of IT initiatives have different origins (see Figure 7.2), Outlines for these initiatives are also initiated in slightly differently ways. On the one hand, fundamental, strategic and local initiatives and respective business needs are identified in advance, reflected in Visions and typically represented as planned IT initiatives in Roadmaps (see Figure 11.2). For example, the planned business need to enable order tracking for customers can be represented in a Roadmap as a corresponding IT initiative and scheduled for execution in the middle of 2018. Accordingly, in the middle of 2018 or a few months beforehand this planned business need from the Roadmap gets elaborated into a new instance of the Initiative Delivery process (see Figure 6.1) and Outlines are developed as the first step of this process to discuss in more detail how exactly order tracking can be enabled. On the other hand, urgent initiatives and corresponding business needs are unpredictable and not reflected in any Visions. For example, the urgent business need to be able to provide specific compliance reports to a regulatory agency from the beginning of the next financial year can emerge unexpectedly as a result of a recent legislative change. In this case, a new instance of the Initiative Delivery process is launched instantly to address this business need in a timely manner and corresponding Outlines are immediately developed to describe how exactly this need can be addressed. Additionally, architectural initiatives and respective technical needs are usually identified in advance and often represented as planned IT initiatives in IT Roadmaps (see Figure 12.4). For example, the planned technical need to decommission unsupported legacy databases and migrate their records to newer database platforms can be represented in an IT Roadmap as a corresponding IT initiative and scheduled for execution at the end of 2018. Accordingly, closer to the end of 2018 this planned technical need from the IT Roadmap gets elaborated into a new instance of the Initiative Delivery process and Outlines are developed to discuss in more detail how exactly it can be accomplished. However, for architectural initiatives senior IT managers usually act instead of business leaders as their key stakeholders, approvers and sponsors.

During the development of Outlines for an IT initiative architects are guided by technical rationalization suggestions resulting from the Technology Optimization process (see Figure 6.1). In particular, architects refer to Standards to select the most appropriate technologies and implementation approaches for the new IT initiative. Architects also leverage Landscapes to understand how the new IT solution can be integrated with the existing IT systems and which IT assets may be reused or decommissioned as part of the initiative. At the same time, architects and senior business stakeholders collaboratively ensure the alignment of the new IT initiative to the established strategic direction for IT reflected in Considerations and Visions. If the proposed initiative deviates from the approved long-term IT investment strategy, then it should be considered as tactical and justified accordingly with a strong emphasis on the expected short-term benefits. In this case Outlines may include an estimation of the introduced architecture debt and describe the appropriate corrective measures to be taken in the future to eliminate this debt, as discussed later in Chapter 18 (Instruments for Enterprise Architecture).

Outlines are often developed in parallel with **business cases** for proposed IT initiatives. Similarly to Outlines, business cases are usually created at the early stages of IT initiatives to justify the corresponding IT investments. Both Outlines and business cases are often required to approve the implementation of any IT initiative. However, Outlines and business cases are significantly different in their nature and focus on different aspects of IT initiatives. On the one hand, Outlines are IT-specific architectural documents. They provide high-level overviews of proposed IT solutions, explain their business value in qualitative terms and help assess their costs. For instance, Outlines allow architects to estimate necessary license fees, hardware equipment and development efforts, or to send the descriptions of proposed IT solutions to appropriate vendors and get their tentative estimations.

On the other hand, business cases are mostly IT-agnostic business documents. They focus specifically on the financial side of IT initiatives, attempt to estimate their business value more accurately using formal quantitative valuation methods (e.g. discounted cash flow (DCF), net present value (NPV) or internal rate of return (IRR)) and calculate the total return on investments (ROI)[3], though far from all benefits of IT solutions can be easily quantified. Essentially, Outlines are intended to justify IT initiatives from the conceptual perspective, while business cases are intended to justify them from the purely financial point of view. Outlines and business cases are closely related and complementary to each other. For their financial calculations business cases typically use the estimates of time and cost provided by Outlines for proposed IT solutions. At the same time, business cases also inform the decision-making around Outlines and allow comparing possible high-level solution implementation options from the perspective of their alignment to the original business motivation behind these IT initiatives. Due to their natural interrelationship, Outlines and business cases are usually developed together during the initiation steps of all IT initiatives.

After being finalized, Outlines are used by business executives and architects to assess, approve and fund specific IT initiatives. Specifically, Outlines and corresponding business cases for proposed IT initiatives usually undergo a formal approval and sign-off governance procedure involving senior business and IT stakeholders responsible for making IT investment decisions, as discussed later in Chapter 17 (Architecture Functions in Organizations). As part of this procedure Outlines and business cases for IT initiatives are evaluated from different perspectives including, but not limited to, the following essential criteria:

- Tactical and strategic business value of the IT initiative
- Expected financial returns from the IT initiative
- Conceptual alignment of the IT initiative to Considerations and Visions
- Technical alignment of the IT initiative to key Standards and Landscapes
- Timelines, costs and risks associated with the IT initiative

Based on a comprehensive analysis of these and other aspects of proposed IT initiatives, senior business and IT stakeholders make the final investment decision regarding each initiative. As a result, senior decision-makers either approve the IT initiative and allocate the necessary funding to implement it, or reject the initiative as inexpedient and unworthy.

Outlines are temporary EA artifacts (see Table 2.2) with a limited lifetime developed specifically to discuss high-level implementation options for proposed IT initiatives and make informed investment decisions regarding these initiatives. Agreed Outlines provide the basis for developing more detailed Designs during the further implementation steps of IT initiatives. Small and medium IT initiatives are typically delivered as separate IT projects and require only single Designs to be implemented. However, large IT initiatives often imply complex IT solutions consisting of multiple different components. These IT solutions are usually delivered step-by-step as a series of several closely related IT projects and require multiple different Designs for their implementation, i.e. one implementable Design for each project. If the approved IT solutions are developed in-house, then internal architects and project teams are engaged to convert their conceptual Outlines into technical Designs and then start their implementation. Otherwise, Outlines of required IT solutions may be sent to tenders in order to choose best implementation partners, receive official price quotations and sign the delivery contracts.

After Outlines are approved and elaborated into more detailed technical Designs they essentially lose their value as EA artifacts and get archived. However, these Outlines may be retrieved and used later (e.g. a few years after completion of corresponding IT initiatives) together with their business cases for the purposes of post-implementation benefit review. During these reviews architects and senior business sponsors of IT initiatives revisit their original Outlines and business cases and assess to what extent the initially declared benefits have been realized and whether the estimated ROI has been actually achieved. Post-implementation reviews can increase the business value of IT investments and bring a number of other benefits to organizations[4]. Firstly, they can add more realism to future value estimations and improve their accuracy, discourage business sponsors from exaggerating benefits or submitting overstated initiative proposals and increase the general credibility of IT. Secondly, post-implementation reviews can ensure business ownership, commitment and accountability for delivering the claimed benefits, e.g. for changing corresponding business processes to fully leverage the potential capabilities of new IT systems. The business success of any IT initiative cannot be guaranteed by the IT department alone merely via delivering the requested system on time and budget, but also requires senior management involvement and leadership to change the business accordingly[5]. Finally, post-implementation reviews enable organizational learning, help eliminate systematic bias in benefit and cost estimations and eventually increase the overall management satisfaction with IT.

Role and Benefits

Outlines essentially represent benefit, time and price tags for proposed IT initiatives. To senior business stakeholders they provide the most essential business information regarding each proposed IT initiative: expected business value, completion times and estimated costs. In other words, Outlines explain to business executives what business value will be delivered if the IT initiative is approved, when and for what price. Outlines typically explain both the strategic and tactical business value expected from the implementation of the IT initiative. Cost estimates provided in Outlines often include the initial financial investments required to deliver the IT initiative, or capital expenses (CAPEX), the recurring financial expenditures required to support the IT solution in the future, or operating expenses (OPEX), as well as the overall direct and indirect costs of the solution during its complete lifecycle, or total cost of ownership (TCO).

The general purpose of all Outlines is to help estimate the overall business impact and value of proposed IT initiatives. The use of Outlines for describing proposed IT initiatives allows business executives to evaluate the advantages and disadvantages of specific initiatives, compare different IT investments based on their anticipated benefits and costs, prioritize them based on their perceived importance and make informed investments decisions regarding these IT initiatives at their early stages. Outlines help business leaders select and fund only the most valuable IT initiatives with maximum payoff from the overall pool of all proposed initiatives. Essentially, Outlines are intended to "sell" corresponding IT initiatives to potential business sponsors.

The proper use of Outlines leads to improved efficiency and ROI of IT investments. Using Outlines for prioritizing IT initiatives allows filtering out inefficient initiatives, which do not deliver reasonable business value for their money, and investing only in initiatives with demonstrated qualitative and quantitative returns. Outlines help business executives consciously approve each IT investment, understand how the IT budget is spent, control IT expenditures and ensure that each IT dollar is invested wisely and profitably.

Difference from the Adjacent Types

Outlines, as business-focused changes EA artifacts, are adjacent to Visions and Designs (see Figure 8.1). Although Visions also provide some high-level business-oriented descriptions similar to Outlines, the descriptions offered by Visions are more conceptual, abstract and global. While Visions focus on describing the long-term organization-wide direction for IT, Outlines describe in detail specific short-term IT initiatives essentially representing distinct actionable steps towards the global strategic direction provided by Visions. In other words, Visions suggest what IT initiatives are desirable for the whole organization, while Outlines provide more detailed separate descriptions of these initiatives. Outlines often describe the changes in specific business processes affected by corresponding IT initiatives, whereas Visions usually "talk" in terms of higher-order abstractions, e.g. business capabilities or activities. Unlike Visions, which typically use only rough qualitative assessments (e.g. large and small) and do not calculate money, Outlines normally contain some financial estimations and quantitative figures for proposed IT initiatives. Put it simply, Visions usually have no business cases, while Outlines are closely associated with respective business cases.

Although Designs also provide some narrow-scoped descriptions of specific IT initiatives similar to Outlines, the descriptions offered by Outlines are intended primarily for executive-level business audience. While Designs are very technical EA artifacts containing extensive implementation-specific details, Outlines are pretty abstract and avoid using "scary" IT-specific terminology incomprehensible to most senior business stakeholders. Unlike Designs, Outlines describe IT solutions at the conceptual level and largely from the business perspective, i.e. emphasizing their business impact, value and costs, rather than their low-level technical details. The key purpose of Outlines is to support the initial decision-making around IT initiatives, while the main purpose of Designs is to facilitate their subsequent practical implementation.

Specific Enterprise Architecture Artifacts Related to Outlines

Articulate subtypes of Outlines often used in established EA practices include Solution Overviews, Options Assessments and Initiative Proposals. Solution Overviews can be considered as essential EA artifacts, Options Assessments as common EA artifacts, while Initiative Proposals as uncommon EA artifacts.

Solution Overviews (Essential)

Solution Overviews (can be also called solution outlines, conceptual architectures, preliminary solution architectures, conceptual designs, solution briefs, etc.) are specific Outlines providing high-level descriptions of specific proposed IT solutions understandable to business leaders. Solution Overviews can be considered as an essential subtype of Outlines found in the majority of successful EA practices.

Solution Overviews represent finalized descriptions of proposed IT solutions agreed with their business sponsors. They are the most elaborate and detailed of all Outlines. Solution Overviews usually describe what new IT systems will be installed, how current business processes will be modified, where the necessary data will come from and other aspects of IT solutions important from the business perspective. In other words, Solution Overviews typically include conceptual technical architectures as well as high-level business process models. In order to explain the nature of the proposed changes more clearly, Solution Overviews often show both the current and expected "to-be" states of affected business operations and emphasize the beneficial contrast between these states.

Besides describing the conceptual structure and process impact of proposed IT solutions, Solution Overviews typically also provide the most essential supporting information regarding the IT initiatives including, but not limited to, the following aspects:

- Goals and objectives of the IT initiative
- Business benefits expected from the IT initiative
- Key business stakeholders and sponsors of the IT initiative
- Essential requirements for the IT solution
- Third parties involved in the implementation of the IT solution

- Estimates of time and cost for the IT solution
- Identified risks associated with the IT solution

Additionally, Solution Overviews often provide a capability "footprint" of the IT solution, i.e. explain which business capabilities will be uplifted if the solution is implemented. Capability footprints help business executives evaluate the alignment of proposed IT initiatives to the general strategic direction reflected in Visions. For instance, they allow mapping specific IT initiatives to Business Capability Models (see Figure 11.1) in order to assess their capability impact and contribution to the strategic business capabilities.

Implementation of large IT solutions as single big-bang IT projects is often considered as too risky, impractical and undesirable. Instead, IT solutions of a considerable size are usually split into several smaller interrelated IT projects and delivered step-by-step. In these cases Solution Overviews may also include mini-roadmaps explaining when and in what sequence different components of the whole IT solution will be delivered as separate projects. However, multi-project IT solutions usually still have single business cases justifying entire solutions, rather than their separate sub-projects one-by-one.

Solution Overviews are often represented as plain MS Word documents with simple intuitive diagrams and textual descriptions typically of ~15-30 pages long. In some cases they may use customized and simplified versions of the BPMN modeling language for describing the proposed process changes. The schematic graphical representation of Solution Overviews is shown in Figure 13.1.

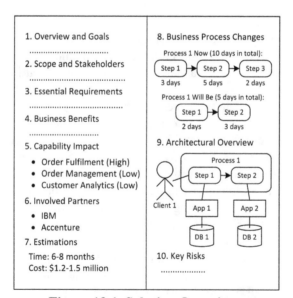

Figure 13.1. Solution Overviews

Solution Overviews are typically completed during the later stages of initiation steps of all IT initiatives to represent the finalized versions of proposed IT solutions agreed with their business sponsors. They are used by senior business and IT stakeholders participating in decision-making committees to make final investment decisions regarding proposed IT initiatives. Once Solution Overviews are approved by IT investment committees, corresponding IT initiatives proceed further to their implementation steps and the development of technical Designs for these initiatives begins.

Options Assessments (Common)

Options Assessments (can be called options analyses, options papers, solution options, solution assessments, discussion papers, etc.) are specific Outlines providing lists of available high-level implementation options for specific IT initiatives with their pros and cons. Options Assessments can be considered as a common subtype of Outlines often found in successful EA practices.

Options Assessments represent high-level descriptions of multiple possible IT solutions addressing the same specified business need, i.e. different approaches for solving the same business problem with IT. In some organizations architects are expected to propose and analyze at least three different conceptual options for addressing any business need. In some cases, the "do nothing" option may be also included into the list of possible options to explicitly explore the consequences of not implementing any solution at all.

Besides briefly describing potential implementation options for a specific IT initiative, Options Assessments also provide the essential supporting information regarding each of these options including its advantages, disadvantages, costs and risks. For example, if business executives articulated a specific business need to enable order tracking for customers, then architects can offer different options for addressing this business need (e.g. develop a mobile app, create an order tracking page on the website or upgrade the existing system to automatically send status notifications via SMS) and explain the pros and cons of these options from the business perspective in Options Assessments.

In order to ease the selection of the most suitable alternatives out of multiple available options, these options are often formally scored according to a number of important criteria including, but not limited to, the following aspects:

- Business functionality provided by the proposed IT solution
- Technical feasibility of the proposed IT solution
- Time, effort and cost estimates of the proposed IT solution
- Security, risks and potential problems associated with the proposed IT solution
- Alignment of the proposed IT solution to the general strategic direction
- Estimated overall bottom-line impact of the proposed IT solution

Based on the scoring of each option according to these and other relevant criteria, total resulting scores can be calculated for all options (e.g. as a sum of weighted scores according to each criterion) and the most desirable implementation option can be selected. Moreover, often senior business sponsors of IT initiatives are asked to prioritize and weight different business requirements based on their perceived importance and then proposed IT solutions can be scored against the list of weighted business requirements separately in order to provide a more accurate scoring for each of the available options. The use of a systematic and consistent scoring mechanism helps business leaders choose the best possible implementation options for new IT initiatives.

However, for many IT initiatives Options Assessments cannot be developed simply because no reasonable alternative solutions can be offered to address the requested business need, only a single implementation option seems to be available. In these cases IT initiatives may immediately proceed further towards the implementation. For instance, more detailed Solution Overviews can be developed to elaborate the only available option and inform the IT investment decision.

Options Assessments are usually represented as MS Word documents or MS PowerPoint presentations with simple intuitive diagrams and textual descriptions for each option. The schematic graphical representation of Options Assessments is shown in Figure 13.2.

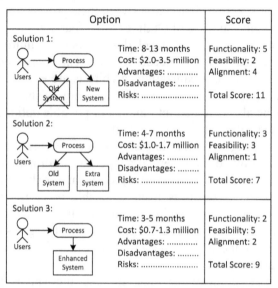

Figure 13.2. Options Assessments

Options Assessments are typically developed during the initiation steps of IT initiatives to facilitate the discussion between business executives and architects regarding the available solution implementation options. They are used by senior business and IT stakeholders to select the most appropriate implementation options for proposed IT initiatives based on the analysis of their advantages and disadvantages. After a certain solution implementation option is selected and approved by business leaders, corresponding IT initiatives may either be further elaborated into more detailed Solution Overviews for their final approval, or proceed immediately to the development of technical Designs required to implement these initiatives.

Initiative Proposals (Uncommon)

Initiative Proposals (can be also called solution proposals, initiative summaries, investment cases, idea briefs, etc.) are specific Outlines providing very early idea-level descriptions of proposed IT initiatives and their justifications. Initiative Proposals can be considered as an uncommon subtype of Outlines relatively rarely found in EA practices.

Initiative Proposals represent very abstract descriptions of specific IT initiatives that might be worth implementing. They are the most brief, simple and conceptual of all Outlines. Initiative Proposals usually describe the general idea of the proposed IT initiative, its expected business value and conceptual solution. They might also provide some broad estimates of time and cost, but these estimations are often based only on best guess.

Initiative Proposals, if used in an organization, are the first EA artifacts developed for specific IT initiatives. They are typically created to secure the initial seed funding for proposed IT initiatives to be able to explore the preliminary immature ideas more thoroughly and then produce more detailed descriptions of these initiatives with their more accurate estimations, often in the form of Options Assessments or Solution Overviews.

Initiative Proposals are usually represented as MS PowerPoint presentations or MS Word documents with a few simple diagrams and textual descriptions typically of several pages long. The schematic graphical representation of Initiative Proposals is shown in Figure 13.3.

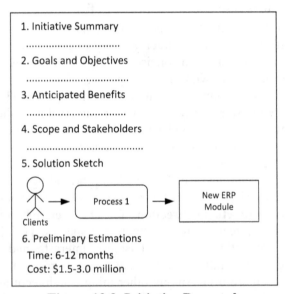

Figure 13.3. Initiative Proposals

Initiative Proposals are typically produced at the very early stages of initiation steps of all IT initiatives to describe the general ideas behind these initiatives, their motivations and envisioned solutions. Initiative Proposals are used to discuss proposed IT initiatives at their earliest stages with senior business stakeholders in order either to get the preliminary approval of these initiatives as "good ideas" and elaborate them further, or to get the initiatives rejected immediately as "bad ideas" without investing any additional efforts in worthless ventures. Initiative Proposals help filter out futile IT initiatives at their earliest stages and focus on more promising initiatives instead.

Less Popular Enterprise Architecture Artifacts Related to Outlines

Besides Solution Overviews, Options Assessments and Initiative Proposals described above, some other noteworthy subtypes of Outlines are occasionally found in organizations practicing enterprise architecture. Firstly, some organizations actively use supplementary EA artifacts summarizing the key decisions made during the development of Solution Overviews or other Outlines, which may be called as **key decisions for Outlines**. These EA artifacts provide one-page textual digests with bullet-point lists of the most significant planning decisions regarding specific IT initiatives and their justifications. For example, key decisions for IT initiatives may include, among many others, the following important decisions:

- Decision to select a specific implementation approach from a number of multiple available options
- Decision to limit the scope of an IT initiative to certain business functionality
- Decision to depart from the established Principles (see Figure 9.1) due to some strong reasons
- Decision to deviate from the desired Target States (see Figure 11.3) due to a compelling business case or other tactical benefits

Technically, these EA artifacts do not contain any new information or planning decisions missing in other EA artifacts, but rather extract the very essence of other EA artifacts related to respective IT initiatives and present it in a concise and digestible manner. For this reason they are always produced after or in parallel with the corresponding full-fledged Outlines. Key decisions for Outlines provide convenient points of discussion around specific IT initiatives and facilitate the communication between business executives and architects during their initiation steps. They help better understand the real impact and value of new IT initiatives for the business of an organization and make informed approval decisions regarding these initiatives as part of formal endorsement and governance procedures.

Secondly, some organizations use EA artifacts providing architectural directions to architects working on developing Solution Overviews or other Outlines for new IT initiatives, which may be called as **architectural directions for Outlines**. Essentially, these EA artifacts represent very high-level architectural requirements for specific IT initiatives, including both conceptual requirements reflecting essential business interests and technical requirements reflecting the most significant rationalization suggestions resulting from the Technology Optimization process (see Figure 6.1). Among other things, architectural directions for Outlines often include subsets of all existing Considerations and key Standards directly applicable to respective IT initiatives. For example, these directions may include, among many others, the following high-level requirements to a new IT solution:

- The IT solution should be suitable for all points of presence according to the established Principles (see Figure 9.1)
- The IT solution should adhere to the national privacy Policies (see Figure 9.2)
- The IT solution should use certain technologies from Technology Reference Models (see Figure 10.1)
- The IT solution should be based on a particular strategic system from Enterprise System Portfolio (see Figure 12.3)

Along with basic business requirements, architectural directions for Outlines provide an input for the Initiative Delivery process (see Figure 6.1). They are developed at the very early stages of IT initiatives to convey key architectural requirements for the corresponding IT solutions. Architectural directions help connect global organization-wide IT planning decisions with local initiative-specific IT planning decisions and essentially offer formalized documents-based communication interfaces between different types of architects, e.g. between enterprise architects and solution architects, as discussed later in Chapter 16 (Architects in Enterprise Architecture Practice).

Thirdly, some organizations actively use EA artifacts providing very simple one-page graphical views of specific IT initiatives, which may be called as **one-page initiative overviews**. These EA artifacts describe the high-level conceptual structure of proposed IT solutions in an informal and intuitive manner. One-page initiative overviews are conceptually similar to organization-wide Context Diagrams (see Figure 11.5), but limited in their scope to separate initiatives and focus exclusively on describing the essence of proposed IT solutions. Due to their inherent simplicity, these diagrams are appealing and easily understandable to a wide circle of business stakeholders. One-page overviews of IT initiatives are typically developed at their very early stages, usually as first Outlines produced for specific initiatives. They can be created very quickly and then used to collect an early feedback from all relevant stakeholders, produce some rough "T-shirt size" estimates (e.g. small, medium or large) and support a collective decision to elaborate respective initiatives further towards their implementation. From this perspective, these diagrams of IT initiatives may be considered as condensed, purely graphical Initiative Proposals.

Fourthly, some organizations use separate temporary mini-roadmaps for large and multi-project IT initiatives (e.g. complex transformation programs), which may be called as **initiative roadmaps**. These roadmaps are conceptually similar to regular Roadmaps (see Figure 11.2), but developed specifically for particular IT initiatives and then discarded after these initiatives are implemented. They typically describe when specific components of entire IT solutions will be delivered as separate IT projects. The use of initiative roadmaps allows business executives and architects agree on the priority and timelines for the delivery of different solution components. Mini-roadmaps for large IT initiatives might be either created as separate EA artifacts or, as noted earlier, included in regular Solution Overviews of these initiatives.

Fifthly, some organizations use separate **analytical papers** for specific IT initiatives implying significant and far-reaching technology choices. These EA artifacts typically analyze in detail the available technical offerings with their long-term impact, advantages and disadvantages to support decision-making at the early stages of IT initiatives. For example, if a particular IT initiative requires introducing a new major technology or expensive product, then an analytical paper can be developed to evaluate the existing vendors on the market and select the most appropriate one according to the organizational needs. From this perspective, these initiative-specific analytical papers are complementary to regular Options Assessments. Analytical papers present a very conceptual analysis of available technology selection options, while Options Assessments present a more specific and down-to-earth analysis of possible solution implementation approaches. Essentially, these EA artifacts might be considered as local, initiative-specific Analytical Reports (see Figure 9.5), or as purely analytical versions of Options Assessments. Analytical papers are developed collaboratively by architects and relevant business stakeholders when required for specific IT initiatives and may provide the basis for preparing corresponding vendor agreements, procurement contracts or tender documents.

Additional Concerns Regarding Outlines

The single biggest threat associated with the practical use of Outlines is arguably the attempts to develop highly detailed Outlines which might be redundant and too "heavyweight" for preliminary decision-making purposes. All Outlines are developed during the initiation steps of IT initiatives (see Figure 6.1) and their general purpose is mostly to help making substantiated investment decisions regarding these initiatives. For each IT initiative corresponding Outlines should provide sufficient information to decide whether an organization will benefit if the initiative is implemented taking into account its expected business impact and cost. From this perspective, all Outlines should largely focus on three key aspects of proposed IT initiatives. Firstly, Outlines should describe the anticipated business value of proposed IT solutions and explain how this value will be realized. Secondly, Outlines should clearly communicate potential risks, problems and other possible negative consequences associated with proposed IT solutions. Thirdly, Outlines should estimate the cost of proposed IT solutions with a certain reasonable degree of accuracy.

On the one hand, in most cases there are no practical reasons for elaborating Outlines further to the next level of detail required in implementable Designs. Moreover, as suggested by the EA uncertainty principle (see Figure 5.6), these attempts might be even unachievable. On the other hand, voluminous Outlines with superfluous descriptions may complicate the assessment of proposed IT initiatives, distract the attention from the most critical questions and eventually even reduce the quality of decision-making. Put it simply, Outlines should be detailed enough to adequately evaluate proposed IT initiatives, but no more detailed than necessary for this purpose.

Chapter Summary

This chapter discussed Outlines as a general type of EA artifacts from the perspective of their informational contents, development, usage, purpose and benefits and then described in more detail popular narrow subtypes of Outlines including Solution Overviews, Options Assessments and Initiative Proposals. The key message of this chapter can be summarized into the following essential points:

- Outlines provide high-level descriptions of separate IT initiatives understandable to business leaders essentially representing benefit, time and price tags for proposed IT investments
- Outlines are temporary decisions EA artifacts that are developed at the early stages of IT initiatives collaboratively by architects and business leaders, used to evaluate, approve and fund specific initiatives and then archived
- Outlines help estimate the overall business impact and value of proposed IT initiatives eventually leading to improved efficiency and ROI of IT investments
- Solution Overviews are essential Outlines providing high-level descriptions of specific proposed IT solutions in business language and helping business leaders and architects negotiate, evaluate and approve the implementation of corresponding solutions
- Options Assessments are common Outlines providing lists of available high-level implementation options for specific IT initiatives with their pros and cons and helping business executives and architects select the most preferable alternatives for corresponding initiatives
- Initiative Proposals are uncommon Outlines providing very early idea-level descriptions of proposed IT initiatives with their justifications and helping business leaders and architects initially select only the most promising initiatives for their further elaboration

Chapter 14: Designs

The previous chapter focused on Outlines as the fifth general type of EA artifacts defined by the CSVLOD model of enterprise architecture. This chapter discusses in great detail various aspects of Designs as the next general type of EA artifacts (IT-focused changes) as well as their more specific subtypes often used in EA practices. In particular, this chapter starts from describing the common properties of all Designs including their type-specific informational contents, development and usage scenarios, role in an EA practice and associated organizational benefits. Then, this chapter discusses in detail popular narrow subtypes of Designs including Solution Designs and Preliminary Solution Designs. Finally, this chapter provides additional concerns and recommendations regarding the practical use of Designs as part of an EA practice.

Designs as a General Type of Enterprise Architecture Artifacts

Designs are IT-focused changes EA artifacts (see Figure 8.1). They provide low-level technical descriptions of specific IT projects developed collaboratively by architects and IT project teams and share the essential common properties of both IT-focused EA artifacts and changes EA artifacts. Specific examples of EA artifacts related to Designs include Solution Designs, Preliminary Solution Designs and some other similar, but less popular EA artifacts (see Figure 8.2)[1].

Informational Contents

Designs provide detailed technical and functional descriptions of separate IT projects actionable for project teams. Essentially, Designs describe what exactly should be implemented as part of a particular IT project and how exactly it should be done. The IT-oriented descriptions provided by Designs address the following and similar project-related questions:

- What specific business requirements should be met by the IT project?
- What infrastructure should be provided to implement the IT project?
- What hardware and software should be installed to implement the IT project?
- What applications should be developed to implement the IT project?
- Which data entitles should be used in the new IT system?
- How exactly should different system components communicate and interact with each other?
- How exactly should the new IT system interact with the surrounding environment?
- How exactly should current business processes be modified as a result?

Most of these questions reflect very IT-specific concerns irrelevant and even incomprehensible to the vast majority of business stakeholders. Business sponsors of IT projects are typically indifferent to how exactly these projects are implemented from the technical perspective, as long as all their essential business requirements are fulfilled. Accordingly, business stakeholders are concerned only with validating the detailed business requirements specified in Designs, often indirectly through professional business analysts acting as their representatives, but not interested in most other purely technical parts of Designs. However, Designs are of direct interest to IT project teams including project managers and various IT specialists responsible for delivering the corresponding projects on time and budget. For this reason, all Designs can be considered as dual EA artifacts (see Figure 2.4) relevant to both architects and project teams. They reflect architecturally significant project-level planning decisions as well as lower-level implementable prescriptions.

Designs usually describe most of the typical EA domains including business, applications, data, infrastructure and security domains, as well as their interrelationship (see Figure 2.2). They are intended to provide end-to-end descriptions of entire IT projects detailed enough to start their actual implementation. Essentially, Designs usually depict the entire IT project stack starting from the "top" business domain (e.g. business requirements, use cases and business processes) and ending with the "bottom" infrastructure domain (e.g. underlying hardware, operating systems and networks). However, not all EA domains may be relevant to every IT project.

Designs are the "last" EA artifacts in the EA delivery chain. All information systems in organizations practicing enterprise architecture are implemented by means of Designs. They provide the most specific, detailed and implementation-ready descriptions of information systems of all types of EA artifacts. Designs are influenced by all other "previous" types of EA artifacts and reflect essential architectural decisions embodied in more generic and high-level types of EA artifacts. In particular, Designs are compliant with conceptual and technical rules defined by Considerations and Standards, aligned to the general strategic direction reflected in Visions, integrate with the existing IT environment described in Landscapes and based on conceptual solutions approved by business leaders via Outlines.

Importantly, Designs are still pretty high-level architectural documents. They focus largely on stipulating significant project-related decisions of organization-wide importance, rather than all possible project-related decisions. In other words, Designs tend to define only what is really important from the perspective of the whole organization, while all minor decisions negligible in the overall organizational context are normally omitted. For instance, Designs often specify what technologies are used in the IT project, how exactly various organization-wide Policies (see Figure 9.2) and Guidelines (see Figure 10.2) are taken into account, which shared data entities are used, how exactly the new IT system fits into the current IT landscape and which Patterns (see Figure 10.3) have been selected to address the availability, recoverability or other critical requirements. However, numerous less important local decisions with no organization-wide impact are often left to the discretion of project team members who, if necessary, may produce more detailed and low-level design documents for their IT projects, which are typically not considered as EA artifacts and not discussed in this book. Essentially, Designs as EA artifacts are equivalent to what is typically called as "system architecture", i.e. architecture of a single IT system. Hence, Designs in the context of this book should be understood as full-fledged system architectures, rather than merely as "designs"[2].

Designs usually focus on the short-term future up to one year ahead, rarely on longer-term planning horizons for large IT projects. Since all Designs describe some approved and funded IT projects planned for implementation, they naturally focus on the future. However, the implementation of most IT systems cannot be planned with the necessary level of detail for a horizon of longer than one year. For this reason, Designs normally focus only on the immediately actionable future, where all the critical implementation-specific details of new IT systems can be planned with a reasonable accuracy, while a longer-term planning of specific IT initiatives is typically accomplished via more abstract Outlines.

Designs are usually expressed as a mix of text, tables and complex diagrams. Since Designs are expected to describe all the architecturally significant implementation-specific details of new IT projects, they can use any suitable representation formats to provide the required details with the appropriate level of granularity. For instance, Designs often include long textual descriptions of specific business requirements for IT projects, extensive configuration tables with various technical parameters and numerous complex IT-specific diagrams explaining the interaction between different system components in minute detail, often using specialized formal modeling notations, e.g. UML or ArchiMate, less often BPMN or ARIS. Unsurprisingly, Designs of large IT projects can be very voluminous, especially in organizations with more "heavyweight" project implementation approaches. Physically, Designs are almost always created and distributed as ordinary MS Word documents.

Development and Usage

Designs represent collective planning decisions (see Table 2.1) on how exactly specific IT projects should be implemented. They are developed for all approved IT projects at the implementation step of the Initiative Delivery process (see Figure 6.1) collaboratively by architects, IT project teams and business representatives (see Figure 2.6) based on the corresponding Outlines previously agreed with business executives. Specifically, high-level IT solutions described in Outlines are taken as the starting point for developing Designs and further elaborated with more implementation-specific technical details. For small and medium IT solutions, which might be delivered as single IT projects, Designs typically describe entire end-to-end solutions. In these cases Designs might be produced merely by extending Outlines, i.e. by adding new, more detailed technical sections to existing Outlines, rather than as completely new documents. However, for large IT solutions, which often require multiple projects to be delivered, Designs usually describe specific components of these solutions representing separate IT projects. Designs are typically developed in parallel with project management plans for corresponding IT projects.

Each of the three parties participating in the development of Designs for a new IT project has its own articulate interests and concerns. Firstly, architects are concerned with the conformance of Designs to the established Standards and their seamless integration into the existing Landscapes. Architects also aim to incorporate into Designs relevant technical rationalization suggestions resulting from the Technology Optimization process (see Figure 6.1). Secondly, IT project teams are concerned with the feasibility, practicality and credibility of the resulting Designs from their down-to-earth implementation-centric perspective. Project managers also ensure the adequacy of delivery schedules and availability of necessary resources. Thirdly, business representatives, who may be either actual business stakeholders of the new IT project or professional business analysts acting on their behalf, are concerned with specifying correct, consistent and complete functional requirements and their inclusion into Designs. The discussions of Designs between architects, project teams and business representatives typically revolve around specific business requirements to new IT systems (see Table 5.1), which are often organized and prioritized according to the so-called MoSCoW (must have, should have, could have and will not have) framework. While business representatives normally specify the expected behavior of new IT systems and determine the relative importance of particular system functions, architects and project teams propose best possible ways to implement the requested functionality with technology. Designs are developed through continuous discussions between these three parties and refined iteratively until a mutually agreed solution satisfying the essential interest of all parties is found and approved. In cases when IT projects are delivered via outsourcing arrangements with external third parties, Designs serve as the key instruments enabling effective communication between internal and external architects and other specialists.

All developed Designs are typically peer-reviewed by other architects to ensure their logical fit into Landscapes and compliance with Standards and then undergo the governance procedure of a formal approval and sign-off, as discussed later in Chapter 17 (Architecture Functions in Organizations). However, in practice not all Designs can be fully compliant with Standards and reasonable justified deviations from Standards in untypical cases are usually tolerated. These deviations are often registered and the consequences of these deviations may be analyzed in the future to enable organizational learning and facilitate the evolution of Standards in the right direction. In case of departure from Standards the incurred architecture debt may be estimated and recorded, as discussed later in Chapter 18 (Instruments for Enterprise Architecture). In some highly regulated industries (e.g. banking and finance) finalized Designs for new IT solutions might also need to be sent to national regulatory bodies for their compliance verification and formal endorsement. Importantly, at the Designs stage of IT initiatives the fundamental investment decisions to implement these initiatives have already been made by senior business and IT stakeholders based on their high-level Outlines, while the role of Designs is only to clarify specific business requirements and explain how exactly the corresponding IT solutions should be implemented to address these requirements.

After being developed and approved, Designs are used by project teams to implement IT projects. Designs are cornerstones of IT projects defining what exactly needs to be done to deliver these projects. Moreover, when projects are implemented by contractors or outsourcers, their Designs often serve as formal contracts between client organizations and delivery partners specifying the criteria against which their work can be assessed, validated and accepted. Designs are actively used by project managers, software developers, database administrators, infrastructure engineers, testers and other project team members to coordinate their implementation activities. In some cases project teams may produce more detailed technical documentation for IT projects based on their architectural Designs in order to provide even more fine-grained implementation plans. However, the design documents produced by project teams within IT projects are considered as purely implementation-specific documents, not as EA artifacts, and therefore are out of the scope of this book and not discussed in detail[3].

During the whole period of project implementation architects supervise IT project teams to ensure that the prescriptions of Designs are actually followed as well as to identify potential inconsistencies between recommended architectural approaches and real-world practical needs on the ground. Direct participation of architects in the project delivery activities helps align Standards to the actual practical needs and avoid the "ivory tower" syndrome. After IT projects are successfully implemented, they are handed over to IT operations and support teams for their further maintenance in an operating mode. At this moment the corresponding IT systems enter from the delivery phase into the realm of IT service management. During the completion of IT projects, architects update respective Landscapes to incorporate the resulting modifications of the IT landscape into relevant current-state descriptions. However, Landscapes based on configuration management databases (CMDBs), most often Inventories (see Figure 12.2), are usually updated directly by IT operations and support teams as part of the project transition into the maintenance phase.

Designs are temporary EA artifacts (see Table 2.2) with a limited lifetime developed specifically to deliver approved IT projects. After IT projects are implemented and released, their Designs are no longer actively used and largely lose their value as EA artifacts. However, Designs of implemented IT systems can still be found useful in the future as passive reference materials on the current state of the organizational IT landscape. For this purpose, Designs are often updated after completion of corresponding IT projects in order to reflect the actual "as-implemented" state taking into account the deviations from the initial Designs that occurred in the course of the project implementation. In some cases additional lower-level details of the delivered IT systems might be also added to the final post-implementation versions of their Designs to capture their internal structure more accurately. Then, updated Designs are typically stored in organizational document repositories for future reference. These Designs might be retrieved and used later, for instance, for user training purposes or by IT operations and support teams to monitor, maintain and troubleshoot running IT systems. From this perspective, Designs of completed IT projects, as reference materials on the current IT landscape, are complementary to Landscapes. While Landscapes describe at a high level what IT systems constitute the IT landscape and how these systems are connected to each other, Designs describe in great detail how exactly each of these systems works internally.

Role and Benefits

Designs represent communication interfaces between architects and IT project teams. Essentially, Designs provide a link between architectural efforts and subsequent implementation efforts. They help ensure the connection between high-level planning decisions and low-level implementation. Designs allow architects to balance global organization-wide architectural concerns (e.g. selection of proper technologies, reuse of appropriate IT assets, centralization of certain types of data, etc.) and local project-specific needs and requirements. Generally, the use of Designs for delivering IT projects is the only existing mechanism in an EA practice to convert all intangible architectural decisions reflected in other types of EA artifacts into tangible IT systems. Without using Designs to enforce the alignment between specific IT projects and instructions of other types of EA artifacts, these instructions remain merely good wishes. As a result, in the absence of peer-reviewed Designs most other EA artifacts are often ignored, while the money invested in these artifacts are usually wasted.

The general purpose of all Designs is to help implement approved IT projects according to business and architectural requirements. Business requirements to IT projects typically include both functional and non-functional requirements to new systems, while architectural requirements to IT projects usually include key architectural suggestions regarding the implementation of these systems significant from the organization-wide perspective. Designs help stipulate in advance all the essential requirements from both the business and IT perspectives and then ensure the compliance with these requirements during the project implementation. Thereby, Designs enable clear traceability between the specified business requirements and the actual functional capabilities of delivered IT systems as well as between the recommended global Standards and the actual implementation approaches followed in these systems.

The proper use of Designs leads to improved quality of the IT project delivery. Using Designs for planning specific IT projects allows identifying potential risks and possible problems with their future delivery and proposing time-proven implementation approaches and risk mitigation strategies beforehand. Designs also help avoid confusion and misunderstanding between various stakeholders of the IT project. They serve as common reference points for all project participants and essentially provide a "single source of truth" to different team members. Thereby, Designs help de-risk IT projects, minimize their deviation from the agreed budgets and timelines, and make their delivery more predictable and smooth.

Difference from the Adjacent Types

Designs, as IT-focused changes EA artifacts, are adjacent to Landscapes and Outlines (see Figure 8.1). Although Landscapes also provide some technical descriptions of specific IT instances similar to Designs, the descriptions offered by Landscapes are broader in their scope and more abstract in their granularity. Designs focus on describing separate IT projects in great detail, while Landscapes provide general higher-level descriptions of the organizational IT landscape. In other words, Designs are limited in their scope to specific IT systems, but do not describe the surrounding IT environment around these systems. Moreover, Landscapes focus mostly on depicting the current IT environment, while Designs describe what only will be delivered in the near future. Essentially, Designs explain how exactly separate changes in Landscapes are going to be implemented.

Although Outlines also provide some narrow-scoped descriptions of specific IT initiatives similar to Designs, the descriptions offered by Designs are more elaborate, detailed and technical in nature. While Outlines focus on presenting and "selling" entire IT solutions to senior business stakeholders, Designs may be developed for separate components of these solutions if they are too large to be delivered as single IT projects. Unlike Outlines, which provide only conceptual requirements to IT solutions, Designs specify detailed business requirements, explain how exactly these business requirements should be met and describe how exactly resulting IT systems should work. Designs stipulate all significant technical decisions related to IT projects and provide sufficient low-level details to start their actual implementation.

Specific Enterprise Architecture Artifacts Related to Designs

Articulate subtypes of Designs often used in established EA practices include Solution Designs and Preliminary Solution Designs. Solution Designs can be considered as essential EA artifacts, while Preliminary Solution Designs as uncommon EA artifacts.

Solution Designs (Essential)

Solution Designs (can be also called detailed designs, technical designs, physical designs, high-level designs, project-start architectures, solution architectures, full solution architectures, solution definitions, solution specifications, etc.) are specific Designs providing detailed technical and functional specifications of approved IT solutions actionable for project teams.

Solution Designs can be considered as an essential subtype of Designs found in the majority of successful EA practices.

Solution Designs represent finalized implementation-ready technical descriptions of IT projects approved by all project stakeholders. Solution Designs typically describe detailed functional and non-functional business requirements, business processes and use cases supported by IT projects as well as all layers of their technology stacks. Usually they cover all relevant EA domains, including business, applications, data, infrastructure and security, in fair detail sufficient to start the actual project implementation. Moreover, Solution Designs are often structured into different sections corresponding to these EA domains.

Solution Designs can vary in their size depending on the size and complexity of an IT project. Naturally, large and complex IT projects tend to have more voluminous Solution Designs, while small and simple projects tend to have more brief ones. Furthermore, the level of detail and volume of Solution Designs usually also depend on the preferred project delivery methodology and can be very organization-specific. On the one hand, organizations practicing agile delivery methodologies tend to develop brief and lean Solution Designs providing only the most critical technical information regarding IT projects, e.g. the list of key technologies to be used, main system components to be created and their integration with external applications and data sources. On the other hand, organizations following more traditional and rigid, waterfall-like delivery methodologies, which imply substantial upfront planning, often develop extensive Solution Designs providing detailed project implementation plans[4]. However, "average" Solution Designs can be somewhere around ~25-50 pages long, while in extreme cases they can reach a few hundred pages.

Solution Designs are typically represented as MS Word documents with complex technical diagrams, extensive tables and rich textual descriptions. The schematic graphical representation of Solution Designs is shown in Figure 14.1.

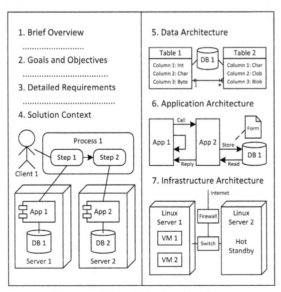

Figure 14.1. Solution Designs

Solution Designs are the most detailed EA artifacts developed for specific IT initiatives. They are used directly by IT project teams as an actionable guidance for the project implementation. After IT projects are completed, Solution Designs are usually updated to reflect all the deviations from the original plans which occurred during the project implementation, if any, and then stored for future reference in searchable document repositories.

Preliminary Solution Designs (Uncommon)

Preliminary Solution Designs (can be also called preliminary solution architectures, solution architectures, logical designs, etc.) are specific Designs providing preliminary high-level technical and functional designs of specific approved IT solutions. Preliminary Solution Designs can be considered as an uncommon subtype of Designs relatively rarely found in EA practices.

Preliminary Solution Designs represent high-level technical descriptions of IT projects with pretty accurate estimates of their time and cost. They can be considered as more technically elaborate versions of corresponding business-focused Solution Overviews (see Figure 13.1). Preliminary Solution Designs usually cover at a high level both the business side of IT projects and all layers of their technology stacks including all typical EA domains (i.e. applications, data, infrastructure and security) when they are relevant.

Preliminary Solution Designs are intermediate "halfway" EA artifacts between Outlines, which are used by business executives to approve proposed IT initiatives, and Solution Designs, which provide detailed implementation plans for these approved initiatives. The main purpose of Preliminary Solution Designs in this context is to refine and reaffirm the earlier Outlines-based estimates of time and cost for the approved IT projects.

Preliminary Solution Designs are typically represented as MS Word documents with high-level technical diagrams, tables and textual descriptions. Although the length of these EA artifacts can be very project-specific and even organization-specific, as in the case of Solution Designs, "average" Preliminary Solution Designs are often of ~20-40 pages long. The schematic graphical representation of Preliminary Solution Designs is shown in Figure 14.2.

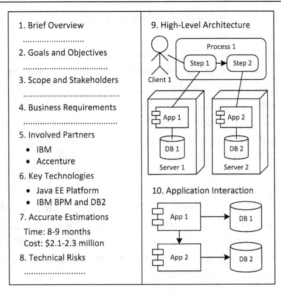

Figure 14.2. Preliminary Solution Designs

Preliminary Solution Designs are typically produced at the early stages of implementation steps of IT initiatives to refine their earlier, less precise time, cost and risk estimates. If the refined estimates confirm the original Outlines-based estimates, or at least do not differ from them significantly, then corresponding IT projects can smoothly proceed further to developing more detailed Solution Designs in a regular manner. However, if the updated estimates for IT projects are dramatically different from the earlier estimates produced during their initiation steps, then these projects may need to be renegotiated with their executive business sponsors and even the very decision to implement these projects might need to be reconsidered.

Less Popular Enterprise Architecture Artifacts Related to Designs

Besides Solution Designs and Preliminary Solution Designs described above, some other noteworthy subtypes of Designs are occasionally found in organizations practicing enterprise architecture. Firstly, some organizations actively use auxiliary EA artifacts summarizing the key decisions made during the development of Solution Designs or Preliminary Solution Designs, which are often called as **key design decisions (KDDs)**. Similarly to the analogous EA artifacts for Outlines described earlier, these artifacts provide one-page summaries of the most significant technical planning decisions regarding specific IT projects and their justifications. For example, these KDDs may include, among many others, the following important decisions:

- Decision to select a specific technical implementation approach or reuse a proven Pattern (see Figure 10.3)
- Decision to implement an IT project based on some existing IT assets from the current Inventories (see Figure 12.2)
- Decision to use a non-standard technology missing in Technology Reference Models (see Figure 10.1) due to the unsuitability of currently supported technologies for unique project needs

- Decision to deviate from the typical best practice Guidelines (see Figure 10.2) due to a highly specific nature of the project

Similarly to the key decisions for Outlines, KDDs do not contain any new planning decisions, but merely present the most critical technical decisions regarding new IT projects reflected in their full-fledged Designs and produced after or in parallel with these Designs. KDDs provide convenient points of discussion around specific IT projects and facilitate the communication between architects and other IT stakeholders during their implementation steps. They help better understand the overall technical fitness of new IT projects for the organizational IT landscape and make informed approval decisions regarding the proposed Designs of these projects.

Secondly, some organizations use EA artifacts providing architectural directions to architects working on developing Designs for new IT projects, which may be called as **architectural directions for Designs**. Similarly to architectural directions for Outlines, these EA artifacts offer high-level architectural requirements for specific IT projects. However, architectural directions for Designs are purely technical in nature and generally represent explicitly documented technical rationalization suggestions relevant to particular IT projects resulting from the Technology Optimization process (see Figure 6.1). Besides other things, architectural directions for Designs typically include the subsets of all established Standards directly applicable to respective IT projects. For example, these directions may include, among many others, the following technical requirements to a new IT system:

- The IT system should store specific data entities in the format defined by Logical Data Models (see Figure 10.5)
- The IT system should follow a number of critical data encryption Guidelines (see Figure 10.2)
- The IT system should interact with some existing systems shown in Landscape Diagrams (see Figure 12.1)
- The IT system should not reuse certain types of IT assets included in Inventories (see Figure 12.2)

Along with detailed functional business requirements, these architectural directions provide an input for developing Designs. They are developed at the very beginning of the implementation step of the Initiative Delivery process (see Figure 6.1) to communicate key architectural requirements for the corresponding IT systems. Similarly to the analogous EA artifacts for Outlines, architectural directions for Designs also offer formal communication interfaces between the architects carrying out the organization-wide Technology Optimization process and the architects responsible for planning specific IT projects. Thereby, these architectural directions help connect global technical decision-making with local project-level IT planning decisions.

Thirdly, some organizations use EA artifacts providing highly technology-specific **supplementary materials** for particular types of IT projects complementary to their general-purpose Designs. For example, for all new IT projects modifying the corporate ERP system, along with their regular Designs, some organizations may also develop separate configuration documents explaining how exactly the configuration of the ERP platform should be changed as part of the project. For all new IT projects modifying the organization-wide integration middleware, along with their regular Designs, some organizations may also develop separate documents or even platform-specific XML files defining how exactly the routing rules of the integration bus should be changed as part of the project. Essentially, these EA artifacts address some critically important, but very narrow and technology-specific aspects of IT projects. They are developed collaboratively by architects and subject-matter experts in specific technologies together with the regular Designs for respective IT projects and then provide an actionable guidance for IT specialists involved in the project implementation. The explicit separation of general-purpose Designs and technology-specific supplementary materials helps better organize the architectural documentation for IT projects and make this documentation more convenient to use.

Fourthly, some lean organizations that completely outsource their IT delivery functions to external partners use EA artifacts which can be considered as **release designs**. These EA artifacts describe the proposed technical designs of all IT projects which are going to be delivered during the next release cycle by the same partner and modifying the same part of the organizational IT landscape. For example, if an organization follows a quarterly release cycle for all organization-wide IT projects and outsourced the support and development of the entire ERP platform to its vendor, then a new release design might be produced every quarter to describe all the proposed changes of the ERP platform to be implemented by the vendor for the next release, even if these changes belong to logically unrelated IT projects sponsored by different business units. Essentially, release designs bundle together all the quarterly changes from all IT projects modifying the same IT platform and implemented by the same partner. While regular Designs normally describe separate and complete IT projects (i.e. produced on a per-project basis), release designs describe all changes of a specific IT platform delivered in one release by a particular partner (i.e. produced on a per-release, per-partner and per-platform basis). The use of bundled release designs instead of typical project-specific Designs may provide a more convenient way of communicating between internal architects and external third parties. Similarly to regular intra-organizational Designs, release designs also provide communication interfaces between architects and IT project teams, but these interfaces are inter-organizational. Release designs may help organizations better structure and manage their outsourcing arrangements with partners, vendors and professional IT service companies.

Additional Concerns Regarding Designs

The single biggest threat associated with the practical use of Designs is arguably the attempts to develop excessively detailed Designs due to the inability to distinguish the practical border between "architecture" and "design". On the one hand, very detailed, fine-grained and voluminous Designs are hard to develop since they typically require unreasonable investments of time and effort. Moreover, practical attempts to create very detailed upfront Designs often end up in a well-known situation of analysis paralysis, when a very large number of different available planning options merely overwhelm planners, prevent them from making any specific decisions and stop any real progress towards completing the plans. The development of new information systems is widely considered to be a "wicked problem", where the perfect solution simply cannot be found upfront by any analytical means. On the other hand, meticulous Designs providing the descriptions of required IT systems in minute detail, even if developed, are often considered as too rigid, inflexible and bureaucratic by project teams. Due to these reasons, overly detailed Designs should be avoided as impractical.

As noted earlier, despite their focus on technical implementation-specific details, pragmatic Designs are still pretty high-level architectural documents. Unlike detailed design documents, which might be produced at the later stages by IT project teams as part of the actual project implementation, architectural Designs describe only the key requirements to new IT systems considered as significant from the organization-wide perspective. For instance, Designs may stipulate core technologies to be used in new IT systems, explain how exactly these systems should support specific business processes or describe critical connections between these systems and their environment. However, Designs normally do not define any lower-level implementation details (e.g. specific database schemas or particular programming patterns), unless these details are critically important for the overall consistency of the IT landscape. In other words, practical Designs should not intend to describe new IT systems in all imaginable details, but rather focus only on architecturally significant elements.

Unfortunately, the strict difference between "architecture" and "design" is extremely hard to define. Since this distinction is always blurred, it is impossible to specify what exactly should be included in Designs of IT projects and what exactly should be left out. However, some general guidelines helping differentiate architecture from design still can be formulated. For instance, notable distinctions between architecture and design include, but are not limited to, the following differences[5]:

- Architectures are concerned with the fitness for purpose, while designs are concerned with the engineering optimization
- Architectures consist of choices dictated by needs, while designs consist of choices compliant with architectures
- Different architectures address different basic needs, while different designs can address the same basic need

Additionally, the volume and granularity of architectural Designs significantly depends on the project delivery methodology adopted in a particular organization. Generally, organizations with more formal, rigid and waterfall-like project methodologies naturally include more details in their Designs, while organizations with more agile and flexible project methodologies (e.g. Scrum) tend to stipulate in their Designs only the most critical architectural decisions.

Chapter Summary

This chapter discussed Designs as a general type of EA artifacts from the perspective of their informational contents, development, usage, purpose and benefits and then described in more detail popular narrow subtypes of Designs including Solution Designs and Preliminary Solution Designs. The key message of this chapter can be summarized into the following essential points:

- Designs provide detailed technical and functional descriptions of separate IT projects actionable for their implementers representing communication interfaces between architects and project teams
- Designs are temporary decisions EA artifacts that are developed at the later stages of IT initiatives collaboratively by architects, IT project teams and business representatives, used by project teams to implement IT projects and then archived

- Designs help implement approved IT projects according to business and architectural requirements eventually leading to improved quality of the project delivery
- Solution Designs are essential Designs providing detailed technical and functional specifications of approved IT solutions and helping architects and project teams plan their implementation and then deliver these solutions
- Preliminary Solution Designs are uncommon Designs providing preliminary high-level technical and functional designs of approved IT solutions and helping architects and project teams plan their implementation and refine their earlier time and cost estimates

Chapter 15: The CSVLOD Model Revisited

The previous chapters described the overarching CSVLOD model of enterprise architecture and discussed in great detail each of the six corresponding types of EA artifacts. This chapter revisits the CSVLOD model and offers an in-depth discussion of advanced, more subtle aspects of the model omitted earlier. In particular, this chapter starts from explaining the continuous nature of the CSVLOD classification taxonomy and mapping specific EA artifacts to their more accurate positions in the taxonomy. Then, this chapter discusses the concept of EA-based decision paths, the descriptive emphasis and known exceptions to the CSVLOD model of enterprise architecture. Finally, this chapter introduces "Enterprise Architecture on a Page" as a convenient one-page view of enterprise architecture and EA artifacts summarizing the most essential information presented in this book.

Continuous Nature of the CSVLOD Taxonomy

Earlier Chapter 8 formally introduced the CSVLOD taxonomy conceptually explaining the notion of enterprise architecture and defining six general types of EA artifacts: Considerations, Standards, Visions, Landscapes, Outlines and Designs (see Figure 8.1). This taxonomy classifies all EA artifacts used in EA practices along two orthogonal dimensions based on *what* these artifacts describe (rules, structures or changes) and *how* these artifacts describe (in a business-focused or IT-focused manner). However, under a more closer scrutiny both these dimensions of the CSVLOD taxonomy can be considered as continuous axes along which all EA artifacts can be positioned.

The first dimension (What?) can be considered as a continuous axis with two opposite extremes: generic and specific. On the one hand, EA artifacts at the very generic extreme describe some intangible norms related to entire organizations. They focus on general concepts and are essentially timeless. Accordingly, EA artifacts gravitating towards the generic extreme tend to describe more broad-scoped, less tangible and precise objects less associated with certain points in time. Put it simply, more generic EA artifacts tend to provide more abstract suggestions and be more related to general ideas. For example, Policies and IT Principles can be positioned very close to the generic extreme. Rules EA artifacts generally gravitate towards the generic extreme. On the other hand, EA artifacts at the very specific extreme describe some tangible instances related to concrete projects. They focus on accurate details and exact time instants. Accordingly, EA artifacts gravitating towards the specific extreme tend to describe more narrow-scoped, tangible and precise objects more associated with certain points in time. In other words, more specific EA artifacts tend to provide more concrete suggestions and be more related to specific initiatives. For example, Solution Overviews and Solution Designs can be positioned very close to the specific extreme. Changes EA artifacts generally gravitate towards the specific extreme.

The second dimension (How?) can be considered as a continuous axis with two opposite extremes: business and IT. On the one hand, EA artifacts at the very business extreme are completely technology-neutral and use pure business language. They discuss money, customers, capabilities, business goals, competitive advantages and other business-related notions. Accordingly, EA artifacts gravitating towards the business extreme tend to be less technical in nature and use more business-specific language. Put it simply, more business-related EA artifacts tend to focus more on business aspects and be more relevant to C-level business executives. For example, Principles and Value Chains can be positioned very close to the business extreme. Business-focused EA artifacts generally gravitate towards the business extreme. On the other hand, EA artifacts at the very IT extreme are purely technical and use very IT-specific language. They discuss systems, applications, databases, platforms, networks and other IT-related notions. Accordingly, EA artifacts gravitating towards the IT extreme tend to be more technical in nature and use more IT-specific language. In other words, more IT-related EA artifacts tend to focus more on IT aspects and be more relevant to ordinary IT specialists. For example, Guidelines and Landscape Diagrams can be positioned very close to the IT extreme. IT-focused EA artifacts generally gravitate towards the IT extreme.

Consequently, the two-dimensional CSVLOD taxonomy can be interpreted as a continuous "coordinate plane" for EA artifacts, while the differences between the six general types of EA artifacts should not be considered as strict black-and-white distinctions. The continuous CSVLOD taxonomy is shown in Figure 15.1.

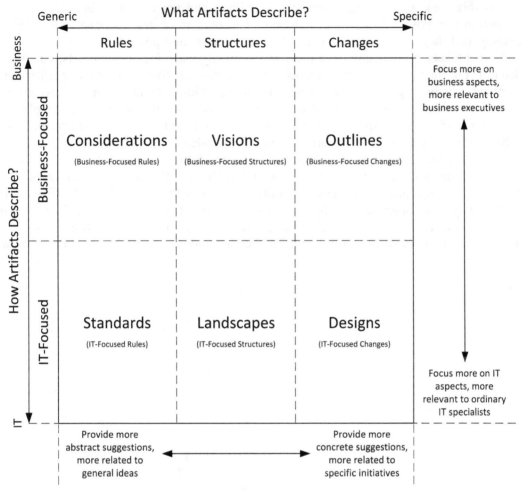

Figure 15.1. The continuous CSVLOD taxonomy

Mapping of Specific EA Artifacts to the CSVLOD Taxonomy

The CSVLOD model of enterprise architecture defines the six general types of EA artifacts and each of the 24 subtypes of EA artifacts discussed earlier can be allocated to one of these six general types (see Figure 8.2). However, the continuous nature of the CSVLOD taxonomy discussed above (see Figure 15.1) allows mapping the 24 narrow subtypes of EA artifacts to more specific positions, or dots, on the coordinate plane. Even though the exact positions of different subtypes of EA artifacts in the continuous CSVLOD taxonomy may be rather approximate, highly subjective and debatable, the placement of specific EA artifacts at certain positions in the taxonomy still helps better understand their main properties and conceptual differences from each other.

Although various non-EA-specific documents having some relationship to information systems planning (e.g. business strategy documents, business cases and project management plans) in this book are not considered as EA artifacts and not discussed in detail, for purely demonstrative purposes of this chapter these documents can be also mapped to the CSVLOD taxonomy as if they were EA artifacts in order to illustrate their possible positions in relation to "real" EA artifacts. Specifically, five types of commonly used documents can be conditionally added to EA artifacts and loosely positioned on the continuous coordinate plane together with all EA artifacts. Firstly, organizational mission and values defining the most fundamental attitude of an organization can be loosely related to Considerations. Secondly, strategic goals, objectives, KPIs and balanced scorecards (BSCs) indicating some long-term targets for an organization can be also loosely related to Considerations. Thirdly, high-level strategic business plans (e.g. to launch new products, enter particular markets or expand into new geographies) providing some general directions for action can be loosely related to Visions. Fourthly, business cases with the numerical financial analysis of proposed IT initiatives can be loosely related to Outlines. Fifthly, project management plans (e.g. budgeting, resourcing and scheduling) prepared to implement specific IT projects can be loosely related to Designs. The 24 subtypes of EA artifacts and five types of documents described above mapped to the continuous CSVLOD taxonomy are shown in Figure 15.2.

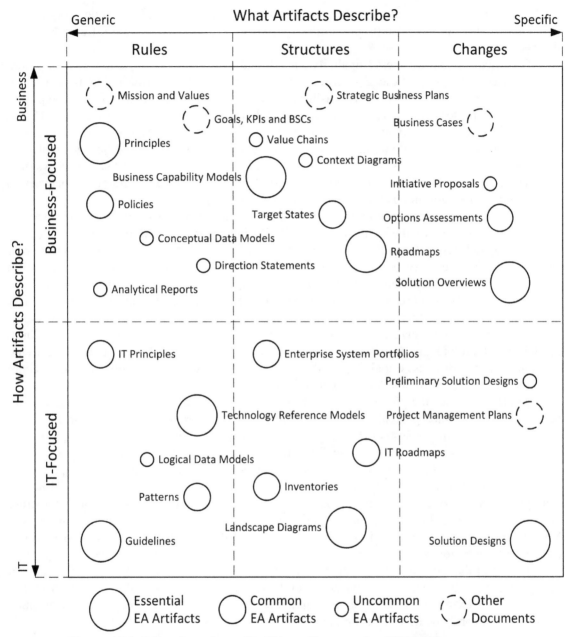

Figure 15.2. Mapping of specific EA artifacts to the CSVLOD taxonomy

Importantly, positions of some EA artifacts in the continuous CSVLOD taxonomy can be fairly considered as approximate, subjective and debatable. However, even the approximate mapping of EA artifacts to the taxonomy can help clarify the properties of these artifacts and explain the differences between distinct subtypes of EA artifacts inside their general types. While all EA artifacts related to any single general type share a number of common row-specific, column-specific and type-specific properties, they can still also have notable differences within their general type.

For instance, both Business Capability Models and Roadmaps belong to the Visions general type. Consequently, both these EA artifacts share common row-specific, column-specific and type-specific properties. Firstly, as business-focused EA artifacts, both of them represent communication interfaces between business and IT helping business executives manage IT (see Figure 8.1). Secondly, as structures EA artifacts, both of them describe high-level structures of an organization or its parts helping understand what changes are desirable and how to implement them (see Figure 8.1). Thirdly, as Visions EA artifacts, both of them represent shared views of an organization and its future agreed by business and IT helping achieve the alignment between IT investments and long-term business outcomes (see Figure 8.2).

However, despite these commonalities Business Capability Models and Roadmaps also have notable differences within the Visions type. While Business Capability Models only highlight the business capabilities that should be uplifted with IT in the future, Roadmaps describe what specific IT initiatives may be necessary to uplift these capabilities and when these initiatives should be implemented. Consequently, Business Capability Models provide more abstract suggestions and focus more on business aspects than Roadmaps and, therefore, are positioned closer to the generic extreme and closer to the business extreme. On the contrary, Roadmaps provide more concrete suggestions and focus more on IT aspects than Business Capability Models and, therefore, are positioned closer to the specific extreme and closer to the IT extreme. Even though both Business Capability Models and Roadmaps belong to Visions, they still occupy the opposite corners within the Visions general type (see Figure 15.2).

At the same time, the proximity between specific subtypes of EA artifacts related to a single general type and other general types also helps clarify the properties of these artifacts. For instance, both Enterprise System Portfolios and Landscape Diagrams belong to the Landscapes general type. Consequently, both these EA artifacts share common type-specific properties of Landscapes, i.e. represent a knowledge base of reference materials on the IT landscape helping understand, analyze and modify the structure of the landscape (see Figure 8.2). However, Enterprise System Portfolios are positioned very close to the Visions general type and, therefore, are also somewhat influenced by the essential properties of Visions. For example, similarly to Visions, Enterprise System Portfolios provide very high-level conceptual views and might be occasionally used for communicating with business executives to determine the IT investment priorities, even though it is not their primary purpose. On the contrary, Landscape Diagrams are very distant from the Visions general type and, therefore, are very dissimilar to Visions in their properties. For example, unlike Visions, Landscape Diagrams provide pretty detailed technical views and can hardly be used for communication with business stakeholders.

Decision Path of the EA-Enabled Strategy Execution

Putting all subtypes of EA artifacts on the common coordinate plane also helps illustrate the general flow of decisions taking place between the strategy formulation and strategy execution. In other words, the mapping of specific EA artifacts to the CSVLOD taxonomy (see Figure 15.2) allows tracing the full **decision path** from the general business strategy to the actual implementation of specific IT initiatives supporting this strategy.

A business strategy in organizations is turned into optimal IT solutions through the Strategic Planning and Initiative Delivery EA-related processes (see Figure 6.1). The Strategic Planning process translates relevant fundamental factors of the external business environment into the general directions for IT and revolves around Considerations and Visions. The Initiative Delivery process translates specific business needs into tangible IT solutions and revolves around Outlines and Designs. Hence, the EA-based decision path from the strategy planning to strategy implementation "lies" through Considerations, Visions, Outlines and Designs. Essential EA artifacts related to these general types include Principles, Business Capability Models, Roadmaps, Solution Overviews and Solution Designs respectively.

Firstly, as part of Strategic Planning business executives and architects decide how an organization needs to work to execute its business strategy and formulate these fundamental strategic requirements as overarching Principles. Secondly, as part of Strategic Planning senior business leaders and architects decide which business capabilities should become the focus of future IT investments to execute the business strategy and highlight these strategic capabilities in Business Capability Models. Thirdly, as part of Strategic Planning business executives and architects come up with specific IT initiatives intended to uplift the strategic business capabilities, decide when these capability increments should be implemented to execute the business strategy and place them as planned IT investments in Roadmaps. Fourthly, as part of Initiative Delivery business leaders and architects decide how each planned IT initiative should be implemented to execute the business strategy and describe corresponding high-level IT solutions as Solution Overviews. Finally, as part of Initiative Delivery architects and project teams decide how exactly the approved IT solutions should be implemented in a technically optimal manner and document their detailed implementation plans as Solution Designs. These five main types of IT-related planning decisions supported by respective EA artifacts are aligned to the EA uncertainty principle (see Figure 5.6) and rather closely correspond to the five key discussion points between business and IT stakeholders relevant for different organizational scopes and time horizons, i.e. to an operating model, business capabilities, specific business needs, business processes and business requirements (see Table 5.1).

As an output from the EA-based decision path described above organizations produce implementable Solution Designs for new IT systems which are compliant with the fundamental strategic requirements described in Principles, uplift the strategic business capabilities highlighted in Business Capability Models, delivered according to the strategic priorities reflected in Roadmaps and based on strategically preferable IT solutions described in Solution Overviews. Therefore, this decision path explains how the general business strategy of an organization is translated step-by-step into specific implementable plans for new IT systems supporting this strategy.

Since the decision-making flow described above is based only on essential EA artifacts used in most organizations, this decision path can be considered as a typical EA-based decision path and is generally correct for most EA practices. The typical decision path of the EA-enabled strategy execution described above is shown in Figure 15.3.

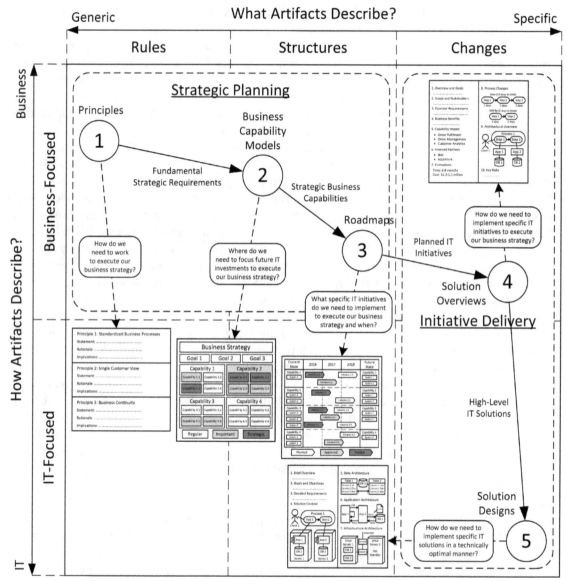

Figure 15.3. The typical decision path of the EA-enabled strategy execution

The EA-based decision path shown in Figure 15.3 clarifies the general flow of the most critical planning decisions occurring as part of the EA-related Strategic Planning and Initiative Delivery processes (see Figure 6.1). In particular, it explains where key IT-related planning decisions are made, which EA artifacts facilitate these decisions and how optimal IT solutions are initiated and planned.

However, this simplified decision path explains only the roles of the five essential EA artifacts in decision-making processes and represents the most general EA-based decision path, whereas real organizations usually use unique organization-specific constellations of EA artifacts supporting their Strategic Planning and Initiative Delivery processes, i.e. unique sets of EA artifacts related to Considerations, Visions, Outlines and Designs. For this reason, most organizations have their own customized, slightly different and more sophisticated decision paths which often incorporate other EA artifacts as well or, in some cases, do not include some of the essential EA artifacts.

For example, Target States may be developed on the way from Business Capability Models to Roadmaps in order to explicitly describe the desired future state required to uplift strategic business capabilities and then use this desired state as the basis for developing Roadmaps. Likewise, Options Assessments may be produced on the way from Roadmaps to Solution Overviews in order to present available implementation options for planned IT initiatives to business executives and then develop Solution Overviews based on the preferred options. Preliminary Solution Designs may be created on the way from Solution Overviews to Solution Designs in order to refine the tentative time and cost estimates and update corresponding business cases for IT initiatives.

Descriptive Nature of the CSVLOD Model

As noted earlier, this book is purely analytical and descriptive in nature. The CSVLOD model of enterprise architecture, specific subtypes of EA artifacts and their classification into essential, common and uncommon ones merely summarize the existing situation in industry and aggregate current EA best practices in different organizations. Essentially, they provide only important lessons from which other organizations and individual EA practitioners can learn how to use enterprise architecture, but they do not offer universal one-size-fits-all prescriptions or recipes suitable for all organizations. Any prescriptions based on the lessons from other organizations should be derived with caution.

On the one hand, the classification of EA artifacts on essential, common and uncommon merely shows that some EA artifacts are used in more organizations than other EA artifacts. However, it does not automatically suggest that more popular EA artifacts are "better" or more important for EA practices. The relative popularity of EA artifacts can be considered only as a proxy for their applicability. For instance, it would be unfair to say that all the eight essential EA artifacts (Principles, Technology Reference Models, Guidelines, Business Capability Models, Roadmaps, Landscape Diagrams, Solution Overviews and Solution Designs) should necessarily be used in all EA practices. In fact, many successful EA practices do not use some of these EA artifacts because of sound organization-specific reasons. For example, some organizations do not use Technology Reference Models because of their heavy reliance on the products of particular strategic vendors, who essentially make all the technology-related choices for their products instead of organizations. Some organizations do not use Business Capability Models, but instead prefer to use Value Chains for the same purposes because of their better acceptance and easier adoption by business audience. Some organizations do not use Solution Overviews, but prefer to develop Designs based directly on Options Assessments or even on Initiative Proposals because this approach is considered to be more agile and lightweight. Some organizations "invent" unique organization-specific EA artifacts and successfully use them instead of some essential EA artifacts. However, the list of eight essential EA artifacts can arguably be used as a reasonable benchmark for EA practices. Even if it is not absolutely necessary to use all the eight essential EA artifacts, organizations at least should be able to clearly explain why some of these artifacts are unnecessary or inappropriate for them, if any.

On the other hand, it would be arguably fair to say that all the six general types of EA artifacts (i.e. Considerations, Standards, Visions, Landscapes, Outlines and Designs) should be present in mature EA practices, although specific EA artifacts representing these general types can vary. In other words, all mature EA practices should use some Considerations to maintain conceptual consistency of all IT-related planning decisions, some Standards to define recommended implementation approaches and technologies, some Visions to focus and guide future IT investments, some Landscapes to capture the current structure of the organizational IT landscape, some Outlines to facilitate the discussion of specific IT initiatives at their early stages and some Designs to support the implementation of these initiatives at their later stages.

Importantly, the maturity of EA practices cannot be assessed or measured simply by counting the number of adopted EA artifacts. As noted earlier, successful EA practices typically use pragmatic sets of ~10-15 value-adding EA artifacts, or about a half of all the 24 different subtypes of EA artifacts often found in EA practices (see Figure 15.2). Hence, using a large number of different EA artifacts does not necessarily signify a mature EA practice, while using a small number of different EA artifacts does not necessarily signify an immature EA practice, as long as all the six general types of EA artifacts are adequately represented.

Exceptions to the CSVLOD Model

The CSVLOD model (see Figure 8.2) provides a convenient research-based conceptualization of enterprise architecture, which explains the notion of enterprise architecture as a set of six general types of EA artifacts: Considerations, Standards, Visions, Landscapes, Outlines and Designs. However, every conceptual model always represents only a simplified and idealized version of the infinitely complex empirical reality. Despite the reasonable accuracy and explanatory power of the CSVLOD model, this model also has a number of inherent limitations that should be clearly understood.

Firstly, the CSVLOD model focuses only on key EA artifacts representing consistent deliverables, or products, which underpin successful EA practices. Essentially, these EA artifacts can be considered as the core supporting pillars of an EA practice. However, besides the full-fledged EA artifacts described by the CSVLOD model, numerous disposable architectural diagrams are also routinely created in EA practices for various purposes. These diagrams are temporary in nature, have no consistent meaning and developed occasionally on an ad hoc basis as part of an EA practice. Often they represent limited extracts from "true" EA artifacts, slices of EA artifacts providing specific narrow views or modified versions of "master copies" of EA artifacts adapted for particular needs. These temporary architectural diagrams are typically intended for discussions and presentations to satisfy the information demands of specific audiences or cover unusual viewpoints important for particular stakeholders and may be included into corresponding stakeholder engagement packs. For instance, custom diagrams may be very helpful for debating the pros and cons of separate architectural decisions and collecting stakeholder feedback. The CSVLOD model does not, and cannot, explain the meaning of all imaginable architectural drawings that might be created for highly specific purposes as part of an EA practice.

Secondly, some rare EA artifacts used in real organizations can combine the contents of two adjacent general types of EA artifacts and, therefore, cannot be allocated to any single general type defined by the CSVLOD model. For example, some organizations combine Principles and IT Principles into a single list of diverse high-level imperatives that can be related to both Considerations and Standards. For better convenience some organizations place Principles in Roadmaps producing EA artifacts that can be related to both Considerations and Visions. Some organizations, and especially small ones, can place architectural initiatives, which are normally placed on separate IT Roadmaps, in business-focused Roadmaps along with regular business initiatives (i.e. fundamental, strategic and local, see Table 7.1) producing EA artifacts that can be related to both Visions and Landscapes. Some organizations combine Technology Reference Models and Enterprise System Portfolios into a single EA artifact showing both technical functions with the underlying technologies and business functions with the underlying applications, which can be related to both Standards and Landscapes. In some organizations Designs are based on the same document templates as Outlines and developed simply by filling in new technical sections in the previously approved Outlines. In these cases Designs might be considered essentially as extended versions of Outlines and represent EA artifacts that can be related to both Outlines and Designs.

Thirdly, some EA artifacts used in real organizations can combine the contents of two different subtypes of EA artifacts related to a single general type. For instance, in some organizations very broad and abstract IT Principles can be mixed with very narrow and specific Guidelines into a single list of diverse IT-specific recommendations. In organizations using specialized software tools for enterprise architecture the information on the current IT landscape can be stored in a comprehensive architectural repository which often contains the list of available IT assets, detailed properties of specific assets and connections between different assets essentially combining the properties of both Landscape Diagrams and Inventories, as discussed later in Chapter 18 (Instruments for Enterprise Architecture).

Importantly, even if some rare EA artifacts cannot be strictly related to any single general type defined by the CSVLOD model, these artifacts still can be related to multiple general types, and almost always specifically to two *adjacent* general types, which demonstrates the overall conceptual soundness of the model. Consequently, all practical EA artifacts can be explained within the boundaries of the CSVLOD model, no EA artifacts go beyond the limits of the model.

Enterprise Architecture on a Page

In order to provide a comprehensive but convenient explanatory view of enterprise architecture, all the 24 narrow subtypes of EA artifacts with their schematic graphical representations (see Figure 9.1 to Figure 14.2) can be placed together on a single page, color-coded according to their relative popularity (i.e. essential, common and uncommon), structured around the overarching CSVLOD model of enterprise architecture and related to the corresponding general types of EA artifacts: Considerations, Standards, Visions, Landscapes, Outlines or Designs (see Figure 8.2). The resulting holistic one-page view of enterprise architecture and EA artifacts can be titled simply as **Enterprise Architecture on a Page**[1]. The full version of Enterprise Architecture on a

Page is freely available to download at http://eaonapage.com. A simplified schematic view of Enterprise Architecture on a Page is shown in Figure 15.4.

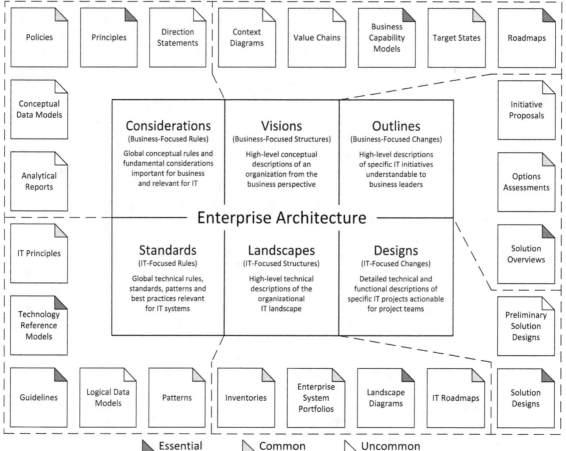

(Schematic view only, visit http://eaonapage.com for the full version)

Figure 15.4. Enterprise Architecture on a Page (schematic view only)

Enterprise Architecture on a Page provides a dense concentrated view of the most essential information on enterprise architecture and EA artifacts contained in this book. In particular, it provides clear, evidence-based and concise answers to the following critical questions regarding an EA practice:

- What EA artifacts are useful?
- What information do they provide?
- What do they look like?
- For what purpose are they developed?
- How exactly are they used?
- What benefits do they bring?

Enterprise Architecture on a Page can be considered as an intuitive visual model of enterprise architecture and as a convenient catalogue of EA artifacts. It can be used as a sense-making instrument or as a tool for thinking around enterprise architecture. It can be freely distributed and used as a common reference point for EA-related discussions. It can be printed, used as a poster and pinned on the wall. It can be helpful to various people dealing with enterprise architecture including aspiring and practicing architects in organizations as well as EA teachers and students in universities. Enterprise Architecture on a Page can be downloaded at http://eaonapage.com.

Chapter Summary

This chapter revisited the CSVLOD model of enterprise architecture, provided an advanced discussion of several important aspects of this model including the continuous nature of the classification taxonomy, the mappings of specific EA artifacts and decision paths to the taxonomy, the descriptive emphasis and known exceptions to the model and finally introduced Enterprise Architecture on a Page as a convenient one-page view of enterprise architecture and EA artifacts. The key message of this chapter can be summarized into the following essential points:

- The two dimensions of the CSVLOD taxonomy, what and how, can be considered as two continuous axes where different EA artifacts can be positioned somewhere between the opposite extremes, generic vs. specific and business vs. IT respectively, essentially turning the taxonomy into a coordinate plane for EA artifacts
- More generic EA artifacts tend to provide more abstract suggestions and be more related to general ideas, while more specific EA artifacts tend to provide more concrete suggestions and be more related to specific initiatives
- More business-related EA artifacts tend to focus more on business aspects and be more relevant to C-level business executives, while more IT-related EA artifacts tend to focus more on IT aspects and be more relevant to ordinary IT specialists
- All subtypes of EA artifacts can be roughly mapped to specific dots on the continuous coordinate plane and the relative proximity of their positions to the six main "poles" represented by general types of EA artifacts helps better understand their essential properties
- Mapping EA artifacts to specific positions on the coordinate plane can be also helpful for illustrating decision paths, i.e. sequences or flows of IT-related planning decisions supported by EA artifacts translating higher-level suggestions into more lower-level plans
- The CSVLOD model is purely descriptive in nature and provides only a "food for thought" for architects, rather than a set of strict prescriptions regarding the selection and usage of EA artifacts in organizations
- Some rare EA artifacts used in real organizations can be considered as exceptions to the CSVLOD model and related to more than one general type of EA artifacts, but even these exceptional EA artifacts in most cases can still be related to two adjacent general types

- Enterprise Architecture on a Page offers a convenient one-page view of the most essential information on enterprise architecture and EA artifacts contained in this book that can be freely downloaded at http://eaonapage.com and publicly distributed

PART III: Other Aspects of Enterprise Architecture

Part III of this book provides a high-level discussion of other important aspects of enterprise architecture and an EA practice. This part addresses diverse secondary facets of an EA practice omitted in the previous chapters including architects, architecture functions, architecture governance, EA tools and modeling languages, EA-related measurements, initiation and maturity of an EA practice as well as the relationship between an internal EA practice and EA consulting.

Part III consists of four consecutive chapters. Chapter 16 discusses the role and skills of architects, common architecture positions often found in organizations, their differences and relationship. Chapter 17 discusses the general role and structure of architecture functions in organizations as well as the roles and different types of architecture governance bodies. Chapter 18 discusses specialized modeling languages and software tools for enterprise architecture, templates for EA artifacts, architecture debt and quantitative measurements for an EA practice. Chapter 19 discusses the initiation of an EA practice in organizations, maturity of an EA practice and the role of external consultancies in an EA practice.

Chapter 16: Architects in Enterprise Architecture Practice

The previous chapters discussed in detail various aspects of an EA practice including EA artifacts and EA-related processes. This chapter focuses specifically on the role and responsibilities of architects as the key actors of an EA practice and chief owners of EA artifacts. In particular, this chapter starts from discussing the general skills and desirable qualities of all architects regardless of their specific architecture positions. Then, this chapter describes five common archetypes of architects often found in organizations, their differences, similarities and relationship to each other. Finally, this chapter provides an organizational mapping of different archetypes of architects based on the planning areas they cover and explains the roles of corresponding architects in the three key EA-related processes.

General Skills and Qualities of Architects

Architects are the key actors, facilitators and organizers of an EA practice. They are also the chief owners and producers of EA artifacts (see Figure 2.7). Architects are relatively sparsely represented specialists in organizations. Organizations often employ only one architect for every 20-30 employees working in their IT departments[1]. All architects working in an organization are typically the employees of its architecture function.

As discussed earlier in Chapter 2, the essential responsibilities of architects in organizations include, but are not limited to, communicating with various business and IT stakeholders, facilitating the dialog between these stakeholders, proposing optimal planning decisions satisfying their essential concerns and developing different EA artifacts, i.e. decisions EA artifacts and facts EA artifacts (see Figure 2.6). Even though architecture functions in different organizations can have different organization-specific positions for architects implying different responsibilities, all architecture positions require approximately the same set of basic skills, qualities and attitudes to carry out typical tasks of architecture functions. In particular, all architecture positions regardless of their seniority have five general requirements: broad expertise, communicability, orientation to teamwork, innovativeness and the ability to provide a "big picture" view. In order to fit these requirements, all architects need to possess highly specific qualities and skills, including good understanding of business and IT, effective communication and collaboration, innovative mindset and systems thinking[2]. In other words, ideal architects are effective team players and communicators, proactive innovators and systems thinkers knowledgeable in both business and IT.

Knowledge of Business and IT

As highly qualified professionals intended to bridge the gap between business and IT, architects are expected to possess a broad knowledge of both business and IT. On the one hand, from the business perspective ideal architects should have a reasonably good, or at least basic, understanding of how organizations work in their different aspects. Specifically, architects should be business-savvy enough to understand typical business terminology and participate in discussions with diverse business stakeholders working at different organizational levels. Architects should be able to explain the implications of various IT-related planning decisions for the business of an organization to a wide business audience. For that purpose, architects should feel comfortable speaking about business strategy, competitive advantages, business capabilities and processes. Ideally architects should be familiar with various business decision supporting tools (e.g. SWOT analysis, value chain, BCG matrix, etc.) and other classic MBA topics. It is also desirable for architects to be aware of popular investment calculation and business case assessment techniques. Additionally, architects are expected to have some feel of organizational politics and culture to be able to effectively promote their decisions and cope with potential resistance.

On the other hand, from the IT perspective ideal architects should have a deep and broad knowledge of the whole IT domain. Firstly, architects are expected to have a significant hands-on working experience in IT that includes fulfilling, among others, the following typical tasks:

- Developing new IT systems using programming languages
- Creating new and administrating existing databases
- Participating in different types of IT projects in different roles
- Preparing various contracts and tender documentation
- Monitoring latest technical trends, assessing and selecting technologies

Secondly, architects are expected to have an overall understanding of the essential IT-related processes and common IT management best practices in different areas including, among others, the following IT-related topics:

- Project management – delivering new IT projects in a well-organized and predictable manner on time and budget
- Release management – organizing the system rollout through different stages and environments, e.g. development, testing and production
- Change management – establishing standardized and repeatable procedures for handling ongoing changes in the IT environment
- Configuration management – keeping track of the configuration and versions of all deployed system components
- Service management – controlling the quality of provided IT services, e.g. service level agreements (SLAs)

Thirdly, architects are expected to have a comprehensive understanding of the external IT environment including, but not limited to, significant knowledge in the following areas:

- What technologies are available or emerging today and what potential they provide to the business
- What types of IT systems exist on the market and what business problems they can solve
- What vendors are present on the IT market and what products or services they offer

Architecture positions generally require very substantial knowledge and understanding of IT. Unsurprisingly, the vast majority of architects have IT backgrounds and move into architecture roles from other IT-related positions by mastering necessary business-related knowledge and skills. Since the role of an architect requires significant and broad previous expertise in IT, IT specialists normally advance into architecture positions only after having ~8-12 years of active practical experience with IT. It is arguably very hard for a business manager to become an architect.

Effective Communication

As highly qualified professionals focused on finding balanced planning decisions satisfying the essential interests of diverse stakeholders, architects are expected to be excellent communicators. The job of an architect is searching for globally and locally optimized planning decisions rational from the perspective of both business and IT. Since all planning decisions reflected in decisions EA artifacts (see Table 2.1) should be understood and approved by their key stakeholders, architects should be able to convey and explain these decisions to all relevant stakeholder groups and collect their feedback. Ideal architects are eager communicators. On the contrary, architects doing the planning work alone locked inside their rooms and unwilling to communicate with real stakeholders usually only waste their time creating useless paperwork.

As discussed earlier, the key stakeholders of Considerations, Visions and Outlines are various business executives, the key stakeholders of Standards are mostly other architects and subject-matter experts, while the key stakeholders of Designs are various members of IT project teams (see Figure 8.2). Unless approved and committed to by their key stakeholders, all these decisions EA artifacts are likely to be ignored and eventually piled up in "ivory towers". In order to use any of these EA artifacts successfully, architects should be able to find a common language with their essential stakeholders to negotiate the corresponding planning decisions. Only facts EA artifacts (i.e. most Landscapes and some Standards), which merely document the current state as is and do not contain any planning decisions (see Table 2.1), can be safely developed by architects alone without involving other stakeholders (see Figure 2.6).

The essential skills required to communicate with diverse business and IT stakeholders of various decisions EA artifacts include, among others, the following abilities:

- Finding appropriate words for a verbal conversation with different general stakeholder groups as well as with specific individuals representing these groups
- Finding appropriate representation formats for EA artifacts easily understandable to their intended audience
- If necessary, finding appropriate arguments for demonstrate the value of using specific EA artifacts to their stakeholders
- If necessary, finding appropriate arguments for explaining the benefits of a disciplined information systems planning approach in general

An effective dialog between architects and any stakeholders requires an understanding of the following and similar essential questions:

- What do the stakeholders generally want to achieve?
- What are the essential concerns and interests of the stakeholders?
- What specific problems do the stakeholders see?
- What limitations do the stakeholders have?

Communication is the core activity of architects. Hence, it is a direct responsibility of architects to establish effective communication with the relevant stakeholders of EA-related planning decisions. The inability of an architect to achieve a productive dialog with a particular stakeholder should be considered as the architect's fault. Stakeholders should not be blamed for communication problems.

Collaborative Attitude

As highly qualified professionals responsible for making significant IT-related planning decisions in the best interests of an entire organization, architects are expected to have a highly collaborative attitude. The vast majority of organizations, with the exception of the smallest ones, employ multiple architects collectively responsible for carrying out all IT planning activities. All architects in an EA practice actively communicate with each other and essentially work as a single unified planning team. The job of an architect always implies teamwork and collaboration, rather than an independence and autonomy.

Any organization-wide planning decision is always a product of negotiation and trade-off between many different stakeholders, rather than a creation of a single brilliant brain. Decisions EA artifacts (see Table 2.1) are not perfect masterpieces created by genius individuals, but rather results of an effective teamwork and collaboration of multiple ordinary people. Collaborative planning in its turn requires the ability to find and accept compromises. For instance, purchasing several different products or technologies fulfilling the same technical function might be desirable from the perspective of separate business units, but undesirable from the organization-wide perspective. Some global Standards might be undesirable for specific IT projects, but desirable for an entire organization to restrain complexity and maintain the overall consistency of the IT landscape.

On the one hand, productive collaboration as part of an EA practice requires from architects possessing the following personal traits:

- Readiness for finding the middle ground between conflicting opinions and needs
- Willingness to trade local advantages for global benefits
- Preference for mutually agreed decisions over the most "intelligent" ones
- Readiness to follow and commit to collective decisions, plans and courses of action regardless of a personal opinion

On the other hand, excessive individualism of architects might be detrimental for an EA practice. Even though architects should primarily concentrate on fulfilling their own individual responsibilities, an overly narrow focus on their own personal interests essentially undermines the general goal of an EA practice to enable optimal organization-wide planning. The inability to concede and commit to the decisions made by other people only provokes conflict and creates tension between architects. Similarly, heated semi-religious disputes are also typically counterproductive for an EA practice.

Innovative Mindset

As highly qualified professionals responsible for planning the IT support of the business, architects are expected to have highly innovative mindset. Technology develops very rapidly and constantly opens new, and sometimes breakthrough, business opportunities for organizations. Cutting-edge technologies can enable previously unavailable ways to cut redundant costs, address existing customer needs, create completely new needs or even pursue radically different business strategies. In order to be able to leverage latest technological developments to benefit business, architects should be aware of the current trends in the evolution of IT and assess the relevancy of these trends to their organization. In particular, it is essential for architects to understand how the newest technologies can be utilized in an organization to address specific business needs or improve general business capabilities. Moreover, architects should also strive to identify in a timely manner potentially disruptive technologies that might have a profound impact on the business of an organization to secure enough time for accommodating with these technologies, e.g. adopting them, waiting for further evidence or rejecting them as unsuitable.

Since architects are the chief planners of IT, their role implies acting as drivers of IT-related innovation and proponents of adopting new technologies for business purposes. Along with senior IT executives, architects are responsible for ensuring that their organization stays relevant with the latest IT trends and leverages these trends when appropriate. For instance, architects should be eager to proactively propose using new technologies for addressing current business problems as well as following new approaches to utilizing IT for enhancing the overall business model and performance. In other words, architects should be able to see the business potential of specific innovative technologies, find appropriate business opportunities for applying these technologies and advocate their organizational adoption. Ideal architects can be considered as pioneers of IT-driven innovation in organizations and leaders of IT-enabled business transformations.

Systems Thinking

As highly qualified professionals responsible for planning the IT landscape of an entire organization in its full complexity, architects are expected to be insightful systems thinkers. An effective systems thinking enables the understanding of numerous explicit and implicit relationships and dependencies existing between various elements constituting the whole organization. This understanding helps architects predict how specific changes in separate elements of the organizational system spread and ripple through the entire system. Thereby, the systems thinking skills allow architects to evaluate the consequences and implications of various local planning decisions for the whole organization on both the short-term and long-term time horizons.

Specifically, ideal architects should be able to see the complex interrelationships between generic and specific, abstract and detailed, global and local, tactical and strategic, business and IT, internal and external elements including, among others, the following connections:

- Connections between generalized patterns and their specific instantiations
- Connections between high-level and low-level abstraction levels
- Connections between global and local needs, problems and directions
- Connections between existing tactical bottlenecks and possible future strategies
- Connections between current and future needs of an organization and specific technologies
- Connections between recent industry trends and corresponding organizational opportunities

Besides understanding the nature of various qualitative relationships between different elements of an organization, architects should be capable of thinking about these relationships in terms of evaluative quantitative approximations. Ideal architects are able not only to discern the existence of particular relationships, but also to estimate the relative significance and magnitude of these relationships. The ability to assess and compare conceptual notions allows architects to distinguish essential from inessential, critical from negligible, major from minor, primary from secondary. As a result, effective architects are able to articulate the very gist of existing problems and their solutions.

Additionally, constructing a consistent broad view of an entire organization often requires rapid refocusing and switching the level of abstraction between high-level visions and low-level details. A complete understanding of the organizational "big picture" implies a reasonably good understanding of its separate elements. Consequently, ideal architects should be capable of seeing the whole "forest" as well as its separate "trees". In order to achieve this view, architects should be able to quickly zoom in and zoom out their brain lenses when necessary.

Five Common Archetypes of Architects

Previously in this book all employees of architecture functions have been titled simply as "architects", while architecture functions in organizations have been viewed merely as homogeneous teams of equivalent architects. In real organizations architecture functions often employ different types of architects with significantly different responsibilities. However, concrete architecture positions in different architecture functions are very organization-specific and highly depend on the size, structure and complexity of an organization.

Despite their variety, typical architecture positions in architecture functions can be usually differentiated by their scopes and domains. Firstly, different types of architects may be responsible for different organizational scopes. For instance, some architects may focus on planning separate IT initiatives, some architects may focus on planning all IT systems in a separate business unit, whereas other architects might be focused on an organization-wide IT planning. Secondly, different types of architects may be responsible for different EA domains, e.g. business, applications, data, integration, infrastructure and security. For instance, some architects may focus on planning single EA domains (e.g. only data or only infrastructure), some architects may focus on planning several related domains (e.g. applications, data and integration), while other architects might be focused on planning the entire stack of EA domains from business to security (see Figure 2.2). Generally, architects responsible for more narrow scopes and domains are expected to provide more detailed planning and possess deeper expertise in their subject areas, and vice versa.

Even though architecture positions can be very organization-specific and even unique, four general common archetypes of architects can be articulated from the perspective of their organizational scope and domain expertise: solution architects, domain architects, business unit architects and enterprise architects. As the employees of architecture functions, architecture managers can be also considered as a special fifth archetype of architects. Although these five common archetypes are certainly not the only possible types of architects, they are often found in architecture functions of many organizations. However, the corresponding positions can have different, and often peculiar, formal titles in different organizations. The titles of architecture positions provided above and used further in this book represent either the most common established titles for these positions, or the most descriptive titles conveying the actual meaning of these positions. Moreover, these architecture positions can have slightly different sets of responsibilities in different organizations and same architects may even combine the responsibilities of multiple different positions. For this reason, the five types of architects described below should be considered only as pure archetypes among the wide variety of possible architecture positions.

Solution Architects

Solution architects are the most "narrow" architects. They focus predominantly on planning separate IT initiatives with limited scopes. Solution architects are usually specialized in concrete technologies and, therefore, are automatically aligned to respective technical EA domains, e.g. applications, data, integration, infrastructure or security (see Figure 2.2). Furthermore, sometimes they are also assigned to particular business functions or lines of business if their work requires substantial contextual knowledge of highly specific business operations and processes. The formal titles of solution architects in organizations often reflect their core specialization. For instance, their positions may be titled as application solution architects, infrastructure solution architects or security solution architects. Solutions architects are typically the most widely represented architects in architecture functions and may be found in virtually every EA practice.

Solution architects carry out only the Initiative Delivery process and essentially do not participate in the Strategic Planning and Technology Optimization processes (see Figure 6.1). They are usually responsible for providing an end-to-end architectural support to specific IT initiatives, from the initial idea-level business need to the final deployment of a working IT solution. Naturally, solution architects develop mostly EA artifacts describing specific change initiatives or projects, i.e. Outlines and Designs (see Figure 8.2). Firstly, during the initiation steps of IT initiatives solution architects communicate mostly with their executive business sponsors, discuss high-level solution implementation options based on Outlines and achieve required executive approvals. Secondly, during the implementation steps of IT initiatives solution architects communicate mostly with project teams, discuss preferred technical implementation approaches based on Designs and then ensure compliance with the agreed Designs. Solution architects actively use existing Considerations, Standards, Visions and Landscapes for developing Outlines and Designs for new IT initiatives. Even though they may also contribute to these types of EA artifacts (e.g. propose new Standards or update current Landscapes after their IT projects are completed), Considerations, Standards, Visions and Landscapes are usually provided to solution architects by other types of architects directly responsible for their development.

Domain Architects

Domain architects focus primarily on an organization-wide planning of separate EA domains, e.g. business, applications, data, integration, infrastructure or security. Usually they are responsible for a single EA domain or, in some cases, for a few closely related "adjacent" domains, e.g. data and integration or infrastructure and security. The formal titles of domain architects in organizations often refer to their key areas of expertise. For instance, their positions may be titled as business architects, data architects, integration architects or infrastructure architects. All architects focused on an organization-wide planning of specific technology layers (e.g. storage, servers or networks) can be loosely related to domain architects as well. Domain architects are more often found in EA practices of centralized organizations. Essentially, these architects are subject-matter experts in their narrow areas intended to improve the corresponding EA domains in an entire organization. However, their typical responsibilities are very domain-specific and significantly different for domain architects focused on business-supporting EA domains (e.g. integration, infrastructure and security, see Figure 2.2) and domain architects focused on business-enabling EA domains (e.g. business, applications and data, see Figure 2.2).

On the one hand, **business-supporting domain architects** (e.g. integration architects, infrastructure architects and security architects) carry out the Technology Optimization process and also participate in the Initiative Delivery process (see Figure 6.1). They are typically responsible for setting consistent organization-wide standards, selecting best technologies, planning future improvements and formulating technical rationalization suggestions for their domains. Naturally, the work of business-supporting domain architects largely revolves around developing, updating and rationalizing corresponding Standards and Landscapes. Since these domain architects are more focused on the technical side of an organization, they usually get business-focused Considerations and Visions from other architects when it is necessary to understand the desired future business direction. They also actively communicate with other business-supporting domain architects to coordinate the plans for their domains with the plans for other related EA domains. The role of business-supporting domain architects in the Initiative Delivery process is limited to supervising solution architects during the planning of new IT initiatives. Firstly, they consult solution architects regarding the available technologies, IT assets and best practices in their domains and provide relevant Standards and Landscapes. Secondly, they provide relevant technical rationalization suggestions to solution architects in order to incorporate these suggestions into new IT solutions and thereby improve the overall quality of the IT landscape. Thirdly, they review and approve all Outlines and Designs for IT initiatives to achieve compliance with the recommended approaches and ensure that new initiatives are implemented properly from the technical perspective.

On the other hand, the role of **business-enabling domain architects** (e.g. business architects, application architects and data architects) is more complex. They carry out the Strategic Planning process, contribute to the Technology Optimization process and participate in the Initiative Delivery process (see Figure 6.1). Firstly, business-enabling domain architects communicate with senior business executives to understand their strategic vision, propose appropriate long-term development strategies for their domains, negotiate these strategies with business leaders and document the achieved agreements regarding the long-term direction for their domains as Considerations and Visions. Secondly, they work with corresponding Standards and Landscapes to establish best practices, select appropriate technologies, plan future improvements and formulate technical rationalization suggestions for their domains. Thirdly, they review and approve all Outlines and Designs for IT initiatives to ensure that these initiatives are aligned to the long-term strategic Considerations and Visions approved by business executives and incorporate relevant rationalization suggestions for their domains. They also actively communicate with other domain architects in order to coordinate the strategic plans for their domains with the strategic plans for other related EA domains.

Business Unit Architects

Business unit architects focus primarily on an end-to-end IT planning for a single or a few closely related major business units, capabilities or areas, e.g. lines of business, business functions or divisions. Essentially, they are intended to plan narrow parts of an organization across the full stack of EA domains, from business and applications to infrastructure and security (see Figure 2.2), and therefore can be considered as "local" enterprise architects. The formal titles of business unit architects in organizations often reflect the respective lines of business or functional areas they cover. For example, their positions may be titled as retail architects, wholesale architects, payments architects or supply chains architects. All architects focused on an end-to-end planning of major IT systems or platforms closely associated with certain business functionality (e.g. ERP, CRM or BI) can be loosely related to business unit architects as well. Business unit architects are more often found in EA practices of large and decentralized organizations, while in small and centralized organizations these positions are usually missing.

Business unit architects carry out the Strategic Planning and Technology Optimization processes for their business units and also participate in the Initiative Delivery process (see Figure 6.1). Firstly, they communicate with the heads of their business units to understand their local strategies, develop corresponding long-term plans for IT, negotiate these plans with local business leaders and document the agreed plans for IT as Considerations and Visions relevant for their business units. Secondly, they review relevant Standards and Landscapes, analyze current technologies, implementation approaches and IT assets existing in their business units, plan their future improvements and formulate technical rationalization suggestions for their business units. Thirdly, they review and approve Outlines and Designs for all IT initiatives in their business units to ensure that these initiatives are aligned to their local Considerations and Visions and incorporate relevant rationalization suggestions. They also actively communicate with other business unit architects to enable global optimization of strategic IT-related decisions.

Enterprise Architects

Enterprise architects are the most "wide" architects. They focus on an overarching organization-wide IT planning of all EA domains, including business, applications, data, integration, infrastructure and security. Essentially, enterprise architects are generalists intended to plan all layers of an entire organization. Their formal positions in architecture functions are usually titled as enterprise architects or less often as chief architects. Enterprise architects are typically found either in EA practices of small organizations, where specialized domain and business unit architects are missing, or in large and complex organizations, where they complement specialized domain and business unit architects.

On the one hand, in small organizations, where dedicated positions for domain architects and business unit architects are missing, enterprise architects usually fulfill the responsibilities of both domain and business unit architects. In particular, they carry out the Strategic Planning and Technology Optimization processes for the whole organization across all EA domains and participate in the Initiative Delivery process by supervising solution architects (see Figure 6.1).

On the other hand, in large and complex organizations, which employ specialized domain architects, business unit architects or both, enterprise architects typically act as chief integrators of local and domain-specific planning efforts of all other architects. By communicating with all other architects during the Strategic Planning, Technology Optimization and Initiative Delivery processes, enterprise architects facilitate truly organization-wide and cross-cutting IT planning. They help develop comprehensive strategic plans for IT taking into account and balancing all local, domain-specific and global interests. For instance, as part of the Strategic Planning process enterprise architects can develop aggregate Considerations and Visions based on the global organization-wide strategic vision of senior business executives and local Considerations and Visions of different business units. Similarly, as part of the Technology Optimization process enterprise architects can develop a consolidated technology portfolio and articulate the most important technical rationalization suggestions based on domain-specific recommendations and local rationalization suggestions proposed by business unit architects. Since enterprise architects are concerned with an organization-wide planning of all typical EA domains, they naturally work with all EA artifacts of organization-wide significance, i.e. Considerations, Standards, Visions and Landscapes (see Figure 8.2).

Architecture Managers

Architecture managers are the employees of architecture functions who are in charge of managing other architects and organizing the effective work of their architecture functions. Organizationally, they are often the official heads of architecture functions and leaders of EA practices reporting directly to CIOs or other equivalent top-level IT executives, e.g. CTOs or vice-presidents of IT.

Architecture managers are typically the least represented employees of architecture functions. Even large organizations usually employ only one or a few full-time architecture managers, while in EA practices of small and medium-sized organizations dedicated positions for architecture managers may be missing altogether. In these cases the formal role of an architecture manager is often fulfilled on a part-time basis by the most senior architect or even directly by the CIO.

The key responsibilities of architecture managers include, but are not limited to, the following activities:

- Defining specific architecture roles and their responsibilities
- Defining the overall structure and size of their architecture functions
- Improving the quality of EA artifacts and EA-related processes
- Allocating resources and assigning architects to IT initiatives
- Interviewing, hiring and promoting architects

Architecture managers organize all the three main EA-related processes (see Figure 6.1). They may also participate in these processes as observers or analysts to identify the potential problems, bottlenecks and opportunities for improvements. Even though architecture managers often do not develop and use any EA artifacts directly, they can be considered as meta-architects, i.e. architects of architecture functions and EA-related processes.

Hierarchy of Architecture Positions

The common archetypes of architects described above, with the exception of architecture managers, can be represented as a hierarchy of architecture positions. Specifically, the four main architecture positions, solution architects, domain architects, business unit architects and enterprise architects, can be ranged based on their organizational scope and domain expertise from specialists to generalists. Specialists cover limited organizational scopes and possess narrow domain expertise, while generalists cover wide organizational scopes and possess broad domain expertise. From this perspective, solution architects can be considered as specialists with the most narrow scopes and expertise, enterprise architects can be considered as generalists with the widest scopes and expertise, while domain architects and business unit architects can be considered as the middle ground between specialists and generalists. The resulting hierarchy of architecture positions is shown in Figure 16.1.

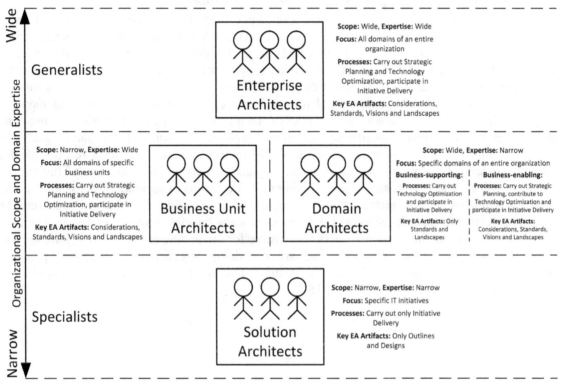

Figure 16.1. The hierarchy of architecture positions

The positions in the hierarchy shown in Figure 16.1 correlate with the seniority of the corresponding archetypes of architects. Architects typically start as solution architects, then rise to domain architects or business unit architects and finally to enterprise architects. In other words, the career path of most architects goes up the hierarchy of architecture positions, i.e. from solution architects to enterprise architects.

Additionally, besides the four main archetypes of architects constituting the hierarchy of architecture positions many organizations also employ specialized technology **designers** sometimes called as technical architects. Essentially, these designers are technical subject-matter experts experienced in specific technologies or vendor products, possessing very narrow and deep expertise and often associated with the respective centers of excellence, e.g. SAP or Oracle. Organizationally, technical designers typically belong to IT delivery functions, rather than to architecture functions. Although they usually inform relevant architectural decisions (e.g.

contribute to the development of Designs and, to a lesser extent, Outlines for specific IT initiatives as well as to the formation of organization-wide Standards), designers still work predominantly on the delivery side as part of project teams implementing requested IT solutions. For this reason, in the context of this book these technical designers, or architects, are not considered as "real" architects and not discussed in detail, though they can be fairly placed somewhere below solution architects in the hierarchy of architecture positions (see Figure 16.1).

Organizational Mapping of Architecture Positions

The difference between the five common archetypes of architects can be clearly illustrated graphically by mapping these architecture positions to the schematic structure of an organization. The whole organization can be represented as a two-dimensional matrix with its rows corresponding to typical EA domains (e.g. business, applications, data, integration, infrastructure and security) and its columns corresponding to different business units (e.g. business unit A, business unit B and business unit C). This graphical representation can be used to map the responsibilities of the common archetypes of architects and help illustrate the essential differences between them. Specifically, enterprise architects responsible for planning all EA domains of an entire organization cover the whole matrix. Domain architects responsible for planning specific EA domains across an entire organization cover different rows of the matrix. Business unit architects responsible for planning all EA domains of separate business units cover different columns of the matrix. Solution architects responsible for planning concrete IT initiatives related to specific technical EA domains in some business units cover different cells of the matrix. Finally, architecture managers responsible for organizing an architecture function and defining other architecture positions, but are not doing any actual architectural planning themselves can be placed outside of the matrix. The resulting organizational mapping of architecture positions is shown in Figure 16.2.

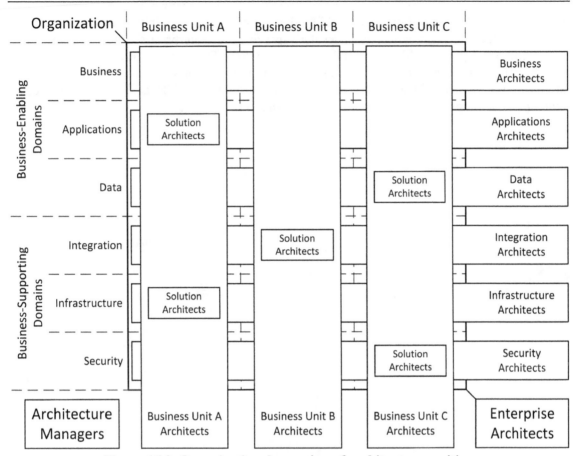

Figure 16.2. Organizational mapping of architecture positions

The mapping of the common architecture positions to the schematic organizational structure shown in Figure 16.2 demonstrates that architecture functions generally can be considered as matrix structures with overlapping but complementary responsibilities of domain and business unit architects. On the one hand, business unit architects are responsible for tying together all EA domains of separate business units. The work of business unit architects intends to facilitate local flexibility, decision-making autonomy and responsiveness to specific needs of different business units. On the other hand, domain architects are responsible for tying together specific EA domains across all business units. The work of domain architects intends to facilitate global consolidation and optimization of an entire organization.

Process Mapping of Architecture Positions

The roles of the common archetypes of architects, with the exception of architecture managers, can be also clarified by mapping these architecture positions to the three main EA-related processes: Strategic Planning, Initiative Delivery and Technology Optimization (see Figure 6.1). Specifically, the Strategic Planning process is carried out collaboratively by enterprise architects, business unit architects and business-enabling domain architects. The Initiative Delivery process is carried out by solution architects under the supervision of enterprise architects, business unit architects and domain architects. Finally, the Technology Optimization process is carried out collaboratively by enterprise architects, business unit architects and business-supporting domain architects and also contributed to by business-enabling domain architects. The resulting process mapping of common architecture positions is shown in Figure 16.3.

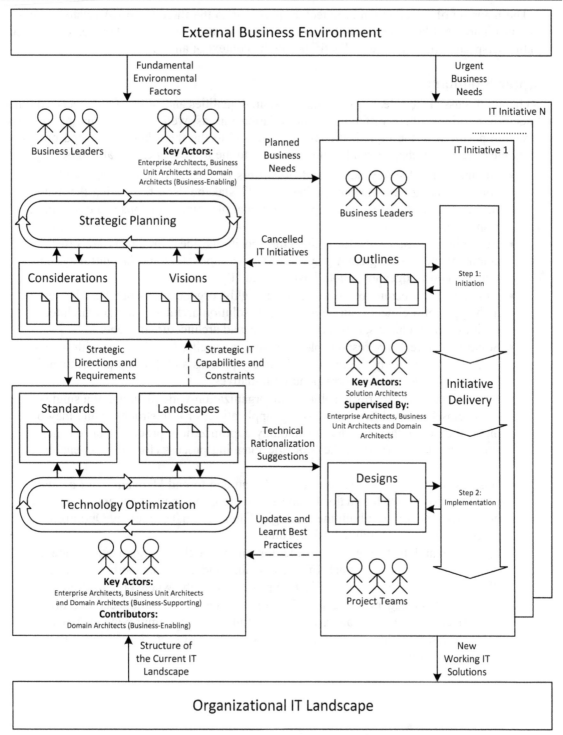

Figure 16.3. Process mapping of common architecture positions

The mapping of the common architecture positions to the three main EA-related processes shown in Figure 16.3 helps better understand the roles of the common archetypes of architects from the perspective of their essential activities in the context of an EA practice.

Chapter Summary

This chapter discussed the role, responsibilities, desired qualities and skills of architects, common architecture positions, their differences and relationship as well as the mapping of these architecture positions to the organizational structure and to the three key EA-related processes. The key message of this chapter can be summarized into the following essential points:

- Architects are the key actors and organizers of an EA practice responsible for communicating with various business and IT stakeholders, facilitating the dialog between these stakeholders, proposing optimal planning decisions and developing respective EA artifacts
- Regardless of their specific architecture positions, ideal architects are effective communicators, strong team players, proactive innovators and insightful systems thinkers knowledgeable in both business and IT
- Although architecture positions can be highly organization-specific, five pure archetypes of architects can be articulated: solution architects, domain architects, business unit architects, enterprise architects and architecture managers
- Solution architects are responsible for planning specific IT initiatives with limited scopes, carry out only the Initiative Delivery process and develop predominantly Outlines and Designs for corresponding initiatives
- Domain architects are responsible for an organization-wide planning of a single or a few closely related EA domains (e.g. applications or infrastructure) and may be more focused either on the Technology Optimization process (for business-supporting domains) or on the Strategic Planning process (for business-enabling domains)
- Business unit architects are responsible for an end-to-end IT planning of a single or a few closely related major business units (e.g. business functions or lines of business) and carry out both the Strategic Planning and Technology Optimization processes for corresponding business units
- Enterprise architects are responsible for an overarching organization-wide IT planning across the full stack of EA domains and carry out both the Strategic Planning and Technology Optimization processes for the whole organization
- Architecture managers are responsible for managing other architects, organizing the effective work of an architecture function and improving EA-related processes, rather than for performing these processes or developing any EA artifacts directly

Chapter 17: Architecture Functions in Organizations

The previous chapter discussed the role of architects in an EA practice as well as common archetypes of architects often found in organizations. This chapter focuses specifically on the role of architecture functions in organizations, their structures and governance mechanisms. In particular, this chapter starts from describing the general role and position of an architecture function in the organizational context and its relationship to other key IT-related functions. Then, this chapter discusses the structure and composition of architecture functions and their dependence on the organizational size and degree of decentralization. Finally, this chapter describes the role of architecture governance bodies, different types of architecture governance committees, their responsibilities and structure as well as corresponding exemption and escalation procedures.

The Role of Architecture Functions in Organizations

An architecture function is a specialized organizational function responsible for an EA practice and a "home" of all architects in an organization. The main role of an architecture function is to enable effective information systems planning in an organization. As a supporting organizational function, an architecture function itself does not deliver any tangible results, but produces only the optimal plans for new IT systems intended to support critical business activities.

Architecture functions usually belong to IT departments and report directly to CIOs[1]. Along with the IT delivery and IT support functions, architecture functions implement one of the three key IT-related organizational capabilities: planning, implementation and maintenance. Essentially, an architecture function provides a "front door" to the IT department for business leaders. As a subunit of the IT department responsible for organization-wide IT planning, an architecture function translates abstract business considerations incoming from business executives into specific implementable designs of new IT solutions. These implementable designs are "consumed" by the IT delivery function, which is responsible for developing new IT systems according to the incoming designs. Finally, the running IT systems developed by the IT delivery function are handed over to the IT support function, which is responsible for continuous monitoring and maintenance of the newly delivered systems. The role of architecture functions in IT departments is shown in Figure 17.1.

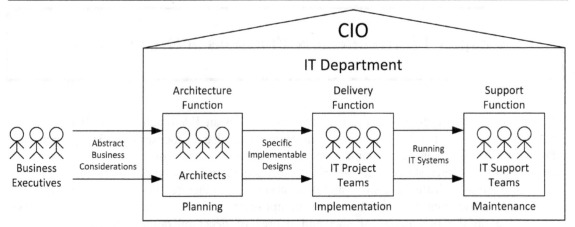

Figure 17.1. The role of architecture functions in IT departments

Architecture functions are complex organizational functions with diverse activities. They are closely interrelated with many other organizational functions, which often report their specific needs for new IT systems to architecture functions. Key responsibilities of architecture functions in organizations include:

- Establishing effective communication with other organizational functions and clarifying their IT-related demands and requirements
- Achieving a sufficient level of engagement with business executives, IT project teams and other relevant stakeholders of all IT planning decisions
- Producing required decisions EA artifacts in a timely manner and getting them approved by their key stakeholders (see Figure 2.6)
- Ensuring compliance with the planning decisions documented in decisions EA artifacts and approved by their stakeholders
- Producing required facts EA artifacts when necessary (see Figure 2.6) and maintaining them up-to-date
- Continuously optimizing the format, content and size of EA artifacts based on the feedback and information needs of their main stakeholders and users
- Institutionalizing and fine-tuning EA-related decision-making and approval processes around decisions EA artifacts
- Maintaining appropriate software toolsets for producing, storing, publishing and searching EA artifacts
- Creating appropriate architecture positions and defining their responsibilities, i.e. sizing, structuring and adapting themselves to better serve the needs of an organization
- Organizing effective peer-review mechanisms and adequate knowledge exchange between different architects
- Advocating and explaining the value of a disciplined information systems planning to all involved stakeholders

All these EA-related activities in organizations are carried out largely by architects, who are the core specialists of architecture functions possessing the necessary skill sets and knowledge to perform them. As discussed earlier, architecture functions may have different organization-specific architecture positions, but the most common archetypes of architects include solution architects, domain architects, business unit architects, enterprise architects and architecture managers (see Figure 16.2).

All architects in architecture functions are linked with each other via reporting and supervisory relationships. They intensively exchange knowledge and closely collaborate during all architectural decision-making processes. Architecture functions organize the work of different architects and structure the EA-related processes carried out by these architects. Architecture functions typically achieve a meaningful collaboration between architects by means of creating appropriate architecture positions, defining their position-specific responsibilities in the context of an EA practice and establishing effective internal structures facilitating their communication. Similarly to specific positions for architects, the structures of architecture functions may be very organization-specific and highly depend on particular organizational needs.

The Structure of Architecture Functions

Previously in this book architecture functions in organizations have been considered essentially as abstract teams of architects of an indefinite size. In real organizations architecture functions consist of concrete numbers of architects occupying specific positions and have certain internal structures adapted to the particular needs of these organizations. The internal structures of architecture functions, as well as architecture positions in these functions, are largely determined by two different organizational factors. Firstly, the structure of an architecture function in an organization is determined by the size of the organization and its IT department. Secondly, the structure of an architecture function in an organization is influenced by the degree of decentralization of the organization.

Dependence on the Size of an Organization

The first significant factor defining the structure of an architecture function is the size of an organization. As noted earlier, organizations on average usually employ one architect for every 20-30 employees working in their IT departments. In other words, architects often constitute around ~3-5% of IT staff. Consequently, the size of an architecture function is directly proportional to the size of an organization and its IT department[2]. At the same time, larger architecture functions require more sophisticated structures and wider diversity of architecture positions, and vice versa. Since organizations can vary dramatically in their size and complexity from local one-man businesses to multinational giants employing millions of people around the globe, architecture functions can vary accordingly in their size and complexity from trivial one-architect functions to very complex multi-level functions employing hundreds of architects.

While organizations employing less than 20-30 IT specialists might not need architecture functions at all, organizations with at least 30-40 IT staff can arguably benefit from practicing enterprise architecture. For instance, these organizations may employ a single enterprise architect responsible for all aspects of organization-wide IT planning. On the one hand, this enterprise architect may carry out the Strategic Planning and Technology Optimization processes for an entire organization. On the other hand, this enterprise architect may be also involved in the

Initiative Delivery process. Depending on the situation, as part of Initiative Delivery the enterprise architect can either act as a solution architect and develop Outlines and Designs for IT initiatives, or merely review and approve Outlines and Designs produced by the third parties engaged by an organization to deliver IT solutions.

Organizations employing a hundred or a couple hundred IT specialists may employ several solution architects, who might be described as "20% enterprise and 80% solution" architects. These architects may spend 80% of their time developing Outlines and Designs for specific IT initiatives as part of the Initiative Delivery process. However, during the remaining 20% of their time they may act essentially as enterprise architects and collectively carry out the Strategic Planning and Technology Optimization processes for an entire organization.

Organizations employing a few hundred IT specialists may employ a single enterprise architect and a dozen solution architects. The enterprise architect may carry out the Strategic Planning and Technology Optimization processes for an entire organization, while solution architects may focus on the Initiative Delivery process under the supervision of the enterprise architect. In this case the enterprise architect may also act essentially as an architecture manager for solution architects as well as for the architecture function in general.

Organizations employing several hundred IT specialists may employ a few domain architects and a couple dozen solution architects. Domain architects may focus on an organization-wide planning of main EA domains (e.g. business, applications, data and infrastructure) and carry out the Strategic Planning and Technology Optimization processes. Domain architects may also act essentially as architecture managers for the solution architects related to their domains. These solution architects may carry out the Initiative Delivery process under the supervision of the corresponding domain architects.

Organizations employing a thousand or a couple thousand IT specialists may employ a single architecture manager, a few business unit architects, several domain architects and tens of solution architects. Business unit architects may focus on an end-to-end IT planning for their business units, while domain architects may focus on an organization-wide planning of their domains. Both business unit architects and domain architects may carry out the Strategic Planning and Technology Optimization processes, while solution architects may carry out the Initiative Delivery process under their supervision. The architecture manager may manage business unit architects and domain architects, while business unit architects may also act essentially as architecture managers for the solution architects related to their business units.

Organizations employing a few thousand or more IT specialists may have even more sophisticated architecture functions. For instance, these organizations may employ a couple of architecture managers, a few enterprise architects, several business unit architects, a dozen domain architects and a large pool of solution architects. Business unit architects and domain architects may focus on a comprehensive IT planning of their business units and domains, while enterprise architects may focus on an organization-wide harmonization of all local and domain-specific plans. Solution architects may focus on planning specific IT initiatives under the supervision of the corresponding business unit architects and domain architects. Architecture managers may manage enterprise architects and business unit architects, enterprise architects may manage domain architects, while business unit architects may manage solution architects related to their business units. The dependence of the structure of an architecture function on the size of an organization with sample architecture positions and structures is shown in Figure 17.2.

	Approximate Scale	Sample Positions	Sample Structure
Small ↑	<40 IT Employees 1 Architect	1 Enterprise Architect (EA)	EA
	100-200 IT Employees 4-8 Architects	4-8 Solution Architects (SAs)	SAs
Size	250-400 IT Employees 10-15 Architects	1 Enterprise Architect (EA) 10-15 Solution Architects (SAs)	EA SAs
	500-800 IT Employees 20-30 Architects	3-5 Domain Architects (DAs) 15-25 Solution Architects (SAs)	DAs SAs
	1200-2000 IT Employees 50-80 Architects	1 Architecture Manager (AM) 3-5 Business Unit Architects (BUAs) 4-8 Domain Architects (DAs) 40-70 Solution Architects (SAs)	AM DAs BUAs SAs
Large ↓	>2500 IT Employees >100 Architects	2-3 Architecture Managers (AMs) 3-5 Enterprise Architects (EAs) 4-8 Business Unit Architects (BUAs) 10-15 Domain Architects (DAs) 80-120 Solution Architects (SAs)	AMs EAs BUAs DAs SAs

Figure 17.2. The dependence of the structure on the size of an organization

The continuum of architecture functions shown in Figure 17.2 demonstrates the critical dependence of the structure of an architecture function on the size of an organization. Larger organizations naturally require larger and more complex architecture functions. Importantly, the scales and samples of architecture positions and structures provided in Figure 17.2 are far from strict and exhaustive. These samples are intended merely to illustrate some possible options for organizing architecture functions in organizations of different sizes.

The samples of architecture functions described above also demonstrate that specific architecture positions in organizations can be very diverse. On the one hand, architecture functions in different organizations may employ different types of architects. For instance, EA practices often even have no dedicated positions for enterprise architects, but instead employ other denominations of architects collectively responsible for organization-wide IT planning. On the other hand, architecture positions in different organizations often deviate from the five pure archetypes of architects described earlier (see Figure 16.2). For example, enterprise architects often act as architecture managers and, in small organizations, even as solution architects.

Similarly, business unit architects and domain architects often manage solution architects allocated to their business units or domains. In some cases, business unit architects responsible for particular business units may also act as domain architects providing expertise in specific EA domains and responsible for their organization-wide planning. Domain architects may often act as business unit architects as well. By combining the responsibilities of different archetypes of architects simultaneously or at least periodically rotating architects occupying different architecture positions, especially positions at different levels of the architectural hierarchy (see Figure 16.1), organizations can facilitate effective knowledge exchange between architects, remove the boundaries between different levels of architecture and avoid the "ivory tower" syndrome[3].

Dependence on the Degree of Decentralization

The second significant factor defining the structure of an architecture function is the degree of decentralization of an organization[4]. Centralized organizations benefit from the global optimization of IT systems and processes, consolidation of technology portfolios and shared reuse of available IT assets, while decentralized organizations benefit from the local flexibility of IT systems and processes, swift responsiveness to unit-specific business needs and better adaptability to the changing environment. The degree of decentralization in most organizations highly correlates with the preferred operating models adopted by these organizations. Specifically, the unification model can be considered as the most centralized operating model, whereas the diversification model can be considered as the most decentralized operating model (see Figure 5.3)

As noted earlier, domain architects generally facilitate global optimization of the whole organization by consolidating respective EA domains across all its business units, while business unit architects more often facilitate local autonomy and flexibility of separate business units by increasing the organizational responsiveness to their critical business needs (see Figure 16.2). Consequently, more centralized organizations tend to employ more domain architects and grant them more authority over IT planning decisions, while more decentralized organizations tend to employ more business unit architects and grant them more authority over IT planning decisions.

For instance, very centralized medium-sized organizations (e.g. organizations with the unification or replication operating model) may employ only domain architects (besides solution architects) and grant them full authority over the Strategic Planning and Technology Optimization processes for an entire organization. This approach facilitates total global consolidation and optimization required by very centralized organizations, but does not allow any local flexibility or decision-making autonomy in different business units.

Centralized medium-sized organizations (e.g. organizations with the coordination operating model) may employ domain architects for the data, integration, infrastructure and security domains as well as some business unit architects for their major business units. Domain architects might be granted authority over the Strategic Planning and Technology Optimization processes in their domains for an entire organization, while business unit architects might be granted authority over the Strategic Planning process for their business units, but only in the business and applications domains having no specialized organization-wide domain architects. This approach facilitates global consolidation and optimization of most EA domains required by centralized organizations, but still allows some local flexibility in business-enabling EA domains (see Figure 2.2) of different business units.

Decentralized medium-sized organizations (e.g. organizations with the diversification operating model) may employ business unit architects for their major business units as well as some domain architects for the infrastructure and security domains. Domain architects might be granted authority over the Technology Optimization process in their domains for an entire organization, while business unit architects might be granted authority over the Strategic Planning and Technology Optimization processes for their business units, with the exception of the infrastructure and security domains having specialized organization-wide domain architects. This approach facilitates significant local flexibility in different business units required by decentralized organizations, but still allows some global consolidation and optimization of business-supporting EA domains (see Figure 2.2).

Finally, very decentralized medium-sized organizations (e.g. organizations with the diversification operating model), or holding companies controlling completely independent subsidiary businesses, may employ only business unit architects and grant them full authority over the Strategic Planning and Technology Optimization processes for their business units. This approach facilitates total decision-making autonomy and local flexibility in different business units required by very decentralized organizations, but does not allow any global consolidation and optimization of the IT landscape. The dependence of the structure of an architecture function on the degree of decentralization with sample architecture positions and structures is shown in Figure 17.3.

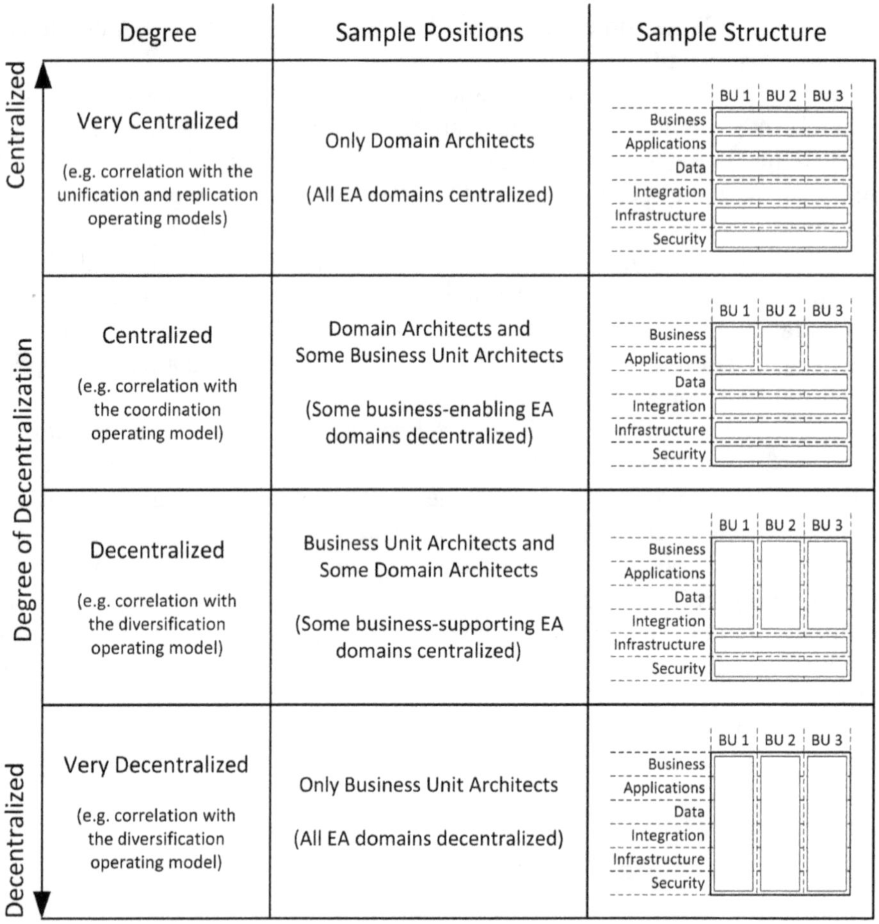

	Degree	Sample Positions	Sample Structure
Centralized	**Very Centralized** (e.g. correlation with the unification and replication operating models)	Only Domain Architects (All EA domains centralized)	BU 1 / BU 2 / BU 3 Business Applications Data Integration Infrastructure Security
	Centralized (e.g. correlation with the coordination operating model)	Domain Architects and Some Business Unit Architects (Some business-enabling EA domains decentralized)	BU 1 / BU 2 / BU 3 Business Applications Data Integration Infrastructure Security
	Decentralized (e.g. correlation with the diversification operating model)	Business Unit Architects and Some Domain Architects (Some business-supporting EA domains centralized)	BU 1 / BU 2 / BU 3 Business Applications Data Integration Infrastructure Security
Decentralized	**Very Decentralized** (e.g. correlation with the diversification operating model)	Only Business Unit Architects (All EA domains decentralized)	BU 1 / BU 2 / BU 3 Business Applications Data Integration Infrastructure Security

(Left axis label: Degree of Decentralization)

Figure 17.3. The dependence of the structure on the degree of decentralization

The continuum of architecture functions shown in Figure 17.3 demonstrates a significant dependence of the structure of an architecture function on the degree of decentralization in general and on the preferred operating model in particular. Importantly, the samples of architecture positions and structures provided in Figure 17.3 are far from strict and exhaustive. These samples are intended merely to illustrate some possible options suitable for organizing architecture functions in centralized and decentralized organizations.

Governance Bodies of Architecture Functions

Besides having specific architecture positions (see Figure 16.2), architecture functions typically also host a set of architecture governance bodies[5]. These governance bodies are EA-related decision-making committees involving architects and other representatives of business and IT.

The Role of Governance Committees

Governance committees in architecture functions are formal committees of decision-makers. They include key representatives of architects and other relevant business and IT stakeholder groups. The main responsibilities of architecture governance committees in organizations include the following activities:

- Conducting periodical meetings on a regular basis
- Organizing discussions of relevant EA-related questions
- Inviting all essential stakeholders of specific discussions
- Ensuring sufficient engagement between different stakeholder groups
- Making and approving key EA-related decisions in a collective manner
- Formally reviewing and officially endorsing decisions EA artifacts (see Table 2.1)

Approvals by architecture governance committees represent the final and most formal step, or milestone, in the overall approval process for all decisions EA artifacts (see Figure 2.6). Importantly, before presenting any EA-related decisions to governance committees for their formal approval, these decisions should be already discussed and informally agreed with their key stakeholders. Significant EA-related decisions should not be new and surprising for participants of governance committees. Moreover, all decisions EA artifacts should be also peer-reviewed by other architects, often by more senior architects, to ensure their adequacy and quality. From this perspective, the bulk of architecture governance is usually accomplished unofficially at the peer-review level before the involvement of governance committees. The key role of governance committees is not to provide a forum for discussions or disputes, but rather to make sure that all relevant stakeholders are fully aware of all important EA-related decisions, do not object to these decisions and ready to act on them. Ideally, architecture governance committees only finalize the decision-making processes by officially authorizing the resulting decisions EA artifacts tentatively approved earlier by their direct stakeholders.

As discussed earlier, all new decisions EA artifacts usually start their existence from informal preliminary discussions with their key stakeholders. Later, in the course of iterative refinements and further clarifications these EA artifacts mature, get completed and informally approved by their direct stakeholders. Only then they are presented at the governance committee meetings for their formal endorsement. For example, normally by the time they are presented to relevant governance committees, new Standards should be already agreed between architects and subject-matter experts, updated Visions should be already approved by business executives, while Designs for new IT projects should be already agreed with their project teams. The role of architecture governance committees in the development of decisions EA artifacts is shown in Figure 17.4.

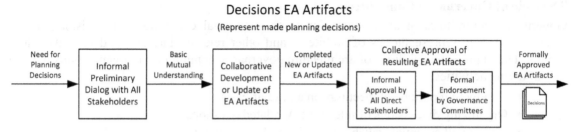

Figure 17.4. The role of governance committees in the development of decisions EA artifacts

All new and substantially updated decisions EA artifacts (i.e. all Considerations, most Standards, all Visions, some Landscapes, all Outlines and all Designs) undergo corresponding governance procedures and get formally approved by architecture governance committees before they take any effect. Only facts EA artifacts (i.e. most Landscapes and some Standards), which intend merely to document the current state and do not imply any new decisions (see Table 2.1), do not require their approval by governance committees. In order to ensure a comprehensive inspection and exhaustive scrutiny of all decisions EA artifacts and respective EA-related planning decisions, architecture governance committees typically include a broad circle of diverse stakeholders, which is often much wider than the circle of direct stakeholders of specific EA artifacts.

Four Types of Governance Committees

Different governance committees in architecture functions focus on different types of EA-related questions and decisions. Depending on their focus, these governance committees may discuss different decisions EA artifacts, meet with different periodicity and invite different stakeholders (besides architects). All governance committees in architecture functions can be classified along two orthogonal dimensions according to their main focus.

Firstly, all governance committees can be classified into business committees and IT committees. On the one hand, business committees focus on the questions and decisions having a direct impact on the business of an organization and approve all business-focused EA artifacts, i.e. all Considerations, Visions and Outlines (see Figure 8.1). Besides architects, these committees typically include numerous business stakeholders and only the most senior IT stakeholders. On the other hand, IT committees focus on the technical questions and decisions having no direct impact on the business of an organization and approve necessary IT-focused EA artifacts, i.e. most Standards, some Landscapes and all Designs. Besides architects, these committees typically include numerous IT stakeholders, including both managers and technical subject-matter experts.

Secondly, all governance committees can be classified into strategic committees and tactical committees. On the one hand, strategic committees focus on the questions and decisions of strategic importance with significant long-term consequences. These committees approve necessary rules and structures EA artifacts, i.e. all Considerations, most Standards, all Visions and some Landscapes (see Figure 8.1). They typically meet less often, but include more senior business and IT stakeholders. On the other hand, tactical committees focus on the questions and decisions of tactical importance having only a short-term impact. These committees approve all changes EA artifacts, i.e. all Outlines and Designs. They typically meet more often, but include less senior business and IT stakeholders.

The intersection of the two orthogonal dimensions described above produces four different types of architecture governance committees. Specifically, strategic business committees can be collectively titled as strategy committees since these committees focus on the EA-related questions and decisions relevant directly to the business strategy of an organization. Strategic IT committees can be collectively titled as technology committees since these committees focus on the EA-related questions and decisions relevant directly to the technology portfolio and IT landscape of an organization. Tactical business committees can be collectively titled as investment committees since these committees focus on the EA-related questions and decisions relevant to the business value of specific IT investments. Finally, tactical IT committees can be collectively titled as design committees since these committees focus on the EA-related questions and decisions relevant to the technical designs of specific IT projects. However, these four types of governance committees can have different organization-specific titles in different organizations. The titles of architecture governance committees provided above and used further in this book represent the most descriptive titles conveying the actual meaning of these committees, regardless of their various formal titles in organizations.

Strategy committees (can be titled as strategic architecture forums, enterprise architecture councils, architecture governance councils, IT steering committees, executive forums, etc.) discuss the EA-related decisions of immediate strategic importance for the business of an entire organization. These committees typically involve senior architects, multiple senior business stakeholders and some of the most senior IT stakeholders. In particular, the invited architects may include enterprise architects, business unit architects and business-enabling domain architects (see Figure 16.1), the invited business stakeholders may include the CEO, other C-level executives and heads of major business units, while the invited IT stakeholders may include the CIO and other senior IT managers. Strategy committees usually discuss and approve significant changes in all Considerations and Visions. For instance, these committees often endorse the introduction of new Principles and Direction Statements, major amendments in established Policies, refocus of Business Capability Models and changes in desired Target States. Strategy committees often meet monthly or convened on an as-necessary basis.

Technology committees (can be titled as technology architecture forums, architecture steering committees, IT architecture boards, IT strategy councils, domain architecture councils, etc.) discuss the EA-related decisions of immediate strategic importance for the entire organizational IT landscape. These committees typically involve senior architects and multiple senior IT stakeholders. Specifically, the invited architects may include enterprise architects, business unit architects and domain architects, while the invited IT stakeholders may include the CIO, other senior IT managers and subject-matter experts. Technology committees usually discuss and approve substantial changes in most Standards and some Landscapes. For example, these committees often endorse the identification of emerging and unsupported technologies in Technology Reference Models, introduction of new Patterns, selection of strategic and legacy IT systems in Enterprise System Portfolios and rearrangements of IT Roadmaps. At the same time, ordinary improvements of narrow Guidelines and Logical Data Models or regular updates of the current state in Landscape Diagrams and Inventories normally do not need to be endorsed regardless of their significance. Technology committees often meet monthly or convened on an as-necessary basis.

Investment committees (can be titled as investment forums, project investment boards, funding committees, innovation forums, portfolio boards, etc.) discuss the EA-related decisions regarding the approval of specific proposed IT investments. Essentially, investment committees are the key decision-makers approving or rejecting the implementation of specific IT initiatives. These committees typically involve architects, senior business stakeholders and some senior IT stakeholders. In particular, the invited architects may include enterprise architects, relevant business unit and domain architects and some solution architects, the invited business stakeholders may include the CEO, CFO, executive business sponsors of proposed IT initiatives and other senior business managers, while the invited IT stakeholders may include the CIO and other senior IT managers. Investment committees usually discuss and approve all Outlines and business cases for proposed IT initiatives, i.e. make investment decisions regarding specific IT investments. For instance, these committees often study Initiative Proposals and Solution Overviews together with their business cases and decide whether the corresponding IT initiatives are worth to be implemented, elaborated further or modified. They also ensure the basic alignment of the proposed IT initiatives to Considerations, Visions, key Standards and Landscapes. Investment committees often meet monthly or biweekly.

Design committees (can be titled as design authorities, architecture review boards, architecture review panels, architecture review meetings, technology architecture review forums, technical review boards, etc.) discuss the EA-related decisions regarding the implementation of specific IT projects. These committees typically involve architects, some business representatives and multiple IT stakeholders. Specifically, the invited architects may include some enterprise, business unit or domain architects, solution architects and in some cases even external vendor architects specialized in relevant technologies, the invited business stakeholders may include either direct business owners of IT projects or business analysts acting on their behalf, while the invited IT stakeholders may include project managers, subject-matter experts and senior IT operations and support specialists. Design committees usually discuss and approve all Designs for proposed IT projects. For example, these committees often study Preliminary Solution Designs and Solution Designs and decide whether the proposed project implementation plans are appropriate from the technical perspective. In particular, they ensure that all new IT projects are based on the technologies, approaches and best practices recommended by Standards and properly fit into the existing IT environment described in Landscapes. They also ensure that all relevant technical rationalization suggestions resulting from the Technology Optimization process (e.g. to reuse or decommission specific IT assets, see Figure 6.1) are incorporated into Designs of new IT projects. Design committees often meet biweekly, weekly or more often if necessary, depending on the number of active IT projects. The four main types of architecture governance committees described above are shown in Figure 17.5.

	Strategic Committees	Tactical Committees	
Business Committees	**Strategy Committees** **Decisions:** Decisions of strategic importance for the business of an entire organization **Participants:** Senior architects, multiple senior business stakeholders and some of the most senior IT stakeholders **Approve:** Significant changes in all Considerations and Visions **Meet:** Monthly or on an as-necessary basis	**Investment Committees** **Decisions:** Decisions regarding the approval of specific proposed IT investments **Participants:** Architects, senior business stakeholders and some senior IT stakeholders **Approve:** All Outlines and business cases for proposed IT initiatives **Meet:** Monthly or biweekly	**Decisions:** Decisions having direct impact on the business of an organization **Participants:** Architects, numerous business stakeholders and only the most senior IT stakeholders
IT Committees	**Technology Committees** **Decisions:** Decisions of strategic importance for the entire organizational IT landscape **Participants:** Senior architects and multiple senior IT stakeholders **Approve:** Significant changes in most Standards and some Landscapes **Meet:** Monthly or on an as-necessary basis	**Design Committees** **Decisions:** Decisions regarding the implementation of specific IT projects **Participants:** Architects, some business representatives and multiple IT stakeholders **Approve:** All Designs for proposed IT projects **Meet:** Biweekly, weekly or more often if necessary	**Decisions:** Technical decisions having no direct impact on the business of an organization **Participants:** Architects, numerous IT stakeholders, including both managers and subject-matter experts
	Decisions: Decisions of strategic importance with significant long-term consequences **Participants:** More senior stakeholders **Meet:** Less often	**Decisions:** Decisions of tactical importance having only a short-term impact **Participants:** Less senior stakeholders **Meet:** More often	

Figure 17.5. Four types of architecture governance committees

Besides the four main types of governance committees shown in Figure 17.5, architecture functions may also organize specialized forums intended to facilitate communication and knowledge sharing between architects. These forums provide an opportunity for all interested architects to discuss promising technology trends, disseminate innovative ideas and merely share interesting EA-related thoughts. Unlike the four types of architecture governance committees shown in Figure 17.5, these forums are largely informal bodies. Usually they have optional attendance, no formal decision-making responsibilities and no governance authority.

Exemption and Escalation Procedures

Sometimes Outlines and Designs developed for new IT initiatives are not fully compliant with the suggestions of established Considerations, Standards, Visions and Landscapes. For instance, proposed Outlines might be inconsistent with some Considerations or deviate from the approved strategic direction reflected in Visions, while proposed Designs might reuse some IT assets marked as undesirable in Landscapes or deviate from the technical implementation approaches prescribed by Standards. In these cases, investment committees for Outlines and design committees for Designs have to decide whether the corresponding IT initiatives should be approved or rejected taking into account both the perceived business importance of these initiatives and the significance of their deviations. If the deviations of proposed Outlines or Designs for reasonably important IT initiatives are considered as insignificant and have sound underlying justifications, then the respective governance committees may grant an **exemption** to these initiatives, i.e. approve their implementation despite some deviations from the established rules and plans. Exemptions for IT initiatives may imply formal obligations to do a certain work some time later in the future to minimize the negative effects of these deviations, e.g. permit to implement a required IT solution now based on a deprecated technology with a documented obligation to migrate the solution to a strategic technology during the next year. Usually all exemptions given to IT initiatives and their reasons are logged to enable the post-implementation analysis of their long-term consequences and facilitate organizational learning. In mature EA practices the notion of architecture debt is often used to estimate the magnitude of deviations, inform the exemption decision and record the corrective actions necessary to "redeem" the debt in a special register, as discussed later in Chapter 18 (Instruments for Enterprise Architecture).

However, if the deviations of proposed Outlines or Designs for very important IT initiatives are considered to be significant and might have substantial far-reaching consequences for an entire organization, then the decisions regarding the corresponding initiatives may need an **escalation** higher to more authoritative governance committees for their consideration. In this situation the higher-level governance committees can decide to reject the proposed Outlines or Designs as completely inappropriate for an organization, still grant an exemption to these Outlines or Designs despite their significant deviations or even reconsider and modify the existing Considerations, Standards, Visions and Landscapes in light of new circumstances. For example, the higher-level governance committees can decide to readjust the established Principles, change the existing implementation Guidelines, reorganize the agreed Roadmaps or reconsider the long-term value of specific IT assets in Inventories. Similarly to exemption decisions, escalation decisions may be also informed by the volume of a potential architecture debt.

For instance, if proposed Designs for new IT projects require the purchase, introduction and subsequent technical support of new technologies or vendor products missing in Technology Reference Models, depart from the established IT Principles or conflict with the approved IT Roadmaps, then the decisions regarding these Designs might need to be escalated from design committees to more authoritative technology committees. Unlike design committees, technology committees are mandated to make organization-wide strategic technology-related decisions and, therefore, may authoritatively approve or reject the proposed Designs, or even revise and modify the respective Standards and Landscapes. Essentially, all the decisions on IT projects having significant unplanned implications for the entire IT landscape are delegated from design committees to technology committees.

If proposed Designs for new IT projects are unable to capture all the required business data according to the agreed Conceptual Data Models or deviate in some aspects from the desired long-term Target States, then the decisions regarding these Designs might need to be escalated from design committees to more authoritative investment committees. Unlike design committees, investment committees are mandated to make IT investment decisions and, therefore, may authoritatively reconsider the very need to implement the corresponding IT initiatives or even request completely reworked Outlines and business cases to reassess the business value of these initiatives from scratch. All the decisions on IT projects having significant unplanned implications for their business value are delegated from design committees to investment committees.

If proposed Outlines for new IT initiatives are not compliant with critical Policies, deviate from the approved Direction Statements or do not uplift any business capabilities marked as strategic or important in Business Capability Models, then the decisions regarding these Outlines might need to be escalated from investment committees to more authoritative strategy committees. Unlike investment committees, strategy committees are mandated to make organization-wide strategic business decisions and, therefore, may authoritatively approve or reject the corresponding IT initiatives, or even revisit and modify the respective Considerations and Visions. Essentially, all the decisions on IT initiatives having significant unplanned implications for the whole organization are delegated from investment committees to strategy committees.

Likewise, all the decisions of technology committees having significant unplanned implications for the business strategy of an entire organization are delegated to strategy committees. For instance, if the decisions regarding an optimal technology portfolio desirable from the technical perspective conflict with the suggestions of Analytical Reports or the decisions regarding the reuse of specific IT assets desirable from the technical perspective conflict with the heatmapped business activities on Value Chains, then these decisions might need to be escalated from technology committees to more authoritative strategy committees. Unlike technology committees, strategy committees are mandated to make technology-related strategic business decisions and, therefore, may authoritatively influence the strategic evolution of the entire IT landscape or even realign the current business strategy to the actual IT capabilities. The escalation procedures between different architecture governance committees described above are shown in Figure 17.6.

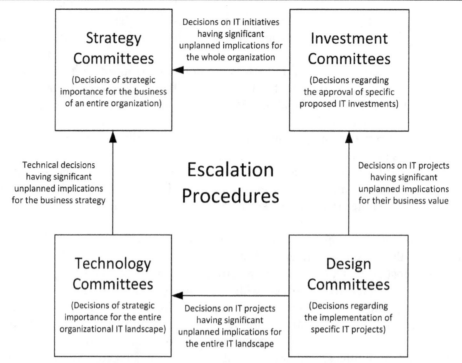

Figure 17.6. Escalation procedures between architecture governance committees

Generally, all possible resolutions of architecture governance committees regarding the approval of new or updated decisions EA artifacts can be summarized into four main categories: endorsement, rejection, exemption and escalation. The endorsement decision represents the unconditional approval of an EA artifact and certifies its overall alignment to relevant higher-level planning decisions reflected in other EA artifacts endorsed earlier, e.g. alignment of a new Design to the established Standards. The rejection decision represents the disapproval of an EA artifact due to its considerable misalignment with higher-level planning decisions. The exemption decision represents the approval of an EA artifact despite its misalignment with higher-level planning decisions, sometimes with an obligation to take certain corrective actions in the future (exemptions with obligations are often considered as conditional endorsements) or a registration of the corresponding architecture debt. Finally, the escalation decision represents the inability of a governance committee to resolve the contradictions related to an EA artifact with a subsequent delegation of the respective decision to more authoritative governance committees for their consideration (see Figure 17.6).

The Structure of Governance Committees

While the structure of an architecture function highly depends on the size and complexity of an organization (see Figure 17.2), the structure of architecture governance committees in its turn highly depends on the size and complexity of an architecture function. Consequently, organizations of different sizes can have different numbers of governance committees fulfilling different decision-making responsibilities. However, regardless of a particular structure and number of architecture governance committees in an organization, the decision-making responsibilities of all the four main types of governance committees should be fulfilled (see Figure 17.5). In other words, the four types of governance committees can be implemented differently from the organizational perspective, but all the four types should be implemented.

For instance, in small organizations the decision-making responsibilities of all the four types of governance committees might be fulfilled by a single architecture committee. This committee might be chaired by the most senior enterprise architect and invite different sets of participants depending on the actual questions being discussed. For example, for all strategy-related discussions the committee may invite the CEO and other executives, while for all design-related discussions the committee may invite the project manager, solution architects and relevant subject-matter experts.

In medium organizations the decision-making responsibilities of the four types of governance committees might be fulfilled by two different committees: business committee and IT committee. The business committee may combine the responsibilities of both strategy and investment committees, while the IT committee may combine the responsibilities of both technology and design committees. This two-committee pattern is arguably the most popular structure of architecture governance committees commonly found in many organizations. The business committee (e.g. IT steering committee) is responsible for setting the overall strategy in relation to IT and approving all IT investments. The IT committee (e.g. architecture review board) is responsible for defining organization-wide technical standards and ensuring the adherence to these standards in all IT projects. All major decisions with significant business implications are escalated from the lower-level IT committee to the higher-level business committee.

In large organizations the decision-making responsibilities of the four types of governance committees might be fulfilled by four separate committees. Finally, in very large and highly decentralized organizations the decision-making responsibilities of each type of governance committees might be fulfilled by multiple different committees. For example, the responsibilities of strategy and investment committees might be fulfilled by several different committees aligned to major business units (e.g. lines of business, business functions or divisions) and chaired by the corresponding business unit architects, while the responsibilities of technology and design committees might be fulfilled by several different committees aligned to different technical EA domains (e.g. applications and infrastructure, see Figure 2.2) and chaired by the corresponding domain architects.

Moreover, besides local committees aligned to specific business units or domains, very large organizations may also have global strategy and technology committees chaired by enterprise architects, responsible for making respective organization-wide decisions and providing the escalation points for all the local committees. In some organizations all IT investments exceeding a certain amount of money are automatically escalated for their approval from local investment committees directly to the executive committee or even to the board of directors. The sample structure of architecture governance committees in different organizations is shown in Figure 17.7.

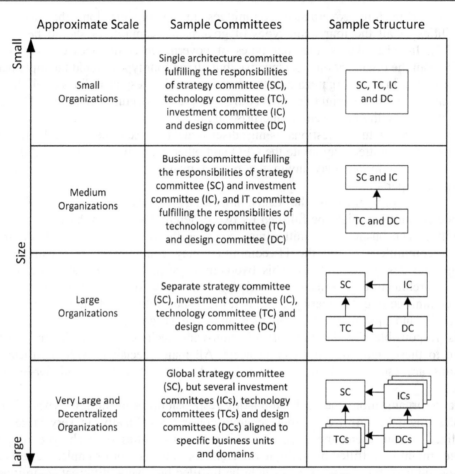

Figure 17.7. The structure of governance committees in different organizations

Although organizationally the responsibilities of the four types of governance committees (see Figure 17.5) often can be implemented by one or two more general architecture committees inviting different sets of stakeholders for different types of discussions, the explicit separation of governance committees may be beneficial for an EA practice. In particular, the direct separation of the decision-making responsibilities between different governance committees helps set separate agenda for different meetings, minimize deviations from the agenda, focus discussions on relevant issues and better structure an EA practice in general. Establishing different governance committees for discussing different questions allows clearly separating, for instance, organization-wide from initiative-level discussions as well as purely technical from business-related discussions.

Chapter Summary

This chapter discussed the general role of architecture functions in organizations, the dependence of their structure on the organizational size and degree of decentralization, the roles and different types of architecture governance bodies as well as corresponding exemption and escalation procedures. The key message of this chapter can be summarized into the following essential points:

- An architecture function is a specialized supporting organizational function usually materialized as a separate subunit of the IT department reporting directly to the CIO, responsible for an EA practice and IT planning, housing all architects and providing a "front door" to the IT department for business executives
- Key responsibilities of architecture functions include enabling knowledge exchange between different architects, establishing effective communication with other organizational functions, achieving sufficient engagement with all stakeholders of IT-related planning decisions and then ensuring compliance with the planning decisions documented in respective EA artifacts
- The size and complexity of an architecture function is directly proportional to the size of an organization, architecture functions can range from trivial one-architect functions to very sophisticated multi-level functions employing hundreds of architects
- More centralized organizations tend to employ more domain architects to facilitate global optimization and consolidation of specific EA domains across all business units, while more decentralized organizations tend to employ more business unit architects to facilitate local flexibility and responsiveness of separate business units
- Architecture governance bodies are formal committees of decision-makers involving architects as well as other business and IT stakeholders and responsible for conducting periodical meetings, approving key EA-related planning decisions and endorsing corresponding decisions EA artifacts
- Depending on their main focus, all architecture governance committees can be classified into four different types: strategy committees (most authoritative ones), technology committees, investment committees and design committees (least authoritative ones)
- If specific planning decisions deviate from the established architectural rules and plans, these decisions depending on their significance and impact can be either granted exemptions or escalated higher to more authoritative governance committees for their consideration

Chapter 18: Instruments for Enterprise Architecture

The previous chapter discussed the role of architecture functions in organizations, their structures and governance mechanisms. This chapter addresses purely "technical" aspects of an EA practice including specialized modeling languages and software tools for enterprise architecture, templates for EA artifacts, architecture debt and quantitative measurements for an EA practice. In particular, this chapter starts from discussing various modeling languages and software tools relevant to enterprise architecture, their practical applicability and roles in an EA practice. Then, this chapter describes the use of templates for creating standardized EA artifacts and the use of so-called "straw-man" architectures for facilitating early discussions around decisions EA artifacts. Finally, this chapter discusses the concept of architecture debt as a measure of architectural deviations as well as aggregate quantitative measurements that proved helpful for monitoring, managing and controlling decision-making flows in the context of an EA practice.

Modeling Languages for Enterprise Architecture

Most EA artifacts, especially Visions, Landscapes, Outlines and Designs, are expressed in graphical formats. These EA artifacts usually depict some aspects of the relationship between business processes, information systems, data entities and underlying infrastructure. The need to describe these and similar relationships occurs very often in the course of information systems planning. Unsurprisingly, a number of specialized modeling notations have been developed to provide a standardized means for creating different models and diagrams. Even though countless modeling languages have been proposed to describe various aspects of information systems, widely known modeling notations relevant from the perspective of enterprise architecture today include ArchiMate, UML, BPMN and ARIS[1].

ArchiMate[2]

ArchiMate is a comprehensive modeling language intended specifically for enterprise architecture. ArchiMate was initiated in 2002 by the Telematica Instituut (later renamed to Novay in 2009) in the Netherlands, but subsequently the ownership of ArchiMate was transferred to The Open Group in 2008.

The ArchiMate core language provides specialized notations for representing various objects in the business, application and technology layers, which loosely map to the stack of common EA domains (see Figure 2.2), as well as their interrelationship. Specifically, the business layer deals mostly with business services, processes and actors, the application layer deals predominantly with application services and underlying applications, while the technology layer focuses on processing, storage and communication services, underlying system software and hardware. For each of these three layers ArchiMate offers a set of graphical elements for describing their active structure, behavior and passive structure aspects. The active structure aspect represents the structural subjects of activity including business actors, application components and hardware devices. The behavior aspect represents specific behavior of the corresponding active subjects including processes, services and events. Finally, the passive structure aspect represents the structural objects on which the behavior of active subjects is performed including information objects, data objects and even physical objects.

Besides the core three layers and three aspects described above, ArchiMate also provides additional graphical notations for representing the elements of a business strategy (e.g. capabilities and resources), elements of implementation and migration plans (e.g. gaps, packages and deliverables), physical elements (e.g. facilities, materials and equipment) as well as the elements of motivation behind architectural decisions (e.g. drivers, goals and stakeholders). ArchiMate is a relatively new modeling language which is arguably still gaining popularity, but is already rather widely adopted by the EA community. Typical examples of ArchiMate diagrams are shown in Figure 18.1.

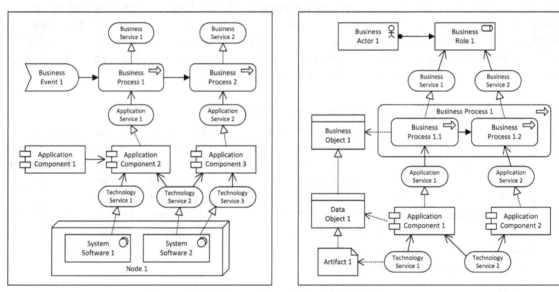

Figure 18.1. Examples of ArchiMate diagrams

UML[3]

Unified Modeling Language (UML) is a very well-known general-purpose modeling language for software engineering. UML originated in 1994 at Rational Software (later acquired by IBM in 2009) in the United States with an intention to standardize diverse notations and modeling approaches used in the software industry for system design purposes. However, in 1997 UML was adopted by the Object Management Group (OMG) and in 2005 published by the International Organization for Standardization (ISO) as an established global industry standard. UML was designed specifically for the needs of software engineering and provides many different types of diagrams for describing various aspects of software systems, which can be generally separated into two broad categories: structural diagrams and behavioral diagrams.

On the one hand, structural UML diagrams offer some static views of the internal structure of software systems explaining what components these systems consist of and how exactly these components are organized. Specific subtypes of structural diagrams provided by UML include class diagrams (depict object-oriented class hierarchies and inheritance relationships), component diagrams (depict connections and interfaces between different system components), composite structure diagrams (depict the internal structure of a class and collaborations enabled by this structure), deployment diagrams (depict the physical deployment of system components on hardware nodes), object diagrams (depict specific instances of objects with their attributes and relationships between each other), package diagrams (depict the dependencies between software packages) and profile diagrams (depict the meta-model with stereotypes and profiles).

On the other hand, behavioral UML diagrams offer some dynamic views of the temporal behavior of software systems explaining how these systems work and how exactly their components interact with each other. Specific subtypes of behavioral diagrams provided by UML include activity diagrams (depict detailed workflows of step-wise activities and actions), communication diagrams (depict the interactions between system components in terms of sequential messages), interaction overview diagrams (depict high-level workflows with the nodes consisting of more detailed interaction diagrams), sequence diagrams (depict how system components interact with each other and in what sequence), state machine diagrams (depict possible states of a system and allowed transition paths between these states), timing diagrams (depict the interactions between system components focusing specifically on accurate time intervals and constraints) and use case diagrams (depict system use cases as possible interactions between the system and its users). UML is an established, very popular and widely used modeling language familiar to the majority of architects and other experienced IT specialists. Typical examples of UML diagrams (class diagrams and sequence diagrams) are shown in Figure 18.2.

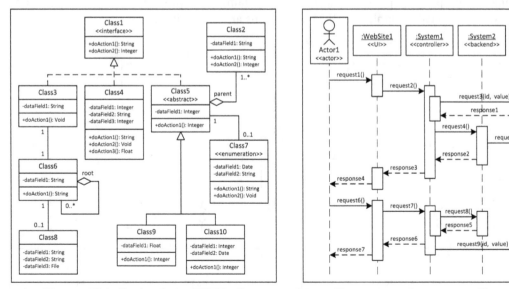

Figure 18.2. Examples of UML diagrams (class diagrams and sequence diagrams)

BPMN[4]

Business Process Model and Notation (BPMN) is a popular graphical modeling language intended predominantly for describing business processes. BPMN was initially developed in 2004 by the Business Process Management Initiative (BPMI), but eventually maintained by the Object Management Group (OMG) since 2005 when these organizations merged. As a modeling language designed specifically for business modeling purposes, BPMN naturally provides powerful notations for specifying business processes and their various aspects, but does not offer any specific notations for describing other EA domains, e.g. applications, data or infrastructure.

BPMN diagrams describe the flow of a business process as a step-wise sequence of its underlying activities or tasks. BPMN diagrams often organize the activities constituting a particular business process according to different "swimlanes" representing corresponding organizational actors (e.g. individual employees, generic roles or even entire business units) responsible for accomplishing these activities. Besides ordinary process activities, which typically represent either simple tasks or more complex sub-processes, BPMN diagrams can also contain other elements for defining the process flow including events, gateways and artifacts. Events represent specific process points where something significant happens, e.g. process starts, process finishes, message arrives, time elapses or right moment comes. Gateways represent specific process points of forking or merging where different process flows can start or converge, e.g. parallel flows or alternative flows. Artifacts normally represent some clarifications of the process flow intended to improve the general readability of corresponding diagrams. For instance, artifacts may show what data is produced or consumed by a process activity, provide an explanatory annotation or textual comment, or merely group a number of logically related activities under a common title. Despite being a relatively new modeling language, BPMN has already gained widespread popularity and is arguably familiar to most practicing architects and business analysts. Typical examples of BPMN diagrams are shown in Figure 18.3.

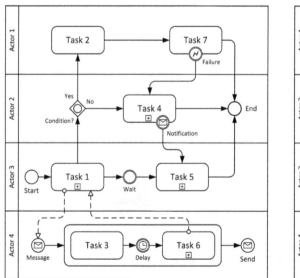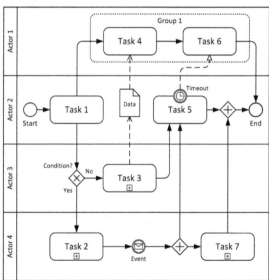

Figure 18.3. Examples of BPMN diagrams

ARIS[5]

Architecture of Integrated Information Systems (ARIS) is an established holistic approach to enterprise modeling addressing both the business and IT sides of organizations. ARIS initially emerged in the 1980s from the academic research of August-Wilhelm Scheer and was owned by his software company IDS Scheer. However, later in 2009 IDS Scheer was acquired by Software AG and the ownership of ARIS was transferred accordingly.

ARIS offers a standard set of specialized notations for describing the relationship between business processes and information systems. It covers the complementary functional, organizational and data views of an organization as well as the control view integrating the three former views. The functional view focuses primarily on business processes, activities, their relationship and hierarchy. The organizational view focuses on organizational actors, roles, units, locations, their relationship and hierarchy. The data view focuses predominantly on data entities, attributes and their relationship. Finally, the control view focuses on the interrelationship between the functional, organizational and data views. This view combines the three other views, provides an integrated picture of organizational business processes and explains their general logical flow. In particular, it describes what business activities are performed as part of a business process and in what sequence, which employees or organizational units accomplish these activities, what information is produced or consumed by these activities and which information systems or IT infrastructure support these activities. ARIS is a mature and rather widely adopted modeling language familiar to many architects. However, currently it is arguably losing its popularity in the EA community. Typical examples of ARIS diagrams are shown in Figure 18.4.

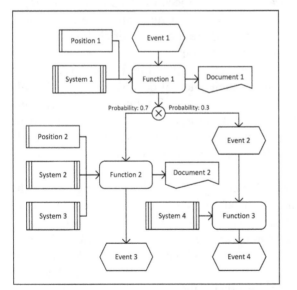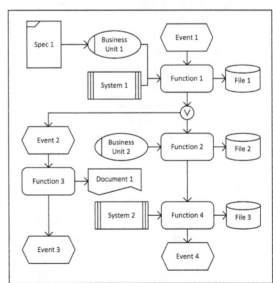

Figure 18.4. Examples of ARIS diagrams

Applicability of Modeling Languages

Despite the variety of available modeling languages that can be used to describe EA artifacts, the practical applicability of these modeling languages in an EA practice is rather limited. The common problem of all popular modeling notations in the context of an EA practice is their focus on specific details and overly formal modeling attitude.

For instance, ArchiMate, though being a relatively high-level modeling language, is still too detailed for executive-level diagrams required in Target States and other Visions. Moreover, even though ArchiMate provides the necessary notations for describing business goals, capabilities and processes, these notations are too formal and technical in nature to be comprehensible to most business stakeholders. Senior business stakeholders of EA artifacts usually find ArchiMate diagrams excessively complex and do not understand them. As a result, ArchiMate in most cases cannot be used in any business-focused EA artifacts. However, ArchiMate may be a good choice for creating purely technical diagrams required in Designs and Landscapes, especially Landscape Diagrams. Although ArchiMate is positioned and widely promoted as a specialized language for enterprise architecture, its real practical applicability is largely limited only to Landscapes and Designs.

UML, as a modeling language created specifically for software engineering, is naturally very detailed, technical and formal. These qualities make UML virtually incomprehensible to most business stakeholders and totally inapplicable to any business-focused EA artifacts. Furthermore, due to its focus on minute details of various software components UML can hardly be used even for Landscapes, which require a higher level of abstraction. However, UML is widely used in practice for creating low-level diagrams describing the internal details of specific IT projects required in Designs, especially in Solution Designs.

BPMN, as a modeling language created specifically for describing business processes, is naturally focused on the low-level details of separate business processes. This narrow, in-depth focus on specific business processes with their internal activities, events and gateways makes BPMN essentially inapplicable to Visions and Landscapes, where much higher abstraction levels are required. Visions usually provide very conceptual descriptions which more often focus on business capabilities and rarely mention concrete business processes, while Landscapes, even if mention specific business processes, still rarely mention their internal details. However, BPMN may be used in Outlines and Designs to explain the impact of new IT solutions on the existing business processes and describe how exactly the flow of specific operating procedures will be modified as a result of particular IT initiatives. Since most business stakeholders barely understand sophisticated modeling notations, simplified and cut-down versions of BPMN are often used in Outlines.

ARIS, as a relatively high-level and comprehensive enterprise modeling language, might be useful for creating technical diagrams required in Designs and Landscapes. However, similarly to ArchiMate diagrams, ARIS diagrams are too formal, detailed and technical for most business stakeholders. Due to these qualities ARIS diagrams can hardly be used in Visions and Outlines.

Hence, the practical applicability of the available modeling languages in an EA practice is limited only to specific types of EA artifacts. On the one hand, popular modeling languages can be used for Designs, Landscapes and Outlines. On the other hand, Visions require more high-level, intuitive and conceptual diagrams not offered by any modeling languages, while Considerations and Standards are expressed largely in textual formats and often do not require any full-fledged diagrams. The typical applicability of popular modeling languages to different types of EA artifacts is shown in Figure 18.5.

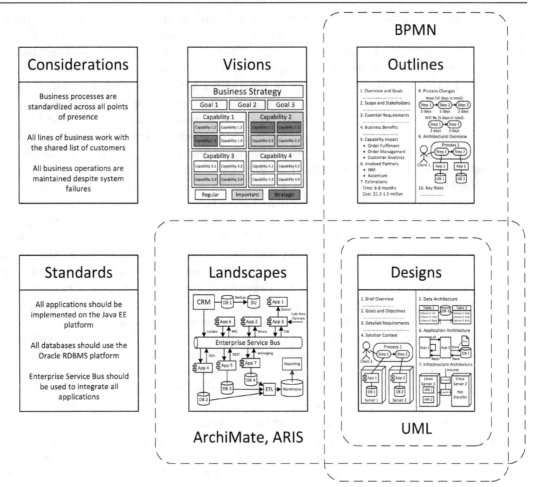

Figure 18.5. Applicability of popular modeling languages to different types of EA artifacts

The Role of Modeling Languages

Specific modeling languages play only a secondary role in an EA practice. Even though the importance of various modeling languages is often emphasized by their authors, trainers and tool vendors, their real value for an EA practice should not be exaggerated. The success or failure of an EA practice cannot be attributed to the usage or non-usage of any specific modeling languages because of several different reasons.

Firstly, perfectly correct modeling is not necessary for an EA practice. As noted earlier, creating accurate descriptions of organizations is not the goal of an EA practice. Most diagrams and models in the context of an EA practice are intended merely to facilitate communication and document the achieved agreements between different stakeholders, rather than to provide strict drawings of information systems. From this perspective, the usefulness of any EA models is wholly determined by their ability to support communication and decision-making, not by their adherence to certain modeling notations.

Secondly, the most critical stakeholders of EA artifacts are business executives responsible for making strategic IT-related decisions. These business stakeholders prefer simple and intuitive diagrams, but generally do not understand any formal modeling languages of technical origin. Consequently, popular modeling languages essentially cannot be used for creating critical business-focused EA artifacts, most notably for creating Visions and Outlines, with the exception of using simplified BPMN for describing business processes. Despite the existence of multiple modeling languages and even specialized EA-oriented modeling languages, these languages do not provide any standardized notations suitable for creating Outlines and Visions and, therefore, do not address the essential needs of an EA practice. Fortunately, Business Capability Models, Roadmaps and Value Chains are usually expressed in common, widely known and informally standardized formats shown in Figure 11.1, Figure 11.2 and Figure 11.4 respectively.

Thirdly, drawing stakeholder-friendly and especially business-friendly diagrams is more art than engineering or science. The selection of appropriate representation formats, modeling approaches and notations for EA artifacts is a direct responsibility of architects, which requires significant practical experience, creativity and taste. As a non-trivial problem, the selection of convenient formats for EA artifacts cannot be resolved automatically or reduced merely to choosing specific modeling languages for drawing diagrams and models. Creating useful EA artifacts is a much more complex task than simply following certain modeling notations.

Fourthly, full versions of most modeling languages are rarely used in practice. Even if used for drawing EA diagrams, different modeling languages are typically simplified and reduced to their most essential elements since their full versions are usually found excessively complex. Sophisticated details of most modeling languages are simply unnecessary and redundant for typical practical purposes. There is no pragmatic value in studying and following a specific modeling notation in every minute detail. Using complete versions of most modeling languages in their full complexity is usually an impractical approach to modeling.

Finally, the obsessive desire to use modeling languages "properly" and create perfectly correct diagrams can even be harmful for an EA practice. Focusing on the details of specific modeling languages can only distract the attention of architects from solving real problems and further complicate an EA practice. Moreover, the excessive focus on formal modeling substitutes the genuine goal of an EA practice (i.e. facilitating communication between stakeholders) with the false goal of creating accurate models. While the proper use of modeling languages alone cannot guarantee the success of an EA practice, the obsession with proper modeling can easily guarantee its failure.

Due to these reasons, many organizations with established EA practices do not use any branded modeling languages, or use them loosely and inconsistently. Most EA artifacts in successful EA practices usually use intuitively understandable ad hoc notations, rather than formal modeling languages with strictly defined rules. The selection of the most appropriate modeling notations and representation formats for particular EA artifacts is often left to the discretion of individual architects. Generally, the use of specific modeling languages should not be considered as a critical aspect of an EA practice.

Software Tools for Enterprise Architecture

An EA practice implies controlling and manipulating numerous objects and entities important for information systems planning. These objects may include business capabilities, processes, initiatives, systems, applications, databases, data entities, servers and any other objects relevant from the perspective of business and IT alignment. Moreover, the relationships between these objects often might be even more important than the objects themselves. Managing a large number of diverse and interrelated objects can be a difficult task, especially in large organizations routinely running hundreds or even thousands of information systems supporting a commensurable number of business processes and capabilities. Unsurprisingly, a number of specialized software tools for enterprise architecture have been developed by different global and local vendors to ease this task. These tools can help architects keep track, store and manage the information on numerous organizational objects relevant to an EA practice and to information systems planning in general. The most popular and widely known specialized software tools for enterprise architecture currently available on the market include Abacus (Avolution), Alfabet (Software AG), Enterprise Architect (Sparx Systems), Enterprise Studio (BiZZdesign), HOPEX (MEGA International), iServer (Orbus), System Architect (UNICOM Systems, former IBM Rational System Architect), Troux (Planview) and some other tools[6].

Capabilities of Specialized Software Tools

Most specialized software tools for enterprise architecture available on the market offer a number of pretty similar capabilities to facilitate the management of EA artifacts and other aspects of an EA practice. These EA tools, though may significantly differ in some vendor-specific details of their implementation, focus predominantly on the storage, visualization and analysis of relevant architectural information[7].

Firstly, software tools for enterprise architecture typically provide specialized **architectural repositories** for storing, organizing and accessing all architectural information in a convenient manner. These repositories can store all the architecturally significant elements related to different EA domains (e.g. business, applications, data and infrastructure, see Figure 2.2) as well as all the relationships existing between these elements. For instance, an architectural repository can capture the fact that the business process A is enabled by the application B, which is based on the technology C, interacts with the applications D and E, stores the data entity F in the database G and runs on the server H. Ideally, an EA repository should store the entire comprehensive network, or graph, of all architecturally significant elements constituting the organizational IT landscape and business capabilities it supports. Architectural repositories are usually organized according to certain meta-models defining the key types of objects that can be stored, their essential properties and the possible types of relationships between different objects. Technically, EA tools are often based on the client-server model, where client applications running on the personal computers of architects access the central repository server storing all the architectural information in an underlying relational database. Via using client applications provided by the EA tools, architects can search, navigate, retrieve, modify and update the information stored in their organizational EA repositories. Currently, many tool vendors offer both on-premise and cloud-based repository deployment options.

Secondly, software tools for enterprise architecture typically offer powerful modeling and visualization capabilities. On the one hand, EA tools provide convenient modeling environments where architects can create various architectural diagrams using common modeling notations and languages (e.g. ArchiMate, UML or ARIS) referring to the existing objects stored in their repositories. For instance, with an EA tool an architect can create a UML diagram explaining how exactly the applications A, B and C described in the repository interact with each other. On the other hand, EA tools provide the functionality for visualizing the relationships between different elements from the repository. Most EA tools can automatically generate structured architectural diagrams or even entire documents in different formats (e.g. HTML or MS Word) representing narrow "slices" of the repository and covering particular areas of the organizational IT landscape. For example, an EA tool can generate a complex diagram explaining all layers of the IT landscape related to a specific business capability or a relationship matrix showing the mapping between the existing applications and data entities. Moreover, many EA tools can also automatically publish required architectural information on the designated web pages for its easier distribution among stakeholders.

Thirdly, software tools for enterprise architecture typically provide strong analytical capabilities. Specifically, EA tools enable an effective multi-purpose analysis of the architectural information available in the repository. One of the most important analytical capabilities offered by EA tools is arguably the impact analysis capability. For instance, architects leveraging the analytical functionality of an EA tool can easily determine which specific business processes and elements of the IT landscape can be affected if the application A is improved or decommissioned. Similarly, if the installed server operating system needs to be upgraded to the next version, architects empowered by an EA tool can quickly identify which exactly servers the corresponding operating system is running on, which applications might need to be stopped to upgrade the operating system and finally which business processes might be disrupted as a result of this operation.

Besides the essential capabilities related to storage, visualization and analysis of architectural information, most software tools for enterprise architecture also provide a number of additional functional and non-functional features. For instance, most EA tools offer some querying and reporting functions which allow extracting the necessary information from the architectural repository and presenting it in textual, graphical and even executable forms, e.g. BPEL. Many tools support the import and export of information to and from the repository in XML and other open or proprietary formats. Most EA tools also provide some mechanisms to enable their effective usage in multi-user collaborative environments including access control, versioning, auditing, locking for concurrent modifications, check-out, check-in and change reconciliation functions. Some tools provide rather advanced capabilities for workflow and change management. These features may include the support of customizable flows, discussion threads, triggered alerts, change notifications, review and approval mechanisms. Additionally, EA tools normally provide a set of routine administrative functions including the control of user roles, permissions and authorization. Many EA tools are flexible, easily configurable and allow fine-tuning their functionality (e.g. the meta-model of a repository) to the specific needs of an organization.

Applicability of Software Tools

Although specialized software tools for enterprise architecture offer powerful capabilities for managing architectural information and creating EA artifacts, these tools alone are typically insufficient for an EA practice. Due to a number of reasons successful EA practices, even if leverage some capabilities of EA-specific tools, are still based more on the popular standard applications of the MS Office suite, most importantly on Word, Visio, PowerPoint and Excel.

On the one hand, most EA artifacts are decisions EA artifacts developed collaboratively by all their stakeholders (see Table 2.1 and Figure 2.6). These EA artifacts need to be easily accessible, distributable, discussable and sometimes also editable by all the stakeholders involved in their development and subsequent usage. However, most EA tools are intended specifically for architects, but largely unsuitable for a broad use among diverse stakeholder groups. They are naturally considered as too technical, complex and inconvenient by business stakeholders and may require considerable learning even for most IT stakeholders, e.g. IT executives, project managers and software developers. Moreover, EA tools typically require installation, configuration and may be priced on a per-user basis according to their license agreements. These qualities make specialized EA tools essentially inaccessible and unusable for all non-architects. Consequently, these tools can be considered only as internal tools used by the narrow group of architects for managing architectural information inside the architecture function, but not as an appropriate mechanism for communicating with the "outer" organizational world. Even if EA tools are often used by architects as modeling environments for creating architectural diagrams, these diagrams are then usually "wrapped" in common file formats (e.g. MS Word or PowerPoint) and distributed among stakeholders in these formats. In other words, resulting EA artifacts in most cases are ordinary MS Office files, even when some of their internal diagrams are generated via sophisticated EA tools.

On the other hand, many EA artifacts can hardly benefit from the capabilities provided by specialized EA tools. For instance, Principles, Policies and other Considerations are essentially unrelated to the technical information stored in architectural repositories and can be easier created as plain MS Word documents. Likewise, most conceptual graphical diagrams intended for executive-level audience, which often do not require references to specific IT assets, can be easier created in MS Visio or PowerPoint without using any complex EA-specific tools. For example, there is arguably little or no value in creating Business Capability Models and Options Assessments in specialized EA tools when these EA artifacts can be more easily created in MS Visio and PowerPoint respectively. For this reason, Visions and Outlines with some exceptions are usually created using standard MS Office tools. At the same time, Designs usually require more detailed descriptions than the ones typically stored in tool-based EA repositories. For this reason, they are also usually created as regular MS Word documents with pretty detailed textual descriptions and diagrams, though some of these diagrams may be backed by EA tools and produced with their assistance. Consequently, many or even most types of EA artifacts simply cannot leverage the power of specialized EA tools in any real sense and can be more easily created in familiar and ubiquitous MS Office applications.

The key value proposition of specialized software tools for enterprise architecture is arguably an architectural repository which helps architects capture the structure of the IT landscape including the properties of different IT assets and relationships between them. Essentially, the unique capability offered exclusively by EA tools is the ability to store, analyze and manage the information on the existing IT landscape in a convenient manner. For this reason, the true power of these tools naturally lies in dealing with facts EA artifacts (i.e. most Landscapes and some Standards), which focus on the current state, provide reference materials for planning and in most cases owned solely by architects (see Table 2.1). A tool-based EA repository can effectively substitute many Landscapes and Standards EA artifacts and enable the synergy between them. For example, an architectural repository can store the list of all IT assets with their properties (i.e. Inventories, see Figure 12.2), relationships between these assets (i.e. Landscape Diagrams, see Figure 12.1), the list of all technologies used in an organization (i.e. Technology Reference Models, see Figure 10.1) and structures of key data entities (i.e. Logical Data Models, see Figure 10.5). Moreover, a repository can also capture the interrelationships between the information from different types of EA artifacts, e.g. the relationship between systems, technologies and data types. This ability to capture, store and share the architectural information between architects makes EA tools ideal for fulfilling the general role of Landscapes as a common knowledge base of reference materials on the IT landscape. By providing a comprehensive information repository bundled with the impact analysis functionality, specialized EA tools can also significantly boost the analytical and planning capabilities of architects. In particular, EA tools help architects accomplish typical activities closely associated with using Landscapes, i.e. identify inefficiencies, redundancies and bottlenecks in the current IT landscape, plan architectures of new IT initiatives as well as the further evolution of the landscape in general. However, even Landscapes and Standards can still be created and maintained "manually" with standard MS Office applications. For instance, Landscape Diagrams and Enterprise System Portfolios are often created as simple drawings in MS Visio, while Inventories are often maintained as ordinary spreadsheets in MS Excel. Similarly, Guidelines, Patterns, IT Principles and even Logical Data Models can be easily described in MS Word documents.

Another broad class of software tools relevant from the perspective of enterprise architecture is configuration management databases (CMDBs)[8]. CMDBs are specialized software tools intended to enable smooth, uninterrupted and incident-free work of organizational IT infrastructure. They are typically used by IT operations and support teams to track and control the configuration of deployed IT systems and hardware. Similarly to specialized EA tools, CMDBs also provide organization-wide or federated configuration repositories for storing the information on the available IT assets (typically called as configuration items (CIs) in the commonly accepted CMDB terminology) and their interdependence. Moreover, usually they also offer some impact analysis capabilities. However, despite their apparent conceptual similarity CMDBs and EA-specific tools are still intended for different purposes and have a number of important ensuing differences[9]. While EA tools are intended to facilitate information systems planning and improve business and IT alignment, CMDBs are intended to facilitate IT support and improve the quality of IT service. Unlike EA tools, which offer a rather abstract view of the IT landscape focusing only on its architecturally significant elements, CMDBs offer a very detailed view focusing on specific physical components, devices and other "nuts and bolts" of the landscape. Although both EA tools and CMDBs are capable of storing the properties of IT assets as well as their interrelationships, EA tools are arguably still more focused on presenting the relationships between different assets in a convenient graphical form and, therefore, are conceptually closer to Landscape Diagrams, while CMDBs are more focused on accurately capturing the properties and attributes of specific assets and, therefore, are conceptually closer to Inventories. Furthermore, EA tools capture the information on very diverse elements from the entire spectrum of typical EA domains (see Figure 2.2) including information systems, business processes and data structures, but CMDBs are largely limited only to the applications and infrastructure domains, i.e. capture predominantly the technical information on specific applications, equipment and hardware with little or no focus on logical elements from other EA domains, e.g. business processes and data entities. The exclusive owners and users of specialized EA tools are architects, whereas CMDBs are usually owned and maintained primarily by IT operations and support teams.

Despite their primary focus on the operational side of IT, very detailed and purely technical view of the IT landscape, limited visualization, presentation and modeling capabilities, CMDBs still can be considered as important and valuable tools for an EA practice. Analogously to Landscapes and architectural repositories of EA tools, CMDBs provide a shared knowledge base and common repository of the available IT assets, their properties and relationships. Moreover, from the perspective of capturing knowledge CMDBs even have a number of significant advantages over tool-based EA repositories. The first notable advantage of CMDBs is their rather powerful automated discovery, or auto-discovery, capabilities. Many CMDBs are able to scan the IT environment, automatically identify existing hardware and software assets and collect their essential properties, e.g. network structure, server hardware, system software, running applications, network communication and traffic patterns, etc. The auto-discovery capability helps initially populate and then automatically update configuration repositories according to the ongoing changes of the IT landscape. Although some EA tools also offer limited auto-discovery capabilities, tool-based EA repositories typically have to be populated and updated manually by architects, which requires considerable efforts and often results in potentially outdated information that needs to be double-checked with the actual owners of corresponding IT assets. The second advantage of CMDBs is their integration with regular change management, release and deployment management, asset management and other standard IT service management processes[10]. Since CMDBs are owned by IT operations and support teams responsible for accomplishing in a disciplined manner all change procedures related to the IT landscape, all ongoing modifications are routinely synchronized with CMDBs when they happen, even if they cannot be auto-discovered. The third advantage of CMDBs is that they can provide a single source of truth on the current structure of the IT landscape to architects, IT operations and support teams. While tool-based EA repositories in most cases can be used only by architects and essentially create additional architecture-specific knowledge repositories, CMDBs can be used by both architects and IT operations staff as a common knowledge database. The use of a CMDB as a shared repository helps reduce redundancy, inconsistency and duplication of information, avoid extra license fees for EA-specific tools, facilitate collaboration and overall simplicity. In this case a CMDB might be updated solely by IT operations and support teams as they deploy new changes in production, while architects may act only as information consumers and use the CMDB in a "read-only" mode.

The use of a CMDB as a central repository of architectural current-state information by architects also solves another common problem. As noted earlier, minor changes of the IT landscape are often implemented without any architectural involvement. These changes, though gradually modify the structure of the IT landscape, are essentially invisible for architects and, therefore, cannot be properly synchronized with EA-specific repositories. However, these changes are still tracked by IT operations and support teams responsible for their deployment and normally get synchronized with CMDBs, manually or automatically. As a result of these beneficial properties, CMDBs are likely to contain more accurate and up-to-date information than specialized EA repositories, though this information may need to be extracted and mentally "digested" to the appropriate level of abstraction by architects to be useful for the purposes of architectural planning. In other words, the information from CMDBs tends to be in a less convenient format for architectural purposes, but more accurate and up-to-date. Due to these advantages some organizations and EA practices prefer to consider CMDBs as the primary sources of information on the current structure of their IT landscapes complementing, or even instead of, EA-specific repositories.

Generally, all the needs of an EA practice cannot be satisfied with any single tool, but only with a complementary set of different tools including general-purpose MS Office tools, operational CMDB tools and specialized EA tools. Even the software tools developed specifically for the needs of an EA practice do not address effectively the entire spectrum of all EA-related requirements. These tools can only complement, but not completely substitute standard MS Office applications. Moreover, each tool that can be used to support an EA practice is typically applicable to, or closely associated with, only specific types of EA artifacts and irrelevant to others. At the same time, many EA artifacts, and especially Landscapes, can be supported by different tools. The typical applicability of popular software tools to different types of EA artifacts is shown in Figure 18.6.

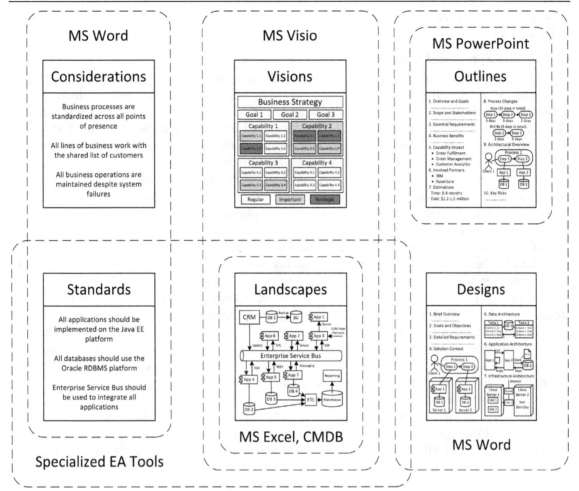

Figure 18.6. Applicability of popular software tools to different types of EA artifacts

Since most EA artifacts are usually ordinary files of standard MS Office formats (e.g. Word, PowerPoint or Visio), they need to be stored in convenient locations enabling easy access, quick distribution and effective collaboration. For this purpose organizations typically use any appropriate collaboration software including popular enterprise portals (e.g. MS SharePoint), wiki-based platforms (e.g. Atlassian Confluence), issue tracking systems (e.g. Atlassian Jira), simple could-based file storage (e.g. Google Drive) and even protected folders on shared network drives. Tool-based EA repositories can be also used for storing regular files representing EA artifacts.

Logically, stored EA artifacts can be structured in multiple different ways into a hierarchy of nested folders. For instance, many EA artifacts can be organized according to respective business capabilities defined in Business Capability Models. Furthermore, Outlines and Designs are usually separated into current and completed IT initiatives, while other types of EA artifacts can be loosely organized according to their EA domains, e.g. applications, data and infrastructure.

The Role of Specialized Software Tools

Specialized software tools for enterprise architecture generally play only a supporting role in an EA practice. Although the use of EA-specific tools may be beneficial and facilitate an EA practice, these tools are still not critically necessary to practice enterprise architecture since all the six general types of EA artifacts can be developed and used with acceptable effectiveness even via standard MS Office applications (see Figure 18.6). Around two-thirds of organizations use some specialized EA tools, while the remaining one third of organizations still rely only on general-purpose, non-EA-specific tools for managing architectural information and creating EA artifacts[11]. For this reason, the role of specialized EA tools for an EA practice, as well as the role of all software tools in general, should not be overemphasized. Similarly to modeling languages, the success or failure of an EA practice cannot be attributed to the usage or non-usage of any specific software tools because of several related reasons.

Firstly, the general meaning of enterprise architecture is to provide an effective means of communication for all relevant actors involved in strategic decision-making and implementation of IT systems (see Figure 2.1). The typical communication problems existing between these actors can be solved only through finding proper communication approaches, mutually understandable common language, convenient discussion points and appropriate representation formats for corresponding EA artifacts. These challenges are simply unrelated to any software tools and can hardly be addressed by means of better tool support. In other words, software tools cannot help architects establish effective communication with relevant stakeholders and make balanced planning decisions.

Secondly, a successful EA practice always represents a complex set of interrelated processes, actors and documents (see Figure 6.1). Establishing an EA practice requires a deliberate organizational effort to involve all relevant stakeholders, institutionalize decision-making processes and develop appropriate sets of EA artifacts to underpin these processes. None of these challenges can be addressed and even facilitated by any software tools. These challenges represent a multifaceted mix of various organizational, political and even psychological issues that can be addressed only by people constituting an organization. Put it simply, software tools cannot organize an EA practice for people.

Thirdly, even from the perspective of EA artifacts specialized EA tools essentially address only the "technical" part of an EA practice. They can certainly help organize and manage the architectural information typically contained in facts EA artifacts (i.e. most Landscapes and some Standards), which are typically valuable as comprehensive reference materials on the current state of the IT landscape and intended to provide an accurate baseline information to architects. However, the value of decisions EA artifacts is realized largely in the process of their collaborative development (see Figure 2.6). These EA artifacts are intended more to enable communication and decision-making, than to store some information for future reference. For these EA artifacts the timely involvement of right stakeholders is far more critical than accuracy and comprehensiveness, but this involvement cannot be ensured by any software tools. Consequently, the value of specialized EA tools for decisions EA artifacts is largely limited to providing modeling environments and supporting technical information understandable mostly to architects. Put it simply, the capabilities of EA tools highly correlate with the key purpose of facts EA artifacts, but do not correlate with the key purpose of decisions EA artifacts.

Due to these reasons specialized software tools for enterprise architecture arguably should not be introduced at the outset of an EA practice, but only at its later stages when the need for these tools is widely understood and the corresponding requirements and expectations are clear[12]. For example, organizations can initially start their EA practices with using simple MS Visio drawings for Landscape Diagrams and MS Excel spreadsheets for Inventories, but then migrate their contents into a tool-based EA repository if at some moment maintaining consistency of these files is found too burdensome and a clear "business case" for introducing an EA tool can be presented. If an organization already has a fully populated CMDB in place, which is actively used by IT operations staff and integrated with established IT service management processes, then installing an additional EA-specific tool may be not worthwhile due to its minimal potential added value. In this case an organization may consider leveraging its existing CMDB as the primary source of architectural information on the current IT landscape instead of establishing a separate EA-specific repository from scratch[13].

Generally, specialized software tools for enterprise architecture should be introduced only when specific reasons justifying their introduction can be articulated. If an EA practice does not work as expected, software tools are the last candidates to blame. EA tools also should not "wag the dog" by dictating how an EA practice should be organized, what EA artifacts should be used and how exactly they should be created. Specialized EA tools are arguably more important for large organizations with extensive IT landscapes.

Templates for Enterprise Architecture Artifacts

Many EA artifacts have pretty diverse informational contents and complex representation formats. In order to standardize the contents and formats of all instances of these EA artifacts, organizations often develop and maintain a set of common reusable **templates** defining their high-level structure. These templates are used by architects as the basis for creating new instances of EA artifacts and as the reference models for updating and reformatting existing EA artifacts.

Templates are typically developed for EA artifacts having multiple different instances in an organization. Ideal candidates for creating templates are all temporary EA artifacts (see Table 2.2) developed specifically for particular IT initiatives and projects (i.e. Outlines and Designs) since these artifacts naturally have numerous instances and their new instances are continuously developed. However, templates can be also created for some permanent EA artifacts as well. For instance, organizations developing separate Roadmaps and Target States for different business areas can create common templates for these EA artifacts to standardize their formats and contents across all business areas. At the same time, templates for Business Capability Models and Enterprise System Portfolios are rarely, if ever, created since most organizations employ only a single instance of each of these EA artifacts.

Templates usually define the representation formats, schematic structures and informational contents of EA artifacts. Essentially, templates of EA artifacts provide a "single source of truth" regarding the desirable structure of all instances of these artifacts. Sample templates of Target States (see Figure 11.3) and Solution Designs (see Figure 14.1) are shown in Figure 18.7.

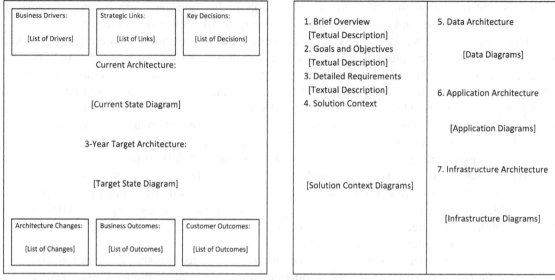

Figure 18.7. Templates of EA artifacts (Target States and Solution Designs)

The use of templates for developing EA artifacts may be highly beneficial to an EA practice. Specifically, templates help architects accelerate the development of new EA artifacts, produce standardized high-quality EA artifacts in a timely manner, provide consistent "look and feel" and predictable stakeholder experience, achieve repeatable and institutionalized EA-related processes. Moreover, templates of EA artifacts are usually improved and optimized based on the feedback provided by the stakeholders of these artifacts. Over time templates essentially accumulate the experience-based EA best practices of a particular organization. Thereby, the use of templates facilitates continuous improvement of an EA practice and organizational learning in general.

Straw-Man Architecture

As discussed earlier, all new decisions EA artifacts, or updated versions of existing decisions EA artifacts, start their lifecycle from informal preliminary discussions of architectural decisions and only then get formalized into tangible documents, approved by their stakeholders and finally endorsed by architecture governance committees (see Figure 17.4). In order to facilitate early discussions of key architectural decisions with their stakeholders, organizations sometimes use the technique often called as "straw-man" architecture. **Straw-man architecture** is an early architectural draft of an EA artifact which can be produced quickly and used to discuss main planning decisions and available alternatives.

Essentially, straw-man architectures can be considered as brief, informal and tentative sketches of full-fledged decisions EA artifacts, or as their hypothetical proof-of-concept versions. Usually straw-man architectures are represented in more simple and lightweight formats than the corresponding "real" EA artifacts. For instance, if a resulting EA artifact is intended to be an MS Word document, then the corresponding straw-man architecture might be represented as an MS PowerPoint presentation. Similarly, if a resulting EA artifact is intended to be an MS PowerPoint presentation, then the corresponding straw-man architecture might be even represented as a set of photographed whiteboard drawings.

Straw-man architectures serve as an intermediate link between the initial discussions of planning decisions with their stakeholders and the finalized EA artifacts formally documenting these decisions. The role of straw-man architectures in the development of decisions EA artifacts is shown in Figure 18.8.

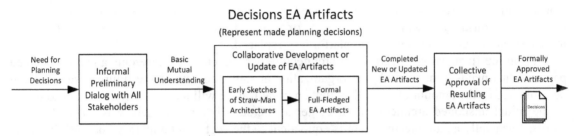

Figure 18.8. The role of straw-man architectures in the development of decisions EA artifacts

Straw-man architecture can be a valuable instrument of an EA practice. The use of straw-man architectures for decisions EA artifacts helps involve relevant stakeholders at the early stages of their development, collect timely feedback, exclude unfeasible alternatives as soon as possible and avoid spending time on elaborating inappropriate planning options.

Architecture Debt

An **architecture debt**, or a technical debt, is a temporary deviation from the ideal long-term architectural direction. It happens when a specific EA-related planning decision motivated by compelling short-term benefits is misaligned with the agreed strategic architectural plans and requires certain corrective measures to be taken later in the future to return back to the normal strategic path. Put it simply, an architecture debt represents a step in the architectural direction opposite to strategic, which distances an organization from its ultimate destination. Architecture debts are accumulated as a result of making tactically desirable, but strategically sub-optimal planning decisions. The volume of an architecture debt associated with a single planning decision is a measure of deviation from the optimum introduced by this decision, while the cumulative volume of an architecture debt represents the degree of overall architectural deterioration ensuing from all the previously made planning decisions.

Typically an architecture debt occurs when some local initiative-related decisions reflected in Outlines and Designs contradict global planning decisions reflected in Considerations, Standards, Visions or Landscapes, but are given exemptions by respective architecture governance committees (see Figure 17.5) based on their tactical business value. For example, in order to benefit from transient market opportunities, an investment committee may endorse the delivery of an IT solution that departs from Considerations and Visions, e.g. violates regular Policies or contravenes the strategic Target State. Likewise, a design committee may approve the implementation of an IT system that deviates from the suggestions of Standards and Landscapes, e.g. uses an unsupported vendor product or leverages some IT assets that should be retired. These and similar planning decisions and exemptions create an architecture debt that needs to be "paid" by an organization some time later in the future[14].

An architecture debt is a dual notion characterized by the actions necessary to roll back the architecturally undesirable changes in the IT landscape as well as by the estimated financial costs of these corrective actions[15]. From the actions perspective, an architecture debt implies a certain work that needs to be accomplished in the future in order to return back to the ideal strategic trajectory from the architectural perspective. For instance, an IT solution deviating from Considerations or Visions in the long run needs to be reworked or even decommissioned, while an IT system misaligned with the suggestions of Standards and Landscapes sooner or later needs to be moved to a newer technological platform or replaced.

From the financial perspective, an architecture debt essentially represents a certain delayed payment that needs to be made by an organization at some moment in the future. Usually it can be estimated as the amount of IT dollars that an organization will need to spend in order to return to the initial unspoiled architectural state, i.e. to the state before the debt was taken. In other words, financially an architecture debt is equivalent to the cost of a temporary "detour" from the main strategic "highway". For instance, in the case of the IT solution deviating from Considerations or Visions an architecture debt may be evaluated as the presumptive cost of adjusting the solution to strategic requirements or removing it from the IT landscape. Similarly, in the case of the IT system misaligned with the suggestions of Standards and Landscapes an architecture debt may be calculated as the amount of money necessary to migrate the system to supported technologies, products and assets. However, often the monetary value of an architecture debt cannot be easily quantified in a straightforward manner and may be assessed based only on a "guesstimation".

The multifaceted concept of architecture debt has important implications for both the Initiative Delivery and Technology Optimization processes (see Figure 6.1). On the one hand, the financial aspect of an architecture debt is more relevant to Initiative Delivery. Specifically, applying the assessment of an incurred architecture debt to EA-related decision-making processes facilitates more objective evaluation of proposed IT initiatives and their possible implementation options at the initiation step of the Initiative Delivery process. Essentially, an architecture debt is an instrument that helps organizations uncover the hidden delayed costs of IT solutions, make better informed IT investment decisions based on their full costs and eventually improve the quality of IT investment portfolios. For instance, for a more realistic assessment of the value of proposed IT initiatives the volume of their architecture debts may be estimated based on their Outlines and then added to their total costs (i.e. subtracted from their business cases) in order to explicitly take into account the postponed future payments. Similarly, estimations of architecture debt can inform the decision-making at the subsequent implementation step of the Initiative Delivery process.

The financial side of an architecture debt can be also used to guide governance and escalation procedures around IT initiatives (see Figure 17.6) as part of the Initiative Delivery process. In many organizations governance arrangements require IT investments and other planning decisions with higher levels of architecture debt to be endorsed by more authoritative governance committees. Moreover, governance policies may formally specify multiple thresholds of architecture debt and corresponding governance procedures to be applied to the decisions exceeding these thresholds. For example, an organizational governance policy may stipulate that the planning decisions with a small architecture debt (e.g. less than 100,000 dollars) can be approved at the discretion of a design committee, the decisions with a moderate debt must be escalated either to an investment committee or technology committee, while all the IT investments introducing high levels of architecture debt (e.g. exceeding one million dollars) must be authorized directly by a strategy committee.

On the other hand, the actions aspect of an architecture debt is relevant mostly to Technology Optimization. In particular, existing architecture debts is one of the core drivers of the Technology Optimization process. All architecture debts taken by organizations (i.e. all exemptions approved by architecture governance committees) are typically recorded by architects into specialized **architecture debt registers** to be tracked, managed and addressed in the future. These registers often capture the description of architecture debts, necessary corrective actions, their financial estimates and the deadlines when these debts should be redeemed, if any, as well as classify all architecture debts into different categories (e.g. minor, medium and major) according to their significance. Since all the corrective measures associated with architecture debts represent certain desirable technical optimizations of the organizational IT landscape, debt registers essentially serve as one of the sources for technical rationalization suggestions resulting from the Technology Optimization process. As noted earlier, these suggestions may be implemented either opportunistically as part of regular IT initiatives or, in some cases, as separate architectural initiatives (see Table 7.1). The schematic graphical representation of architecture debt registers is shown in Figure 18.9.

Debt	Description	Actions	Estimate	Deadline
Debt 1	....	....	$350k	Q1 2018
Debt 2	....	....	$40k	N/A
Debt 3	....	....	$1.6m	Q4 2018
Debt 4	....	....	$200k	N/A
Debt 5	....	....	$90k	Q4 2016
Debt 6	....	....	$25k	Q3 2017
Debt 7	....	....	$600k	Q2 2018
Debt 8	....	....	$65k	N/A
Debt 9	....	....	$50k	Q2 2017
Debt 10	....	....	$1.1m	Q3 2018
Debt 11	....	....	$30k	N/A
Debt 12	....	....	$280k	N/A
Debt 13	....	....	$20k	Q1 2017
Minor		Medium		Major

Figure 18.9. Architecture debt registers

Architecture debt registers describe the existing deficiencies of the organizational IT landscape as well as the planned activities to address these deficiencies. They are owned solely by architects and used to rationalize the IT environment and plan new IT initiatives. From this perspective, architecture debt registers can be considered as a special type of Landscapes somewhat resembling IT Roadmaps also showing planned technical improvements of the IT landscape.

An architecture debt provides a helpful metaphor for explaining the negative long-term consequences of shortsighted EA-related decisions and shortcuts to non-IT-savvy business leaders. Generally, a clear understanding that "all debts must be paid" allows avoiding myopic thinking and irresponsible architectural "borrowing", i.e. implementing tactical IT solutions that ultimately undermine the future strategic positioning of an organization from the architectural perspective. The awareness, evaluation and proactive management of architecture debts helps organizations stay on a strategic track, control architectural deviations from the "theoretical" norm and maintain the quality of their IT landscapes. The use of the concept of architecture debt is more typical for rather mature EA practices.

Measurements in Enterprise Architecture Practice

Mature EA practices often introduce a system of aggregate numerical measurements helping monitor and control the flow of IT-related planning decisions over time[16]. A comprehensive quantitative assessment of certain trends in an EA practice allows detecting anomalies and optimizing the entire mechanism of information systems planning. These quantitative indicators often address two aspects of an EA practice: the quality of IT investments and the magnitude of technical deviations.

Firstly, mature EA practices often evaluate the overall quality of all undertaken IT investments. These quantitative measurements are usually intended to estimate the total percentage of IT investments considered as strategic or desirable from the organizational perspective. Typical aggregate measurements of the quality of IT investments include, but are not limited to, the following indicators:

- The percentage of IT investments contributing to Target States and uplifting the business capabilities heatmapped in Business Capability Models – IT investments building the desired IT platform and improving the required capabilities are considered as strategic, while all other investments are considered as non-strategic, i.e. a higher percentage indicates better strategic focus of IT investments
- The percentage of IT investments in the strategic information systems and IT assets indicated in Enterprise System Portfolios and Inventories – IT investments developing strategic systems and assets are considered as strategic, while all other investments are considered as non-strategic, i.e. a higher percentage indicates better strategic focus of IT investments
- The ratio of IT investments in improving existing assets to IT investments in creating new assets – IT investments in existing assets might be considered as more preferable, while investments in new assets might be considered as less preferable, i.e. higher ratios indicate better utilization and reuse of available IT assets
- The ratio of planned IT investments from Roadmaps fulfilling foreseen business needs to unplanned IT investments addressing urgent needs (see Figure 7.2) – planned IT investments are considered as more important, while unplanned

investments are considered as less important, i.e. higher ratios indicate better quality of planning and IT investments

- A more detailed breakdown of all IT investments according to their origin and motivation (e.g. into fundamental, strategic, local, urgent and architectural, see Table 7.1) – some types of IT investments (e.g. fundamental and strategic) are considered as more desirable, while other types of investments (e.g. urgent and architectural) are considered as undesirable, i.e. a higher focus on desirable types indicates better overall quality of IT investments
- Any other organization-specific classifications of IT investments considered as informative and useful for assessing the overall quality, focus and meaning of these investments[17]

Additionally, periodical mapping of all IT investments undertaken over a certain period of time, often during the last financial year, to Business Capability Models and more rarely to Value Chains helps business executives understand where the IT budget was spent and evaluate the actual alignment between the incurred IT expenses and the declared business strategy. A sample mapping of the undertaken IT investments to Business Capability Models is shown in Figure 18.10.

Figure 18.10. Mapping of IT investments to Business Capability Models

Secondly, mature EA practices often evaluate the overall magnitude of technical deviations of implemented IT projects from the suggestions of Standards and Landscapes. These quantitative measurements are usually intended to estimate the total percentage of IT projects implemented unusually from the technical perspective (i.e. following exotic implementation approaches), but given exemptions by architecture governance committees. Typical aggregate measurements of the technical deviations of IT projects include, but are not limited to, the following indicators:

- The percentage of IT projects based on unusual technologies missing in Technology Reference Models or tagged as retiring – these projects are considered as deviating, i.e. a higher percentage indicates a higher degree of technological heterogeneity
- The percentage of IT projects inconsistent with the established Guidelines, Patterns and IT Principles – these projects are considered as deviating, i.e. a higher percentage indicates a higher degree of general technical diversity

- The percentage of IT projects reusing IT assets marked as undesirable in Landscapes – these projects are considered as deviating, i.e. a higher percentage indicates a higher degree of overall "toxicity" of the IT landscape

Conducting a post factum analysis of the quality of undertaken IT investments and technical deviations of implemented IT projects helps audit and monitor the effectiveness of an EA practice in focusing investments and restraining complexity. On the one hand, a low percentage of strategic and desirable IT investments, a decreasing trend in this percentage or its recent plummeting may indicate potential problems and signify that a considerable portion of the whole IT budget is spent ineffectively. On the other hand, a high ratio of deviating IT projects, an increasing trend in this ratio or its recent skyrocketing may also indicate potential problems and signify that the current technology portfolio and implementation approaches might be inadequate for the actual business needs.

Organizations can produce periodical yearly and even quarterly reports with the quantitative indicators described above to track the efficacy of an EA practice in achieving its key objectives on a nearly real-time basis. Naturally, organizations strive to increase the proportion of strategic IT investments by better focusing their investments on strategically important business areas and decrease the percentage of deviating IT projects by adapting their technology portfolios and implementation standards to the genuine business needs.

If necessary, organizations can also "invent" and introduce some more sophisticated, organization-specific measurement approaches to control the work of their EA practices. For example, these measurements may address the quality of EA artifacts, coverage of EA artifacts, complexity of the IT landscape, reuse of IT assets, technologies and platforms, organizational awareness and penetration of an EA practice, percentage of the IT budget spent on maintenance of the existing systems, the overall volume of an accumulated architecture debt or yearly changes in this volume, as discussed earlier, as well as other relevant indicators[18].

Quantitative EA-related measurements and indicators are the attributes of advanced EA practices, as discussed later in Chapter 19 (The Lifecycle of Enterprise Architecture Practice). These measurements are rarely found in organizations with emerging or immature EA practices. The use of any numerical indicators cannot be considered as essential for an EA practice. However, these indicators may be beneficial to mature EA practices with institutionalized EA-related procedures, repeatable processes and established organization-specific sets of EA artifacts for further optimization and fine-tuning.

Chapter Summary

This chapter discussed formal modeling languages for enterprise architecture, specialized software tools for enterprise architecture, standardized templates for EA artifacts, so-called "straw-man" architectures and quantitative measurements for an EA practice. The key message of this chapter can be summarized into the following essential points:

- Most widely known general-purpose and EA-specific formal modeling languages and notations that can be used for drawing EA diagrams and creating graphical EA artifacts include ArchiMate, UML, BPMN and ARIS
- Due to their formal attitude and focus on specific details, the applicability of specialized modeling languages and notations in the context of an EA practice is

limited and covers essentially only Designs, Landscapes and to some extent Outlines

- Successful EA practices require diverse toolsets often consisting of standard general-purpose MS Office applications (mostly Word, Visio, PowerPoint and Excel), operational CMDB systems and specialized EA tools, but no single software tool can satisfy all the EA-related needs
- Specialized software tools for enterprise architecture can address only the technical part of an EA practice (e.g. storage, analysis and management of facts EA artifacts), but they cannot establish consistent decision-making processes and automatically improve communication between business and IT stakeholders
- The use of standardized templates defining the formats, structures and informational contents of EA artifacts can accelerate the development of new EA artifacts, help achieve more predictable stakeholder experience and facilitate continuous improvement and learning
- Straw-man architecture is a preliminary architectural draft of an EA artifact which can be produced rather quickly, used to discuss main planning decisions at their early stages, collect timely feedback from stakeholders and exclude unfeasible alternatives as soon as possible
- Architecture debt is a temporary deviation from the ideal architectural direction that implies necessary corrective actions and respective expenses in the future, providing a helpful instrument for assessing the true costs of IT solutions, improving decision-making during Initiative Delivery and driving Technology Optimization
- Mature EA practices often establish a system of aggregate numerical measurements in order to evaluate and manage the overall quality of IT investment portfolios, the magnitude of technical deviations in IT projects or other more sophisticated indicators related to coverage, reuse and complexity

Chapter 19: The Lifecycle of Enterprise Architecture Practice

The previous chapter discussed the technical side of an EA practice including relevant modeling languages, software tools and some other useful techniques. This chapter focuses on different phases of the lifecycle of an EA practice including the initiation of an EA practice in organizations, achieving maturity of an EA practice and leveraging external EA consultancies to enhance an EA practice. In particular, this chapter starts from discussing the most appropriate approaches for establishing an EA practice in organizations from scratch. Then, this chapter describes different ways of facilitating the organizational acceptance of an EA practice, the signs of mature EA practices and the role of maturity as a factor of sustainable competitive advantage. Finally, this chapter discusses three types of productive EA consulting engagements as well as different types of counterproductive relationships between client organizations and EA consultancies.

Establishing Enterprise Architecture Practices in Organizations

As it should be evident from the previous chapters, an EA practice represents a very complex mix of interrelated processes, people and EA artifacts (see Figure 6.1) supported by sophisticated techniques and various specialized and general-purpose software tools (see Figure 18.6). An EA practice implies profound and far-reaching changes in organizations. In particular, it redistributes power and authority among organizational actors, modifies most IT-related decision-making procedures and requires organic integration with regular management processes.

Due to its inherent complexity and considerable organizational impact, a full-fledged EA practice cannot be introduced in an organization quickly in one day, one week and even in one month. Instead, EA practices are established gradually over time and in some cases may take several years to mature to a reasonable level, especially in large organizations. They require intensive organizational learning and often go through a long and rough evolutionary path from limited local activities to comprehensive organization-wide practices. Organizing a mature EA practice takes significant time and effort to initiate necessary EA-related processes, adjust them to organizational realities and institutionalize them, i.e. make these processes an essential part of routine organizational activities, or "the way we do things around here"[1].

Moreover, even though an EA practice needs architects, it cannot be instantly "switched on" simply by hiring an architecture team. EA practices can hardly be initiated by the efforts of architects alone. Instead, establishing an EA practice requires strong organizational mandate, executive commitment and an active participation of business leaders in respective EA-related processes. At the same time, since an EA practice represents the whole organizational system of disciplined decision-making, it is impossible to become an architect in isolation from the organizational system (e.g. merely by obtaining EA certifications or creating EA artifacts in an organization that is not eager to start practicing enterprise architecture) in the same way in which it is impossible to become a politician in a country without any political institutes and elections.

Essentially, the very job of architects exists only within the context of an EA practice and does not exist apart from it. For this reason, the problem of establishing an EA practice in an organization can be considered as a "chicken and egg" problem which requires initiative from both sides simultaneously, i.e. executive mandate at the top to sponsor the introduction of EA-related processes and the presence of skilled architects on the ground capable of organizing and carrying out these processes.

However, seemingly every organization with the IT landscape of a considerable size can benefit from using enterprise architecture and establish an EA practice, at least in some form. As noted earlier, currently enterprise architecture is widely adopted in very diverse organizations of various sizes and industries operating all over the world. From this perspective, adopting an EA practice by an organization can be compared to studying a foreign language by a person. Both tasks are beneficial and perfectly doable, but require commitment, hard work and should not be approached superficially.

Arguably the most practical way to establish an EA practice in an organization is to gradually introduce its elements into the organizational organism via mastering and institutionalizing the usage of corresponding types of EA artifacts step-by-step under the general guidance of a designated EA leader responsible for organizing an EA practice, e.g. the CIO, architecture manager or experienced architect with an executive mandate. It seems more reasonable and safe to focus on mastering a single type of EA artifacts, or a small manageable number of EA artifacts, at a time. In this case, a mature EA practice can be established smoothly over time as a series of incremental organizational improvements encompassing no more than one or a few types of EA artifacts in parallel. Since mastering each type of EA artifacts requires substantial individual and organizational learning, the attempts to introduce too many different EA artifacts at once can overwhelm the involved stakeholders, exceed their change capacity and undermine the entire effort.

In order to introduce, master and institutionalize the organizational usage of EA artifacts of a specific type, the following key aspects of their usage should be addressed:

- Senior executive support and mandate for introducing these EA artifacts should be secured, e.g. the mandate of the CIO for IT-focused EA artifacts and the mandate of chief business executives for business-focused EA artifacts (see Figure 8.1)
- Commitment of relevant stakeholders to use these EA artifacts for a disciplined decision-making should be obtained
- Architects should be appointed to own this type of EA artifacts and take general responsibility for their usability, e.g. via creating and polishing their standardized templates (see Figure 18.7)
- Consistent processes around these EA artifacts should be organized, e.g. periodical development, update, review and re-approval with the involvement of all key stakeholders
- Architecture governance bodies officially approving and endorsing these EA artifacts should be established and their regular meetings scheduled (see Figure 17.5), if no governance committees exist in an organization appropriate for this purpose

- Appropriate enforcement mechanisms for the planning decisions represented by these EA artifacts should be introduced (only for decisions EA artifacts, see Table 2.1), e.g. formal governance procedures, peer-reviews of "downstream" EA artifacts or direct supervision of IT project teams
- Valuable organizational benefits achieved from using these EA artifacts should be felt, understood and widely acknowledged

For example, if an organization wants to introduce and master Business Capability Models, then the commitment of senior business executives to adopt Business Capability Models for focusing and prioritizing IT investments should be obtained and some architects should be assigned or hired to create and maintain these EA artifacts. The collective process of priorities identification involving all business leaders should be organized and consistently carried out to heatmap Business Capability Models. A C-level strategy committee should be established to formally endorse Business Capability Models and corresponding investment priorities. Finally, the existing IT investment selection and approval procedures should be modified to take into account the strategic priorities reflected in Business Capability Models. After the improved effectiveness and transparency of the new IT investment prioritization approach are acknowledged and business executives start to believe that "it works", the use of Business Capability Models can be considered as fully mastered.

Likewise, if an organization wants to introduce and master Technology Reference Models, then the commitment of the CIO and other senior IT stakeholders to adopt Technology Reference Models for standardizing and consolidating the technology portfolio should be secured and some architects should be nominated as owners of these EA artifacts. The periodical technology assessment and review process should be organized and performed on a regular basis to identify emerging and retiring technologies based on collective intelligence and then update Technology Reference Models accordingly. An organization-wide technology committee chaired by the CIO should be established to formally endorse Technology Reference Models and respective recommendations regarding the selection and use of technologies in new IT projects. Finally, informal peer-review, formal approval and exception management procedures should be introduced to ensure the compliance of all IT initiatives with the suggestions of Technology Reference Models. When better cost-effectiveness, reduced risks and other organizational benefits of the new disciplined technology selection approach are appreciated and become self-evident, the use of Technology Reference Models can be considered as fully mastered. The overall process of establishing an EA practice via gradually introducing and mastering new types of EA artifacts in a step-wise manner is shown in Figure 19.1.

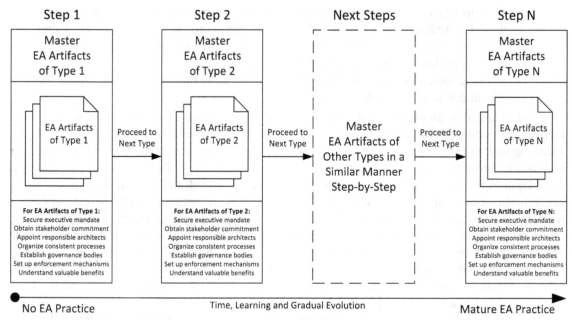

Figure 19.1. Establishing an EA practice via introducing new types of EA artifacts

In large organizations it might be also more practical to introduce and master necessary EA artifacts in a single business unit first and only then replicate these practices to other business units and uplift them to the organization-wide level. Since introducing any large-scale organizational changes is often associated with significant risks, gradual proliferation of EA-related planning practices across different departments, geographies or lines of business may be considered as a more preferable and safer approach to establishing an EA practice.

The consecutive process of mastering new types of EA artifacts shown in Figure 19.1 outlines only the general recommended approach to introducing and evolving an EA practice in organizations, but it does not specify which particular types of EA artifacts should be introduced first or last. From the perspective of the sequence of introducing different types of EA artifacts, arguably two different approaches, or paths, to establishing an EA practice can be articulated: historical path and deliberate path. The historical path represents the historical evolution of EA practices in many leading-edge organizations that have been using enterprise architecture in some or the other form for decades, while the deliberate path represents a more conscious approach to establishing an EA practice enabled by the existence of proven EA best practices and the availability of experienced architects able to reproduce these best practices.

The Historical Path to Establishing Enterprise Architecture Practice

The **historical path** to establishing an EA practice reflects the historical development patterns of an EA practice in many early-adopter organizations (e.g. large banks and insurance companies) that have been using or experimenting with what is now known as enterprise architecture for a long time, possibly under various earlier once-popular titles, e.g. information systems plans or information systems architecture. These organizations were essentially at the forefront of enterprise architecture progress and seemingly developed many of the current EA best practices based on their own harsh practical lessons and negative experience with numerous widely promoted formal architecture-based planning methodologies, e.g. BSP, Information Engineering, EAP and then TOGAF[2], as discussed earlier in Chapter 3 (the historical evolution of formal architecture-based planning methodologies from BSP to TOGAF and the problems associated with these methodologies are also described in great detail in Appendix). The historical path of these organizations arguably represents the mainstream path taken by the industry as a whole and corresponds to the historical formation of the entire EA discipline in its current form and respective best practices[3]. As noted earlier, the EA best practices described in this book emerged and matured in industry. These best practices seemingly reflect the present state of the continuous evolutionary process that went along this historical path.

The historical path naturally developed from more simple to more complex activities and planning practices[4]. Put it simply, historically the simplest practices emerged and had been adopted in organizations first, while the most sophisticated practices appeared and became widely accepted last. Specifically, the most basic EA-related practices evidently relate to the local and limited-scope architectural planning of separate IT initiatives, i.e. to the usage of Outlines and Designs as part of the Initiative Delivery process (see Figure 6.1). These practices imply developing business cases for IT initiatives to ensure their positive business value and establishing a consistent step-wise solution delivery methodology with a number of decision-making gates, or control checkpoints, informed by the corresponding EA artifacts to achieve predictable quality of the resulting IT systems. These planning practices are often collectively called simply as solution architecture. From the historical perspective, these practices seemingly appeared and had been mastered in organizations first.

More complex EA-related practices relate to the global architectural planning of the technical aspects of the entire IT landscape, i.e. to the usage of Standards and Landscapes as part of the Technology Optimization process. These practices imply a centralized organization-wide selection of preferable technologies and approaches, a formal architectural review, approval and subsequent supervision of all IT initiatives as well as a separate funding mechanism for architectural initiatives (see Table 7.1). These planning practices are often collectively called simply as enterprise, or enterprise-wide, IT architecture. From the historical perspective, these practices seemingly appeared and had been mastered after solution architecture practices.

The most sophisticated EA-related practices relate to the global architectural planning of the business aspects of the whole organization, i.e. to the usage of Considerations and Visions as part of the Strategic Planning process. These practices imply effective strategic dialog between senior business and IT stakeholders, collective prioritization of proposed IT investments and direct architecture governance at the chief executive level. These planning practices are often collectively called as "true" enterprise architecture. From the historical perspective, these practices evidently appeared last and currently are still not fully mastered even in many organizations with rather mature EA practices. The historical path to establishing an EA practice described above is shown in Figure 19.2.

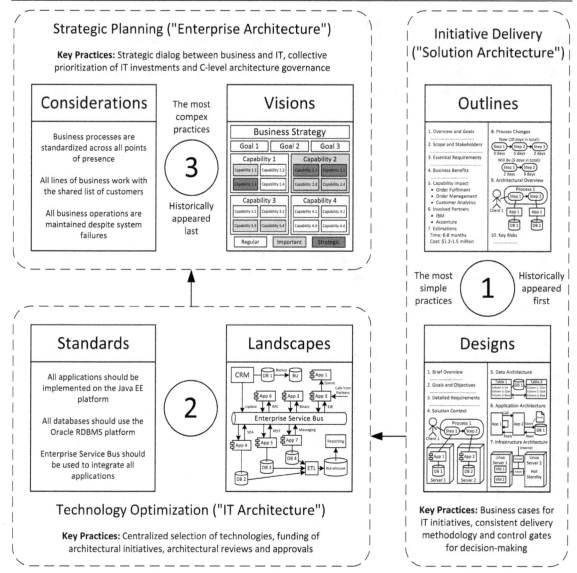

Figure 19.2. The historical path to establishing an EA practice

Since the historical path shown in Figure 19.2 reflects the natural progression from the simplest activities to the most complex planning practices, this path arguably might be the easiest and least risky one for organizations to follow, i.e. start from mastering Outlines and Designs, then gradually adopt Standards and Landscapes and finally introduce Considerations and Visions (see Figure 19.1).

The Deliberate Path to Establishing Enterprise Architecture Practice

Historically organizations adopted EA-related planning practices as these practices slowly emerged and spread across the industry over the years. Leading-edge organizations seemingly introduced new types of EA artifacts and respective planning activities as soon as these practices became widely acknowledged and accepted by the architecture community. Essentially, in the past organizations were largely limited in their choices of EA-related planning approaches due to the absence of consistent EA best practices in many areas. From this perspective, historically organizations had to start their EA practices from mastering specifically Outlines and Designs simply because more advanced planning practices, for instance associated with using Considerations and Visions for a global long-range planning, were non-existing, insufficiently understood or poorly developed at that time. However, the current understanding of acknowledged EA best practices enables a more conscious selection of appropriate planning approaches and opens the possibility for a better path to initiating an EA practice in organizations from scratch.

The **deliberate path** to establishing an EA practice is a newer path that benefits from the existence of a large body of proven EA best practices, the clear understanding of their practical applicability and the availability of experienced architects acquainted with these best practices on the job market. Essentially, this path leverages many known trails "trodden" previously by many organizations and architects through the unexplored and dangerous territory of information systems planning.

The newer and arguably more effective, though potentially also more risky, deliberate path to establishing an EA practice is based on the idea of using EA artifacts for problem solving, when different types of EA artifacts are considered as instruments for solving corresponding business problems. Specifically, Outlines and Designs provide appropriate tools for solving the business problems related to inefficient, unpredictable and late delivery of IT initiatives and misunderstanding of their real business impact and value. Standards and Landscapes help address the business problems related mostly to exorbitant IT expenditures and risks, low organizational agility and excessive dependence on legacy systems. Finally, Considerations and Visions offer suitable instruments for solving the business problems related to insufficient effectiveness and transparency of IT investments, poor data availability and the overall strategic misalignment between business and IT.

Since each type of EA artifacts helps solve a particular business problem or a set of closely related problems, organizations can start practicing enterprise architecture from introducing EA artifacts that directly address their most pressing business problems according to their perceived priority. In particular, senior business and IT executives should firstly determine the most critical IT-related issues troubling their organization by collectively answering the following question: "What is our biggest business problem in relation to IT?" Further steps and the general path of an EA practice highly depend on the answer to this question.

If the primary concern of senior executives is that their IT budget is spent mostly on keeping the available systems up and running[5], that new IT systems are expensive to introduce while existing systems are extremely hard to modify, that IT is unable to accommodate with the growing business demands or that the current IT landscape consisting of numerous legacy applications (e.g. inherited from earlier acquisitions of other companies) poses considerable business risks, then the organization should consider starting its EA practice from introducing and mastering Standards and Landscapes to address these business problems via reducing overall complexity of the landscape, i.e. start from initiating and institutionalizing the Technology Optimization process. For example, the organization may need to create Inventories and

Technology Reference Models to keep track of the available IT assets and utilized technologies, sketch out Landscape Diagrams to understand the dependencies between the existing applications and databases, develop general IT Principles and more specific Guidelines to standardize the preferred approaches to building and organizing IT systems. The organization may also need to develop IT Roadmaps for platform simplification and consolidation purposes to plan the retirement of duplicated IT assets and obsolete technologies. If the improved data integration is required, then the organization may consider creating Logical Data Models to standardize the structure of key data entities across the entire IT landscape.

If the topmost concern of senior executives is that the business does not understand what IT is doing and how IT dollars are spent, that IT investments have little or no strategic impact, that the existing IT landscape is unable to support the realization of envisioned strategic plans or that the overall contribution of IT to the business goals is marginal, then the organization should consider starting its EA practice from introducing and mastering Considerations and Visions to address these business problems via improving strategic alignment and consistency between business and IT, i.e. start from initiating and institutionalizing the Strategic Planning process. For example, the organization may need to develop overarching Principles to articulate the most fundamental requirements to IT, create Business Capability Models or Value Chains to enable disciplined decision-making around the long-term priorities for IT investments and develop more detailed investment Roadmaps. If rather significant changes in the IT landscape are required, then the organization may consider developing explicit Target States to indicate where future IT investments should lead to in the long run. The need for better security or regulatory compliance can be addressed via maintaining Policies explicitly stipulating the necessary norms for IT.

Finally, if the predominant concern of senior executives is that too many IT initiatives fail to realize the anticipated business improvements and benefits, that most IT projects dramatically exceed their original time and cost estimates, that the track record of unsuccessful projects is very extensive or that the IT department is often unable to deliver on its commitments, then the organization should consider starting its EA practice from introducing and mastering Outlines and Designs to address these business problems via improving the initial evaluation and subsequent delivery of IT initiatives, i.e. start from "fixing" and achieving better predictability of the Initiative Delivery process. For example, for every IT initiative the organization may need to start developing firstly Options Assessments to determine the preference of business leaders regarding the available initiative implementation options, then more detailed Solution Overviews to enable informed decision-making based on the benefits and costs of the initiative, then rather technical Preliminary Solution Designs to refine and confirm the earlier estimations and finally low-level Solution Designs to describe how exactly corresponding business requirements should be addressed.

Based on the identification and prioritization of the most acute business problems related to IT, organizations can select and introduce appropriate types of EA artifacts helping address these problems, as described in the examples above. In this approach, the actual development path of an EA practice is always organization-specific, driven directly by the respective business problems and closely aligned to the specific needs of an organization. Unlike the linear historical path to establishing an EA practice (see Figure 19.2), the deliberate path is flexible and adaptive in nature. It offers no predefined best sequence of EA artifacts that should be mastered in organizations to establish an EA practice, but rather suggests that different EA artifacts should be introduced based on the perceived organizational necessity to solve corresponding problems. The deliberate path to establishing an EA practice described above is shown in Figure 19.3.

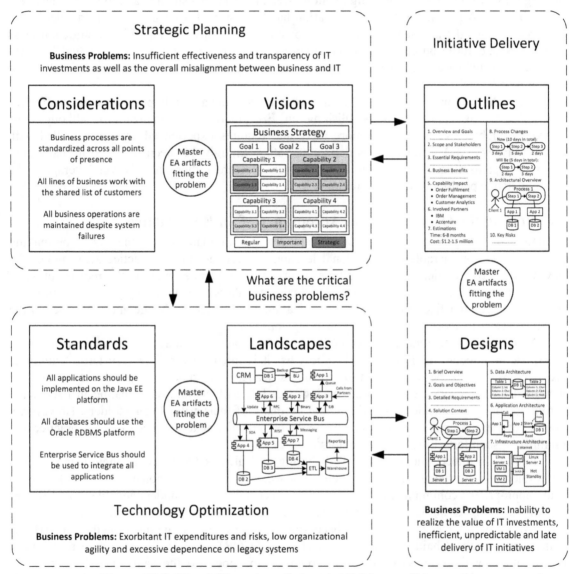

Figure 19.3. The deliberate path to establishing an EA practice

Starting an EA practice from addressing the most pressing business problems allows collecting "low hanging fruits" and achieving rather quick wins required to kindle the interest to enterprise architecture among senior executives. Using EA artifacts to solve concrete high-priority business problems helps immediately prove the business value of an EA practice and uplift the credibility and authority of architects in the eyes of business leaders. By demonstrating their ability to improve business, architects can gain the reputation of trusted and valuable business partners. At the same time, starting an EA practice from irrelevant activities and inappropriate EA artifacts can easily ruin the entire initiative. For instance, if business executives are eager to improve the strategic alignment between their IT investments and long-term business goals, but an EA practice in their organization has been started from introducing Standards and Landscapes, then the incipient EA effort may be considered only as an additional burden, useless paperwork and futile bureaucracy, rather than as a productive solution of the actual business problems. In this case, the executive support and sponsorship of an EA practice is likely to be discontinued.

The deliberate path based on the idea of problem solving arguably provides a more effective and value-adding approach to establishing an EA practice in organizations, although this approach might be considered as more risky and requires experienced architects skilled with different types of EA artifacts. This deliberate path seemingly has been followed in many late-majority organizations that adopted enterprise architecture rather recently via leveraging the accumulated expertise of the EA community.

Facilitating the Organizational Acceptance of an EA Practice

Initiating an EA practice requires significant changes in many established decision-making processes and considerable organizational learning. Moreover, an EA practice also implies the buy-in and active participation of multiple diverse stakeholders as well as the redistribution of power among different business and IT decision-makers. Unsurprisingly, the attempts to introduce an EA practice often face the organizational resistance to change and reluctance of the involved actors to adopt corresponding planning approaches.

Many relevant actors, and especially business managers, may barely understand what enterprise architecture is, how it works and what it is intended for. The very term "enterprise architecture" might be interpreted by business leaders as something purely technical and unrelated to their work. As a result, working with EA artifacts and participating in EA-related activities might be considered as frightening by many of their critical stakeholders. However, a number of measures can be taken to facilitate the organizational acceptance of an EA practice and minimize discomfort of the involved actors[6].

Firstly, architects should avoid IT-babbling and always try to adapt their language and terminology to the specific needs of their audience. It is a direct responsibility of architects to find appropriate communication approaches acceptable and understandable to different stakeholders. For example, if senior business stakeholders actively use certain decision-making frameworks or reference models for discussing their problems (e.g. the growth-share (BCG) matrix or Supply Chain Operations Reference (SCOR) model), then architects in their conversations with business executives should try to appeal to the same models and terms. Ideally, architects should act essentially like chameleons able to easily change their color to fit the surrounding environment. This adaptability allows different stakeholders, and especially senior business leaders, to comfortably participate in EA-related activities using their regular vocabulary.

Secondly, with the exception of highly specialized EA artifacts intended exclusively for architects, the developed EA artifacts should use simple and intuitive representation formats, avoid excessive clumsiness and complexity. All EA artifacts should be easily understandable to their essential stakeholders, whereas incomprehensible EA artifacts can only scare away the people and lead to general disappointment with enterprise architecture. This concern is especially relevant in relation to senior business leaders, who usually hardly understand formal diagrams and models. For this reason all EA artifacts intended for business audience should be as intuitive as possible. Creating simple and easily consumable EA artifacts can minimize overall confusion and learning required to master the usage of EA artifacts by their stakeholders.

Thirdly, each new type of EA artifacts should be introduced with a sound underlying motivation behind it. Since most "general-purpose" EA artifacts eventually turn into useless paperwork, it should always be clearly understood why a particular EA artifact is created, who is going to use it, how, when and what kind of planning decisions this artifact intends to facilitate. Furthermore, EA artifacts should be constantly optimized for their typical audiences and purposes, e.g. necessary information commonly sought by their stakeholders should be added, while irrelevant, incomprehensible or redundant sections removed. Developing EA artifacts with a clear idea regarding their future usage can put an EA practice on more pragmatic "rails", ensure the usability and usefulness of resulting artifacts and avoid the common problem of producing architecture for the sake of architecture.

Fourthly, as discussed earlier, organizations should master new types of EA artifacts gradually and do not attempt to introduce more than one or a few different types of EA artifacts simultaneously (see Figure 19.1). This approach can help the involved actors stay largely within their normal comfort zones, minimize the associated stress and uncertainty, avoid excessive organizational disturbance and secure enough time for the full institutionalization of respective planning practices[7].

Fifthly, when it is possible, architects should try to leverage and adapt the existing documents used as part of current decision-making processes for EA-related purposes, rather than sweeping these documents aside and replacing them with completely new EA artifacts. For example, if an organization already uses some form of non-architectural proposal papers for justifying new IT projects, then these documents can be leveraged and turned via adding new sections with architectural information either into brief Initiative Proposals or even into full-fledged Solution Overviews with minimal process changes and organizational disturbance. Similarly, if value chains are already used in an organization as the instrument of strategic communication between its business executives, then these value chains can be leveraged by architects and elaborated into the instrument of strategic communication between business and IT, i.e. turned into architectural Value Chains. Due to their familiarity to business leaders, these adapted Value Chains might be eagerly accepted by their stakeholders as helpful decision-making tools and used to focus and prioritize IT investments, which may be a much better approach to establishing the strategic dialog between business and IT than introducing unfamiliar Business Capability Models for the same purpose. Leveraging existing documents and converting them into EA artifacts may ease their organizational acceptance, flatten the learning curve and facilitate smooth adoption of respective planning practices.

Sixthly, as noted earlier, organizations arguably should not start an EA practice from installing specialized software tools for enterprise architecture, unless the involved architects are already experienced in using these tools. Problems and risks associated with using sophisticated but unfamiliar software tools may divert the focus of architects from solving real organizational problems (e.g. how to achieve adequate stakeholder participation) to purely technical questions of secondary importance (e.g. how to setup and configure the tool properly)[8]. Moreover, most organizations already have some basic software support sufficient for the early stages of an EA practice, e.g. MS Office suite as a tool for creating EA artifacts, MS SharePoint as a shared document repository for storing EA artifacts or a CMDB as a comprehensive database of the existing IT assets (see Figure 18.6).

Seventhly, the organizational acceptance of an EA practice may be also facilitated via organizing appropriate trainings in order to inform all the involved actors on the goals of an EA practice as well as on their specific roles in corresponding planning activities[9]. An organization should be able to provide timely support to all stakeholders of EA artifacts and answer all their questions regarding an EA practice.

Finally, as noted earlier, starting an EA practice from identifying and addressing the most critical business problems related to IT (see Figure 19.3) helps achieve early wins, demonstrate the business value of enterprise architecture and gain increased support and sponsorship at the senior executive level. In other words, the realization of tangible benefits from an EA practice raises enthusiasm among senior business stakeholders that in its turn fuels further progress of an EA practice.

Maturity of Enterprise Architecture Practice

As a complex and comprehensive organizational practice, an EA practice cannot be simply "brought in" or established quickly in limited timeframes. Building a mature EA practice requires considerable time and effort to adapt the practice to organizational needs, optimize the set of used EA artifacts, deeply institutionalize the corresponding processes around these artifacts and fully integrate them with other decision-making processes. In other words, building a mature EA practice implies completing the full path of mastering necessary EA artifacts (see Figure 19.2 and Figure 19.3) and then further fine-tuning the practice to perfectly fit the organization in all aspects, e.g. structure, culture and style. This process can be a lengthy one and is typically measured in years, rather than in months or weeks. For instance, in small organizations it may take around two years to establish a reasonably mature EA practice from scratch, while in large organizations this process may require up to several years of persistent work of multiple people. However, mature EA practices pay off and bring significant benefits to organizations[10].

Signs of Mature Enterprise Architecture Practices

The overall maturity of an EA practice is extremely hard to measure or evaluate objectively[11]. On the one hand, from the perspective of the core meaning and goals of an EA practice, its maturity is determined mostly by the genuine quality of engagement and partnership between business and IT stakeholders, rather than by any formal factors or criteria, e.g. presence of some EA artifacts, execution of some processes or existence of some architecture governance bodies. All the typical EA artifacts, processes and governance bodies might be in place, but the actual engagement can still remain rather poor because of multiple subtle reasons. The quality of collaboration between business and IT that an EA practice aims to improve is very multifaceted, intangible and partly subjective in nature. For this reason, it cannot be reliably measured with simplistic checkbox lists, structured questionnaires or surveys, even though a certain correlation between observable external factors and genuine internal quality may definitely exist.

On the other hand, the maturity of an EA practice in organizations is often uneven across two different "orthogonal" dimensions. Firstly, some types of EA artifacts can be mastered significantly better than other types. As a result, some of the three EA-related processes constituting an EA practice (see Figure 6.1) can be far more mature than others. Since different types of EA artifacts and associated processes represent largely independent components of a full EA practice, they essentially have their own type-specific and process-specific maturity. For example, an organization may fully master Standards, Landscapes, Outlines and Designs (i.e. have rather mature Technology Optimization and Initiative Delivery processes), but still did not master the usage of Considerations and Visions (i.e. have an immature Strategic Planning process). Moreover, due to the historical reasons discussed earlier (see Figure 19.2), in most organizations Initiative Delivery tends to be the most mature EA-related process, while Strategic Planning tends to be the least mature process. From this perspective, it makes more sense to discuss the maturity of each of the three key EA-related processes instead of discussing the maturity of an EA practice in general.

Secondly, in many organizations, and especially in large and decentralized ones, EA practices have different maturity levels in different business units or areas. For example, in some lines of business all the three EA-related processes may be mature, whereas in other lines only Initiative Delivery and Technology Optimization, or even only Initiative Delivery, may be reasonably mature. In highly decentralized organizations an EA practice is often highly decentralized as well and carried out by different groups of architects closely aligned to respective business units (see Figure 17.3), which allows introducing different EA-related planning practices in different business units based on their unit-specific needs and problems. Furthermore, in large organizations EA-related planning practices are rarely introduced in all business units simultaneously, but more often piloted and tested in some business units and only then propagated to other business units, as noted earlier, which naturally leads to unequal maturity of an EA practice across different parts of the organization. In these cases, it makes more sense to discuss the maturity of an EA practice in specific business units, rather than its organization-wide maturity.

Due to the problems with evaluating the maturity of an EA practice in organizations described above, the maturity of an EA practice remains a rather conditional and elusive notion. However, the maturity of an EA practice is arguably manifested in several important signs that still might be used to assess the overall progression of EA practices in organizations towards the right direction.

Firstly, in mature EA practices all the six general types of EA artifacts defined by the CSVLOD model (i.e. Considerations, Standards, Visions, Landscapes, Outlines and Designs) are mastered. As noted earlier, specific EA artifacts related to each of these general types may be highly organization-specific, but all the six types should be adequately represented by some artifacts fulfilling the corresponding roles. Importantly, the maturity of an EA practice implies mastering and using a reasonable number of appropriate types of EA artifacts necessary for addressing key IT-related organizational problems (see Figure 19.3), often ten to fifteen different types, rather than as many different types of EA artifacts as possible. Put it simply, the maturity means using "just enough" of right EA artifacts, rather than more EA artifacts.

Secondly, in mature EA practices all EA-related processes are predictable and repeatable. Every EA-related process is clearly defined and associated with specific standardized types of

EA artifacts serving as its regular inputs or outputs. Moreover, every EA-related process is consistently followed with the involvement all relevant decision-makers and enables adequate engagement between business and IT stakeholders. In mature EA practices all participants of EA-related processes clearly understand the meaning and purpose of these processes as well as the roles of the underlying EA artifacts in these processes. Many actors of a mature EA practice are able to accurately and unambiguously describe the respective processes and EA artifacts[12].

Thirdly, mature EA practices pay significant attention to optimization of EA artifacts and EA-related processes. In particular, the quality of existing EA artifacts and processes is formally reviewed and assessed within the architecture function on a periodical basis, often yearly. As part of these discussions inefficiencies and opportunities for improvements are identified and corrective actions are planned accordingly. Regular reviews of current EA artifacts and their templates help align their informational contents and representation formats to the information needs of their stakeholders and maintain their overall adequacy.

Fourthly, in mature EA practices the overall ratio of urgent and local initiatives (see Table 7.1) in IT investment portfolios tends to be lower than in their less mature counterparts from the same industry sector. On the one hand, in mature EA practices more business needs are identified in advance during the Strategic Planning process and placed as planned IT initiatives in corresponding Roadmaps. Due to the better engagement with business stakeholders, mature EA practices essentially convert many urgent initiatives into foreseen local initiatives (see Figure 7.2) and ensure their alignment with the existing strategic plans. On the other hand, mature EA practices facilitate proactive identification of strategic opportunities for future IT investments and launch more IT initiatives in a top-down manner (i.e. strategic and fundamental initiatives) thereby reducing the number of reactive local initiatives. However, urgent and local initiatives still cannot be avoided completely regardless of the maturity level, especially in dynamic industries, e.g. retail.

Finally, in mature EA practices the total percentage of strategic IT investments tends to be higher than in their less mature counterparts from the same industry sector[13]. The business value of all proposed IT initiatives is better assessed and understood at their outset. As a result, the initiatives with a considerable strategic contribution are stimulated, while the initiatives bringing only marginal long-term benefits are discouraged. Moreover, as noted earlier, mature EA practices more often explicitly manage architecture debts (see Figure 18.9) and employ some numerical measurements of the quality of investment portfolios to be able to quantitatively estimate, monitor and control the overall ratio of strategic IT investments (see Figure 18.10). These efforts maximize the portion of the IT budget invested strategically, though non-strategic IT investments still cannot be completely avoided.

Importantly, the maturity of an EA practice is manifested mostly not in doing some special activities, following more sophisticated processes or creating more advanced EA artifacts, but rather in doing ordinary things better, more systematically and in a more predictable manner. From this perspective, a mature EA practice can be metaphorically compared with a well-oiled, fine-tuned and self-optimizing clockwork mechanism, where all operations are simple, but decently honed, properly scheduled and perfectly coordinated with each other.

Maturity of an EA Practice as a Factor of Sustainable Competitive Advantage

In the 21st century packaged systems, hardware infrastructure and outsourced IT services essentially became standard commodity readily available to all market players for a relatively cheap price. Due to their ubiquity, these resources on their own cannot provide significant competitive advantage to any organization[14]. Custom strategic information systems and innovative applications of technology may bring considerable business benefits and improve competitive positions of organizations on the market. However, in most cases these IT systems and innovations can be rather quickly copied or simulated by competing organizations giving their original creators only temporary bursts of competitive advantage[15]. Moreover, the same logic is also valid for specific business products and services. After being introduced as highly innovative or strategic by a leading organization, these new products or services are readily imitated by all major market players and become industry-standard mainstream offerings gradually losing their strategic value for the organization that initially invented and introduced them to the market.

For this reason, sustainable competitive advantage today comes not from specific IT systems, business products or services, but rather from the ability to consistently outperform competitors in various aspects of business performance, e.g. understand customer needs better, respond to these needs more quickly, provide better service quality or deliver cheaper products. Essentially, in the 21st century the competition between organizations is a competition between their management models and approaches, rather than between their products and services as it was before[16]. Currently the overall quality of management can be considered as the single most important competitive factor defining the organizational performance in the long run.

Similarly, sustainable competitive advantage from using IT today also comes predominantly from the ability to manage IT better than competitors or, in other words, from having a more developed IT capability[17]. Furthermore, due to the actual convergence of business and IT in modern organizations, IT management nowadays represents an essential part of general organizational management. The quality of IT management is an integral component of the overall management quality. An EA practice, in its turn, represents a critical element of IT management and the quality of an EA practice, along with the quality of IT delivery and support (see Figure 17.1), defines the organizational IT capability and contributes to the overall quality of IT management[18]. Via boosting the quality of management, an EA practice allows organizations to surpass their competitors in a systematic manner and achieve lasting competitive benefits on the market, e.g. operational excellence, customer intimacy or product leadership (see Figure 3.1). From this perspective, the maturity of an EA practice can be considered as one of the multiple factors determining enduring competitive advantage of organizations. The role of the maturity of an EA practice as a factor of sustainable competitive advantage is shown in Figure 19.4.

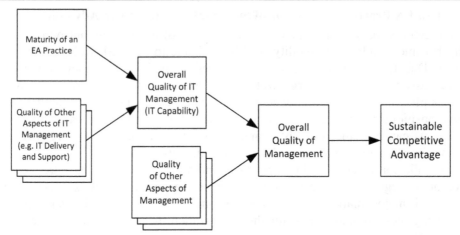

Figure 19.4. Maturity of an EA practice as a factor of sustainable competitive advantage

As a source of sustainable competitive advantage, the maturity of an EA practice essentially represents a valuable organizational asset, or resource, that can be obtained only with deliberate and persistent effort. Moreover, it requires considerable time investments to be developed or cultivated. Unlike specific business ideas, products or services, it cannot be easily acquired, copied, mimicked or "stolen" from other organizations. For these reasons, in the 21st century the maturity of an EA practice can be considered as a full-fledged factor of sustainable competitive advantage and as one of the constituents of competitive success on the market.

Enterprise Architecture Practice and Enterprise Architecture Consulting

Historically, enterprise architecture was very closely associated with consulting practice[19]. As noted earlier, all the widely known comprehensive information systems planning methodologies had been driven by consultancies. Starting from the seminal BSP methodology introduced by IBM in the late 1960s, all subsequent architecture-based planning methodologies had been promoted by consulting companies and individual consultants, e.g. Method/1 by Arthur Andersen and Information Engineering by James Martin, Clive Finkelstein and affiliated consultancies. Similarly, the first widely known BSP-based planning methodology explicitly using the term "enterprise architecture", Enterprise Architecture Planning (EAP), had been also promoted by consultants. At that time many or even most organizations did not have their own internal architects or dedicated IT planners[20].

From the perspective of consultancies, the practice of information systems planning, and later the practice of enterprise architecture, were essentially equivalent to time-limited consulting engagements, or one-shot planning projects, where the consultants guided by corresponding step-wise planning methodologies (e.g. BSP or EAP), studied client organizations, analyzed their business strategies and IT landscapes, developed idealistic architectures defining desired long-term target states and got paid merely for creating comprehensive documents or EA artifacts[21]. Unsurprisingly, consultants at that time often proclaimed the necessity for organizations to "have" architecture and promoted the benefits of having architecture, rather than using it for communication and decision-making, as if the very existence of detailed architectures somehow automatically benefited organizations[22]. However, as noted earlier, the very planning approach embodied in various slightly different formal architecture-based planning methodologies from BSP to TOGAF proved ineffective and in most cases produced only the heaps of cryptic architectural documents of little or no value to client organizations[23]. From the financial point of view, these planning engagements represented sheer losses for client organizations, but riskless profits for consulting companies[24]. For this reason, such consulting services were very actively promoted by consultancies on the market despite their evident practical ineffectiveness[25].

Moreover, this consultants-driven engagement-based planning approach essentially implied complete outsourcing of organizational information systems planning to external consultancies and opened numerous uncontrolled opportunities for consultants to manipulate and even abuse their clients. Firstly, often the relationships between consultancies and client organizations were rather short-term and ended after the stipulated architectural documents were completed. In these cases consultancies were naturally motivated only to "sell" more documents, rather than improve information systems planning in any real sense. As a result, consultants essentially cared neither of how these documents were used, nor of their actual quality[26].

Secondly, in case of long-lasting relationships between consultancies and their clients these information systems, and later enterprise architecture, planning engagements were often used by consultancies as a means of selling more of their own products and services. For example, vendor-related consultancies often used discounted or even free planning engagements as a pre-sale opportunity for recommending their own software products or hardware equipment. Likewise, large IT service companies often used planning engagements to secure further profitable contracts for the development and support of the IT systems prescribed by the architectural plans they created[27].

Thirdly, consulting companies often abused the trendy buzzword "enterprise architecture", as well as previous popular buzzwords like "information engineering", to market and sell whatever services they provided under the latest catchy titles to increase their chances of winning and signing contracts[28]. As a result, a wide spectrum of various IT services were positioned on the market as EA consulting sometimes having little or no connection between what was promoted and what was actually offered[29]. Essentially, anything starting from the development of comprehensive organization-wide architectural plans and ending with the planning and implementation of separate IT projects could have been marketed and sold under the attractive brand of enterprise architecture creating considerable confusion around this term[30].

However, at the present time the industry situation with EA consulting is seemingly changing for the better. On the one hand, the fundamental ineffectiveness of the formal planning approach pioneered almost 50 years ago by BSP and currently represented by multiple derivative step-by-step EA methodologies still actively promoted by many consultancies and gurus (e.g. TOGAF) is arguably widely understood in organizations. Even though many successful EA practices today are still operating under the "signboard" of TOGAF and other popular EA frameworks, the actual prescriptions of these frameworks are never treated seriously by architects and do not affect their real activities in any sense[31]. Instead of following archaic step-wise EA methodologies for producing unusable documentation, the EA community finally developed a set of consistent planning best practices described in this book that proved their efficacy in organizations.

On the other hand, the very nature of the EA discipline has changed significantly as well. From the initial consulting-driven discipline based predominantly on short-term planning engagements, enterprise architecture turned into a full-fledge and established internal organizational practice[32]. Most companies realized that they can outsource only information systems delivery, but not their strategic planning. Furthermore, today it is seemingly also widely acknowledged in industry that any static architectural plans, even of the highest quality, bring only a limited value at best, while the real value of planning can be achieved only via embedding a disciplined planning process into the organizational decision-making mechanism[33]. As a result, the majority of large and even medium organizations in developed countries now tend to host their own permanent architecture teams responsible for information systems planning instead of relying on the services of external consultancies to carry out the planning on their behalf.

Despite the general historical ineffectiveness of pre-EA and EA consulting practices, currently EA consulting still plays an important role in the EA discipline and forms a separate multibillion dollar global market[34]. Various EA consulting services are offered by many, or even most, international vendors and consultancies including, among others, IBM, Accenture and EY[35]. However, the practical role of EA consulting now is significantly different from its previous, historically discredited, traditional role. In particular, EA consultants today are usually engaged to complement internal architects, rather than to accomplish the planning instead of them. Architecture functions in many organizations now employ both internal and external architects collaborating together and forming a synergistic partnership beneficial for organizations[36]. Internal architects constitute the permanent core of an architecture team, understand the needs and specifics of their organization and protect its interests from external manipulations, while consulting architects offer a broader outlook, understand latest industry trends, best practices and technologies and able to enrich the organization with their expertise.

From the perspective of their goals, meaning and organizational impact, productive relationships between client organizations and EA consultancies can be loosely classified into three main types of consulting engagements: initiative-based engagements, strategic engagements and developmental engagements.

Initiative-Based Engagements

Initiative-based engagements are EA consulting engagements when external architects are hired by a client organization to plan and then supervise the implementation of specific IT initiatives. In these cases consulting architects are typically engaged either because of their deep knowledge of particular technologies for which the organization lacks adequate in-house expertise, or simply to add more capacity and accommodate with the transient peaks of commencing IT initiatives in the periods of massive IT investments and intense IT-driven transformations. These consulting engagements essentially represent a rather expensive way for organizations to temporarily extend their workforce with additional manpower possessing necessary skills and experience.

In this type of engagements EA consultants essentially fulfill the role of solution architects (see Figure 16.1), work under the supervision of internal enterprise architects, business unit architects and domain architects and involved only in the Initiative Delivery process (see Figure 16.3). Their role implies leading the development of Outlines and then Designs for separate IT initiatives addressing specific business needs suggested by Visions, leveraging existing Landscapes and aligning to organization-wide Considerations and Standards. Moreover, the role of EA consultants in these engagements usually also implies participating in the actual solution implementation activities at least in some form, often via supervising and supporting project teams delivering corresponding IT solutions. The ultimate outcome of these consulting engagements is either deployed and functioning IT systems, or at least systems at the later stages of their development cycle when all architecturally significant questions and risks have been fully addressed.

Initiative-based engagements allow organizations to fill their knowledge gaps in highly specific, exotic types of solutions, products or technologies, attract experienced architects with the required competence on an as-necessary basis and quickly adapt to the high "seasonal" workload. This type of engagements can be considered as the most basic, short-term and common form of relationship between client organizations and EA consultancies.

Strategic Engagements

Strategic engagements are EA consulting engagements when external architects are hired by a client organization to help plan its long-term development or a global reorganization of its IT landscape. In these cases consulting architects are usually engaged either because of their significant experience with large IT-driven transformations in specific businesses and industry sectors, or because of their good understanding of the strategic business potential of particular innovative or disruptive technologies. These consulting engagements provide excellent opportunities for organizations to get acquainted with the latest industry trends in using IT for enabling business operations and rethink the general role of IT in their business models.

In this type of engagements EA consultants essentially fulfill the role of enterprise architects, business unit architects or domain architects (see Figure 16.1), work in a close collaboration with internal architects and actively participate in the Strategic Planning and Technology Optimization processes (see Figure 16.3). Their role implies contributing to the development of Considerations and Visions by proposing effective long-term strategies aligned with the global industry directions as well as contributing to the evolution of Standards and Landscapes leveraging their broad knowledge of the recent technological developments, vendor offerings and respective best practices in these areas. Although these consulting engagements often result in the creation or update of some EA artifacts and launch of some IT initiatives, the most critical outcome expected from these engagements is the knowledge transfer from EA consultants to internal architecture teams.

Strategic engagements allow organizations to be part of ongoing global industry transformations, stay relevant with the latest waves and revolutions of the technological progress, augment and update the skills of their internal architecture teams with valuable external competence. This type of engagements can be considered as a rather advanced and even strategic form of collaboration between client organizations and EA consultancies.

Developmental Engagements

Developmental engagements are EA consulting engagements when external architects are hired by a client organization to help establish, evolve or improve its internal EA practice, architecture function and EA-related processes. In these cases consulting architects are usually engaged because of their knowledge of existing industry best practices in using enterprise architecture, previous experience in organizing architecture functions, enhancing EA-related processes and improving the quality of the dialog between business and IT. These consulting engagements naturally support organizations in their endeavors to start practicing enterprise architecture or evolve their current EA practices to a higher level of maturity, e.g. optimize existing EA artifacts or establish a full-fledged Strategic Planning process (see Figure 19.2).

In this type of engagements EA consultants essentially fulfill the role of architecture managers organizing the effective work of an EA practice, defining appropriate architecture positions and their responsibilities, establishing and fine-tuning the Strategic Planning, Initiative Delivery and Technology Optimization processes (see Figure 16.3). Their role implies governing, managing and often even hiring internal architects for different architecture positions, involving all relevant stakeholders into EA-related decision-making processes and achieving good quality of all corresponding EA artifacts supporting these processes. The ultimate outcome of these consulting engagements is the qualitative improvements in the organizational EA practice and its processes as well as the knowledge transfer from EA consultants to internal EA leaders.

Developmental engagements allow organizations to start practicing enterprise architecture from scratch when their in-house EA expertise is insufficient or lacking altogether, improve already existing EA-related processes and adopt latest industry approaches and best practices. However, as noted earlier, an EA practice requires deliberate organizational learning and cannot be established or improved merely by engaging even best EA consultants for a limited period of time without a genuine commitment of internal actors. This type of engagements can be considered as the most advanced form of partnership between client organizations and EA consultancies. Besides helping individual organizations boost their EA practices, developmental engagements also facilitate the knowledge exchange within the broader EA community, propagation of practical experience across the entire industry and accumulation of consistent EA best practices.

Productive and Counterproductive Relationships with Consultancies

As discussed above, productive relationships between client organizations and EA consultancies can be loosely categorized into initiative-based engagements, strategic engagements and developmental engagements. These three types of productive EA consulting engagements mapped to the corresponding EA-related processes are shown in Figure 19.5.

Developmental Engagements

(Consultants are engaged to help establish, evolve or improve the internal EA practice in an organization)

Consulting Architects

Motivation: Establish an EA practice from scratch or improve the existing practice in the absence of adequate in-house EA expertise

Role: Consultants act as architecture managers of an EA practice

Outcomes: Qualitative improvements in an EA practice as well as the knowledge transfer from consultants to internal EA leaders

Strategic Engagements

(Consultants are engaged to help plan the long-term development or reorganization of the IT landscape)

Motivation: Stay relevant with the waves of technological progress and latest industry trends

Role: Consultants act as enterprise architects, business unit architects or domain architects

Outcome: Knowledge transfer from consulting architects to internal architecture teams

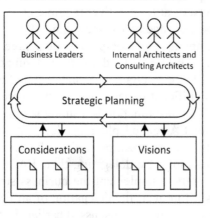

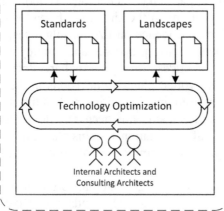

Initiative-Based Engagements

(Consultants are engaged to plan and supervise the implementation of specific IT initiatives)

Motivation: Fill knowledge gaps in highly specific technical areas or accommodate with the temporary peaks of workload

Role: Consultants act as solution architects

Outcome: Implemented IT solutions, or solutions at the later development stages

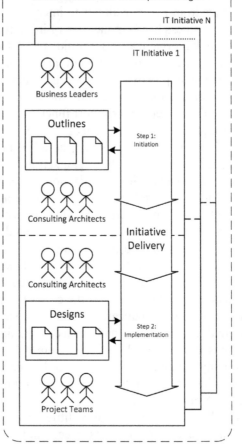

Figure 19.5. Three types of productive EA consulting engagements

Although EA consulting can provide a valuable intellectual input, deliver significant benefits to organizations, complement and enrich their in-house EA expertise and support their internal EA practices, some types of relationships with EA consultancies can be considered as unproductive or even detrimental to client organizations. These types of engagements are seemingly still rather widely offered by many EA consultancies and gurus, but in most cases should be avoided by organizations as non-value-adding at best and harmful at worst.

Firstly, many consultancies still capitalize on promoting and selling project-based documentation-oriented EA consulting highly resembling infamously known old-style BSP studies, i.e. when consultants analyze the organization for several months, produce a comprehensive set of required documents, collect their paychecks and leave the organization. As noted earlier, this approach never worked particularly well, at least for client organizations, and most often results only in the heaps of useless documentation[37]. This type of EA consulting can only waste money, discredit the very word "architecture" and even undermine all further attempts to establish an EA practice in an organization[38]. For this reason, organizations should avoid EA consulting engagements where architectural documents are positioned as the key output[39]. Instead, successful consulting engagements result primarily in the transfer of knowledge and competence from EA consultants to internal architects, or at least deliver tangible IT solutions for particular business needs in the case of initiative-based engagements (see Figure 19.5).

Secondly, organizations should avoid the temptation to completely outsource their EA practices to external consulting companies in a way similar to IT delivery and support[40]. This type of partnership between client organizations and EA consultancies is unequal and essentially puts these organizations in the inferior position of significant dependence on their consultancies. Unlike the IT delivery and support functions, an architecture function is a strategic organizational function that should not be outsourced. Since many EA-related planning decisions are highly strategic in nature, these decisions should be made by the organization itself, rather than by some third parties on behalf of the organization[41]. Put it simply, by delegating their EA practices to external EA consultancies organizations essentially start to implement the business strategies of these consultancies, rather than their own strategies. Moreover, the delegation of an EA practice to external consultancies creates ample opportunities for abuse, as discussed earlier. For instance, if an EA consulting company is associated with a particular technology vendor, then this company is likely to lead its dependent client organizations to the situation of vendor lock-in[42]. For this reason, organizations should avoid excessive dependence on EA consultancies, limit the influence of consultants on their EA-related decision-making processes and employ their own permanent architecture teams as the core of their EA practices. Strong internal architecture teams can assert genuine organizational interests, stop uncontrolled planning decisions in the interests of external consultancies and protect organizations from manipulations and authority of EA consultants and gurus. Essentially, internal architecture teams are necessary to maintain the "sovereignty" of an organization from the perspective of information systems planning. As a rule, most members of an architecture team should be permanent employees of an organization, not external EA consultants.

Thirdly, there are arguably little or no reasons to engage external EA consultants for developing facts EA artifacts (see Table 2.1), e.g. current-state Landscape Diagrams or Inventories. These EA artifacts are conceptually simple, do not imply any planning decisions and can be developed in a rather straightforward manner merely by documenting the existing IT environment (see Figure 2.6). Although their initial development may be time-consuming and tedious, it does not require much specific knowledge, deep expertise or particularly high qualification. Since external EA consultants tend to be more expensive for organizations than internal architects, engaging EA consultants for developing facts EA artifacts in most cases is economically inefficient and may be justified only when the in-house EA expertise is insufficient even for this simple activity, e.g. any experience with specialized software tools among internal architects is missing.

Chapter Summary

This chapter discussed the initiation, acceptance and maturity of an EA practice in organizations as well as the role of external consultancies in an EA practice, different types of EA consulting engagements, productive and counterproductive relationships between client organizations and EA consultancies. The key message of this chapter can be summarized into the following essential points:

- An EA practice in an organization cannot be instantly "switched on" by hiring architects, but requires considerable effort, intensive organizational learning and may take up to several years to establish and mature necessary EA-related processes
- The most practical way to establish an EA practice is to gradually introduce its elements into the organizational organism via mastering and institutionalizing the usage of corresponding types of EA artifacts step-by-step under the guidance of a designated EA leader
- The historical path to establishing an EA practice reflects the natural evolution of EA-related activities from simple to more complex ones, while the deliberate path represents a more proactive approach enabled by the availability of experienced architects and proven EA best practices
- Organizational acceptance of an EA practice can be facilitated by a number of measures including avoiding unnecessary IT-babble, using intuitive representation formats for EA artifacts, leveraging existing decision-making documents, avoiding sophisticated EA tools, providing appropriate trainings and demonstrating early wins
- Mature EA practices master all the six general types of EA artifacts, establish consistent and repeatable EA-related processes, continuously optimize EA artifacts and procedures and minimize the number of urgent initiatives in their IT investment portfolios
- As a resource that cannot be easily acquired, copied or imitated by other companies, the maturity of an EA practice represents a full-fledged strategic asset and can be considered as an important contributing factor of sustainable competitive advantage
- Productive EA consulting engagements can be classified into initiative-based engagements (consultants plan and supervise the implementation of separate IT initiatives), strategic engagements (consultants help plan the long-term

development of an organization) and developmental engagements (consultants help establish or improve the internal EA practice)

- Project-based documentation-oriented engagements, engagements focused on facts EA artifacts and complete outsourcing of EA practices to external consultancies can be considered as counterproductive relationships between client organizations and consulting companies

Afterword

In this book I made a pretty bold effort to analyze established industry best practices in using enterprise architecture as well as to provide a refreshing look at the EA discipline in general. This book debunks many wide-spread myths surrounding enterprise architecture and offers a comprehensive description of an EA practice based on the empirical evidence collected from tens of real organizations.

Firstly, this book criticizes the mainstream ideas and views aggressively promoted by numerous commercially motivated EA "experts", i.e. popular EA frameworks and other similar flawed planning approaches. Secondly and much more importantly, this book provides a sound evidence-based alternative to the heaps of faddish EA-related recipes having little or no relationship to the practical realities of information systems planning. In this book I attempted to present a consistent fads-free conceptualization and rich description of current EA best practices based directly on the first-hand empirical data from industry.

Hopefully, this book offers a more adequate, realistic and actionable description of an EA practice than the ones provided by most other available sources on enterprise architecture, the description that was necessary to systematize, codify and explain existing EA best practices, the description that the EA community, practitioners and students truly deserve. This long-awaited description arguably can move the entire EA discipline forward and eventually transform it from the inscrutable craft understandable only to experienced architects into a demystified and mature profession.

As a sole author of this book, I am the only one to be blamed or praised for the quality of ideas and materials presented here. I would be happy to receive any questions, comments, opinions, feedback and even criticism from the readers of this book. Finally, I would be very grateful if the readers could send me their own views, ideas, suggestions for improvement, samples of real EA artifacts or any other materials that can help improve the quality of this book and prepare the second updated edition in the future.

Best regards,
Svyatoslav Kotusev (kotusev@kotusev.com)

Appendix: The Origin of EA and Modern EA Best Practices

The main chapters of this book provided a comprehensive description of the existing industry best practices in using enterprise architecture for improving business and IT alignment. This appendix discusses in great detail the long and complex history of the modern EA discipline, explains the origination of the established EA best practices in their current form and clarifies their relationship to widely discussed EA frameworks. In particular, this appendix starts from describing the historical evolution of formal architecture-based planning methodologies from the 1960s to the present days. Then, this appendix discusses the three common problems of all formal architecture-based planning methodologies, demonstrates their practical ineffectiveness and analyzes the actual prevalence of these methodologies in organizations. Finally, this appendix concludes that the modern EA best practices described in this book emerged in industry and have no real relationship to widely promoted EA frameworks.

The Origin of Enterprise Architecture: Myths and Facts

The longstanding and widely accepted myth existing in the EA community suggests that the entire EA discipline originates from the breakthrough article of John Zachman titled "A Framework for Information Systems Architecture" published in 1987 in the IBM Systems Journal[1], which subsequently provided the basis for current EA best practices reflected in modern frameworks, most importantly in TOGAF[2]. Ironically, but an evidence-based analysis of the current and historical literature on information systems planning clearly shows that nothing could be farther from the truth, while the real origin of the EA discipline in its current form and corresponding best practices described in this book seemingly can be best explained by the following quote of renowned management scholars:

> "Classics [in management] typically arise not from the writings of academics or consultants but emerge out of practitioner responses to economic, social, and competitive challenges" (Miller and Hartwick, 2002, p. 27)

On the one hand, numerous architecture-based information systems planning approaches and methodologies have been proposed by various consultancies, gurus and experts since the very early days of computing long before 1987. On the other hand, all these proposed approaches and methodologies never proved effective and current EA best practices are essentially unrelated to these approaches beyond trivial common-sense generalities, e.g. development of some EA artifacts.

The History of Architecture-Based Planning Methodologies

The idea of deliberate information systems planning is far from new and dates back to the 1960s when the first planning approaches had been proposed. Since then, the discourse around organization-wide IT planning has gradually evolved from information systems plans to information systems architecture and finally to enterprise architecture[3]. However, the fundamental tenets and assumptions of corresponding architecture-based planning methodologies still stayed largely the same for the last half of a century and remained essentially unchanged from the 1960s to the present days.

Information Systems Plans Epoch

Since the beginning of the commercial use of computers in large organizations, numerous approaches had been proposed to plan, design and organize corporate information systems. These early planning approaches offered various recommendations on how to plan organization-wide information systems based on a business strategy, goals and objectives[4], products and markets[5], overall organizational system[6], data flows between departments[7], suppliers and orders[8], ends and means[9], vertical and horizontal classifications[10], critical success factors[11], management decisions[12], information requirements[13] and even generic soft systems problem solving methodology (SSM)[14]. Many of these approaches implied some form of modeling to understand the required structure of information systems as well as the creation of some explicit information systems plans.

However, the earliest rudiments of the step-wise planning methodology currently advocated by TOGAF and other EA frameworks can be seemingly traced back to the article of Marshall K. Evans and Lou R. Hague titled "Master Plan for Information Systems" published in 1962 in Harvard Business Review[15]. This article proposed to use various modeling techniques including information flows, input-output matrices and layout charts for creating the "master plan" defining the structure of required information systems (prototype of modern enterprise architecture)[16]. More importantly, the article also outlined a high-level five-step approach to information systems planning strongly resembling the general logic of all subsequent architecture-based planning methodologies. This step-wise planning approach proposed in the article, presumably the earliest published approach to information systems planning, is shown in Figure A.1.

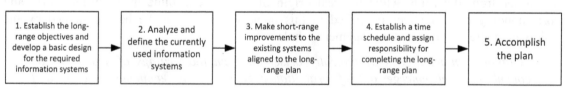

Figure A.1. The earliest step-wise approach to information systems planning (1962)[17]

Later a more detailed step-by-step approach to information systems planning based on very similar ideas had been published in Datamation magazine by M. Herbert Schwartz in 1970[18]. The step-wise planning approach proposed by Schwartz is shown in Figure A.2.

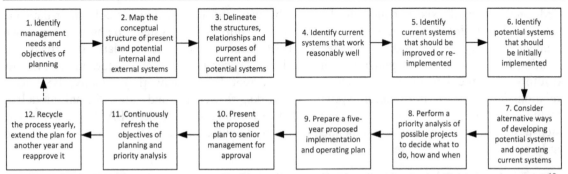

Figure A.2. The approach to information systems planning proposed by Schwartz (1970)[19]

Seemingly the first detailed structured methodology for organization-wide information systems planning was the Study Organization Plan (SOP) methodology introduced by IBM in the early 1960s and later supplemented with more extensive descriptions and teaching materials[20]. The SOP methodology was carried out by a specialized team of planners in a sequential manner and implied studying an organization and its operations by means of interviewing its business managers, then specifying requirements for the necessary information systems and finally designing the actual systems. Each of these activities, or phases, produced corresponding formal written reports using various forms, standardized sheets and simple modeling techniques. In the late 1960s similar planning methodologies had been also proposed by some other companies and experts[21]. The step-wise planning approach recommended by the SOP methodology is shown in Figure A.3.

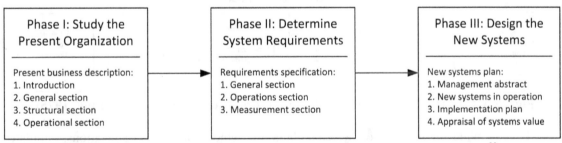

Figure A.3. IBM Study Organization Plan (SOP) methodology (1968)[22]

However, the earliest full-fledged, comprehensive and commercially promoted step-by-step information systems planning methodology that undoubtedly shaped modern EA frameworks was the Business Systems Planning (BSP) methodology[23] initiated by IBM in the late 1960s and led by P. Duane ("Dewey") Walker[24]. The first edition of BSP officially issued in 1975 introduced many novel ideas easily found in current EA frameworks and methodologies. For instance, the BSP methodology was implemented in a step-wise manner starting from identifying business objectives, defining business processes and data, analyzing the existing IT landscape and ending with developing a desired future information systems plan, preparing a detailed action plan and communicating it (prototype of the steps found in most current EA methodologies including, among others, TOGAF architecture development method). BSP activities were carried out by a dedicated group of experts called the BSP study team and responsible for collecting data via interviewing business managers and then developing information systems plans in a top-down manner (prototype of modern architects). BSP information systems plans described the relationship between an organization, its business processes, data and information systems (prototype of the key domains found in most current EA frameworks). Finally, BSP used relationship matrices, information systems networks, flowcharts and other formal modeling techniques to describe processes, systems and data (prototype of modern EA diagrams)[25]. The step-wise planning approach recommended by the first edition of the BSP methodology is shown in Figure A.4.

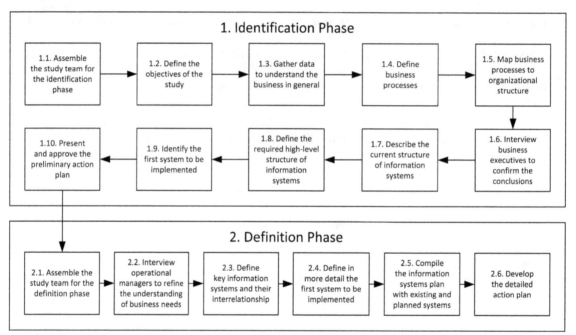

Figure A.4. IBM Business Systems Planning (BSP) methodology (1st edition, 1975)[26]

High demand for information systems planning methodologies in organizations stimulated the supply of these methodologies by consultancies[27]. As a result, after the introduction of the seminal BSP methodology by IBM, a number of similar BSP-like planning approaches quickly emerged on the market[28]. On the one hand, other BSP-based methodologies have been proposed by IBM itself, e.g. Information Quality Analysis (IQA) as a lightweight and automated version of original BSP developed by IBM Belgium[29]. On the other hand, highly similar planning methodologies had been also readily proposed by other consulting companies and experts essentially emulating and mimicking BSP in all the core aspects, i.e. step-wise, top-down and formal planning approaches producing comprehensive plans for required information systems[30].

For example, one of the most widely known BSP-like information systems planning methodologies was Method/1 promoted by Arthur Andersen (now Accenture)[31]. Method/1 advocated the same planning approach as BSP with very similar steps including studying an organization and its business strategy, analyzing the current IT landscape, developing desired data, application and technology plans and finally producing the action plan defining necessary IT projects. The step-wise planning approach recommended by the late version of the Method/1 methodology is shown in Figure A.5.

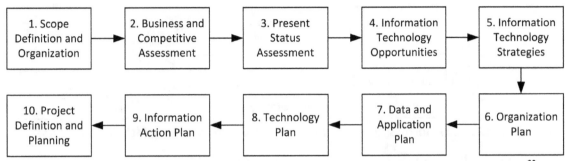

Figure A.5. Arthur Andersen Method/1 planning methodology (version 8.0, 1987)[32]

Information Systems Architecture Epoch

During the further evolution of the information systems planning consulting market the word "architecture" gained widespread popularity in the lexicon of consultants[33]. As a result, previous information systems plans had been renamed to "newer" information systems architecture, data architecture or information architecture. This shift stimulated active discussions on how exactly architecture should be structured and first taxonomies for organizing architecture, or architecture frameworks[34], had been proposed accordingly including the early architectural model of Caroline Wardle in 1984[35], the PRISM framework in 1986[36] and only then the famous Zachman Framework in 1987[37], which gained its reputation of the first EA framework seemingly only because of its effective promotion to the masses.

After the main focus in the information systems planning discourse shifted to architecture, the corresponding methodologies had been renamed accordingly to architecture planning methodologies. For instance, the BSP methodology, which initially focused on old-fashioned "information systems plans" (see Figure A.4), in the later versions switched to more trendy "information architecture" to describe the relationship between business processes and data classes. The step-wise planning approach recommended by the fourth edition of the BSP methodology is shown in Figure A.6.

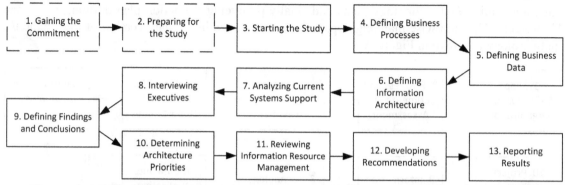

Figure A.6. IBM Business Systems Planning (BSP) methodology (4th edition, 1984)[38]

Highly similar architecture planning methodologies had been also offered by other prominent consultancies including, among others, the 4FRONT methodology by Deloitte & Touche (now Deloitte), the Summit S methodology by Coopers & Lybrand (now part of PwC)[39], the Information System Master Architecture and Plan (ISMAP) methodology by Atkinson, Tremblay & Associates (now defunct)[40] and the analogous architecture planning methodology by Nolan, Norton & Company (now part of KPMG)[41]. For example, the step-wise planning approaches recommended by Atkinson, Tremblay & Associates and Nolan, Norton & Company are shown in Figure A.7 and Figure A.8 respectively.

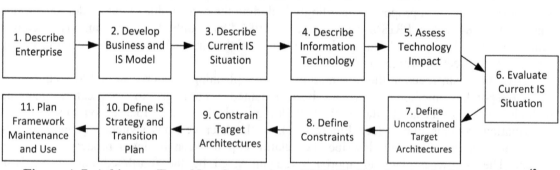

Figure A.7. Atkinson, Tremblay & Associates ISMAP planning methodology (1990)[42]

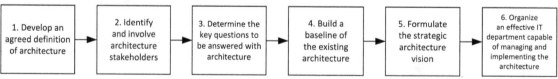

Figure A.8. Nolan, Norton & Company architecture planning methodology (1987)[43]

Besides major consulting companies, similar architecture planning methodologies had been also actively promoted by individual consultants and gurus including Edwin E. Tozer[44], Thomas E. Gallo[45], Denis A. Connor[46], Claire M. Parker[47], William H. Inmon, now better known as an expert in data warehousing[48], and even by some academics[49]. All these methodologies advocated essentially the same planning approach as BSP that implied interviewing business leaders, determining their business strategies, goals and information needs, assessing the current information systems support, describing the desirable architecture of future information systems and eventually formulating actionable implementation plans. For example, the step-wise planning approaches recommended by Edwin E. Tozer and Thomas E. Gallo are shown in Figure A.9 and Figure A.10 respectively.

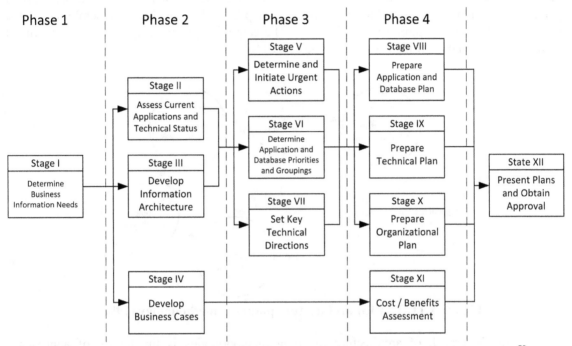

Figure A.9. The architecture planning methodology proposed by Tozer (1988)[50]

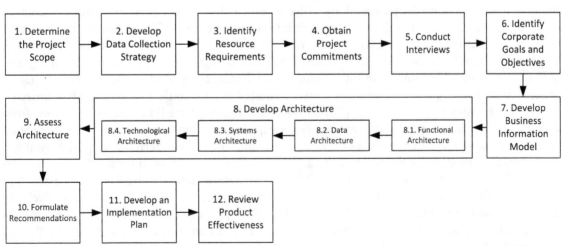

Figure A.10. The architecture planning methodology proposed by Gallo (1988)[51]

Being widely promoted in commercial private sector companies, architecture planning methodologies also started to expand into U.S. public sector and governmental organizations[52]. The Department of Defense was one of the first U.S. government agencies to develop its own architecture planning methodology. Specifically, based on the earlier approaches to architecture, the Defense Information Systems Agency (DISA) composed the Technical Architecture Framework for Information Management (TAFIM)[53]. TAFIM defined a comprehensive formal planning methodology with a familiar top-down step-by-step logic highly resembling all the previous architecture planning methodologies. The step-wise planning approach recommended by the late version of TAFIM is shown in Figure A.11.

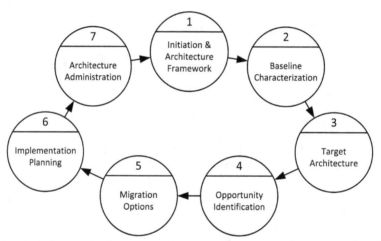

Figure A.11. TAFIM architecture planning methodology (1996)[54]

A notable branch of architecture planning methodologies is the family of approaches collectively titled as Information Engineering. The original Information Engineering methodology was initially proposed by IBM alumni Clive Finkelstein and James Martin in 1981[55], but later Information Engineering split into several slightly different sub-branches offered by various consultancies and gurus[56]. The most widely known sub-branch of the Information Engineering family is the sibling approach titled as Strategic Data/Information Planning and actively promoted by James Martin[57]. Information Engineering shifted the primary focus of architectural planning from business processes and applications to data as a "first-class citizen". While most previous architecture planning methodologies started the planning effort from identifying business processes or applications, Information Engineering recommended developing comprehensive data architecture first and only then deriving required systems, processes and procedures from this data architecture. Proponents of Information Engineering argued that data entities tend to be more stable in nature than the business processes that manipulate these entities and data-driven planning approaches, therefore, are more likely to produce sound, reliable and long-living architecture[58]. For example, the late versions of Information Engineering recommended by Arthur Young consultancy (now part of EY) and Clive Finkelstein are shown in Figure A.12 and Figure A.13 respectively.

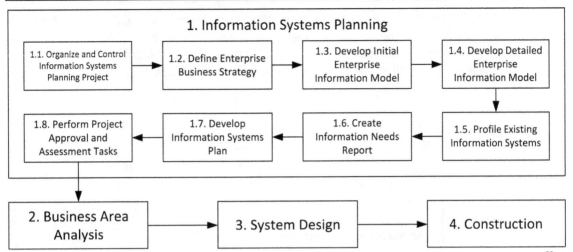

Figure A.12. Information Engineering methodology proposed by Arthur Young (1988)[59]

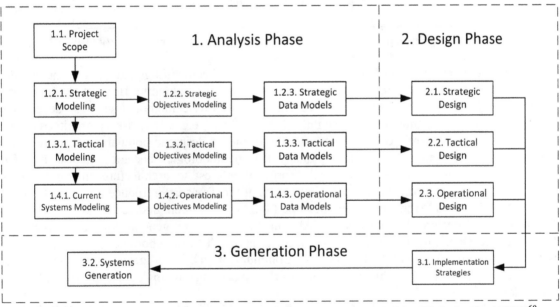

Figure A.13. Information Engineering methodology proposed by Finkelstein (1989)[60]

In the 1990s the entire Information Engineering branch had faded away, while the "trunk" of architecture planning approaches continued its active growth and further evolution towards modern enterprise architecture methodologies.

Enterprise Architecture Epoch

In the beginning of the 1990s the newer term "enterprise architecture" became in vogue[61]. The first planning methodology explicitly referring to enterprise architecture and titled simply Enterprise Architecture Planning (EAP) was proposed by consultants Steven H. Spewak and

Steven C. Hill in 1992[62]. EAP was based on BSP (see Figure A.4 and Figure A.6) and recommended essentially the same formal top-down step-wise approach to develop comprehensive enterprise architecture[63]. The step-wise planning approach recommended by the EAP methodology (the so-called "wedding cake") is shown in Figure A.14.

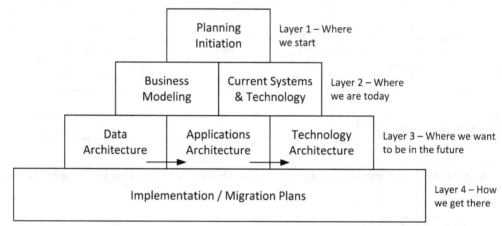

Figure A.14. Enterprise Architecture Planning (EAP) methodology (1992)[64]

The "brand new" notion of enterprise architecture had been willingly adopted by the broader consulting community. As a result, other consultants and gurus including Bernard H. Boar[65] and Melissa A. Cook[66] proposed their own, very similar step-wise methodologies for developing enterprise architecture, though under slightly different titles, e.g. enterprise IT architecture and enterprise information architecture. Also, after the further widespread popularization of the term "framework" within the EA community many EA methodologies became positioned as EA frameworks[67]. These trends excited a new surge of interest to architecture among the U.S. government agencies. For instance, the Department of the Treasury introduced its own Treasury Information Systems Architecture Framework (TISAF) and then updated it to the Treasury Enterprise Architecture Framework (TEAF) in line with the general industry direction[68]. Likewise, the Department of Defense replaced its earlier TAFIM approach (see Figure A.11) with the Command, Control, Computers, Communications, Intelligence, Surveillance and Reconnaissance (C4ISR) architecture framework advocating an analogous six-step planning methodology[69].

In 1999, as a reaction to the Clinger-Cohen Act obliging all agencies of the U.S. Federal Government to develop consistent enterprise architectures, the U.S. Federal CIO Council initiated the Federal Enterprise Architecture (FEA) program and published the corresponding FEA Framework (FEAF) to guide the program[70]. FEAF was based on the EAP methodology (see Figure A.14), prescribed the same step-wise planning approach, but recommended to develop enterprise architecture in a segmented manner[71]. Later essentially the same enterprise architecture planning approach was repeated and presented as a continuous iterative process in a series of articles in IT Professional magazine authored by Frank J. Armour, Stephen H. Kaisler and Simon Y. Liu, contributors to the FEA program[72]. The step-wise planning approach recommended by Armour, Kaisler and Liu is shown in Figure A.15.

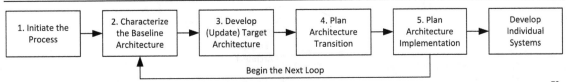

Figure A.15. The EA planning methodology proposed by Armour, Kaisler and Liu (1999)[73]

The next generation of highly similar EA methodologies, and now EA frameworks, promoted by both individual EA consultants and major consulting companies had emerged in the 2000s. On the one hand, this stream encompassed numerous slightly different EA methodologies proposed by prominent gurus from different countries including Christophe Longepe[74], Jane A. Carbone[75], Scott A. Bernard[76], Fenix Theuerkorn[77], Klaus D. Niemann[78], Jaap Schekkerman[79] and Samuel B. Holcman, a former business partner of John Zachman[80]. For example, the four-phase 20-step enterprise architecture implementation methodology recommended by Scott A. Bernard and the eight-step iterative approach to enterprise architecture recommended by Jaap Schekkerman are shown in Figure A.16 and Figure A.17 respectively.

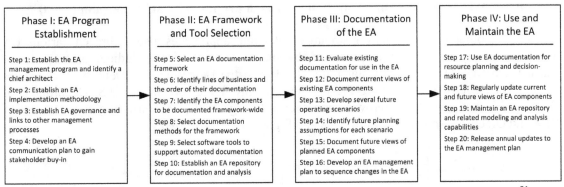

Figure A.16. The EA implementation methodology proposed by Bernard (2004)[81]

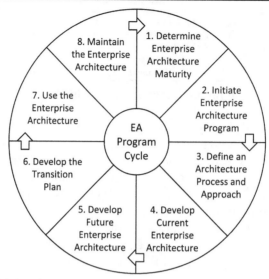

Figure A.17. The EA implementation approach proposed by Schekkerman (2008)[82]

On the other hand, the newer stream of planning approaches also embraced various EA methodologies and frameworks promoted by major consultancies including, among others, Gartner[83], IBM[84], Oracle[85] and Capgemini[86], and even the Department of Defense Architecture Framework (DoDAF) superseding the previous C4ISR framework in the U.S. Department of Defense[87]. For example, the step-wise approaches to organizing EA consulting engagements of IBM and Oracle are shown in Figure A.18 and Figure A.19 respectively.

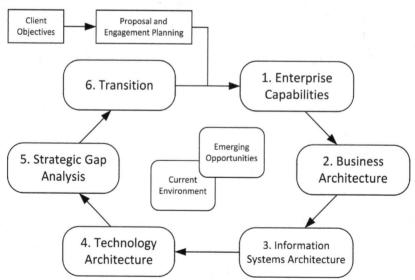

Figure A.18. IBM enterprise architecture consulting method (2006)[88]

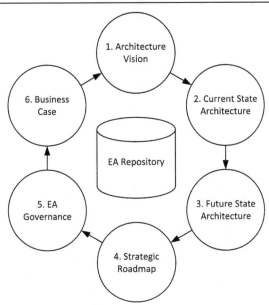

Figure A.19. Oracle enterprise architecture development process (2009)[89]

Finally, in the 2010s The Open Group Architecture Framework (TOGAF) gained widespread popularity in the EA community[90]. Originally based on TAFIM (see Figure A.11), TOGAF has evolved through a number of incremental improvements from the initial version 1.0 introduced in 1995 to the current version 9.2 published in April 2018. Recently TOGAF reached the status of the most popular EA framework[91] and now positioned by The Open Group as a definitive global standard in enterprise architecture[92]. The step-wise architecture development method (ADM) recommended by TOGAF is shown in Figure A.20.

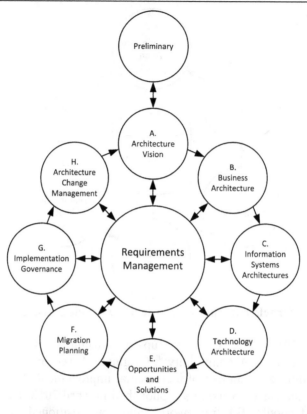

Figure A.20. TOGAF architecture development method (ADM) (2018)[93]

Conclusions of the Historical Analysis

The analysis of the long historical evolution of architecture-based planning methodologies from the early days of computing to the present days provided above (see Figure A.1 to Figure A.20) clearly shows that the latest EA methodologies and frameworks cannot be considered as new planning approaches in any real sense. Instead, the historical analysis demonstrates an undeniable connection of TOGAF and other modern EA methodologies to the earliest five-decades-old information systems planning approaches (see Figure A.1 to Figure A.3), and especially to BSP (see Figure A.4 and Figure A.6). Essentially, current EA methodologies and frameworks embody the high-level planning approach initially proposed by Marshall K. Evans and Lou R. Hague in 1962 and borrow many lower-level details from the BSP methodology.

Moreover, this lineage is evident and can be clearly traced at the level of general ideas, involved companies and even at the level of specific personalities. From the perspective of general ideas, all architecture-based planning methodologies, whether referring to information systems plans, information systems architecture or enterprise architecture, were based on the same basic principles. In particular, all these methodologies prescribed a formal, top-down and step-wise planning approach starting with the analysis of an organization and its business strategy and ending with some organization-wide plans, or architectures, describing the structure of required information systems[94]. Certainly, various architecture-based planning methodologies offered a multitude of different "flavors" (e.g. process, system or data emphasis), different sequences of steps (e.g. the future state is described before the current state or vice versa), different attitudes (e.g. one-shot projects or iterative processes) and different terminology better aligned to the popular buzzwords of respective time periods (e.g. Information Engineering appealed to the then-popular ideas of data normalization and computer-aided software engineering (CASE)). However, despite their continuous restyling and rewording, fundamentally all these methodologies represented only slightly different variations of the same analysis-synthesis documentation-oriented core planning paradigm inspired by traditional industrial engineering methods. All these methodologies from the 1960s to the present days inherited the same pivotal ideas, e.g. first developing comprehensive plans for information systems in some or the other form and then implementing these plans. Furthermore, in some cases this "genealogy" was openly admitted by the authors of corresponding methodologies. For instance, it was explicitly acknowledged that FEAF is based on EAP which, in its turn, is based on BSP[95], thereby directly confirming the existing connection between modern EA frameworks and the 50-years-old BSP methodology. Likewise, it is officially declared that TOGAF was derived from the earlier materials of TAFIM[96].

From the perspective of involved companies, many or even most architecture-based planning methodologies introduced to the market since the 1970s were products of the same narrow group of competing consulting companies, e.g. various predecessors of current "Big Four" consultancies (Deloitte, EY, KPMG and PwC) and most importantly IBM, or their former employees. For example, IBM alumni Clive Finkelstein, James Martin and John Zachman were among the most prominent individual contributors to the stream of formal architecture-based planning methodologies. Similarly, Edwin E. Tozer started his consulting career at Arthur Andersen and then worked for James Martin's consulting company James Martin Associates, while William H. Inmon worked for Coopers & Lybrand.

Finally, the strong link between the latest EA methodologies and the earliest information systems planning approaches of the 1960s-1970s is easily traceable even at the level of specific personalities involved in their promotion. Most importantly, John Zachman joined IBM as a marketing specialist in the 1960s, successfully promoted BSP in the 1970s-1980s[97], published his famous framework for information systems architecture in 1987, then became the "father" of enterprise architecture in the 1990s and recently acquired the Federal Enterprise Architecture Certification (FEAC) Institute to sell FEAF and DoDAF trainings[98]. Similarly, Clive Finkelstein began his career at IBM in the 1960s, founded his own consultancy during the early BSP period in the 1970s, "fathered" Information Engineering in the 1980s, then started mentioning "enterprise information engineering" in the early 1990s[99] and finally also switched to promoting enterprise architecture[100].

The comprehensive historical analysis of architecture-based planning methodologies proposed by various companies and information systems experts since the 1960s allows making two curious conclusions important for the entire EA discipline. Firstly, the historical analysis provided above clearly debunks the popular myth that the discipline of enterprise architecture originates from the Zachman Framework. As the analysis unambiguously demonstrates, current EA methodologies and frameworks are evident descendants of the earliest information systems planning approaches of the 1960s. In fact, the Zachman Framework neither influenced architecture-based planning methodologies in any real sense, nor even was the first published architecture framework[101]. However, John Zachman himself still was among the most active promoters of architecture-based planning methodologies and specifically BSP.

Secondly, the historical analysis provided above allows grouping all the discussed architecture-based planning methodologies into a single family, or pedigree, of conceptually similar planning approaches. Essentially, all formal, top-down and step-wise planning methodologies promoted by various consultancies and gurus over the last half of a century from BSP to TOGAF can be considered merely as different elements of a single long-lasting and persistent global effort to "sell" the same planning approach under various titles. Although these methodologies significantly differed in their presentation style and terminology (e.g. initially referred to information systems plans, then to information systems architecture and finally to enterprise architecture), their real essence and fundamental meaning stayed unchanged and always implied the same analysis-synthesis documentation-oriented plan-then-implement mechanistic attitude towards information systems planning. The historical analysis of the family of formal architecture-based planning methodologies provided above is summarized in Figure A.21.

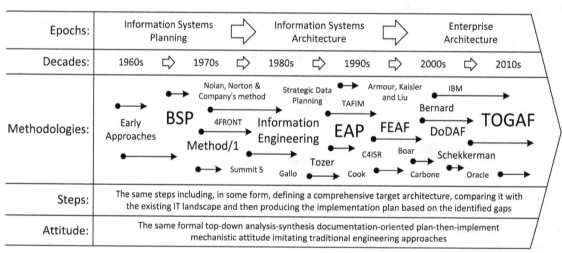

Figure A.21. The family of formal architecture-based planning methodologies

Despite the evident conceptual similarity of all the proposed architecture-based planning methodologies from BSP to TOGAF, some general trends in the historical evolution of these methodologies still can be noticed. Firstly, architecture-based methodologies evolved from one-shot planning projects often called as architecture studies (e.g. BSP and Method/1) to continuous iterative processes where the next planning iteration, or project, starts as soon as the previous iteration is completed (e.g. TAFIM and TOGAF).

Secondly, architecture-based methodologies evolved from rather conceptual planning focused mostly on the logical aspects of architecture (e.g. processes, data and systems) to more "deep" planning also encompassing the underlying physical aspects of architecture (e.g. hardware, infrastructure and technology). For example, BSP and Information Engineering were largely abstracted from the technical details of architecture, while EAP and TOGAF explicitly cover the technology domain as well.

Thirdly, architecture-based methodologies evolved from using relationship matrices as a means to capture and represent architecture to using more conventional graphical notations for this purpose. For example, BSP, Strategic Data/Information Planning and even EAP extensively relied on process/data class (CRUD), process/organization, organization/system and other types of matrices to describe the relationship between various elements of architecture, while TOGAF and other modern EA methodologies rely primarily on graphical diagrams and models to depict architecture.

Finally, architecture-based methodologies evolved from the planning approaches having a certain sophisticated theoretical basis to conceptually simple, largely atheoretical approaches. In other words, the historical evolution of architecture-based methodologies went towards the simplification of their theoretical foundations. For instance, BSP implied a set of rigid, sequential and conceptually justified analytical procedures (essentially an optimization algorithm) that allowed deriving an ideal architecture almost automatically from the information collected during the interviews with senior business stakeholders via grouping closely related business processes and data classes into cohesive IT systems. Likewise, Information Engineering leveraged the data normalization theory developed by Edgar F. Codd as a conceptual foundation to derive normalized, "mathematically" optimal, non-redundant architectures. However, all modern EA methodologies including TOGAF only suggest that the desired target architecture should be defined, but without specifying how exactly this architecture should be derived from the input information and how to ensure the optimality of the resulting architecture. Put it simply, early architecture-based planning methodologies tended to have some "ideological" underpinning and sound theoretical justifications for their procedures and outcomes, while modern methodologies are more theoretically shallow.

The Application of Architecture-Based Planning Methodologies

Despite being positioned as "best practices" in information systems planning and aggressively promoted by commercially motivated consultancies and gurus, formal architecture-based planning methodologies rarely fulfilled their promise and usually did not meet the expectations of organizations. Moreover, these methodologies were consistently found to be impractical, much less effective and popular than pragmatic and flexible homegrown architecture-based approaches to information systems planning.

Problems of Architecture-Based Planning Methodologies

The first attempts to investigate the practical effectiveness of formal architecture-based planning methodologies seemingly date back to the end of the 1980s[102]. The analogous efforts had been also undertaken later in the 1990s[103]. Then, during the following enterprise architecture epoch, similar studies and reports appeared in the late 2000s[104] and more recently in the 2010s[105]. All these studies and field reports unanimously conclude that the practical implementation of architecture-based planning methodologies is associated with a number of considerable problems. Although these problems are rather diverse and multifaceted, they can be grouped into three core issues raised in some or the other form by most empirical studies of formal architecture-based methodologies: enormous planning efforts, poor quality of the resulting plans and disconnection from the rest of the organization. These three issues are largely independent from each other, "orthogonal" in nature and can be clearly attributed specifically to the very essence of corresponding planning methodologies, rather than to some other more general factors, e.g. lack of management commitment and support, inadequate leadership, unclear business direction or shortage of skilled personnel.

Firstly, the proper execution of architecture-based planning methodologies requires substantial investments of time, effort and managerial attention. The creation of comprehensive plans, or architectures, formally describing an organization and its desired future state as recommended by architecture-based planning methodologies may take several months of full-time work for a dedicated team of people or even longer. The corresponding development process is often further complicated by a wide organizational scope, dynamic context, high complexity and a large number of stakeholders involved in the process. Moreover, comparable efforts are also required later to maintain the existing plans or architectures up to date in order to accommodate with the ongoing changes in an organization and its environment.

Secondly, the planning documents or EA artifacts resulting from the execution of architecture-based planning methodologies are often found incomprehensible for their stakeholders and unable to support decision-making. Common reasons of this problem include irrelevant informational contents, inconvenient presentation formats and inappropriate levels of abstraction and granularity of architectural plans. Furthermore, strict architectural plans recommended by most architecture-based methodologies are often considered as too complex and technical by senior business stakeholders, especially by stakeholders unfamiliar with formal modeling notations and techniques. Another factor contributing to this problem and undermining the usefulness of architectural plans is their constant obsolescence. Frequent shifts in business priorities quickly render comprehensive architectures outdated and make them essentially irrelevant to decision-makers.

Thirdly, architecture-based planning methodologies imply a separate standalone planning lifecycle essentially isolated from the surrounding organizational context. These methodologies are executed in a step-by-step manner in their own "time zone" and guided by their own internal logic, but do not enable adequate integration between the respective architecture planning activities and normal organizational activities, e.g. strategic planning, portfolio budgeting and project delivery. As a result, existing architectures are not leveraged during regular decision-making processes and the architectural input is simply ignored. In fact, none of the architecture-based planning methodologies clearly explains when exactly resulting architectures should be used. The most common natural outcome of this disconnection between methodology-driven architecture planning processes and the rest of the organization is disbanded architecture teams and shelved architectural plans.

The three inherent problems with formal architecture-based planning methodologies described above represent permanent problems. The very same problems in some or the other form have been consistently identified by different observers at different time periods regarding all generations of architecture-based planning methodologies from BSP to TOGAF[106], which is unsurprising taking into account conceptual similarity or even equivalency of these methodologies, as demonstrated earlier. The problems associated with these methodologies are natural, rather than accidental and result from their flawed design, rather than from their poor execution. These problems stem directly from the very essence of corresponding methodologies, i.e. top-down, step-wise, documentation-oriented, plan-then-implement mechanistic approach imitating classical engineering.

Unsurprisingly, over a long period of time many disinterested researchers, observers and analysts unanimously concluded that formal architecture-based planning methodologies are deficient and ineffective[107]. Moreover, independent observers at different time periods also concluded that the problems with these methodologies are fundamental in nature and called for rethinking the very approach to information systems planning[108]. As opposed to "heavyweight", rigid and mechanistic architecture-based methodologies executed mostly by specialized planners or architects on behalf of an organization, many authors consistently argued for more pragmatic, flexible, participative and organic approaches to information systems planning[109].

Interestingly, the actual direction of the historical evolution of architecture-based planning methodologies discussed earlier (i.e. the evolution from more conceptual and theoretically substantiated planning projects creating relationship matrices to more technical and atheoretical iterative processes producing graphical diagrams) was essentially orthogonal to the empirically suggested development direction towards greater flexibility, pragmatism and stakeholder involvement. As a result, decades of this misdirected evolution driven seemingly only by chaotic commercial interests of competing consultancies and gurus, rather than by objective analysis and common sense, did not solve any of the three core practical problems associated with these methodologies described above[110].

Prevalence of Architecture-Based Planning Methodologies

Besides branded information systems planning methodologies widely promoted by global consultancies (e.g. BSP and Method/1), other types of planning approaches also "quietly" existed since the early days of computing and had been actively used in organizations. Specifically, many organizations developed their own internal, homegrown approaches to information systems planning[111]. These approaches were established in-house, customized for the needs of particular organizations, never promoted publicly and had no specific well-known "loud" titles.

Historically, homegrown approaches to information systems planning prevailed in organizations, while BSP and similar architecture-based methodologies, despite being very widely discussed, were actually used only in about one-fifth of all organizations[112]. Moreover, many of these homegrown approaches proved much more effective in practice than formal architecture-based planning methodologies[113]. At the same time, the very idea of using some form of architecture to describe the relationship between business and IT was found helpful and promising by information systems planners, though with substantial deviations from the original prescriptions of popular architecture-based methodologies[114]. Taking into account the significant problems with formal architecture-based planning methodologies discussed above, it would be fair to say that genuine best practices in information systems planning, and even in architecture-based planning, historically were outside of the conspicuous zone of commercial architecture-based planning methodologies (e.g. BSP and Information Engineering), but instead were embodied in effective homegrown planning approaches developed in-house. However, these best practices stayed essentially invisible to the outer world, i.e. worked in leading organizations without being formally described, studied, conceptualized or widely promoted[115].

During the current enterprise architecture epoch the actual prevalence of formal architecture-based planning methodologies, which are promoted today mostly as popular EA frameworks including TOGAF, is much harder to estimate since the very concept of enterprise architecture for many people became inextricably associated with EA frameworks essentially blurring the boundary between practicing enterprise architecture and using EA frameworks. At the first glance, most organizations practicing enterprise architecture indeed report on using some EA frameworks, though about one-third of all organizations still do not use any of them[116]. However, a closer scrutiny immediately reveals the curious fact that in most cases the usage of EA frameworks is only formally declared, but their original prescriptions are not followed in any real sense[117].

In other words, at the present moment many successful EA practices operate under the "signboards" of EA frameworks without even trying to implement any of their actual recommendations, but instead carrying out some homegrown EA-based planning approaches unrelated to frameworks that proved effective in practice. Taking into account the abundant and sharp criticism of EA frameworks[118], it would be arguably fair to say that the general impracticality of EA frameworks is now commonly acknowledged in the EA community and most architects do not treat their recommendations seriously any longer[119], while the overwhelming majority of organizations "using" EA frameworks simply ignore their essential prescriptions and rely on proven EA-based planning practices spreading across the industry. Analogously to the similar situation observed earlier during the previous pre-EA epoch described above, the current situation in the enterprise architecture epoch again clearly indicates that genuine EA best practices actually lay outside of the conspicuous zone of popular EA frameworks (e.g. TOGAF, FEAF and DoDAF), but instead are embodied in effective homegrown EA-based planning approaches quickly disseminating from organizations to organizations. These EA best practices are analyzed in this and some other earlier evidence-based books on enterprise architecture[120].

Conclusions of the Application Analysis

The analysis of the practical application of architecture-based planning methodologies provided above clearly shows that these methodologies never represented mainstream best practices in information systems planning. On the one hand, the entire family of formal architecture-based planning methodologies from BSP to TOGAF (see Figure A.21) proved impractical and much less effective than pragmatic homegrown architecture-based approaches to information systems planning developed in many organizations and then spread across the industry. All these step-by-step methodologies never worked particularly well and were always associated with the three major practical problems described earlier. From this perspective, formal architecture-based methodologies can be even considered as proven worst practices in information systems planning.

On the other hand, formal architecture-based planning methodologies never represented even mainstream planning practices. As discussed above, during the previous pre-EA epoch these methodologies were used only in the minority of organizations, while during the current enterprise architecture epoch the usage of these methodologies in the overwhelming majority of cases is purely declarative, i.e. the use of EA frameworks is proclaimed, but their actual recommendations are simply ignored or in the most extreme cases are not even studied. Essentially, all architecture-based planning methodologies were only widely promoted and briskly discussed in literature, but rarely practiced and never represented "average" mainstream planning approaches actually used in real organizations. In other words, these methodologies, as well as their successes, always existed mostly on paper rather than in practice[121].

The comprehensive analysis of the practical application of formal architecture-based planning methodologies allows making two curious conclusions important for the entire EA discipline. The first conclusion is that all well-known architecture-based planning methodologies from BSP to TOGAF essentially reflect only a small visible tip of the huge planning "iceberg". All these methodologies represent evident management fads aggressively promoted by commercially motivated consultancies and widely discussed in literature, but rarely actually used in practice and even more rarely with successful results for organizations. Although these methodologies always attracted considerable attention, created significant hype and essentially defined the discourse around information systems planning, information systems architecture and then enterprise architecture over the last half of a century, they never worked well in practice, never were widely used in organizations and never represented real best practices in information systems planning. Seeking best practices in these intentionally promoted but inherently ineffective architecture-based planning methodologies can be ironically compared to searching for keys under the lamppost because this is where the light is, even though the keys had been definitely lost somewhere else.

At the same time, genuine best practices in architecture-based planning belong to an invisible underwater part of the planning "iceberg". These best practices seemingly emerged as rudimentary homegrown planning approaches developed in-house, evolved in leading organizations over decades (arguably according to the approximate historical path discussed earlier, see Figure 19.2), gradually disseminated across the industry without being formally described or actively promoted on a commercial basis and currently matured to their present form analyzed in this book[122]. Unlike conspicuous but faddish and flawed architecture-based planning methodologies (e.g. BSP, Information Engineering, FEAF and TOGAF), real best practices worked "silently" in organizations and never were widely discussed, but constituted the actual body of knowledge on information systems planning stored mostly in the heads of practicing architects. The persistent disparity between widely promoted architecture-based planning methodologies and actual architecture-based planning best practices clearly demonstrates the existence of a dramatic gap between what is superficially discussed and what actually works in organizations[123].

The second conclusion is that genuine EA best practices described in this book have no relationship to EA frameworks. Moreover, the lack of any connection between actual EA best practices and EA frameworks is evident from both the conceptual and practical perspectives. From the conceptual perspective, the development of genuine EA best practices and EA frameworks was motivated by different and essentially unrelated goals. While real EA best practices were obviously sought by organizations interested in improving the quality of their information systems planning, EA frameworks were seemingly motivated only by the commercial interests of consultancies and gurus eager to continuously resell the same "old wine in new bottles", i.e. promote new and new fresh-looking methodologies via replicating the same 50-years-old flawed ideas of BSP and other early planning approaches regardless of the well-known problems of these methodologies and a common understanding that more pragmatic, flexible and participative approaches are required[124].

From the practical perspective, the recommendations of EA frameworks do not overlap with proven EA best practices beyond very high-level common-sense generalities, e.g. some form of architectural planning is desirable, some diagrams and models can be useful, both the present situation and future goals should be taken into account, business, applications, data and technology aspects should be addressed, etc. At the same time, none of the frameworks-specific prescriptions proved useful in practice[125]. For instance, recommended taxonomies for organizing EA artifacts, long lists of specific EA artifacts, sequences of steps in which these artifacts should be created and even the general plan-then-implement approach advocated by EA frameworks all proved either impractical or harmful. Instead, successful EA practices are based on different sets of EA artifacts (see Figure 15.4), require diverse and continuous communication processes (see Figure 6.1), avoid detailed planning of the future state (see Figure 5.6) and even imply no strict separation of EA artifacts into different EA domains (see Figure 2.2) as suggested by EA frameworks. Furthermore, the vast majority of useful EA artifacts and planning techniques constituting successful EA practices cannot be traced to any EA frameworks that proposed them. Most notably, ubiquitously used Business Capability Models (see Figure 11.1) are not even mentioned in any existing EA frameworks or methodologies. Even when useful EA artifacts are included in EA frameworks (e.g. Principles (see Figure 9.1) and some other useful EA artifacts are listed in TOGAF), these frameworks only mention them among numerous useless EA artifacts and do not explain how exactly these artifacts should be used, when and why.

Historically, formal architecture-based planning methodologies and actual architecture-based planning best practices essentially form two different streams that evolved in parallel independently of each other driven by different forces. These streams are disparate in nature and should not be confused. On the one hand, the stream of formal architecture-based planning methodologies (see Figure A.1 to Figure A.20) was driven by consultancies and gurus. The corresponding prescriptive methodologies, and now EA frameworks, were created artificially simply by repacking the same ideas in different packages and "reselling" them again and again without taking into account their evident practical problems. These methodologies were always widely promoted and discussed in literature, but rarely worked successfully in practice and, therefore, represent only classical management fads of little or no practical value. On the other hand, the stream of real architecture-based planning best practices described in its current form in this book was driven by information systems planners in organizations. These planning approaches naturally evolved from simple to more complex practices and spread across the industry. Although never deliberately promoted and rarely discussed in literature, these planning approaches work successfully in numerous companies and, therefore, represent the genuine body of knowledge on information systems planning. The comparison between the two streams of architecture-based planning approaches described above is summarized in Table A.1.

Stream	Formal architecture-based planning methodologies (see Figure A.21)	Real architecture-based planning best practices (this book)
Origin	Consulting companies and gurus	Information systems planners in organizations
Nature	Artificial, prescribed and imposed	Natural, industry-born and spontaneous
Evolution	Same approach replicated many times under different titles with insignificant changes	Gradual evolution from simple to more complex practices
Approaches of the information systems planning epoch	BSP, Method/1 and earlier approaches (see Figure A.1 to Figure A.5)	Proven planning practices of these epochs are poorly studied and documented, no reliable sources or sound conceptualizations available, but seemingly loosely aligned to the historical evolutionary path discussed earlier (see Figure 19.2)
Approaches of the information systems architecture epoch	BSP, Information Engineering, TAFIM and other methodologies (see Figure A.6 to Figure A.13)	
Approaches of the current enterprise architecture epoch	EAP, FEAF, TOGAF and other frameworks and methodologies (see Figure A.14 to Figure A.20)	Proven planning practices described in this book and earlier evidence-based books on enterprise architecture
Core ideas	Analysis-synthesis approach based on sequential steps and formal descriptions	Effective communication and continuous decision-making at different levels
Key features	Heavyweight, rigid, mechanistic and arcane	Pragmatic, flexible, organic and participative
Practicality	Impractical, associated with significant fundamental problems	Practical, work more or less successfully in numerous diverse organizations
Prevalence	Widely promoted and discussed in literature, but rarely used in practice	Rarely promoted and discussed in literature, but widely adopted in industry
Metaphor	Visible tip of the iceberg	Invisible body of the iceberg
Essence	Classical management fads of little or no practical value	Genuine body of knowledge on information systems planning
Role	Provided the initial inspiration for real best practices, but never actually defined them	Actual best practices defining the discipline of enterprise architecture in its current form

Table A.1. Two streams of architecture-based planning approaches

Due to their incessant and irresponsible promotion by commercially motivated consultancies and gurus, EA frameworks became a prominent phenomenon of the modern EA discipline that cannot be simply ignored despite their irrationality, practical uselessness and evident faddish nature. Essentially, EA frameworks now are a curious fact of life that undeservingly attracts significant attention in the EA discourse and occupies a considerable part of the entire information field. For this reason, this appendix will finish with the following brief advice for dealing with EA frameworks:

- Do not believe that EA frameworks are important, they are not
- Do not think that EA frameworks reflect best practices, they do not
- Do not try to implement EA frameworks, it cannot be done

- Ignore gurus promoting EA frameworks, they are bluffing
- Avoid discussing EA frameworks, think in a frameworks-free manner

Although framework certifications can improve the CVs of EA practitioners and comparisons of frameworks can enrich the publication records of EA academics, EA frameworks are not related to the current discipline of enterprise architecture in any real sense and represent extremely harmful management fads that should be eradicated[126].

Appendix Summary

This appendix analyzed the long history of the EA discipline, the evolution of formal architecture-based planning methodologies, the origination of modern EA best practices described in this book and their relationship to widely discussed EA frameworks. The key message of this chapter can be summarized into the following essential points:

- The roots of the current step-wise planning methodology recommended by TOGAF and other modern EA frameworks can be traced back to the early information systems planning approaches introduced in the 1960s and especially to the BSP methodology promoted by IBM
- After being introduced in a rudimentary form in the 1960s, formal architecture-based planning methodologies slowly evolved over the last half of a century through three different epochs initially positioned as information systems planning, then as information systems architecture and now as enterprise architecture
- Despite their apparent stylistic differences, all architecture-based planning methodologies from BSP to TOGAF are based on the same core ideas, advocate a very similar analysis-synthesis plan-then-implement attitude imitating traditional engineering and essentially represent a single family of planning approaches
- The entire family of formal architecture-based planning methodologies proved impractical and even fundamentally flawed due to their common tendency to require significant investments of time and effort and producing only the heaps of cryptic documents largely useless for decision-making purposes
- Despite being highly conspicuous and widely promoted, formal architecture-based planning methodologies were actually used only in the minority of organizations, while most companies developed their own homegrown architecture-based planning approaches and many of these homegrown approaches proved much more effective than branded methodologies
- Current EA best practices described in this book seemingly descend from the homegrown architecture-based planning approaches that emerged in leading organizations, proved their practical effectiveness, gradually spread across the industry and matured over time, but have no real relationship to widely discussed faddish EA frameworks

Preface

[1] The citation analysis of Simon et al. (2013) demonstrates that popular EA frameworks (i.e. TOGAF, Zachman, FEAF and DoDAF) are indeed the most highly cited and influential EA publications

[2] Most authors, for instance Sessions (2007), Simon et al. (2013) and Lohe and Legner (2014) to name a few among many others, argue that the entire EA discipline emerged from the seminal work of Zachman (1987)

[3] Specifically, I mean the approaches to enterprise architecture recommended by Wagter et al. (2005) (DYA) and Ross et al. (2006) (MIT). These two approaches propose significantly different ways of practicing enterprise architecture inconsistent with the suggestions of popular EA frameworks (Kotusev, 2016b; Kotusev, 2017a; Kotusev et al., 2015a)

[4] For instance, Wagter et al. (2005) criticize the approaches recommended by popular EA frameworks for producing useless "paper tigers" instead of working architecture, while Ross et al. (2006, p. vii) criticize these approaches for "their remoteness from the reality of the business and their heavy reliance on mind-numbing detail represented in charts that look more like circuit diagrams than business descriptions and that are useful as little more than doorstops"

[5] As Wierda (2015, p. 65) puts it, "for a subject that is over thirty years old, there is pretty little empirical proof that any of the proposed methods of frameworks actually work". For example, regarding the famous and well-known Zachman Framework Ylimaki and Halttunen (2006, p. 189) correctly notice that it is "hard to find scientific studies on applying or utilizing the Zachman framework". "We made a considerable effort in searching for scientific research on the Zachman framework. As a result, it seems that there is a lack of scientific studies on the application of the Zachman framework – and analyzing its applicability – in practice" (Ylimaki and Halttunen, 2006, p. 190). Similar observations have been made about TOGAF as well: "There is a pressing need for some detailed worked examples and use cases. Although these were requested, they were not forthcoming from TOGAF trainers or The Open Group" (Anderson et al., 2009, p. 66). My own comprehensive literature search also did not identify any documented examples of the practical implementation of EA frameworks (Kotusev, 2017e)

[6] The impracticality of EA frameworks is consistently reported by different authors (Buckl et al., 2009; Gaver, 2010; Gerber et al., 2007; Holst and Steensen, 2011; Lohe and Legner, 2014). "Most EA methods and frameworks claim that [their prescriptions] can be applied to the development of an EA for an entire organization, but attempts to develop architecture on this scope routinely fail" (Trionfi, 2016, p. 40). As Wierda (2015, p. 31) puts it, "let's face our own inconvenient truth: enterprise architecture doesn't really work the way we have assumed for thirty years it would"

[7] Numerous case studies demonstrate that successful EA practices have nothing to do with EA frameworks and their recommendations (Ahlemann et al., 2012c; Erder and Pureur, 2006; Gerber et al., 2007; Haki et al., 2012; Holst and Steensen, 2011; Murer et al., 2011; Ross et al., 2006; Smith et al., 2012; Tamm et al., 2015). For instance, Holst and Steensen (2011, p. 18) report that "most noticeable was the absence of formalized EA documentation work of as-is based on a framework, as recommended in a large part of the EA literature"

[8] For instance, a relatively well-known EA guru and consultant Vish Viswanathan provides the following cryptic explanation of the practical usage of TOGAF: "Organizations start with an open framework like the TOGAF framework, but as it gets customized and tailored, it adapts to an organization's culture to become their own "personalized" enterprise architecture model. As enterprise architecture matures in an organization, the

TOGAF framework is still inside and powering their enterprise architecture but no longer very visible" (Viswanathan, 2015, p. 16)

[9] The same conclusion is reported, for instance, by Winter et al. (2010, p. 6): "While analyzing EA management literature, it became apparent that adapting an approach to company-specific needs is neglected in all investigated EA management approaches except TOGAF, which only states that the ADM should be adapted without specifying how"

[10] My historical analysis of EA frameworks and their origin is thoroughly described in Kotusev (2016e) and in the appendix of this book (The Origin of EA and Modern EA Best Practices)

[11] The practical problems with BSP and other similar planning methodologies are widely discussed in literature (Beynon-Davies, 1994; Goodhue et al., 1992; Goodhue et al., 1988; Kim and Everest, 1994; Lederer and Sethi, 1988; Lederer and Sethi, 1992; Shanks, 1997). Firstly, these methodologies require considerable time and human resources to produce recommended architectural plans. Secondly, the resulting plans are often found too conceptual, overly technical and generally useless for business decision-making purposes. Thirdly, the resulting plans are either carried out only partially, or even not used at all in any real sense and shelved

[12] The practical problems with popular EA frameworks are widely discussed in literature (Ambler, 2010; GAO, 2015; Gaver, 2010; Hauder et al., 2013; Kotusev et al., 2015b; Lohe and Legner, 2012; Lohe and Legner, 2014; Roth et al., 2013; Seppanen et al., 2009; Trionfi, 2016). These problems are essentially the same as the previously reported problems with the BSP-like planning approaches. Firstly, extraordinary efforts are required to develop and maintain recommended EA artifacts. Secondly, the resulting EA artifacts are usually found too complex, improperly detailed and do not address the real information needs of their stakeholders. Thirdly, the resulting EA artifacts are poorly integrated into regular decision-making and planning processes and eventually end up in an "ivory tower"

[13] The ineffectiveness of BSP and other similar planning approaches was consistently reported by researchers. For instance, Lederer and Sethi (1988, p. 455) concluded that "given their great expense and time consumption, [our] findings seriously challenge the utility of [BSP and similar] planning methodologies". Goodhue et al. (1988, p. 383) reported that "the approach is too expensive, its benefits are too uncertain, and it is organizationally difficult to implement". Lederer and Sethi (1992, p. 76) concluded that "in summary, strategic information systems planners are not particularly satisfied with [the BSP-like planning approach]. After all, it requires extensive resources. Top management commitment is often difficult to obtain. When the [BSP-like] study is complete, further analysis may be required before the plan can be executed. The execution of the plan might not be very extensive"

[14] The very phenomenon of management fads is far from new and widely studied in the management literature (Abrahamson, 1991; Abrahamson, 1996; Abrahamson and Fairchild, 1999; Aldag, 1997; Carson et al., 1999; Donaldson and Hilmer, 1998; Gill and Whittle, 1992; Kieser, 1997; Miller and Hartwick, 2002; Miller et al., 2004)

[15] Although the practical usefulness of EA frameworks was consistently questioned (Bloomberg, 2014; Buckl et al., 2009; Gaver, 2010; Gerber et al., 2007; Holst and Steensen, 2011; Lohe and Legner, 2014; Molnar and Proper, 2013; Trionfi, 2016; Tucci, 2011), they have never been previously recognized as management fads (Kotusev, 2016c)

[16] Numerous once-popular and widely promoted management techniques have been later recognized to be ineffective and largely useless. The list of these commonly acknowledged management fads includes business process reengineering (BPR), Japanese management (Theory Z), job enrichment, management by objectives (MBO), quality circles (QC), self-managed teams (SMT), T-groups, total quality management (TQM) and many other former "silver bullets" (Abrahamson and Fairchild, 1999; Carson et al., 1999; Carson et al., 2000; Gibson and Tesone, 2001; Kieser, 1997; Miller et al., 2004)

[17] For instance, Wierda (2015, pp. 28-29) describes this situation in the following way: "Now, here is our very inconvenient truth: Enterprise Architecture as a discipline has so far largely failed to produce the intended results. This is reflected in many ways. The most important one is of course that the same sort of chaos that

enterprise architecture is meant to prevent still exists everywhere, regardless of the fact that we now have had the concept of enterprise architecture for approximately thirty years. Something is clearly not working"

[18] My analysis of the historical problems of EA frameworks and previous analogous approaches to information systems planning is thoroughly described in Kotusev (2016c) and in the appendix of this book (The Origin of EA and Modern EA Best Practices)

[19] Unfortunately, even in scientific management research some faddish ideas are often taken for granted without appropriate empirical validation. For instance, Aldag (1997, p. 13) argues that "[management] fads, in fact, often are seen [by academics] as self-evidently correct, somehow above the need for empirical proof". Similarly, Donaldson and Hilmer (1998, p. 18) argue that "faddism in management studies has created an impediment to greater intellectual productivity by allowing unproven and incorrect ideas to go unchallenged"

[20] I consider the evident inconsistency between mainstream views on the role of EA frameworks and empirical realities of using EA frameworks as one of the critical problems of the entire EA discipline (Kotusev, 2017b)

[21] See Kotusev (2017e)

[22] The list of organizations using TOGAF was removed from The Open Group website in June 2016, but is still available in the Internet archive (The Open Group, 2016a). Accidently or not, this list was removed shortly after the publication of my articles sharply criticizing TOGAF (Kotusev, 2016a; Kotusev, 2016d)

[23] Numerous EA methodologies recommended by various gurus and consultancies (Armour et al., 1999b; Bernard, 2012; Bittler and Kreizman, 2005; Boar, 1999b; Carbone, 2004; Holcman, 2013; IBM, 2006; Longepe, 2003; Niemann, 2006; Schekkerman, 2008; Spewak and Hill, 1992; Theuerkorn, 2004), though not explicitly positioned or classified as EA frameworks, advocate essentially the same flawed planning approaches

[24] My comparative analysis of the imaginary and real worlds of enterprise architecture is thoroughly described in Kotusev (2016h). The existence of two different worlds of enterprise architecture has been also acknowledged earlier by Wierda (2015, p. 30): "Another clear sign [of the problems in the EA discipline] is the lack of true success stories at (enterprise architecture) conferences and in the literature. Enterprise architecture conferences are never about real enterprise architectures in whatever form. They are generally about enterprise architecture frameworks, tools and techniques. [...] The conferences consist of people active in the field talking about methodology that should work but that has never been proven to work. [...] It is as if the enterprise architecture world is a world separate from the real world of organizations, some sort of abstraction of it"

[25] As Wierda (2015, p. 85) puts it, "why, after thirty years, is nobody shouting that the emperor is not wearing clothes?"

[26] For instance, renowned management scholars Pfeffer and Sutton (2006a, p. 66) argue that "a big part of the problem [with flawed management practices] is consultants, who are always rewarded for getting work, only sometimes rewarded for doing good work, and hardly ever rewarded for evaluating whether they have actually improved things"

[27] As fairly noticed by Gill and Whittle (1992, p. 288), "consultancies are generally resistant to independent evaluation or systematic monitoring of their work and there is predictably little published, critical examination of their efforts which would enable improved understanding of what works, what does not and why". Likewise, Brickley et al. (1997, p. 30) argue that "because of their interest in promoting their products, consultants are likely, for example, to provide detailed information on companies where their techniques appeared to work and less information on those where the techniques failed"

[28] The critical importance of publishing research in the top-tier scientific journals for academic promotion and tenure is widely recognized (Athey and Plotnicki, 2000; Dean et al., 2011; Dennis et al., 2006)

[29] The excessive theoretical emphasis of the current system of academic journals, peer-reviews and promotions in information systems, as well as in management in general, is widely acknowledged (Bennis and O'Toole, 2005; Davenport et al., 2003a; Hambrick, 2007; Jennex, 2001; Kock et al., 2002). For instance, Michael Myers argues that "despite many proclamations about the value of IS research being practical, the reality is it does not matter. [...] I advise young IS researchers not to take these proclamations too seriously. The

most practical thing they can do is to focus on their research. That way they are far more likely to succeed in having their research articles published in peer-reviewed academic journals. And that way they are far more likely to get promotion and tenure in a good school" (Kock et al., 2002, p. 340). Similarly, John Rockart, one of the founders and the longtime director of the MIT Center for Information Systems Research (CISR), argues that "every untenured faculty member needs to know what the real rules of gaining tenure are and should not listen to the siren of "relevance", especially if he is on the faculty of one of the "top" schools. Developing new theory or extending old in major ways is what is rewarded... no matter what is stated" (Kock et al., 2002, p. 341). The resulting poor practical relevance of the academic research in information systems and other management-related disciplines is also widely acknowledged rather long ago (Benbasat and Zmud, 1999; Davenport and Markus, 1999; Gill and Bhattacherjee, 2009; Gray, 2001; Kock et al., 2002; Moody, 2000; Paper, 2001; Robey and Markus, 1998). For instance, Davenport et al. (2003a, p. 81) even argue that "the realm of business academia [for the most part] is a wasteland for the practicing manager"

[30] Arguably the most vivid demonstration of this curious fact is the recent publication of Bui (2017) in the Communications of the Association for Information Systems, a rather prestigious peer-reviewed scientific journal. This publication provides yet another speculative, highly "theoretically sound" comparison of the existing EA frameworks, while the very fact that none of these frameworks has any documented examples of its successful practical implementation is merely neglected by the author, reviewers and editors, even when previous empirical research in real organizations concluded that "the frameworks appear theoretical and impossible to implement" (Buckl et al., 2009, p. 15)

[31] Active academic research on enterprise architecture started arguably around 2002-2003 (Kotusev, 2017e; Simon et al., 2013)

[32] For instance, Wierda (2015, p. 14) describes this situation in the following way: "Sadly, we must conclude that enterprise architecture has not been a success story. True, the field is established, there are methods, frameworks, conferences, books, specialists, departments, and so forth, all very busy with enterprise architecture. But ask most organizations that do something with enterprise architecture, and you will not find many that are very satisfied with the results"

[33] Unsurprisingly, various authors report that as much as 40% (Zink, 2009), 66% (Roeleven, 2010), 80% (DiGirolamo, 2009) or even more than 90% (Jacobson, 2007) of all EA initiatives fail to deliver business value

[34] Primarily I mean the excellent works of Wagter et al. (2005), Ross et al. (2006), Murer et al. (2011) and Ahlemann et al. (2012c)

[35] For instance, Holst and Steensen (2011, p. 19) fairly notice that a "successful EA [practice] is difficult to create based on a large part of the established and commonly accepted mechanistic inspired EA literature". Interestingly, the previous pre-EA wave of literature on information systems planning and architecture also provided little meaningful empirical studies and evidence-based descriptions of successful planning practices, but offered mostly a collection of prescriptive approaches of questionable origin, their theoretical comparisons and other speculative conceptual arguments highly resembling the current EA literature revolving primarily around EA frameworks (Galliers, 1987a; Galliers, 1987b; Galliers, 1987c; Galliers, 1988; Periasamy, 1994). For example, regarding the analogous pre-EA concept of information architecture Periasamy (1994, p. iv) reported that "literature suggests significant advocacy [of information architecture] with inadequate supporting evidence on its existence, application or value. The available limited research evidence generally presents unsatisfactory information architecture experience. Notwithstanding the unresolved issues and reported unsatisfactory experience, information architecture continues to be referenced as an important information management issue". "[Information architecture] has continued to hold sway in the practitioner's world and there has been no lack of literature on [information architecture] [...]. The usage, benefits, problems and limitations attributed to [information architecture] in these publications tend to be based on perception, inference and anecdote rather than research" (Periasamy, 1994, p. 29)

[36] For instance, Wierda (2015, p. 15) describes this situation in the following way: "Enterprise architecture today is like someone who has entered that room and doesn't know that his approach is doomed. He needs to retrace his steps and go elsewhere"

[37] For instance, one of the interviewed architects fairly compared the current EA discipline with the craft of blacksmiths, where the only way to become a blacksmith is to join the blacksmiths guild as an apprentice and then learn the necessary skills from your master

[38] As noticed by Miller and Hartwick (2002, p. 27), simple, prescriptive, easy to "cut and paste" recommendations indicating specific actions to be taken are the true signs of management fads, while real management classics are "complex, multifaceted, and applied in different ways to different businesses. The [management] classics don't come with simple primers on how to make the changes they propose nor do they have simple rules everyone must follow"

[39] As noted by many prominent scholars of management innovations and fads (Birkinshaw and Mol, 2006; Davenport et al., 2003a; Hamel, 2006; Miller and Hartwick, 2002; Miller et al., 2004; Pfeffer and Sutton, 2006b), true management innovations and genuine best practices are usually developed over time by the collective mind in industry as a reaction to pressing business problems, rather than result from the works and "proposals" of specific consultancies, experts or lonely gurus

[40] For instance, even the most widely known conceptual models of the EA discipline, including the Zachman Framework and TOGAF architecture development method (ADM), have no demonstrated examples of their successful practical implementation in real organizations and, therefore, cannot be used to analyze or explain EA practices

[41] For instance, Lapkin and Allega (2010, p. 3) describe this common consulting approach in the following way: "Consultants tend to treat client engagements as "projects". One characteristic of a project is that it has a defined start and a defined end. If you and your consultant are treating EA as a project, then, typically, there comes a time when EA is declared "finished". At that point, the EA deliverables are stamped "complete", put on a shelf and (in most cases) completely ignored. [...] Taking a "project-centric" approach to the EA effort invariably leads to a significant expenditure on the part of the client for shelfware that never delivers value to the enterprise"

[42] The fundamental difference in the perspectives of EA consultants and client organizations is discussed in more detail in Kotusev (2016h)

[43] There is no single commonly accepted definition of enterprise architecture (Kappelman et al., 2008; Kotusev et al., 2015a; Lapalme, 2012; Radeke, 2010; Schoenherr, 2008; Simon et al., 2013). For instance, Saint-Louis et al. (2017) found in literature 145 diverse definitions of the term "enterprise architecture". Moreover, there is even no consensus on whether enterprise architecture is a "noun" or "verb". For example, Simon et al. (2013, p. 2) define enterprise architecture as "a structured and aligned collection of plans [...]". Ahlemann et al. (2012a, p. 16) define enterprise architecture as "the fundamental organization of an enterprise [...]". Gartner defines enterprise architecture as "the process of translating [...]" (Lapkin et al., 2008, p. 4). The Federation of Enterprise Architecture Professional Organizations (FEAPO) defines enterprise architecture as "a well-defined practice [...]" (FEAPO, 2013, p. 1). Bernard (2006, p. 13) even defines enterprise architecture as "both a management program and a documentation method [...]". However, arguably the most obscure definition of enterprise architecture is provided by Schekkerman (2008, p. 31): "Enterprise Architecture is about understanding all of the different elements that go to make up the Enterprise and how those elements inter-relate"

[44] For example, arguably the most paradoxical opinion rather often heard now in EA-related discussions is that the Zachman Framework is actually not a framework at all, while TOGAF is actually only a solution architecture framework

Chapter 1: Introduction

[1] For instance, see Withington (1974), Somogyi and Galliers (1987) and Rockart (1988)

[2] These statistical numbers are provided by Laudon and Laudon (2013) (Chapter 1)

[3] These statistical numbers are provided by Kappelman et al. (2018)

[4] For instance, Moore's law suggests that the computing power of microprocessors doubles approximately every two years, while the law of mass digital storage suggests that the volume of digital data that can be stored for one dollar doubles approximately every fifteen months (Laudon and Laudon, 2013)

[5] Other examples of information systems that might be used in organizations to support different functional areas are provided, for instance, by Valacich and Schneider (2011) (Chapters 1 and 2)

[6] The complex and multifaceted nature of the organizational changes required to benefit from the use of information systems is fairly emphasized, for instance, by Laudon and Laudon (2013)

[7] These three areas of competitive advantage loosely correspond to the three generic strategies identified by Porter (1980) and to the three value disciplines identified by Treacy and Wiersema (1997)

[8] For example, proliferation of the Internet profoundly influenced industry structure and the very nature of competition (Porter, 2001)

[9] The most "classic" description and analysis of the phenomenon of disruptive technologies is provided by Christensen (1997)

[10] Other examples of innovative disruptive technologies and corresponding displaced or marginalized technologies are provided, for instance, by Laudon and Laudon (2013) (Chapter 3) and Valacich and Schneider (2011) (Chapter 2)

[11] Some implications of new disruptive technologies for organizational business strategies are discussed, for instance, by McGahan (2004) and Adner and Snow (2010)

[12] The need for business executives to actively manage IT had been widely acknowledged rather long ago (Jarvenpaa and Ives, 1991; Martin et al., 1995; Rockart, 1988; Rockart and Crescenzi, 1984). As John Rockart puts it, business executives must incorporate IT into their "theory of the business" (Martin et al., 1995, p. 166)

[13] Organizations are often conceptualized as complex systems consisting of diverse but mutually interrelated elements ranging from "hard" elements (e.g. strategy, structure and processes) to "soft" elements (e.g. motivation, culture and skills) in different theoretical models. For example, since the initial discovery of a strong interconnection between strategy and structure by Chandler (1962), a number of more sophisticated models have been proposed by different authors for analyzing organizational systems including the "diamond" model (task, structure, technology and people) (Leavitt, 1965), "star" model (task, structure, processes, rewards and people) (Galbraith, 1977), McKinsey 7S model (structure, strategy, systems, style, staff, skills and superordinate goals) (Waterman et al., 1980), MIT90s model (strategy, structure, management processes, people and technology) (Rockart and Scott Morton, 1984; Scott Morton, 1991) and some other less popular models (Burke and Litwin, 1992; Nadler and Tushman, 1980). However, for the purposes of this book organizations can be considered as socio-technical systems consisting primarily of business capabilities, processes, IT systems and infrastructure

[14] All theoretical models conceptualizing organizations as complex systems consisting of diverse elements emphasize the need for harmony, mutual alignment and dynamic equilibrium between all the constituting elements, e.g. strategy, structure, culture, technology and processes (Galbraith, 1977; Leavitt, 1965; Nadler and Tushman, 1980; Scott Morton, 1991; Waterman et al., 1980). However, this book focuses mostly on the alignment between business activities and IT landscapes

[15] Business and IT alignment has been recognized as an imperative for organizations long ago, for instance, by Rockart et al. (1996)

[16] Here and further in this book business and IT alignment is understood mostly in a broad sense as the alignment in a narrow sense (i.e. the ability of IT to meet current and future business needs) plus IT efficiency (i.e. the ability of IT to meet these needs with minimal costs and delays)

[17] Business and IT alignment is usually conceptualized according to the seminal alignment model proposed by Henderson and Venkatraman (1993) as the mutual consistency between four key elements: business strategy, IT strategy, organizational infrastructure and processes, and IT infrastructure and processes (Avison et al., 2004; Baets, 1992; Broadbent and Weill, 1993; Burn, 1996; Burn and Szeto, 2000; Chan and Reich, 2007; Coltman et al., 2015; Gerow et al., 2014; Gerow et al., 2015; Grant, 2003; Luftman et al., 1993; Sabherwal et al., 2001).

This model resulted from the "Management in the 1990s" research program conducted by the MIT Center for Information Systems Research (CISR) (Venkatraman, 1991) and essentially represents a narrow "slice" of the more comprehensive MIT90s model (Scott Morton, 1991). However, this alignment model has been questioned by Ciborra (1997)

[18] The positive influence of business and IT alignment on the overall organizational performance is confirmed by numerous studies (Byrd et al., 2006; Chan, 2002; Chan et al., 1997; Chan and Reich, 2007; Chan et al., 2006; Cragg et al., 2002; Gerow et al., 2016; Gerow et al., 2014; Gerow et al., 2015; Kearns and Lederer, 2000; Luftman et al., 2017; Schlosser et al., 2015; Tallon, 2007; Tallon, 2011; Tallon and Pinsonneault, 2011; Wagner et al., 2014; Yayla and Hu, 2012)

[19] Specific cultural differences between business and IT stakeholders hindering effective communication are discussed in more detail, for instance, by Ward and Peppard (1996)

[20] The lack of effective communication, mutual understanding and partnership between business and IT stakeholders is widely recognized as one of the most significant inhibitors of business and IT alignment (Lederer and Mendelow, 1989a; Luftman and Brier, 1999; Luftman et al., 2006; Luftman and McLean, 2004; Luftman et al., 1999)

[21] This model is largely inspired by the work of Fonstad (2006b) and other related research on the IT engagement model conducted by the MIT Center for Information Systems Research (CISR) (Fonstad, 2006a; Fonstad, 2007; Fonstad and Robertson, 2004; Fonstad and Robertson, 2005; Fonstad and Robertson, 2006a; Fonstad and Robertson, 2006b; Ross et al., 2006)

[22] Year after year since 1980 countless U.S. and international surveys of IT executives consistently demonstrate that improving information systems planning and achieving better business and IT alignment are considered among the top key issues of IT management, usually as the single most important issue (Badri, 1992; Ball and Harris, 1982; Brancheau and Wetherbe, 1987; Broadbent et al., 1989; Caudle et al., 1991; Dickson et al., 1984; Galliers et al., 1994; Hartog and Herbert, 1986; Herbert and Hartog, 1986; Kappelman et al., 2014; Kappelman et al., 2016; Kappelman et al., 2018; Kappelman et al., 2017; Kappelman et al., 2013; Luftman, 2005; Luftman and Ben-Zvi, 2010a; Luftman and Ben-Zvi, 2010b; Luftman and Ben-Zvi, 2011; Luftman and Derksen, 2012; Luftman et al., 2015; Luftman and Kempaiah, 2008; Luftman et al., 2006; Luftman et al., 2009; Luftman and McLean, 2004; Luftman and Zadeh, 2011; Luftman et al., 2012; Luftman et al., 2013; Moores, 1996; Moynihan, 1990; Niederman et al., 1991; Parker and Idundun, 1988; Pervan, 1994; Wang, 1994; Wang and Turban, 1994; Watson, 1989; Watson and Brancheau, 1991; Watson et al., 1997)

[23] Effective communication, mutual understanding and partnership between business and IT stakeholders are widely recognized among the most significant enablers of business and IT alignment (Chan and Reich, 2007; Kuruzovich et al., 2012; Lederer and Mendelow, 1989a; Luftman and Brier, 1999; Luftman et al., 2006; Luftman and McLean, 2004; Luftman et al., 1999; Nath, 1989; Preston and Karahanna, 2009; Reich and Benbasat, 2000; Schlosser et al., 2015; Schlosser and Wagner, 2011; Teo and Ang, 1999; Wagner et al., 2014; Wagner and Weitzel, 2012)

[24] From the sociological perspective, EA documents can be considered as boundary objects between different communities of business and IT stakeholders (Abraham, 2013; Abraham et al., 2015; Abraham et al., 2013; Dreyfus, 2007; Korhonen and Poutanen, 2013; Magalhaes et al., 2007; Poutanen, 2012; Valorinta, 2011), i.e. special objects which help diverse social communities cooperate, collaborate and successfully pursue shared goals despite their different expertise, concerns and backgrounds (Star, 2010; Star and Griesemer, 1989)

[25] From the sociological perspective, an organization using enterprise architecture can be considered as a complex actor-network where various stakeholders interact via using EA artifacts, i.e. inscribe their interests into EA artifacts and get influenced by the interests of other stakeholders inscribed into EA artifacts (Sidorova and Kappelman, 2010; Sidorova and Kappelman, 2011). For instance, Sidorova and Kappelman (2011, p. 39) argue that "enterprise architecture work helps to achieve agreement and thus alignment of the interests of internal actors within the context of enterprise interests and inscribes such agreement into architectural artifacts"

Chapter 2: The Concept of Enterprise Architecture

[1] As noted earlier, there is no single commonly accepted definition of enterprise architecture (Kappelman et al., 2008; Kotusev et al., 2015a; Lapalme, 2012; Radeke, 2010; Saint-Louis et al., 2017; Schoenherr, 2008; Simon et al., 2013). The definition provided here emphases the real practical meaning of enterprise architecture and is consistent with the purpose and structure of this book

[2] As noted earlier, EA documents, or artifacts, can be considered as boundary objects between diverse social communities enabling effective communication and collaboration between them (Abraham, 2013; Abraham et al., 2015; Abraham et al., 2013; Dreyfus, 2007; Korhonen and Poutanen, 2013; Magalhaes et al., 2007; Poutanen, 2012; Valorinta, 2011)

[3] The analogy between enterprise architecture and building architecture was initially promoted by the former IBM marketing specialist and chief EA guru John Zachman (Sowa and Zachman, 1992a; Zachman, 1987; Zachman, 1996; Zachman, 2001; Zachman, 2003; Zachman, 2006; Zachman, 2007; Zachman, 2010a; Zachman, 2010b) and subsequently exploited by many other less prominent EA gurus (Bernard, 2012; Boar, 1999b; Holcman, 2013; Schekkerman, 2006a). For example, Sowa and Zachman (1992a, p. 591) argued that "when applied to an information system, the word architecture is a metaphor that compares the construction of a computer system to the construction of a house [...]. It compares the perspectives in describing an information system to the perspectives produced by an architect in designing and constructing a building". "It makes little difference whether the object is physical, like an airplane, or conceptual, like an Enterprise. The challenges are the same. How do you design and build it piece-by-piece such that it achieves its purpose without dissipating its value and raising its cost" (Zachman, 1996, p. 4). Later Zachman (2006, p. 37) argued that "architecture is architecture is architecture. It doesn't matter what the architecture is for: buildings, airplanes, automobiles, computers, whatever. The underlying order of the descriptive representations is the same". However, this analogy is completely inappropriate and can be considered only as a deceptive marketing trick unrelated to empirical realities of information systems planning. For example, Doug McDavid argues that the "flawed concept [promoted by John Zachman] is that building enterprise information systems is just like building airplanes. In fact, an enterprise information system is much more like the nervous system of a living organism" (Greene et al., 1997, p. 9). "We may call aircraft design and enterprise modeling both modeling. We must, however, not lose sight of the fundamental differences that lie between them. An aircraft can be "frozen" in time and space, whereas an enterprise, like any social organization, cannot. It is recreated every day. The way in which processes are carried out and procedures are followed changes continuously, sometimes without the persons involved even noticing it" (Stecher, 1993, p. 285). As fairly noticed by Gaver (2010, p. 72), "the analogy to classical architecture first made by John Zachman is faulty and incomplete. [...] We need to reexamine the analogy and correct it". Renowned management scholars Pfeffer and Sutton (2006b, p. 35) argue that "yet another flaw with the marketplace for business ideas is that it is filled with sloppy analogies that somehow win managers over"

[4] The ideas of the discipline of enterprise engineering (Bernus, 2009; Bernus and Nemes, 1996; CIMOSA, 1993; Dietz et al., 2013; Doumeingts, 1989; Kosanke et al., 1999; Mertins and Jochem, 2005; Williams, 1994) seemingly can be applied only to computer-integrated manufacturing (CIM) assembly lines or industrial factories, but not to post-industrial customer-focused enterprises. As fairly noticed by Bloomberg (2014, p. 1), "the enterprise isn't an ordinary system like a machine or a building, and can't be architected or engineered as such"

[5] The attempts to analyze the evolution, lifecycles, possible growth and decline trajectories of organizations as living entities had been made long ago, for instance, by Greiner (1972), Adizes (1988) and Miller (1992)

[6] The organic, rather than mechanistic, nature of successful EA practices is emphasized, for instance, by Holst and Steensen (2011, p. 20): "The scientific EA discipline needs to become more organic in its approach. The empirical findings [from successful EA practices] confirmed this with an absence of the mechanistic concept

of a large formalized documentation framework, and the lack of any theoretically-based concept of gap analysis or detailed as-is and to-be architecture"

[7] The idea of creating comprehensive architectural descriptions of organizations analogous to building architectures is consistently found to be impractical (Basten and Brons, 2012; Beeson et al., 2002; Erder and Pureur, 2006; Kim and Everest, 1994; Lohe and Legner, 2014; Schmidt and Buxmann, 2011). "While some authors have stressed the necessity for a complete set of architectural descriptions (e.g., Zachman, 1987), this has generally not been feasible in practice due to the high efforts associated with the creation and maintenance of such models" (Schmidt and Buxmann, 2011, p. 174). "The companies recognized that complete EA documentation was not feasible due to the many different stakeholders, the overall organizational complexity, and the too large scope" (Lohe and Legner, 2014, p. 115). As correctly noticed by Beeson et al. (2002, p. 320), "in most cases, the complexity and volatility of the business environment, and of the internal IS development context, coupled with the usually complex legacy of IT systems in situ, make a stable or fully articulated business model and IS architecture impossible to achieve"

[8] This view of enterprise architecture as an instrument for managing the evolution of organizations is inspired by the excellent book of Murer et al. (2011)

[9] The current popularity of the term "enterprise architecture" arguably can be attributed primarily to the aggressive, persistent and irresponsible promotion of the flawed analogy between organizations and physical engineering objects by numerous EA gurus over the last decades. For instance, this speculative analogy was very actively exploited for promoting and popularizing the Zachman Framework by the most widely known EA guru John Zachman (Sowa and Zachman, 1992a; Zachman, 1987; Zachman, 2006; Zachman, 2010a; Zachman, 2010b). "Since the Zachman Framework classification was observed empirically in the structure of the descriptive representations (that is, "architecture") of buildings, airplanes, and other complex industrial products, there is substantial evidence to establish that the Framework is the fundamental structure for Enterprise Architecture and thereby yields the total set of descriptive representations relevant for describing an Enterprise" (Zachman, 2010b, p. 61). "The [Zachman] Framework for Enterprise Architecture simply defines what enterprise architecture looks like. It is not mysterious how I figured this out. I went back to the Industrial Age products and tried to understand what Architecture was relative to industrial products, and then I simply assigned enterprise names to the set of design artifacts that were created for describing anything, including enterprises" (Zachman, 2006, p. 37). "This is the same total set of descriptive representations relevant for describing airplanes, locomotives, buildings, computers, all industrial products. I simply put the Enterprise names on the descriptive representations because I was interested in engineering and manufacturing Enterprises" (Zachman, 2010a, p. 41). "Why would anyone think that the descriptive representations for enterprises are going to be any different from the descriptive representations of anything else that has ever been created?" (Zachman, 2010a, p. 41)

[10] For instance, Fehskens (2015, p. 26) explains the metaphorical nature of the term "enterprise architecture" in the following way: "We need to accept that the use of the word "Architecture" in "Enterprise Architecture" is at best a metaphor rather than an assertion of isomorphism [...]. If we want to argue that "EA is to an enterprise as building architecture is to a building" then we have to be able to argue that "EA is to building architecture as an enterprise is to a building". Comparing and contrasting enterprises and buildings shows that they have little more in common than that they are both artifacts that are designed, made, and used by people". Similarly, Bente et al. (2012, p. 35) fairly notice that "in contrast to the traditional architecture practices, which primarily look at pure technical systems such as a bridge, a car, or a plane, EA deals with a socio-technical system [...]. The people element brings complex behavioral attributes into the functioning of an enterprise [...]. Hence, the term architecture does not literally apply to the enterprise in the same way as it has been traditionally applied to technical systems". Potts (2013, p. 29) argues that "from an architectural perspective, enterprises offer a particular challenge because they are self-determining. Enterprises can constantly re-design their own architectures in ways that other kinds of entities cannot". For these reasons, no analogy between enterprise architecture and classical architecture is appropriate. Instead of trying to simulate or learn from classical architecture, as suggested by some authors (Kerr, 1989; Pavlak, 2006; von Halle, 1992; von Halle, 1996), the unique nature of enterprise architecture should be clearly acknowledged and understood

[11] There are no consistent or commonly accepted definitions of an EA practice

[12] At the present moment there are arguably no books or conceptual models providing comprehensive, systematic, evidenced-based and consistent descriptions of an EA practice with all its various aspects. This book attempts to offer such a description

[13] Most real organizational improvements, e.g. introducing an ERP system (Davenport, 2000) or even improving the management of IT risk (Westerman and Hunter, 2007), require complex and coordinated changes in the corresponding people, process and technology aspects of an organization. Laudon and Laudon (2013) also emphasize the complex and multifaceted nature of all organizational changes related to information systems

[14] The need to integrate an EA practice with other organizational processes, the essential requirements for this integration and the problems of disintegration are widely known (Lohe and Legner, 2012; Lohe and Legner, 2014). The integration of an EA practice with specific organizational processes is also widely studied (Ahlemann and El Arbi, 2012; Blomqvist et al., 2015; Fonstad and Robertson, 2006b; Legner and Lohe, 2012; Lux and Ahlemann, 2012; Radeke and Legner, 2012)

[15] There is no common consensus on which exactly documents should be and should not be considered as EA artifacts. In this book all documents used during organizational IT planning activities, from organization-wide planning to project-level planning, and providing more or less specific suggestions regarding the structure of information systems are considered to be EA artifacts. For instance, business strategy documents, business cases and project management plans, though may be important in the context of an EA practice, are not considered to be EA artifacts since these documents typically do not provide any real suggestions regarding the structure of information systems. Similarly, various procedural documents regulating the work of architecture functions in organizations including architecture mandates, governance responsibilities, reporting structures and other documents that can be related to "meta-architecture" (i.e. architecture of architecture functions) are not considered to be EA artifacts in the context of this book by the same reason

[16] From the sociological perspective, specifically this duality makes EA artifacts effective boundary objects facilitating cooperation between diverse social communities (Abraham, 2013; Abraham et al., 2015; Abraham et al., 2013; Dreyfus, 2007; Korhonen and Poutanen, 2013; Magalhaes et al., 2007; Poutanen, 2012; Valorinta, 2011)

[17] From the perspective of the sociological actor-network theory, the collaborative development of decisions EA artifacts by their stakeholders represents a perfect example of interests inscription, when human actors inscribe their essential interests into physical objects which then represent these interests in the future and shape subsequent decision-making processes (Hanseth and Monteiro, 1997; Sidorova and Kappelman, 2010; Sidorova and Kappelman, 2011; Walsham, 1997)

[18] Here and further this book intentionally uses the generic term "architects" without distinguishing different types of architects (e.g. enterprise architects and solution architects) until Chapter 16 (Architects in Enterprise Architecture Practice) where the differences between these types of architects are discussed in great detail

[19] As noted earlier, organizations using enterprise architecture can be viewed as complex actor-networks where various stakeholders inscribe their interests into corresponding EA artifacts (Sidorova and Kappelman, 2010; Sidorova and Kappelman, 2011)

Chapter 3: The Role of Enterprise Architecture Practice

[1] The imperative nature of the productive partnership between business and IT has been recognized long ago, for instance, by Rockart et al. (1996)

[2] Boundary objects are often developed naturally in the process of collaboration between people from heterogeneous communities (Nicolini et al., 2012) since these objects help represent and transform knowledge on the boundaries of these communities (Carlile, 2002; Carlile, 2004). Unsurprisingly, some forms of boundary objects are widely used in many different areas to facilitate communication between the groups of diverse

stakeholders, for example in aerospace engineering (Bergman et al., 2007), software development (Smolander et al., 2008) and project management (Doolin and McLeod, 2012)

[3] These benefits have been confirmed statistically by the survey of Ross and Weill (2005)

[4] These benefits have been confirmed statistically by the surveys of Bradley et al. (2011) and Bradley et al. (2012)

[5] These benefits have been confirmed statistically by the survey of Ross and Weill (2005)

[6] For instance, Holst and Steensen (2011) argue that measuring the exact value of enterprise architecture is either impossible or irrelevant

[7] A number of authors (Lyzenski, 2008; Rico, 2006; Schekkerman, 2005a) propose some approaches for calculating ROI and making business cases for enterprise architecture. These approaches are arguably no more than speculations

[8] For instance, a practicing architect describes this attitude in the following way: "We have never worried about whether it is actually profitable to [practice enterprise architecture] or not, but I would like to say that we never have measured whether it pays off to have a management either. EA is just a set of tools which management utilizes and if we didn't have EA, management would just do something else to govern this area" (Holst and Steensen, 2011, p. 18)

[9] The value of an EA practice can be also explained in a way similar to the following well-known joke: "If you think education is expensive, try ignorance"

[10] For instance, see Gerber et al. (2007), Gonzalez (2011), Murer et al. (2011), Hungerford (2007), Hungerford (2009), Smith et al. (2012), Smith and Watson (2015), Tamm et al. (2015), Kotusev et al. (2016), Toppenberg et al. (2015) and Richardson et al. (1990) respectively

[11] For instance, see Venkatesh et al. (2007), Anderson et al. (2009), Rees (2011), Janssen and Hjort-Madsen (2007), Pheng and Boon (2007), Alsoma et al. (2012), Kiat et al. (2008), Findlay (2006), Lynch (2006), Gregor et al. (2007) and Rauf (2013) respectively

[12] The survey of 374 organizations from North America, Europe and Asia Pacific region by Ambler (2010) shows that among the organizations employing more than 100 IT specialists 63% of organizations practice enterprise architecture and 6% of organizations thinking about starting their EA practices

[13] For instance, see Laudon and Laudon (2013) (Chapter 5)

[14] See Lewis (1957), Whisler and Leavitt (1958), Hoos (1960), Anshen (1960) and Garrity (1963). For instance, Lewis (1957, p. 84) argues that despite the initial hype and inflated expectations around computers, "it is evident that the future role of computers is a tremendous one"

[15] See Taylor and Dean (1966) and Dean (1968)

[16] For instance, see the early approaches to information systems planning described by Evans and Hague (1962), SOP (1963b), Dearden (1965), Glans et al. (1968b), Hartman et al. (1968), Honeywell (1968), Kriebel (1968), Blumenthal (1969), Thompson (1969), Schwartz (1970) and Zani (1970). A more general idea of deliberately designing organizations is far from new as well (Galbraith, 1973; Galbraith, 1977)

[17] As noted earlier, countless U.S. and international surveys of IT executives from 1980 (Ball and Harris, 1982) to 2017 (Kappelman et al., 2018) consistently demonstrate the pressing need for better information systems planning and business and IT alignment

[18] The historical evolution of information systems planning methodologies and EA frameworks is analyzed in detail in Kotusev (2016e) and in the appendix of this book (The Origin of EA and Modern EA Best Practices)

[19] See BSP (1975), Orsey (1982a), Vacca (1983), BSP (1984), Lederer and Putnam (1986) and Lederer and Putnam (1987)

[20] See Arthur Andersen (1979), Arthur Andersen (1987), Lederer and Gardiner (1992a) and Lederer and Gardiner (1992b)

[21] See Martin and Finkelstein (1981), Arthur Young (1987), Inmon (1988), Finkelstein (1989), Martin (1989) and Davids (1992)

[22] See Martin (1982b) and Martin and Leben (1989)

[23] See Spewak and Hill (1992) and Spewak and Tiemann (2006)

[24] See TAFIM (1996a) and TAFIM (1996b)

[25] See FEAF (1999) and FEAF (2013)

[26] See Perks and Beveridge (2003) and TOGAF (2018)

[27] The chronic ineffectiveness of all these step-wise information systems planning methodologies, and later EA frameworks, was consistently demonstrated by numerous studies during their entire history (Beynon-Davies, 1994; Bloomberg, 2014; Davenport, 1994; GAO, 2015; Gaver, 2010; Goodhue et al., 1992; Goodhue et al., 1986; Goodhue et al., 1988; Holst and Steensen, 2011; Kemp and McManus, 2009; Kim and Everest, 1994; Lederer and Sethi, 1988; Lederer and Sethi, 1992; Lohe and Legner, 2014; Periasamy, 1994; Shanks, 1997; Shanks and Swatman, 1997; Trionfi, 2016). Moreover, researchers and practitioners at different time periods consistently concluded that the problems with these methodologies are fundamental in nature (Gaver, 2010; Goodhue et al., 1992; Hamilton, 1999; Stegwee and van Waes, 1990)

[28] For instance, see GAO (2002), GAO (2003b), GAO (2006), Gaver (2010) and Kotusev (2016c). In particular, Gaver (2010, p. 52) reports that "literally more than a billion dollars have been spent so far on Enterprise Architecture by the federal government, and much, if not most of it has been wasted". "Most departments and agencies [of the U.S. Federal Government] reported they expect to realize the benefits from their respective enterprise architecture programs [...] sometime in the future. What this suggests is that the real value in the federal government from developing and using enterprise architectures remains largely unrealized" (GAO, 2011, p. 64)

[29] For instance, architects from government agencies even found it beneficial to avoid using the "A" word altogether: "Architecture is not a well-regarded practice in many [government] agencies. Attendees reported that terms, such as "business transformation imperatives", were more helpful in garnering support" (James, 2008, p. 1). Similarly, Jeanne Ross tells the following story about architecture: "I was actually asked to go into a non-profit [organization] and give a speech on architecture, but "please don't use the word architecture. It's a bad word here" (Kappelman, 2010, p. 12). "In fact, architecture has become a bad word in some companies, mostly because architects in those companies are seen as more of an obstacle than a problem solver" (Ross et al., 2014, p. 1). Gartner reports that "many restarted programs find that the negative "baggage" associated with the term "EA" is too strong to overcome, and it is simply easier and more effective to call it something else" (Bittler and Burton, 2011, p. 4)

[30] As Miller and Hartwick (2002, p. 27) put it, "[management] classics typically arise not from the writings of academics or consultants but emerge out of practitioner responses to economic, social, and competitive challenges". Birkinshaw and Mol (2006, p. 84) also argue that real management innovations are usually born in organizations and motivated by pressing business needs: "Dissatisfaction can be framed as a future threat, a current problem or a means to escape a crisis. But the important point is that management innovation is generally a response to some form of challenge facing the organization. Unlike technological innovations, which are sometimes created in a laboratory without much thought as to what problem they might solve, management innovations tend to emerge through necessity"

[31] From the early days of using IT in business many organizations developed their own homegrown approaches to information systems planning (Carter et al., 1990; Carter et al., 1991; Cerpa and Verner, 1998; Corbin, 1988; Davies and Hale, 1986; Flynn and Hepburn, 1994; Martinsons and Hosley, 1993; McFarlan, 1971; McLean and Soden, 1977; Palmer, 1993; Penrod and Douglas, 1988; Periasamy, 1994; Reponen, 1993; Rush, 1979; Sporn, 1978; van Rensselaer, 1979; van Rensselaer, 1985). These approaches were generally much more prevalent in organizations than BSP and other widely promoted branded methodologies (Earl, 1993; Finnegan and Fahy, 1993; Flynn and Goleniewska, 1993; Galliers, 1986; Galliers, 1987b; Galliers, 1987c; Galliers, 1988; Goodhue et al., 1988; Hoffman and Martino, 1983; Periasamy, 1994; Premkumar and King, 1991; Vitale et al., 1986). Moreover, many of these homegrown approaches worked more effectively than BSP and similar formal planning methodologies (Doherty et al., 1999; Earl, 1990; Earl, 1993; Earl, 1996; Goodhue et al., 1988; Periasamy, 1994; Segars and Grover, 1999). At the same time, the very concept of architecture was generally

considered as promising and useful, though with significant deviations from the original prescriptions of BSP and other architecture-based methodologies (Hamilton, 1999; Periasamy, 1993; Periasamy, 1994; Periasamy and Feeny, 1997). Historically, many organizations established successful in-house approaches to information systems planning and architecture through trial and error, ample experimentation, countless failures, reorganizations and restarts (Burton and Bittler, 2011; Earl, 1996; Hobbs, 2012; Holst and Steensen, 2011; Wierda, 2015; Zink, 2009)

[32] For instance, renowned management scholars Pfeffer and Sutton (2006c, p. 91) argue that "a focus on gurus masks how business knowledge is and ought to be developed and used. Knowledge isn't generated by lone geniuses who magically produce brilliant new ideas in their gigantic brains. This is a dangerous fiction"

[33] Birkinshaw and Mol (2006, p. 82) argue that the purely inspirational, rather than prescriptive, role of external ideas is very typical for management innovations: "[In the studied management innovations external change agents including academics, consultants and management gurus] often provided the initial inspiration for a management innovation, and they frequently helped to shape and legitimize the innovation as it took hold. These external agents rarely if ever actually developed the new practices per se, but they offered important inputs to both the process of experimentation and to the subsequent stage of validation"

[34] As Haki et al. (2012, p. 1) fairly notice, "[EA] frameworks have been suggested as guidelines to [EA] implementation, but our experience indicates that very few companies follow the steps prescribed by such frameworks"

[35] Arguably the most perfect examples of pure speculations around an EA practice are the widely known and highly cited publications by Schekkerman (2004) and Sessions (2007). Both these publications proclaim the importance of frameworks for an EA practice and then discuss their advantages, disadvantages, strengths, weaknesses, limitations and applicability. However, neither of these publications appeals to any empirical evidence on the use of EA frameworks in real organizations. As a result, both these publications can be considered only as a science fiction unrelated to real EA practices

[36] As noted earlier, real best practices are usually complex, multifaceted and cannot be reduced to simplistic, easily repeatable step-by-step procedures applicable to all organizations (Miller and Hartwick, 2002; Miller et al., 2004)

[37] For instance, Ross et al. (2006) in Chapter 3 describe an example of Delta Air Lines which went bankrupt because of an excellent EA-driven implementation of a flawed business strategy

[38] The danger of delegating architectural planning to a dedicated group of architects is illustrated, for instance, by Ross et al. (2006, p. 65): "In many companies enterprise architecture design is the responsibility of a small IT staff sequestered in a back room for several months, emerging only after drawing a book's worth of diagrams. [...] Most of these architecture exercises end up abandoned on a shelf"

[39] For instance, Gartner gives the following recommendation: "Remember that EA is not a "project" with a defined start and a defined end, but rather an ongoing, iterative process that never ends" (Lapkin and Allega, 2010, p. 1)

[40] As Dwight Eisenhower famously noted, "plans are nothing, planning is everything"

[41] As fairly noticed by Beeson et al. (2002, p. 320), business and IT alignment in organizations results not from an overarching plan or model, but rather "from a continuous process of adjustment and readjustment of plans and goals, in which local and relatively short-term plans are formulated and weighed against current understanding of the business's key interests"

[42] The importance of actually using architecture for decision-making, rather than merely producing and "having" architecture is vividly illustrated, for instance, by Thomas et al. (2000, p. 2): "The prevailing belief was that if one built the architecture, the owners and operators would come. History has shown, however, that few organizations actually "operationalized" the architecture – and the owners and operators did not come. The inherent flaw from the beginning was the lack of a standard framework or methodology that allows the architecture to be inserted into the decision making process"

[43] For example, Lankhorst (2013) essentially equates an EA practice with enterprise modeling, which is not the case for successful EA practices

[44] As Basten and Brons (2012, p. 225) put it, "EA modeling activities should always focus on benefits. Practically, this means considering the benefits of all the artifacts and models that will be modeled"

[45] The danger of excessive modeling for its own sake is vividly illustrated by the following story (Hobbs, 2012, p. 85): "An organization that shall remain nameless established a large, award-winning architecture, which it documented in minute detail (the architecture diagrams alone covered four walls of a conference room from floor to ceiling!), and appeared to cover every conceivable eventuality. There was just one problem: It was so involved and complicated that no one attempting to use it had any idea where to start. The teams that did attempt to use the elaborate architecture ended up significantly over-engineering the solution, which led to major scope, time and cost overruns. [...] After several well-publicized project failures, with multimillion dollar consequences, the organization eventually reorganized its EA efforts and put new leadership into place. They discarded the elaborate target architecture in favor of a much simpler and more pragmatic approach". Interestingly, almost identical conclusions had been also made long time ago regarding the earlier popular "fashion" of comprehensive computer-based mathematical modeling of organizations (Hayes and Nolan, 1974)

[46] The importance of selecting simple, stakeholders-oriented and intuitively understandable presentation formats for EA artifacts is illustrated, for instance, by Blumenthal (2007, p. 63): "The problem is EA information often is unintelligible. The necessary data might be there, but the presentation is so poor that the decision-maker's ability to use it is impaired. If information is not understandable, accessible and easily navigable, then it quickly becomes "shelfware", meaning it sits on a shelf collecting dust. Of course, the result is unsatisfied stakeholders"

[47] As noted earlier, enterprise architecture is very different in its nature from the traditional architecture of buildings and other complex engineering objects (Bente et al., 2012; Bloomberg, 2014; Fehskens, 2015; Gaver, 2010; Potts, 2013)

[48] Some EA gurus (Bernard, 2009; Boar, 1999a; Boar, 1999b) argue for developing formal and complete sets of strict EA artifacts resembling engineering drawings. These recommendations are impractical, unrealistic and completely inconsistent with empirical realities of information systems planning. Similarly, as fairly noticed by Niemi and Pekkola (2017, p. 325), "the analysis of EA [artifacts is] much simpler in practice than suggested by the myriad of complex technical analysis methods presented in the literature"

[49] As noted earlier, successful EA practices are organic, not mechanic, in nature (Holst and Steensen, 2011)

[50] As noted earlier, the ideas of the discipline of enterprise engineering (Bernus, 2009; Bernus and Nemes, 1996; CIMOSA, 1993; Dietz et al., 2013; Doumeingts, 1989; Kosanke et al., 1999; Mertins and Jochem, 2005; Williams, 1994) cannot be applied to the vast majority of post-industrial organizations

[51] My analysis of the harmful and faddish nature of popular EA frameworks is thoroughly described in Kotusev (2016c)

[52] For example, see Gaver (2010), Lohe and Legner (2014) and Trionfi (2016)

[53] Specifically, five organizations included in the list of TOGAF users provided by The Open Group (The Open Group, 2016a) have been studied as part of the research underpinning this book, but none of these organizations followed the key prescriptions of TOGAF in any real sense (Kotusev, 2016a; Kotusev, 2016d)

[54] As noted earlier, the very idea of creating comprehensive architectural descriptions of entire organizations was consistently found to be impractical (Basten and Brons, 2012; Beeson et al., 2002; Erder and Pureur, 2006; Kim and Everest, 1994; Lohe and Legner, 2014; Schmidt and Buxmann, 2011). The origin and problems of popular EA frameworks are discussed in detail in Appendix (The Origin of EA and Modern EA Best Practices)

[55] As noted earlier, real management innovations and best practices typically emerge over time in leading organizations or communities of practitioners, rather than get "created" by some consultancies, academics and thought leaders (Birkinshaw and Mol, 2006; Davenport et al., 2003a; Hamel, 2006; Miller and Hartwick, 2002; Miller et al., 2004; Pfeffer and Sutton, 2006b)

Chapter 4: Enterprise Architecture and City Planning

[1] As noted earlier, the commonly used analogy between enterprise architecture and building architecture is conceptually flawed and inadequately represents the general meaning of an EA practice (Bente et al., 2012; Bloomberg, 2014; Fehskens, 2015; Gaver, 2010; Potts, 2013)

[2] An EA practice is often compared to city planning (FEAPO, 2013; Robertson, 2010; Schulte, 2002; Sessions, 2007; Sessions and de Vadoss, 2014). However, even the most elaborate available comparisons still do not go beyond general ideas or very high-level conceptual analogies (Ahlemann et al., 2012a; Burke, 2003; Schmidt and Buxmann, 2011)

[3] From the perspective of the sociological boundary objects theory, this dual architecture principle provides a perfect example of a boundary object having different meanings for the representatives of different social communities and facilitating their communication (Carlile, 2002; Carlile, 2004; Nicolini et al., 2012; Star, 2010; Star and Griesemer, 1989)

[4] From the perspective of the sociological boundary objects theory, this dual business capability map also provides a good example of a boundary object between different social communities (Carlile, 2002; Carlile, 2004; Nicolini et al., 2012; Star, 2010; Star and Griesemer, 1989)

[5] From the perspective of the sociological actor-network theory, the alignment of new Outlines to the established Considerations and Visions previously approved by business executives is a perfect example of the interests representation, when physical objects with the inscribed interests of human actors protect these interests on behalf of the human actors (Hanseth and Monteiro, 1997; Sidorova and Kappelman, 2010; Sidorova and Kappelman, 2011; Walsham, 1997)

[6] From the perspective of the sociological actor-network theory, the alignment of new Designs to the previously agreed Outlines is also a good example of the interests inscription and representation (Hanseth and Monteiro, 1997; Sidorova and Kappelman, 2010; Sidorova and Kappelman, 2011; Walsham, 1997)

[7] These relationships between Considerations, Standards, Visions, Landscapes, Outlines and Designs have been described earlier in Kotusev (2017f)

[8] The CSVLOD model of enterprise architecture has been initially presented in a series of brief articles (Kotusev, 2016g; Kotusev, 2017c; Kotusev, 2017f) and is based on the earlier higher-level model defining four general types of EA artifacts: Principles, Visions, Standards and Models (Kotusev, 2016f; Kotusev et al., 2017)

Chapter 5: The Dialog Between Business and IT

[1] Many EA gurus (Bernard, 2012; Finkelstein, 2006a; Holcman, 2013; Longepe, 2003; Parker and Brooks, 2008) argue that architectural plans for IT can and should be derived by architects directly from the business strategy, goals and objectives. Schekkerman (2006a, p. 6) formulates this idea in the most striking way: "No strategy, no enterprise architecture". These suggestions are inconsistent with empirical realities of information systems planning

[2] This problem with the business strategy is widely known for a long time and discussed by numerous authors (Baets, 1992; Banaeianjahromi and Smolander, 2016; Brown, 2010; Campbell, 2005; Cantara et al., 2016a; Cantara et al., 2016b; Chan and Reich, 2007; Flynn and Hepburn, 1994; Galliers, 1986; Hackney et al., 2000; Lederer and Mendelow, 1986; Lederer and Mendelow, 1987; Lederer and Mendelow, 1988; Lederer and Mendelow, 1989a; Lederer and Mendelow, 1989b; Rosser, 2000; Segars and Grover, 1996; Slater, 2002; Vitale et al., 1986)

[3] For instance, Campbell (2005, p. 657) reports that "the results [of my study] indicate that the major concern of practitioners when considering alignment is coping with the ambiguity surrounding the business strategies that are actually in use"

[4] For instance, Baets (1992, p. 206) reports that "preliminary research undertaken by the author in a well ranked European bank showed quite clearly that many of its middle managers, charged with carrying out the corporate strategy on behalf of the bank, were unable to define the corporate strategy"

[5] For instance, the Gartner survey shows that "two-thirds of business leaders are unclear about what their business strategy is and what underlying assumptions it is based on" (Cantara et al., 2016a, p. 2). Similarly, Slater (2002, p. 85) reports that the survey by Cutter Consortium found that "almost a third of the respondents had no formally articulated business plan at all". Earlier Lederer and Mendelow (1989a, p. 11) reported that "nine IS executives stated that sometimes top business executives have no clearly defined mission, objectives, and priorities, and do not know their plans for the coming year"

[6] For instance, Lederer and Mendelow (1989b, p. 16) report that "some interviewees [IT executives] maintained that top [business] executives preferred flexibility which is lost when a plan is written. Written plans are more difficult to change"

[7] For instance, the survey by Hauder et al. (2013) shows that 84.8% of European and U.S. organizations consider unclear business goals as a significant challenge to their EA practices

[8] This problem with the business strategy is widely acknowledged and discussed by many authors (Lederer and Mendelow, 1986; Lederer and Mendelow, 1987; Lederer and Mendelow, 1988; Lederer and Mendelow, 1989a; Lederer and Mendelow, 1989b; Ross, 2005; Ross et al., 2006; Segars and Grover, 1996; Slater, 2002; Weill and Ross, 2008)

[9] As Lederer and Mendelow (1987, p. 393) put it, "top management fails to communicate corporate objectives in a way to which IS personnel can relate"

[10] As Ross et al. (2006, p. 6) put it, "general statements about the importance of "leveraging synergies" or "getting close to the customer" are difficult [for IT] to implement". Likewise, Slater (2002, p. 86) fairly notices that "business strategies are typically written at a very high level. They frequently talk about markets, sales and distribution channels, and growth targets, but rarely address how the company gets its work done". Earlier Lederer and Mendelow (1989b, p. 16) reported that "in other cases, the corporate plans were glittering generalities or mere financial targets which could not be translated into IT plans"

[11] For instance, Lederer and Mendelow (1987, p. 393) describe this situation in the following way: "For example, top management told one interviewee that the organization's major objective was to increase sales by a given percentage and that IS should provide systems to help do so. This provided little substantive direction as to what specific systems to develop". Similarly, "Finance Vice President stated that his objective was to "maximize the financial flexibility of the organization" but could not articulate how this should be done. This objective was too general to permit the [IT] director to formulate a supporting plan for [information systems]" (Lederer and Mendelow, 1989a, p. 11)

[12] For instance, Lederer and Mendelow (1988, p. 74) describe this situation in the following way: "For example, an objective to "increase market share by a specified percentage" does not define a computer application, leaving systems managers to draw their own, sometimes erroneous, conclusions"

[13] By analogy with the object-relational impedance mismatch, i.e. the difficulty of translation between object-oriented programming languages and relational databases (Ireland et al., 2009), the difficulty of translation between business and IT plans can be called as the business-IT impedance mismatch

[14] This problem with the business strategy is widely acknowledged and discussed by many authors (Kotusev et al., 2016; Lederer and Mendelow, 1987; Lederer and Mendelow, 1988; Lederer and Mendelow, 1989a; Lederer and Mendelow, 1993; Ross, 2005; Ross et al., 2006; Sauer and Willcocks, 2002; Segars and Grover, 1996; Vitale et al., 1986; Wierda, 2015)

[15] As Lederer and Mendelow (1989a, p. 11) put it, "even if top executives know their plans in sufficient detail, an unstable environment might render them inapplicable"

[16] For instance, an architect at a very dynamic retail organization vividly illustrates this situation: "The problem with an organization like this is that in twelve months the organization has changed direction three or four times. So, you're not going to get that kind of stability that fits those timeframes" (Kotusev et al., 2016, p.

34). Sauer and Willcocks (2002, p. 41) report that "most [surveyed CEOs and CIOs of e-business companies] were responding to an increasingly volatile business environment by shrinking their development and planning cycles. Half don't extend plans beyond a year, and half of those with infrastructure plans update them quarterly". Unsurprisingly, the survey by Hauder et al. (2013) shows that 71.4% of European and U.S. organizations consider quickly changing organizational environment as a significant challenge to their EA practices

[17] For instance, an architect at a large U.S. financial organization vividly illustrates this problem: "We did a thorough job of aligning ourselves with organizational strategy. We felt confident in our analysis and proceeded to operate within the enterprise models developed. However, we did not do a good enough job of ensuring that these models were maintained. It only took a period of months before critical aspects of strategy and the business had changed" (Segars and Grover, 1996, p. 388)

[18] This problem with the business strategy is not acknowledged very widely, but still discussed by some authors (Ross, 2005; Ross et al., 2006; Shpilberg et al., 2007; Weill and Ross, 2008; Weill and Ross, 2009; Wierda, 2015)

[19] For instance, Wierda (2015, p. 134) argues that "what people seldom realize that if you build a landscape of elements that have an average life span of fifteen years with a strategy that changes direction every few years, chances are that you end up with a mess". "Ironically, one of the most pregnant uncertainties is the strategy of the company itself. Systems have an average life time of fifteen years. The strategy of a company manages maybe four. In other words: in the time that the architecture of a system and a large part of its surrounding systems exists, the organization's strategy will have changed four times, and often such changes are pretty radical" (Wierda, 2015, pp. 140-141). This problem with different lifespans of business strategies and information systems has been also identified and actively discussed by MIT researchers (Mocker, 2012; Ross, 2011). For example, Mocker (2012) explains it by saying that IT exists in a different "time zone" from business

[20] For instance, Shpilberg et al. (2007, p. 52) describe the situation of "alignment trap" at Charles Schwab in the following way: "The company's various divisions were driving independent initiatives, each one designed to address its own competitive needs. IT's effort to satisfy its various (and sometimes conflicting) business constituencies created a set of Byzantine, overlapping systems that might satisfy individual units for a while but did not advance the company's business as a whole"

[21] Weill and Ross (2008, p. 1) describe this situation in the following way: "IT organizations attempt to build capabilities while addressing a laundry list of immediate business needs. The result, in most cases, is IT spaghetti – with ever increasing maintenance costs and slow time to market"

[22] Ross (2005, p. 1) describes this situation in the following way: "IT is left to align with individual strategic initiatives – after they are announced. Thus, IT becomes a persistent bottleneck"

[23] I consider the evident inconsistency between the mainstream views on the role of a business strategy in an EA practice and empirical realities of the strategy-based IT planning as one of the critical problems of the entire EA discipline (Kotusev, 2017b)

[24] For instance, Wierda (2015, pp. 141-142) explains the role of a business strategy in an EA practice in the following way: "It is therefore a fundamental flaw in many enterprise architecture approaches that one starts from the (current) business strategy and/or a set of principles that may be derived from that strategy. Such a waterfall almost never works. That does of course not mean that the current strategy plays no role whatsoever. We should certainly not devise solutions that are in conflict with it. But simply taking the current strategy and hand that to the architects to turn it into the starting point of enterprise architecture will almost certainly fail, because the strategy is going to change long before the results of enterprise architecture are visible. What it does mean, is that the board of a company must steer enterprise architecture more directly. It must take a longer view so it can direct matters that do not immediately depend on just the current strategy and current environment"

[25] This section and all further discussions of the operating model in this book are based on the research of Ross et al. (2006) and other related research on the operating model conducted by the MIT Center for Information Systems Research (CISR) (Mocker, 2012; Robertson, 2007; Ross, 2005; Ross and Weill, 2006; Weill and Ross, 2008; Weill and Ross, 2009). However, somewhat similar ideas have been also discussed by Reese (2008) and much earlier by Gunton (1989)

[26] The notion of operating model is formally defined by Ross et al. (2006, p. 25) as "the necessary level of business process integration and standardization for delivering goods and services to customers". Unfortunately, the term "operating model" is widely used by various authors to mean very different things. For example, Treacy and Wiersema (1997) also use this term, but define it as a complementary and synergistic combination of business processes, organizational structures, management systems, information systems and culture implementing a particular value discipline. "Operating models are made up of operating processes, business structure, management systems, and culture, all of which are synchronized to create a certain superior value" (Treacy and Wiersema, 1997, p. 32). Consequently, this term in the context of this book should not be confused with any other "operating models" discussed by other authors. In other words, the term "operating model" used in this book should be understood exactly as defined by Ross et al. (2006), i.e. as the necessary level of organization-wide process standardization and integration

[27] The fundamental importance of these decisions for IT planning has been acknowledged long ago by Gunton (1989). For instance, Gunton (1989) (Chapter 2) argues that an organization-wide planning of IT infrastructure should start from deciding on the necessary level of autonomy (a close opposite analog of process standardization) and coupling (a close analog of data integration) of its end users. These two planning decisions together determine one of the four generic strategies for information systems: end-user computing environment (an analog of diversification), distributed information system (an analog of coordination), office utility network (an analog of replication) and corporate information engine (an analog of unification). Historically, decisions on centralization, decentralization and distribution of computing resources across business units played a significant role for information systems planning in large organizations (van Rensselaer, 1979; van Rensselaer, 1985)

[28] The architecture of ERP systems, or enterprise systems, typically implies standardization of business processes and integration of data (Davenport, 1997; Davenport, 2000; Ross, 1999). Consequently, these systems are naturally suitable for the unification operating model

[29] Weill and Ross (2009) argue that organizations should specify an operating model at each level where they report performance

[30] As noted by Weill and Ross (2009), when different operating models are adopted at different organizational levels, an operating model of a subunit must be at least as standardized and at least as integrated as the operating model of its parent business unit. Put it simply, operating models of subunits can shift only towards the upper right corner of the taxonomy (see Figure 5.3). An example of the complex organization combining all the four operating models at different organizational levels is discussed, for instance, by Robertson (2007)

[31] For instance, an operating model of an organization shapes its IT governance arrangements and mechanisms (Weill and Ross, 2004; Weill and Ross, 2008; Weill and Ross, 2009)

[32] For example, an operating model of an organization arguably correlates with its key organization-wide value discipline (Treacy and Wiersema, 1993; Treacy and Wiersema, 1997; Weill and Ross, 2004). Specifically, the discipline of operational excellence, which is largely based on standardized low-cost transaction systems, naturally highly correlates with the replication and unification models. The discipline of customer intimacy, which is largely based on shared customer databases and knowledge repositories, highly correlates with the coordination model. Finally, the discipline of product leadership, which is largely based on flexibility, creativity and person-to-person communications, arguably somewhat correlates with the diversification model. Very similar correlations can be also observed between the four operating models and the three generic strategies identified by Porter (1980), i.e. cost leadership, focus and differentiation. A more complex analysis of the relationship between business drivers, organizational workflows and the degree of autonomy and coupling of IT infrastructure is provided by Gunton (1989)

[33] Ross et al. (2006, p. 28) argue that "every company should position itself in one of these quadrants [shown in Figure 5.3] to clarify how it intends to deliver goods and services to customers"

[34] A digitized platform is defined by Weill and Ross (2009, p. 4) as "an integrated set of electronic business processes and the technologies, applications, and data supporting those processes". More information

on planning, building and leveraging digitized platforms is provided by Ross et al. (2006) and Weill and Ross (2009)

[35] Business capabilities, as convenient discussion points for business and IT stakeholders, are widely discussed in literature (Greski, 2009; Keller, 2015; King, 1995; Scott, 2009; Swindell, 2014)

[36] For instance, Hadaya and Gagnon (2017) consider business capabilities as abstract composites consisting of eight core underlying elements: business functions, business processes, organizational units, know-how assets, information assets, technology assets, natural resource deposits and brands

[37] Development, documentation and management of detailed business requirements for IT systems is discussed in detail, for instance, by Wiegers and Beatty (2013) and Wiegers (2005)

[38] On the one hand, the list of possible, but less popular discussion points between business and IT stakeholders is very long, potentially infinite. For example, at the organization-wide level these discussion points include, among others, critical success factors which proved useful long ago as convenient abstractions for translating high-level strategic goals into more specific demands for IT (Boynton and Zmud, 1984; Bullen and Rockart, 1981; Munro and Wheeler, 1980; Rockart, 1979; Shank et al., 1985), while at the level of separate IT solutions these discussion points include, among others, information required to execute business processes. On the other hand, not all of the five key discussion points can be relevant in all cases. For example, new IT solutions may intend not to improve existing business processes, but to deliver some other improvements having no obvious process implications, e.g. provide more accurate and timely information for decision-making purposes

[39] Ross et al. (2006, p. 26) argue that "the operating model is a choice about what strategies are going to be supported"

[40] The relationship between an organizational level and the length of a planning horizon appropriate at this level is discussed, for instance, by Jaques (1990) and Jaques and Clement (1994)

[41] The title "enterprise architecture uncertainty principle" is inspired by the loose analogy to Heisenberg's uncertainty principle existing in physics, which suggests that either the position or momentum of an elementary particle can be accurately measured at any one moment in time, but both the position and momentum cannot be accurately measured at the same time

[42] For example, Tamm et al. (2015, p. 190) clearly illustrate the EA uncertainty principle in action by reporting that in a successful EA practice "a high-level EA vision was created upfront[, but] the finer-level architectural details were defined on an as-needed basis during the transformation program". At the same time, the idea of considering enterprise architecture as "a complete expression of the enterprise" promoted, among others, by Schekkerman (2004, p. 13) is conceptually flawed and practically unachievable (Basten and Brons, 2012; Beeson et al., 2002; Erder and Pureur, 2006; Kim and Everest, 1994; Lohe and Legner, 2014; Schmidt and Buxmann, 2011)

Chapter 6: Processes of Enterprise Architecture Practice

[1] Many popular EA frameworks and methodologies (Armour et al., 1999b; Bernard, 2012; FEAF, 1999; Schekkerman, 2008; Spewak and Hill, 1992; TOGAF, 2018) prescribe detailed step-by-step processes to practice enterprise architecture, but these step-wise processes are unrealistic and never followed in successful EA practices. As Haki et al. (2012, p. 2) fairly notice, "our practical experience [...] shows that companies apply very diverse approaches in adopting [EA], and seldom follow the steps prescribed by [EA] frameworks or methodologies". For instance, as I reported earlier (Kotusev, 2016d; Kotusev, 2016f; Kotusev et al., 2017), the steps of the TOGAF architecture development method (ADM) are not followed even in the organizations included in the list of TOGAF users provided by the Open Group (The Open Group, 2016a). The origin and problems of modern step-wise EA methodologies including TOGAF are discussed in detail in Appendix (The Origin of EA and Modern EA Best Practices)

[2] These three processes are EA-specific processes defined in this book. They should not be confused with other organizational processes with same or similar titles unrelated to enterprise architecture

[3] As noted earlier, the EA-specific Strategic Planning process should not be confused with regular "normal" strategic planning, i.e. with a definition of a business strategy, goals and objectives accomplished as part of strategic management

[4] A detailed discussion of the activities corresponding to the Strategic Planning process similar to the one described here is also provided by Radeke and Legner (2012)

[5] Some critical IT-related decisions that should be made by senior business executives as part of Strategic Planning are discussed, for instance, by Ross and Weill (2002b)

[6] It has been acknowledged long ago that senior business managers have very "chaotic" jobs and spend most of their time in scheduled and unscheduled meetings and conversations (Kotter, 1982; Mintzberg, 1971; Mintzberg, 1973; Mintzberg, 1975)

[7] Unlike Strategic Planning and Technology Optimization, the Initiative Delivery process exists in some form even in organizations not practicing enterprise architecture. In these organizations IT initiatives are implemented simply without a disciplined architectural planning, i.e. without using any EA artifacts

[8] A detailed discussion of the activities constituting the Initiative Delivery process described here is also provided by Wagter et al. (2005) and Lux and Ahlemann (2012)

[9] The Initiative Delivery process deals only with architecturally significant IT initiatives introducing considerable changes to the organizational IT landscape, e.g. developing new or decommissioning existing IT systems. At the same time, numerous small changes in separate IT systems (e.g. reconfigurations, bug fixes or minor functional improvements) usually can be registered as routine change requests at the service desk and then implemented by relevant IT specialists alone without any architectural involvement and oversight. These small changes are not the subject of the Initiative Delivery process and largely irrelevant in the context of an EA practice. In order to better distinguish architecturally significant changes from insignificant ones, organizations often develop formal checklists with specific assessment criteria helping estimate the magnitude and architectural significance of required changes

[10] These or similar project lifecycle phases are recommended by most project delivery methodologies including the Rational Unified Process (RUP) (Kruchten, 2003), PRINCE2 (OGC, 2009) and PMBOK (PMI, 2013)

[11] As noted earlier, business cases are typically not considered as EA artifacts since they do not provide any architectural information on IT systems. However, business cases still play an important role in the context of an EA practice

[12] Shpilberg et al. (2007) call the situations caused by these negative side effects as the "alignment trap", analyze them in more detail and suggest a potential solution through technology optimization

[13] Developing architecture for the sake of architecture is considered as a significant problem of the entire EA discipline (Kappelman, 2010). For instance, the chief architect at BT (former British Telecom) vividly illustrates this problem: "Architectures, like fondue sets and sandwich makers, are rarely used. We occasionally dig them out and wonder why we ever spent the money on them. [Our] experience resonates with that of many other large corporations: architectures have emerged as erudite, elegant abstractions of the world, but they gain no momentum, unable to find traction in a world they profess to model" (Fonstad and Robertson, 2004, pp. 1-2)

Chapter 7: IT Initiatives and Enterprise Architecture

[1] Not all business needs in organizations require changes in their IT landscapes. Many important business initiatives may be simply unrelated to IT. For example, changing the selection criteria for assessing and prioritizing proposed investments or changing the HR strategy regarding staff recruitment and promotion may not require any significant modifications of the existing IT landscape. Consequently, it would be more correct to say that the typical purpose of an IT initiative is to address a specific business need with a certain IT component. At the same time, specific business needs without any IT components, though may be very important for an organization, are irrelevant and essentially invisible from the perspective of an EA practice

[2] See Ross et al. (2006) and Weill and Ross (2009) for more detail on planning, building and leveraging digitized platforms

[3] The inability to take into account the local needs of business units during the Strategic Planning process often leads to the proliferation of so-called "feral" information systems developed locally on an ad hoc basis without any disciplined planning (Tambo and Baekgaard, 2013)

[4] All foreseen business needs identified in advance, but still not taken into account during the Strategic Planning process (e.g. because of the immaturity of an EA practice or any other reasons) can be also considered as urgent needs from the perspective of an EA practice when they become urgent for their business stakeholders

[5] The overall percentage of urgent initiatives in IT investment portfolios of different organizations is seemingly very industry-specific and varies dramatically across various industries. For instance, this percentage has been roughly estimated by the interviewed architects to be near ~10-20% in the utilities, energy and education industry sectors, near ~40-50% in the banking and insurance industry sectors and up to 80% in the retail industry sector

[6] Sometimes even purely technical changes in the IT landscape may have a very clear meaning for business stakeholders and address specific business needs. For example, an infrastructure-related initiative to consolidate datacenters and migrate some applications or databases into a new, PCI-compliant datacenter may enable the business to process larger volumes of credit card payment transactions. This and other similar infrastructure-related IT initiatives should not be considered as architectural initiatives, even if most changes in IT infrastructure are purely technical, do not offer any new business functionality and generally irrelevant to business stakeholders

[7] This classification of IT initiatives into five different types highly correlates with the more coarse-grained classification into three different types proposed by Radeke and Legner (2012): strategic business and IT initiatives, strategic architecture initiatives and emergent initiatives. Specifically, strategic business and IT initiatives correspond to fundamental, strategic and local initiatives, strategic architecture initiatives correspond to architectural initiatives, while emergent initiatives correspond to urgent initiatives

[8] For instance, Wierda (2015) fairly compares launching new IT initiatives with making good chess moves intended to improve your overall position on the chessboard against the inherent uncertainty of the future

Chapter 8: The CSVLOD Model of Enterprise Architecture

[1] As noted earlier, the CSVLOD model of enterprise architecture has been initially presented and published in a series of short articles (Kotusev, 2016g; Kotusev, 2017c; Kotusev, 2017f)

[2] Since the scope of all EA artifacts related to changes is limited to separate change initiatives, formally these artifacts represent what is typically called as "solution architecture", i.e. architecture of separate IT solutions. However, due to a number of conceptual and practical reasons solution architecture should be better considered merely as a narrow subset of broader enterprise architecture. From this perspective, all solution architecture artifacts (i.e. changes) should be viewed only as special types of EA artifacts

[3] It has been acknowledged long ago, for instance by Gorry and Scott Morton (1971) and Mintzberg (1972), that senior business managers in their decision-making rely mostly on "soft" and loosely structured information (e.g. verbal communication, educated opinions and aggregate views), rather than on formal detailed documents and reports

[4] This classification of EA artifacts into essential, common and uncommon is based on their reported usage in the 27 studied non-consulting organizations with established and reasonably mature EA practices

Chapter 9: Considerations

[1] As noted earlier, non-EA-specific strategy documents are not considered as EA artifacts in the context of this book. However, if these documents are still considered to be EA artifacts, then an organizational mission, strategic goals and objectives can be also loosely related to Considerations

[2] Considerations often reflect some of the critical IT-related business decisions discussed by Ross and Weill (2002b)

[3] Principles are among the earliest and most widely known EA artifacts, which can be traced back to the work of King (1978). They were actively discussed in the late 1980s (Davenport et al., 1989; PRISM, 1986; Richardson et al., 1990), then a decade later in the form of maxims (Broadbent and Kitzis, 2005; Broadbent and Weill, 1997; Weill and Broadbent, 1998) and still attract significant attention in the EA literature (Greefhorst and Proper, 2011)

[4] Principles, or maxims, have been recognized long ago as effective instruments for establishing required synergies between different business units in terms of global process standardization and data integration (Broadbent and Kitzis, 2005; Broadbent and Weill, 1997; Davenport et al., 1989; van Rensselaer, 1985; Weill and Broadbent, 1998)

[5] The implications and potential benefits of the Sarbanes-Oxley Act for organizations are discussed, for instance, by Wagner and Dittmar (2006)

[6] The implications of various regulatory requirements on organizational information systems are discussed, for instance, by Laudon and Laudon (2013) (Chapter 8)

[7] The notion of a hype cycle was developed and popularized by Gartner (Fenn and Raskino, 2008)

[8] For example, see the ThoughtWorks technology radar (ThoughtWorks, 2017)

[9] For instance, Fenn and Raskino (2008) describe a detailed method for tracking, assessing, prioritizing and introducing technology innovations in organizations (the STREET process)

[10] See Gartner (2017) and Forrester (2017) respectively

[11] The desirable properties of good Principles are discussed in more detail, for instance, by Beijer and de Klerk (2010)

[12] As Davenport et al. (1989, p. 133) put it, "good principles reflect the organization that created them"

[13] Pretty detailed recommendations on developing effective Principles, or maxims, can be found in the works of many authors (Broadbent and Kitzis, 2005; Broadbent and Weill, 1997; Davenport et al., 1989; PRISM, 1986; Weill and Broadbent, 1998)

[14] For instance, Treacy and Wiersema (1997) argue that the organizations mastering the discipline of operational excellence require the IT capabilities for integrated low-cost transaction processing, the organizations mastering the discipline of product leadership require the IT capabilities for enabling person-to-person communication, cooperation and knowledge management, while the organizations mastering the discipline of customer intimacy require the IT capabilities for sharing customer information and expertise. Similarly, Ross and Weill (2002a) identify five general architectural styles corresponding to different strategic drivers: high-volume transaction processing (corresponds to product efficiency drivers), real-time response (corresponds to customer responsiveness drivers), analytical and decision support (corresponds to market segmentation and risk management drivers), work group support (corresponds to knowledge sharing drivers) and enterprise system (corresponds to integration and standardization drivers). Similar ideas have been also promoted by Gartner (Rosser, 2002a; Rosser, 2002b)

[15] The importance of IT-related business decisions on the desired levels of fault tolerance and security is emphasized, for instance, by Ross and Weill (2002b)

[16] Some considerations informing the adoption decisions regarding the cloud and big data technologies are discussed, for instance, by McAfee (2011) and Ross et al. (2013) respectively

Chapter 10: Standards

[1] The concept of architectural patterns, as reusable solutions to commonly occurring design problems, seemingly originated from classical architecture (Alexander et al., 1977), then expanded to software architecture (Gamma et al., 1994), enterprise application architecture (Fowler, 2002), enterprise integration architecture (Hohpe and Woolf, 2004) and finally to enterprise architecture (Perroud and Inversini, 2013)

Chapter 11: Visions

[1] As noted earlier, non-EA-specific strategy documents are not considered as EA artifacts in the context of this book. However, if these documents are still considered to be EA artifacts, then more or less actionable strategic business plans can be also loosely related to Visions

[2] Visions often reflect some of the critical IT-related business decisions discussed by Ross and Weill (2002b)

[3] Some of the interviewed architects argued that the planning horizon is constantly shrinking and planning for five years ahead may no longer be realistic

[4] The usage of Business Capability Models, or maps, for strategic information systems planning is widely discussed in literature (Burton, 2010; Burton, 2012; Greski, 2009; Keller, 2015; Khosroshahi et al., 2018; Scott, 2009; Swindell, 2014; Weldon and Burton, 2011; Wijgunaratne and Madiraju, 2016)

[5] For instance, Swindell (2014, p. 5) argues that "an ideal rule of thumb is that there should be no more than 12-20 level 1 business capabilities to enable business and technology executives to see how key business capability should be organized to tell and deliver the organizational story". Gartner recommends to limit the number of nested sub-capabilities to 8-10 at each level of the model (Cantara et al., 2016a)

[6] These generic reference models include, among others, the Process Classification Framework (PCF) (APQC, 2017), Business Process Framework (eTOM) (TM Forum, 2017), BIAN Service Landscape (BIAN, 2017) and Supply Chain Operations Reference (SCOR) model (APICS, 2017)

[7] This approach is recommended, for instance, by Gartner (Rayner, 2012; Swanton, 2012b)

[8] The popular faddish EA literature recommends developing rather detailed explicit descriptions of the desired target state and considers these descriptions as the essential part of enterprise architecture (Bernard, 2012; Carbone, 2004; Holcman, 2013; Schekkerman, 2008; Spewak and Hill, 1992; Theuerkorn, 2004; TOGAF, 2018; van't Wout et al., 2010). However, empirical evidence shows that describing the long-term target state in detail is impractical. Instead, some organizations develop only rather abstract Target States, whereas the majority of organizations do not create any explicit descriptions of the target state at all and plan their long-term future only via highlighting the required business capabilities in Business Capability Models and placing corresponding IT initiatives in Roadmaps

[9] A good example of the Target State used for consolidation of IT is provided by Tamm et al. (2015, p. 185)

[10] Even though value chains are pretty commonly used in business departments for communication between different business stakeholders, they are relatively rarely used specifically as EA artifacts, i.e. as documents facilitating communication between business and IT stakeholders. For this reason Value Chains are considered to be an uncommon subtype of Visions

[11] The concept of a value chain was seemingly first introduced by Porter (1985)

[12] The usage of Value Chains for strategic information systems planning is described, for instance, by Laudon and Laudon (2013) (Chapter 3)

[13] Although the use of core diagrams is reported and highly recommended by Ross et al. (2006), they have not been identified in the organizations studied as part of the research underpinning this book. Core diagrams, as well as their development, usage and purpose, are comprehensively described by Ross et al. (2006). Importantly, Ross et al. (2006, p. 47) focus on enterprise architecture in a very narrow sense, as "the organizing logic for business processes and IT infrastructure reflecting the integration and standardization requirements of the company's operating model", and consider enterprise architecture and core diagrams as very closely related concepts, i.e. core diagrams encapsulate enterprise architecture. This narrow understanding of enterprise architecture as a one-page executive-level view of an entire organization adopted by Ross et al. (2006) should not be confused with the broader understanding of enterprise architecture adopted in this book as a collection of all documents used for information systems planning, ranging from global organization-wide planning to local project-level planning. In other words, enterprise architecture, as it is defined by Ross et al. (2006), is a subset of

enterprise architecture discussed in this book. Specifically, enterprise architecture of Ross et al. (2006) directly corresponds to Visions, but is not related to any other types of EA artifacts discussed in this book (Ross et al., 2006, pp. 47-50)

[14] See Ross et al. (2006) and Weill and Ross (2009) for more detail on planning, building and leveraging digitized platforms

[15] A detailed description of the concept of business model canvas is provided by Osterwalder and Pigneur (2010)

[16] Similarly to Value Chains, these types of documents are commonly used in business departments for communication between different business stakeholders, but they are rarely used specifically as EA artifacts, i.e. as instruments facilitating communication between business and IT stakeholders. For this reason these EA artifacts are considered to be an unpopular subtype of Visions

[17] For instance, Vivek Kundra, the former federal CIO of the United States, vividly illustrates this problem: "[Architects] focus on documenting the current state or what the future state should be. By the time they are done with their architectural artifact, a new technology has already killed whatever they are working on" (Tucci, 2011, p. 1)

[18] As Ross et al. (2006, p. 65) put it, "detailed architectural drawings of business processes and systems applications – apart from a specific business process initiative [initially described at a high level in Outlines and then in more detail in Designs] – can make companies feel as if someone is doing something about complexity, but they are rarely acted upon"

[19] Quick obsolescence and practical uselessness of detailed long-term information systems plans has been recognized long ago, for instance, by Lasden (1981). The recommended approach is not to plan "in any more detail that is necessary for you to determine what to do in the short term" (Lasden, 1981, p. 112)

[20] For example, Lasden (1981, p. 102) reports the following story: "In 1971, the company [Trans World Airlines] underwent some major changes, switching dp [date processing] hardware vendors and moving headquarters from New York to Kansas City. As a result, its two-volume LRP [long-range information systems plan], specifying five years worth of hardware, software, and applications, ended up in the wastebasket"

Chapter 12: Landscapes

[1] For example, applications in Inventories can be classified based on their expected pace of change, as recommended by Gartner (Carlton, 2012; Carlton et al., 2012)

Chapter 13: Outlines

[1] As noted earlier, non-EA-specific business documents are not considered as EA artifacts in the context of this book. However, if these documents are still considered to be EA artifacts, then business cases for IT initiatives can be also loosely related to Outlines

[2] The importance of planning entire customer journeys is emphasized, for instance, by Rawson et al. (2013) and Edelman and Singer (2015)

[3] Specific recommendations on developing effective business cases for IT initiatives are provided, for instance, by Maholic (2013), Ward et al. (2008) and Valacich and Schneider (2011) (Chapter 9)

[4] The advantages of post-implementation benefit reviews are discussed in more detail, for instance, by Ward and Daniel (2008)

[5] The critical importance of senior business ownership, involvement and responsibility for realizing the business value of IT initiatives is emphasized, for instance, by Ross and Weill (2002b) and Peppard et al. (2007)

Chapter 14: Designs

[1] As noted earlier, non-EA-specific project documents are not considered as EA artifacts in the context of this book. However, if these documents are still considered to be EA artifacts, then various project management plans can be also loosely related to Designs

[2] The boundary between architecture and design is still not completely clear and debated in the IT literature (Beijer and de Klerk, 2010; Rivera, 2007)

[3] For example, these implementation-specific documents may often describe more detailed software architecture of new IT systems (Daigneau, 2011; Fowler, 2002; Gamma et al., 1994; Len et al., 2012)

[4] Organizations can also follow different project delivery methodologies for different types of IT projects. For instance, the survey of Manwani and Bossert (2016) shows that 23.3% of organizations do not use agile delivery, 27.2% use agile delivery for most projects and 49.5% use agile delivery only for fast-moving applications

[5] These and other differences between architecture and design are described in more detail by Rivera (2007) and Beijer and de Klerk (2010)

Chapter 15: The CSVLOD Model Revisited

[1] Enterprise Architecture on a Page has been presented and published online some time earlier (Kotusev, 2017d)

Chapter 16: Architects in Enterprise Architecture Practice

[1] This number is based on the statistics collected from the studied organizations and highly correlates with the earlier statistical findings of the global Infosys and McKinsey EA surveys (Aziz and Obitz, 2005; Manwani and Bossert, 2016; Obitz and Babu, 2009) as well as with the recommendations regarding the right size of an architecture team provided by Gartner (Short and Burke, 2010)

[2] Experienced architects are hard to find on the job market. For instance, 87.2% of European and U.S. organizations surveyed in 2013 reported that the lack of experienced architects represents a significant challenge to their EA practices (Hauder et al., 2013)

Chapter 17: Architecture Functions in Organizations

[1] This observation is based on the data collected from the studied organizations and consistent with the earlier findings of the global Infosys and McKinsey EA surveys, which also demonstrate that architecture functions usually report to the CIO or other similar roles, e.g. the CTO or director of IT (Aziz and Obitz, 2005; Aziz and Obitz, 2007; Manwani and Bossert, 2016; Obitz and Babu, 2009)

[2] The size of an organization from the perspective of an EA practice can be most accurately measured arguably by its effective full-time equivalent number of IT employees, including all permanent staff, temporary contractors and involved third parties. At the same time, other common measures typically used to estimate the size of organizations (e.g. the overall number of employees, total assets or gross revenue) may poorly correlate with the scale of the organizational IT landscape and, therefore, can be generally misguiding for EA-related purposes. For example, average IT expenses as a percentage of total revenue can range from less than 2.5% in the manufacturing, retail and energy industry sectors to more than 7.5% in the financial, consulting and education industry sectors (Kappelman et al., 2018; Kappelman et al., 2017; Weill et al., 2009). The percentage of IT staff in the workforce can also vary significantly across different industries, often ranging from less than 2% in retail to more than 20% in finance. Likewise, typical financial measures, including total assets and turnover, are highly industry-specific and hardly indicate the size of the organizational IT landscape

[3] The benefits of combining the responsibilities of architects from different levels of the architectural hierarchy (e.g. enterprise and business unit architects or domain architects and solution architects) are noted by Murer et al. (2011) and Smith et al. (2012)

[4] A detailed discussion of centralized and decentralized structures of architecture functions is also provided by Hobbs (2012)

[5] A detailed discussion of architecture governance bodies is also provided by Hobbs (2012)

Chapter 18: Instruments for Enterprise Architecture

[1] This observation is based on the data collected from the studied organizations and loosely correlates with the earlier findings of EA surveys (Ambler, 2010; Schekkerman, 2005b). The once popular IDEF family of modeling languages (Marca and McGowan, 2005) is arguably no longer widely used. At the same time, proprietary organization-specific modeling notations can be also developed and used (Frank, 2002; Rohloff, 2005)

[2] A comprehensive description of ArchiMate is provided by the official ArchiMate specification (ArchiMate, 2016) and Lankhorst (2013)

[3] A comprehensive description of UML is provided by the official UML specification (UML, 2015) and other popular sources (Booch et al., 2005; Fowler, 2003). Holt and Perry (2010) specifically discuss the application of UML to enterprise architecture

[4] A comprehensive description of BPMN is provided by the official BPMN specification (BPMN, 2011) and other sources (Silver, 2012; White and Miers, 2008)

[5] There is no publicly accessible specification of ARIS, but the description of ARIS is provided, for instance, by Scheer (1992)

[6] An overview, analysis and comparison of major EA tool vendors and their offerings is provided, for instance, by Gartner (McGregor, 2016; Searle and Kerremans, 2017) and Forrester (Barnett, 2015; Barnett, 2017)

[7] A detailed analysis and comparison of EA tools and their capabilities is provided, for instance, by Gartner (McGregor, 2015; Searle and Allega, 2017)

[8] A detailed discussion of configuration management databases (CMDBs) is provided, for instance, by O'Donnell and Casanova (2009). CMDB solutions are offered by several global vendors including BMC Atrium, CA Technologies, HP, IBM Tivoli and ServiceNow (Colville, 2012). A detailed analysis and comparison of CMDB solutions and their capabilities is provided, for instance, by Gartner (Colville and Greene, 2014b)

[9] The differences, similarities and potential synergy between specialized EA tools and CMDBs are discussed in more detail, for instance, by Gartner (Colville and Greene, 2014a; James and Colville, 2006)

[10] Change management, service asset and configuration management, release and deployment management processes, as well as their integration with a configuration management system (CMS) or CMDB, are described in detail by the ITIL Service Transition volume (Rance et al., 2011)

[11] This observation is based on the data collected from the studied organizations and rather consistent with the earlier findings of the EA surveys demonstrating the growing adoption of specialized EA tools over the years (Aziz and Obitz, 2005; Aziz and Obitz, 2007; Obitz and Babu, 2009; Schekkerman, 2005b)

[12] This suggestion is consistent with the earlier recommendations of Lapkin and Allega (2010) and Basten and Brons (2012)

[13] About one-third of all the studied organizations actively used CMDBs as major, or even primary, sources of architectural information on the current IT landscape. This observation highly correlates with the findings of the earlier study of eighteen German organizations by Buckl et al. (2009)

[14] Importantly, far from all deviations, exemptions and unplanned actions imply an architecture debt, but rather only planning decisions that go against the established long-term course of action. For example, an unplanned installation of a new CRM system introduces an architecture debt arguably only if an organization

plans to consolidate all its CRM systems into one in the future, but entails no debt when no global consolidation of CRM systems is planned. Likewise, the use of a particular technology in a new IT system implies an architecture debt arguably only if this technology is planned to be removed from the IT landscape in the long run

[15] In situations when organizations are capped in their IT delivery capacity and cannot quickly augment their workforce (e.g. via engaging external providers and contractors), an architecture debt may imply the time aspect as well

[16] As noted earlier, the actual resulting business value realized from using enterprise architecture can hardly be quantified or measured. For instance, Holst and Steensen (2011, p. 18) fairly notice that it is "either impossible or irrelevant" to measure the value of an EA practice because "the value of the EA effort is a subjective thing, as long as it is perceived by management as being valuable, because it helps them realize their strategy and govern the enterprise. While the needs of management are satisfied, the demand for value measurement is overlooked". Birkinshaw and Mol (2006) argue that the benefits of most management innovations cannot be evaluated numerically based on hard data

[17] For example, MIT researchers propose to classify all IT investments into four different types: transformation (investments in building new strategy-enabling shared infrastructure with a long-term payoff), renewal (investments in upgrading existing shared infrastructure with a short-term payoff), process improvement (investments in business applications supporting immediate business needs with a short-term payoff) and experiments (investments in innovative or experimental business applications with a long-term payoff) (Ross and Beath, 2001; Ross and Beath, 2002). Another classification proposed by MIT researchers categorizes all IT assets and corresponding IT investments into four different types: infrastructure (intended to provide a reusable shared base of IT services), transactional (intended to cut costs or increase throughput via automation), informational (intended to provide information for decision-making purposes) and strategic (intended to introduce innovation or gain a competitive advantage) (Aral and Weill, 2007; Weill and Aral, 2003; Weill and Aral, 2004a; Weill and Aral, 2004b; Weill and Aral, 2005a; Weill and Aral, 2005b; Weill and Aral, 2006; Weill et al., 2007; Weill and Broadbent, 1998; Weill and Johnson, 2005; Weill and Ross, 2009; Weill et al., 2009; Weill et al., 2008). Gartner analysts propose to classify all IT systems and corresponding IT investments according to the so-called "pace-layered" model into three different types: systems of record (systems with a long lifecycle supporting standard transaction processing capabilities), systems of differentiation (systems with a medium lifecycle enabling unique organization-specific processes) and systems of innovation (systems with a short lifecycle addressing new business opportunities) (Mangi and Gaughan, 2015; Shepherd, 2011; Swanton, 2012a). These and other similar classification approaches might be used for analyzing IT investment portfolios in organizations and assessing their overall fitness to the organizational needs

[18] These and some other advanced measurements for an EA practice are discussed in more detail by Legner and Lohe (2012) and Murer et al. (2011) (Chapter 7)

Chapter 19: The Lifecycle of Enterprise Architecture Practice

[1] The positive relationship between institutionalization and effectiveness of an EA practice is confirmed statistically by Weiss et al. (2013)

[2] Countless evidence suggests that many organizations experimented with enterprise architecture, struggled to establish their EA practices through a series of unsuccessful attempts and undertook multiple reorganizations of the approaches to architecture before building a successful EA practice in its current form. EA initiatives in these organizations failed, seemingly misguided by the flawed advice of EA frameworks, but have been restarted again due to the high perceived potential of enterprise architecture (Zink, 2009). For example, Holst and Steensen (2011, p. 17) report that despite the initial failures of EA endeavors "none of the EA initiatives [in the four studied organizations] have been completely shut down, instead they have been redesigned or reprioritized. This could indicate that organizations can see the potential of EA, but are having difficulties in realizing it". "After several well-publicized [EA] project failures, with multimillion dollar consequences, the organization eventually reorganized its EA efforts and put new leadership into place" (Hobbs, 2012, p. 85). Likewise, Wierda (2015, p. 29) reports that he has "seen at one organization that, within six years, the central enterprise

architecture function was reorganized four (!) times. [...] And this pattern is seen everywhere". In 2011 Gartner estimated that "as many as 25% of all organizations may be in this restart situation" (Burton and Bittler, 2011, p. 2). Interestingly, very similar observations regarding approaches to information systems planning had been also reported previously by Earl (1996, p. 55): "Many firms that have adopted the organizational approach [which proved to be most effective], however, got there almost by trial and error – after other approaches had failed"

[3] It is arguably impossible now to trace where and when exactly specific practices constituting the current body of EA best practices originated because of at least three different reasons. Firstly, there are no credible empirical studies of proven architecture-based planning practices at different historical periods. Secondly, an EA practice essentially represents a collection of multiple related sub-practices that seemingly emerged sequentially over a long period of time, rather than simultaneously as a single big-bang management innovation. Thirdly, the introduction of management innovations is typically a gradual and diffuse process with no definite start and end points. For instance, Birkinshaw and Mol (2006, p. 82) report that "most management innovations [we studied] took several years to implement, and in some cases it was impossible to say with any precision when the innovation actually took place"

[4] The historical path to establishing an EA practice described here was confirmed by a number of veteran architects and highly correlates with the EA maturity stages and corresponding architecture management practices described by Ross et al. (2006) (Chapters 4 and 5)

[5] Different survey-based sources provide different estimates of the percentage of IT budget spent in an average organization on sustaining IT investments required to maintain the existing systems and "keep the lights on" including 40%, 42%, 54% (Kappelman et al., 2018; Kappelman et al., 2017), 62% (Weill et al., 2009), 63% (Weiss and Rosser, 2008), 66% (Weill et al., 2008), from 60% to 69% (Weill and Woerner, 2010) and 71% (Weill and Ross, 2009)

[6] Some other approaches to facilitating acceptance and coping with the resistance to an EA practice are provided by Ahlemann et al. (2012b)

[7] From the perspective of the organizational theory, the ability of an organization to change and adopt new practices is limited and determined by its absorptive capacity (Cohen and Levinthal, 1990; Szulanski, 1996; Zahra and George, 2002)

[8] As noted earlier, this suggestion is consistent with the recommendations of Lapkin and Allega (2010) and Basten and Brons (2012). For instance, Lapkin and Allega (2010, p. 8) "advise first-time EA efforts to avoid investments in EA tools, as this tends to encourage focus on the tool, rather than on the architecture". Likewise, Basten and Brons (2012, p. 220) argue that starting an EA practice with simple tools is desirable for "maintaining the focus of those involved [actors] on the EA concept rather than on new software"

[9] The positive relationship between training and the organizational acceptance of enterprise architecture is confirmed statistically by Hazen et al. (2014)

[10] The positive relationship between the maturity of an EA practice (though the criteria of maturity can be interpreted differently and rather loosely) and various benefits resulting from the use of enterprise architecture is confirmed statistically by a number of surveys (Bradley et al., 2012; Bradley et al., 2011; Burns et al., 2009; Lagerstrom et al., 2011; Ross and Beath, 2011; Ross and Beath, 2012; Ross and Weill, 2005)

[11] A number of EA maturity models defining different EA maturity levels have been proposed (DoC, 2007; EAAF, 2009; GAO, 2003a; GAO, 2010; NASCIO, 2003; OMB, 2007; Schekkerman, 2006b; Vail, 2005). However, these maturity models are purely speculative and non-empirical in nature, have no examples of their successful practical application, largely based on the flawed ideas of EA frameworks and can be considered only as a science fiction for all practical purposes. At the same time, the four-stage EA maturity model described by Ross et al. (2006), though evidence-based and empirically substantiated, evaluates architectural maturity of the organizational IT landscape, rather than maturity of an EA practice itself as a set of EA-related processes and their quality. Moreover, this model seemingly correlates only with the historical path followed earlier by numerous organizations (see Figure 19.2), but might be unfit for the organizations following the newer deliberate path (see Figure 19.3)

[12] This observation very highly correlates with the earlier finding that the single most important predictor of effective IT governance is the percentage of senior executives able to accurately describe their IT governance (Weill, 2004; Weill and Broadbent, 2002; Weill and Ross, 2004; Weill and Ross, 2005)

[13] For example, Gartner estimates that "organizations with mature EA teams spend 20% less on "keeping the lights on" and 28% more on transformational projects" (Burke and Smith, 2009, p. 1)

[14] The rapid commoditization of the most basic IT resources as well as the vanishing competitive value of these computing resources is discussed in detail, for instance, by Carr (2003)

[15] In the early 1980s specific strategic information systems and innovative applications of technology were considered as a potential source of competitive advantage for organizations (Benjamin et al., 1984; Cash and Konsynski, 1985; Clemons, 1986; Ives and Learmonth, 1984; McFarlan, 1984; Parsons, 1983; Rackoff et al., 1985; Wiseman, 1988; Wyman, 1985). However, later due to their susceptibility to imitation a transient nature of this advantage had been widely acknowledged (Hopper, 1990; Peppard and Ward, 1999; Peppard and Ward, 2004; Ross et al., 1996)

[16] For instance, Pfeffer (1994, pp. 16-17) argues that "as other sources of competitive success have become less important, what remains as a crucial, differentiating factor is the organization, its employees, and how they work". Likewise, Davenport et al. (2003b, p. 60) fairly notice that "product innovations are copied quickly and easily today, leaving managerial innovation as an important way for companies to differentiate themselves"

[17] This fact had been also acknowledged rather long ago, for instance, by Hopper (1990), Ross et al. (1996), Peppard and Ward (1999) and Peppard and Ward (2004)

[18] For instance, Feeny and Willcocks (1998) long ago identified architecture planning as one of the nine core capabilities required to manage IT

[19] The strong historical relationship between enterprise architecture and consulting has been also noticed earlier by other researchers. For instance, the review of early EA publications by Langenberg and Wegmann (2004) concluded that the EA discipline is driven largely by consulting companies. Similarly, Khoury and Simoff (2004, p. 65) argued that "contemporary approaches to [enterprise architecture] have been largely hijacked by the consulting classes". The earlier survey by Meiklejohn (1986) demonstrated that in the United Kingdom alone at least 26 medium and large consulting companies provided information systems planning services in some or the other form. Moreover, the information systems planning consulting market was booming: "Practically 60% of consultancies report a growth in [planning] assignments of up to 50% over the past three years, with over 40% reporting even higher growth rates. In 1985 alone, growth rates of up to 50% were reported by over 90% of the consultancies" (Galliers, 1988, p. 188). Later Spewak and Hill (1992) in Appendix B provided a "partial list" of 33 global and local companies that offered enterprise architecture consulting services

[20] For instance, the survey of 334 U.S. organizations practicing systematic information systems planning by Cresap, McCormick and Paget (Hoffman and Martino, 1983) showed that only 14% of these organizations employed dedicated IT planners, while in the majority of these organizations information systems planning was the responsibility of senior IT managers. A decade later the survey of 105 large Irish companies by Finnegan and Fahy (1993) demonstrated that permanent information systems planning groups existed in 43.6% of these companies

[21] For example, the survey of 26 U.K. consultancies by Meiklejohn (1986) showed that information systems planning consulting engagements usually lasted from three weeks to one year, several months on average, and typically implied interviewing 20 to 30 people from client organizations as part of the engagement. Likewise, the survey of 131 U.K. companies by Galliers (1988) demonstrated that these information systems planning "studies" more often took 3-5 months to complete. Later the survey of 105 IT planners who participated in information systems planning studies by Lederer and Sethi (1996, p. 48) found that "the average duration of each study was 6.9 months"

[22] For example, Kanter and Miserendino (1987, p. 25) proclaim that "having an architecture is more important than ever". In a similar vein, Cheung (1990), a manager of the Information Engineering consulting practice at Ernst and Young (now EY), in his discussion of the pitfalls of information systems planning essentially equates the problem of planning with the problem of creating proper architectural plans (e.g.

obtaining management support, defining the planning methodology and its deliverables, selecting the right scope and level of detail), but completely ignores the questions related to the subsequent usage of the resulting plans as irrelevant

[23] For instance, regarding the early architecture-based planning methodologies Tozer (1988, p. 61) reported that "mistakes were made in the 1970s, when major "architecture projects" were mounted without a clear definition of the outcome, and in some cases ran for two years or more without producing anything of business value". Then, Osterle et al. (1993, p. xi) reported a very similar situation observed during the next decade: "In the 1980s many enterprises (usually with the help of external consultants) [...] developed enterprise-wide information system architectures at great cost, and now find their position has scarcely changed: an application backlog, dissatisfied user departments [and other problems]. Added to this is the disappointment that the information system architecture has not solved the problems". Reponen (1993, p. 202) provided the following description of a BSP study conducted by external consultants in one large Finnish company: "Finnpap's data processing department underwent a comprehensive BSP-analysis in 1984, carried out by outside consultants. [However,] the results of the BSP-analysis had not been used effectively. Representatives of the business side had found the analysis laborious; they remembered the interviews and the drawing of pictures, but not the results of all the work. There had been neither a high degree of involvement and interaction, nor sufficient reality. Consequently the plans had been put away on shelves and forgotten". Later exactly the same story was repeated by Vivek Kundra regarding the FEAF-based Federal Enterprise Architecture (FEA) program: "I kept pushing the person [in charge of the project], "What did we get, what did we get, what did we get?" And ultimately it ended up being this book [enterprise architecture]" (Tucci, 2011, p. 1). Another government CIO also reported an analogous story: "Yes, we have an EA. It is sitting in a binder gathering dust on my shelf" (Burton, 2011, p. 6). The survey of 105 IT planners by Hartono et al. (2003) statistically demonstrates that the involvement of external consultants in information systems planning efforts and the use of formal planning methodologies negatively correlate with the actual implementation of the resulting plans. Interestingly, the tendency of comprehensive architectural plans to end up on shelves is acknowledged even by consultants themselves, for instance, by Atkinson (1992). The problems with formal architecture-based planning methodologies from BSP to TOGAF are discussed in detail in Appendix (The Origin of EA and Modern EA Best Practices)

[24] For instance, Galliers (1987c) indicates that only 35% of the surveyed consultancies reported that their information systems planning efforts had been evaluated by client organizations. Unsurprisingly, only 7% of external consultants considered their planning efforts as unsuccessful from the senior management viewpoint, while among internal IT planners the same estimate varied from 42% to 59% (Galliers, 1986; Galliers, 1988)

[25] The impressive "effectiveness" of flawed architecture-based planning methodologies for consulting companies and their total ineffectiveness for client organizations is discussed in more detail in Kotusev (2016h)

[26] For instance, Kemp and McManus (2009, p. 21) describe this consulting approach in the following way: "[Enterprise architecture] can be generated relatively quickly. A five-year IT strategy can be generated by an EA team in 3-6 months, perhaps. What happens then? Do the [enterprise architects] start to test their EA by monitoring its adoption by various projects? In our experience, they do not"

[27] For instance, Gartner still warns organizations of these and similar "tricks" of consulting companies (Blosch and Short, 2012; Blosch and Short, 2013; Lapkin and Allega, 2010). "The challenge with consulting organizations from large system integrators is that they are often looking for (and positioning the EA toward) the follow-on projects that they have the capability to deliver. A different challenge from vendor organizations is that they view an EA engagement, which is often delivered for free, as a presales activity to understand the client's needs for their product" (Blosch and Short, 2013, p. 3). One of the recommended ways to address this problem is to "inform the consultant at the outset, preferably written into the contract, that by taking on the EA engagement the consultant is disqualified from implementation projects that may result from the EA work" (Blosch and Short, 2012, pp. 4-5)

[28] Similar effects often happen with many "hot" buzzwords on the management consulting market. For instance, in the early 1990s, at the very peak of the hype around a then-popular management fad of business process reengineering promoted by Hammer and Champy (1993), reengineering was also equated to very diverse

management practices and was even defined by astute managers as "any project you want to get funded" (Davenport and Stoddard, 1994, p. 121)

[29] For instance, in order to avoid confusion when dealing with EA consulting companies Gartner recommends first to "make sure that candidate [EA consultancies] use a definition of EA that is consistent with your own; otherwise, you may end up with technology standards for one division when you really wanted better data management related to your enterprisewide critical business processes" (Lapkin and Allega, 2010, p. 3)

[30] Permanent confusion, inconsistent use and even the absence of a commonly accepted definition of the term "enterprise architecture" arguably result from the excessive hype around enterprise architecture and from the ongoing irresponsible abuse of this term by numerous commercially motivated consultancies and gurus. As noted earlier, enterprise architecture has a countless number of very diverse definitions (Saint-Louis et al., 2017) and it is still debated whether enterprise architecture represents a plan (Simon et al., 2013), project (Alaeddini and Salekfard, 2013), process (Lapkin et al., 2008), practice (FEAPO, 2013) or fundamental structure of an organization (Ahlemann et al., 2012a)

[31] I discussed this phenomenon in more detail in some of my earlier articles (Kotusev, 2016a; Kotusev, 2016d; Kotusev, 2018)

[32] For instance, in 2012 Gartner reported that only 20.8% of organizations practicing enterprise architecture used the services of EA consultancies (Burton et al., 2012). Later in 2014 it was reported that 51.0% of respondents in the United States and 49.8% of respondents in EMEA (Europe, the Middle East and Africa) were either already using or planning to use EA consultancies (Brand, 2014)

[33] As discussed earlier, all decisions EA artifacts must be developed collaboratively by all relevant stakeholders and their value is realized largely during the development process, i.e. a disciplined collective decision-making process itself is more important than the resulting artifacts (see Figure 2.6)

[34] For instance, in 2013 Gartner estimated the combined revenue of the top ten global EA consultancies to be about two billion dollars, while in 2015 the total revenue of the nine leading EA consultancies (Accenture, CSC, Deloitte, EY, HP, IBM, Oracle, PwC and TCS) was estimated to be about three billion dollars (Brand, 2015). Similarly, Forrester in 2015 estimated the overall volume of the EA consulting market to be about four billion dollars (Peyret and Barnett, 2015). An overview, analysis and comparison of largest EA consultancies is provided, for instance, by Gartner (Brand, 2015) and Forrester (Peyret and Barnett, 2015)

[35] Interestingly, the very same companies, or their legal predecessors, previously were among the most active "inventors" and promoters of the most widely known flawed architecture-based planning methodologies of the pre-EA epoch. Specifically, IBM previously promoted BSP (BSP, 1975; BSP, 1984), Arthur Andersen (now Accenture) previously promoted Method/1 (Arthur Andersen, 1979; Arthur Andersen, 1987), while Arthur Young (now part of EY) previously promoted Information Engineering (Arthur Young, 1987)

[36] The critical importance of collaboration between internal client architects and external EA consultants is emphasized, for instance, by Gartner: "Gartner has observed [...] clients who have derailed the EA effort (and any subsequent attempts) through improper use of consultants. This usually happens when the client engages a consultant to do the architecture "to them" rather than "with them". Without the active participation of the client in the EA effort, the critical link to the business is lost" (Lapkin and Allega, 2010, p. 3). The attempts of external EA consultants to develop some architectural plans for a client organization are essentially equivalent to the attempts to develop decisions EA artifacts on behalf of their real stakeholders without their active participation and naturally doomed to failure (see Figure 2.6)

[37] For instance, Lapkin and Allega (2010, p. 6) describe these project-based documentation-oriented EA consulting engagements in the following way: "EA is not a "project" and should not be treated as such. However, many consultants have a "project" orientation to their client engagements. They want to come in, produce some deliverables, get paid and leave (or go on to the next project in your enterprise). This is not an appropriate orientation for an EA engagement. We see many organizations spend considerable money with consultants in EA "projects". In most cases, the project-oriented attitude of the consultant bleeds over into the customer, and when the consultant leaves, the client organization regards the architecture effort as "complete".

The deliverables are put on a shelf and ignored until the next "refresh cycle". The net result is that considerable money is spent with little or no value delivered to the enterprise"

[38] As noted earlier, historically the concept of architecture was largely discredited and the very word "architecture" even became a bad word in many organizations (Bittler and Burton, 2011; James, 2008; Kappelman, 2010; Ross et al., 2014)

[39] These EA consulting engagements might still be better than having no systematic IT planning whatsoever and can arguably be beneficial to some very special types of organizations, e.g. small, simple and static organizations with lagging IT departments and underdeveloped IT management practices. For instance, this view was expressed earlier regarding BSP studies by Gunton (1989). However, these types of consulting engagements are very inefficient, unfit for the vast majority of modern organizations and cannot be considered as mainstream EA "best practice"

[40] This suggestion is consistent with the earlier recommendation of Gartner to "use an [EA consultancy] to supplement your EA initiative, but never outsource your EA effort completely" (Lapkin and Allega, 2010, p. 1)

[41] For instance, Lapkin and Allega (2010, p. 3) describe this attitude in the following way: "Although many processes and functions of the enterprise can be outsourced, EA cannot be. Turning the responsibility and accountability for this critical strategic function over to a third party is tantamount to abdicating the responsibility for the realization of the business strategy. It is never advisable, because EA is so critical to business success"

[42] For instance, Lapkin and Allega (2010, p. 4) describe this situation in the following way: "Many software or hardware vendors have captive consultancies that represent themselves as having an EA framework and process that is independent and agnostic to final results. In truth, most of these frameworks offer predefined end states that presume your business needs are a perfect match for their offerings. Architecture engagement with this type of [EA consultancy] should be approached with extreme caution. [...] The process of EA is designed to discover the best fit of products given the desired target states, not the target state given a vendor's product portfolio. [...] Never abdicate the discovery of answers about your enterprise's future state to vendors that are selling products that may or may not be a fit to your changing needs"

Appendix: The Origin of EA and Modern EA Best Practices

[1] For instance, Simon et al. (2013, p. 2) formulate this belief in the most striking way: "The discipline of enterprise architecture (EA) has evolved enormously since John Zachman ignited its flame in 1987 (Zachman, 1987)". Similarly, Plessius et al. (2014, p. 2) describe the origin of enterprise architecture in the following way: "The concept of Enterprise Architecture (EA) was introduced in 1987 by Zachman with the words: "With increasing size and complexity of the implementations of information systems, it is necessary to use some logical construct (or architecture) for defining and controlling the interfaces and the integration of all of the components of the system." (Zachman, 1987, p. 276)"

[2] For instance, TOGAF is considered as a de facto industry standard in enterprise architecture by many authors (Brown and Obitz, 2011; Dietz and Hoogervorst, 2011; Gosselt, 2012; Lankhorst et al., 2010; Sarno and Herdiyanti, 2010; Sobczak, 2013)

[3] In my previous publications discussing the history of enterprise architecture (Kotusev, 2016c; Kotusev, 2016e) I used a slightly different classification and articulated the following three periods of information systems planning methodologies: pre-EA (BSP), early enterprise architecture and modern enterprise architecture. A much earlier attempt to analyze the history and evolution of approaches to information systems planning has been presented by Stegwee and van Waes (1990)

[4] See Kriebel (1968) and Strategy Set Transformation (SST) (King, 1978; King, 1983; King, 1984)

[5] See DeFeo (1982)

[6] See Siegel (1975)

[7] See Blumenthal (1969) and Statland (1982)

[8] See Business Information Analysis and Integration Technique (BIAIT) (Carlson, 1979) and Business Information Characterization/Control Study (BICS) (Kerner, 1979; Kerner, 1982)

[9] See Wetherbe and Davis (1982)

[10] See Dearden (1965)

[11] See Rockart (1979) and Bullen and Rockart (1981)

[12] See Zani (1970) and Henderson and West (1979)

[13] See King and Cleland (1975) and Ghymn and King (1976)

[14] See Checkland (1981) and Le Fevre and Pattison (1986)

[15] See Evans and Hague (1962)

[16] The history of countless formal modeling techniques for processes and systems can be traced back at least to the early 1900s (Couger, 1973), while the article of Evans and Hague (1962) is only the first identified application of these techniques to organization-wide information systems planning

[17] Based on Evans and Hague (1962)

[18] See Schwartz (1970)

[19] Based on Schwartz (1970)

[20] See Glans et al. (1968b), Glans et al. (1968a) and a series of earlier IBM manuals where the SOP methodology was originally described (SOP, 1961; SOP, 1963a; SOP, 1963b; SOP, 1963c; SOP, 1963d; SOP, 1963e), as well as some rudimentary works of IBM on total system studies (Ridgway, 1961)

[21] For example, see the ARDI (Analysis, Requirements determination, Design and development, Implementation and evaluation) end-to-end systems planning and development methodology with analogous steps and deliverables developed by Philips (Hartman et al., 1968), the BISAD (Business Information Systems Analysis and Design) methodology developed by Honeywell (Honeywell, 1968) and a similar high-level approach proposed by Thompson (1969)

[22] Based on Glans et al. (1968b)

[23] See BSP (1975), Orsey (1982a), Orsey (1982b), Orsey (1982c), Vacca (1983), BSP (1984), Lederer and Putnam (1986) and Lederer and Putnam (1987)

[24] The origination of current EA frameworks and methodologies from BSP is acknowledged by some authors (Harrell and Sage, 2010; Hermans, 2015; Holcman, 2014; Sidorova and Kappelman, 2010; Spewak and Hill, 1992; Veryard, 2011) and even by John Zachman himself (Spewak and Hill, 1992; Zachman, 2015; Zachman and Ruby, 2004; Zachman and Sessions, 2007). For instance, John Zachman explicitly refers to Dewey Walker and BSP: "I acknowledge Dewey Walker, [...], as the "grandfather" of architecture methodologies. It was his internal IBM experience in Information Architecture that later became known as Business Systems Planning (BSP)" (Spewak and Hill, 1992, p. xv). Likewise, Holcman (2014, p. 4) describes the origin of enterprise architecture in the following way: "In 1970, [Dewey] Walker was commissioned to establish a national marketing approach for IBM. That assignment resulted in a highly successful program called Business Systems Planning (BSP), for which Walker received IBM's Outstanding Contribution Award in 1973". However, by some reason the lineage of popular EA frameworks from BSP is still largely ignored by the EA community

[25] Later BSP was also supported by specialized software tools and databases for capturing the data collected as part of BSP studies and then reporting on this data (Sakamoto, 1982; Sakamoto and Ball, 1982). These tools and databases can be considered as a prototype of modern EA tools and architectural repositories discussed earlier in Chapter 18

[26] Based on BSP (1975)

[27] As noted earlier, an insatiable market demand for improving business and IT alignment in organizations is demonstrated by countless yearly surveys of IT executives starting from 1980 (Ball and Harris, 1982)

[28] The fact that most subsequent information systems planning methodologies had been spawned and derived from BSP is widely acknowledged in literature (Adriaans and Hoogakker, 1989; Davenport, 1994; Lederer and Putnam, 1986; Lederer and Putnam, 1987; Stegwee and van Waes, 1990; Sullivan, 1985; Sullivan,

1987; Vacca, 1983; Wiseman, 1988; Zachman, 1982). As Vacca (1983, p. 11) puts it, "while BSP, developed in 1970, is not the only strategic planning methodology around today, it is the root from which the others have evolved"

[29] See Vacca (1984) and Vacca (1985)

[30] For example, see the Corporate Data Plan (CDP) methodology proposed by Cohn (1981) and the Business Information Systems Planning (BISP) methodology proposed by Levy (1982), which even mimicked BSP's title

[31] See Arthur Andersen (1979), Arthur Andersen (1987), Lederer and Gardiner (1992a) and Lederer and Gardiner (1992b)

[32] Based on Arthur Andersen (1987)

[33] The first use of the word "architecture" in relation to organization-wide information systems planning seemingly can be traced back to the article of Walker and Catalano (1969). Wardle (1984, p. 206) argues that "the term "architecture" is clearly attractive because of its association with structure and integration"

[34] Originally the word "framework" in relation to architecture was essentially synonymous to the word "taxonomy". For instance, the chief evangelist of EA frameworks John Zachman initially defined an EA framework as "a logical structure for classifying and organizing the descriptive representations of an Enterprise that are significant to the management of the Enterprise as well as to the development of the Enterprise's systems" (Zachman, 1996, p. 2). Accordingly, most early EA publications (Bernard, 2004; Boar, 1999b; Carbone, 2004; Spewak and Hill, 1992) very clearly distinguished frameworks, as taxonomies for organizing EA artifacts, and methodologies, as sets of actions necessary to create EA artifacts, i.e. to fill the cells of frameworks. However, later the term "EA framework" has been blurred to the extent of full vagueness and now essentially lost any definite meaning altogether. For example, numerous very diverse entities have been recently considered as "EA frameworks" by different authors including, among others, the Enterprise Architecture Planning methodology of Spewak and Hill (1992) (Matthes, 2011), the book of Ross et al. (2006) (Bui, 2012; Bui, 2017), ArchiMate and ARIS modeling languages (Kallgren et al., 2009; Matthes, 2011), various EA maturity models (Matthes, 2011), the POSIX open-system environment reference model (Matthes, 2011) and even ITIL and COBIT (Aziz and Obitz, 2007; Gall, 2012; Obitz and Babu, 2009). All these entities have no real relationship to the original meaning of the term "EA framework" and some of them even have no relationship to enterprise architecture. From this perspective, the term "EA framework" now can be formally defined only as "any arbitrary set of EA-related or non-EA-related recommendations", or even recursively as "anything that can be considered by someone to be an EA framework". See Appendix F in Kotusev (2017e) for a more detailed discussion of the confusion around the term "EA framework". In this book "EA frameworks" in most contexts refer specifically to the limited set of popular EA-related publications explicitly titled as "frameworks", primarily to TOGAF, Zachman, FEAF and DoDAF

[35] The architectural model proposed by Wardle (1984) classifies components of architecture into twelve distinct categories according to four domains (data, applications, communications and technology) and three levels (conceptual, logical and design guidelines & boundaries). The study of Wardle (1984) was supported financially and organizationally by Nolan, Norton & Company

[36] The PRISM (Partnership for Research in Information Systems Management) framework classifies components of architecture into sixteen distinct categories according to four domains (infrastructure, data, application and organization) and four types (inventory, principles, models and standards) (PRISM, 1986). The corresponding PRISM research project was sponsored by a group of companies including IBM (Davenport, 1986)

[37] See Zachman (1987), Zachman (1988), Zachman (1989), Sowa and Zachman (1992a) and Sowa and Zachman (1992b)

[38] Based on BSP (1984)

[39] See Remenyi (1991) (Appendices 4-11)

[40] See Parker et al. (1989) (Part 3) and Atkinson and Montgomery (1990)

[41] See Nolan and Mulryan (1987)

[42] Based on Atkinson and Montgomery (1990)

[43] Based on Nolan and Mulryan (1987)

[44] See Tozer (1986b), Tozer (1986a), Tozer (1988) and Tozer (1996)

[45] See Gallo (1988)

[46] See Connor (1988). This architecture planning methodology was seemingly the first methodology that used an architecture framework, namely the so-called STRIPE matrix, to organize its outputs. The STRIPE matrix classifies architecture deliverables into fifteen distinct categories according to five domains (business, data, application, technical environment and type of plan) and three planning levels (strategic, tactical and operational)

[47] See Parker (1990)

[48] See Inmon (1986) and Inmon and Caplan (1992)

[49] See the planning methodology developed at the University of Minnesota (Vogel and Wetherbe, 1984; Vogel and Wetherbe, 1991; Wetherbe and Davis, 1983) and the similar "belated" approaches proposed by Rowley (1994), Mentzas (1997), Min et al. (1999) and Li and Chen (2001)

[50] Based on Tozer (1988)

[51] Based on Gallo (1988)

[52] See GAO (1992) and GAO (1994)

[53] See TAFIM (1996a) and TAFIM (1996b)

[54] Based on TAFIM (1996b)

[55] See Finkelstein (1981) and Martin and Finkelstein (1981)

[56] See Arthur Young (1987), Inmon (1988), Finkelstein (1989), Martin (1989), Davids (1992), Finkelstein (1992), Finkelstein (2006b) and a similar high-level planning approach proposed by Spencer (1985)

[57] See Martin (1982b) and Martin and Leben (1989)

[58] For instance, Finkelstein (1981, p. 2) explained that "Information Engineering identifies and models the data that is the organization. And that data generally changes less frequently than the procedures that utilize the data". Analogously, Martin (1982a, p. 29) argued that "the procedures change rapidly (or should); the computer programs, processes, networks and the hardware change; but the basic types of data are relatively stable. [...] Because the basic data types are stable, whereas procedures tend to change, data-oriented techniques succeed if correctly applied where procedure-oriented techniques have failed"

[59] Based on Arthur Young (1987)

[60] Based on Finkelstein (1989)

[61] The term "enterprise architecture" seemingly was first used consistently by Rigdon (1989), though without any specific definition of its meaning. Later this term was formally defined by Richardson et al. (1990, p. 386) as an architecture that "defines and interrelates data, hardware, software, and communications resources, as well as the supporting organization required to maintain the overall physical structure required by the architecture" and then further popularized by Spewak and Hill (1992). However, the phrase "enterprise architecture" was once mentioned earlier, arguably accidentally, by Zachman (1982, p. 32). See Kotusev (2016e) for a more detailed discussion of the origin of the term "enterprise architecture"

[62] See Spewak and Hill (1992) and Spewak and Tiemann (2006)

[63] Spewak and Hill (1992, p. 53) explicitly admit that "EAP has its roots in IBM's BSP". Moreover, "Strategic Data Planning, Information Engineering, [...] have also contributed techniques and ideas to EAP" (Spewak and Hill, 1992, p. 53)

[64] Based on Spewak and Hill (1992)

[65] See Boar (1999b)

[66] See Cook (1996)

[67] As noted earlier, in their original narrow meaning architecture frameworks represented only logical structures, or taxonomies, for organizing architectural descriptions (PRISM, 1986; Wardle, 1984; Zachman, 1987). However, later the meaning of the term "EA framework" had been significantly broadened to represent, among other things, even full-fledged EA methodologies. While some of the "new" EA frameworks, e.g. E2AF (Schekkerman, 2006a) and EA Grid (Pulkkinen, 2006), still conform to the original definition of architecture frameworks (i.e. provide only taxonomies for architectural descriptions), most of the current EA frameworks including TOGAF, FEAF and DoDAF provide comprehensive EA methodologies with recommended steps, deliverables and other aspects of an EA practice

[68] See TEAF (2000)

[69] See C4ISR (1997) and Sowell (2000)

[70] See FEAF (1999), FEA (2001), FEA (2007), FEA (2012) and FEAF (2013)

[71] See FEAF (1999, pp. 20-22)

[72] See Armour et al. (1999a), Armour et al. (1999b) and Armour and Kaisler (2001)

[73] Based on Armour et al. (1999b)

[74] See Longepe (2003)

[75] See Carbone (2004)

[76] See Bernard (2004)

[77] See Theuerkorn (2004)

[78] See Niemann (2006)

[79] See Schekkerman (2008)

[80] See Holcman (2013)

[81] Based on Bernard (2004)

[82] Based on Schekkerman (2008)

[83] See Bittler and Kreizman (2005)

[84] See IBM (2006)

[85] See Covington and Jahangir (2009)

[86] See van't Wout et al. (2010)

[87] See Wisnosky and Vogel (2004), DoDAF (2007a), DoDAF (2007b), DoDAF (2007c), DoDAF (2009) and Dam (2015)

[88] Based on IBM (2006)

[89] Based on Covington and Jahangir (2009)

[90] See Perks and Beveridge (2003) and TOGAF (2018)

[91] As noted earlier, TOGAF is often considered as a de facto industry standard in enterprise architecture (Brown and Obitz, 2011; Dietz and Hoogervorst, 2011; Gosselt, 2012; Lankhorst et al., 2010; Sarno and Herdiyanti, 2010; Sobczak, 2013)

[92] For instance, The Open Group claims that TOGAF is "a proven Enterprise Architecture methodology and framework" as well as "the most prominent and reliable Enterprise Architecture standard in the world" which is used in 80% of companies from the Global 50 list and in 60% of companies from the Fortune 500 list (The Open Group, 2016b, p. 1)

[93] Based on TOGAF (2018)

[94] The strong conceptual similarity between all early architecture-based planning methodologies has been noticed previously by Stegwee and van Waes (1990, pp. 11-12): "There exist many methodologies for [information systems planning] which stem from BSP [...], like Information Engineering [...]. In essence they all follow the [same] main lines [...]. First, the business strategy is determined by means of mission statements, organizational goals, and critical success factors. Next, the trends and opportunities in the field of information

technology are analyzed in order to identify new application areas and alternative technical architectures. Then, an overview is given of the current information system support [...]. The information architecture is specified by means of a process model, developed for the organization, an entity model, summarizing the data to be stored, and a matrix showing which data is created, retrieved, updated, or deleted by which processes. The logical information architecture is then manipulated to form the systems architecture, specifying individual information systems to be discerned [...]. A transition path has to be provided in order to indicate how to reach the new situation, as described by the architectures [...]. From these results a project portfolio and plan can be developed for the short to mid-range period". Similarly, Wiseman (1988, p. 82) also noticed that "most of the other general-purpose approaches to information systems planning (e.g., [...] James Martin's information engineering, and those offered by large accounting firms [e.g. 4FRONT by Deloitte & Touche and Summit S by Coopers & Lybrand]) are lineal descendants of BSP"

[95] See FEAF (1999, pp. 20-22) and Spewak and Hill (1992, p. 53)

[96] For instance, TOGAF (2018, p. 3) states that "the original development of TOGAF Version 1 in 1995 was based on the Technical Architecture Framework for Information Management (TAFIM), developed by the US Department of Defense (DoD). The DoD gave The Open Group explicit permission and encouragement to create Version 1 of the TOGAF standard by building on the TAFIM, which itself was the result of many years of development effort and many millions of dollars of US Government investment". In its turn, TAFIM was based on some earlier models initiated in 1986 (Golden, 1994)

[97] See Zachman (1977), Zachman (1982) and Marenghi and Zachman (1982)

[98] See Zachman International (2012)

[99] See Finkelstein (1991)

[100] See Finkelstein (2006a)

[101] As noted earlier, the architectural taxonomy proposed by Wardle (1984) and the PRISM framework (PRISM, 1986) had been published before the Zachman Framework (Zachman, 1987)

[102] See Goodhue et al. (1986), Goodhue et al. (1988), Lederer and Sethi (1988) and Lederer and Sethi (1989)

[103] See Goodhue et al. (1992), Lederer and Sethi (1992), Beynon-Davies (1994), Davenport (1994), Kim and Everest (1994), Periasamy (1994), Segars and Grover (1996), Shanks (1997), Shanks and Swatman (1997) and Hamilton (1999)

[104] See Kemp and McManus (2009), Seppanen et al. (2009) and Gaver (2010)

[105] See Holst and Steensen (2011), Tucci (2011), Lohe and Legner (2012), Bloomberg (2014), Lohe and Legner (2014), GAO (2015) and Trionfi (2016)

[106] For example, exactly the same problems had been reported earlier specifically regarding TAFIM, the direct and officially acknowledged predecessor of TOGAF, and eventually lead to its retirement due to impracticality of the proposed approach: "TAFIM most certainly required a large investment of both time and money", "the elapsed time required to produce the architecture makes it close to obsolete before completion", "the end result is normally incomprehensible to a business-oriented audience and is harder to trace to the business strategy" and "due to some of these flaws, the TAFIM was abruptly cancelled" (Perks and Beveridge, 2003, p. 79)

[107] The adequacy of formal architecture-based planning methodologies was consistently questioned by many authors including Goodhue et al. (1988), Lederer and Sethi (1988), Goodhue et al. (1992), Davenport (1994), Kim and Everest (1994), Periasamy (1994), Shanks (1997), Hamilton (1999), Kemp and McManus (2009), Gaver (2010), Holst and Steensen (2011), Tucci (2011), Bloomberg (2014), Lohe and Legner (2014) and Trionfi (2016). For instance, significant doubts regarding the efficacy of the earliest formal information systems planning methodology, Study Organization Plan (SOP), were expressed long ago by Head (1971, p. 23): "It is interesting to speculate why SOP was not widely accepted. Its methodology was somewhat cumbersome, and its full implementation in many cases required documentation efforts of questionable value". Later Vitale et al. (1986, p. 271) concluded that "high levels of environmental turbulence cast shadows on the utility of the top

down planning process as an instrument for [information systems planning]". Lederer and Mendelow (1988, p. 75) reported that "many systems managers say [formal architecture-based] planning methodologies require too much time and thought by both line and systems managers. In addition, the systems-planning cycle takes too long, and major business changes can make the final plan irrelevant". Bock et al. (1992, p. 14) expressed a similar opinion: "Numerous methodologies have been proposed for implementing enterprisewide modeling, including IBM's business systems planning method, [...] and Martin's strategic data planning approach. In each case, these methods require extensive planning exercises. In reality, however, most organizations do not construct enterprisewide models. One IS director [...] stated that he knew of no corporation in [his industry] that could claim significant success in enterprisewide modeling". Davenport (1994, p. 121) argued that "information architecture [advocated by BSP] has never achieved its promise. Enterprise models of information types, uses, and responsibilities are too broad and arcane for nontechnical people to comprehend – and they can take years to build". Earl (1996, p. 55) concluded that "the general verdict on this [formal architectural] approach [...] was negative. It typically takes large amounts of resources, including management time, and in one company user managers found it hard to grasp the meaning of the blueprint generated or to see which elements mattered most. As a result, though some elements can be useful, the overall blueprint is often axed or aborted". As Ross et al. (2006, p. vii) put it, "the historic ineffectiveness of IT architecture efforts in large organizations has troubled us for years. In presentations we have railed against traditional IT architecture efforts for their remoteness from the reality of the business and their heavy reliance on mind-numbing detail represented in charts that look more like circuit diagrams than business descriptions and that are useful as little more than doorstops". Gunton (1989, pp. 137-138) provided a fair summary of the typical problems and outcomes of formal architecture-based planning methodologies: "The traditional approach [to information systems planning] is exemplified by [formal architecture-based] planning techniques such as IBM's Business Systems Planning (BSP) and updated variants such as James Martin's Strategic Data Planning. [...] They produce a blueprint or map of the systems and/or the information that the business needs, based on a methodical process of analysis. The drawbacks of this approach are that the analysis process is very expensive and difficult to organize. It demands the commitment of senior managers who really understand the business, which is often difficult to obtain. Even where this difficulty can be overcome, the blueprint that is produced can easily prove so complex and unwieldy that its value as a strategic corporate overview is obscured by a mass of detail. And, since analysis invariably focuses on today's operations, it is always vulnerable to unanticipated changes in markets or in organization. I know of far more organizations that have developed a strategic data model, then shelved it or adopted only a small part of it, than have successfully carried a substantial part of the model through to implementation in the form of databases and applications"

[108] For instance, Stegwee and van Waes (1990, p. 16) argued that "looking back to the developments concerning ISP [information systems planning] we can conclude that [...] the time has arrived to change our attitudes towards ISP fundamentally". Likewise, Goodhue et al. (1992, p. 28) concluded that "the evidence of the nine [organizations that tried BSP and similar planning methodologies] presented here strongly supports the need for a fundamental rethinking of IS planning methodologies". Hamilton (1999, p. 81) concluded that "findings from the study suggest strongly that the prescriptive approach to architecture-driven planning at the portfolio level is fundamentally flawed". Finally, Gaver (2010, p. 10) concluded that "EA often doesn't work well anywhere because the problems with Enterprise Architecture [frameworks] are fundamental in nature"

[109] Calls for more pragmatic, flexible, collaborative and evolutionary planning approaches were consistently incoming from many authors including Goodhue et al. (1988), Stegwee and van Waes (1990), Goodhue et al. (1992), Beynon-Davies (1994), Kim and Everest (1994), Earl (1996), Shanks (1997), Holst and Steensen (2011), Lohe and Legner (2012) and Lohe and Legner (2014)

[110] By analogy with the "garbage can" model of organizational choice, i.e. the model describing decision-making in organizations as a semi-anarchic process characterized by almost random interactions between problems, solutions and decision makers (Cohen et al., 1972), the historical evolution of architecture-based planning methodologies can be described as a "garbage can" of chaotic mutations

[111] Descriptions of some early homegrown approaches to information systems planning of the 1970s are provided, for instance, by McFarlan (1971), McLean and Soden (1977), Sporn (1978), Rush (1979) and van

Rensselaer (1979). Some homegrown planning approaches of the 1980s are described, for instance, by van Rensselaer (1985), Davies and Hale (1986), Corbin (1988) and Penrod and Douglas (1988). Descriptions of some later homegrown planning approaches of the 1990s are provided, for instance, by Carter et al. (1990), Carter et al. (1991), Martinsons and Hosley (1993), Palmer (1993), Reponen (1993), Flynn and Hepburn (1994), Periasamy (1994) and Cerpa and Verner (1998)

[112] In the late 1980s and the 1990s systematic information systems planning had been practiced seemingly in about a half of all medium and large organizations in developed countries (Ang and Teo, 1997; Conrath et al., 1992; Falconer and Hodgett, 1997; Falconer and Hodgett, 1998; Galliers, 1987b; Galliers, 1987c; Galliers, 1988; Pavri and Ang, 1995; Teo et al., 1997). However, the vast majority of these companies used some homegrown planning approaches and only ~15-25% of them used formal architecture-based planning methodologies. For instance, the survey of 334 U.S. organizations by Cresap, McCormick and Paget (Hoffman and Martino, 1983) showed that only 23% of these organizations used BSP-like planning methodologies, while 78% used their own homegrown planning approaches (answers were not mutually exclusive). Out of the sixteen "random" U.S. CIOs surveyed by Vitale et al. (1986) who had, or planned to have, systematic information systems planning processes only four reported that they used BSP-like planning approaches. The survey of 209 U.K. and Australian companies by Galliers (1987b) demonstrated the predominance of in-house planning approaches over well-known architecture-based methodologies and in the United Kingdom "in-house approaches outnumber the well-known, proprietary methodologies by over 3:1" (Galliers, 1986, p. 36). The study of 31 information systems planning efforts in different U.S. companies by Goodhue et al. (1988, p. 380) showed that only five of the examined efforts used BSP or similar planning methodologies and "none of these firms saw the kind of success envisioned in the literature". The survey of 245 U.S. organizations by Premkumar and King (1991, p. 46) concluded that "only 22 per cent of the respondents use a commercial [information systems] planning methodology, while the rest use an in-house developed methodology". Specifically, only 12% of the surveyed organizations used Information Engineering and only 8% used BSP. The study of 27 U.K. companies by Earl (1993) demonstrated that only four of them used formal architecture-based planning methodologies. The survey of eighteen U.K. organizations by Flynn and Goleniewska (1993) indicated that only one of them used Information Engineering. The survey of 105 Irish companies by Finnegan and Fahy (1993, p. 132) demonstrated that only 21% of these companies used BSP and only 11% used Information Engineering, but "over 78% of respondents had the IS planning methodology developed or adapted internally". The survey of 76 U.K. organizations by Fidler et al. (1993) showed that only 18% of these organizations used BSP. Finally, the survey of 294 U.K. companies by Periasamy (1994) of which 194 practiced information systems planning demonstrated that only 12% of these companies used Information Engineering, only 3% used BSP and only 3% used Method/1, while 73% used homegrown planning approaches. At the same time, the available detailed case studies of organizations using formal architecture-based methodologies, e.g. BSP (Gill, 1981; Wahi et al., 1983), Method/1 (Mainelli and Miller, 1988) and Information Engineering (Adriaans and Hoogakker, 1989; Brown et al., 1990), show that the prescriptions of these methodologies were actually followed in practice to develop comprehensive architectures, which sharply contrasts with the purely declarative use of EA frameworks prevalent in industry today, as discussed later in this chapter

[113] For instance, the qualitative comparative studies of information systems planning approaches by Goodhue et al. (1988), Earl (1990), Earl (1993), Periasamy (1994) and Earl (1996) unanimously demonstrated the superiority of pragmatic, flexible and participative homegrown planning approaches over formal architecture-based planning methodologies promoted by consultancies. In particular, Periasamy (1994, p. 264) reports that "the [six] case studies provide support for the "organizational approach" [identified previously by Earl (1993)] as the form of IS planning appropriate for integrated strategy development and business planning [...]. No formal IS planning methodology is used and there is emphasis on management processes and cooperation. In this IS planning arrangement, IT and other functional level planning activities are ongoing". The subsequent quantitative surveys by Falconer and Hodgett (1998), Doherty et al. (1999) and Segars and Grover (1999) also confirmed that the clusters of planning approaches highly correlating with the "organizational" approach (characterized by the continuous dialog between business and IT) are most effective, while the clusters correlating with the "method-driven" and "technological" approaches identified by Earl (1993) (characterized by

the focus on formal methodologies and architectures respectively) are among least effective. Interestingly, it was explicitly acknowledged that TOGAF represents specifically the "technological" approach considered by Earl (1993) as one of the least promising: "The architectural approach to planning described in this book [TOGAF version 6.0] has its roots in Earl's Technical Approach" (Perks and Beveridge, 2003, p. 51)

[114] For example, the survey of 294 U.K. organizations by Periasamy (1994, p. 69) demonstrated that "72% of those who practiced in-house [information systems planning] methodologies had [architecture], and 69% of [architecture] utilizers had adopted in-house methodologies". The concept of architecture was considered as promising and useful, but in a form significantly different from the one advocated by formal architecture-based planning methodologies (Hamilton, 1999; Periasamy, 1993; Periasamy, 1994; Periasamy and Feeny, 1997). Most importantly, the studies of Periasamy (1994) and Periasamy and Feeny (1997) demonstrate that comprehensive architectural models and relationship matrices recommended by architecture-based planning methodologies were found largely useless in practice, while more simple, high-level and easy-to-understand architectures depicting the relationship between business and IT in an intuitive graphical form "invented" in-house proved very useful for facilitating communication between business and IT stakeholders. "Involvement and participation by senior management and functional management were viewed as being more important than usage of an [architecture-based planning] methodology. Though formal methodology was considered to be of only marginal relevance to the planning process, IT architecture and IS models were perceived to be of some value" (Periasamy, 1994, p. 225). Many organizations went through numerous unsuccessful attempts, failures and disappointments with architecture before establishing successful homegrown architecture-based planning practices (Burton and Bittler, 2011; Earl, 1996; Hobbs, 2012; Holst and Steensen, 2011; Wierda, 2015; Zink, 2009). As noted earlier, branded architecture-based methodologies proposed by consultancies and gurus might have provided only the initial inspiration for using architecture, but did not define the actual best practices in this area (Birkinshaw and Mol, 2006)

[115] Arguably the most comprehensive available description of homegrown architecture-based planning approaches and best practices of the early 1990s is offered by Periasamy (1994)

[116] Around 2010 enterprise architecture had been practiced seemingly in about two-thirds of all medium and large organizations in developed countries (Ambler, 2010) and numerous industry surveys (Ambler, 2010; Aziz and Obitz, 2007; Buckl et al., 2009; Cameron and McMillan, 2013; Gall, 2012; Obitz and Babu, 2009; Schekkerman, 2005b; Schneider et al., 2015) reported varying statistics regarding the usage of EA frameworks, but a significant portion of organizations in every survey still either explicitly acknowledged that no EA frameworks were used, or provided some other elusive answers, e.g. used homemade, blended or hybrid EA frameworks

[117] This curious fact was noticed previously by other researchers and then completely supported by the field research underpinning this book. For example, the study of eighteen German organizations by Buckl et al. (2009) shows that 64% of these organizations used some EA frameworks, but only in a "simplified" form or even only as idea contributors. The case study of Chubb Insurance by Smith et al. (2012) also shows that even though TOGAF was used as the basis for its EA practice, no TOGAF-specific recommendations could be actually observed in the resulting EA practice. Likewise, many organizations studied as part of this research nominally used some EA frameworks and five of these organizations were even included in the official list of TOGAF users (The Open Group, 2016a). However, none of the studied organizations followed the prescriptions of TOGAF or other EA frameworks in any real sense (Kotusev, 2016a; Kotusev, 2016d; Kotusev, 2018). Interestingly, many of the interviewed architects reported that they used EA frameworks, but at the same time were unable to explain clearly how exactly these frameworks were used. Even more interestingly, some of the interviewed architects never read the original TOGAF text, but were still convinced that their EA practices were TOGAF-based

[118] The impracticality of EA frameworks is very widely acknowledged (Bloomberg, 2014; Gerber et al., 2007; Holst and Steensen, 2011; Lohe and Legner, 2014; Trionfi, 2016). For instance, Buckl et al. (2009, p. 15) argue that "the frameworks appear theoretical and impossible to implement". Vivek Kundra, the former federal CIO of the United States, reportedly argued that "enterprise architecture frameworks are worse than useless" (Tucci, 2011, p. 1)

[119] For instance, Evernden (2015, p. 29) fairly argues that "many practitioners see frameworks as theoretical or conceptual rather than a highly practical everyday device for managing and thinking about architectures"

[120] Primarily I mean the previous books of Wagter et al. (2005), Ross et al. (2006), Murer et al. (2011) and Ahlemann et al. (2012c)

[121] For example, the study of six large companies considered as rather advanced IT users by Periasamy (1994) arguably presents a fair historical snapshot of architecture-based planning practices in different organizations, which clearly illustrates both the prevalence of respective planning approaches and their contrasting outcomes: five of these companies successfully used pragmatic homegrown architecture-based planning approaches, while the sixth company tried to use Information Engineering and failed

[122] This process very highly correlates with the research-based model of management innovations developed by Birkinshaw and Mol (2006): the innovation typically starts from the dissatisfaction with "status quo" (persistent problems with business and IT alignment) and the inspiration from external sources (architecture-based planning methodologies and later EA frameworks proposed by consultancies and gurus), then the innovation is actually "invented" within organizations (emergence of homegrown architecture-based planning approaches), acknowledged as effective by internal and external actors (in-house IT planners and architecture consultants) and finally diffuses to other organizations (currently EA best practices quickly disseminate across the industry by countless migrating architects)

[123] The evident disparity between popular EA frameworks and genuine EA best practices is discussed in more detail in Kotusev (2016h)

[124] For instance, Earl (1996, p. 58) even reports that in many organizations more or less successful homegrown approaches to information systems planning had been replaced with flawed approaches imposed by consultancies: "We usually find that much of the organizational approach [which worked successfully] was then already in place, but it was thrown out as firms listened to the prescriptions of the IT and consulting industries"

[125] Interestingly, exactly the same conclusion had been made previously by Earl (1996, p. 56) regarding approaches to information systems planning: "Paradoxically, the organizational approach [which proved to be most successful] does not closely match the usual prescriptions for IS planning. The literature recommends, for example: basing IS plans on established business goals; using strategy analysis techniques to discover IT applications that will yield a competitive advantage; using formal planning methods and information engineering techniques; and assiduously following resource-planning and project-control procedures"

[126] As Donaldson and Hilmer (1998, p. 7) put it, "many techniques truly deserve the pejorative label, "fad", and deserve to be strenuously combated"

References

Abraham, R. (2013) "Enterprise Architecture Artifacts as Boundary Objects - A Framework of Properties", In: van Hillegersberg, J., van Heck, E. and Connolly, R. (eds.) *Proceedings of the 21st European Conference on Information Systems*, Utrecht, The Netherlands: Association for Information Systems, pp. 1-12.

Abraham, R., Aier, S. and Winter, R. (2015) "Crossing the Line: Overcoming Knowledge Boundaries in Enterprise Transformation", *Business and Information Systems Engineering*, Vol. 57, No. 1, pp. 3-13.

Abraham, R., Niemietz, H., de Kinderen, S. and Aier, S. (2013) "Can Boundary Objects Mitigate Communication Defects in Enterprise Transformation? Findings from Expert Interviews", In: Jung, R. and Reichert, M. (eds.) *Proceedings of the 5th International Workshop on Enterprise Modelling and Information Systems Architectures*, St. Gallen, Switzerland: Gesellschaft fur Informatik, pp. 27-40.

Abrahamson, E. (1991) "Managerial Fads and Fashions: The Diffusion and Rejection of Innovations", *Academy of Management Review*, Vol. 16, No. 3, pp. 586-612.

Abrahamson, E. (1996) "Management Fashion", *Academy of Management Review*, Vol. 21, No. 1, pp. 254-285.

Abrahamson, E. and Fairchild, G. (1999) "Management Fashion: Lifecycles, Triggers, and Collective Learning Processes", *Administrative Science Quarterly*, Vol. 44, No. 4, pp. 708-740.

Adizes, I. (1988) *Corporate Lifecycles: How and Why Corporations Grow and Die and What to Do About It*, Englewood Cliffs, NJ: Prentice Hall.

Adner, R. and Snow, D. C. (2010) "Bold Retreat: A New Strategy for Old Technologies", *Harvard Business Review*, Vol. 88, No. 2, pp. 76-81.

Adriaans, W. and Hoogakker, J. T. (1989) "Planning an Information System at Netherlands Gas", *Long Range Planning*, Vol. 22, No. 3, pp. 64-74.

Ahlemann, F. and El Arbi, F. (2012) "An EAM Navigator", In: Ahlemann, F., Stettiner, E., Messerschmidt, M. and Legner, C. (eds.) *Strategic Enterprise Architecture Management: Challenges, Best Practices, and Future Developments*, Berlin: Springer, pp. 35-53.

Ahlemann, F., Legner, C. and Schafczuk, D. (2012a) "Introduction", In: Ahlemann, F., Stettiner, E., Messerschmidt, M. and Legner, C. (eds.) *Strategic Enterprise Architecture Management: Challenges, Best Practices, and Future Developments*, Berlin: Springer, pp. 1-33.

Ahlemann, F., Mohan, K. and Schafczuk, D. (2012b) "People, Adoption and Introduction of EAM", In: Ahlemann, F., Stettiner, E., Messerschmidt, M. and Legner, C. (eds.) *Strategic Enterprise Architecture Management: Challenges, Best Practices, and Future Developments*, Berlin: Springer, pp. 229-263.

Ahlemann, F., Stettiner, E., Messerschmidt, M. and Legner, C. (eds.) (2012c) *Strategic Enterprise Architecture Management: Challenges, Best Practices, and Future Developments*, Berlin: Springer.

Alaeddini, M. and Salekfard, S. (2013) "Investigating the Role of an Enterprise Architecture Project in the Business-IT Alignment in Iran", *Information Systems Frontiers*, Vol. 15, No. 1, pp. 67-88.

Aldag, R. J. (1997) "Moving Sofas and Exhuming Woodchucks: On Relevance, Impact, and the Following of Fads", *Journal of Management Inquiry*, Vol. 6, No. 1, pp. 8-16.

Alexander, C., Ishikawa, S. and Silverstein, M. (1977) *A Pattern Language: Towns, Buildings, Construction*, New York, NY: Oxford University Press.

Alsoma, A. S., Hourani, H. M. and Masduki, D. M. S. (2012) "Government Enterprise Architecture: Towards the Inter-Connected Government in the Kingdom of Saudi Arabia", In: Saha, P. (ed.) *Enterprise Architecture for Connected E-Government: Practices and Innovations*, Hershey, PA: Information Science Reference, pp. 121-151.

Ambler, S. W. (2010) "Enterprise Architecture: Reality Over Rhetoric", Dr. Dobb's Journal, URL: http://www.drdobbs.com/architecture-and-design/enterprise-architecture-reality-over-rhe/224600174.

Anderson, P., Backhouse, G., Townsend, J., Hedges, M. and Hobson, P. (2009) "Doing Enterprise Architecture: Enabling the Agile Institution" (#533), Bristol, UK: Joint Information Systems Committee (JISC).

Ang, J. S. and Teo, T. S. (1997) "CSFs and Sources of Assistance and Expertise in Strategic IS Planning: A Singapore Perspective", *European Journal of Information Systems*, Vol. 6, No. 3, pp. 164-171.

Anshen, M. (1960) "The Manager and the Black Box", *Harvard Business Review*, Vol. 38, No. 6, pp. 85-92.

APICS (2017) "SCOR Framework", American Production and Inventory Control Society (APICS), URL: http://www.apics.org/apics-for-business/products-and-services/apics-scc-frameworks/scor/.

APQC (2017) "APQC's Process Classification Framework (PCF)", American Productivity and Quality Center (APQC), URL: https://www.apqc.org/pcf/.

Aral, S. and Weill, P. (2007) "IT Assets, Organizational Capabilities, and Firm Performance: How Resource Allocations and Organizational Differences Explain Performance Variation", *Organization Science*, Vol. 18, No. 5, pp. 763-780.

ArchiMate (2016) "ArchiMate 3.0 Specification", The Open Group, URL: http://pubs.opengroup.org/architecture/archimate3-doc/.

Armour, F. J. and Kaisler, S. H. (2001) "Enterprise Architecture: Agile Transition and Implementation", *IT Professional*, Vol. 3, No. 6, pp. 30-37.

Armour, F. J., Kaisler, S. H. and Liu, S. Y. (1999a) "A Big-Picture Look at Enterprise Architectures", *IT Professional*, Vol. 1, No. 1, pp. 35-42.

Armour, F. J., Kaisler, S. H. and Liu, S. Y. (1999b) "Building an Enterprise Architecture Step by Step", *IT Professional*, Vol. 1, No. 4, pp. 31-39.

Arthur Andersen (1979) "Method/1: Systems Development Practices", Chicago, IL: Arthur Andersen.

Arthur Andersen (1987) "Foundation-Method/1: Information Planning (Version 8.0)", Chicago, IL: Arthur Andersen.

Arthur Young (1987) *The Arthur Young Practical Guide to Information Engineering*, New York, NY: Wiley.

Athey, S. and Plotnicki, J. (2000) "An Evaluation of Research Productivity in Academic IT", *Communications of the Association for Information Systems*, Vol. 3, No. 2, pp. 1-19.

Atkinson, R. A. (1992) "Keeping IS Strategic Plans Off the Shelf", *Information Systems Management*, Vol. 9, No. 1, pp. 68-71.

Atkinson, R. A. and Montgomery, J. (1990) "Reshaping IS Strategic Planning", *Journal of Information Systems Management*, Vol. 7, No. 4, pp. 9-17.

Avison, D., Jones, J., Powell, P. and Wilson, D. (2004) "Using and Validating the Strategic Alignment Model", *Journal of Strategic Information Systems*, Vol. 13, No. 3, pp. 223-246.

Aziz, S. and Obitz, T. (2005) "Infosys Enterprise Architecture Survey 2005", Bangalore, India: Infosys.

Aziz, S. and Obitz, T. (2007) "Infosys Enterprise Architecture Survey 2007", Bangalore, India: Infosys.

Badri, M. A. (1992) "Critical Issues in Information Systems Management: An International Perspective", *International Journal of Information Management*, Vol. 12, No. 3, pp. 179-191.

Baets, W. R. J. (1992) "Aligning Information Systems with Business Strategy", *Journal of Strategic Information Systems*, Vol. 1, No. 4, pp. 205-213.

Ball, L. and Harris, R. (1982) "SMIS Members: A Membership Analysis", *MiS Quarterly*, Vol. 6, No. 1, pp. 19-38.

Banaeianjahromi, N. and Smolander, K. (2016) "Understanding Obstacles in Enterprise Architecture Development", In: Ozturan, M., Rossi, M. and Veit, D. (eds.) *Proceedings of the 24th European Conference on Information Systems*, Istanbul, Turkey: Association for Information Systems, pp. 1-15.

Barnett, G. (2015) "The Forrester Wave: Enterprise Architecture Management Suites, Q3 2015", Cambridge, MA: Forrester.

Barnett, G. (2017) "The Forrester Wave: Enterprise Architecture Management Suites, Q2 2017", Cambridge, MA: Forrester.

Basten, D. and Brons, D. (2012) "EA Frameworks, Modelling and Tools", In: Ahlemann, F., Stettiner, E., Messerschmidt, M. and Legner, C. (eds.) *Strategic Enterprise Architecture Management: Challenges, Best Practices, and Future Developments*, Berlin: Springer, pp. 201-227.

Beeson, I., Green, S., Sa, J. and Sully, A. (2002) "Linking Business Processes and Information Systems Provision in a Dynamic Environment", *Information Systems Frontiers*, Vol. 4, No. 3, pp. 317-329.

Beijer, P. and de Klerk, T. (2010) *IT Architecture: Essential Practice for IT Business Solutions*, Raleigh, NC: Lulu.com.

Benbasat, I. and Zmud, R. W. (1999) "Empirical Research in Information Systems: The Practice of Relevance", *MIS Quarterly*, Vol. 23, No. 1, pp. 3-16.

Benjamin, R. I., Rockart, J. F., Scott Morton, M. S. and Wyman, J. (1984) "Information Technology: A Strategic Opportunity", *MIT Sloan Management Review*, Vol. 25, No. 3, pp. 3-10.

Bennis, W. G. and O'Toole, J. (2005) "How Business Schools Lost Their Way", *Harvard Business Review*, Vol. 83, No. 5, pp. 96-104.

Bente, S., Bombosch, U. and Langade, S. (2012) *Collaborative Enterprise Architecture: Enriching EA with Lean, Agile, and Enterprise 2.0 Practices*, Waltham, MA: Morgan Kaufmann.

Bergman, M., Lyytinen, K. and Mark, G. (2007) "Boundary Objects in Design: An Ecological View of Design Artifacts", *Journal of the Association for Information Systems*, Vol. 8, No. 11, pp. 546-568.

Bernard, S. A. (2004) *An Introduction to Enterprise Architecture (1st Edition)*, Bloomington, IN: AuthorHouse.

Bernard, S. A. (2006) "Using Enterprise Architecture to Integrate Strategic, Business, and Technology Planning", *Journal of Enterprise Architecture*, Vol. 2, No. 4, pp. 11-28.

Bernard, S. A. (2009) "The Importance of Formal Documentation in Enterprise Architectures", *Journal of Enterprise Architecture*, Vol. 5, No. 3, pp. 29-58.

Bernard, S. A. (2012) *An Introduction to Enterprise Architecture (3rd Edition)*, Bloomington, IN: AuthorHouse.

Bernus, P. (2009) "The Future of Enterprise Engineering", In: Doucet, G., Gotze, J., Saha, P. and Bernard, S. (eds.) *Coherency Management: Architecting the Enterprise for Alignment, Agility and Assurance*, Bloomington, IN: AuthorHouse, pp. 431-449.

Bernus, P. and Nemes, L. (1996) "A Framework to Define a Generic Enterprise Reference Architecture and Methodology", *Computer Integrated Manufacturing Systems*, Vol. 9, No. 3, pp. 179-191.

Beynon-Davies, P. (1994) "Information Management in the British National Health Service: The Pragmatics of Strategic Data Planning", *International Journal of Information Management*, Vol. 14, No. 2, pp. 84-94.

BIAN (2017) "BIAN Service Landscape 5.0", Banking Industry Architecture Network (BIAN), URL: http://www.bian.org/deliverables/bian-standards/bian-service-landscape-5-0/.

Birkinshaw, J. M. and Mol, M. J. (2006) "How Management Innovation Happens", *MIT Sloan Management Review*, Vol. 47, No. 4, pp. 81-88.

Bittler, R. S. and Burton, B. (2011) "How to Restart and Re-energize an Enterprise Architecture Program" (#G00214385), Stamford, CT: Gartner.

Bittler, R. S. and Kreizman, G. (2005) "Gartner Enterprise Architecture Process: Evolution 2005" (#G00130849), Stamford, CT: Gartner.

Blomqvist, S., Halen, M. and Helenius, M. (2015) "Connecting Enterprise Architecture with Strategic Planning Processes: Case Study of a Large Nordic Finance Organization", In: Kornyshova, E. (ed.) *Proceedings of the 17th IEEE Conference on Business Informatics*, Lisbon: IEEE, pp. 43-50.

Bloomberg, J. (2014) "Is Enterprise Architecture Completely Broken?", Forbes, URL: http://www.forbes.com/sites/jasonbloomberg/2014/07/11/is-enterprise-architecture-completely-broken/.

Blosch, M. and Short, J. (2012) "Seven Best Practices for Building an Enterprise Architecture Consultant Relationship That Adds Long-Term Value" (#G00233849), Stamford, CT: Gartner.

Blosch, M. and Short, J. (2013) "How to Get Business Value from Enterprise Architecture Consultants" (#G00248517), Stamford, CT: Gartner.

Blumenthal, A. (2007) "The Long View: Enterprise Architecture Plans Are Useless Without Clear, Relevant Information", *Government Executive*, Vol. 39, No. 8, p. 63.

Blumenthal, S. C. (1969) *Management Information Systems: A Framework for Planning and Development*, Englewood Cliffs, NJ: Prentice Hall.

Boar, B. H. (1999a) "A Blueprint for Solving Problems in Your IT Architecture", *IT Professional*, Vol. 1, No. 6, pp. 23-29.

Boar, B. H. (1999b) *Constructing Blueprints for Enterprise IT Architectures*, New York, NY: Wiley.

Bock, D. B., Klepper, R. W. and Sumner, M. R. (1992) "Avoiding the Pitfalls of Implementing Enterprisewide Modeling", *Data Resource Management*, Vol. 3, No. 2, pp. 13-21.

Booch, G., Rumbaugh, J. and Jacobson, I. (2005) *The Unified Modeling Language User Guide (2nd Edition)*, Boston, MA: Addison-Wesley Professional.

Boynton, A. C. and Zmud, R. W. (1984) "An Assessment of Critical Success Factors", *MIT Sloan Management Review*, Vol. 25, No. 4, pp. 17-27.

BPMN (2011) "Business Process Model and Notation (BPMN), Version 2.0", Object Management Group (OMG), URL: http://www.omg.org/spec/BPMN/2.0/.

Bradley, R. V., Pratt, R. M., Byrd, T. A., Outlay, C. N. and Wynn Jr, D. E. (2012) "Enterprise Architecture, IT Effectiveness and the Mediating Role of IT Alignment in US Hospitals", *Information Systems Journal*, Vol. 22, No. 2, pp. 97-127.

Bradley, R. V., Pratt, R. M., Byrd, T. A. and Simmons, L. L. (2011) "The Role of Enterprise Architecture in the Quest for IT Value", *MIS Quarterly Executive*, Vol. 10, No. 2, pp. 73-80.

Brancheau, J. C. and Wetherbe, J. C. (1987) "Key Issues in Information Systems Management", *MIS Quarterly*, Vol. 11, No. 1, pp. 23-45.

Brand, S. (2014) "Market Guide for Business-Outcome-Driven Enterprise Architecture Consulting" (#G00269141), Stamford, CT: Gartner.

Brand, S. (2015) "Magic Quadrant for Enterprise Architecture Consultancies" (#G00276891), Stamford, CT: Gartner.

Brickley, J. A., Smith, C. W. and Zimmerman, J. L. (1997) "Management Fads and Organizational Architecture", *Journal of Applied Corporate Finance*, Vol. 10, No. 2, pp. 24-39.

Broadbent, M., Hansell, A., Dampney, C., Gilmour, P. and Hardy, G. (1989) "Information Systems Management: Strategic Concerns and Priorities", *International Journal of Information Management*, Vol. 9, No. 1, pp. 7-18.

Broadbent, M. and Kitzis, E. (2005) *The New CIO Leader: Setting the Agenda and Delivering Results*, Boston, MA: Harvard Business School Press.

Broadbent, M. and Weill, P. (1993) "Improving Business and Information Strategy Alignment: Learning from the Banking Industry", *IBM Systems Journal*, Vol. 32, No. 1, pp. 162-179.

Broadbent, M. and Weill, P. (1997) "Management by Maxim: How Business and IT Managers Can Create IT Infrastructures", *MIT Sloan Management Review*, Vol. 38, No. 3, pp. 77-92.

Brown, A. and Obitz, T. (2011) "Enterprise Architecture Is Maturing: Findings from the Infosys Enterprise Architecture Survey 2007", Bangalore, India: Infosys.

Brown, D. W., Bell, R. C. and Mountford, J. (1990) "Strategic Planning of Business Operations and Information Systems", *British Telecommunications Engineering*, Vol. 9, No. 2, pp. 16-19.

Brown, I. (2010) "Strategic Information Systems Planning: Comparing Espoused Beliefs with Practice", In: Alexander, T., Turpin, M. and van Deventer, J. P. (eds.) *Proceedings of the 18th European Conference on Information Systems*, Pretoria, South Africa: Association for Information Systems, pp. 1-12.

BSP (1975) "Business Systems Planning: Information Systems Planning Guide (1st Edition)" (#GE20-0527-1), White Plains, NY: IBM Corporation.

BSP (1984) "Business Systems Planning: Information Systems Planning Guide (4th Edition)" (#GE20-0527-4), Atlanta, GA: IBM Corporation.

Buckl, S., Ernst, A. M., Lankes, J., Matthes, F. and Schweda, C. M. (2009) "State of the Art in Enterprise Architecture Management", Munich, Germany: Software Engineering for Business Information Systems (SEBIS).

Bui, Q. N. (2012) "Making Connections: A Typological Theory on Enterprise Architecture Features and Organizational Outcomes", In: Jessup, L. and Valacich, J. (eds.) *Proceedings of the 18th Americas Conference on Information Systems*, Seattle, WA: Association for Information Systems, pp. 1-9.

Bui, Q. N. (2017) "Evaluating Enterprise Architecture Frameworks Using Essential Elements", *Communications of the Association for Information Systems*, Vol. 41, No. 1, pp. 121-149.

Bullen, C. V. and Rockart, J. F. (1981) "A Primer on Critical Success Factors", Cambridge, MA: Center for Information Systems Research (CISR), MIT Sloan School of Management.

Burke, B. (2003) "Enterprise Architecture or City Planning?" (#Delta 2638), Stamford, CT: META Group.

Burke, B. and Smith, M. (2009) "The CFO's Essential Guide to Enterprise Architecture" (#G00167209), Stamford, CT: Gartner.

Burke, W. W. and Litwin, G. H. (1992) "A Causal Model of Organizational Performance and Change", *Journal of Management*, Vol. 18, No. 3, pp. 523-545.

Burn, J. M. (1996) "IS Innovation and Organizational Alignment - A Professional Juggling Act", *Journal of Information Technology*, Vol. 11, No. 1, pp. 3-12.

Burn, J. M. and Szeto, C. (2000) "A Comparison of the Views of Business and IT Management on Success Factors for Strategic Alignment", *Information and Management*, Vol. 37, No. 4, pp. 197-216.

Burns, P., Neutens, M., Newman, D. and Power, T. (2009) "Building Value Through Enterprise Architecture: A Global Study", London: Booz & Company.

Burton, B. (2010) "Eight Business Capability Modeling Best Practices" (#G00175782), Stamford, CT: Gartner.

Burton, B. (2011) "Thirteen Worst EA Practices" (#G00214881), Stamford, CT: Gartner.

Burton, B. (2012) "Eight Business Capability Modeling Best Practices Enhance Business and IT Collaboration" (#G00245455), Stamford, CT: Gartner.

Burton, B. and Bittler, R. S. (2011) "You Are Not Alone: Common Reasons Why EA Efforts Need to Be Restarted" (#G00215131), Stamford, CT: Gartner.

Burton, B., Short, J. and Blosch, M. (2012) "Global Profile of Enterprise Architecture Use of and Spending on EA Consultancies" (#G00231476), Stamford, CT: Gartner.

Byrd, T. A., Lewis, B. R. and Bryan, R. W. (2006) "The Leveraging Influence of Strategic Alignment on IT Investment: An Empirical Examination", *Information and Management*, Vol. 43, No. 3, pp. 308-321.

C4ISR (1997) "C4ISR Architecture Framework, Version 2.0", Arlington County, VA: Department of Defense.

Cameron, B. H. and McMillan, E. (2013) "Analyzing the Current Trends in Enterprise Architecture Frameworks", *Journal of Enterprise Architecture*, Vol. 9, No. 1, pp. 60-71.

Campbell, B. (2005) "Alignment: Resolving Ambiguity within Bounded Choices", In: Wei, C.-P. and Yen, B. (eds.) *Proceedings of the 9th Pacific Asia Conference on Information Systems*, Bangkok: Association for Information Systems, pp. 656-669.

Cantara, M., Burton, B. and Scheibenreif, D. (2016a) "Eight Best Practices for Creating High-Impact Business Capability Models" (#G00314568), Stamford, CT: Gartner.

Cantara, M., Burton, B., Weldon, L. and Scheibenreif, D. (2016b) "Three Things CIOs Can Say to Get CEOs Excited About Business Capability Modeling" (#G00320029), Stamford, CT: Gartner.

Carbone, J. A. (2004) *IT Architecture Toolkit*, Upper Saddle River, NJ: Prentice Hall.

Carlile, P. R. (2002) "A Pragmatic View of Knowledge and Boundaries: Boundary Objects in New Product Development", *Organization Science*, Vol. 13, No. 4, pp. 442-455.

Carlile, P. R. (2004) "Transferring, Translating, and Transforming: An Integrative Framework for Managing Knowledge Across Boundaries", *Organization Science*, Vol. 15, No. 5, pp. 555-568.

Carlson, W. M. (1979) "Business Information Analysis and Integration Technique (BIAIT): The New Horizon", *DATA BASE for Advances in Information Systems*, Vol. 10, No. 4, pp. 3-9.

Carlton, D. (2012) "How to Develop Your Applications Portfolio Using the Pace-Layered Model" (#G00233308), Stamford, CT: Gartner.

Carlton, D., Duggan, J. and Mangi, L. (2012) "Use the Pace-Layered Application Strategy to Understand Your Applications Portfolio" (#G00232225), Stamford, CT: Gartner.

Carr, N. G. (2003) "IT Doesn't Matter", *Harvard Business Review*, Vol. 81, No. 5, pp. 41-49.

Carson, P. P., Lanier, P. A., Carson, K. D. and Birkenmeier, B. J. (1999) "A Historical Perspective on Fad Adoption and Abandonment", *Journal of Management History*, Vol. 5, No. 6, pp. 320-333.

Carson, P. P., Lanier, P. A., Carson, K. D. and Guidry, B. N. (2000) "Clearing a Path Through the Management Fashion Jungle: Some Preliminary Trailblazing", *Academy of Management Journal*, Vol. 43, No. 6, pp. 1143-1158.

Carter, R. B., Nilakanta, S. and Norris, D. (1990) "Information Systems Planning: A Case Study", *Journal of Systems Management*, Vol. 41, No. 7, pp. 10-15.

Carter, R. B., Nilakanta, S. and Norris, D. (1991) "Strategic Planning for Information Systems: The Evidence from a Successful Implementation in an Academic Setting", *Journal of Research on Computing in Education*, Vol. 24, No. 2, pp. 280-288.

Cash, J. I. and Konsynski, B. R. (1985) "IS Redraws Competitive Boundaries", *Harvard Business Review*, Vol. 63, No. 2, pp. 134-142.

Caudle, S. L., Gorr, W. L. and Newcomer, K. E. (1991) "Key Information Systems Management Issues for the Public Sector", *MIS Quarterly*, Vol. 15, No. 2, pp. 171-188.

Cerpa, N. and Verner, J. M. (1998) "Case Study: The Effect of IS Maturity on Information Systems Strategic Planning", *Information and Management*, Vol. 34, No. 4, pp. 199-208.

Chan, Y. E. (2002) "Why Haven't We Mastered Alignment? The Importance of the IT Informal Organizational Structure", *MIS Quarterly Executive*, Vol. 1, No. 2, pp. 97-112.

Chan, Y. E., Huff, S. L., Barclay, D. W. and Copeland, D. G. (1997) "Business Strategic Orientation, Information Systems Strategic Orientation, and Strategic Alignment", *Information Systems Research*, Vol. 8, No. 2, pp. 125-150.

Chan, Y. E. and Reich, B. H. (2007) "IT Alignment: What Have We Learned?", *Journal of Information Technology*, Vol. 22, No. 4, pp. 297-315.

Chan, Y. E., Sabherwal, R. and Thatcher, J. B. (2006) "Antecedents and Outcomes of Strategic IS Alignment: An Empirical Investigation", *IEEE Transactions on Engineering Management*, Vol. 53, No. 1, pp. 27-47.

Chandler, A. D. (1962) *Strategy and Structure: Chapters in the History of the Industrial Enterprise*, Cambridge, MA: MIT Press.

Checkland, P. (1981) *Systems Thinking, Systems Practice*, New York, NY: Wiley.

Cheung, S. C. (1990) "Avoiding the Pitfalls of Information Systems Planning", *Data Resource Management*, Vol. 1, No. 3, pp. 16-22.

Christensen, C. M. (1997) *The Innovator's Dilemma: When New Technologies Cause Great Firms to Fail*, Boston, MA: Harvard Business School Press.

Ciborra, C. U. (1997) "De Profundis? Deconstructing the Concept of Strategic Alignment", *Scandinavian Journal of Information Systems*, Vol. 9, No. 1, pp. 67-82.

CIMOSA (1993) *CIMOSA: Open System Architecture for CIM (2nd Edition)*, Berlin: Springer-Verlag.

Clemons, E. K. (1986) "Information Systems for Sustainable Competitive Advantage", *Information and Management*, Vol. 11, No. 3, pp. 131-136.

Cohen, M. D., March, J. G. and Olsen, J. P. (1972) "A Garbage Can Model of Organizational Choice", *Administrative Science Quarterly*, Vol. 17, No. 1, pp. 1-25.

Cohen, W. M. and Levinthal, D. A. (1990) "Absorptive Capacity: A New Perspective on Learning and Innovation", *Administrative Science Quarterly*, Vol. 35, No. 1, pp. 128-152.

Cohn, A. M. (1981) "Planning the Business Data Environment", *Journal of Systems Management*, Vol. 32, No. 9, pp. 31-33.

Coltman, T., Tallon, P., Sharma, R. and Queiroz, M. (2015) "Strategic IT Alignment: Twenty-Five Years On", *Journal of Information Technology*, Vol. 30, No. 2, pp. 91-100.

Colville, R. J. (2012) "IT Service View CMDB Vendor Landscape, 2012" (#G00230009), Stamford, CT: Gartner.

Colville, R. J. and Greene, J. (2014a) "Build Your CMDB Ecosystem with Your Enterprise Architecture Tool" (#G00268772), Stamford, CT: Gartner.

Colville, R. J. and Greene, J. (2014b) "Critical Capabilities for Configuration Management Database" (#G00258266), Stamford, CT: Gartner.

Connor, D. A. (1988) *Computer Systems Development: STrategic Resource Information Planning and Execution - STRIPE*, Englewood Cliffs, NJ: Prentice Hall.

Conrath, D. W., Ang, J. S. and Mattay, S. (1992) "Strategic Planning for Information Systems: A Survey of Canadian Organizations", *INFOR: Information Systems and Operational Research*, Vol. 30, No. 4, pp. 364-378.

Cook, M. A. (1996) *Building Enterprise Information Architectures: Reengineering Information Systems*, Upper Saddle River, NJ: Prentice Hall.

Corbin, D. S. (1988) "Strategic IRM Plan: User Involvement Spells Success", *Journal of Systems Management*, Vol. 39, No. 5, pp. 12-16.

Couger, J. D. (1973) "Evolution of Business System Analysis Techniques", *Computing Surveys*, Vol. 5, No. 3, pp. 167-198.

Covington, R. and Jahangir, H. (2009) "The Oracle Enterprise Architecture Framework", Redwood Shores, CA: Oracle.

Cragg, P., King, M. and Hussin, H. (2002) "IT Alignment and Firm Performance in Small Manufacturing Firms", *Journal of Strategic Information Systems*, Vol. 11, No. 2, pp. 109-132.

Daigneau, R. (2011) *Service Design Patterns: Fundamental Design Solutions for SOAP/WSDL and RESTful Web Services*, Boston, MA: Addison-Wesley Professional.

Dam, S. H. (2015) *DoD Architecture Framework 2.0: A Guide to Applying Systems Engineering to Develop Integrated, Executable Architectures*, Manassas, VA: SPEC Innovations.

Davenport, T. H. (1986) "What's Worked, What Hasn't", *Computerworld*, Vol. 20, No. 40, pp. 19-20.

Davenport, T. H. (1994) "Saving IT's Soul: Human-Centered Information Management", *Harvard Business Review*, Vol. 72, No. 2, pp. 119-131.

Davenport, T. H. (1997) "Putting the Enterprise into the Enterprise System", *Harvard Business Review*, Vol. 76, No. 4, pp. 121-131.

Davenport, T. H. (2000) *Mission Critical: Realizing the Promise of Enterprise Systems*, Boston, MA: Harvard Business School Press.

Davenport, T. H., Hammer, M. and Metsisto, T. J. (1989) "How Executives Can Shape Their Company's Information Systems", *Harvard Business Review*, Vol. 67, No. 2, pp. 130-134.

Davenport, T. H. and Markus, M. L. (1999) "Rigor vs. Relevance Revisited: Response to Benbasat and Zmud", *MIS Quarterly*, Vol. 23, No. 1, pp. 19-23.

Davenport, T. H., Prusak, L. and Wilson, H. J. (2003a) *What's the Big Idea? Creating and Capitalizing on the Best New Management Thinking*, Boston, MA: Harvard Business School Press.

Davenport, T. H., Prusak, L. and Wilson, H. J. (2003b) "Who's Bringing You Hot Ideas (and How Are You Responding)?", *Harvard Business Review*, Vol. 81, No. 2, pp. 58-65.

Davenport, T. H. and Stoddard, D. B. (1994) "Reengineering: Business Change of Mythic Proportions?", *MIS Quarterly*, Vol. 18, No. 2, pp. 121-127.

Davids, A. (1992) *Practical Information Engineering: The Management Challenge*, London: Pitman Publishing.

Davies, T. R. and Hale, W. M. (1986) "Implementing a Policy and Planning Process for Managing State Use of Information Technology Resources", *Public Administration Review*, Vol. 46, No. Special Issue, pp. 516-521.

Dean, D. L., Lowry, P. B. and Humpherys, S. (2011) "Profiling the Research Productivity of Tenured Information Systems Faculty at U.S. Institutions", *MIS Quarterly*, Vol. 35, No. 1, pp. 1-8.

Dean, N. J. (1968) "The Computer Comes of Age", *Harvard Business Review*, Vol. 46, No. 1, pp. 83-91.

Dearden, J. (1965) "How to Organize Information Systems", *Harvard Business Review*, Vol. 43, No. 2, pp. 65-73.

DeFeo, J. (1982) "Management of a Systems Strategy", In: Goldberg, R. and Lorin, H. (eds.) *The Economics of Information Processing (Volume 1: Management Perspectives)*, New York, NY: Wiley, pp. 32-43.

Dennis, A. R., Valacich, J. S., Fuller, M. A. and Schneider, C. (2006) "Research Standards for Promotion and Tenure in Information Systems", *MIS Quarterly*, Vol. 30, No. 1, pp. 1-12.

Dickson, G. W., Leitheiser, R. L., Wetherbe, J. C. and Nechis, M. (1984) "Key Information Systems Issues for the 1980's", *MIS Quarterly*, Vol. 8, No. 3, pp. 135-159.

Dietz, J. L. and Hoogervorst, J. A. (2011) "A Critical Investigation of TOGAF - Based on the Enterprise Engineering Theory and Practice", In: Albani, A., Dietz, J. L. and Verelst, J. (eds.) *Advances in Enterprise Engineering V*, Berlin: Springer, pp. 76-90.

Dietz, J. L. G., Hoogervorst, J. A. P., Albani, A., Aveiro, D., Babkin, E., Barjis, J., Caetano, A., Huysmans, P., Iijima, J., van Kervel, S., Mulder, H., Op't Land, M., Proper, H. A., Sanz, J., Terlouw, L., Tribolet, J., Verelst, J. and Winter, R. (2013) "The Discipline of Enterprise Engineering", *International Journal of Organisational Design and Engineering*, Vol. 3, No. 1, pp. 86-114.

DiGirolamo, V. (2009) "Gauging the Value of Strategic IT Planning and Enterprise Architecture", *Architecture and Governance Magazine*, Vol. 5, No. 7, pp. 8-10.

DoC (2007) "Enterprise Architecture Capability Maturity Model, Version 1.2", Washington, DC: Department of Commerce.

DoDAF (2007a) "The DoDAF Architecture Framework, Version 1.5 (Volume I: Definitions and Guidelines)", Arlington County, VA: Department of Defense.

DoDAF (2007b) "The DoDAF Architecture Framework, Version 1.5 (Volume II: Product Descriptions)", Arlington County, VA: Department of Defense.

DoDAF (2007c) "The DoDAF Architecture Framework, Version 1.5 (Volume III: Architecture Data Description)", Arlington County, VA: Department of Defense.

DoDAF (2009) "The DoDAF Architecture Framework, Version 2.0", Arlington County, VA: Department of Defense.

Doherty, N. F., Marples, C. G. and Suhaimi, A. (1999) "The Relative Success of Alternative Approaches to Strategic Information Systems Planning: An Empirical Analysis", *Journal of Strategic Information Systems*, Vol. 8, No. 3, pp. 263-283.

Donaldson, L. and Hilmer, F. G. (1998) "Management Redeemed: The Case Against Fads that Harm Management", *Organizational Dynamics*, Vol. 26, No. 4, pp. 7-21.

Doolin, B. and McLeod, L. (2012) "Sociomateriality and Boundary Objects in Information Systems Development", *European Journal of Information Systems*, Vol. 21, No. 5, pp. 570-586.

Doumeingts, G. (1989) "GRAI Approach to Designing and Controlling Advanced Manufacturing System in CIM Environment", In: Nof, S. Y. and Moodie, C. L. (eds.) *Advanced Information Technologies for Industrial Material Flow Systems*, Berlin: Springer, pp. 461-529.

Dreyfus, D. (2007) "Information System Architecture: Toward a Distributed Cognition Perspective", In: Gallupe, B. and Pinsonneault, A. (eds.) *Proceedings of the 28th International Conference on Information Systems*, Montreal, Canada: Association for Information Systems, pp. 1-15.

EAAF (2009) "Enterprise Architecture Assessment Framework v3.1", Washington, DC: Office of Management and Budget.

Earl, M. J. (1990) "Approaches to Strategic Information Systems Planning: Experience in Twenty-One United Kingdom Companies", In: DeGross, J. I., Alavi, M. and Oppelland, H. J. (eds.) *Proceedings of the 11th International Conference on Information Systems*, Copenhagen: Association for Information Systems, pp. 271-277.

Earl, M. J. (1993) "Experiences in Strategic Information Systems Planning", *MIS Quarterly*, Vol. 17, No. 1, pp. 1-24.

Earl, M. J. (1996) "Research Round-Up: 1. Information Systems Strategy... Why Planning Techniques Are Not the Answer", *Business Strategy Review*, Vol. 7, No. 1, pp. 54-58.

Edelman, D. C. and Singer, M. (2015) "Competing on Customer Journeys", *Harvard Business Review*, Vol. 93, No. 11, pp. 88-100.

Erder, M. and Pureur, P. (2006) "Transitional Architectures for Enterprise Evolution", *IT Professional*, Vol. 8, No. 3, pp. 10-17.

Evans, M. K. and Hague, L. R. (1962) "Master Plan for Information Systems", *Harvard Business Review*, Vol. 40, No. 1, pp. 92-103.

Evernden, R. (2015) "The Architect Role - What Kind of Architect Are You?", *Journal of Enterprise Architecture*, Vol. 11, No. 2, pp. 28-30.

Falconer, D. J. and Hodgett, R. A. (1997) "Strategic Information Systems Planning, an Australian Experience", In: Gupta, J. (ed.) *Proceedings of the 3rd Americas Conference on Information Systems*, Indianapolis, IN: Association for Information Systems, pp. 1-4.

Falconer, D. J. and Hodgett, R. A. (1998) "An Australian Evaluation of Earl's Five Strategic IS Planning Approaches", In: Baets, W. R. J. (ed.) *Proceedings of the 6th European Conference on Information Systems*, Aix-en-Provence, France: Association for Information Systems, pp. 1101-1108.

FEA (2001) "A Practical Guide to Federal Enterprise Architecture, Version 1.0", Springfield, VA: Chief Information Officer Council.

FEA (2007) "FEA Practice Guidance", Washington, DC: Office of Management and Budget.

FEA (2012) "The Common Approach to Federal Enterprise Architecture", Washington, DC: Office of Management and Budget.

FEAF (1999) "Federal Enterprise Architecture Framework, Version 1.1", Springfield, VA: Chief Information Officer Council.

FEAF (2013) "Federal Enterprise Architecture Framework, Version 2", Washington, DC: Office of Management and Budget.

FEAPO (2013) "A Common Perspective on Enterprise Architecture", University Park, PA: The Federation of Enterprise Architecture Professional Organizations (FEAPO).

Feeny, D. F. and Willcocks, L. P. (1998) "Core IS Capabilities for Exploiting Information Technology", *MIT Sloan Management Review*, Vol. 39, No. 3, pp. 9-21.

Fehskens, L. (2015) "Len's Lens - Introduction to an Editor's Series", *Journal of Enterprise Architecture*, Vol. 11, No. 1, pp. 23-27.

Fenn, J. and Raskino, M. (2008) *Mastering the Hype Cycle: How to Choose the Right Innovation at the Right Time*, Boston, MA: Harvard Business School Press.

Fidler, C., Rogerson, S. and Spiers, N. (1993) "Current IS Practices within UK-Based Institutions", *Information Management and Computer Security*, Vol. 1, No. 2, pp. 13-20.

Findlay, D. (2006) "Enterprise Architecture in the Federal Aviation Administration Air Traffic Organization", *Journal of Enterprise Architecture*, Vol. 2, No. 2, pp. 28-33.

Finkelstein, C. (1981) "Information Engineering (Reprint of Computerworld Issues Dated May 11, May 25, June 1, June 8 and June 15 of 1981)", Englewood Cliffs, NJ: Prentice Hall.

Finkelstein, C. (1989) *An Introduction to Information Engineering: From Strategic Planning to Information Systems*, Sydney, Australia: Addison-Wesley.

Finkelstein, C. (1991) "Together at Last", *Computerworld*, Vol. 25, No. 50, pp. 91-94.

Finkelstein, C. (1992) *Information Engineering: Strategic Systems Development*, Sydney, Australia: Addison-Wesley.

Finkelstein, C. (2006a) *Enterprise Architecture for Integration: Rapid Delivery Methods and Technologies*, Boston, MA: Artech House.

Finkelstein, C. (2006b) "Information Engineering Methodology", In: Bernus, P., Mertins, K. and Schmidt, G. (eds.) *Handbook on Architectures of Information Systems (2nd Edition)*, Berlin: Springer, pp. 459-483.

Finnegan, P. and Fahy, M. J. (1993) "Planning for Information Systems Resources?", *Journal of Information Technology*, Vol. 8, No. 3, pp. 127-138.

Flynn, D. J. and Goleniewska, E. (1993) "A Survey of the Use of Strategic Information Systems Planning Approaches in UK Organizations", *Journal of Strategic Information Systems*, Vol. 2, No. 4, pp. 292-315.

Flynn, D. J. and Hepburn, P. A. (1994) "Strategic Planning for Information Systems - A Case Study of a UK Metropolitan Council", *European Journal of Information Systems*, Vol. 3, No. 3, pp. 207-217.

Fonstad, N. O. (2006a) "Engagement Matters: Enhancing Alignment with Governance Mechanisms", Cambridge, MA: Center for Information Systems Research (CISR), MIT Sloan School of Management.

Fonstad, N. O. (2006b) "Expanding the Value from Outsourcing: The Role of Engagement Mechanisms", Cambridge, MA: Center for Information Systems Research (CISR), MIT Sloan School of Management.

Fonstad, N. O. (2007) "Enhancing Engagement at BT: An Update", Cambridge, MA: Center for Information Systems Research (CISR), MIT Sloan School of Management.

Fonstad, N. O. and Robertson, D. (2004) "Realizing IT-Enabled Change: The IT Engagement Model", Cambridge, MA: Center for Information Systems Research (CISR), MIT Sloan School of Management.

Fonstad, N. O. and Robertson, D. (2005) "Engaging for Change: An Overview of the IT Engagement Model", Cambridge, MA: Center for Information Systems Research (CISR), MIT Sloan School of Management.

Fonstad, N. O. and Robertson, D. (2006a) "Linking Mechanisms at TD Banknorth", Cambridge, MA: Center for Information Systems Research (CISR), MIT Sloan School of Management.

Fonstad, N. O. and Robertson, D. (2006b) "Transforming a Company, Project by Project: The IT Engagement Model", *MIS Quarterly Executive*, Vol. 5, No. 1, pp. 1-14.

Forrester (2017) "Forrester Wave", Forrester, URL: https://www.forrester.com/marketing/policies/forrester-wave-methodology.html.

Fowler, M. (2002) *Patterns of Enterprise Application Architecture*, Boston, MA: Addison-Wesley Professional.

Fowler, M. (2003) *UML Distilled: A Brief Guide to the Standard Object Modeling Language (3rd Edition)*, Boston, MA: Addison-Wesley Professional.

Frank, U. (2002) "Multi-Perspective Enterprise Modeling (MEMO) - Conceptual Framework and Modeling Languages", In: Sprague, R. H. (ed.) *Proceedings of the 35th Hawaii International Conference on System Sciences*, Big Island, HI: IEEE, pp. 1258-1267.

Galbraith, J. R. (1973) *Designing Complex Organizations*, Reading, MA: Addison-Wesley.

Galbraith, J. R. (1977) *Organization Design*, Reading, MA: Addison-Wesley.

Gall, N. (2012) "Gartner's 2011 Global Enterprise Architecture Survey: EA Frameworks Are Still Homemade and Hybrid" (#G00226400), Stamford, CT: Gartner.

Galliers, R. D. (1986) "A Failure of Direction", *Business Computing and Communications*, Vol. 5, No. 7, pp. 32-38.

Galliers, R. D. (1987a) "Applied Research in Information Systems Planning", In: Feldman, P., Bhabuta, L. and Holloway, S. (eds.) *Information Management and Planning: Database 87, 14-16 April 1987, Craiglockhart Conference Centre, Edinburgh*, Brookfield, VT: Gower Technical, pp. 45-58.

Galliers, R. D. (1987b) "Information Systems Planning in the United Kingdom and Australia - A Comparison of Current Practice", In: Zorkoczy, P. I. (ed.) *Oxford Surveys in Information Technology, Volume 4*, Oxford, UK: Oxford University Press, pp. 223-255.

Galliers, R. D. (1987c) "Information Systems Planning: A Manifesto for Australian-Based Research", *Australian Computer Journal*, Vol. 19, No. 2, pp. 49-55.

Galliers, R. D. (1988) "Information Technology Strategies Today: The UK Experience", In: Earl, M. (ed.) *Information Management: The Strategic Dimension*, Oxford, UK: Clarendon Press, pp. 179-201.

Galliers, R. D., Merali, Y. and Spearing, L. (1994) "Coping with Information Technology? How British Executives Perceive the Key Information Systems Management Issues in the Mid-1990s", *Journal of Information Technology*, Vol. 9, No. 3, pp. 223-238.

Gallo, T. E. (1988) *Strategic Information Management Planning*, Englewood Cliffs, NJ: Prentice Hall.

Gamma, E., Helm, R., Johnson, R. and Vlissides, J. (1994) *Design Patterns: Elements of Reusable Object-Oriented Software*, Boston, MA: Addison-Wesley Professional.

GAO (1992) "Strategic Information Planning: Framework for Designing and Developing System Architectures" (#GAO/IMTEC-92-51), Washington, DC: Government Accountability Office.

GAO (1994) "Executive Guide: Improving Mission Performance Through Strategic Information Management and Technology" (#GAO/AIMD-94-115), Washington, DC: Government Accountability Office.

GAO (2002) "Information Technology: Enterprise Architecture Use Across the Federal Government Can Be Improved" (#GAO-02-6), Washington, DC: Government Accountability Office.

GAO (2003a) "A Framework for Assessing and Improving Enterprise Architecture Management (Version 1.1)" (#GAO-03-584G), Washington, DC: Government Accountability Office.

GAO (2003b) "Information Technology: Leadership Remains Key to Agencies Making Progress on Enterprise Architecture Efforts" (#GAO-04-40), Washington, DC: Government Accountability Office.

GAO (2006) "Enterprise Architecture: Leadership Remains Key to Establishing and Leveraging Architectures for Organizational Transformation" (#GAO-06-831), Washington, DC: Government Accountability Office.

GAO (2010) "A Framework for Assessing and Improving Enterprise Architecture Management (Version 2.0)" (#GAO-10-846G), Washington, DC: Government Accountability Office.

GAO (2011) "Opportunities to Reduce Potential Duplication in Government Programs, Save Tax Dollars, and Enhance Revenue" (#GAO-11-318SP), Washington, DC: Government Accountability Office.

GAO (2015) "DOD Business Systems Modernization: Additional Action Needed to Achieve Intended Outcomes" (#GAO-15-627), Washington, DC: Government Accountability Office.

Garrity, J. T. (1963) "Top Management and Computer Profits", *Harvard Business Review*, Vol. 41, No. 4, pp. 6-12.

Gartner (2017) "Gartner Magic Quadrant", Gartner, URL: http://www.gartner.com/technology/research/methodologies/research_mq.jsp.

Gaver, S. B. (2010) "Why Doesn't the Federal Enterprise Architecture Work?", McLean, VA: Technology Matters.

Gerber, S., Meyer, U. and Richert, C. (2007) "EA Model as Central Part of the Transformation Into a More Flexible and Powerful Organisation", In: Reichert, M., Strecker, S. and Turowski, K. (eds.) *Proceedings of the 2nd International Workshop on Enterprise Modelling and Information Systems Architectures*, St. Goar, Germany: Gesellschaft fur Informatik, pp. 23-32.

Gerow, J. E., Grover, V. and Thatcher, J. (2016) "Alignment's Nomological Network: Theory and Evaluation", *Information and Management*, Vol. 53, No. 5, pp. 541-553.

Gerow, J. E., Grover, V., Thatcher, J. B. and Roth, P. L. (2014) "Looking Toward the Future of IT-Business Strategic Alignment Through the Past: A Meta-Analysis", *MIS Quarterly*, Vol. 38, No. 4, pp. 1059-1085.

Gerow, J. E., Thatcher, J. B. and Grover, V. (2015) "Six Types of IT-Business Strategic Alignment: An Investigation of the Constructs and Their Measurement", *European Journal of Information Systems*, Vol. 24, No. 5, pp. 465-491.

Ghymn, K. I. and King, W. R. (1976) "Design of a Strategic Planning Management Information System", *OMEGA*, Vol. 4, No. 5, pp. 595-607.

Gibson, J. W. and Tesone, D. V. (2001) "Management Fads: Emergence, Evolution, and Implications for Managers", *Academy of Management Executive*, Vol. 15, No. 4, pp. 122-133.

Gill, G. and Bhattacherjee, A. (2009) "Whom Are We Informing? Issues and Recommendations for MIS Research from an Informing Science Perspective", *MIS Quarterly*, Vol. 33, No. 2, pp. 217-235.

Gill, J. and Whittle, S. (1992) "Management by Panacea: Accounting for Transience", *Journal of Management Studies*, Vol. 30, No. 2, pp. 281-295.

Gill, S. (1981) "Information System Planning: A Case Review", *Information and Management*, Vol. 4, No. 5, pp. 233-238.

Glans, T. B., Grad, B., Holstein, D., Meyers, W. E. and Schmidt, R. N. (1968a) *Instructor's Manual for Management Systems*, New York, NY: Holt, Rinehart and Winston.

Glans, T. B., Grad, B., Holstein, D., Meyers, W. E. and Schmidt, R. N. (1968b) *Management Systems*, New York, NY: Holt, Rinehart and Winston.

Golden, C. (1994) "A Standard Satellite Control Reference Model", In: Rash, J. L. (ed.) *Proceedings of the 3rd International Symposium on Space Mission Operations and Ground Data Systems*, Greenbelt, MD: NASA, pp. 1205-1212.

Gonzalez, S. (2011) "An Enterprise Architecture for Banking", *Journal of Enterprise Architecture*, Vol. 7, No. 4, pp. 70-79.

Goodhue, D. L., Kirsch, L. J., Quillard, J. A. and Wybo, M. D. (1992) "Strategic Data Planning: Lessons from the Field", *MIS Quarterly*, Vol. 16, No. 1, pp. 11-34.

Goodhue, D. L., Quillard, J. A. and Rockart, J. F. (1986) "The Management of Data: Preliminary Research Results", Cambridge, MA: Center for Information Systems Research (CISR), MIT Sloan School of Management.

Goodhue, D. L., Quillard, J. A. and Rockart, J. F. (1988) "Managing the Data Resource: A Contingency Perspective", *MIS Quarterly*, Vol. 12, No. 3, pp. 373-392.

Gorry, G. A. and Scott Morton, M. S. (1971) "A Framework for Management Information Systems", *MIT Sloan Management Review*, Vol. 13, No. 1, pp. 55-70.

Gosselt, R. W. (2012) "A Maturity Model Based Roadmap for Implementing TOGAF", In: Wijnhoven, F. (ed.) *Proceedings of the 17th Twente Student Conference on IT*, Enschede, The Netherlands: University of Twente, pp. 1-10.

Grant, G. G. (2003) "Strategic Alignment and Enterprise Systems Implementation: The Case of Metalco", *Journal of Information Technology*, Vol. 18, No. 3, pp. 159-175.

Gray, P. (2001) "Introduction to the Special Volume on Relevance", *Communications of the Association for Information Systems*, Vol. 6, No. 1, pp. 1-12.

Greefhorst, D. and Proper, E. (2011) *Architecture Principles: The Cornerstones of Enterprise Architecture*, Berlin: Springer.

Greene, B., McDavid, D. and Zachman, J. A. (1997) "Back to the Issue of the Century", *Database Programming and Design*, Vol. 10, No. 6, pp. 8-9.

Gregor, S., Hart, D. and Martin, N. (2007) "Enterprise Architectures: Enablers of Business Strategy and IS/IT Alignment in Government", *Information Technology and People*, Vol. 20, No. 2, pp. 96-120.

Greiner, L. E. (1972) "Evolution and Revolution as Organizations Grow", *Harvard Business Review*, Vol. 50, No. 3, pp. 37-46.

Greski, L. (2009) "Business Capability Modeling: Theory & Practice", *Architecture and Governance Magazine*, Vol. 5, No. 7, pp. 1-4.

Gunton, T. (1989) *Infrastructure: Building a Framework for Corporate Information Handling*, New York, NY: Prentice Hall.

Hackney, R., Burn, J. and Dhillon, G. (2000) "Challenging Assumptions for Strategic Information Systems Planning: Theoretical Perspectives", *Communications of the Association for Information Systems*, Vol. 3, No. 3, pp. 1-24.

Hadaya, P. and Gagnon, B. (2017) *Business Architecture: The Missing Link in Strategy Formulation, Implementation and Execution*, Montreal, Canada: ASATE Publishing.

Haki, M. K., Legner, C. and Ahlemann, F. (2012) "Beyond EA Frameworks: Towards an Understanding of the Adoption of Enterprise Architecture Management", In: Pries-Heje, J., Chiasson, M., Wareham, J., Busquets, X., Valor, J. and Seiber, S. (eds.) *Proceedings of the 20th European Conference on Information Systems*, Barcelona, Spain: Association for Information Systems, pp. 1-12.

Hambrick, D. C. (2007) "The Field of Management's Devotion to Theory: Too Much of a Good Thing?", *Academy of Management Journal*, Vol. 50, No. 6, pp. 1346-1352.

Hamel, G. (2006) "The Why, What, and How of Management Innovation", *Harvard Business Review*, Vol. 84, No. 2, pp. 72-84.

Hamilton, D. (1999) "Linking Strategic Information Systems Concepts to Practice: Systems Integration at the Portfolio Level", *Journal of Information Technology*, Vol. 14, No. 1, pp. 69-82.

Hammer, M. and Champy, J. A. (1993) *Reengineering the Corporation: A Manifesto for Business Revolution*, New York, NY: HarperBusiness.

Hanseth, O. and Monteiro, E. (1997) "Inscribing Behavior in Information Infrastructure Standards", *Accounting, Management and Information Technologies*, Vol. 7, No. 4, pp. 183-211.

Harrell, J. M. and Sage, A. P. (2010) "Enterprise Architecture and the Ways of Wickedness", *Information, Knowledge, Systems Management*, Vol. 9, No. 3, pp. 197-209.

Hartman, W., Matthes, H. and Proeme, A. (1968) *Management Information Systems Handbook: Analysis, Requirements Determination, Design and Development, Implementation and Evaluation*, Apeldoorn, The Netherlands: Philips-Electrologica.

Hartog, C. and Herbert, M. (1986) "1985 Opinion Survey of MIS Managers: Key Issues", *MIS Quarterly*, Vol. 10, No. 4, pp. 351-361.

Hartono, E., Lederer, A. L., Sethi, V. and Zhuang, Y. (2003) "Key Predictors of the Implementation of Strategic Information Systems Plans", *DATA BASE for Advances in Information Systems*, Vol. 34, No. 3, pp. 41-53.

Hauder, M., Roth, S., Matthes, F. and Schulz, C. (2013) "An Examination of Organizational Factors Influencing Enterprise Architecture Management Challenges", In: van Hillegersberg, J., van Heck, E. and Connolly, R. (eds.) *Proceedings of the 21st European Conference on Information Systems*, Utrecht, The Netherlands: Association for Information Systems, pp. 1-12.

Hayes, R. H. and Nolan, R. L. (1974) "What Kind of Corporate Modeling Functions Best?", *Harvard Business Review*, Vol. 52, No. 3, pp. 102-112.

Hazen, B. T., Kung, L., Cegielski, C. G. and Jones-Farmer, L. A. (2014) "Performance Expectancy and Use of Enterprise Architecture: Training as an Intervention", *Journal of Enterprise Information Management*, Vol. 27, No. 2, pp. 180-196.

Head, R. V. (1971) "Automated System Analysis", *Datamation*, Vol. 17, No. 16, pp. 22-24.

Henderson, J. C. and Venkatraman, N. (1993) "Strategic Alignment: Leveraging Information Technology for Transforming Organizations", *IBM Systems Journal*, Vol. 32, No. 1, pp. 4-16.

Henderson, J. C. and West, J. M. (1979) "Planning for MIS: A Decision-Oriented Approach", *MIS Quarterly*, Vol. 3, No. 2, pp. 45-58.

Herbert, M. and Hartog, C. (1986) "MIS Rates the Issues", *Datamation*, Vol. 32, No. 22, pp. 79-86.

Hermans, P. (2015) "The Zachman Framework for Architecture Revisited by Paul Hermans", Zachman International, URL: https://www.zachman.com/resources/ea-articles-reference/321-the-zachman-framework-for-architecture-revisited-by-paul-hermans.

Hobbs, G. (2012) "EAM Governance and Organisation", In: Ahlemann, F., Stettiner, E., Messerschmidt, M. and Legner, C. (eds.) *Strategic Enterprise Architecture Management: Challenges, Best Practices, and Future Developments*, Berlin: Springer, pp. 81-110.

Hoffman, J. and Martino, C. (1983) "Information Systems Planning to Meet Business Objectives: A Survey of Practices", New York, NY: Cresap, McCormick and Paget.

Hohpe, G. and Woolf, B. (2004) *Enterprise Integration Patterns: Designing, Building, and Deploying Messaging Solutions*, Boston, MA: Addison-Wesley Professional.

Holcman, S. B. (2013) *Reaching the Pinnacle: A Methodology of Business Understanding, Technology Planning, and Change*, Pinckney, MI: Pinnacle Business Group Inc.

Holcman, S. B. (2014) "State of Practice of Enterprise Architecture" (#0615669875), Pinckney, MI: Pinnacle Business Group Inc.

Holst, M. S. and Steensen, T. W. (2011) "The Successful Enterprise Architecture Effort", *Journal of Enterprise Architecture*, Vol. 7, No. 4, pp. 16-22.

Holt, J. and Perry, S. (2010) *Modelling Enterprise Architectures*, Stevenage: The Institution of Engineering and Technology.

Honeywell (1968) *Business Information Systems Analysis & Design: Student Reference Guide*, Wellesley Hills, MA: Honeywell Inc.

Hoos, I. R. (1960) "When the Computer Takes Over the Office", *Harvard Business Review*, Vol. 38, No. 4, pp. 102-112.

Hopper, M. D. (1990) "Rattling SABRE - New Ways to Compete on Information", *Harvard Business Review*, Vol. 68, No. 3, pp. 118-125.

Hungerford, P. (2007) "The Syngenta Architecture Story", In: Saha, P. (ed.) *Handbook of Enterprise Systems Architecture in Practice*, Hershey, PA: Information Science Reference, pp. 331-350.

Hungerford, P. (2009) "The Evolving Role of Enterprise Architecture within Syngenta", In: Doucet, G., Gotze, J., Saha, P. and Bernard, S. (eds.) *Coherency Management: Architecting the Enterprise for Alignment, Agility and Assurance*, Bloomington, IN: AuthorHouse, pp. 307-328.

IBM (2006) "An Introduction to IBM's Enterprise Architecture Consulting Method", Armonk, NY: IBM Global Services.

Inmon, W. H. (1986) *Information Systems Architecture: A System Developer's Primer*, Englewood Cliffs, NJ: Prentice Hall.

Inmon, W. H. (1988) *Information Engineering for the Practitioner: Putting Theory into Practice*, Englewood Cliffs, NJ: Yourdon Press.

Inmon, W. H. and Caplan, J. H. (1992) *Information Systems Architecture: Development in the 90's*, New York, NY: Wiley.

Ireland, C., Bowers, D., Newton, M. and Waugh, K. (2009) "A Classification of Object-Relational Impedance Mismatch", In: Chen, Q., Cuzzocrea, A., Hara, T., Hunt, E. and Popescu, M. (eds.) *Proceedings of the 1st International Conference on Advances in Databases, Knowledge, and Data Applications*, Gosier, Guadeloupe, France: IEEE, pp. 36-43.

Ives, B. and Learmonth, G. P. (1984) "The Information System as a Competitive Weapon", *Communications of the ACM*, Vol. 27, No. 12, pp. 1193-1201.

Jacobson, I. (2007) "Enterprise Architecture Failed Big Way!", Ivar Jacobson International, URL: http://blog.ivarjacobson.com/ea-failed-big-way/.

James, G. A. (2008) "Findings: Elements for Successful EA in Government Agencies" (#G00157190), Stamford, CT: Gartner.

James, G. A. and Colville, R. J. (2006) "Enterprise Architecture Tools and Configuration Management Databases Are Similar but Different" (#G00137222), Stamford, CT: Gartner.

Janssen, M. and Hjort-Madsen, K. (2007) "Analyzing Enterprise Architecture in National Governments: The Cases of Denmark and the Netherlands", In: Sprague, R. H. (ed.) *Proceedings of the 40th Hawaii International Conference on System Sciences*, Big Island, HI: IEEE, pp. 1-10.

Jaques, E. (1990) "In Praise of Hierarchy", *Harvard Business Review*, Vol. 68, No. 1, pp. 127-133.

Jaques, E. and Clement, S. D. (1994) *Executive Leadership: A Practical Guide to Managing Complexity*, Arlington, VA: Wiley-Blackwell.

Jarvenpaa, S. L. and Ives, B. (1991) "Executive Involvement and Participation in the Management of Information Technology", *MIS Quarterly*, Vol. 15, No. 2, pp. 205-227.

Jennex, M. E. (2001) "Research Relevance - You Get What You Reward", *Communications of the Association for Information Systems*, Vol. 6, No. 1, pp. 49-52.

Kallgren, A., Ullberg, J. and Johnson, P. (2009) "A Method for Constructing a Company Specific Enterprise Architecture Model Framework", In: Kim, H.-K. and Lee, R. (eds.) *Proceedings of the 10th ACIS International Conference on Software Engineering, Artificial Intelligence, Networking and Parallel/Distributed Computing*, Daegu, South Korea: IEEE, pp. 346-351.

Kanter, J. and Miserendino, J. (1987) "Systems Architectures Link Business Goals and IS Strategies", *Data Management*, Vol. 25, No. 11, pp. 17-25.

Kappelman, L., McGinnis, T., Pettite, A. and Sidorova, A. (2008) "Enterprise Architecture: Charting the Territory for Academic Research", In: Benbasat, I. and Montazemi, A. R. (eds.) *Proceedings of the 14th Americas Conference on Information Systems*, Toronto, Canada: Association for Information Systems, pp. 1-10.

Kappelman, L., McLean, E., Johnson, V. and Gerhart, N. (2014) "The 2014 SIM IT Key Issues and Trends Study", *MIS Quarterly Executive*, Vol. 13, No. 4, pp. 237-263.

Kappelman, L., McLean, E., Johnson, V. and Torres, R. (2016) "The 2015 SIM IT Issues and Trends Study", *MIS Quarterly Executive*, Vol. 15, No. 1, pp. 55-83.

Kappelman, L., McLean, E., Johnson, V., Torres, R., Nguyen, Q., Maurer, C. and David, A. (2018) "The 2017 SIM IT Issues and Trends Study", *MIS Quarterly Executive*, Vol. 17, No. 1, pp. 53-88.

Kappelman, L., McLean, E., Johnson, V., Torres, R., Nguyen, Q., Maurer, C. and Snyder, M. (2017) "The 2016 SIM IT Issues and Trends Study", *MIS Quarterly Executive*, Vol. 16, No. 1, pp. 47-80.

Kappelman, L., McLean, E., Luftman, J. and Johnson, V. (2013) "Key Issues of IT Organizations and Their Leadership: The 2013 SIM IT Trends Study", *MIS Quarterly Executive*, Vol. 12, No. 4, pp. 227-240.

Kappelman, L. A. (2010) "The Pioneers of Enterprise Architecture: A Panel Discussion", In: Kappelman, L. A. (ed.) *The SIM Guide to Enterprise Architecture*, Boca Raton, FL: CRC Press, pp. 9-26.

Kearns, G. S. and Lederer, A. L. (2000) "The Effect of Strategic Alignment on the Use of IS-Based Resources for Competitive Advantage", *Journal of Strategic Information Systems*, Vol. 9, No. 4, pp. 265-293.

Keller, W. (2015) "Using Capability Models for Strategic Alignment", In: Simon, D. and Schmidt, C. (eds.) *Business Architecture Management: Architecting the Business for Consistency and Alignment*, Berlin: Springer, pp. 107-122.

Kemp, P. and McManus, J. (2009) "Whither Enterprise Architecture?", *ITNOW Computing Journal*, Vol. 51, No. 2, pp. 20-21.

Kerner, D. V. (1979) "Business Information Characterization Study", *DATA BASE for Advances in Information Systems*, Vol. 10, No. 4, pp. 10-17.

Kerner, D. V. (1982) "Business Information Control Study Methodology", In: Goldberg, R. and Lorin, H. (eds.) *The Economics of Information Processing (Volume 1: Management Perspectives)*, New York, NY: Wiley, pp. 71-83.

Kerr, J. M. (1989) "A Blueprint for Information Systems", *Database Programming and Design*, Vol. 2, No. 9, pp. 60-67.

Khosroshahi, P. A., Hauder, M., Volkert, S., Matthes, F. and Gernegross, M. (2018) "Business Capability Maps: Current Practices and Use Cases for Enterprise Architecture Management", In: Bui, T. X. (ed.) *Proceedings of the 51st Hawaii International Conference on System Sciences*, Big Island, HI: IEEE, pp. 4603-4612.

Khoury, G. R. and Simoff, S. J. (2004) "Enterprise Architecture Modelling Using Elastic Metaphors", In: Hartmann, S. and Roddick, J. F. (eds.) *Proceedings of the 1st Asia-Pacific Conference on Conceptual Modelling*, Dunedin, New Zealand: Australian Computer Society, pp. 65-69.

Kiat, S. E., Chiew, L. H., Hong, P. S. and Fung, C. C. (2008) "The Organization's Compass - Enterprise Architecture", *Journal of Enterprise Architecture*, Vol. 4, No. 1, pp. 11-19.

Kieser, A. (1997) "Rhetoric and Myth in Management Fashion", *Organization*, Vol. 4, No. 1, pp. 49-74.

Kim, Y.-G. and Everest, G. C. (1994) "Building an IS Architecture: Collective Wisdom from the Field", *Information and Management*, Vol. 26, No. 1, pp. 1-11.

King, W. R. (1978) "Strategic Planning for Management Information Systems", *MIS Quarterly*, Vol. 2, No. 1, pp. 27-37.

King, W. R. (1983) "Planning for Strategic Decision Support Systems", *Long Range Planning*, Vol. 16, No. 5, pp. 73-78.

King, W. R. (1984) "Exploiting Information as a Strategic Business Resource", *International Journal of Policy and Information*, Vol. 8, No. 1, pp. 1-8.

King, W. R. (1995) "Creating a Strategic Capabilities Architecture", *Information System Management*, Vol. 12, No. 1, pp. 67-69.

King, W. R. and Cleland, D. I. (1975) "The Design of Management Information Systems: An Information Analysis Approach", *Management Science*, Vol. 22, No. 3, pp. 286-297.

Kock, N., Gray, P., Hoving, R., Klein, H., Myers, M. D. and Rockart, J. (2002) "IS Research Relevance Revisited: Subtle Accomplishment, Unfulfilled Promise, or Serial Hypocrisy?", *Communications of the Association for Information Systems*, Vol. 8, No. 1, pp. 330-346.

Korhonen, J. J. and Poutanen, J. (2013) "Tripartite Approach to Enterprise Architecture", *Journal of Enterprise Architecture*, Vol. 9, No. 1, pp. 28-38.

Kosanke, K., Vernadat, F. and Zelm, M. (1999) "CIMOSA: Enterprise Engineering and Integration", *Computers in Industry*, Vol. 40, No. 2, pp. 83-97.

Kotter, J. P. (1982) "What Effective General Managers Really Do", *Harvard Business Review*, Vol. 60, No. 6, pp. 156-167.

Kotusev, S. (2016a) "The Critical Scrutiny of TOGAF", British Computer Society (BCS), URL: http://www.bcs.org/content/conWebDoc/55892.

Kotusev, S. (2016b) "Different Approaches to Enterprise Architecture", *Journal of Enterprise Architecture*, Vol. 12, No. 4, pp. 9-16.

Kotusev, S. (2016c) "Enterprise Architecture Frameworks: The Fad of the Century", British Computer Society (BCS), URL: http://www.bcs.org/content/conWebDoc/56347.

Kotusev, S. (2016d) "Enterprise Architecture Is Not TOGAF", British Computer Society (BCS), URL: http://www.bcs.org/content/conWebDoc/55547.

Kotusev, S. (2016e) "The History of Enterprise Architecture: An Evidence-Based Review", *Journal of Enterprise Architecture*, Vol. 12, No. 1, pp. 29-37.

Kotusev, S. (2016f) "One Minute Enterprise Architecture", British Computer Society (BCS), URL: http://www.bcs.org/content/conWebDoc/56198.

Kotusev, S. (2016g) "Six Types of Enterprise Architecture Artifacts", British Computer Society (BCS), URL: http://www.bcs.org/content/conWebDoc/57097.

Kotusev, S. (2016h) "Two Worlds of Enterprise Architecture", Melbourne, Australia: Unpublished manuscript.

Kotusev, S. (2017a) "Conceptual Model of Enterprise Architecture Management", *International Journal of Cooperative Information Systems*, Vol. 26, No. 3, pp. 1-36.

Kotusev, S. (2017b) "Critical Questions in Enterprise Architecture Research", *International Journal of Enterprise Information Systems*, Vol. 13, No. 2, pp. 50-62.

Kotusev, S. (2017c) "Eight Essential Enterprise Architecture Artifacts", British Computer Society (BCS), URL: http://www.bcs.org/content/conWebDoc/57318.

Kotusev, S. (2017d) "Enterprise Architecture on a Single Page", British Computer Society (BCS), URL: http://www.bcs.org/content/conWebDoc/58615.

Kotusev, S. (2017e) "Enterprise Architecture: What Did We Study?", *International Journal of Cooperative Information Systems*, Vol. 26, No. 4, pp. 1-84.

Kotusev, S. (2017f) "The Relationship Between Enterprise Architecture Artifacts", British Computer Society (BCS), URL: http://www.bcs.org/content/conWebDoc/57563.

Kotusev, S. (2018) "TOGAF-Based Enterprise Architecture Practice: An Exploratory Case Study", *Communications of the Association for Information Systems*, Vol. 43, No. 1, pp. 321-359.

Kotusev, S., Singh, M. and Storey, I. (2015a) "Consolidating Enterprise Architecture Management Research", In: Bui, T. X. and Sprague, R. H. (eds.) *Proceedings of the 48th Hawaii International Conference on System Sciences*, Kauai, HI: IEEE, pp. 4069-4078.

Kotusev, S., Singh, M. and Storey, I. (2015b) "Investigating the Usage of Enterprise Architecture Artifacts", In: Becker, J., vom Brocke, J. and de Marco, M. (eds.) *Proceedings of the 23rd European Conference on Information Systems*, Munster, Germany: Association for Information Systems, pp. 1-12.

Kotusev, S., Singh, M. and Storey, I. (2016) "Enterprise Architecture Practice in Retail: Problems and Solutions", *Journal of Enterprise Architecture*, Vol. 12, No. 3, pp. 28-39.

Kotusev, S., Singh, M. and Storey, I. (2017) "A Frameworks-Free Look at Enterprise Architecture", *Journal of Enterprise Architecture*, Vol. 13, No. 1, pp. 15-21.

Kriebel, C. H. (1968) "The Strategic Dimension of Computer Systems Planning", *Long Range Planning*, Vol. 1, No. 1, pp. 7-12.

Kruchten, P. (2003) *The Rational Unified Process: An Introduction (3rd Edition)*, Boston, MA: Addison-Wesley Professional.

Kuruzovich, J., Bassellier, G. and Sambamurthy, V. (2012) "IT Governance Processes and IT Alignment: Viewpoints from the Board of Directors", In: Sprague, R. H. (ed.) *Proceedings of the 45th Hawaii International Conference on System Sciences*, Maui, HI: IEEE, pp. 5043-5052.

Lagerstrom, R., Sommestad, T., Buschle, M. and Ekstedt, M. (2011) "Enterprise Architecture Management's Impact on Information Technology Success", In: Sprague, R. H. (ed.) *Proceedings of the 44th Hawaii International Conference on System Sciences*, Kauai, HI: IEEE, pp. 1-10.

Langenberg, K. and Wegmann, A. (2004) "Enterprise Architecture: What Aspects Is Current Research Targeting?" (#IC/2004/77), Lausanne, Switzerland: Ecole Polytechnique Federale de Lausanne.

Lankhorst, M. (2013) *Enterprise Architecture at Work: Modelling, Communication and Analysis (3rd Edition)*, Berlin: Springer.

Lankhorst, M. M., Quartel, D. A. and Steen, M. W. (2010) "Architecture-Based IT Portfolio Valuation", In: Harmsen, F., Proper, E., Schalkwijk, F., Barjis, J. and Overbeek, S. (eds.) *Proceedings of the 2nd Working Conference on Practice-Driven Research on Enterprise Transformation*, Delft, The Netherlands: Springer, pp. 78-106.

Lapalme, J. (2012) "Three Schools of Thought on Enterprise Architecture", *IT Professional*, Vol. 14, No. 6, pp. 37-43.

Lapkin, A. and Allega, P. (2010) "Ten Criteria for Choosing an External Service Provider for Your EA Effort" (#G00174157), Stamford, CT: Gartner.

Lapkin, A., Allega, P., Burke, B., Burton, B., Bittler, R. S., Handler, R. A., James, G. A., Robertson, B., Newman, D., Weiss, D., Buchanan, R. and Gall, N. (2008) "Gartner Clarifies the Definition of the Term 'Enterprise Architecture'" (#G00156559), Stamford, CT: Gartner.

Lasden, M. (1981) "Long-Range Planning: Curse or Blessing?", *Computer Decisions*, Vol. 13, No. 2, pp. 102-113.

Laudon, K. C. and Laudon, J. P. (2013) *Management Information Systems: Managing the Digital Firm (13th Edition)*, Boston, MA: Pearson Education Limited.

Le Fevre, A. and Pattison, L. (1986) "Planning for Hospital Information Systems Using the Lancaster Soft Systems Methodology", *Australian Computer Journal*, Vol. 18, No. 4, pp. 180-185.

Leavitt, H. J. (1965) "Applied Organizational Change in Industry: Structural, Technological and Humanistic Approaches", In: March, J. G. (ed.) *Handbook of Organizations*, Chicago, IL: Rand McNally College Publishing Company, pp. 1144-1170.

Lederer, A. L. and Gardiner, V. (1992a) "The Process of Strategic Information Planning", *Journal of Strategic Information Systems*, Vol. 1, No. 2, pp. 76-83.

Lederer, A. L. and Gardiner, V. (1992b) "Strategic Information Systems Planning: The Method/1 Approach", *Information Systems Management*, Vol. 9, No. 3, pp. 13-20.

Lederer, A. L. and Mendelow, A. L. (1986) "Paradoxes of Information Systems Planning", In: Maggi, L., Zmud, R. W. and Wetherbe, J. C. (eds.) *Proceedings of the 7th International Conference on Information Systems*, San Diego, CA: Association for Information Systems, pp. 255-264.

Lederer, A. L. and Mendelow, A. L. (1987) "Information Resource Planning: Overcoming Difficulties in Identifying Top Management's Objectives ", *MIS Quarterly*, Vol. 11, No. 3, pp. 389-399.

Lederer, A. L. and Mendelow, A. L. (1988) "Information Systems Planning: Top Management Takes Control", *Business Horizons*, Vol. 31, No. 3, pp. 73-78.

Lederer, A. L. and Mendelow, A. L. (1989a) "Coordination of Information Systems Plans with Business Plans", *Journal of Management Information Systems*, Vol. 6, No. 2, pp. 5-19.

Lederer, A. L. and Mendelow, A. L. (1989b) "Information Systems Planning: Incentives for Effective Action", *DATA BASE for Advances in Information Systems*, Vol. 20, No. 3, pp. 13-20.

Lederer, A. L. and Mendelow, A. L. (1993) "Information Systems Planning and the Challenge of Shifting Priorities", *Information and Management*, Vol. 24, No. 6, pp. 319-328.

Lederer, A. L. and Putnam, A. G. (1986) "Connecting Systems Objectives to Business Strategy with BSP", *Information Strategy: The Executive's Journal*, Vol. 2, No. 2, pp. 75-89.

Lederer, A. L. and Putnam, A. G. (1987) "Bridging the Gap: Connecting Systems Objectives to Business Strategy with BSP", *Journal of Information Systems Management*, Vol. 4, No. 3, pp. 40-46.

Lederer, A. L. and Sethi, V. (1988) "The Implementation of Strategic Information Systems Planning Methodologies", *MIS Quarterly*, Vol. 12, No. 3, pp. 445-461.

Lederer, A. L. and Sethi, V. (1989) "Pitfalls in Planning", *Datamation*, Vol. 35, No. 11, pp. 59-62.

Lederer, A. L. and Sethi, V. (1992) "Meeting the Challenges of Information Systems Planning", *Long Range Planning*, Vol. 25, No. 2, pp. 69-80.

Lederer, A. L. and Sethi, V. (1996) "Key Prescriptions for Strategic Information Systems Planning", *Journal of Management Information Systems*, Vol. 13, No. 1, pp. 35-62.

Legner, C. and Lohe, J. (2012) "Embedding EAM into Operation and Monitoring", In: Ahlemann, F., Stettiner, E., Messerschmidt, M. and Legner, C. (eds.) *Strategic Enterprise Architecture Management: Challenges, Best Practices, and Future Developments*, Berlin: Springer, pp. 169-199.

Len, B., Paul, C. and Rick, K. (2012) *Software Architecture in Practice (3rd Edition)*, Boston, MA: Addison-Wesley Professional.

Levy, J. D. (1982) "Bridging the Gap with Business Information Systems Planning", *Infosystems*, Vol. 29, No. 6, pp. 82-84.

Lewis, R. F. (1957) "Never Overestimate the Power of a Computer", *Harvard Business Review*, Vol. 35, No. 5, pp. 77-84.

Li, E. Y. and Chen, H.-G. (2001) "Output-Driven Information System Planning: A Case Study", *Information and Management*, Vol. 38, No. 3, pp. 185-199.

Lohe, J. and Legner, C. (2012) "From Enterprise Modelling to Architecture-Driven IT Management? A Design Theory", In: Pries-Heje, J., Chiasson, M., Wareham, J., Busquets, X., Valor, J. and Seiber, S. (eds.) *Proceedings of the 20th European Conference on Information Systems*, Barcelona, Spain: Association for Information Systems, pp. 1-13.

Lohe, J. and Legner, C. (2014) "Overcoming Implementation Challenges in Enterprise Architecture Management: A Design Theory for Architecture-Driven IT Management (ADRIMA)", *Information Systems and e-Business Management*, Vol. 12, No. 1, pp. 101-137.

Longepe, C. (2003) *The Enterprise Architecture IT Project: The Urbanisation Paradigm*, London: Kogan Page Science.

Luftman, J. (2005) "Key Issues for IT Executives 2004", *MIS Quarterly Executive*, Vol. 4, No. 2, pp. 269-285.

Luftman, J. and Ben-Zvi, T. (2010a) "Key Issues for IT Executives 2009: Difficult Economy's Impact on IT", *MIS Quarterly Executive*, Vol. 9, No. 1, pp. 49-59.

Luftman, J. and Ben-Zvi, T. (2010b) "Key Issues for IT Executives 2010: Judicious IT Investments Continue Post-Recession", *MIS Quarterly Executive*, Vol. 9, No. 4, pp. 263-273.

Luftman, J. and Ben-Zvi, T. (2011) "Key Issues for IT Executives 2011: Cautious Optimism in Uncertain Economic Times", *MIS Quarterly Executive*, Vol. 10, No. 4, pp. 203-212.

Luftman, J. and Brier, T. (1999) "Achieving and Sustaining Business-IT Alignment", *California Management Review*, Vol. 42, No. 1, pp. 109-122.

Luftman, J. and Derksen, B. (2012) "Key Issues for IT Executives 2012: Doing More with Less", *MIS Quarterly Executive*, Vol. 11, No. 4, pp. 207-218.

Luftman, J., Derksen, B., Dwivedi, R., Santana, M., Zadeh, H. S. and Rigoni, E. (2015) "Influential IT Management Trends: An International Study", *Journal of Information Technology*, Vol. 30, No. 3, pp. 293-305.

Luftman, J. and Kempaiah, R. (2008) "Key Issues for IT Executives 2007", *MIS Quarterly Executive*, Vol. 7, No. 2, pp. 99-112.

Luftman, J., Kempaiah, R. and Nash, E. (2006) "Key Issues for IT Executives 2005", *MIS Quarterly Executive*, Vol. 5, No. 2, pp. 81-99.

Luftman, J., Kempaiah, R. and Rigoni, E. H. (2009) "Key Issues for IT Executives 2008", *MIS Quarterly Executive*, Vol. 8, No. 3, pp. 151-159.

Luftman, J., Lyytinen, K. and Ben-Zvi, T. (2017) "Enhancing the Measurement of Information Technology (IT) Business Alignment and Its Influence on Company Performance", *Journal of Information Technology*, Vol. 32, No. 1, pp. 26-46.

Luftman, J. and McLean, E. (2004) "Key Issues for IT Executives", *MIS Quarterly Executive*, Vol. 3, No. 2, pp. 89-104.

Luftman, J., Papp, R. and Brier, T. (1999) "Enablers and Inhibitors of Business-IT Alignment", *Communications of the Association for Information Systems*, Vol. 1, No. 3, pp. 1-33.

Luftman, J. and Zadeh, H. S. (2011) "Key Information Technology and Management Issues 2010-11: An International Study", *Journal of Information Technology*, Vol. 26, No. 3, pp. 193-204.

Luftman, J., Zadeh, H. S., Derksen, B., Santana, M., Rigoni, E. H. and Huang, Z. D. (2012) "Key Information Technology and Management Issues 2011-2012: An International Study", *Journal of Information Technology*, Vol. 27, No. 3, pp. 198-212.

Luftman, J., Zadeh, H. S., Derksen, B., Santana, M., Rigoni, E. H. and Huang, Z. D. (2013) "Key Information Technology and Management Issues 2012-2013: An International Study", *Journal of Information Technology*, Vol. 28, No. 4, pp. 354-366.

Luftman, J. N., Lewis, P. R. and Oldach, S. H. (1993) "Transforming the Enterprise: The Alignment of Business and Information Technology Strategies", *IBM Systems Journal*, Vol. 32, No. 1, pp. 198-221.

Lux, J. and Ahlemann, F. (2012) "Embedding EAM into the Project Life Cycle", In: Ahlemann, F., Stettiner, E., Messerschmidt, M. and Legner, C. (eds.) *Strategic Enterprise Architecture Management: Challenges, Best Practices, and Future Developments*, Berlin: Springer, pp. 141-168.

Lynch, N. (2006) "Enterprise Architecture - How Does It Work in the Australian Bureau of Statistics?", In: Spencer, S. and Jenkins, A. (eds.) *Proceedings of the 17th Australasian Conference on Information Systems*, Adelaide, Australia: Association for Information Systems, pp. 1-14.

Lyzenski, S. (2008) "Making the Business Case for Enterprise Architecture", *Journal of Enterprise Architecture*, Vol. 4, No. 3, pp. 13-27.

Magalhaes, R., Zacarias, M. and Tribolet, J. (2007) "Making Sense of Enterprise Architectures as Tools of Organizational Self-Awareness (OSA)", In: Lankhorst, M. M. and Johnson, P. (eds.) *Proceedings of the 2nd Trends in Enterprise Architecture Research Workshop*, St. Gallen, Switzerland: Telematica Instituut, pp. 61-69.

Maholic, J. (2013) *Business Cases that Mean Business: A Practical Guide to Identifying, Calculating and Communicating the Value of Large Scale IT Projects*, North Charleston, SC: CreateSpace Independent Publishing Platform.

Mainelli, M. R. and Miller, D. R. (1988) "Strategic Planning for Information Systems at British Rail", *Long Range Planning*, Vol. 21, No. 4, pp. 65-75.

Mangi, L. and Gaughan, D. (2015) "How to Develop a Pace-Layered Application Strategy" (#G00276478), Stamford, CT: Gartner.

Manwani, S. and Bossert, O. (2016) "EA Survey Findings: The Challenges and Responses for Enterprise Architects in the Digital Age", *Journal of Enterprise Architecture*, Vol. 12, No. 3, pp. 6-9.

Marca, D. A. and McGowan, C. L. (2005) *IDEF0 and SADT: A Modeler's Guide*, Auburndale, MA: OpenProcess, Inc.

Marenghi, C. and Zachman, J. A. (1982) "Data Design Key to Systems: IBM Consultant", *Computerworld*, Vol. 16, No. 43, pp. 11-12.

Martin, B. L., Batchelder, G., Newcomb, J., Rockart, J. F., Yetter, W. P. and Grossman, J. H. (1995) "The End of Delegation? Information Technology and the CEO", *Harvard Business Review*, Vol. 73, No. 5, pp. 161-172.

Martin, J. (1982a) "An Overall Plan", *Computerworld*, Vol. 16, No. 40, pp. 17-32.

Martin, J. (1982b) *Strategic Data-Planning Methodologies*, Englewood Cliffs, NJ: Prentice Hall.

Martin, J. (1989) *Information Engineering (Book I: Introduction, Book II: Planning and Analysis, Book III: Design and Construction)*, Englewood Cliffs, NJ: Prentice Hall.

Martin, J. and Finkelstein, C. (1981) *Information Engineering (Volumes I and II)*, Carnforth, UK: Savant Institute.

Martin, J. and Leben, J. (1989) *Strategic Information Planning Methodologies (2nd Edition)*, Englewood Cliffs, NJ: Prentice Hall.

Martinsons, M. G. and Hosley, S. (1993) "Planning a Strategic Information System for a Market-Oriented Non-Profit Organization", *Journal of Systems Management*, Vol. 44, No. 2, pp. 14-41.

Matthes, D. (2011) *Enterprise Architecture Frameworks Kompendium: Über 50 Rahmenwerke für das IT-Management*, Berlin: Springer.

McAfee, A. (2011) "What Every CEO Needs to Know About the Cloud", *Harvard Business Review*, Vol. 89, No. 11, pp. 124-132.

McFarlan, F. W. (1971) "Problems in Planning the Information System", *Harvard Business Review*, Vol. 49, No. 2, pp. 75-89.

McFarlan, F. W. (1984) "Information Technology Changes the Way You Compete", *Harvard Business Review*, Vol. 62, No. 3, pp. 98-103.

McGahan, A. M. (2004) "How Industries Change", *Harvard Business Review*, Vol. 82, No. 10, pp. 86-94.

McGregor, M. (2015) "Critical Capabilities for Enterprise Architecture Tools" (#G00274824), Stamford, CT: Gartner.

McGregor, M. (2016) "Magic Quadrant for Enterprise Architecture Tools" (#G00294575), Stamford, CT: Gartner.

McLean, E. R. and Soden, J. V. (1977) *Strategic Planning for MIS*, New York, NY: Wiley.

Meiklejohn, I. (1986) "Who Are the IT Strategists?", *Business Computing and Communications*, Vol. 5, No. 5, pp. 47-55.

Mentzas, G. (1997) "Implementing an IS Strategy - A Team Approach", *Long Range Planning*, Vol. 30, No. 1, pp. 84-95.

Mertins, K. and Jochem, R. (2005) "Architectures, Methods and Tools for Enterprise Engineering", *International Journal of Production Economics*, Vol. 98, No. 2, pp. 179-188.

Miller, D. (1992) "The Icarus Paradox: How Exceptional Companies Bring About Their Own Downfall", *Business Horizons*, Vol. 35, No. 1, pp. 24-35.

Miller, D. and Hartwick, J. (2002) "Spotting Management Fads", *Harvard Business Review*, Vol. 80, No. 10, pp. 26-27.

Miller, D., Hartwick, J. and Le Breton-Miller, I. (2004) "How to Detect a Management Fad - And Distinguish It From a Classic", *Business Horizons*, Vol. 47, No. 4, pp. 7-16.

Min, S. K., Suh, E.-H. and Kim, S.-Y. (1999) "An Integrated Approach Toward Strategic Information Systems Planning", *Journal of Strategic Information Systems*, Vol. 8, No. 4, pp. 373-394.

Mintzberg, H. (1971) "Managerial Work: Analysis from Observation", *Management Science*, Vol. 18, No. 2, pp. 97-110.

Mintzberg, H. (1972) "The Myths of MIS", *California Management Review*, Vol. 15, No. 1, pp. 92-97.

Mintzberg, H. (1973) *The Nature of Managerial Work*, New York, NY: Harper and Row.

Mintzberg, H. (1975) "The Manager's Job: Folklore and Fact", *Harvard Business Review*, Vol. 53, No. 4, pp. 49-61.

Mocker, M. (2012) "2012-07 Enterprise Architecture Research at MIT", MIT Sloan CIO Symposium, Boston, MA, URL: https://www.youtube.com/watch?v=9IGQm4-HheA.

Molnar, W. A. and Proper, H. A. (2013) "Engineering an Enterprise: Practical Issues of Two Case Studies from the Luxembourgish Beverage and Tobacco Industry", In: Harmsen, F. and Proper, H. A. (eds.) *Proceedings of the 6th Working Conference on Practice-Driven Research on Enterprise Transformation*, Utrecht, The Netherlands: Springer, pp. 76-91.

Moody, D. L. (2000) "Building Links Between IS Research and Professional Practice: Improving the Relevance and Impact of IS Research", In: Orlikowski, W. J., Ang, S., Weill, P., Krcmar, H. C. and DeGross, J. I. (eds.) *Proceedings of the 21st International Conference on Information Systems*, Brisbane, Australia: Association for Information Systems, pp. 351-360.

Moores, T. T. (1996) "Key Issues in the Management of Information Systems: A Hong Kong Perspective", *Information and Management*, Vol. 30, No. 6, pp. 301-307.

Moynihan, T. (1990) "What Chief Executives and Senior Managers Want from Their IT Departments", *MIS Quarterly*, Vol. 14, No. 1, pp. 15-25.

Munro, M. C. and Wheeler, B. R. (1980) "Planning, Critical Success Factors, and Management's Information Requirements", *MIS Quarterly*, Vol. 4, No. 4, pp. 27-38.

Murer, S., Bonati, B. and Furrer, F. J. (2011) *Managed Evolution: A Strategy for Very Large Information Systems*, Berlin: Springer.

Nadler, D. A. and Tushman, M. L. (1980) "A Model for Diagnosing Organizational Behavior", *Organizational Dynamics*, Vol. 9, No. 2, pp. 35-51.

NASCIO (2003) "NASCIO Enterprise Architecture Maturity Model, Version 1.3", Lexington, KY: National Association of State Chief Information Officers.

Nath, R. (1989) "Aligning MIS with the Business Goals", *Information and Management*, Vol. 16, No. 2, pp. 71-79.

Nicolini, D., Mengis, J. and Swan, J. (2012) "Understanding the Role of Objects in Cross-Disciplinary Collaboration", *Organization Science*, Vol. 23, No. 3, pp. 612-629.

Niederman, F., Brancheau, J. C. and Wetherbe, J. C. (1991) "Information Systems Management Issues for the 1990s", *MIS Quarterly*, Vol. 15, No. 4, pp. 475-500.

Niemann, K. D. (2006) *From Enterprise Architecture to IT Governance: Elements of Effective IT Management*, Wiesbaden: Vieweg.

Niemi, E. and Pekkola, S. (2017) "Using Enterprise Architecture Artefacts in an Organisation", *Enterprise Information Systems*, Vol. 11, No. 3, pp. 313-338.

Nolan, R. L. and Mulryan, D. W. (1987) "Undertaking an Architecture Program", *Stage by Stage*, Vol. 7, No. 2, pp. 1-10.

O'Donnell, G. and Casanova, C. (2009) *The CMDB Imperative: How to Realize the Dream and Avoid the Nightmares*, Upper Saddle River, NJ: Prentice Hall.

Obitz, T. and Babu, M. (2009) "Infosys Enterprise Architecture Survey 2008/2009", Bangalore, India: Infosys.

OGC (2009) *Managing Successful Projects with PRINCE2 (5th Edition)*, London: The Stationery Office.

OMB (2007) "Federal Enterprise Architecture Program EA Assessment Framework 2.2", Washington, DC: Office of Management and Budget.

Orsey, R. R. (1982a) "Business Systems Planning: Management of Information", *Computer Decisions*, Vol. 14, No. 2, pp. 154-158.

Orsey, R. R. (1982b) "Clarifying BSP", *Computer Decisions*, Vol. 14, No. 7, pp. 173-173.

Orsey, R. R. (1982c) "Methodologies for Determining Information Flow", In: Goldberg, R. and Lorin, H. (eds.) *The Economics of Information Processing (Volume 1: Management Perspectives)*, New York, NY: Wiley, pp. 57-70.

Osterle, H., Brenner, W. and Hilbers, K. (1993) *Total Information Systems Management: A European Approach*, Chichester, UK: Wiley.

Osterwalder, A. and Pigneur, Y. (2010) *Business Model Generation: A Handbook for Visionaries, Game Changers, and Challengers*, Hoboken, NJ: Wiley.

Palmer, S. D. (1993) "A Plan That Cured Chaos", *Datamation*, Vol. 39, No. 1, pp. 77-78.

Paper, D. (2001) "Future IS Research: The Criticality of Relevance", *Journal of Information Technology Case and Application Research*, Vol. 3, No. 3, pp. 1-6.

Parker, C. M. (1990) "Developing an Information Systems Architecture: Changing How Data Resource Managers Think About Systems Planning", *Data Resource Management*, Vol. 1, No. 4, pp. 5-11.

Parker, M. M., Trainor, H. E. and Benson, R. J. (1989) *Information Strategy and Economics: Linking Information Systems Strategy to Business Performance*, Englewood Cliffs, NJ.

Parker, T. and Brooks, T. (2008) "Which Comes First, Strategy or Architecture?", *Journal of Enterprise Architecture*, Vol. 4, No. 4, pp. 46-57.

Parker, T. and Idundun, M. (1988) "Managing Information Systems in 1987: The Top Issues for IS Managers in the UK", *Journal of Information Technology*, Vol. 3, No. 1, pp. 34-42.

Parsons, G. L. (1983) "Information Technology: A New Competitive Weapon", *MIT Sloan Management Review*, Vol. 25, No. 1, pp. 3-14.

Pavlak, A. (2006) "Lessons from Classical Architecture", *Journal of Enterprise Architecture*, Vol. 2, No. 2, pp. 20-27.

Pavri, F. and Ang, J. S. (1995) "A Study of the Strategic Planning Practices in Singapore", *Information and Management*, Vol. 28, No. 1, pp. 33-47.

Penrod, J. I. and Douglas, J. V. (1988) "Strategic Planning for Information Resources at the University of Maryland", *Long Range Planning*, Vol. 21, No. 2, pp. 52-62.

Peppard, J. and Ward, J. (1999) "Mind the Gap: Diagnosing the Relationship Between the IT Organisation and the Rest of the Business", *Journal of Strategic Information Systems*, Vol. 8, No. 1, pp. 29-60.

Peppard, J. and Ward, J. (2004) "Beyond Strategic Information Systems: Towards an IS Capability", *Journal of Strategic Information Systems*, Vol. 13, No. 2, pp. 167-194.

Peppard, J., Ward, J. and Daniel, E. (2007) "Managing the Realization of Business Benefits from IT Investments", *MIS Quarterly Executive*, Vol. 6, No. 1, pp. 1-11.

Periasamy, K. P. (1993) "The State and Status of Information Architecture: An Empirical Investigation", In: DeGross, J. I., Bostrom, R. P. and Robey, D. (eds.) *Proceedings of the 14th International Conference on Information Systems*, Orlando, FL: Association for Information Systems, pp. 255-270.

Periasamy, K. P. (1994) *Development and Usage of Information Architecture: A Management Perspective*, PhD Thesis: University of Oxford, UK.

Periasamy, K. P. and Feeny, D. F. (1997) "Information Architecture Practice: Research-Based Recommendations for the Practitioner", *Journal of Information Technology*, Vol. 12, No. 3, pp. 197-205.

Perks, C. and Beveridge, T. (2003) *Guide to Enterprise IT Architecture*, New York, NY: Springer.

Perroud, T. and Inversini, R. (2013) *Enterprise Architecture Patterns: Practical Solutions for Recurring IT-Architecture Problems*, Berlin: Springer.

Pervan, G. P. (1994) "Information Systems Management: An Australian View of the Key Issues", *Australasian Journal of Information Systems*, Vol. 1, No. 2, pp. 32-44.

Peyret, H. and Barnett, G. (2015) "The Forrester Wave: Enterprise Architecture Service Providers, Q1 2015", Cambridge, MA: Forrester.

Pfeffer, J. (1994) "Competitive Advantage Through People", *California Management Review*, Vol. 36, No. 2, pp. 9-28.

Pfeffer, J. and Sutton, R. I. (2006a) "Evidence-Based Management", *Harvard Business Review*, Vol. 84, No. 1, pp. 63-74.

Pfeffer, J. and Sutton, R. I. (2006b) *Hard Facts, Dangerous Half-Truths and Total Nonsense: Profiting from Evidence-Based Management*, Boston, MA: Harvard Business School Press.

Pfeffer, J. and Sutton, R. I. (2006c) "Management Half-Truths and Nonsense: How to Practice Evidence-Based Management", *California Management Review*, Vol. 48, No. 3, pp. 77-100.

Pheng, T. E. and Boon, G. W. (2007) "Enterprise Architecture in the Singapore Government", In: Saha, P. (ed.) *Handbook of Enterprise Systems Architecture in Practice*, Hershey, PA: Information Science Reference, pp. 129-143.

Plessius, H., van Steenbergen, M. and Slot, R. (2014) "Perceived Benefits from Enterprise Architecture", In: Mola, L., Carugati, A., Kokkinaki, A. and Pouloudi, N. (eds.) *Proceedings of the 8th Mediterranean Conference on Information Systems*, Verona, Italy: Association for Information Systems, pp. 1-14.

PMI (2013) *A Guide to the Project Management Body of Knowledge (5th Edition)*, Newtown Square, PA: Project Management Institute.

Porter, M. E. (1980) *Competitive Strategy: Techniques for Analyzing Industries and Competitors*, New York, NY: The Free Press.

Porter, M. E. (1985) *Competitive Advantage: Creating and Sustaining Superior Performance*, New York, NY: The Free Press.

Porter, M. E. (2001) "Strategy and the Internet", *Harvard Business Review*, Vol. 79, No. 3, pp. 62-78.

Potts, C. (2013) "Enterprise Architecture: A Courageous Venture", *Journal of Enterprise Architecture*, Vol. 9, No. 3, pp. 28-31.

Poutanen, J. (2012) "The Social Dimension of Enterprise Architecture in Government", *Journal of Enterprise Architecture*, Vol. 8, No. 2, pp. 19-29.

Premkumar, G. and King, W. R. (1991) "Assessing Strategic Information Systems Planning", *Long Range Planning*, Vol. 24, No. 5, pp. 41-58.

Preston, D. S. and Karahanna, E. (2009) "Antecedents of IS Strategic Alignment: A Nomological Network", *Information Systems Research*, Vol. 20, No. 2, pp. 159-179.

PRISM (1986) "PRISM: Dispersion and Interconnection: Approaches to Distributed Systems Architecture", Cambridge, MA: CSC Index.

Pulkkinen, M. (2006) "Systemic Management of Architectural Decisions in Enterprise Architecture Planning. Four Dimensions and Three Abstraction Levels", In: Sprague, R. H. (ed.) *Proceedings of the 39th Hawaii International Conference on System Sciences*, Kauai, HI: IEEE, pp. 1-9.

Rackoff, N., Wiseman, C. and Ullrich, W. A. (1985) "Information Systems for Competitive Advantage: Implementation of a Planning Process", *MIS Quarterly*, Vol. 9, No. 4, pp. 285-294.

Radeke, F. (2010) "Awaiting Explanation in the Field of Enterprise Architecture Management", In: Santana, M., Luftman, J. N. and Vinze, A. S. (eds.) *Proceedings of the 16th Americas Conference on Information Systems*, Lima: Association for Information Systems, pp. 1-10.

Radeke, F. and Legner, C. (2012) "Embedding EAM into Strategic Planning", In: Ahlemann, F., Stettiner, E., Messerschmidt, M. and Legner, C. (eds.) *Strategic Enterprise Architecture Management: Challenges, Best Practices, and Future Developments*, Berlin: Springer, pp. 111-139.

Rance, S., Rudd, C., Lacy, S. and Hanna, A. (2011) *ITIL Service Transition (2nd Edition)*, London: The Stationery Office.

Rauf, A. (2013) "Leveraging Enterprise Architecture for Reform and Modernization", *Journal of Enterprise Architecture*, Vol. 9, No. 1, pp. 89-93.

Rawson, A., Duncan, E. and Jones, C. (2013) "The Truth About Customer Experience", *Harvard Business Review*, Vol. 91, No. 9, pp. 90-98.

Rayner, N. (2012) "Applying Pace Layering to ERP Strategy" (#G00227719), Stamford, CT: Gartner.

Rees, A. (2011) "Establishing Enterprise Architecture at WA Police", *Journal of Enterprise Architecture*, Vol. 7, No. 3, pp. 49-56.

Reese, R. J. (2008) *I/T Architecture in Action*, Bloomington, IN: Xlibris Corporation.

Reich, B. H. and Benbasat, I. (2000) "Factors that Influence the Social Dimension of Alignment Between Business and Information Technology Objectives", *MIS Quarterly*, Vol. 24, No. 1, pp. 81-113.

Remenyi, D. (1991) *Introducing Strategic Information Systems Planning*, Manchester, UK: NCC Blackwell.

Reponen, T. (1993) "Information Management Strategy - An Evolutionary Process", *Scandinavian Journal of Management*, Vol. 9, No. 3, pp. 189-209.

Richardson, G. L., Jackson, B. M. and Dickson, G. W. (1990) "A Principles-Based Enterprise Architecture: Lessons from Texaco and Star Enterprise", *MIS Quarterly*, Vol. 14, No. 4, pp. 385-403.

Rico, D. F. (2006) "A Framework for Measuring ROI of Enterprise Architecture", *Journal of Organizational and End User Computing*, Vol. 18, No. 2, pp. i-xii.

Ridgway, A. O. (1961) "An Automated Technique for Conducting a Total System Study", In: Howerton, P. W. and Jackson, T. G. (eds.) *Eastern Joint Computer Conference*, Washington, DC: ACM, pp. 306-322.

Rigdon, W. B. (1989) "Architectures and Standards", In: Fong, E. N. and Goldfine, A. H. (eds.) *Information Management Directions: The Integration Challenge (NIST Special Publication 500-167)*, Gaithersburg, MD: National Institute of Standards and Technology (NIST), pp. 135-150.

Rivera, R. (2007) "Am I Doing Architecture or Design Work?", *IT Professional*, Vol. 9, No. 6, pp. 46-48.

Robertson, B. (2010) "Use Analogies to Market Enterprise Architecture" (#G00129426), Stamford, CT: Gartner.

Robertson, D. (2007) "2009 Robertson Enterprise Architecture Speech (What to Tell the Management)", Seminarium om Affarsdriven SOA, Stockholm, URL: https://www.youtube.com/watch?v=aZha3iL-TJA.

Robey, D. and Markus, M. L. (1998) "Beyond Rigor and Relevance: Producing Consumable Research About Information Systems", *Information Resources Management Journal*, Vol. 11, No. 1, pp. 7-15.

Rockart, J. F. (1979) "Chief Executives Define Their Own Data Needs", *Harvard Business Review*, Vol. 57, No. 2, pp. 81-93.

Rockart, J. F. (1988) "The Line Takes the Leadership - IS Management in a Wired Society", *MIT Sloan Management Review*, Vol. 29, No. 4, pp. 57-64.

Rockart, J. F. and Crescenzi, A. D. (1984) "Engaging Top Management in Information Technology", *MIT Sloan Management Review*, Vol. 25, No. 4, pp. 3-16.

Rockart, J. F., Earl, M. J. and Ross, J. W. (1996) "Eight Imperatives for the New IT Organization", *MIT Sloan Management Review*, Vol. 38, No. 1, pp. 43-55.

Rockart, J. F. and Scott Morton, M. S. (1984) "Implications of Changes in Information Technology for Corporate Strategy", *Interfaces*, Vol. 14, No. 1, pp. 84-95.

Roeleven, S. (2010) "Why Two Thirds of Enterprise Architecture Projects Fail", Darmstadt, Germany: Software AG.

Rohloff, M. (2005) "Enterprise Architecture - Framework and Methodology for the Design of Architectures in the Large", In: Bartmann, D., Rajola, F., Kallinikos, J., Avison, D. E., Winter, R., Ein-Dor, P., Becker, J., Bodendorf, F. and Weinhardt, C. (eds.) *Proceedings of the 13th European Conference on Information Systems*, Regensburg, Germany: Association for Information Systems, pp. 1659-1672.

Ross, J. W. (1999) "Surprising Facts About Implementing ERP", *IT Professional*, Vol. 1, No. 4, pp. 65-68.

Ross, J. W. (2005) "Forget Strategy: Focus IT on Your Operating Model", Cambridge, MA: Center for Information Systems Research (CISR), MIT Sloan School of Management.

Ross, J. W. (2011) "Gaining Competitive Advantage from Enterprise Architecture (Executive Seminar: Enabling IT Value Through Enterprise Architecture)", Case Western Reserve University, Cleveland, OH, URL: https://www.youtube.com/watch?v=ScHG63YmJ2k&t=572.

Ross, J. W. and Beath, C. M. (2001) "Strategic IT Investment", Cambridge, MA: Center for Information Systems Research (CISR), MIT Sloan School of Management.

Ross, J. W. and Beath, C. M. (2002) "Beyond the Business Case: New Approaches to IT Investment", *MIT Sloan Management Review*, Vol. 43, No. 2, pp. 51-59.

Ross, J. W. and Beath, C. M. (2011) "Maturity Still Matters: Why a Digitized Platform Is Essential to Business Success", Cambridge, MA: Center for Information Systems Research (CISR), MIT Sloan School of Management.

Ross, J. W. and Beath, C. M. (2012) "Maturity Matters: Generate Value from Enterprise Architecture", *Journal of Enterprise Architecture*, Vol. 8, No. 1, pp. 22-26.

Ross, J. W., Beath, C. M. and Goodhue, D. L. (1996) "Develop Long-Term Competitiveness Through IT Assets", *MIT Sloan Management Review*, Vol. 38, No. 1, pp. 31-42.

Ross, J. W., Beath, C. M. and Quaadgras, A. (2013) "You May Not Need Big Data After All", *Harvard Business Review*, Vol. 91, No. 12, pp. 90-98.

Ross, J. W., Mocker, M. and Sebastian, I. (2014) "Architect Your Business - Not Just IT!", Cambridge, MA: Center for Information Systems Research (CISR), MIT Sloan School of Management.

Ross, J. W. and Weill, P. (2002a) "Distinctive Styles of IT Architecture", Cambridge, MA: Center for Information Systems Research (CISR), MIT Sloan School of Management.

Ross, J. W. and Weill, P. (2002b) "Six IT Decisions Your IT People Shouldn't Make", *Harvard Business Review*, Vol. 80, No. 11, pp. 84-95.

Ross, J. W. and Weill, P. (2005) "Understanding the Benefits of Enterprise Architecture", Cambridge, MA: Center for Information Systems Research (CISR), MIT Sloan School of Management.

Ross, J. W. and Weill, P. (2006) "Enterprise Architecture: Driving Business Benefits from IT (Selected Research Briefings)", Cambridge, MA: Center for Information Systems Research (CISR), MIT Sloan School of Management.

Ross, J. W., Weill, P. and Robertson, D. C. (2006) *Enterprise Architecture as Strategy: Creating a Foundation for Business Execution*, Boston, MA: Harvard Business School Press.

Rosser, B. (2000) "IT Planning: How to Elicit a Business Strategy" (#TU-11-8194), Stamford, CT: Gartner.

Rosser, B. (2002a) "Architectural Styles and Enterprise Architecture" (#AV-17-4384), Stamford, CT: Gartner.

Rosser, B. (2002b) "What Is an Architectural Style?" (#COM-17-7016), Stamford, CT: Gartner.

Roth, S., Hauder, M., Farwick, M., Breu, R. and Matthes, F. (2013) "Enterprise Architecture Documentation: Current Practices and Future Directions", In: Alt, R. and Franczyk, B. (eds.) *Proceedings of the 11th International Conference on Wirtschaftsinformatik*, Leipzig, Germany: Association for Information Systems, pp. 911-925.

Rowley, J. (1994) "Strategic Information Systems Planning: Designing Effective Systems", *Business Executive*, Vol. 8, No. 50, pp. 154-155.

Rush, R. L. (1979) "MIS Planning in Distributed Data-Processing Systems", *Journal of Systems Management*, Vol. 30, No. 8, pp. 17-25.

Sabherwal, R., Hirschheim, R. and Goles, T. (2001) "The Dynamics of Alignment: Insights from a Punctuated Equilibrium Model", *Organization Science*, Vol. 12, No. 2, pp. 179-197.

Saint-Louis, P., Morency, M. C. and Lapalme, J. (2017) "Defining Enterprise Architecture: A Systematic Literature Review", In: Halle, S., Dijkman, R. and Lapalme, J. (eds.) *Proceedings of the 21st IEEE International Enterprise Distributed Object Computing Conference Workshops*, Quebec City, Canada: IEEE, pp. 41-49.

Sakamoto, J. G. (1982) "Use of DB/DC Data Dictionary to Support Business Systems Planning Studies: An Approach", In: Goldberg, R. and Lorin, H. (eds.) *The Economics of Information Processing (Volume 1: Management Perspectives)*, New York, NY: Wiley, pp. 127-136.

Sakamoto, J. G. and Ball, F. W. (1982) "Supporting Business Systems Planning Studies with the DB/DC Data Dictionary", *IBM Systems Journal*, Vol. 21, No. 1, pp. 54-80.

Sarno, R. and Herdiyanti, A. (2010) "A Service Portfolio for an Enterprise Resource Planning", *International Journal of Computer Science and Network Security*, Vol. 10, No. 3, pp. 144-156.

Sauer, C. and Willcocks, L. P. (2002) "The Evolution of the Organizational Architect", *MIT Sloan Management Review*, Vol. 43, No. 3, pp. 41-49.

Scheer, A.-W. (1992) *Architecture of Integrated Information Systems: Foundations of Enterprise Modelling*, Berlin: Springer.

Schekkerman, J. (2004) *How to Survive in the Jungle of Enterprise Architecture Frameworks: Creating or Choosing an Enterprise Architecture Framework (2nd Edition)*, Victoria, BC: Trafford Publishing.

Schekkerman, J. (2005a) *The Economic Benefits of Enterprise Architecture: How to Quantify and Manage the Economic Value of Enterprise Architecture*, Victoria, BC: Trafford Publishing.

Schekkerman, J. (2005b) "Trends in Enterprise Architecture 2005: How Are Organizations Progressing?", Amersfoort, The Netherlands: Institute for Enterprise Architecture Developments (IFEAD).

Schekkerman, J. (2006a) "Extended Enterprise Architecture Framework Essentials Guide, Version 1.5", Amersfoort, The Netherlands: Institute for Enterprise Architecture Developments (IFEAD).

Schekkerman, J. (2006b) "Extended Enterprise Architecture Maturity Model Support Guide, Version 2.0", Amersfoort, The Netherlands: Institute for Enterprise Architecture Developments (IFEAD).

Schekkerman, J. (2008) *Enterprise Architecture Good Practices Guide: How to Manage the Enterprise Architecture Practice*, Victoria, BC: Trafford Publishing.

Schlosser, F., Beimborn, D., Weitzel, T. and Wagner, H.-T. (2015) "Achieving Social Alignment Between Business and IT - An Empirical Evaluation of the Efficacy of IT Governance Mechanisms", *Journal of Information Technology*, Vol. 30, No. 2, pp. 119-135.

Schlosser, F. and Wagner, H.-T. (2011) "IT Governance Practices for Improving Strategic and Operational Business-IT Alignment", In: Seddon, P. B. and Gregor, S. (eds.) *Proceedings of the 15th Pacific Asia Conference on Information Systems*, Brisbane, Australia: Association for Information Systems, pp. 1-13.

Schmidt, C. and Buxmann, P. (2011) "Outcomes and Success Factors of Enterprise IT Architecture Management: Empirical Insight from the International Financial Services Industry", *European Journal of Information Systems*, Vol. 20, No. 2, pp. 168-185.

Schneider, A. W., Gschwendtner, A. and Matthes, F. (2015) "IT Architecture Standardization Survey", Munich, Germany: Software Engineering for Business Information Systems (SEBIS).

Schoenherr, M. (2008) "Towards a Common Terminology in the Discipline of Enterprise Architecture", In: Feuerlicht, G. and Lamersdorf, W. (eds.) *Proceedings of the 3rd Trends in Enterprise Architecture Research Workshop*, Sydney, Australia: Springer, pp. 400-413.

Schulte, W. R. (2002) "Enterprise Architecture and IT 'City Planning'" (#COM-17-2304), Stamford, CT: Gartner.

Schwartz, M. H. (1970) "MIS Planning", *Datamation*, Vol. 16, No. 10, pp. 28-31.

Scott, J. (2009) "Business Capability Maps: The Missing Link Between Business Strategy and IT Action", *Architecture and Governance Magazine*, Vol. 5, No. 9, pp. 1-4.

Scott Morton, M. S. (1991) "Introduction", In: Scott Morton, M. S. (ed.) *The Corporation of the 1990s: Information Technology and Organizational Transformation*, New York, NY: Oxford University Press, pp. 3-23.

Searle, S. and Allega, P. (2017) "Critical Capabilities for Enterprise Architecture Tools" (#G00319167), Stamford, CT: Gartner.

Searle, S. and Kerremans, M. (2017) "Magic Quadrant for Enterprise Architecture Tools" (#G00308704), Stamford, CT: Gartner.

Segars, A. H. and Grover, V. (1996) "Designing Company-Wide Information Systems: Risk Factors and Coping Strategies", *Long Range Planning*, Vol. 29, No. 3, pp. 381-392.

Segars, A. H. and Grover, V. (1999) "Profiles of Strategic Information Systems Planning", *Information Systems Research*, Vol. 10, No. 3, pp. 199-232.

Seppanen, V., Heikkila, J. and Liimatainen, K. (2009) "Key Issues in EA-Implementation: Case Study of Two Finnish Government Agencies", In: Hofreiter, B. and Werthner, H. (eds.) *Proceedings of the 11th IEEE Conference on Commerce and Enterprise Computing*, Vienna: IEEE, pp. 114-120.

Sessions, R. (2007) "A Comparison of the Top Four Enterprise-Architecture Methodologies", Microsoft, URL: http://web.archive.org/web/20170310132123/https://msdn.microsoft.com/en-us/library/bb466232.aspx.

Sessions, R. and de Vadoss, J. (2014) "A Comparison of the Top Four Enterprise Architecture Approaches in 2014", Redmond, WA: Microsoft.

Shank, M. E., Boynton, A. C. and Zmud, R. W. (1985) "Critical Success Factor Analysis as a Methodology for MIS Planning", *MIS Quarterly*, Vol. 9, No. 2, pp. 121-129.

Shanks, G. (1997) "The Challenges of Strategic Data Planning in Practice: An Interpretive Case Study", *Journal of Strategic Information Systems*, Vol. 6, No. 1, pp. 69-90.

Shanks, G. and Swatman, P. (1997) "Building and Using Corporate Data Models: A Case Study of Four Australian Banks", In: Gable, G. and Weber, R. (eds.) *Proceedings of the 3rd Pacific Asia Conference on Information Systems*, Brisbane, Australia: Association for Information Systems, pp. 815-825.

Shepherd, J. (2011) "How to Get Started With a Pace-Layered Application Strategy" (#G00211245), Stamford, CT: Gartner.

Short, J. and Burke, B. (2010) "Determining the Right Size for Your Enterprise Architecture Team" (#G00206390), Stamford, CT: Gartner.

Shpilberg, D., Berez, S., Puryear, R. and Shah, S. (2007) "Avoiding the Alignment Trap in Information Technology", *MIT Sloan Management Review*, Vol. 49, No. 1, pp. 51-58.

Sidorova, A. and Kappelman, L. A. (2010) "Enterprise Architecture as Politics: An Actor-Network Theory Perspective", In: Kappelman, L. A. (ed.) *The SIM Guide to Enterprise Architecture*, Boca Raton, FL: CRC Press, pp. 70-88.

Sidorova, A. and Kappelman, L. A. (2011) "Better Business-IT Alignment Through Enterprise Architecture: An Actor-Network Theory Perspective", *Journal of Enterprise Architecture*, Vol. 7, No. 1, pp. 39-47.

Siegel, P. (1975) *Strategic Planning of Management Information Systems*, New York, NY: Petrocelli Books.

Silver, B. (2012) *BPMN Method and Style: With BPMN Implementer's Guide*, Aptos, CA: Cody-Cassidy Press.

Simon, D., Fischbach, K. and Schoder, D. (2013) "An Exploration of Enterprise Architecture Research", *Communications of the Association for Information Systems*, Vol. 32, No. 1, pp. 1-72.

Slater, D. (2002) "Strategic Planning Don'ts (and Dos): As You Write Your Company's Next IT Strategic Plan Don't Repeat These Classic Mistakes", *CIO Magazine*, Vol. 15, No. 16, pp. 84-93.

Smith, H. A. and Watson, R. T. (2015) "The Jewel in the Crown - Enterprise Architecture at Chubb", *MIS Quarterly Executive*, Vol. 14, No. 4, pp. 195-209.

Smith, H. A., Watson, R. T. and Sullivan, P. (2012) "Delivering an Effective Enterprise Architecture at Chubb Insurance", *MIS Quarterly Executive*, Vol. 11, No. 2, pp. 75-85.

Smolander, K., Rossi, M. and Purao, S. (2008) "Software Architectures: Blueprint, Literature, Language or Decision", *European Journal of Information Systems*, Vol. 17, No. 6, pp. 575-588.

Sobczak, A. (2013) "Methods of the Assessment of Enterprise Architecture Practice Maturity in an Organization", In: Kobylinski, A. and Sobczak, A. (eds.) *Perspectives in Business Informatics Research*, Berlin: Springer, pp. 104-111.

Somogyi, E. K. and Galliers, R. D. (1987) "Applied Information Technology: From Data Processing to Strategic Information Systems", *Journal of Information Technology*, Vol. 2, No. 1, pp. 30-41.

SOP (1961) "IBM Study Organization Plan: Documentation Techniques" (#SC20-8075-0), White Plains, NY: IBM Corporation.

SOP (1963a) "Basic System Study Guide" (#SF20-8150-0), White Plains, NY: IBM Corporation.

SOP (1963b) "IBM Study Organization Plan: The Approach" (#SF20-8135-0), White Plains, NY: IBM Corporation.

SOP (1963c) "IBM Study Organization Plan: The Method Phase I" (#SF20-8136-0), White Plains, NY: IBM Corporation.

SOP (1963d) "IBM Study Organization Plan: The Method Phase II" (#SF20-8137-0), White Plains, NY: IBM Corporation.

SOP (1963e) "IBM Study Organization Plan: The Method Phase III" (#SF20-8138-0), White Plains, NY: IBM Corporation.

Sowa, J. F. and Zachman, J. A. (1992a) "Extending and Formalizing the Framework for Information Systems Architecture", *IBM Systems Journal*, Vol. 31, No. 3, pp. 590-616.

Sowa, J. F. and Zachman, J. A. (1992b) "A Logic-Based Approach to Enterprise Integration", In: Petrie, C. J. (ed.) *Proceedings of the 1st International Conference on Enterprise Integration Modeling*, Austin, TX: MIT Press, pp. 152-163.

Sowell, P. K. (2000) "The C4ISR Architecture Framework: History, Status, and Plans for Evolution", In: Burns, D. (ed.) *Proceedings of the 5th International Command and Control Research and Technology Symposium*, Canberra: CCRP Press, pp. 1-21.

Spencer, R. A. (1985) "Information Architecture", *Journal of Systems Management*, Vol. 36, No. 11, pp. 34-42.

Spewak, S. H. and Hill, S. C. (1992) *Enterprise Architecture Planning: Developing a Blueprint for Data, Applications and Technology*, New York, NY: Wiley.

Spewak, S. H. and Tiemann, M. (2006) "Updating the Enterprise Architecture Planning Model", *Journal of Enterprise Architecture*, Vol. 2, No. 2, pp. 11-19.

Sporn, D. L. (1978) "Designing an ADP Planning Process", *Long Range Planning*, Vol. 11, No. 1, pp. 43-46.

Star, S. L. (2010) "This is Not a Boundary Object: Reflections on the Origin of a Concept", *Science, Technology and Human Values*, Vol. 35, No. 5, pp. 601-617.

Star, S. L. and Griesemer, J. R. (1989) "Institutional Ecology, 'Translations' and Boundary Objects: Amateurs and Professionals in Berkeley's Museum of Vertebrate Zoology, 1907-39", *Social Studies of Science*, Vol. 19, No. 3, pp. 387-420.

Statland, N. (1982) "The Relationships Between Data Flow and Organization Management", In: Goldberg, R. and Lorin, H. (eds.) *The Economics of Information Processing (Volume 1: Management Perspectives)*, New York, NY: Wiley, pp. 84-95.

Stecher, P. (1993) "Building Business and Application Systems with the Retail Application Architecture", *IBM Systems Journal*, Vol. 32, No. 2, pp. 278-306.

Stegwee, R. A. and van Waes, R. M. C. (1990) "The Development of Information Systems Planning: Towards a Mature Management Tool", *Information Resources Management Journal*, Vol. 3, No. 3, pp. 8-22.

Sullivan, C. H. (1985) "Systems Planning in the Information Age", *MIT Sloan Management Review*, Vol. 26, No. 2, pp. 3-12.

Sullivan, C. H. (1987) "An Evolutionary New Logic Redefines Strategic Systems Planning", *Information Strategy: The Executive's Journal*, Vol. 3, No. 2, pp. 13-19.

Swanton, B. (2012a) "How to Differentiate Governance and Change Management in Your Pace-Layered Application Strategy" (#G00237513), Stamford, CT: Gartner.

Swanton, B. (2012b) "Use a Pace-Layered Application Strategy to Clean Up ERP During Upgrades and Consolidation" (#G00230527), Stamford, CT: Gartner.

Swindell, A. (2014) "Business Capability Models: Why You Might Be Missing Out on Better Business Outcomes", *Architecture and Governance Magazine*, Vol. 10, No. 2, pp. 3-7.

Szulanski, G. (1996) "Exploring Internal Stickiness: Impediments to the Transfer of Best Practices Within the Firm", *Strategic Management Journal*, Vol. 17, No. S2, pp. 27-43.

TAFIM (1996a) "Department of Defense Technical Architecture Framework for Information Management, Volume 1: Overview (Version 3.0)", Arlington County, VA: Defense Information Systems Agency.

TAFIM (1996b) "Department of Defense Technical Architecture Framework for Information Management, Volume 4: DoD Standards-Based Architecture Planning Guide (Version 3.0)", Arlington County, VA: Defense Information Systems Agency.

Tallon, P. P. (2007) "A Process-Oriented Perspective on the Alignment of Information Technology and Business Strategy", *Journal of Management Information Systems*, Vol. 24, No. 3, pp. 227-268.

Tallon, P. P. (2011) "Value Chain Linkages and the Spillover Effects of Strategic Information Technology Alignment: A Process-Level View", *Journal of Management Information Systems*, Vol. 28, No. 3, pp. 9-44.

Tallon, P. P. and Pinsonneault, A. (2011) "Competing Perspectives on the Link Between Strategic Information Technology Alignment and Organizational Agility: Insights from a Mediation Model", *MIS Quarterly*, Vol. 35, No. 2, pp. 463-486.

Tambo, T. and Baekgaard, L. (2013) "Dilemmas in Enterprise Architecture Research and Practice from a Perspective of Feral Information Systems", In: Bagheri, E., Gasevic, D., Halle, S., Hatala, M., Nezhad, H. R. M. and Reichert, M. (eds.) *Proceedings of the 8th Trends in Enterprise Architecture Research Workshop*, Vancouver, Canada: IEEE, pp. 289-295.

Tamm, T., Seddon, P. B., Shanks, G., Reynolds, P. and Frampton, K. M. (2015) "How an Australian Retailer Enabled Business Transformation Through Enterprise Architecture", *MIS Quarterly Executive*, Vol. 14, No. 4, pp. 181-193.

Taylor, J. W. and Dean, N. J. (1966) "Managing to Manage the Computer", *Harvard Business Review*, Vol. 44, No. 5, pp. 98-110.

TEAF (2000) "Treasury Enterprise Architecture Framework, Version 1", Washington, DC: Department of the Treasury.

Teo, T. S. and Ang, J. S. (1999) "Critical Success Factors in the Alignment of IS Plans with Business Plans", *International Journal of Information Management*, Vol. 19, No. 2, pp. 173-185.

Teo, T. S., Ang, J. S. and Pavri, F. N. (1997) "The State of Strategic IS Planning Practices in Singapore", *Information and Management*, Vol. 33, No. 1, pp. 13-23.

The Open Group (2016a) "TOGAF Users by Market Sector", The Open Group, URL: http://web.archive.org/web/20151121161238/http://www.opengroup.org/togaf/users-by-market-sector.

The Open Group (2016b) "TOGAF Worldwide", The Open Group, URL: http://www.opengroup.org/subjectareas/enterprise/togaf/worldwide.

Theuerkorn, F. (2004) *Lightweight Enterprise Architectures*, Boca Raton, FL: Auerbach Publications.

Thomas, R., Beamer, R. A. and Sowell, P. K. (2000) "Civilian Application of the DOD C4ISR Architecture Framework: A Treasury Department Case Study", In: Burns, D. (ed.) *Proceedings of the 5th International Command and Control Research and Technology Symposium*, Canberra: CCRP Press, pp. 1-21.

Thompson, L. A. (1969) "Effective Planning and Control of the Systems Effort", *Journal of Systems Management*, Vol. 20, No. 7, pp. 32-35.

ThoughtWorks (2017) "ThoughtWorks Technology Radar", ThoughtWorks, URL: https://www.thoughtworks.com/radar.

TM Forum (2017) "Business Process Framework (eTOM)", TM Forum, URL: https://www.tmforum.org/business-process-framework/.

TOGAF (2018) "TOGAF Version 9.2" (#C182), Reading, UK: The Open Group.

Toppenberg, G., Henningsson, S. and Shanks, G. (2015) "How Cisco Systems Used Enterprise Architecture Capability to Sustain Acquisition-Based Growth", *MIS Quarterly Executive*, Vol. 14, No. 4, pp. 151-168.

Tozer, E. E. (1986a) "Developing Plans for Information Systems", *Long Range Planning*, Vol. 19, No. 5, pp. 63-75.

Tozer, E. E. (1986b) "Developing Strategies for Management Information Systems", *Long Range Planning*, Vol. 19, No. 4, pp. 31-40.

Tozer, E. E. (1988) *Planning for Effective Business Information Systems*, Oxford, UK: Pergamon Press.

Tozer, E. E. (1996) *Strategic IS/IT Planning*, Boston, MA: Butterworth-Heinemann.

Treacy, M. and Wiersema, F. (1993) "Customer Intimacy and Other Value Disciplines", *Harvard Business Review*, Vol. 71, No. 1, pp. 84-93.

Treacy, M. and Wiersema, F. (1997) *The Discipline of Market Leaders: Choose Your Customers, Narrow Your Focus, Dominate Your Market*, Reading, MA: Addison-Wesley.

Trionfi, A. (2016) "Guiding Principles to Support Organization-Level Enterprise Architectures", *Journal of Enterprise Architecture*, Vol. 12, No. 3, pp. 40-45.

Tucci, L. (2011) "Two IT Gurus Face Off on Value of Enterprise Architecture Frameworks", TotalCIO, URL: http://itknowledgeexchange.techtarget.com/total-cio/two-it-gurus-face-off-on-value-of-enterprise-architecture-frameworks/.

UML (2015) "Unified Modeling Language (UML), Version 2.5", Object Management Group (OMG), URL: http://www.omg.org/spec/UML/2.5/.

Vacca, J. R. (1983) "BSP: How Is It Working?", *Computerworld*, Vol. 17, No. 12, pp. 9-18.

Vacca, J. R. (1984) "BSP IQA: IBM's Information Quality Analysis", *Computerworld*, Vol. 18, No. 50, pp. 45-47.

Vacca, J. R. (1985) "Information Quality Analysis", *Infosystems*, Vol. 32, No. 12, pp. 60-61.

Vail, E. F. (2005) "CMM-Based EA: Achieving the Next Level of Enterprise Architecture Capability and Performance", *Journal of Enterprise Architecture*, Vol. 1, No. 2, pp. 37-44.

Valacich, J. and Schneider, C. (2011) *Information Systems Today: Managing in the Digital World (5th Edition)*, Boston, MA: Prentice Hall.

Valorinta, M. (2011) "IT Alignment and the Boundaries of the IT Function", *Journal of Information Technology*, Vol. 26, No. 1, pp. 46-59.

van't Wout, J., Waage, M., Hartman, H., Stahlecker, M. and Hofman, A. (2010) *The Integrated Architecture Framework Explained: Why, What, How*, Berlin: Springer.

van Rensselaer, C. (1979) "Centralize? Decentralize? Distribute?", *Datamation*, Vol. 25, No. 7, pp. 88-97.

van Rensselaer, C. (1985) "Global, Shared, Local: At Hewlett-Packard, Information Systems Come in Three Flavors", *Datamation*, Vol. 31, No. 6, pp. 105-114.

Venkatesh, V., Bala, H., Venkatraman, S. and Bates, J. (2007) "Enterprise Architecture Maturity: The Story of the Veterans Health Administration", *MIS Quarterly Executive*, Vol. 6, No. 2, pp. 79-90.

Venkatraman, N. (1991) "IT-Induced Business Reconfiguration", In: Scott Morton, M. S. (ed.) *The Corporation of the 1990s: Information Technology and Organizational Transformation*, New York, NY: Oxford University Press, pp. 122-158.

Veryard, R. (2011) "The Sage Kings of Antiquity", Architecture, Data and Intelligence, URL: https://rvsoapbox.blogspot.com/2011/06/sage-kings-of-antiquity.html.

Viswanathan, V. (2015) "Four Questions: Vish Viswanathan", *Journal of Enterprise Architecture*, Vol. 11, No. 2, pp. 15-17.

Vitale, M. R., Ives, B. and Beath, C. M. (1986) "Linking Information Technology and Corporate Strategy: An Organizational View", In: Maggi, L., Zmud, R. W. and Wetherbe, J. C. (eds.) *Proceedings of the 7th*

International Conference on Information Systems, San Diego, CA: Association for Information Systems, pp. 265-276.

Vogel, D. R. and Wetherbe, J. C. (1984) "University Planning: Developing a Long-Range Information Architecture", *Planning and Changing*, Vol. 15, No. 3, pp. 177-191.

Vogel, D. R. and Wetherbe, J. C. (1991) "Information Architecture: Sharing the Sharable Resource", *CAUSE/EFFECT*, Vol. 14, No. 2, pp. 4-9.

von Halle, B. (1992) "Leap of Faith", *Database Programming and Design*, Vol. 5, No. 9, pp. 15-18.

von Halle, B. (1996) "Architecting in a Virtual World", *Database Programming and Design*, Vol. 9, No. 11, pp. 13-18.

Wagner, H.-T., Beimborn, D. and Weitzel, T. (2014) "How Social Capital Among Information Technology and Business Units Drives Operational Alignment and IT Business Value", *Journal of Management Information Systems*, Vol. 31, No. 1, pp. 241-272.

Wagner, H.-T. and Weitzel, T. (2012) "How to Achieve Operational Business-IT Alignment: Insights from a Global Aerospace Firm", *MIS Quarterly Executive*, Vol. 11, No. 1, pp. 25-36.

Wagner, S. and Dittmar, L. (2006) "The Unexpected Benefits of Sarbanes-Oxley", *Harvard Business Review*, Vol. 84, No. 4, pp. 133-140.

Wagter, R., van den Berg, M., Luijpers, J. and van Steenbergen, M. (2005) *Dynamic Enterprise Architecture: How to Make It Work*, Hoboken, NJ: Wiley.

Wahi, P. N., Popp, K. and Stier, S. (1983) "Applications Systems Planning at Weyerhaeuser", *Journal of Systems Management*, Vol. 34, No. 3, pp. 12-21.

Walker, P. D. and Catalano, S. D. (1969) "Where Do We Go from Here with MIS?", *Computer Decisions*, Vol. 1, No. 9, pp. 34-37.

Walsham, G. (1997) "Actor-Network Theory and IS Research: Current Status and Future Prospects", In: Lee, A. S., Liebenau, J. and DeGross, J. I. (eds.) *Information Systems and Qualitative Research*, Boston, MA: Springer, pp. 466-480.

Wang, P. (1994) "Information Systems Management Issues in the Republic of China for the 1990s", *Information and Management*, Vol. 26, No. 6, pp. 341-352.

Wang, P. and Turban, E. (1994) "Management Information Systems Issues of the 1990s in the Republic of China: An Industry Analysis", *International Journal of Information Management*, Vol. 14, No. 1, pp. 25-38.

Ward, J. and Daniel, E. (2008) "Increasing Your Odds: Creating Better Business Cases", *Cutter Benchmark Review*, Vol. 8, No. 2, pp. 5-31.

Ward, J., Daniel, E. and Peppard, J. (2008) "Building Better Business Cases for IT Investments", *MIS Quarterly Executive*, Vol. 7, No. 1, pp. 1-15.

Ward, J. and Peppard, J. (1996) "Reconciling the IT/Business Relationship: A Troubled Marriage in Need of Guidance", *Journal of Strategic Information Systems*, Vol. 5, No. 1, pp. 37-65.

Wardle, C. (1984) "The Evolution of Information Systems Architecture", In: Nunamaker, J., King, J. L. and Kraemer, K. L. (eds.) *Proceedings of the 5th International Conference on Information Systems*, Tucson, AZ: Association for Information Systems, pp. 205-217.

Waterman, R. H., Peters, T. J. and Phillips, J. R. (1980) "Structure Is Not Organization", *Business Horizons*, Vol. 23, No. 3, pp. 14-26.

Watson, R. T. (1989) "Key Issues in Information Systems Management: An Australian Perspective - 1988", *Australian Computer Journal*, Vol. 21, No. 3, pp. 118-129.

Watson, R. T. and Brancheau, J. C. (1991) "Key Issues in Information Systems Management: An International Perspective", *Information and Management*, Vol. 20, No. 3, pp. 213-223.

Watson, R. T., Kelly, G. G., Galliers, R. D. and Brancheau, J. C. (1997) "Key Issues in Information Systems Management: An International Perspective", *Journal of Management Information Systems*, Vol. 13, No. 4, pp. 91-115.

Weill, P. (2004) "Don't Just Lead, Govern: How Top-Performing Firms Govern IT", *MIS Quarterly Executive*, Vol. 3, No. 1, pp. 1-17.

Weill, P. and Aral, S. (2003) "Managing the IT Portfolio (Update Circa 2003)", Cambridge, MA: Center for Information Systems Research (CISR), MIT Sloan School of Management.

Weill, P. and Aral, S. (2004a) "IT Savvy Pays Off", Cambridge, MA: Center for Information Systems Research (CISR), MIT Sloan School of Management.

Weill, P. and Aral, S. (2004b) "Managing the IT Portfolio: Returns from the Different IT Asset Classes", Cambridge, MA: Center for Information Systems Research (CISR), MIT Sloan School of Management.

Weill, P. and Aral, S. (2005a) "IT Savvy Pays Off: How Top Performers Match IT Portfolios and Organizational Practices", Cambridge, MA: Center for Information Systems Research (CISR), MIT Sloan School of Management.

Weill, P. and Aral, S. (2005b) "IT Savvy: Achieving Industry Leading Returns from Your IT Portfolio", Cambridge, MA: Center for Information Systems Research (CISR), MIT Sloan School of Management.

Weill, P. and Aral, S. (2006) "Generating Premium Returns on Your IT Investments", *MIT Sloan Management Review*, Vol. 47, No. 2, pp. 39-48.

Weill, P., Aral, S. and Johnson, A. (2007) "Compilation of MIT CISR Research on IT Portfolios, IT Savvy and Firm Performance (2000-2006)", Cambridge, MA: Center for Information Systems Research (CISR), MIT Sloan School of Management.

Weill, P. and Broadbent, M. (1998) *Leveraging the New Infrastructure: How Market Leaders Capitalize on Information Technology*, Boston, MA: Harvard Business School Press.

Weill, P. and Broadbent, M. (2002) "Describing and Assessing IT Governance - The Governance Arrangements Matrix", Cambridge, MA: Center for Information Systems Research (CISR), MIT Sloan School of Management.

Weill, P. and Johnson, A. (2005) "Managing the IT Portfolio (Update Circa 2005): Where Did the Infrastructure Go?", Cambridge, MA: Center for Information Systems Research (CISR), MIT Sloan School of Management.

Weill, P. and Ross, J. W. (2004) *IT Governance: How Top Performers Manage IT Decision Rights for Superior Results*, Boston, MA: Harvard Business School Press.

Weill, P. and Ross, J. W. (2005) "A Matrixed Approach to Designing IT Governance", *MIT Sloan Management Review*, Vol. 46, No. 2, pp. 26-34.

Weill, P. and Ross, J. W. (2008) "Implementing Your Operating Model Via IT Governance", Cambridge, MA: Center for Information Systems Research (CISR), MIT Sloan School of Management.

Weill, P. and Ross, J. W. (2009) *IT Savvy: What Top Executives Must Know to Go from Pain to Gain*, Boston, MA: Harvard Business School Press.

Weill, P. and Woerner, S. L. (2010) "What's Next: Learning from the Most Digital Industries", Cambridge, MA: Center for Information Systems Research (CISR), MIT Sloan School of Management.

Weill, P., Woerner, S. L. and McDonald, M. (2009) "Managing the IT Portfolio (Update Circa 2009): Infrastructure Dwindling in the Downturn", Cambridge, MA: Center for Information Systems Research (CISR), MIT Sloan School of Management.

Weill, P., Woerner, S. L. and Rubin, H. A. (2008) "Managing the IT Portfolio (Update Circa 2008): It's All About What's New", Cambridge, MA: Center for Information Systems Research (CISR), MIT Sloan School of Management.

Weiss, D. and Rosser, B. (2008) "Focus Enterprise Architecture Metrics on Business Value" (#G00155631), Stamford, CT: Gartner.

Weiss, S., Aier, S. and Winter, R. (2013) "Institutionalization and the Effectiveness of Enterprise Architecture Management", In: Baskerville, R. and Chau, M. (eds.) *Proceedings of the 34th International Conference on Information Systems*, Milan, Italy: Association for Information Systems, pp. 1-19.

Weldon, L. and Burton, B. (2011) "Use Business Capability Modeling to Illustrate Strategic Business Priorities" (#G00217535), Stamford, CT: Gartner.

Westerman, G. and Hunter, R. (2007) *IT Risk: Turning Business Threats into Competitive Advantage*, Boston, MA: Harvard Business School Press.

Wetherbe, J. C. and Davis, G. B. (1982) "Strategic Planning Through Ends/Means Analysis", Minneapolis, MN: Management Information Systems Research Center (MISRC), University of Minnesota.

Wetherbe, J. C. and Davis, G. B. (1983) "Developing a Long-Range Information Architecture", In: Smith, A. N. (ed.) *Proceedings of the 1983 National Computer Conference*, Anaheim, CA: ACM, pp. 261-269.

Whisler, T. L. and Leavitt, H. J. (1958) "Management in the 1980's", *Harvard Business Review*, Vol. 36, No. 6, pp. 41-48.

White, S. A. and Miers, D. (2008) *BPMN Modeling and Reference Guide: Understanding and Using BPMN*, Lighthouse Point, FL: Future Strategies.

Wiegers, K. E. (2005) *More About Software Requirements: Thorny Issues and Practical Advice*, Redmond, WA: Microsoft Press.

Wiegers, K. E. and Beatty, J. (2013) *Software Requirements (3rd Edition)*, Redmond, WA: Microsoft Press.

Wierda, G. (2015) *Chess and the Art of Enterprise Architecture*, Amsterdam: R&A.

Wijgunaratne, I. and Madiraju, S. (2016) "Addressing Enterprise Change Capability, a Constraint in Business Transformation", *Journal of Enterprise Architecture*, Vol. 12, No. 3, pp. 52-63.

Williams, T. J. (1994) "The Purdue Enterprise Reference Architecture", *Computers in Industry*, Vol. 24, No. 2, pp. 141-158.

Winter, K., Buckl, S., Matthes, F. and Schweda, C. M. (2010) "Investigating the State-of-the-Art in Enterprise Architecture Management Methods in Literature and Practice", In: Sansonetti, A. (ed.) *Proceedings of the 4th Mediterranean Conference on Information Systems*, Tel Aviv, Israel: Association for Information Systems, pp. 1-12.

Wiseman, C. (1988) *Strategic Information Systems*, Homewood, IL: Irwin.

Wisnosky, D. E. and Vogel, J. (2004) *DoDAF Wizdom: A Practical Guide to Planning, Managing and Executing Projects to Build Enterprise Architectures Using the Department of Defense Architecture Framework*, Naperville, IL: Wizdom Press.

Withington, F. G. (1974) "Five Generations of Computers", *Harvard Business Review*, Vol. 52, No. 4, pp. 99-108.

Wyman, J. (1985) "Technological Myopia - The Need to Think Strategically About Technology", *MIT Sloan Management Review*, Vol. 26, No. 4, pp. 59-64.

Yayla, A. A. and Hu, Q. (2012) "The Impact of IT-Business Strategic Alignment on Firm Performance in a Developing Country Setting: Exploring Moderating Roles of Environmental Uncertainty and Strategic Orientation", *European Journal of Information Systems*, Vol. 21, No. 4, pp. 373-387.

Ylimaki, T. and Halttunen, V. (2006) "Method Engineering in Practice: A Case of Applying the Zachman Framework in the Context of Small Enterprise Architecture Oriented Projects", *Information, Knowledge, Systems Management*, Vol. 5, No. 3, pp. 189-209.

Zachman International (2012) "Zachman International Closes Acquisition of the FEAC Institute", Zachman International, URL: https://www.zachman.com/press/97-zachman-international-closes-acquisition-of-the-feac-institute.

Zachman, J. A. (1977) "Control and Planning of Information Systems", *Journal of Systems Management*, Vol. 28, No. 7, pp. 34-41.

Zachman, J. A. (1982) "Business Systems Planning and Business Information Control Study: A Comparison", *IBM Systems Journal*, Vol. 21, No. 1, pp. 31-53.

Zachman, J. A. (1987) "A Framework for Information Systems Architecture", *IBM Systems Journal*, Vol. 26, No. 3, pp. 276-292.

Zachman, J. A. (1988) "A Framework for Information Systems Architecture", In: March, S. T. (ed.) *Proceedings of the 6th International Conference on Entity-Relationship Approach*, Amsterdam: North-Holland Publishing, p. 7.

Zachman, J. A. (1989) "The Integration of Systems Planning, Development, and Maintenance Tools and Methods", In: Fong, E. N. and Goldfine, A. H. (eds.) *Information Management Directions: The Integration Challenge (NIST Special Publication 500-167)*, Gaithersburg, MD: National Institute of Standards and Technology (NIST), pp. 63-122.

Zachman, J. A. (1996) "Concepts of the Framework for Enterprise Architecture: Background, Description and Utility", Monument, CO: Zachman International.

Zachman, J. A. (2001) "You Can't "Cost-Justify" Architecture", Monument, CO: Zachman International.

Zachman, J. A. (2003) "The Zachman Framework for Enterprise Architecture: Primer for Enterprise Engineering and Manufacturing", Monument, CO: Zachman International.

Zachman, J. A. (2006) "Enterprise Architecture: Managing Complexity and Change", In: von Halle, B. and Goldberg, L. (eds.) *Business Rule Revolution: Running Business the Right Way*, Cupertino, CA: Happy About, pp. 33-43.

Zachman, J. A. (2007) "Foreword", In: Saha, P. (ed.) *Handbook of Enterprise Systems Architecture in Practice*, Hershey, PA: Information Science Reference, pp. xv-xviii.

Zachman, J. A. (2010a) "Architecture Is Architecture Is Architecture", In: Kappelman, L. A. (ed.) *The SIM Guide to Enterprise Architecture*, Boca Raton, FL: CRC Press, pp. 37-45.

Zachman, J. A. (2010b) "John Zachman's Concise Definition of the Zachman Framework", In: Kappelman, L. A. (ed.) *The SIM Guide to Enterprise Architecture*, Boca Raton, FL: CRC Press, pp. 61-65.

Zachman, J. A. (2015) "A Historical Look at Enterprise Architecture with John Zachman", The Open Group, URL: https://blog.opengroup.org/2015/01/23/a-historical-look-at-enterprise-architecture-with-john-zachman/.

Zachman, J. A. and Ruby, D. (2004) "Erecting the Framework, Part I ", Enterprise Architect Online, URL: http://archive.visualstudiomagazine.com/ea/magazine/spring/online/druby/default_pf.aspx.

Zachman, J. A. and Sessions, R. (2007) "Exclusive Interview with John Zachman, President of Zachman International, CEO of Zachman Framework Associates", Austin, TX: Perspectives of the International Association of Software Architects.

Zahra, S. A. and George, G. (2002) "Absorptive Capacity: A Review, Reconceptualization, and Extension", *Academy of Management Review*, Vol. 27, No. 2, pp. 185-203.

Zani, W. M. (1970) "Blueprint for MIS", *Harvard Business Review*, Vol. 48, No. 6, pp. 95-100.

Zink, G. (2009) "How to Restart an Enterprise Architecture Program After Initial Failure", *Journal of Enterprise Architecture*, Vol. 5, No. 2, pp. 31-41.

Index

4

4FRONT, 338

A

Acceptance of an EA practice, 316-18

Analysis, Requirements determination, Design and development, Implementation and evaluation (ARDI), 389

Analytical papers, 213, *See also* Outlines

Analytical Reports, 136-38, *See also* Considerations

Application interaction diagrams, 194, *See also* Landscapes

Applications domain, 18, *See also* Domains of enterprise architecture

ArchiMate, 281-82, 286

Architects, 27-32, 245-60

Architectural directions for Designs, 224, *See also* Designs

Architectural directions for Outlines, 212, *See also* Outlines

Architectural initiatives, 106-7, 107-10, 192, 203, *See also* IT initiatives

Architectural repository, 289-90, 291

Architecture debt, 274, 299-302

Architecture debt registers, 301, *See also* Architecture debt

Architecture function, 32-33, 250, 254, 261-79

Architecture governance, 268-79, 300, *See also* Architecture governance bodies

Architecture governance bodies, 33, 268-79, *See also* Architecture governance

Architecture managers, 254, 256-57, 263-66, 326, *See also* Architects

Architecture of Integrated Information Systems (ARIS), 285, 286

Architecture-based planning methodologies. *See* History of enterprise architecture

Arthur Andersen, 336, 387

Arthur Young, 340, 387

Artifacts. *See* Enterprise architecture artifacts

Asset roadmaps, 194, *See also* Landscapes

Atkinson, Tremblay & Associates, 338

B

Benefits of enterprise architecture, 12-14, 36-38, 130, 146, 162, 184, 206, 220

Bernard, Scott A., 343

Building architecture, 17

Business actors, 9, *See also* Communication problems

Business and IT alignment, 8-12, 13, 37

Business capabilities, 74-76, 80, 164, *See also* Business Capability Models, *See also* Discussion points

Business Capability Models, 163-67, *See also* Visions

Business cases for IT initiatives, 88, 204, 205

Business domain, 18, *See also* Domains of enterprise architecture

Business executives, 10, 16, 20, 86, 88, 129, 160, 203, *See also* Stakeholders of enterprise architecture

Business Information Analysis and Integration Technique (BIAIT), 389

Business Information Characterization/Control Study (BICS), 389

Business Information Systems Analysis and Design (BISAD), 389

Business model canvases, 176, *See also* Visions

Business Process Model and Notation (BPMN), 284, 286

Business processes, 77-78, 80, 203, *See also* Discussion points

Business requirements, 78-79, 80, 217, *See also* Discussion points

Business strategy, 63-66, 66, 73, 76, 80, 235

Business Systems Planning (BSP), xx, 39, 322, 335, 336, 337, 338, 358, 389, 394

Business unit architects, 253, 254-56, 256-57, 257-60, 263-66, 266-68, 325, *See also* Architects

Business unit managers, 10, 16, 88, 217, *See also* Stakeholders of enterprise architecture

Business-enabling domain architects, 252, *See also* Domain architects

Business-enabling EA domains, 18, *See also* Domains of enterprise architecture

Business-focused EA artifacts, 115-16, 197, *See also* CSVLOD model of enterprise architecture

Business-supporting domain architects, 252, *See also* Domain architects

Business-supporting EA domains, 19, *See also* Domains of enterprise architecture

C

Capital expenses (CAPEX), 206

Changes EA artifacts, 113-15, *See also* CSVLOD model of enterprise architecture

City planning and enterprise architecture, 45-61

Common EA artifacts, 118

Communication problems, 9-12

Compliance acts, 5, 134

Conceptual Data Models, 135-36, *See also* Considerations

Configuration management databases (CMDBs), 292-94, 297

Considerations, 48-49, 86, 118-19, 127-42, *See also* CSVLOD model of enterprise architecture

Consulting. *See* Enterprise architecture consulting

Context Diagrams, 174-75, *See also* Visions

Coordination model, 70, 73, 266, *See also* Operating model

Core diagrams, 176, *See also* Visions

CRUD matrices, 349

CSVLOD model of enterprise architecture, 60-61, 113-25, 229-42, *See also* Enterprise architecture artifacts

Customer journey mapping, 203

D

Data domain, 18, *See also* Domains of enterprise architecture

Data integration, 69, *See also* Operating model

Decision paths, 234-37

Decisions EA artifacts, 23-25, 27-31, 247, 269-70, 298-99, *See also* Enterprise architecture artifacts

Deliberate path to establishing an EA practice, 313, *See also* Initiation of an EA practice

Department of Defense Architecture Framework (DoDAF), 344, *See also* Enterprise architecture frameworks

Design committees, 272, 274, *See also* Architecture governance bodies

Designers, 255, *See also* Architects

Designs, 54-55, 89, 121-22, 215-27, *See also* CSVLOD model of enterprise architecture

Development of EA artifacts, 27-31, 129-30, 144-46, 160-62, 182-84, 203-6, 217-19, *See also* CSVLOD model of enterprise architecture

Developmental consulting engagements, 325-26, 327, *See also* Enterprise architecture consulting

Direction Statements, 138-39, *See also* Considerations

Discounted cash flow (DCF), 204

Discussion points, 66-83, 92, 102, 103

Disruptive technologies, 5, 137, 249, 325

Diversification model, 69, 267, *See also* Operating model

Domain architects, 251-52, 254-56, 256-57, 257-60, 263-66, 266-68, 325, *See also* Architects

Domains of enterprise architecture, 18-19, *See also* Domain architects

Domain-specific landscape diagrams, 194, *See also* Landscapes

Duality of EA artifacts, 21-23, 49, 51, 53, 54, 55, *See also* Enterprise architecture artifacts

E

Enterprise architects, 253-54, 254-56, 256-57, 257-60, 263-66, 266-68, 325, *See also* Architects

Enterprise architecture, 15-19

Enterprise architecture artifacts, 20-26, 47-60, 111-242, *See also* Enterprise architecture

Enterprise architecture consulting, xxv-xxvi, 322-29, *See also* History of enterprise architecture

Enterprise architecture frameworks, xix-xxii, 38-40, 43, 333-56, 390, *See also* Management fads

Enterprise architecture methodologies, 341-46, *See also* Architecture-based planning methodologies

Enterprise Architecture on a Page, 239-41

Enterprise Architecture Planning (EAP), 39, 322, 341, 342, 391

Enterprise architecture practice, 19-20, 40-43, *See also* Processes of an EA practice

Enterprise architecture uncertainty principle, 82-83, 177

Enterprise data portfolios, 195, *See also* Landscapes

Enterprise engineering, 43

Enterprise modeling, 42

Enterprise System Portfolios, 189-91, *See also* Landscapes

Entity-relationship modeling, 154

Escalation procedures, 273-76, 300, *See also* Architecture governance

Essential EA artifacts, 118

Exemption procedures, 273-76, 299, *See also* Architecture governance

Explicit duality, 22, *See also* Duality of EA artifacts

Extended inventories, 196, *See also* Landscapes

External actors, 10, *See also* Communication problems

F

Facts EA artifacts, 23-25, 27-31, 328, *See also* Enterprise architecture artifacts

Federal Enterprise Architecture (FEA), 39, 342

Federal Enterprise Architecture Framework (FEAF), 39, 342, 347, *See also* Enterprise architecture frameworks

Finkelstein, Clive, 340, 341, 347

Frameworks. *See* Enterprise architecture frameworks

Fundamental initiatives, 104, 107-10, 161, 203, *See also* IT initiatives

G

Gallo, Thomas E., 338

General Data Protection Regulation (GDPR), 5, 134, *See also* Compliance acts

Gramm-Leach-Bliley Act (GLBA), 134, *See also* Compliance acts

Guidelines, 150-51, *See also* Standards

H

Health Insurance Portability and Accountability Act (HIPAA), 5, 134, *See also* Compliance acts

Historical path to establishing an EA practice, 310, *See also* Initiation of an EA practice

History of enterprise architecture, 38-40, 333-56

Hype cycle, 137

I

IBM, xx, 38, 322, 335, 340, 344, 347

Implementation step of the Initiative Delivery process, 88-89, 217, *See also* Initiative Delivery process

Implicit duality, 22, *See also* Duality of EA artifacts

Information Engineering, 39, 322, 340, 341

Information Quality Analysis (IQA), 336

Information System Master Architecture and Plan (ISMAP), 338

Infrastructure domain, 18, *See also* Domains of enterprise architecture

Initiation of an EA practice, 307-16

Initiation step of the Initiative Delivery process, 88, 203, *See also* Initiative Delivery process

Initiative Delivery process, 87-89, 93-94, 94-95, 97, 170, 203, 235, 300, 311, 314, 324, *See also* Processes of an EA practice

Initiative Proposals, 210-11, *See also* Outlines

Initiative roadmaps, 213, *See also* Outlines

Initiative-based consulting engagements, 324-25, 327, *See also* Enterprise architecture consulting

Inmon, William H., 338, 347

Integration domain, 18, *See also* Domains of enterprise architecture

Internal actors, 10, *See also* Communication problems

Internal rate of return (IRR), 204

Inventories, 187-89, *See also* Landscapes

Investment committees, 272, 274, 275, *See also* Architecture governance bodies

IT actors, 9, *See also* Communication problems

IT budget, 3, 303, 384

IT capability models, 196, *See also* Landscapes

IT delivery function, 261

IT executives, 10, 16, 106, 204, *See also* Stakeholders of enterprise architecture

IT initiatives, 101-10

IT Principles, 152-54, *See also* Standards

IT project teams, 10, 16, 20, 88, 217, *See also* Stakeholders of enterprise architecture

IT projects. *See* IT initiatives

IT Roadmaps, 191-94, *See also* Landscapes

IT support function, 261

IT target states, 195, *See also* Landscapes

IT-focused EA artifacts, 115-16, *See also* CSVLOD model of enterprise architecture

Ivory tower syndrome, 98, 156, 197, 218, 247, 266, 358

K

Key decisions for Outlines, 211, *See also* Outlines

Key design decisions (KDDs), 223, *See also* Designs

Kundra, Vivek, 380, 386, 396

L

Landscape Diagrams, 185-87, *See also* Landscapes

Landscapes, 52-53, 90, 120-21, 181-99, *See also* CSVLOD model of enterprise architecture

Local initiatives, 105, 107-10, 161, 203, 320, *See also* IT initiatives

Logical Data Models, 154-55, *See also* Standards

M

Management fads, xx, 43, 352-56

Martin, James, 340, 347

Master data maps, 194, *See also* Landscapes

Maturity of an EA practice, 318-22

Measurements in an EA practice, 37, 302-5

Method/1, 39, 322, 336, 337

Methodologies. *See* Architecture-based planning methodologies

Microservices, 42

Microsoft Office suite, 290-91, 295

MoSCoW framework, 218

N

Net present value (NPV), 204

Nolan, Norton & Company, 338, 390

O

One-page initiative overviews, 213, *See also* Outlines

Operating expenses (OPEX), 206

Operating model, 68-74, 80, 132, 266, *See also* Discussion points

Options Assessments, 209-10, *See also* Outlines

Organizational structures, 176, *See also* Visions

Origin of EA best practices. *See* History of enterprise architecture

Outlines, 53-54, 88, 121, 201-14, *See also* CSVLOD model of enterprise architecture

Outsourcing, 166, 218, 225

P

Pace-layered model, 383

Patterns, 151-52, *See also* Standards

Payment Card Industry Data Security Standard (PCI DSS), 134

Permanent EA artifacts, 25, *See also* Enterprise architecture artifacts

Policies, 133-35, *See also* Considerations

Post-implementation benefit reviews, 205

Preliminary Solution Designs, 222-23, *See also* Designs

Principles, 131-33, *See also* Considerations

PRISM framework, 337, 390, *See also* Enterprise architecture frameworks

Problems of architecture-based methodologies, xx, 39, 323, 349-51, *See also* Architecture-based planning methodologies

Process models, 175, *See also* Visions

Process standardization, 69, *See also* Operating model

Processes of an EA practice, 85-99, 102, 103, 109, 259, 327

Product catalogs, 176, *See also* Visions

Project management, 20, 87

R

Release designs, 225, *See also* Designs

Replication model, 70, 73, 266, *See also* Operating model

Responsibilities of architects, 27, 245, *See also* Architects

Return on investments (ROI), 38, 204

Roadmaps, 167-70, *See also* Visions

Rules EA artifacts, 113-15, *See also* CSVLOD model of enterprise architecture

S

Sarbanes-Oxley Act (SOX), 5, 134, *See also* Compliance acts

Schekkerman, Jaap, 343

Security domain, 18, *See also* Domains of enterprise architecture

Service-oriented architecture (SOA), 42

Skills of architects, 27, 245-50, *See also* Architects

Socio-technical systems, 6-8, 17

Solution architects, 251, 254-56, 256-57, 257-60, 263-66, 324, *See also* Architects

Solution Designs, 220-22, *See also* Designs

Solution Overviews, 207-9, *See also* Outlines

Specific business needs, 76-77, 80, 101, 102, 168, *See also* Discussion points

Spewak, Steven H., 341

Stakeholders of enterprise architecture, 10-11

Standards, 49-50, 90, 119, 143-57, *See also* CSVLOD model of enterprise architecture

Strategic actors, 10, *See also* Communication problems

Strategic consulting engagements, 325, 327, *See also* Enterprise architecture consulting

Strategic Data Planning (SDP), 39, 340, 394

Strategic initiatives, 104-5, 107-10, 161, 203, *See also* IT initiatives

Strategic management, 20, 63, 86

Strategic Planning process, 85-87, 93-94, 95-96, 97, 235, 311, 314, 325, *See also* Processes of an EA practice

Strategy committees, 271, 275, *See also* Architecture governance bodies

Strategy Set Transformation (SST), 388

Straw-man architecture, 298-99

STRIPE matrix, 391, *See also* Enterprise architecture frameworks

Structures EA artifacts, 113-15, *See also* CSVLOD model of enterprise architecture

Study Organization Plan (SOP), 335, 393

Summit S, 338

Supplementary materials, 224, *See also* Designs

SWOT analysis, 137

T

Tactical actors, 10, *See also* Communication problems

Target States, 170-72, *See also* Visions

Technical architects. *See* Designers

Technical Architecture Framework for Information Management (TAFIM), 39, 340, 393, *See also* Enterprise architecture frameworks

Technical EA domains, 18, *See also* Domains of enterprise architecture

Technology committees, 271, 274, 275, *See also* Architecture governance bodies

Technology Optimization process, 89-91, 94-95, 95-96, 97, 301, 311, 313, 325, *See also* Processes of an EA practice

Technology radar, 137

Technology Reference Models, 148-50, *See also* Standards

Templates for EA artifacts, 297-98

Temporary EA artifacts, 25, *See also* Enterprise architecture artifacts

The Open Group Architecture Framework (TOGAF), 39, 43, 345, 346, 347, 396, *See also* Enterprise architecture frameworks

Third parties, 11, 16, 218, 225, *See also* Stakeholders of enterprise architecture

Tools for enterprise architecture, 289-97, 317

Total cost of ownership (TCO), 206

Tozer, Edwin E., 338, 347

U

Uncertainty principle. *See* Enterprise architecture uncertainty principle

Uncommon EA artifacts, 118

Unification model, 71, 266, *See also* Operating model

Unified Modeling Language (UML), 282-83, 286

Urgent initiatives, 105-6, 107-10, 203, 320, *See also* IT initiatives

Usage of EA artifacts, 129-30, 144-46, 160-62, 182-84, 203-6, 217-19, *See also* CSVLOD model of enterprise architecture

V

Value Chains, 172-74, *See also* Visions

Vendor analysis, 138

Visions, 50-51, 86, 119-20, 159-79, *See also* CSVLOD model of enterprise architecture

W

Walker, P. Duane (Dewey), 335, 389

Z

Zachman Framework, xix, 337, 347, 357, 365, *See also* Enterprise architecture frameworks

Zachman, John, 333, 347, 348, 364, 365

About the Author

Svyatoslav Kotusev is an independent researcher. Since 2013 he focuses on studying enterprise architecture practices in organizations. Besides this book, he is an author of many articles on enterprise architecture that appeared in various academic journals and conferences, industry magazines and online outlets (visit http://kotusev.com for more information). Svyatoslav received his PhD in information systems from RMIT University, Melbourne, Australia. Prior to his research career he held various software development and architecture positions in industry. He can be reached at kotusev@kotusev.com.

CPSIA information can be obtained
at www.ICGtesting.com
Printed in the USA
LVHW062006300623
751173LV00013B/8